Baptist
Ways

Baptist
Ways

A History

Bill J. Leonard

Judson Press
Valley Forge

Baptist Ways: A History

Judson Press has made every effort to trace the ownership of all quotes. In the event of a question arising from the use of a quote, we regret any error made and will be pleased to make the necessary correction in future printings and editions of this book.

Library of Congress Cataloging-in-Publication Data

Leonard, Bill.
      Baptist ways : a history / Bill J. Leonard.
          p. cm.
          Includes bibliographical references and index.
          ISBN 0-8170-1231-1 (alk. paper)
1. Baptists—History. 2. Baptists—United States—History. I. Title.

BX6231.L46 2003
286'.09—dc21
                                                                        2003047541

Printed in the U.S.A.

10 09 08 07 06 05 04 03

10 9 8 7 6 5 4 3 2 1

To Dr. John Thomas Porter
and the Sixth Avenue Baptist Church, Birmingham, Alabama,
who taught me anew what it means to be a Baptist
and what it means to be free

Contents

Foreword

OVER HALF A CENTURY AGO, JUDSON PRESS PUBLISHED ROBERT G. TORBET'S *A History of the Baptists*. A decade later this was followed with a second edition, and after another decade with a third, such proving the need for and the durability of a general history of Baptists around the world. In fact, Torbet's last edition continues to sell, though in diminished numbers.

In the early 1990s the Board of Managers of the American Baptist Historical Society actively considered whether a further revision of Torbet was called for or was wise. After much deliberation (including discussions with the author, who died in 1995), it was decided that an entirely new history was needed. Not only had historical developments multiplied in number and complexity, but historiographical shifts of major proportion had also occurred. So a new book—which meant, of course, a new author. Here the Board's search ended in a most fortuitous choice: Dr. Bill Leonard, now Dean of the Divinity School at Wake Forest University in Winston-Salem, North Carolina, who graciously agreed to undertake this mammoth task.

After many years of persistent—even dogged—labor, the result is now before you: a fresh and exciting new interpretation and presentation of Baptists worldwide. This panorama offers much to the fortunate reader: personalities (brittle and benevolent); movements (inspired and ill-humored); rapid growth along with—to be sure—rapid firing schism, missionary successes, and sacrifices; tradition and innovation; ecumenism arrayed against sectarianism; and much more.

Leonard's sensitive attention to the indispensable role of women is especially welcome. This includes a careful delineation of the contribution of Women's Missionary Societies both at home and abroad. The author also gives to minorities their due, or more properly speaking, what is long past due. Native Americans, African Americans, Hispanic and Asian Americans find their place—and in their own words—in these pages. The less familiar stories of Baptist developments in Africa and Asia are likewise skillfully unfolded here.

The Baptist dedication to and ambivalence concerning education also find full delineation in Leonard's story. Though resources were painfully few, small communities in country after country somehow found it possible to establish schools and colleges and seminaries. The faithful watched over these institutions with growing pride and, sometimes, with growing suspicion. Loving God with all of one's mind on occasion seemed to dominate loving God with all of one's heart. And for a pietistic people, this could never be allowed.

One theme often neglected in general histories of the Baptists is hymnody. It is not neglected here, as Leonard shows that Baptists (like Methodists) did not leave all the good tunes to the devil. Of course, in the early years the singing of hymns, like so much else, was a matter of controversy and even schism. But eventually the Baptist message sang its way into foreign lands, on the frontiers, among children, who in simplest sincerity could sing together: "Jesus loves me, this I know, for the Bible tells me so."

Which brings us, of course, to the Bible and its place in Baptist life. To say that Baptists are a Bible-believing people is to start the story but hardly to end it. As Leonard's rich history reveals, the Bible has been for Baptists both a platform for proclamation and a battleground for disputation—not for Baptists alone, to be sure, for every Christian group seeks somehow to re-create the New Testament church. But that church is incontrovertibly a first-century institution, whose reconstitution demands adjustments whether in the seventeenth century or in the twenty-first. New manuscript discoveries and new scholarly techniques complicate the picture further. And since no single ecclesiastical authority can provide the official interpretation for Baptists, many authorities offer a plethora of interpretations.

Ecclesiastically speaking, the ultimate authority in Baptist life is the local church. And there are lots of them. So this "congregational polity" produces a democracy—and much noisy confusion. Baptists are free agents, and their churches are free spirits. This leaves much room for the operation of the Holy Spirit, and also much room for the vagaries of human nature to expose and express themselves. But there are church covenants (well delineated herein) that attempt to corral a rampant individualism. Beyond that one finds associations or conventions (but no synods or general assemblies) that are intended to enlarge the voice of the local church, not to stifle it. And in all of this clanging machinery of church governance, it is not surprising that further controversies arise.

It is true that Baptists embrace religious liberty—in their best days for all of humankind. It is also true that Baptists embody religious liberty—in their worst days in the unending multiplicity of denominational tags and labels and nicknames. Of the making of many books, the author of *Ecclesiastes* wearily complained, there is no end. The church historian, and certainly the Baptist historian, can with deep feeling share that sentiment regarding denominations and sects and sub sects—without end.

Leonard faithfully follows those many paths, providing us with the names and places necessary for our understanding of a complex history. But more than that, he reminds us of the vision and the spirit that make the telling of this story so imperative in the first place.

Edwin S. Gaustad
Santa Fe, New Mexico

Preface

THE THESIS OF THIS BOOK IS RELATIVELY SIMPLE. IT SUGGESTS THAT AMID certain distinctives, Baptist identity is configured in a variety of ways by groups, subgroups, and individuals who claim the Baptist name. This identity extends across a theological spectrum from Arminian to Calvinist, from conservative to liberal, from open to closed communionist, and from denominationalist to independent. The book traces significant aspects of Baptist history from the seventeenth through the twentieth centuries. It surveys basic beliefs, events, and experiences evident in Baptist communities. The early chapters are an attempt to pass on information about the ways in which fledgling Baptist communities struggled with identity, ideas, and cultural contexts. Contemporary Baptists continue to struggle with questions of identity: What does it mean to be Baptist? What is the nature of the Baptist role in church and society? At a time when much Baptist identity worldwide is in a state of permanent transition, it is important that we understand something of the diversity and continuity of Baptist life in the initial years of the movement(s).

While a survey of Baptist history requires attention to a multitude of details, names, dates, and movements, the accounts herein are, at best, representative. No doubt, some readers will be distressed that particular stories have not been told. While attention is given to the global Baptist presence, extensive concentration is placed upon the American Baptist experience. Clearly, additional research should be done into the Baptist experiences in Eastern Europe, Asia, Africa, and South America—areas where churches are growing rapidly.

This book took longer to write than either the editors at Judson Press or I ever intended. The research began while I was chair of the department of religion and philosophy at Samford University in Birmingham, Alabama. In 1996, I was invited to become dean and professor of church history at the Divinity School at Wake Forest University, Winston-Salem, North Carolina. At that point the school had no faculty or students, and I was asked to help begin the new endeavor. The Divinity School began in the fall of 1999, and work on the formation of the new school required time and energy that delayed the completion of the manuscript.

Through it all, I am immensely grateful for the patience and encouragement of Randy Frame, editor at Judson Press. Throughout all the frustrating delays, he has maintained patience and concern. I am also grateful to the Center for the Study of American Protestantism and its director, Dr. James Lewis, for a research grant afforded me. Likewise, Samford University provided a faculty research grant that enabled me to pursue research in the Angus Library of Regent's Park College, Oxford. Susan Mills, the director of that superb archive, was of invaluable help in providing materials and friendship. Paul Fiddes, principal of Regent's Park College, also gave significant encouragement and friendship on my visits to Oxford.

Elizabeth Wells, in the Baptist Collection of the Samford University Library, provided valuable research help early in the project. Sharon Snow, research librarian in the Baptist Collection at Wake Forest University, also made those resources available to me. I am also indebted to innumerable Baptist churches throughout the United States, particularly in the American South, that allowed me to talk and write about these issues in ways that helped the book take shape. I am especially grateful to students at the Southern Baptist Theological Seminary, Louisville; Samford University; and Wake Forest University who also allowed me to explore ideas, summarize issues, and "think out loud" about the history and theology of the people called Baptists.

When I began teaching courses in American Christianity at the Southern Baptist Seminary in 1975, I never imagined that I would be invited to write a history of the Baptists or ever be considered a serious student of Baptist history. I was, at least in my own mind, an "Americanist" who would leave the intricacies of Baptist history to others. Unexpectedly, life, academics, and controversy compelled me to become a student of the Baptists. Perhaps this volume really began in June of 1979 when the Southern Baptist Convention took a turn to the right and precipitated events that required many of us to reclaim, rethink, and rely on our Baptist heritage. Writing about those traumatic issues, I began to reflect about Baptist identity in ways that led me to this survey text. Today, I am grateful for the encouragement of innumerable mentors, friends, and colleagues. I honor them here with a list that is illustrative, not definitive. Some, as the old preachers used to say, have "gone on ahead," preparing the way, I hope, for the rest of us. So I am deeply indebted to Thomas Doss, Ed Brooks Bowles, John Loftis, Alice Wonders, William R. Estep, Robert A. Baker, M. R. Leonard, C. C. Goen, James Melvin Washington, Penrose St. Amant, Frank Stagg, Norman Maring, Carlyle Marney, Robert Torbet, Dale Moody, Winthrop Hudson, Lynn May, Sydney Ahlstrom, Eric Rust, Earl Marsalis, Helen Barnett, Kenneth Chafin, and David Duke. My grandmothers, Lula Lee Leonard and Frances Edith Henton; my aunt, Erlene Henton Smith; and my mother, Lavelle Henton Leonard, passed on Baptist identity and piety to me before I ever knew what to call it. Among the living, I have learned from Walter Shurden, Glenn Hinson, Morgan Patterson, Henlee Barnett, Robert Handy, Will Campbell, Karen Smith, Martin Marty, Earl Kent Brown, C. Allyn Russell, Samuel Hill, Wayne Flynt, Charles Reagan Wilson, Howard Dorgan, Edwin Gaustad, Richard Pierard, Helen Lewis, Mary Lee Daugherty, W. T. Edwards, H. Leon McBeth, Frank Tupper, Timothy George, Charles Kimball, Glenn Stassen, Paul Fiddes, B. R. White, David Bebbington, Robert Nash, Douglas Weaver, Andrew Pratt, Andrew Manis, Linda Weaver Williams, James Dunn, William Hull, Phyllis Pleasants, Nancy Ammerman, Ralph Reavis, William Brackney, and John Kinney. These and other persons shaped my understanding of the nature of Christian and Baptist identity across the years.

In January 1993 our family joined the Sixth Avenue Baptist Church, Birmingham, Alabama, an African American congregation whose pastor, John Thomas Porter, is one of the finest examples of Baptist spirit and ministry that I have ever known. Fresh from the Baptist "wars" in Louisville, I found in the Sixth Avenue Baptist Church a community of healing and acceptance. It is a debt that I can never repay. This volume is lovingly dedicated to Dr. Porter, now retired, and to the Sixth Avenue congregation.

Through it all, my spouse, Dr. Candyce Leonard, and our daughter, Stephanie, have sustained me in ways too deep for words to describe. Judson Press will have to forgive me for the many evenings when I should have been working on this book but instead went with Stephanie to Wake Forest basketball games in celebration and hope.

Perched on the edge of the twenty-first century, Baptists, like other religionists, confront a variety of challenges that require them to address history, theology, and identity that inform what it means to be Baptist. How they answer those questions will determine the future of the movement. It is a good time to write a history of the Baptists. It is a good time to revisit Baptist ways, whatever they mean and wherever they appear.

Chapter 1

Baptist Ways: Defining a People

IN *AUTHORITY AND POWER IN THE FREE CHURCH TRADITION*, PAUL HARRISON observed, "It is clear that Baptist history is freighted with ambiguity, and those who strive to establish the singularity of the tradition are on a weak foundation."[1] Any attempt to write a history of the Baptists must begin with such an admonition. From their beginnings in seventeenth-century Europe, Baptists have demonstrated beliefs and practices so diverse as to make it difficult to compile a consistent list of distinctives applicable to all segments of the movement at all times. Brief examples illustrate an interminable dilemma.

Consider the Baptist approaches to the Bible. All Baptist groups affirm an abiding belief in the authority of Scripture as found in the Hebrew and Christian Testaments. Yet numerous churches and individuals disagree on the nature of biblical authority and readily divide over theories of inspiration, doctrines of inerrancy, and methods of interpretation (hermeneutics).

Some utilize modern critical methods of biblical study; others use selected elements of such theories; and still others eschew them all as unorthodox. Even biblical inerrantists—those who believe that the Scriptures are completely without error (in the original manuscripts)—differ over theories of inspiration.[2]

Then there is baptism. While Baptists generally agree that the immersion of Christian believers should be the normative mode, they divide over the identity of proper candidates and the meaning of the act itself. Some congregations require immersion of all who join the church. This includes the "rebaptism" of those who come from nonimmersionist traditions or traditions that practice "alien immersion" (immersion performed in non-Baptist churches). Other churches require immersion only of new converts and those new members who have not previously received immersion. Still other churches administer immersion to new believers but accept the previous baptism of all professing Christians who join their ranks. Debates over admission of nonimmersed Christians to church membership or to communion have divided Baptists since the seventeenth century.

The proper age for baptism is another matter that reflects Baptist diversity. Few, if any, segments of the Baptist family administer baptism to infants.[3] Rather, Baptists insist that baptism must follow a profession of faith in Christ. Yet Baptist communions vary considerably as to the appropriate age of baptismal candidates. Some Baptists permit the immersion of persons only after they have reached adolescence or adulthood.

Others baptize children, some even of preschool age.

Baptist theology also reflects considerable diversity. From the beginning of the movement, Baptist dogmas have covered a spectrum from Arminian to Calvinist. The General Baptists who began in Holland in 1608–1609 were Arminians, affirming prevenient grace, free will, the general atonement of Christ, and the possibility of "falling from grace." By the 1630s, a group of Particular Baptists had formed in London, espousing Reformed theology, with its doctrines of limited atonement, total depravity, predestination, unconditional election, and perseverance of the saints. Since that time, Baptist communions have moved across the Arminian/Calvinist spectrum in a variety of ways.

The role of women in Baptist churches is another matter of controversy. Certain Baptists encourage females to receive theological education with ordination to the pastorate and the diaconate; others vehemently oppose such practice. In some Baptist churches, men and women participate equally in church ministries and government, while others set restrictions on the activities of women in church affairs.

In short, describing particular distinctives that typify Baptist identity requires extensive qualification. Numerous scholars have sought to delineate the essence of the Baptists, with their conclusions often being as diverse as the distinctives they sought to define.

Curtis W. Freeman, James Wm. McClendon Jr., and C. Rosalee Velloso da Silva suggest three approaches for discerning Baptist identity. Some point to doctrinal distinctives as a way of discerning Baptist uniqueness, while others refer to "principles or self-evident axioms." Still others prefer "identifying marks" evident in "characteristic practices," including "biblicism, mission, liberty, discipleship and community."[4] Perhaps certain types of Baptist identity are found in all these "marks" as articulated by scholars, critics, and Baptists themselves.

Shaping Baptist Distinctives

The early critics of the Baptists were quick to delineate the basic tenets of the new sect, often with considerable derision. Most opponents mistakenly equated them with the Continental Anabaptists. In the 1640s, Anglican cleric Daniel Featley offered his perception of the teachings of the "Dippers," rampant in England. They include:

First, that none are rightly baptized but those who are dipt.

Secondly, that no children ought to be baptized.

Thirdly, that there ought to be no set form of Liturgy or prayer by the Book, but onely by the Spirit.

Fourthly, that there ought to be no distinction by the Word of God between the Clergy and the Laity but that all who are gifted may preach the Word, and administer the Sacraments.

Fifthly, that it is not lawful to take an oath at all, no, not though it be demanded by the magistrate.

Sixthly, that no Christian may with good conscience execute the office of civil magistrate.[5]

With the exception of "dipping," Baptist practices paralleled those of numerous seventeenth-century antiestablishment sects, including Quakers, Seekers, and Levellers.

Writing almost 250 years later, Alvah Hovey (1820–1903), American Baptist theologian and educator, listed the unifying principles he found in diverse Baptist communions. He noted, "Several of these principles are asserted by other Christians as earnestly as by ourselves, yet they must be embraced in my statement, because they are central elements of our creed, and cannot be omitted without injury to the strength and beauty of that creed."[6] Specific characteristics might not be unique to the Baptist family, but were combined in peculiarly Baptist ways.

First, Hovey acknowledged Baptists' belief in "the supreme authority of the Scriptures in matters of religion."[7] In their effort to discover proper instruction for Christian belief and practice, Baptists began with the Bible. As Hovey understood it, however, Baptists' knowledge and understanding of the biblical revelation remained partial and conditional. He commented, "The moral and religious truths of our religion have received their ultimate expression in the New Testament, but the full meaning of this expression may not be discovered until the last generation of Christians has finished its course on earth."[8] The truths of the Bible were so extensive, and human understanding so incomplete, that insights about it were always conditional. Other Baptists simply insist that the Bible is true in all, regardless of human understanding.

Second, Hovey acknowledged the Baptist commitment to "personal accountability to God alone in matters purely religious." This "individual accountability" involved nothing less than the obligation of each member "to judge … what is true and right."[9] In this idea was the basis for Baptist support of religious liberty, freedom of conscience, and "the right of free inquiry after truth, though it should lead to change of creed."[10] In their search for truth, Baptists have often amended their beliefs, even when it led to schism in the church or denomination.

Third, Baptists insisted, "Union with Christ [is] essential to salvation."[11] Salvific regeneration is required of all persons who claim Christian faith. In this sense, Baptists were, and generally remain, conversionists in their understanding of the need for personal response to God's love and grace.

Fourth, Baptists demanded "a new kind of life" as evidence of one's personal experience of grace. Sanctification, growing in grace, involves daily Christian experience and discipleship. It is a life nurtured in the community of faith, the church.[12]

Fifth, Hovey suggested that this "new life should be one of unqualified obedience to Christ." Such obedience was demonstrated in ethical behavior, through response to human need, and in receiving the ordinances of believer's baptism and the Lord's Supper.[13]

Hovey's list of distinctives reflects broad ideals that he believed to be the essence of Baptist identity. Specific characteristics—baptism, church membership, religious liberty—grew out of general spiritual categories. If Daniel Featley knew Baptists to be a radical and heretical sect, Alvah Hovey viewed them as a bona fide denomination in the Free Church tradition.

In the first edition of his history of the Baptists, Robert Torbet shortened Hovey's list. It included (1) the authority of Holy Scripture; (2) a regenerate church membership; (3) baptism by immersion as the sign of new life in Christ and membership in the church; (4) the autonomy of the local congregation; (5) the priesthood of all believers; and (6) religious liberty.[14]

Other essayists admit that isolating common particularities among Baptist groups is highly problematic. William Brackney observed, "A major difficulty in any list of Baptist emphases or distinguishing marks is the diversity now existing among Baptists. A profile which may legitimately delineate the character of one group, say the Italian Baptist Association, by no means fits the General Association of Regular Baptists."[15] Brackney suggested that believer's baptism by immersion is "the functional essence of historic Baptist identity."[16] In baptism, Baptists anchored their concern for a regenerate church membership, their identification with the New Testament community, their commitment to Christian discipleship, and their insistence on public profession of faith.[17]

Eric Ohlmann listed the traditional characteristics of the Baptists—biblical authority, religious liberty, soul competency, local autonomy, evangelism and missions, believers' church, discipleship—but warned that "the essence of a movement does not necessarily lie in its most distinctive characteristic."[18] For Ohlmann, Baptists' uniqueness "lies in their soteriology," their understanding of the nature of salvation. This is evident in their view of a church "with greatly diminished authority and power and individual believers with greatly increased choice and responsibility."[19] Baptist ideas on salvation and Christian discipleship were increasingly concerned with free will and the autonomy of the individual in the salvific process.[20]

Karen Smith acknowledged that even common distinctives had "varied interpretation by Baptists." She concluded that in spite of Baptist diversity "on biblical, ethical, and doctrinal matters, there is one central tenet which united Baptists of every theological persuasion: the idea that an individual's experience of faith is nurtured and shared within the context of the wider covenant community. The basis of Baptist life has always been the principle that believers are never believers alone, but bound together in a covenant community."[21] This emphasis on the centrality of covenant to Baptist identity is echoed by a variety of British Baptists. Paul S. Fiddes concluded that English Baptists had some "ambiguity" about the relationship between covenant and confessions of faith. Thus, "Covenant is about relationship, and trust, about 'walking together' which is in some mysterious way part of the very journey of salvation."[22]

Edwin Gaustad suggested that the most distinctive characteristic of the early Baptists was the idea that "baptism be responsible, that is, administered to believers," a practice that early Baptists shared with the Anabaptist movement.[23] Attempts to link them with alleged extravagances of the Radical Reformers often led early Baptist apologists to distance themselves from such comparisons.

Other scholars warn that diversity of belief does not mean that all Baptists are orthodox Christians. Writing in the latter part of the twentieth century, L. Russ Bush and Tom Nettles affirmed the centrality of biblical authority in Baptist life, with particular attention to the presence of the doctrine of biblical inerrancy. They observed, "Historically, Baptists have built their theology on a solid foundation. Holy Scripture was taken to be God's infallible revelation in words.... Scripture has been the cornerstone, the common ground, the point of unity."[24] The inability to articulate central and unifying principles led Paul Harrison to warn that the Baptist emphasis on individualism and free will was one of the great dangers of the tradition. He wrote, "The early heritage of the Baptists contains ambiguities which through the passage of time have been transformed into historical contradictions."[25] Harrison believed that Baptists had undermined their initial concern for the freedom of God through their obsession with the freedom of the individual. Their excessive concern for soul competency in religion created an overly idealized individualism. He concluded, "The Baptist emphasis upon 'soul competency' crystallizes attention upon the possibilities of men rather than upon the power of God."[26] Harrison maintained that by the nineteenth century Baptists were unable to distinguish between the freedom of God and the freedom of the individual will.[27]

Harrison's critique highlights the Baptist emphasis on freedom and the role of the individual in the quest for religious truth. Such a concern is understandable, given the historical context of the earliest Baptist communities and their reaction against the religious establishments. Thus, Baptists, along with others in the Free Church tradition, affirmed the freedom of the individual and the community of faith in determining spiritual and theological ideals in light of biblical norms. Agreeing on those norms was not without divisions, even in the most orthodox contexts.

Historically, the Baptist movement began in a time of great political and religious turmoil when individuals and churches were searching for the ultimate revelation. Many were willing to relinquish once-cherished beliefs and practices when convinced that a greater and more biblical truth had been discovered. Such theological inquisitiveness led Baptist founder John Smyth to move from Anglicanism to Puritan Separatism in his quest for the true church. He then elected to administer believer's baptism to himself—an act that marked the beginning of the Baptist movement. He became convinced that a more valid baptism was to be found with the Dutch Mennonites, left the Baptists, and died while waiting for admission to the Mennonite fellowship. His quest for the true church also created the first schism in the fledgling Baptist communion in Amsterdam.

Roger Williams, the quintessential American dissenter, moved through Puritan Separatism to the Baptists, founding the first Baptist church in America. Shortly thereafter, he became convinced that all revelations were tainted, and he died while awaiting a new word from God.

This continuing search for truth is evident in the introduction to the Somerset Confession of Particular Baptists (1656). It declares: "Wee believe the Lord will daily cause truth more to apeare in the hearts of his Saints, and make them ashamed of their folly in the land of their nativitie, that so they may with one shoulder more studie to lift up the name of the Lord Jesus."[28] This statement did not mean that there were no clear teachings in Scripture. Indeed, the confession set forth specific doctrines in a Calvinistic framework. Rather, it meant that the "Saints" were ever called to search for truth.

Such openness to new insights is known as the "principle of mutability," the idea that individuals or churches were ready to alter their dogmas if convinced that a clearer reading of Scripture had been discovered.[29] For example, the First London Confession of Particular Baptists (1644) states, "We confesse that we know but in part, and that we are ignorant of many things which we desire and seek to know; and if any shall doe us that friendly part to shew us from the Word of God that we see not, we shall have cause to be thankful to God and them."[30]

This biblicism led many Baptists to adhere to a strenuous "primitivism," a belief that the true church in any era is the one that best replicates the New Testament church. Determining the marks of the true church, even in the New Testament, is no easy matter, and Baptists themselves divided over which distinguishing qualities were most biblical.

These attitudes led certain Baptists to reject other ecclesial or denominational traditions as nonbiblical, corrupt, or even apostate. B. R. White wrote of the biblicism of General Baptist founder, John Smyth: "Smyth, in his own eyes at least, had a clear case for reconstituting the Church, its ministry, and its baptism, afresh in a situation of total apostasy. When all other Christian communities had wandered off into the darkness of error, as had even the Separatists on the all-important matter … of baptism, his duty, he believed and argued, was clear enough."[31] Smyth, believing that all other churches were corrupt, determined to found a faith community that would conform to the biblical norm. White commented that Smyth was "convinced that he and his followers stood alone in the context of a totally apostate Christendom."[32] When he decided that the Mennonites had the proper authority for baptism, Smyth abandoned his newly formed church for what seemed a more biblical way.

Perhaps another way to describe the similarities and disparities in Baptist identity is to view classic distinctives as dynamics moving in tandem across a wide spectrum of belief and practice. Common beliefs may be given varying emphases by diverse Baptist communities and individuals. Baptist uniqueness is found less in the specific doctrines they promote than in the way (or ways) those precepts may be combined. Particular rubrics do not stand alone but are interrelated, each creating inevitable tension amid the unceasing and elusive struggle for balance. Certain doctrines cannot be understood apart from related concepts and ideals. This involves the following eight dialectics.

The Authority of Scripture and the Liberty of Conscience. Like other Christians, Baptists understand the Bible to be the Word of God, the authoritative revelation for Christian belief and practice.[33] The Standard Confession, composed by the British General Baptists in 1660, states "that the holy Scriptures is the rule whereby Saints both in matters of Faith, and conversation are to be regulated."[34]

Theories of biblical inspiration abound in Baptist life, sometimes creating debate and division, yet all affirming the centrality of the Bible for faith and practice.[35] Biblical authority is mediated through individual and communal interpretation based on liberty of conscience. The Standard Confession says, "That it is the will, and mind of God (in these Gospel times) that all men should have the free liberty of their own Consciences in matters of Religion, or Worship, without the least oppression, or persecution."[36]

In their battle for religious liberty, Baptists suggested that God alone was judge of conscience and all persons were accountable only to God for their religious beliefs and practices. The individual was responsible for interpreting Scripture according to the dictates of conscience. In short, Baptists suggested that the people could be trusted to interpret Scripture aright through the inner guidance of the Holy Spirit within the community of faith.

The emphasis on conscience did not mean that each person was free to believe anything at all and still remain a Baptist. Rather, individual interpretation was pursued under the guidance of the Holy Spirit, within the congregation of believers. At best, biblical authority kept liberty of conscience from degenerating into antinomianism. Liberty of conscience kept biblical authority from deteriorating into "corpse-cold" literalism.[37]

The Church: Local Autonomy and Associational Cooperation. Baptists began with a radical congregationalism and the idea that the authority of Christ was mediated not through pope, bishop, or king but through the congregation of believers. The congregation bore the authority for administering the ordinances (sacraments), preaching, ordaining, and determining the nature of its own ministry. Yet no sooner was the movement underway than individual Baptist churches reached out to other like-minded churches in fellowship, encouragement, and other associational expressions. Early associations in Britain and America sometimes developed extensive influence, exercising authority over member churches and individuals. An uneasy tension often existed between local congregations and associations, particularly when local autonomy appeared threatened by authoritarian bureaucracies. Whatever its forms, Baptist polity retained an elusive quality. In 1947, Henry Cook acknowledged, "Strictly speaking there is no such thing as 'Baptist church polity,' because Baptists by their own fundamental principle are committed to accepting the Church polity of the New Testament, and no-one can really say with positive certainty what that actually is."[38]

The Ministry: Laity and Clergy. Baptists place great emphasis on the Reformation doctrine of the priesthood of all believers, insisting that each individual may encounter God's grace directly, without clerical or ecclesiastical mediation. They contend that every believer is a minister in service in the church and in the world. Some early Baptists offered the laying on of hands to the newly baptized as an outward sign of their calling to service and ministry. At the same time, Baptists set aside certain individuals for specific ministry in and through the community of faith.

Ordination of both pastors (clergy) and deacons (laity) as congregational officers illustrates the effort to balance leadership in the church. In one sense, all are ministers; in another sense, pastoral leadership is entrusted to a specific group of duly ordained ministers.

In spite of associational and other denominational connections, local autonomy, individual freedom, and congregational polity have combined to make schism, debate, and division an ever-present reality of Baptist communal relationships. In her study of American frontier religion, Christine Leigh Heyrman described the tendency of Baptist churches to split over ministerial and lay authority. Heyrman observed, "The absence of any authoritative higher body left the Baptists with no means of settling disputes among the clergy, generational or otherwise." She concluded that when conflicts arose, "the Baptists could only wait and hope for a resolution after the blood-letting over contested leadership engulfed and then exhausted their churches. Given their abiding devotion to congregational independence, a veritable icon of lay adoration, the Baptists could not have handled matters differently and still remained Baptists."[39] Debates and divisions seem inescapable, perhaps integral, to Baptist life.

Regeneration: Dramatic Event and Sustaining Process. For Baptists, the church is composed of believers who have experienced grace through the regenerating power of God. The Orthodox Creed (1679) states that those who "are united unto Christ by effectual faith, are regenerated, and have a new heart and spirit created in them through the virtue of Christ his death, resurrection, and intercession, and by the efficacy of the holy spirit, received by faith."[40]

The terms of regeneration vary with individuals and churches. Some suggest that such an episode involves a dramatic conversion when the sinner confronts a powerful spiritual and moral struggle, "accepts Christ," and receives salvation. The Standard Confession (1660) defined the converted as those who could "assent to the truth of the Gospel, believing with all their hearts, that there is remission of sins, and eternal life to be had in Christ."[41]

Amid conversion rhetoric, most Baptist communions insist on nurturing young people to faith. Many report that they were drawn to faith early in life through gentle guidance and instruction provided by ministers, teachers, and spiritual mentors. Their conversion came less by dramatic event than by gradual nurture into faith. While these two approaches may complement each other, they may also create differences concerning the nature of conversion, its proper process, and its authentic recipients.

Ordinances: Sacraments and Symbols. Baptists generally speak of baptism and the Lord's Supper as "ordinances" of the church. This means that they are symbolic observances commanded by Christ and linking contemporary Christians with the church throughout history. While most Baptists have used the word "ordinance" in describing these two communal celebrations, some of the early confessions of faith referred to them as "sacraments," outward and visible signs of an inward grace. The Orthodox Creed (1679) used both terms, noting, "Those two sacraments, viz. Baptism, and the Lord's-supper, are ordinances of positive, sovereign, and holy institution, appointed by the Lord Jesus Christ."[42] The Lord's Supper was a sign of "our communion and union each with other, in the participation of this holy sacrament."[43] The document repudiated both the "popish doctrine of transubstantiation" (the Catholic belief that the bread and wine literally become the body and blood of Christ) and the Lutheran idea of "real presence" whereby Christ is both physically and spiritually present with the bread and wine.[44] While Baptist confessions reject the sacramentalism of other traditions and stress the symbolic nature of the ordinances, they describe them as powerful symbols of spiritual events. The Second London Confession (1677) reflected the Calvinist idea that the Lord's Supper was an experience of Christ's spiritual presence. It acknowledged, "Worthy receivers, outwardly partaking of the visible Elements in this Ordinance, do then also inwardly by faith, really and indeed, yet not carnally, and corporally, but spiritually receive and feed upon Christ crucified."[45]

While all Baptists practice baptism and the Lord's Supper, they interpret them in various ways. Some have demonstrated a more sacramental approach, while others have stressed the essentially symbolic nature of the ordinances.

Doctrinal Statements: Invariably Confessional, Selectively Creedal. Some Baptists insist that their tradition is "confessional, not creedal"—statements of belief that are not equal with Scripture or binding on individual conscience. Confessions are guidelines, whereas creeds are imposed. This statement is admirable but not always accurate.

From the beginning of their movement, many Baptists used confessions of faith to delineate basic doctrines. Others rejected them all together. Some used them as guides, while others applied them more uniformly. Separate Baptists rejected written confessions as conformist and detrimental to the centrality of Scripture. Nonetheless, many Baptist churches organized themselves around confessional statements.

Some qualified such statements with preambles aimed at permitting dissent without creating schism. The Virginia Association of Regular and Separate Baptists united in 1787 with a confession and a preamble that delineated its use: "We do not mean that every person is bound to the strict observance of everything therein contained; yet that it holds forth the essential truths of the gospel ... [that] ought to be believed by every Christian and maintained by every minister of the gospel."[46]

Likewise, the Baptist Faith and Message, the official confession of the Southern Baptist Convention, in its 1925 and 1963 editions, included a preamble stating, "We do not regard them as complete statements of our faith, having any quality of finality or infallibility.... That the sole authority for faith and practice among Baptists is the Scriptures of the Old and New Testaments. Confessions are only guides in interpretation, having no authority over the conscience. That they are statements of religious convictions, drawn from the Scriptures, and are not to be used to hamper freedom of thought or investigation in other realms of life."[47] In spite of these disclaimers, Baptists often have used confessions of faith as a basis for organizing congregations, excluding members, dealing with questions of orthodoxy, and ordaining ministers. Sometimes the effort to impose uniformity led to schism and the creation of new Baptist churches or movements.

William Lumpkin wrote, "The Baptist Movement has traditionally been non-creedal in the sense that it has not erected authoritative confessions of faith as official bases of organization and tests of orthodoxy. An authority that could impose a confession upon individuals, churches, or larger bodies, has been lacking, and the desire to achieve uniformity has never been strong enough to secure adoption of a fixed creed even if the authority for imposing it had existed. Still, Baptists have recognized the valuable uses to which confessions of faith might be put."[48] In short, confessions of faith have had multiple uses among Baptists. Efforts to impose them on the constituency have met with varying responses.

Religious Liberty and Christian Citizenship. Baptists were among the first to call for radical religious liberty in the modern state. From the earliest period of their history, many Baptists challenged prevailing religious and political establishments, insisting that the state could judge neither the heretic nor the atheist. In this way they moved beyond a call for simple religious toleration of groups outside the established church to a complete antiestablishment position. Writing in 1612, Baptist leader Thomas Helwys argued that the state could not act punitively in religious matters against the heretic, the non-Christian, or the atheist. Some suggest that this was the first statement of radical religious freedom to be published in English.[49]

Most Baptists readily affirm their loyalty to the state. The Orthodox Creed (1679) declared that God had "ordained civil magistrates to be under him, over the people for his own glory, and the public good."[50] They would be loyal citizens of the state as long as the state did not try to compel them to violate their sacred consciences and their commitment to Christ.

Diversity: Theological and Ecclesial. Baptist theology covers a wide spectrum of sometimes contradictory theological affirmations from Calvinist to Arminian, from fundamentalist to liberal. This diversity is evident in varying views on the doctrine of the atonement. Some Baptist confessions of faith affirm the general atonement (Christ's death for all humankind), while others insist on limited atonement (Christ's death for the elect). Those who press either one of these dogmas as the only genuine Baptist way will find no support in history. While congregationalism is at the center of their ecclesial order, diverse Baptist groups demonstrate varying degrees of connectionalism in their denominational alliances. National, regional, and local relationships are evident throughout the worldwide Baptist community, yet no genuine uniformity prevails. Some Baptist bodies demonstrate an elaborate denominational connectedness, while others flee such affiliations like the plague. Theological diversity, congregational autonomy, and freedom of conscience create environments in which debate, controversy, and schism are not merely possible but inevitable. In a sense, Baptists created an ecclesiastical and theological framework that ensured controversy, dispute, and division.

Such continued division inside Baptist systems was not lost on certain Baptist leaders. John Clifford, nineteenth-century British Baptist pastor and theologian, observed of the Baptist penchant for controversy, "Living men differ. It is the dead who agree. Poor shattered fragments that we are! Why truth would have no chance at all on the earth if each man were nothing but a sibilant echo of his fellow. God sets men at different angles to the truth, so that one may see what others cannot, and, thereby, more of her virginal beauty and perennial loveliness be revealed.... Pluck the fruits of controversy from the New Testament tree, and you have not only stripped it of its most precious growths, but left the branches so bare that they cease to be a sheltering home for the wearied nations of the earth."[51] Many Baptists seem surprised when disputes arise in their churches or denominational communities.

While they well might be saddened by the divisions that have resulted from these confrontations, they should not be surprised. Dissent is one of the Baptist ways.

Theories of Baptist Origins

Where did Baptists come from? The quest for origins is one of the more colorful and widely debated aspects of the Baptist story. Isolating an appropriate explanation of Baptist beginnings is no easier than explicating common distinctives. Theories of Baptist origins abound and are based on several factors.

First, Baptists have no single founder whose life and thought identifies the historical and theological origins of the movement. They cannot point to a Martin Luther, a John Calvin, or a John Wesley as the source of their lineage. John Smyth and Roger Williams, founders of the first Baptist churches in Holland and America, respectively, remained Baptist for a limited time. Thomas Helwys, John Murton, and other early British General Baptists died relatively soon after they assumed leadership of the fledgling churches. Calvinist or Particular Baptist beginnings in London may be traced to several persons, not one seminal figure.

Second, historians have offered varying explanations about the roots of the movement. These include: (1) a successionist effort to trace Baptist lineage to the first-century church; (2) the influence of, or "kinship" with, the sixteenth-century Anabaptists; (3) the development of Baptist groups directly from segments of English Puritanism; and (4) a combination of several of these ideas.

Third, Baptists themselves have affirmed continuity with classic Christian traditions. Often accused of being merely an antiestablishment sect, Baptists have attempted to prove that their doctrines are those of classic Christian orthodoxy.

Fourth, even if they could not prove historic continuity, many Baptists have attempted to connect their movement to the New Testament and the earliest Christian communities. They have insisted that theirs was a continuation of the work and witness of the true New Testament church.

Fifth, doctrinal disputes have led some Baptists to search for their theological origins. Differences over dogma inside the Baptist family have led many to examine the historic beliefs and practices that gave the movement its birth.

Baptist Successionism. The successionist theory represents an attempt to trace Baptists beginnings through a succession of churches dating from the first century. Robert Torbet used the phrase "Jerusalem-Jordan-John" to describe the successionist theory based on the belief that Baptists began with Jesus' baptism by John (the Baptizer) in the river Jordan, and that the first church in Jerusalem was essentially Baptist in nature (some have said that it was Baptist in everything but name).

In its most forthright expressions, successionism suggests that Baptist churches alone possess the marks of the true church and have endured through a series of crypto-Baptist communities from the early church to the present. Writers such as Thomas Crosby, David Benedict, G. H. Orchard, J. T. Christian, and other successionists have promoted these views. Crosby, labeled by some as "the first Baptist historian," produced a four-volume work entitled *The History of the English Baptists*. His successionism focused on the practice of believer's baptism, a rite that he traced all the way back to the first-century church. He tracked Baptist movements back to the medieval "reformer" John Wycliffe.[52]

In 1838, G. H. Orchard introduced his *Concise History of Baptists* with this successionist statement: "Our design is, to trace and record the existence and practice of those Christian societies, which scripturally administered the ordinance of believers' baptism, and this, we hope to do, from the Jewish Jordan to the British Thames."[53] Successionists such as Orchard traced a series of dissenting groups—Montanists, Donatists, Novatianists, Cathari, Waldenses, and Anabaptists—whose members were Baptist in everything but name, or at least crypto-Baptist in their beliefs and practices. This theory suggested that Baptists could claim the ultimate historic founder, Jesus Christ. Advocates thus resisted efforts to link Baptists with the Protestant Reformation and insisted that the Baptist tradition had existed since the New Testament, predating and anticipating the Reformation church. To this day, some Baptists still refuse to refer to their movement as being Protestant.

Successionist historiography linked Baptists directly to the New Testament church. These links included the following points: (1) Baptists could trace their origins directly to Jesus and John the Baptizer; (2) New Testament principles and churches (therefore Baptist churches) had been preserved throughout history by means of a faithful remnant of dissenting movements; (3) Baptist churches alone were the true churches of Christ; and (4) Baptists predated the Reformation and therefore should not properly be considered Protestant.

While the successionist hypothesis remains popular in some Baptist churches, few, if any, contemporary historians accept it as a credible approach for explaining Baptist roots. Direct linkage cannot be proven historically, nor were the dissenting groups Baptist in everything but name. The most that might be said is that Baptists paralleled other antiestablishment, dissenting groups in Christian history.

Anabaptist "Kinship." Successionists claimed that direct links existed between the Anabaptist and Baptist traditions. Other historians disputed that assertion but have supported a kind of "kinship" between the Dutch Anabaptists and the early Baptist communities. Still other scholars have denied that there was significant Anabaptist influence on the original Baptist movement. Some have seen the modern Baptist movement, like the Anabaptist revival before it, as a restoration of true New Testament Christianity long lost through the Constantinian and Roman Catholic corruption of the church. This meant that the "fall" of the church occurred in the early fourth century, when Christianity became the official, and therefore privileged, religion of the Roman Empire. This union of church and state, along with the resulting Roman Catholic hegemony in Europe, created a false church. Albert Newman wrote, "If the apostolic churches were Baptist churches, the churches of the second century were not. Still less were those of the third and the following centuries."[54]

Anabaptist is the name given to a large and diverse group of radical believers in the sixteenth century. One of the first Anabaptist groups began in Zurich with a group of "radicals" influenced by, but differing from, the beliefs and practices of Ulrich Zwingli, the Swiss reformer. While accepting many of Zwingli's reformist views—biblical authority, separation from Rome, faith alone for salvation—the Swiss Brethren, as they were called, moved beyond their mentor on issues of baptism and church-state relations. They affirmed the baptism of adult believers, rejected infant baptism, and called for freedom of worship beyond state control. Persecuted by Protestant and Catholic establishments alike as both heretics and traitors, the Swiss Brethren were soon jailed, exiled, or executed.

While some were attracted to apocalyptic speculation, the more enduring strain took the name of the Dutch Anabaptist Menno Simons (1496–1561), and these were popularly known as Mennonites. Divisions after Simons's death led to the development of what E. A. Payne called "certain more progressive congregations" in the Waterland region of the Netherlands. Although these Anabaptists are known as Waterlander Mennonites, they called themselves Doopsgezinde, "baptism-minded people."[55] Baptist scholars remain divided over the Anabaptist-Baptist relationship. Successionists link Anabaptists and Baptists in direct lineage with little or no distinction between the two traditions. Others point to certain shared ideals joining the two groups in a "spiritual affinity." Still others have denied substantial Anabaptist impact on Baptist origins. Advocates of the "kinship" theory point to certain commonalities of belief and practice as well as early contacts between Dutch Mennonites and early English Baptists.[56]

John Smyth, one of the founders of the movement, utilized the early Mennonite method of baptism by affusion (pouring). Smyth soon left his Baptist colleagues, convinced that the Mennonites held the true baptismal succession.

Some analysts have suggested that the only shared doctrine of the Anabaptist-Baptist connection was in the repudiation of infant baptism, while others have noted a variety of common beliefs: authority of the New Testament, believers' church, believer's baptism, congregational polity, and religious liberty.[57] William R. Estep, an advocate of Anabaptist-Baptist connections, acknowledged differences on the taking of oaths and on Christian participation in government. He insisted, "Both Smyth and Helwys were dependent on the Mennonites for the determinative features of what was to become known as Baptist faith and practice."[58] James Mosteller resolved the matter by arguing for two "distinct theological strains within the Baptist body…. One came through the Calvinistic position within Puritanism, that of the Particular Baptists; the other is directly from the Continental Anabaptists due to Smyth's association with them, that of the General Baptists."[59]

James R. Coggins traced Smyth's theological journey and insisted that his move from Calvinist to Anabaptist theology was the surest sign of Anabaptist influence upon him. Coggins wrote, "Maybe to avoid the frightening prospect of damned children, Smyth became a theological Anabaptist. He decided that all children were definitely saved on the grounds that there was no original sin."[60]

Glen Stassen maintained that Menno Simons's best-known work, *The Foundation of Christian Doctrine,* "laid the foundation of the Particular Baptist origin."[61] Stassen compared the *First London Confession* (1644) with Simons's *Foundation-Book* and noted that while portions of the document came from the "Brownist Congregational church" (Separatist) and from William Ames's *The Marrow of Theology,* other sections on baptism and discipleship mirror those of the *Foundation-Book.* He concluded, "But I believe the evidence is already overwhelming that the first Particular Baptists, in their initial decision to become Baptists and in their authoritative confessions during the seventeenth century, drew significantly from Menno Simons's *Foundation of Christian Doctrine.*"[62] As a result, Stassen urged Baptists to accept Simons as a significant "parent." He insisted that the traditional emphases regarding Baptist identity did not go "deep enough," by failing to "name our Baptist Christ-centeredness" and the centrality of Christian discipleship.[63]

Not all historians accept the Anabaptist-Baptist connection. Winthrop Hudson asserted that there was no direct influence, arguing that the seventeenth-century Baptists sought to separate themselves from any association with the Anabaptist tradition. He cited the complaints of Smyth and his colleagues "against the term *Anabaptist,* as a name of *reproach* unjustly cast upon them."[64] Both General and Particular Baptist groups alike distinguished their kind of Christianity from Anabaptism. A 1660 statement of faith from the General Baptists was entitled "A Brief Confession or Declaration of Faith, set forth by many of us who are (falsely) called Ana-Baptists."[65]

Particular Baptist confessions published in 1644 and 1646 used similar qualifying statements. Baptists generally rejected Anabaptist opposition to the taking of oaths in civil or religious matters, as well as their theology of the "celestial flesh of Christ"—the idea that Jesus' physical body was not tainted by original sin passed on by his mother. Hudson wrote that the Baptists repudiated any common links with the Anabaptists and "condemned the distinctive Anabaptist doctrines as errors." They utilized the Westminster Confession and Catechism as their primary theological guides and were drawn from the ranks of Congregationalists and Separatists in their origins. He concluded, "The insistence upon believer's baptism was a logical corollary drawn from the Reformation emphasis upon the necessity for an explicit faith and from the Congregational concept of a gathered church, as well as from the common storehouse of Biblical precept and example, rather than being the result of any supposed Anabaptist influence."[66]

B. R. White's survey of the English Separatist tradition rejected any direct link between Anabaptism and English Separatism. He wrote, "It may, therefore, be fairly claimed that, when a plausible source of Separatist views is available in Elizabethan Puritanism and its natural developments, the onus of proof lies upon those who would affirm that the European Anabaptists had any measurable influence upon the shaping of English Separatism."[67]

Puritanism. Most scholars agree that the most explicit connection between Baptists and other Christian traditions comes from seventeenth-century Puritanism, particularly in its Separatist form. Puritanism developed in England with individuals who sought to "purify" the Anglican Church of certain "trappings of popery," which included kneeling at communion, making the sign of the cross, and elaborate clerical vestments. They refused to conform to many of the rubrics in the *Book of Common Prayer,* which they found to be too "popish." Many were strongly committed to the tenets of Reformed theology.

They differed, however, over things such as the validity of the Anglican Church and the appropriate form of church government. "Nonseparating" Puritans affirmed the Church of England as a true, albeit corrupt, tradition, while Separatist Puritans denounced it as a false communion in which no true Christian should remain. Some nonseparating Puritans favored Presbyterian or Congregational church polity, in contrast to the prevailing episcopal system of Anglicanism.

John Smyth, Thomas Helwys, and their group of General (Arminian) Baptists (1608–1609) were directly related to Separatist communities in England and the Netherlands. The Particular Baptists who formed congregations in London in the 1630s were connected to the Jacob-Lathrop-Jessey Church, a nonseparating Puritan congregation. The decision to reject infant baptism in favor of the baptism of adult believers distinguished Baptists from their Puritan counterparts.

An Evolving History

This study indicates that Baptists have understood and articulated their theology and practice in a variety of ways. While there are clear distinctives shared by most, if not all, Baptist groups, these distinctives are fused in a variety of ways of being Baptist. Those who seek to understand Baptist life and thought might consider the following.

First, any attempt to delineate Baptist distinctives must begin with a confession that any effort to hold certain dynamic, sometimes contradictory, ideals in balance is a noble, but nearly impossible, task. Some Baptist groups were in the vanguard of the modern mission movements, while others rejected missionary activity altogether. Some have supported the ordination of women, while others have rejected it entirely. Some have demanded various degrees of creedal uniformity, while others have eschewed all creeds and confessions.

Biblicism—the attempt to conform to biblical authority and practices—has led some Baptists to modify or relinquish certain views when convinced that others were more scriptural. Biblicism has led some Baptists to modify the list of imperatives regarding missions, revivals, foot washing, and the laying on of hands. Biblicism has created divisions when individuals and churches differed over the meaning and application of specific texts.

Second, the tension between the individual and the community, between conscience and congregationalism, has meant that schism is an inescapable element of Baptist life. The right of the individual to interpret the nature of the church's life and work anticipated controversy as persons and churches pressed specific doctrines to the breaking point. Individuals dissatisfied with one Baptist congregation could simply leave and establish their own church.

Third, Baptists' theological positions remain exceedingly diverse. Like few other denominations, Baptist groups occupy a spectrum that runs from Calvinist to Arminian. General and Particular Baptists and their heirs maintained a variety of common distinctives—regenerate church membership, congregational polity, believer's baptism, and religious liberty—but within a theological framework that was sometimes Calvinist, sometimes Arminian, sometimes a creative and resourceful combination of those and other doctrinal views. Baptist groups that desire to establish a systematic theology can, with legitimacy, claim various theological traditions for defining Baptist dogma.

Fourth, the compelling ideal that informs Baptist identity theologically and pragmatically seems to be the belief that the people can be trusted to interpret Scripture aright, in the context of community and under the guidance of the Holy Spirit.

Fifth, perhaps a more realistic way of understanding Baptists' origins is to suggest that they exhibit an evolving history, shaped by archetypal beliefs but adapting through a variety of social and cultural contexts. While it is important for all religious communions to understand their origins, they are compelled to acknowledge that movements, like families, are never static. The quest for origins may imply that if contemporary Baptists could simply discover and duplicate what the founders believed, they then would be the true representatives of the Baptist ideal. Given Baptist diversity, that would require delineating which type of "original" Baptist one wished to be.

Amidst the search for origins, contemporary Baptist groups reflect the impact of multiple trends and experiences. In North America, for example, many Baptists have been shaped by revivalism, dispensationalism, the social gospel, the civil rights movement, or the megachurch phenomenon. In other countries, communism, socialism, Catholicism, and an abiding minority status have shaped the sense of identity in a variety of ways. For instance, while many Baptists in the former Soviet Union opposed communism, other Baptists in Italy embraced it in their dissent against the Catholic establishment.

Studies of Baptist history must take into account the culture of origins that shaped specific Baptist groups. In short, although Baptists share certain commonalities of belief and practice, many traceable to their seventeenth-century forebears, they also are heirs of their own peculiar historical and social circumstances.

Finally, it is clear that even the writing of Baptist history is not without controversy. In 1890, William Whitsitt, president of the Southern Baptist Theological Seminary, in Louisville, Kentucky, wrote, "I am casting about to begin writing a work on American Baptist History. It is an herculean task, and I must keep it all to myself. Baptist History is a department in which 'the wise man concealeth knowledge.' It is likely I shall not be able to publish the work while I live, but I can write it out in full and make arrangements to publish it after my death, when I shall be out of the reach of bigots and fools."[68]

Those who write and read the elusive history of the Baptists would do well to avoid the fallacy of origins—the belief that one might find authority for contemporary procedures by determining the beliefs and practices of the earliest communities and duplicating them in the present. Even if such replications were possible, Baptist diversity itself requires decisions as to which kind of Baptist tradition might be considered normative. Present and future Baptists are compelled to ask: What kind of Baptists do we wish to be? What historical, theological, spiritual, and communal realities inform the nature of Baptist life in a particular context? Those who wish to discover what it means to be Baptist will be obliged to determine what principles and practices are worth retaining and how best to apply them in the unending transitions of the church and world.

Notes

1. Paul M. Harrison, *Authority and Power in the Free Church Tradition* (Carbondale: Southern Illinois University Press, 1959), 33.
2. David S. Dockery, *The Doctrine of the Bible* (Nashville: Convention Press, 1991), 86–87. Dockery sets forth six variant positions found among biblical inerrantists.
3. Some Baptists in the European country of Georgia administer baptism to infants as a sign of dedication to God.
4. Curtis W. Freeman, James Wm. McClendon Jr., and C. Rosalee Velloso da Silva, *Baptist Roots: A Reader in the Theology of a Christian People* (Valley Forge, Pa.: Judson Press, 1999), 5–6.
5. Daniel Featley, *The Dippers Dipt, or, The Anabaptists Duck'd and Plung'd over Head and Eares, at a Disputation at Southwark* (London: Nicholas Bourne and Richard Royston, 1646), 36. Some of these, particularly the latter two tenets, probably reflect Featley's confusion of the Baptists with many of the Continental Anabaptists.
6. Alvah Hovey, *Restatement of Denominational Principles* (Philadelphia: American Baptist Publication Society, 1892), 3.
7. Ibid., 4.
8. Ibid., 5.
9. Ibid., 8.
10. Ibid.
11. Ibid., 10.
12. Ibid., 11.
13. Other distinctives of the Old Baptists are described in John Watson, *The Old Baptist Test; or, Bible Signs of the Lord's People* (Nashville: Republican Banner Press, 1855).
14. Robert G. Torbet, *A History of the Baptists* (Philadelphia: Judson Press, 1950), 15–34. Torbet omitted the list of distinctives from later editions. See also Bill J. Leonard, ed., *Dictionary of Baptists in America* (Downers Grove, Ill.: InterVarsity Press, 1994), 4. Other Baptist scholars who set forth Baptist distinctives include H. Wheeler Robinson, *The Life and Faith of the Baptists* (London: Methuen, 1927), 1–19; Walter B. Shurden, *The Baptist Identity: Four Fragile Freedoms* (Macon, Ga.: Smyth & Helwys, 1993).

15. William Brackney, "'Commonly (Though Falsely) Called': Reflections on the Search for Baptist Identity," in *Perspectives in Churchmanship: Essays in Honor of Robert G. Torbet*, ed. David Scholer (Macon, Ga.: Mercer University Press, 1986), 71.

16. Ibid., 80.

17. Ibid., 79–80.

18. Eric Ohlmann, "The Essence of the Baptists," in Scholer, ed., *Perspectives in Churchmanship*, 99.

19. Ibid.

20. Ibid.

21. Karen Smith, "The Covenant Life of Some Eighteenth-Century Calvinistic Baptists in Hampshire and Wiltshire," in *Pilgrim Pathways: Essays in Baptist History in Honour of B. R. White*, ed. William H. Brackney and Paul S. Fiddes (Macon, Ga.: Mercer University Press, 1999), 165.

22. Paul S. Fiddes, "Theology and a Baptist Way of Community," in *Doing Theology in a Baptist Way*, ed. Paul S. Fiddes (Oxford: Whitley, 1999), 25.

23. Edwin S. Gaustad, ed., *Baptists, the Bible, Church Order and the Churches: Essays from Foundations, a Baptist Journal of History and Theology* (New York: Arno Press, 1980), 30.

24. L. Russ Bush and Tom Nettles, *Baptists and the Bible* (Chicago: Moody Press, 1980), 18.

25. Harrison, *Authority and Power*, 21.

26. Ibid., 22.

27. Ibid., 23.

28. Gaustad, ed., *Baptists*, 31.

29. Ibid., 34.

30. Ibid., 34.

31. B. R. White, *The English Separatist Tradition* (London: Oxford University Press, 1971), 137–38.

32. Ibid.

33. Walter B. Shurden, "I Am the Bible in Baptist History," *Baptist History and Heritage* 19 (July 1984): 4–6.

34. In William L. Lumpkin, *Baptists Confessions of Faith* (Chicago: Judson Press, 1959), 232.

35. During the latter part of the twentieth century, some Baptists debated issues of biblical inerrancy with particular vehemence. The debate is evident in numerous volumes, including Bush and Nettles, *Baptists and the Bible*; Ralph H. Elliott, The "Genesis Controversy" and *Continuity in Southern Baptist Chaos: A Eulogy for a Great Tradition* (Macon, Ga.: Mercer University Press, 1992); Robison B. James, ed., *The Unfettered Word: Southern Baptists Confront the Authority-Inerrancy Question* (Waco, Tex.: Word, 1987); Robison B. James and David S. Dockery, eds., *Beyond the Impasse? Scripture, Interpretation, and Theology in Baptist Life* (Nashville: Broadman, 1992).

36. Lumpkin, *Baptist Confessions of Faith*, 232.

37. Debates over biblical authority and conscience were particularly evident in Southern Baptist controversies in the latter part of the twentieth century. See Paul A. Basden, ed., *Has Our Theology Changed? Southern Baptist Thought Since 1845* (Nashville: Broadman & Holman, 1994); Shurden, *The Baptist Identity*.

38. Henry Cook, *What Baptists Stand For* (London: Kingsgate Press, 1947) (cited in Brian Stanley, "Planting Self-Governing Churches," *Baptist Quarterly* 34 [October 1992]: 66).

39. Christine Leigh Heyrman, *Southern Cross: The Beginnings of the Bible Belt* (New York: Knopf, 1997), 97.

40. Lumpkin, *Baptist Confessions of Faith*, 316.

41. Ibid., 226.

42. Ibid., 317.

43. Ibid., 321.

44. Ibid., 321–22.

45. Ibid., 293.

46. David Benedict, *A General History of the Baptist Denomination in America* (New York: Colby, 1848), 652; Steve McNeely, "Early Baptists in the South: The Formation of a 'Folk Religion,'" *Quarterly Review* 9 (October–December 1974): 71.

47. Lumpkin, *Baptist Confessions of Faith*, 392–93. The confession was revised in 2000 and has been used more uniformly by the Southern Baptist Convention.

48. Ibid., 16–17.

49. Thomas Helwys, *A Short Declaration of the Mystery of Iniquity* (1611/1612), ed. Richard Groves (Macon, Ga.: Mercer University Press, 1998).

50. Lumpkin, *Baptist Confessions of Faith*, 331.

51. Sydnor L. Stealey, ed., *A Baptist Treasury* (New York: Crowell, 1958), 100.

52. W. Morgan Patterson, *Baptist Successionism: A Critical View* (Valley Forge, Pa.: Judson Press, 1969), 19–20.

53. Cited in James Leo Garrett, "Restitution and Dissent among Early English Baptists: Part 1," *Baptist History and Heritage* 12 (October 1977): 200.

54. Albert H. Newman, *A History of Anti-Pedobaptism from the Rise of Pedobaptism to A.D. 1609* (Philadelphia: American Baptist Publication Society, 1897), 1–14; see Garrett, "Restitution and Dissent," 202.

55. Ernest A. Payne, "Contacts between Mennonites and Baptists," *Foundations* 4 (1961): 41.

56. Glen H. Stassen, "Anabaptist Influence in the Origin of the Particular Baptists," *Mennonite Quarterly Review* 36 (October 1962): 324–33; William R. Estep, *The Anabaptist Story* (Nashville: Broadman, 1963), 197–222.

57. James D. Mosteller, "Baptists and Anabaptists II," *The Chronicle* 20 (July 1957): 109–11.

58. Estep, *The Anabaptist Story*, 218.

59. James D. Mosteller, "John Smyth and the Dutch Mennonites," *The Chronicle* 20 (July 1957): 112.
60. James R. Coggins, "The Theological Positions of John Smyth," *Baptist Quarterly* 30 (1984): 254.
61. Stassen, "Anabaptist Influence," 322–48; idem, "Opening Menno Simons's *Foundation-Book* and Finding the Father of Baptist Origins Alongside the Mother—Calvinist Congregationalism," *Baptist History and Heritage* 33 (spring 1998): 34.
62. Stassen, "Menno Simons's *Foundation-Book,*" 43. Stassen's views have been challenged in James M. Renihan, "An Examination of the Possible Influence of Menno Simons' *Foundation Book* upon the Particular Baptist Confession of 1644," *American Baptist Quarterly* 15 (September 1996): 190–207.
63. Glen H. Stassen, "Revisioning Baptist Identity by Naming Our Origin and Character Rightly," *Baptist History and Heritage* 33 (spring 1998): 52–53.
64. Winthrop Hudson, "Baptists Were Not Anabaptists," *The Chronicle* (October 1953): 171.
65. Ibid., 171.
66. Ibid., 176.
67. White, *The English Separatist Tradition,* 164.
68. Thomas R. McKibbens, "The Life, Writings, and Influence of Morgan Edwards," *Quarterly Review* 11 (January–March 1976): 68.

Chapter 2
Baptist Beginnings: The Historical Context

The Reformation Churches

Whatever else may be said of them, Baptists are a Reformation people. They were born of ideas and incidents that flourished in Europe and Britain in the great religious and political upheavals of the sixteenth century. To say that the Reformation began with Martin Luther (1483–1546) is not to suggest that he was the first to call for changes in Catholic dogma and practice, but to acknowledge Luther's seminal work as controversialist and churchman, theologian and prophet. Luther built on the work of innumerable reformists who preceded him. These include the contributions of British theologian John Wycliffe (ca.1330–1384) and the Bohemian preacher John Huss (ca.1372–1415). In their respective regions these individuals challenged papal authority, promoted a stronger national church, and questioned the doctrine of transubstantiation as the theological definition of Christ's presence in the Eucharist.

The Lutheran Reformation
Luther's contribution to the Reformation began with his opposition to certain practices of the Catholic church of his day, specifically the selling of indulgences and what he viewed as an attempt to commercialize divine grace. With the declaration of his famous Ninety-Five Theses in Wittenberg in 1517, Luther challenged not only the immediate sale of indulgences, but also the very authority of the pope to offer remission of sin on earth or in purgatory. This theological challenge to papal authority, combined with the German political dissatisfaction toward the pope's temporal claims, created confrontations that brought about Luther's excommunication in 1521 and the first of several schisms in the *corpus Christianum*, that unity of church and state which had dominated European life for centuries.

Luther's legacy to Baptists and other heirs of the Reformation included the three classic concepts of *sola fide, sola scriptura,* and *sola gratia*—faith alone, Scripture alone, and grace alone. His concern for the primary authority of Scripture, the priesthood of all believers, and the evangelical dimension of faith had profound impact on the Baptist understanding of the nature of Christian belief. Luther continued to link infant baptism and citizenship, extending the medieval relationship between church and state—a concept that would be rejected by Anabaptists and Baptists alike. While eschewing transubstantiation, Luther retained the idea of Christ's real presence in the Lord's Supper.

Ulrich Zwingli

Martin Luther was not the only sixteenth-century religious leader to challenge the theology and practice of the Catholic establishment. In Zurich, Switzerland, a priest named Ulrich Zwingli (1484–1531) led a movement that turned that canton (city-state) to Protestantism. Zwingli repudiated indulgences, transubstantiation, and papal authority. He taught that the Lord's Supper was not a transformation of bread and wine into Christ's body and blood, but a memorial through which the believing community recalled Christ's sacrifice for the sins of the world. Many Baptists later affirmed Zwingli's theology of the Lord's Supper. Like Luther, Zwingli retained the practice of infant baptism and its relationship to citizenship. As Zwingli understood it, to relinquish the baptism of infants would mean the loss of the moral and spiritual fabric in both church and society.

Radical Reformers: The Swiss Brethren

Zwingli's views on infant baptism brought him into conflict with certain individuals who initially had supported his efforts and ideals. These Swiss Brethren studied with Zwingli and agreed with his renunciation of the Roman Catholic Church. Yet they differed with him on infant baptism, and they insisted that the New Testament knew only a believers' church. Baptism was to be given only to those who had repented and professed faith in Christ—an action impossible for infants. They rejected the unity of baptism and citizenship—a belief that their critics saw as both heresy and treason. These practices led their detractors to label the group *Wiedertäufer*, or Anabaptists (rebaptizers).

Persecution was swift and sure. Many of their early leaders, including Conrad Grebel (d. 1526), Felix Manz (1498?–1526), and George Blaurock (1491–1529) were executed or died in prison. Manz was drowned in Zurich's Limmat River by order of the city council—an act that made him the first Protestant to be martyred by Protestants. Many men and women died in continuing persecution.[1]

Militant Revolts

The Radical Reformation was also associated with political unrest and armed rebellions that occurred in sixteenth-century Europe. In Germany, Thomas Müntzer (ca.1490–1525) scorned infant baptism, the established churches (both Lutheran and Catholic), and the exploitation of the peasants. He was killed in the Peasants' Revolt of 1525.

Anabaptist views also were promoted by the millennialists Jan of Leyden and Jan Mattys, who led the takeover of the German town of Munster in 1535. Lutheran and Catholic princes joined in recapturing the city, and the rebels were executed. The scandal of Munster was ever after used to undermine the reputations of Anabaptists, and Catholics and Protestants alike dismissed them as religious and political anarchists.

Balthasar Hübmaier

Balthasar Hübmaier (1480?–1527), an Anabaptist theologian martyred in 1527, wrote an important treatise on church and state in 1524. Entitled *Concerning Heretics and Those*

Who Burn Them, it suggested that God was the sole judge of the religious decisions of every individual. The state, Hübmaier believed, had no right to punish either the heretic or the atheist. He wrote, "We should pray and hope for repentance, as long as man lives in this misery.... A Turk or a heretic is not convinced by our act, either with the sword or with fire, but only with patience and prayer; and so we should await with patience the judgment of God."[2] Hübmaier's libertarian views moved beyond mere toleration to radical religious freedom. Such ideas later were echoed in the seventeenth century by Baptists Thomas Helwys in England and Roger Williams in the American colonies.

The Mennonites

The Swiss Brethren were only one segment of the Radical Reformation. Perhaps the best known and most enduring of the Anabaptist groups are the Mennonites, who took their name from the Dutch preacher Menno Simons (1496–1561). Simons promoted Anabaptist dogmas with particular emphasis on church discipline, discipleship, refusing oaths, and passive resistance. He promulgated a doctrine known as "celestial flesh," which suggested that Christ did not receive any physical attributes or sinful nature but passed through Mary like water through a tube. The Mennonites divided into numerous subgroups spread throughout the Netherlands and around Europe.

Anabaptist Beliefs

As already noted, debates continue about the impact of the Anabaptist tradition on the people called Baptists. Because of that discussion, it is important to survey certain basic Anabaptist, particularly Mennonite, beliefs. Like Luther, the Anabaptists affirmed the authority of the Bible, the priesthood of all believers, and the importance of faith alone for salvation. They rejected the claims of the Roman Catholic Church regarding councils, popes, and bishops. They suggested that the church is composed only of true believers, those who can testify to an experience of grace through repentance and faith. This profession is followed by baptism—a rite administered to believers only. The church is governed by the authority of Christ passed on to the community of believers.

Anabaptists stressed the importance of Christian discipleship—following Christ in daily life and devotion. Discipleship involved commitment to pacifism, resistance to taking oaths, opposition to capital punishment, and refusal to serve as agents of the state. They generally advocated complete religious liberty for heretic and atheist alike.

John Calvin and the Church in Geneva

In Geneva, Switzerland, the Reformation took shape through the leadership of John (or Jean) Calvin (1509–1564). Born in France, Calvin was exiled from Paris in 1535 because of his participation in certain Protestant activities. Traveling through Geneva in 1536, he was compelled to remain by the fiery preacher William Farel (1489–1565), who had introduced Reformation ideas into the city. From that day forward, Calvin's life was entwined with Geneva, a city that became a seedbed of the Reformed faith. Calvin's written works included commentaries, sermons, and other scholarly writings. His seminal work, *Institutes of the Christian Religion,* was first published in 1536.

Calvin's ideas were grounded in the Reformation concepts of *sola scriptura* and *sola fide.*

His training was shaped by Christian humanism and its concern to return to the classic sources of Scripture, literature, and history. Calvinist orthodoxy included doctrines of the total depravity of all humanity, God's unconditional election of certain persons for salvation, Christ's sacrificial atonement for the sins of the elect, the power of grace to bring the elect to salvation, and the perseverance of all who receive God's grace. Undergirding these doctrines was the sovereignty of God in all things.

Calvin retained infant baptism as a sign of the covenant with God and as the Christian equivalent of Jewish circumcision. His approach to the Lord's Supper stressed the spiritual presence of Christ in the elements as a means of grace. Some early Baptists used similar language in describing the Lord's Supper. Likewise, Calvin supported the close connection between the church and the state, without which, he believed, moral and spiritual chaos would prevail. The Genevan experiment became a model for many Protestants, among them the Scot John Knox (1513?–1572).

Jacob Arminius: Freedom of the Will

Calvin's doctrines of election and predestination were not without controversy. In the early seventeenth century, a Dutch theologian named Jacob Arminius (1560–1609) offered a response to Calvin's views, challenging the dogmas of limited atonement, unconditional election, perseverance of the saints, and other Calvinist dicta. He suggested that while all persons were inherently sinful, prevenient, or enabling, grace made possible the exercise of human free will in the process of salvation. Through enabling grace, sinners could freely choose to accept God's gift of salvation. Christ's death on the cross was for all human beings. All persons were potentially elected and could actualize election through repentance and faith. Since all could freely accept salvation, they also could determine to fall away from grace along the way. In 1610, Arminius's views were affirmed by some forty-six Dutch Protestant pastors in a document entitled the "Remonstrance." Arminian theology was evident in elements of seventeenth-century Anglicanism as well as the General Baptists in Amsterdam and London. It also was the theological position affirmed by John Wesley and the Methodists in the eighteenth century. The Synod of Dort (1619), a gathering dominated by Dutch Calvinists, condemned Arminian dogmas.

The Anglican Church

The English decision to break with the Roman Catholic Church in the 1530s was the culmination of a long and stormy relationship that began in 597 when the Benedictine monk Augustine founded a church at Canterbury and became Britain's first bishop. Canterbury became the center of Roman Christianity in Britain, and, after Thomas Becket's martyrdom in 1170, its most popular shrine. Becket's conflict with his friend and monarch Henry II over church-state prerogatives was but one of numerous controversies that challenged the power of the pope to control matters of church and state in Britain. These contentions reached their climax when Pope Clement VII refused the request of the Tudor monarch Henry VIII (1491–1547) for a divorce from his wife, the Spanish princess Catherine of Aragon (d. 1536). Henry's efforts to secure a male heir led him to divorce Catherine, break with Rome, and reconstitute the English church with the king as "the only supreme head in earth of the Church of England" *(Ecclesia Anglicana)*.

Thomas Cranmer (1489–1556), whom Henry appointed archbishop of Canterbury, strengthened Anglicanism through the publication of the *Book of Common Prayer,* the basic sourcebook of Anglican prayer and worship to this day.

This Reformation period also witnessed the appearance of the so-called Anabaptist heresy in England. While certain individuals may have been proponents of actual Anabaptist views, many religious nonconformists were tarred with the Anabaptist name, since it was used as a catchall term for religious dissenters.

Henry was succeeded in 1547 by his ailing son, Edward VI, who ruled only until 1553. A minor, he was aided successively by two "Protectors," the dukes of Northumberland and Warwick, both men of strong Protestant sentiments. The editions of the *Book of Common Prayer* published in 1549 and 1552 reflected strong Protestant sentiments.

At Edward's death, his elder sister Mary Tudor (1516–1558) acceded to the throne, bringing her Catholicism with her. The daughter of Catherine of Aragon, she was determined to restore Catholic control of the English church. Her efforts contributed to the death of some three hundred Protestants, including Archbishop Cranmer. The long-term results of Mary's efforts were less than successful, and her reign was relatively brief.

When Mary died in 1558, Elizabeth I (1533–1603), the daughter of Henry and Anne Boleyn, ascended the throne and began efforts to restore Protestantism. A master politician, Elizabeth I sought to make Anglicanism a *via media,* or middle way, between Protestant theology and Catholic liturgy. She also changed the ecclesiastical title of the British monarch from "supreme head" to "supreme governor" of the church on earth in England, in an effort to avoid offending those who claimed Christ or the pope as head of the church on earth.

During Elizabeth's forty-five-year reign, her policies created conflicts not only with Catholics but also with many Protestants who felt that she had retained too many "trappings of popery." These Puritans refused to conform to certain requirements regarding clergy vestments, certain rites such as kneeling at communion or making the sign of the cross, and other outward signs of religious conformity. Their attempts to purify the church led to controversy, even persecution, from the Anglican establishment and the English crown.

Elizabeth died childless in 1603 and was succeeded by her second cousin James Stuart (1566–1625). The son of Mary Stuart (the Scottish queen executed in 1587 for treason by her cousin Elizabeth), he was heir to both the Scottish and English thrones. Educated by Scottish Protestants, James initially was welcomed by Puritans who hoped that he would be sympathetic to their concerns. They greeted his arrival with petitions for a modified prayer book, fewer liturgical regulations, and a new translation of the Bible. Although James rejected their other suggestions, he did authorize a new biblical translation, and the King James Version appeared in 1611. He affirmed his commitment to the episcopal system with the simple declaration "No bishop, no king!" and instigated actions against those who did not conform to the regulations.

At James's death in 1625, his son Charles I (d. 1649) became king. Even less tolerant than his father, Charles appointed William Laud (1573–1645) as archbishop of Canterbury and charged him with enforcing Anglican uniformity. Laud was a zealot in this cause, and he persecuted nonconformists so rigorously that multitudes of exiles fled to Europe and America in what came to be known as the "Laudian persecution."

Puritan Subgroups

The Puritans were not a homogeneous group, and they divided over questions such as the relationship with Anglicanism, the nature of church government, and the observance of New Testament practices. Some "nonseparating" Puritans continued to affirm that although the Church of England was a true church of Christ, it needed purification from its last vestiges of Roman Catholicism. They wanted a prayer book that was less restrictive and less Roman. Many desired to replace the episcopal system (a church governed by bishops) with other types of ecclesiastical government, but they could not agree on the specific form. Some preferred a Presbyterian system in which clergy and laity shared governance through a presbytery composed of pastors, teachers, deacons, and elders. Others, known as Independents, favored a system in which the congregation was the primary source of authority and elected pastors (or elders) and deacons as leaders. Another group, known as Separatists, insisted that the Church of England was a false church, with no possibility of reform. They called true believers to abandon Anglicanism. In *A Treatise for Reformation without Tarrying for Anie*, published in 1580, Separatist leader Robert Browne (1550?–1633) defined the church as a body of believers bound to Christ by means of a covenant. Through Christ's authority, the congregation selects its leaders and institutes its ministries. The persecution of Separatists in England forced Browne to flee to the Netherlands and led to the execution of Separatist leaders John Greenwood and Henry Barrow in 1593 under a charge of sedition. Browne himself later returned to the Church of England, but Separatism continued to influence Protestants in England and America.

These events indicate that the world into which the Baptists came was characterized by religious upheaval, ecclesial innovation, and a quest for the "true church." Baptists were a significant part of this religious tumult and the early stages of Protestant denominationalism.

John Smyth and Baptist Beginnings

Although John Smyth was reared in the Church of England, he "became Puritan, Separatist, and then a Baptist Separatist," and he ended his days seeking admission to the Mennonites.[3] Smyth (1570?–1612) graduated from Cambridge and was ordained as an Anglican, but he was one with Puritan sentiments. He was appointed "City Preacher" in Lincoln, where his frustrations with Anglicanism escalated. Smyth left the Church of England in 1606 for a Separatist congregation at Gainsborough. One participant described the church's purpose: "As the Lord's free people, they joined themselves by a covenant of the Lord into a church estate, in the fellowship of the gospel, to walk in all His ways, made known or to be made known unto them."[4]

As the Gainsborough Separatist community grew, the group divided, and one segment moved to Leyden, in the Netherlands, under the leadership of John Robinson and William Brewster. Certain members of that congregation eventually embarked for the New World on the *Mayflower* in 1620. They settled at Plymouth, and are known in American history as the Pilgrims.

The persecution of religious nonconformists in England led another faction of the Gainsborough church to migrate to Amsterdam in 1608. The trip probably was funded by John

Smyth's friend and associate Thomas Helwys. Educated in London, Helwys (1550?–1616?) was one of the lesser gentry and was a person of some financial means. With Smyth, he also became a leader of the Separatist congregation. After arriving in Amsterdam, Smyth and his company worshiped for a time with the Separatist Congregation of English expatriates led by Francis Johnson (1562–1618), Smyth's former tutor at Cambridge. Johnson's little band was sometimes known as the "Ancient Church" because of its concern to observe the teachings and practices of the New Testament community. B. R. White contended that Smyth and Helwys arrived in Amsterdam as "convinced" Separatists in their polity and Calvinists in their theology.[5] If so, they would soon change, even moving toward Arminianism.

White proposed that both General and Particular Baptist groups "inherited" many of their views from the Separatists. These included churches founded on the basis of a covenant as well as congregational appointment of leaders as "prescribed in his Word." Congregational authority enabled the community to exercise discipline and act under the authority of Christ.[6]

From the beginning, Smyth objected to many of Johnson's Separatist beliefs. These included the abolition of books, Scriptures, and psalms from public worship, the use of a single pastoral elder in place of ruling elders, and a congregational treasury to which only believers were to contribute.[7]

Concerning the use of Scripture in public worship, Smyth suggested that the Word of God should be free and spiritual, not limited to translated texts. He wrote, "We hold that the worship of the new testament properly so called is spirituall proceeding originally from the heart: & that reading out of a booke (though a lawfull ecclesiastical action) is no part of spirituall worship, but rather the invention of the man of sin it being substituted for a part of spiritual worship."[8] He objected not only to the reading of Scripture without comment, as practiced in the Church of England, but also to the use of biblical translations in worship.[9]

Smyth concluded, "All the arguments used against the reading of homilies & prayers may be applyed against the reading of translations in tyme of worship."[10] He listed ten "reasons proving the Originals [of Scripture] not to be given as helps before the eye in worship." He maintained that Christ's coming signified "that ceremony of bookworship, or the ministerie of the lettre was now expired, & finished."[11] Spiritual worship went beyond the public reading of books because, among other things, "upon the day of Pentecost fiery cloven tongues did appear, not fiery cloven bookes."[12] These declarations illustrate Smyth's radical biblicism and his reaction against the liturgical practices prescribed in the *Book of Common Prayer*.

Smyth asserted that only members of the congregation should contribute to its financial support, and no funds should be received from nonbelievers. His theology seems to have been in constant flux as he searched for clearer revelations from the Bible.

In a 1609 treatise entitled *The Character of the Beast, or The False Constitution of the Church*, Smyth's Baptist views were first evident. Here he set forth two propositions: first, that "infants are not to be baptized"; and second, that "Antichristians converted are to be admitted into the true Church by baptism."[13] The church, he said, was a community of believers who had signified their faith by baptism. Infants could not exercise faith and thus were not proper baptismal candidates. Since infant baptism was outside the biblical norm, Smyth declared that all churches that perpetuated it were false.[14]

As his theology evolved, Smyth rejected the idea of hereditary guilt, or original sin. He concluded that infants were born into a state of innocence that did not require immediate baptism. They would not be damned should they die in infancy.[15]

Ultimately, Smyth moved toward believer's baptism and the formation of a new religious community. He affirmed the right of the congregation to exercise authority received from Christ to elect its officers and establish its mission in covenant relationship. He became convinced that baptism should be given only to those who manifested repentance from sin and faith in Christ. Around 1609, he concluded that the little band should be reconstituted as a true church of Christ on the basis of faith and believer's baptism.

In a classic passage, A. C. Underwood described the beginning of the new ecclesial community: "Pastor and deacons laid down their office, the church disbanded or avowed itself no church, and all stood as private individuals, unbaptized. All being equal, Smyth proposed that Helwys their social leader should baptize them, but he deferred to his spiritual leader. Smyth baptized himself, then baptized Helwys and the others. The mode was apparently trine affusion, pouring water three times in the name of the Father, the Son and the Holy Ghost. The first Baptist church in the world was born with John Smyth's self-baptism."[16]

Many were scandalized by this self-baptism. B. R. White observed, "When the news got out it caused, as Smyth must have known it would, a chorus of shocked horror erupted from every part of the theological spectrum from Episcopalian to Separatist." Separatist Richard Clifton, Smyth's contemporary, challenged, "Resolve me how you can baptize yourself into the Church being out of it, yea and where there was no church."[17] Smyth responded that the absence of a true church required a radical act—a self-baptism—in order to begin the church over again.

Smyth's restless spirit was not sated by his self-baptism. He entered into conversations with the Waterlanders, a Mennonite community that had practiced believer's baptism since the sixteenth century. He concluded that his own self-baptism was invalid and requested membership among the Mennonites, convinced that they had a baptismal tradition worthy of the New Testament church. Although he died awaiting admission, others of his flock became Mennonites. Thomas Helwys and others retained their baptism and their Baptist commitments.

Smyth's understanding of the nature of religious authority illustrates something of his quest for truth. On the one hand, he appeared to be an uncompromising biblicist, even literalist, in his effort to follow the teachings of the Scriptures. He wrote, "The holy Scriptures viz, the Originalls Hebrew & Greek are given by Divine Inspiration & in their first donation were without error most perfect & therefore Canonicall."[18] On the other hand, as James Leo Garrett observed, Smyth believed that "regenerate persons receive direct inward revelation from the Father, the Son, and the Holy Spirit without biblical mediation and that for the regenerate such revelation from the Trinity makes the Bible less essential."[19] His biblicism took him through many Protestant communities in a search for the fullest revelation available.

Thomas Helwys and the General Baptists

Thomas Helwys and others disagreed with Smyth's decision to join the Mennonites. They excommunicated Smyth and declared themselves to be the true church.[20] Returning to

London in 1612, they founded the first Baptist church in England at Spitalfield. Their Arminian theology and its emphasis on Christ's general atonement led to their designation as General Baptists.

Helwys was not a sophisticated theologian. Nonetheless, his advocacy of religious freedom was unique for his era. His work *A Short Declaration of the Mystery of Iniquity,* written in 1612, was the first statement of absolute religious liberty to be written in English. It was addressed to King James I, who, as Helwys noted, "hath no power over ye immortall soules of his subjects, to make lawes & ordinances for them, and to set spirituall Lords over them."[21] In perhaps his most famous passage, Helwys wrote, "Let the King judge, it not most equal that men should choose their religion themselves, seeing they only must stand themselves before the judgment seat of god to answer for themselves, when it shall be no excuse for them to say, We were commanded or compelled to be of this religion by the king or by them that had authority from him."[22]

He maintained that religious liberty was an absolute right not only for Christian dissenters and nonconformists, but also for believer and unbeliever, for heretic and atheist alike. Helwys went beyond John Smyth, who suggested, "The magistrate is not by virtue of his office to meddle in religion, or matters of conscience … but to leave Christian religion free."[23] As Richard Groves observed, "Helwys argued that religious liberty must be available to everyone: 'Let them be heretics, Turks, Jews, or whatsoever, it appertains not to the earthly power to punish them in the least measure.'"[24]

In 1615, Helwys and his congregation published an unsigned treatise entitled *Persecution for Religion Judged and Condemned,* which set forth certain Baptist ideals, including their belief "that every man has a right to judge for himself in matters of religion, and that to persecute any on that account is illegal and antichristian."[25] They permitted the taking of oaths and rejected other "strange opinions" held by the Anabaptists, with whom they were often equated. Helwys's views, published and sent to the king, led to his imprisonment in London's Newgate Prison. He died there, probably in 1616.

Leonard Busher

Little is known of the life of Leonard Busher, another of Helwys's colleagues. W. T. Whitley suggested that he was Dutch, that he was a companion of Smyth and Helwys in Amsterdam, and that he was naturalized on moving to England. His treatise *Religions Peace: or, A Plea for Liberty of Conscience* (1614) reaffirmed his loyalty to king and country.[26]

Like similar Baptist documents, the treatise was addressed to King James I. Busher wrote, "No king nor bishop can, or is able to command faith; That is the gift of God, who worketh in us both the will and the deed of his own good pleasure (Eph 2.8)."[27] He noted, "And as kings and bishops cannot command the wind, so they cannot command faith; … You may force men to church against their consciences, but they will believe as they did afore, when they come there; for God giveth a blessing only to his own ordinance, and abhorreth antichrist's."[28] He warned, "Bishops should know, that error and heresy cannot be killed by the fire and sword, but by the word and Spirit of God."[29]

Busher set out seventeen reasons for opposing the persecution of religious dissenters. For one thing, it cost the nation many of its best citizens. He wrote, "For through forcing men to church by persecution, the true-hearted subjects are forced out of the land, and out of the world. Some [are] banished, others burned, hanged, and imprisoned to death."[30] Persecution was a negative witness to non-Christians, undermining the possibility of their conversion. Furthermore, it encouraged them—"Jews, Turks, and Pagans"—to persecute Christians.[31] Busher concluded with a call for freedom of the press and an admonition to the government: "Again, therefore, I humbly pray his majesty and parliament, to repeal and make void all popish laws and canons, and to see the moral and judicial law of God both firmly enacte and carefully practised, after the mind of Christ."[32] Busher's work further illustrates the Baptist commitment to complete religious liberty.

Thomas Helwys: Another Treatise

Thomas Helwys is the supposed author of a lesser-known but equally forthright pamphlet written in two segments. One section of *Persecution for Religion Judged and Condemned* was published in 1615 and the other added in 1620. The treatise was republished in 1827 with a preface by the Baptist historian Joseph Ivimey.[33] The essay itself is a dialogue between two characters, Anti-Christian and Christian. It declares that monarchs (states) cannot compel faith by means of persecution and that the English had rejected the "bloody religion" of the papists only to replace it with their own violent religion.[34] God alone would punish heresy and immorality. The work concludes, "The whole New Testament throughout in all the doctrines and practices of Christ and his disciples, teach no such thing as compelling men by persecution and afflictions to obey the Gospel, but the direct contrary."[35] This treatise illustrates another effort by Baptists to address the role of religion in the public sphere.

John Murton and Arminianism

John Murton (d. 1625?), another of the early General Baptists, extended the call for religious liberty in a 1615 work entitled *Objections Answered by Way of Dialogue*. Baptized by Smyth, Murton returned to England with Helwys and was a leader in the Spitalfield church. In 1620, he published *A Description of What God Hath Predestinated Concerning Man*. It illustrates the Arminian views of the early General Baptists.

Murton began by noting that the Council (Synod) of Dort had affirmed Calvin's doctrine of predestination as infallible orthodoxy. Yet, unlike Catholics, Protestants believe that councils can err and "therefore ought to be no further beleeued, then euery mans Conscience can iudge them to accord with the meaning of God in the Scriptures."[36] All persons who received God's "Grace by Faith in his Sonne, them, in this his eternall Predestination, he elected."[37] Concerning divine foreknowledge, Murton commented, "Though God fore-seeth all thinges, yet doth he not will all thinges, for his foresight doth extend both to good and evil, but his will is only of things that be good, as God fore-seeth the death of a sinner, and the cause thereof namely his wickedness, but he willeth it not."[38] He contended, "A man having true Grace may fall away, even as Esau lost his earthly inheritance which he had right unto; so may the Saints loose their heavenly inheritance which they have right unto."[39]

Murton and other General Baptists articulated an Arminian theology that challenged the Calvinism of English Puritanism. They also linked theological diversity to religious liberty for believer and nonbeliever alike. Mere toleration of dissent was not sufficient.

Baptist Identity: Six Principle Baptists

By 1615, Baptists in England were attempting to distinguish themselves from the Continental Anabaptists, with whom they often were linked. They also delineated their own identity, distinct from that of other Protestant communions. Thomas Crosby concluded that these Baptists affirmed the "magistracy to be God's ordinance, were willing to take an oath, dismissed the papist idea that excommunicated monarchs could be murdered by their subjects, acknowledged that Christ took the flesh of Mary [Mennonites claimed he did not], and rejected the association with 'Anabaptists.'"[40]

By the middle of the seventeenth century, many General Baptists had accepted a doctrinal statement based on the "Six Principles" taken from Hebrews 6:1-2. The passage reads: "Therefore leaving the principles of the doctrine of Christ, let us go on unto perfection; not laying again the foundation of repentance from dead works, and of faith toward God, of the doctrine of baptisms, and of laying on of hands, and of resurrection of the dead, and of eternal judgment" (KJV). These doctrines were affirmed by Particular Baptists as early as 1644. In 1655, John Griffith published *God's Oracle and Christ's Doctrine, or The Six Principles of the Christian Religion*. William Lumpkin contended that this work became "the textbook of the Six-Principle churches."[41]

Of special importance to the Six Principle churches was the practice of the laying on of hands, administered to all the newly baptized and also to those set aside for specific ministry in the church. Not all accepted the Six Principle approach, and the General Assembly (a gathering of General Baptist churches) often divided over those issues. During the 1660s, some compromise was reached by utilizing dual confessions: the General Baptist confession of 1660 and the Six Principles taken from the book of Hebrews. That agreement was short-lived, however, and the resulting schism led to the formation of a separate assembly of English Six Principle Baptists in 1690.[42]

Particular Baptists: Beginnings

Calvinistic Baptists in England developed from the Independent/Congregational movement as represented in an Independent London congregation known variously as the Jacob-Lathrop-Jessey (-Barebone) Church, in honor of its first pastors. Henry Jacob (1563–1624) graduated from Oxford and was ordained in the Anglican Church. He traveled to Middelburg, Holland, in the 1580s, where apparently he met Separatists Robert Browne and Francis Johnson. On his return to England in 1603, Jacob was thrown "in the Clink," a local prison, for his nonconformist sentiments. On his release, he petitioned the king for greater tolerance, but to no avail. He then returned to the Netherlands, this time to Leyden, where he met John Robinson, leader of the Separatist/Pilgrim congregation.[43]

Back in England in 1616, Jacob helped constitute a congregation in Southwark. After a time of prayer and fasting, they "joyned both hands each with other Brother and stood in a Ringwise; ... Then they Covenanted togeather to walk in all Gods Ways as he had revealed or should make known to them."[44]

The new congregation then ordained Jacob as pastor. Jacob served "about 9 years" (probably 1616–1624/5) and then departed for Virginia.[45] The congregation then chose John Lathrop, or Lathorp (d. 1653), as pastor, and he served "about 9 years to their great comfort." During this period, several members broke away from the church over the question of infant baptism. In 1632, increased persecution led to the imprisonment of Lathrop and several other church members, some for up to two years.[46] Lathrop was succeeded by Henry Jessey (1601–1663), another minister of Congregational sentiments.

The Particular Baptists seem to have developed from two distinct segments of the Jacob-Lathrop-Jessey Church. One was served by Jessey, the other by a Puritan Independent named Praise-God Barebone. Church records describe the division as it occurred around 1633: "There haveing been much discussing these denying Truth of ye parish Churches, & ye Church being now become so large yt it might be prejudicial, these following desired dismission that they might become an Entire Church, & further ye comunion of those Churches in Order amongst themselves, which at last was granted to them & and performed Sept 12. 1633."[47] The new group included some nineteen or twenty persons, among them Richard Blunt and Samuel Eaton, soon to become leaders of the church's Baptist contingent. The two were among those who would soon receive "a further baptism."[48]

The "Kiffin Manuscript" details the beginnings of the Baptist segment of the church. Attributed to Baptist William Kiffin (b. 1616), it describes the division of the church (1633–1638) and the decision of some fifty-three of the members in the two different groups—Samuel Eaton's and John Spilsbury's—to accept "dipping" as the biblical mode for baptism. It suggests that these individuals "believed that baptism was not rightly administered to infants, so they look'd upon the baptism they had received in that age as invalid: whereupon most or all of them received a new baptism."[49]

A 1638 entry reads, "These also being of ye same Judgment with Sam. Eaton & desiring to depart & not to be censured our interest in them was remitted wth Prayer made in their behalf June 8th 1638. they having first forsaken Us and Joyned with Mr Spilsbury."[50] Initially, this church was distinct from Eaton's congregation.

Ultimately, the group decided to pursue believer's baptism:

> 1640. 3rd Mo: The Church became two by mutal consent just half being with Mr P. Barboyne, & ye other half with Mr H. Jessey Mr Richard Blunt with him being convinced of Baptism yet also it ought to be by diping ye Body into ye Water, resembling Burial & rising again. 2 Col: 2.12 Rom: 6.4. Had sober conference about in ye Church, & then with some of the forenamed who also were so convinced: And after Prayer & conference about their so enjoying it, none having then so practised in England to professed Believers, & hearing that some in ye Nether Lands had so practised they agreed & sent over Mr Rich. Blunt [who understood Dutch] with Letters of Comendation, who was kindly accepted there, & returned with Letters from them.[51]

Blunt returned in January 1641 and instituted a ceremony of "dipping" described as follows: "Mr Blunt Baptized Mr Blacklock yt was a Teacher amongst them, & Mr Blunt being Baptized, he & Mr Blacklock Baptized ye rest of their friends that ware so minded, & many being added to them they increased much."[52] Forty-one persons were baptized at that time. Soon there were as many as seven such churches in London.[53] These represent the first Particular, or Calvinist, Baptists.

The decision to immerse may have been influenced by the Collegiant Mennonites located in the Rhynsburger region of Holland. The early source materials are not precise enough to determine exactly that Blunt received immersion at their hands. Prominent Baptist historians disagree over the matter. Underwood concluded that Blunt did receive baptism from the Collegiants, sometime in 1641.[54] Robert Torbet suggested that Blunt was not baptized until he returned to England. Torbet believed that Blunt and Blacklock baptized each other and then immersed their colleagues.[55] Leon McBeth accepted the idea that Blunt was immersed by the Mennonites, as evidenced in the phrase "Mr Blunt being baptized."[56] B. R. White offered still another opinion: "Although the evidence is somewhat ambiguous … it seems likely that Blunt first baptized himself and then baptized Blacklock."[57] The sources do not offer evidence enough to support any of these conclusions completely.

Praise-God Barebone

Praise-God Barebone, or Barebon, who became pastor to one group that divided from the Jacob Church in 1640, was himself an example of the religious diversity of seventeenth-century England. This group of believers met in Barebone's house, "The Lock and Key," located on Fleet Street.[58] He was one of three brothers, each of whom took a name as a testimony to his Christian faith (reportedly, the others chose the names "Christ-came-into-the-world-to-save Barebone" and "If-Christ-had-not-died-thou-hadst-been-damned Barebone"). Praise-God Barebone was a leather seller by trade, and he was such a formidable member of one of Cromwell's parliaments that the body sometimes was referred to as the "Barebones Parliament."

Barebone believed that baptism in the Church of England was valid, although administered by a false church.[59] In 1645, he published *A Defence of the Lawfulnesse of Baptizing Infants*, a response to John Spilsbury's critique of infant baptism, yet later his name is listed with a 1654 declaration of Baptists signed by twenty-two persons identified "as of the church that walked with Mr. Barebone."[60]

The Civil War and the Commonwealth

Religious life in England was affected substantively by the civil war that shook the country during the 1640s and created turmoil that lasted until the revolution of 1688 and the dissolution of the Stuart monarchy. Military actions began when Charles I sent an army on an invasion of Scotland. The king's request for funding from Parliament created further turmoil at home. Parliament, controlled by Puritans, rejected many of the king's demands and imprisoned Archbishop William Laud (1573–1645) on a charge of treason. Charles's attempt to arrest five members of Parliament led to armed confrontation in 1642.

Ultimately, the king was arrested, charged with treason, and beheaded in 1649. The army, led by Oliver Cromwell (1599–1658), gained primary governmental authority. Holding the title of "Lord Protector," Cromwell extended support to elements of Puritanism, particularly those in the Reformed tradition. The Westminster Assembly, a gathering dominated by Presbyterians, produced the Westminster Confession of Faith, one of the historic creeds of Reformed Christianity. During the 1640s, Presbyterianism was declared by many to be the "official" expression of the Church of England, but it met with limited acceptance throughout the country.

While the Cromwell Protectorate offered a certain degree of toleration, the revolutionary period was a time of great religious ferment. Sectarianism flourished with groups such as the millenarian Fifth Monarchy movement, the antinomian Ranters, the "socialist" Levellers, and the inspirationalist Quakers and Seekers. Some Baptists were caught up in these developments as religiously ardent individuals continued to search for newer, fuller revelations. This religious pluralism was viewed as a genuine threat to the traditional union of church and state in England. The relationship would never be the same.[61]

The civil war was an important time for Baptists. Many served in the army and supported Cromwell with the hope of greater religious freedom. Amidst the plurality of religious sectarians, Baptists sought to affirm the nature of their faith and the shape of their ecclesiastical life. In 1644, for example, Particular Baptists in London produced their first *Confession of Faith*—a guide to Calvinist Baptists in England and in the New World.

Particular Baptist Leaders

During the turmoil of the civil war, Baptists sought guidance from a variety of leaders, including the Particular Baptist Hanserd Knollys. Knollys (1599?–1691) was a member of the Jacob-Lathrop-Jessey Church in London and was among those who came to accept believer's baptism.[62]

Born in Lincolnshire, a stronghold of Puritanism, Knollys attended Cambridge in 1629, received Anglican ordination, and became master of a school in Gainsborough. Persecution against Puritans caused him to flee to Massachusetts, but he returned to England in 1641. He soon renounced his Anglican orders and was imprisoned in Newgate Prison for preaching Puritan views. During the 1640s, Knollys and his friend William Kiffin joined the Jessey Church, rejected infant baptism, and moved toward the Baptists.

In 1645, Knollys received believer's baptism and baptized Henry Jessey. Church records note, "After that H. Jessey was convinced also, the next morning early after that which had been a day of Solemne Seeking ye Lord in fastg & prayer (That if Infants Baptism were unlawfull & if we should be further baptized &c the Lord would not hide it from us, but cause us to know it) First H. Jessey was convinced against pedobaptisme, & then that himself should be baptized … and was baptized by Mr Knollys, and then by degrees he Baptized many of ye Church, when convinced they desired it."[63]

In 1648, Knollys published *The Rudiments of the Hebrew Grammar in English,* a lexicon to aid Christians in understanding "the Bible in the original tongues." Known as "the scholar's companion," it contained "all the interpretations of the Hebrew and Greek Bible." Knollys stated that book was "not only for the ear of the learned, but also that the unlearned may come to the knowledge of both testaments in the original tongues." This book and others like it indicate the educational level of some of the early English Baptists.[64]

Of Knollys's death, on September 19, 1691, Kiffin commented, "He was chosen an Elder to a congregation in London, with whom he laboured for near fifty years, under many difficulties that attended him; but neither the poverty of the church, nor the persecutions that he endured, were any temptation to him to neglect his duty towards them, but was willing to be poor with them in their poverty, and to suffer with them in their sufferings."[65]

Knollys, Benjamin Keach, and other Baptist ministers founded the first identifiable assembly of Particular Baptists in 1689.[66] Some one hundred churches sent representatives to the initial gathering. At that meeting, Baptists determined to develop a fund to support ministers and aid candidates in ministerial preparation. However, it would be twenty-eight years before the Particular Baptist Fund was created.

William Kiffin, Hanserd Knollys, and others helped to write "A Confession of Faith of Seven Congregations or Churches of Christ in London, which are commonly (but unjustly) called Anabaptist." The confession was published in 1646, "For the vindication of the Truth, and information of the ignorant; likewise for the taking off of those aspersions which are frequently both in Pulpit and Print unjustly cast upon them."

The confession was both a statement of basic beliefs and an attempt to distinguish Baptists from the oft-persecuted Continental Anabaptists. Of the Anabaptists, the confession noted, "And although they [Anabaptists] acknowledge with us, that the truth is not fully discovered, yet they will tie all future discovery to a former light, and conceive they do well in so doing. But God will by his truth shew their error, and exalt Jesus Christ the chiefe cornerstone, which the builders so much reject.... And although we be distinct in our meetings, for conveniency; yet are we one in faith, fellowship and communion, holding Jesus Christ for our Head and Law-giver under whose Rule and government we desire to walk." The document was signed by representatives of the seven English congregations and "a French congregation of the same judgement."[67]

Kiffin and other Baptists did not hesitate to challenge the actions of other sectarian groups. In 1650, Kiffin, John Spilsbury, and others signed a document entitled *Heart Bleedings for Professors Abominations*. The work attacked certain antinomian or charismatic sects of the day, such as the Ranters and the Quakers, who stressed the inner light of God in each person. It warned that many "poor souls through temptations" have "quit their professions" and have been "taken with their snares." It rejected the idea that each soul is God; that each soul is incarnate in a body and is therefore a Christ. It also attacked the antinomianism of the Ranters, who claimed that the redeemed were free to indulge in fleshly activities—cursing, drinking, "uncleanness."

Of Scriptures, the document noted, "That the Scriptures which do declare this great mystery of Jesus Christ and His Gospel, be the holy Scriptures, and the infallible Word of God, for it could never have enterred into the heart of man to have known or manifested those hidden mysteries, had not God himself by his own Word revealed them from heaven; now the Scriptures are Gods Word, ... and therefore not to be slighted and undervalued, as a dead Letter, a bare History, a carnal empty Story."[68]

Apparently, the presence of Baptists in certain Ranter-inspirationalist groups led to the criticism that all Baptists were guilty of Ranter excesses. Baptists responded that many had departed their ranks for such heretical communions, but conceded, "We do acknowledge though some eminent Professors [believers] of the same truth with us have fallen fouly (which hath been occasion of much grief to us) yet it hath been hitherto and we hope ever shall be our care (as they have been by the righteous judgment of God discovered) according to our duty to put them from amongst us, endeavouring to preserve our selves from all iniquity, and not to have fellowship with the unprofitable works of darkness, but rather to reprove them."[69] Spilsbury, Kiffin, Joseph Sanson, Ralph Prentice, and twelve other representatives of churches attached their names to the document.

The Fifth Monarchy and Persecution

Baptists were present in the Fifth Monarchy movement, a radical millenarian sect that developed out of the religious and political ferment of the civil war in England, "based on intense belief in the imminence of the 'Fifth Monarchy' or universal rule of God's people on earth, as gathered from revelations contained in the apocalyptic book of Daniel."[70] It flourished during the Commonwealth period to such an extent that one scholar commented, "There is … a sense in which the great majority of (religious) Englishmen at that time might be called Fifth Monarchists."[71] The movement was a sectarian remnant whose actions and ideas were dominated by apocalyptic anticipation and were evident in Cromwell's army as early as 1645.[72] After the execution of Charles I and the beginning of the Cromwell Protectorate, Fifth Monarchists were not content to wait on patient providence and gradual change, but sought to take up the sword to hasten the kingdom.

While Baptists such as Christopher Feake were outspoken Fifth Monarchists, others in London sought to dissociate themselves from the movement. William Kiffin criticized Fifth Monarchy gatherings in Blackfriars, London, and their belief that policies on war or peace should be determined by "a spirit stirred up … by God to throw down potentates and powers."[73]

Baptists of various types were connected to the Fifth Monarchists. In 1649, Baptist James Toppe declared his belief in "Christ's monarchial and personall reign uppon earth over the kingdoms of the world … in which is also shewed the time when this kingdom shall begin and where it shall be."[74] Many Seventh Day Baptists were so prominent in the movement that some historians were convinced that the Sabbatarian Baptists came directly from the Fifth Monarchy.[75] Benjamin Keach, hauled into court for his Baptist views, was silenced by the judge in this way: "You are a fifth monarchy man, and you can preach as well as write books, and you would preach here if I would let you; but I shall take such order, as you shall do no more mischief."[76]

Fearing anarchy, Oliver Cromwell moved to suppress the movement. Its leaders were arrested and its assemblies disbanded. Many of its members turned to the Baptists or the Quakers. Following the Stuart Restoration, members of the Fifth Monarchy movement revolted against the state. Led by Thomas Venner, they staged an unsuccessful rebellion in early 1660. The failed attempt led to legislation aimed at the "sectaries," which included Quakers and Baptists. They were accused of plotting to disturb the peace.

Hanserd Knollys and other Baptist leaders were imprisoned as a result of these laws. Knollys apparently was involved in the Fifth Monarchy movement. His views on the end of the age were published in a 1681 volume entitled *The World That Now Is and the World That Is to Come,* an exposition of "several prophecies" yet to be fulfilled. The first part of the work contained theological speculation on the nature of Christ's work on behalf of humanity. The second half also dealt with Christ's return, which Knollys believed would occur "personally, visibly and suddenly; that he will set up his kingdom and will reign, raise the dead and judge both the quick and the dead. 2 Tim. 4.1." He concluded that fires and other catastrophes of the late seventeenth century were evidence of the end time and the need for immediate repentance.[77]

John Sturgion insisted that the falsely imprisoned Baptists had repudiated Thomas Venner's violent chiliastic movement. Their only crime was their firm belief in God. Sturgion offered this plea to the monarch: "And may it further please your majesty, to consider your afflicted and innocent subjects, how they have been haled from their peaceable habitations, and thrust into prisons, almost in all counties in England, and many are still detained to the utter undoing of themselves and families. And most of them are poor men, whose livelihood, under God, depends upon the labour of their hands.... And whilst they suffer here, some of their wives and tender babes want bread at home."[78]

Seventh Day Baptists

The continuing quest for the true church led some Baptists to reflect on Old Testament implications of church order. They concluded that Saturday, the Jewish Sabbath, was the divinely appointed day of worship. Others charged that the Sabbatarians were returning to the old law of "works." Some churches included members of both Sabbatarian and non-Sabbatarian sentiments.[79]

Controversy over the proper day for worship in the Church of England arose as early as 1595 in a work entitled *The Doctrine of the Sabbath,* by Nicolas Bownde. It concluded that "the Sabbath must needs be still upon the seventh day as it alwais hath beene."[80] The book was banned by the established church, but debate over the Sabbath continued among the Puritans. Another Anglican, James Ockford, published *The Doctrine of the Fourth Commandment, Deformed by Popery, Reformed & Restored to Its Primitive Purity* (1650), in which he insisted that the Jewish Sabbath must be maintained in the Christian church.[81] These books had a significant influence on Seventh Day Baptists.

Historians of the Seventh Day Baptist movement suggest that there were at least two such churches in England by the end of the 1650s. In 1661, a Seventh Day Baptist preacher named John James was executed for his participation in the Fifth Monarchy movement. At his execution, he affirmed his belief in the Sabbath as the true Lord's Day.[82]

Edward Stennett was patriarch of a family of Seventh Day Baptist ministers and church leaders. Stennett's *The Royal Law Contended For* (1658) asserted that the divine law of the Hebrew covenant was not abrogated by Christ's incarnation. Don Sanford notes that Stennett was "a leading voice for the Seventh Day Baptists in England for over thirty years."[83]

Many of the early Sabbatarians came from the ranks of the General Baptists and were often permitted to retain that membership. There seems to have been significant interaction among the early Baptist congregations. Thomas Grantham, prominent General Baptist leader, refused to dismiss members who did not accept the doctrine of the general atonement. Some General Baptist churches allowed members to affirm Christ's limited atonement as long as they did not disrupt the fellowship.[84]

The Stuart Restoration

When Charles II was restored to the English throne in 1660, the Baptists were among the first groups to present their grievances to the crown. On July 26, 1660, Lincolnshire Baptists implored the king to extend liberty to religious minorities, noting, "We have been much abused as we pass in the streets, and as we sit in our houses."[85] That same day, London Baptists presented Charles with "An Humble Apology," detailing abuses and calling for freedom for worship. Nonetheless, sanctions against nonconformists continued, as evidenced in the Clarendon Code, a series of laws directed against dissenters.[86]

The Clarendon Code

The Clarendon Code contained numerous provisions aimed at regulating nonconformist activities. The Corporation Act (1661) required office holders to renounce any connections to Scottish Presbyterians made during the Protectorate, take an oath of nonresistance to the crown, and receive the sacrament under Anglican rites.[87] The Act of Uniformity (1662) exacted compliance to the revised *Book of Common Prayer* and its liturgical rubrics. Clergy who violated this law were removed from their parishes.[88] The Conventicle Act (1664) brought sanctions against "seditious sectaries," those persons over the age of sixteen who participated in nonconformist worship services. The Five Mile Act (1665) required nonconformist ministers to remain at least five miles from any town where they had earlier performed pastoral functions. The Test Act (1673) was intended to keep Roman Catholics out of public life. It required office holders to receive communion in the Church of England.[89]

Baptists were not immune to these sanctions. John Bunyan, Bedford pastor and author of *Pilgrim's Progress,* was imprisoned for twelve years (1660–1672) during this persecution. An account published by the clerk of the peace in 1670 stated, "One Bonyon was indicted upon the Statute of 35 Elizabeth, for being at a Conventicle [nonconformist meeting]. He was in prison, and was brought into Court and the indictment read to him; and because he refused to plead to it, the court ordered me to record his confession, and he hath lain in prison upon that conviction, ever since Christmas Sessions."[90]

In 1660, Baptists in the county of Kent, some of whom were imprisoned in the Maidstone Gaol, issued "The Humble Petition and Representation of the Sufferings of Several Peaceable, and Innocent Subjects Called by the Name of Anabaptists." They affirmed their allegiance to the king and urged him to end religious persecution, stating, "Not only our own lives are in danger, but also an irresistible destruction cometh on our wives and little ones, by that violence which is now exercised upon us."[91] They insisted, "And now, O King, that no man as he is a Christian, hath power to be a lord over another's faith, or by outward force to impose any thing in the worship of God."[92] They supported their position with these assertions: (1) neither Christ nor his disciples compelled anyone to believe; (2) the apostles and elders of the church could have used such power in first century, but rejected it; (3) in the parable of the wheat and the tares, Jesus forbids "any force to be exercised upon false worshippers";[93] (4) Christ himself was crucified because religious people mistakenly sought to punish blasphemy; and (5) religious persecution inhibited Jewish immigration, thereby eliminating the possibility that they would hear the gospel. The document concluded, "Furthermore, it is too well known that the Jews are the greatest blasphemers against our Lord Jesus Christ that are on the earth, yet it is not the mind of the Lord they should be destroyed from the face of the earth; for how then should the scripture be fulfilled, wherein God hath promised to call them, and make them the most glorious nation in the world?"[94]

For themselves, the Baptists noted, "Many of us that are now prisoners cannot take the oath of allegiance, because we cannot swear at all, the Lord Christ having forbidden, in the fifth of Matthew, 33rd verse, compared with James v. 12, not only vain oaths, but also such swearing as was delivered of old time, persuaded, and therefore before now, under former powers, have denied to swear."[95]

The presence of informers in the Baptist ranks led to the development of extraordinary measures aimed at protecting ministers from arrest. The records of the church in Bristol reported, "To prevent Spies that might come in ye Roome as hearers,—and yet that noe strangers, or persons we knew not, might be hindered from coming into our Meeting, whether good or Bad, to hear ye Gospell,—we Contrived a Curtaine to be hung in ye Meeting place, that did enclose as much room as above 50 might sit within it, and among those men, he that preached should stand; that so if any Informer was private in ye Room as a hearer he might hear him that spake, but could not see him, and thereby not know him."[96] When "Informers or Officers" appeared, the preacher sat down and the congregation sang a psalm, "so they could not find any one preaching, but all Singing."[97]

Nonetheless, persecution was a reality. The Bristol church minutes lamented, "Our Ministers being taken from us, one dead, and ye rest Imprisoned, and we feared their death likewise in such a Bad Prison, and we being pursued closely every meeting, hardly one Escaped."[98]

Toleration Secured

Some Baptists assured authorities that they were not fanatics or improper citizens. In 1654, Baptist minister William Britten wrote a treatise defending the beliefs and practices of the oft-persecuted communion. Titled *The Moderate Baptist,* it stressed the Baptist commitment to orthodoxy and peace.[99]

In 1667, Charles II included Protestant dissenters in his efforts to extend greater toleration to English Catholics. On his way to becoming a Catholic, James II issued the "Declaration of Indulgence" (1672), a statement of religious freedom that created controversy throughout the nation. In response, Parliament passed the Test Act (1673), requiring oaths to the monarch and to the Church of England along with repudiation of transubstantiation. William Kiffin was appointed a London alderman, but he refused the office because it would have required him to receive Anglican sacraments. Threatened with imprisonment, he accepted the title of alderman but declined to fulfill his duties.[100]

Legal toleration was secured only after the demise of the Stuart monarchy and the accession of William and Mary to the English throne in 1688. The Toleration Act of 1689 exempted "their Majesties' Protestant subjects dissenting from the Church of England from the penalties of certain laws."[101] While such toleration was given only to Protestants whose ministers affirmed thirty-six of the thirty-nine articles of the Anglican Church's *Confession of Faith,* required continued tithes to the established church, and continued other formal sanctions, it provided for significant protection for dissenting communions, including Baptists.[102]

Baptists in Ireland

The earliest Baptists in Ireland were soldiers in Oliver Cromwell's army who arrived in the 1640s during the English Civil War. Most were Particular Baptists who advocated Reformed theology, believer's immersion, and closed communion.[103] Thomas Patient and Christopher Blackwood were two of the earliest Baptist ministers in Ireland. Patient's Dublin congregation constructed a meeting house in 1653.[104] That same year a "letter" issued by Irish Baptists acknowledged that there were "churches of Christ in Ireland walking together in the faith and order of the Gospell ... resident in severall places." These churches were located in Dublin, Waterford, Clonmel, Kilkenny, Cork, Limerick, Galway, Wexford, and Kerry. [105] Each church agreed "to sett apart one day in every month, solemnly to seeke the face of our God and, by fasting and praying, humbly to mourne before him." Fasting was instituted, in part, because of "our little laying to heart the great breaches the Lord hath made amongst us by removing many righteous ones from us and from the evill to come," and "Our want of spirituall wisedome to reprove sin plainly in all without respect of persons."[106]

These early congregations were vilified by their Irish neighbors not only for their beliefs and practices, but also for their affiliations with British (Baptist) soldiers. With the Stuart Restoration, however, Irish Baptists reasserted their loyalty to the crown, and turned attention to the development of their fledgling congregations.[107]

Dublin was the center of the early Baptist presence in Ireland. A letter from Joseph Pettit to Elisha Callender of Boston, written in November 1725, reported that there were eleven Baptist churches, nine of which comprised the Irish Baptist Association (IBA). The two remaining congregations included a strict Calvinist and strict Arminian communion. At that time the mother church in Swift's Alley, Dublin, claimed a membership of up to two hundred persons.[108]

Baptists in Scotland

As in Ireland, the Baptist presence in Scotland began with Baptists in Cromwell's army who took up residence there after the defeat of the Scots in 1650. While no permanent congregations were formed from these emigres, the Baptist presence did not go unnoticed. A Declaration of Toleration was issued at Dalkeith in 1652. It was also reported, "This yeir (1653) Anabaptistes daylie increst in this natioun, quhair [where] nevir name was of befoir...."[109] In spite of these early activities, a formal Baptist presence was not established in Scotland until the eighteenth century.

Baptists in Wales

Baptists have a long history in Wales, with significant numerical growth extending into the early twentieth century. Joshua Thompson contended that the first Welsh Baptist church began on the "borders of Herefordshire about the year 1633."[110] This early Baptist presence in Wales is difficult to document with certainty. Thus the twentieth century historian T. M. Bassett concluded that "even after extending the evidence to its utmost, would be that there were few, if any, Baptists in Wales before the First (English) Civil War."[111]

Origins of a wider Baptist presence came from various sources. Two General Baptists, Hugh Evans and Jeremy Ives, were among the first Baptists to preach in Wales, beginning in the 1640s. John Miles (1621–1683) and Thomas Proud were the first Particular Baptists to work as missionaries in Wales as early as 1649. The two began a congregation in Ilston. In 1650 that church and two others organized the first Particular Baptist general assembly in Wales.[112]

Puritan victories in the Civil War led to legal actions that impacted the early Welsh Baptists. "An Act for the Better Propagation and Preaching of the Gospel in Wales" (1650) allowed nonconformist ministers, including Baptists, to secure the dismissal of certain Anglican ministers who were perceived to be ineffective and to draw their "livings," or salaries, for themselves. Thus Baptist ministers received some state funds for ministerial support. Such practices were clearly in direct contradiction to later "historic" Baptist opposition to state support. T. M. Bassett defended this action by the early Welsh Baptists as evidence of "the utter hopelessness with which they viewed the religious state of their native country." Baptists were not uniform in their response to the use of state funds. In 1655 the Abergavenny church repudiated any connection with ministers who received support from the state.[113]

An association of Baptist churches was founded in November 1650 in Ilston, near Swansea. The membership came from three churches—Ilston, Hay, and Llantrisant (Glamorgan). The minutes of the initial associational meeting acknowledged the shortage of ministers and advocated programs for raising funds to provide for the financial needs of pastors.

The associational minutes acknowledged the persistence of certain disputes by which "the adversary" (Satan) sought "to withdraw, if it were possible, the very elect from their steadfastness [sic]." Churches were encouraged "to take especiall care to stopp and quench all divideings principles, that shal be broached by or among, and of the brethren, and that shall or may in any wise tend to the subversione, or hinderinge of right order, and discipline among them."[114] Associations took an active part in Welsh Baptist life.

Differences of opinion, both internal and external, created schism among the fledgling Baptist congregations. For example, some differed over hymn singing and "Psalme singing," while others debated whether the newly baptized should receive the laying on of hands. Still others differed over open and closed communion.[115]

As with most Baptist communities, Welsh Baptists divided over open membership policies. In 1651 the Ilston church took action to separate pastor Thomas Proud from its membership for "having grievously sinned against God by broaching that destructive opinion maintaining the mixed communion of baptized and unbaptized (unimmersed) in visible church fellowship, and haveing endevoured to draw other to the same judgment by several wayes and meanes and soe to rend and divide the church."[116] Proud evidently saw the error of his ways and offered "full satisfaction in all particulars to the church." He was restored to fellowship after only fourteen weeks.[117] The question of open membership nonetheless remained a matter of contention among the earliest Welsh Baptists.

A decision to enter the Baptist fold was not without consequences. Pastor Morgan Jones (1662?–1730?) married a woman named Griffiths who was disowned by her family for becoming a Baptist. Indeed, "they deprived her of what was her right and equity of her own" and defended their action because "she had left the established church, and turned to be a phanatic." Sources suggest that "Mrs. Jones bore an excellent character every way, but she died young and left children; yet her parents absolutely refused to the last to give or leave her rights, either to her or to her children, though on her death bed she solemnly charged them as they were to answer before God not to deprive her husband and her motherless children of what was their just due."[118]

Morgan Jones was no stranger to controversies brought on by his Baptist views. One such confrontation involved the following exchange between Jones and a Welsh Catholic:

> *Catholic: I say, that the church of Rome is the true Catholic Apostolic Church, and that the Church of England and all you phanatics, are but bastards of that church. Jones: Softly neighbor, boast not too much, for if the children be all bastards, then the mother must needs be a whore, you know.*[119]

Church Offices among Welsh Baptists

Minutes of the sixth associational gathering in 1654 provide an explanation of specific offices in the early Welsh Baptist churches. These include pastors, teachers, "Helps, or those who rule," and deacons. The first three are all known as "Elders, Bishops, Watchmen, etc." They cared for the church, "consult on controversies," "order things in the church," "advise in matters of doubt," "govern," visit the sick, and "care for the distribution of collections." Pastors were specifically charged to exhort, "reprove with all authority," "cast out," "lead the sheep," "watch," administer the ordinances," "give himself wholly to the word and doctrine," and to "rule well, which consists in right ordering of questions and disorderly speakings, (and) in preserving purity of doctrine and discipline."[120]

Teachers were to "wait on teaching, to expound scriptures, and confute errors." Ruling elders oversaw "the lives and manners of men," while deacons served the Lord's table, "and the tables of all others in the church, that shall want his service." Likewise, "for the assistance of the deacons there are widows," who served the church, primarily "the poor and sick." Prophets held forth "as permitted" by the churches for the "edification, exhortation and comfort."[121] Such offices are illustrative of the Particular, or Calvinistic, orientation of these churches.

Some were ordained and others without ordination served as "ministering helpers." Several churches included "ordained assistants" and "other acceptable preachers." Some lay preachers worked "when needful, to prevent more vacancies."[122] Many seventeenth- and early eighteenth-century ministers were known for their ability to preach in both English and Welsh. John James (d. 1760), pastor of the church at Rhydwilim, was described as "a godly, solid, experimental preacher," whose "method ... was not so taking with young people as some others were."[123]

Ministers officiated at wedding ceremonies in Welsh Baptist churches and devised their own marriage rituals, distinct from those of the established church. Carried out in the company of the congregation, the ceremony included a lengthy sermon, prayers, and hymns. A certificate of marriage was given to the new wife. One document from the church in Rhydwilim read:

> *We whose names are hereto subscribed do certify whom it may concern, that L.P. and E.J. of the parish of Ll. [probably Llanglydwen] did, in the presence of God, and of us this people, enter into the honorable state of matrimony, to live together according to his holy ordinance, until death shall them both separate.*

The document was signed by the ministers present and dated July 1, 1682.[124]

The Restoration Brings Persecution

The Stuart Restoration brought an end to Nonconformist influence on the state and resulted in extensive persecution against Welsh Baptists under the Clarendon Code. Churches were closed, fines were imposed, and unbaptized infants were refused burial in hallowed ground. By the 1670s, Baptists were permitted to secure licenses to worship under specific guidelines. Barrett noted that the church at Carmarthen, one of the earliest in Wales, "disappeared completely."[125]

Relations with America

Persecution led many Welsh Baptists to emigrate to the American colonies. The first Baptist church in Massachusetts was founded by Welsh Baptists in the 1660s. Those who remained behind soon formed ties to those American churches. Sources indicate that they sent "letters" vouching for their members who journeyed to the New World, as evidenced in a document dated July 30, 1710. It identified the church at Swansea, in Glamorganshire, as "teaching believers baptism, laying on of hands, the doctrine of personal election, and final perseverance." The letter is addressed, "To any church of Christ Jesus in the province of Pennsylvania, in America, of the same faith and order to whom this may concern." The letter listed numerous Baptists who had emigrated to Pennsylvania, and admonished:

> This is to testify unto you, that all the above names are in full communion with us, and we commit them, all of them to your Christian care, beseeching you therefore to receive them in the Lord, watch over them, and perform all Christian duties toward them as becommeth Christians to their fellow members.[126]

Churches obviously were concerned to give good accounts of their members as they journeyed to other congregations, even in far-off America.

Organizational Activities

Associational relationships languished among Welsh Baptists during the period of the great persecution, but the Act of Toleration (1689) created opportunity for a renewed connectionalism. London Baptist churches invited Welsh representatives to a meeting in September 1689. The gathering produced a confession of faith and Welsh participation in the London Association. Six Welsh churches joined the association. The relationship endured until 1692, when they joined the Western Association. In 1700, these nine Welsh Baptist churches formed their own association. Other congregations, fearing a threat to localism, refused to participate in the endeavor.[127]

Baptist Identity: The Shape of Things

Baptist communities took shape in the seventeenth century as they developed theological and organizational identity. Some gave emphasis to free will and falling from grace, while others stressed election and predestination. All these churches were organized around covenants that bound believers to God and to one another. Individual churches soon created associations of churches for fellowship, encouragement, and help in times of crisis.

These early Baptists responded to the political and social upheavals of their times, often participating in the army or militant millenarian groups. They wrote confessions of faith to delineate their beliefs, and they established procedures for ordaining ministers. Frequently persecuted by the state, they were passionate advocates of religious liberty for believer and unbeliever alike.

Notes

1. George Hunston Williams, *The Radical Reformation* (Philadelphia: Westminster Press, 1962); William R. Estep, *The Anabaptist Story* (Nashville: Broadman, 1963).
2. Estep, *The Anabaptist Story*, 53.
3. Alfred C. Underwood, *A History of the English Baptists* (London: Baptist Union Publishing Department, 1947), 33.
4. W. T. Whitley, *A History of British Baptists*, rev. ed. (London: Kingsgate Press, 1932), 20.
5. B. R. White, *The English Baptists of the Seventeenth Century*, rev. ed. (Didcot, England: Baptist Historical Society, 1996), 18.
6. Ibid., 17–18.
7. James Leo Garrett, "Restitution and Dissent among Early English Baptists: Part II," *Baptist History and Heritage* 13 (April 1978): 19–20.
8. John Smyth, *The Differences of the Churches of the Separation* (London, 1608), in *The Works of John Smyth*, ed. W. T. Whitley, 2 vols. (Cambridge: Cambridge University Press, 1915), 1:269–70.
9. Whitley, ed., *Works of John Smyth*, 1:279.
10. Ibid., 1:292.
11. Ibid.
12. Ibid.
13. Ibid., 1:20 (citing 2:565).
14. Ibid.
15. Underwood, *English Baptists*, 27.
16. Ibid., 37–38.
17. B. R. White, "The Frontiers of Fellowship between English Baptists, 1609–1660," *Foundations* 11 (July–September 1968): 245.
18. John Smyth, *Churches of the Separation*, in Whitley, ed., *Works of John Smyth*, 1:279.
19. James Leo Garrett, "Sources of Authority in Baptist Thought," *Baptist History and Heritage* 13 (July 1978): 41.
20. Underwood, *English Baptists*, 39.
21. Thomas Helwys, *The Mistery of Iniquity* (1612; facsimile reprint, London: Kingsgate Press, 1935), 4, 7.
22. Whitley, *British Baptists*, 33.
23. Richard Groves, introduction to Thomas Helwys, *A Short Declaration of the Mystery of Iniquity* (1611/1612), ed. Richard Groves (Macon, Ga.: Mercer University Press, 1998), xxxii (citing William L. Lumpkin, *Baptist Confessions of Faith* [Chicago: Judson Press, 1959], 140).
24. Groves, introduction to Helwys, *Mystery of Iniquity*, xxxii.
25. Thomas Crosby, *The History of the English Baptists*, 4 vols. (London: 1738–40), 1:273. Crosby's history provides numerous primary source citations from Baptists during the seventeenth and eighteenth centuries.
26. W. T. Whitley, *Transactions of the Baptist Historical Society* 1 (1908–9): 111.
27. Leonard Busher, *Religions Peace: or, A Plea for Liberty of Conscience* (1616; republished 1646; reprinted in Edward B. Underhill, ed., *Tracts on Liberty of Conscience and Persecution, 1614–1661* [London: T. Haddon, 1846], 17).
28. Ibid., 17–18.
29. Ibid., 22.
30. Ibid., 30.
31. B. R. White, "Early Baptist Arguments for Religious Freedom: Their Overlooked Agenda," *Baptist History and Heritage* 24 (October 1989): 6–7.
32. Busher, *Religions Peace*, 69.
33. Thomas Helwys, *Persecution for Religion Judged and Condemned* (London: Wightman and Cramp, 1827).
34. Ibid., 19–20, 23–24.
35. Ibid., 25.
36. John Murton, *A Description of What God Hath Predestined Concerning Man* (London: 1620).
37. Ibid, 3.
38. Ibid., 18.
39. Ibid., 79.
40. Crosby, *English Baptists*, 1:124–25.
41. Lumpkin, *Baptist Confessions of Faith*, 222.
42. Ibid., 222–23.

43. "Records of the Jacob-Lathrop-Jessey Church, 1616–1641," *Transactions of the Baptist Historical Society* 1 (1908–9): 206–8.
44. Ibid., 209.
45. Ibid., 212.
46. Ibid., 218.
47. Ibid., 220.
48. Ibid. (Eaton was buried in Bunhill Fields Cemetery, outside the walls of London, on August 25, 1638. Two hundred people attended the burial, but no Anglican clergy would officiate.)
49. Crosby, *English Baptists,* 1:148–49. Kiffin joined an Independent congregation in 1638 and was "dipped" sometime later. He was one of the Baptists who debated Daniel Featley at Southwark in 1642.
50. "Jacob-Lathrop-Jessey Church," 221.
51. William Kiffin, "Kiffin Manuscript," reproduced in "The Rise of Particular Baptists in London, 1633–1644," *Transactions of the Baptist Historical Society* 1 (1908–9): 232–33.
52. Ibid., 234.
53. Ibid., 235.
54. Underwood, *English Baptists,* 59.
55. Robert G. Torbet, *A History of the Baptists,* 3rd ed. (Valley Forge, Pa.: Judson Press, 1973), 43.
56. H. Leon McBeth, *The Baptist Heritage* (Nashville: Broadman, 1987), 46; *A Sourcebook for Baptist Heritage* (Nashville: Broadman, 1990), 27 n.
57. White, *English Baptists,* 61.
58. Torbet, *History of the Baptists,* 41.
59. John Taylor, *New Preachers New!* (London, 1641), republished as *A Word to Fanatics, Puritans, and Sectaries; or, New Preachers New!* (London: Baynes & Son, 1821).
60. Torbet, *History of the Baptists,* 41.
61. White, *English Baptists,* 25–26.
62. I. Mallard, "The Hymns of Katherine Sutton," *Baptist Quarterly* (January 1963): 23.
63. "Debate on Infant Baptism, 1643," *Transactions of the Baptist Historical Society* 1 (1908–9): 45.
64. Hanserd Knollys, *The Rudiments of the Hebrew Grammar in English* (London: M. Bell, 1648).
65. William Kiffin, with Hanserd Knollys, *The Life and Death of That Old Disciple of Jesus Christ, and Eminent Minister of the Gospel, Mr. Hanserd Knollys* (1692; reprint, London: E. Huntington, 1812), 5.
66. The Particular Baptist Confession of 1644 reflected the beliefs of an early gathering or assembly of churches that came together but formed no permanent association.
67. Handwritten notes in this second edition, located at Regent's Park College, Oxford, suggest that five of the names do not appear in the first edition. These include Hanserd Knollys, Thomas Holms, Benjamin Cockes (or Cox), and the two French ministers. The confession is included in Lumpkin, *Baptist Confessions of Faith,* 156–171.
68. William Kiffin et al., *Heart Bleedings for Professors Abominations* (London, 1650), 11. This statement clearly refers to Ranter claims to immediate inspiration.
69. Ibid., 14–15.
70. "The Fifth Monarchy Movement," *Transactions of the Baptist Historical Society* 2 (1910–11): 166.
71. Ibid., 167.
72. Ibid.
73. Ibid., 174.
74. Don A. Sanford, *A Choosing People: The History of Seventh Day Baptists* (Nashville: Broadman, 1992), 56.
75. Ibid., 56–57.
76. Crosby, *English Baptists,* 1:199.
77. Hanserd Knollys, *The World That Now Is and the World That Is to Come* (London: Thomas Snowden, 1681), 48.
78. Underhill, ed., *Tracts on Liberty,* 327–28. In another document, "To the King of These Nations, by Several Societies Called Anabaptists" (1660), it reads: "Such is the portion of many of us, to be taken out of our houses, and from our employments, beaten and abused in the streets by the rude multitude, haled before the justices and other officers, and then having nothing to charge us with, they put us to the oath, and upon refusal, though Christ hath prohibited swearing at all, especially any promissory oath, are we sent to prison, to the impoverishing and ruin of us, our lives, and children" (ibid., 328 n).
79. White, "Frontiers of Fellowship," 251–52.
80. Sanford, *A Choosing People,* 47.
81. Ibid., 58–59.
82. Seventh Day Baptist General Conference, *Seventh Day Baptists in Europe and America,* 2 vols. (1910; reprint, New York: Arno Press, 1980), 1:69.
83. Sanford, *A Choosing People,* 73.
84. E. P. Winter, "The Lord's Supper," *Baptist Quarterly* 17 (1957–58): 268.
85. Underhill, ed., *Tracts on Liberty,* 292.
86. Edward Terrill, *The Records of a Church of Christ in Bristol, 1640–1687,* ed. Roger Hayden (Bristol: Bristol Record Society, 1974), 59.
87. Ibid.
88. Ibid., 60.

89. Ibid., 61–65.
90. "Bunyan's Imprisonments," *Transactions of the Baptist Historical Society* 6 (1918–19): 5.
91. Underhill, ed., *Tracts on Liberty,* 298.
92. Ibid., 301.
93. Ibid., 302.
94. Ibid., 305.
95. Ibid., 307.
96. Terrill, *Records of a Church,* 150–51.
97. Ibid., 151.
98. Ibid., 150.
99. Crosby, *English Baptists,* 1:254.
100. Underwood, *English Baptists,* 109–10.
101. White, *English Baptists,* 163.
102. Ibid.
103. Joshua Thompson, "Baptists in Ireland 1792–1922, A Dimension of Protestant Dissent" (unpublished D.Phil. thesis, Regents Park College, Oxford, 1988), 4.
104. Ibid., 5, citing B. R. White, "Thomas Patient in England and Ireland," *Irish Baptist Historical Society Journal* 2 (1969–70), 36–48.
105. B. R. White, ed., *Association Records of Particular Baptists in England, Wales and Ireland to 1660,* Part 2 (London: The Baptist Historical Society, 1973), 119–120.
106. Ibid., 119.
107. Ibid., 6–8.
108. Ibid., 9.
109. D. W. Bebbington, ed., *The Baptists in Scotland: A History* (Glasgow: The Baptist Union of Scotland, 1988), 10. This is probably a reference to Baptists.
110. Rev. Dr. (Joshua) Thomas, "The Baptist Denomination in Wales," in *The Baptist Denomination in England, Wales, Scotland and Ireland* (London: J. Heaton and Son, 1863), 14.
111. T. M. Bassett, *The Welsh Baptists* (Swansea: Ilston House, 1977), 14.
112. Albert W. Wardin, ed., *Baptists around the World* (Nashville: Broadman & Holman Publishers, 1995), 191.
113. T. M. Bassett, *The Welsh Baptists,* 16, 31.
114. B. R. White, ed., *Association Records of the Particular Baptists of England, Wales and Ireland to 1660,* Part 1 (London: The Baptist Historical Society, 1971), 4.
115. Ibid., 5.
116. Ibid.
117. Joshua Thompson, *The American Baptist Heritage in Wales,* Part 1 (Lafayette, Tenn.: Church History Research and Archives Affiliation, 1976), 51.
118. Ibid., 71–72.
119. Ibid., 75–76.
120. Ibid., 11.
121. Ibid., 11–12.
122. Ibid., 114–115.
123. Ibid., 115.
124. Ibid., 92.
125. T. M. Bassett, *The Welsh Baptists,* 40.
126. Ibid., 76.
127. Ibid., 49–51.

Chapter 3
English Baptists: The Seventeenth Century

FROM THE EARLY DAYS OF THE BAPTIST MOVEMENT, ECCLESIOLOGY WAS CENTRAL to unity. Baptists united around a vision of the church as a community of believers, celebrating baptism and the Lord's Supper, preaching the gospel, and organizing congregational life. The authority for the church's mission and ministry came from Christ as mediated through the community of believers.

Questions of belief and practice distinguished English Baptists from the Anglican establishment, from other Protestant nonconformists, and often from each other. B. R. White noted that the formation of the early Baptist churches created numerous theological inquiries that generated discussion, debate, and schism. Many of these issues would continue to haunt Baptists in the next centuries. They included: How would Baptists relate to other churches, especially those that baptized infants? Was baptism administered by those churches to be considered valid? Could persons baptized as infants receive communion in Baptist churches? Was rebaptism required of all nonimmersed persons who joined Baptist churches? Where might the authority for believer's baptism be secured? What was the proper mode of baptism?[1]

In seeking answers to these questions, seventeenth-century Baptists went to the Bible. The diversity of their responses reflected not a lack of conviction but rather a passion for determining what was the most appropriate reading of Scripture. They were also influenced by the religious ferment of the times and the populism of their own congregational system. A survey of some of those issues reveals both the uniformity and the divergence of Baptist outlooks.

Baptists and Church Covenants

Covenantal relationships were essential to early Baptist ecclesiology. The covenant theology of the Separatist group at Gainsborough had significant influence on the Baptists who came out from them. This community, like the Baptists who would follow, constituted a church "gathered" around "a covenant or solemn agreement both with God and with each other."[2]

Paul S. Fiddes describes four ways in which Baptists understood the meaning of covenant. First, it described God's "covenant of grace" with "human beings and angels for their salvation in Jesus Christ." Second, it could mean a transaction inside the Godhead "in which the Son is envisaged as consenting to the will of the Father to undertake the work of the salvation of the elect." Third, it was an "agreement God makes corporately" with the whole church or with specific congregations. Fourth, covenant could mean an agreement by believers who formed a particular congregation and required of all who joined that community of faith.[3] Karen Smith noted that covenantal agreements gave great attention to questions of practical application rather than "doctrinal unanimity." She concluded that the emphasis was on the church as "a visible community of saints" whose members pledged to participate together in "worship, prayer for one another, attendance for the ordinances, and participation in the discipline and government of the congregation."[4]

While General Baptists utilized covenants, such documents were especially important to Particular Baptist congregations. Even Particular Baptists did not always agree on their use. John Spilsbury, for example, favored the use of church covenants as a declaration of unity between God and humanity, a statement around which churches were united, a sign of Christian identity, and the agreement around which a church is constituted under God.[5] Spilsbury's contemporary Hanserd Knollys opposed covenants on the grounds that they had no precedent in the New Testament and were not used by all Baptist churches as a basis for organization. According to Knollys, churches were to be constituted on the basis of faith, repentance, and baptism.[6]

Later on, Benjamin Keach expanded the use of covenants to include baptism, the formation of new congregations, and the admission of new converts to membership. In 1697, Keach observed that when new members were admitted, "they must solemnly enter into a covenant, to walk in the fellowship of that particular congregation, and submit themselves to the care and discipline thereof."[7]

As Charles Deweese has shown, covenants included categories such as "church fellowship, church discipline, public worship and personal devotion, and pastoral and lay care."[8] Although they required affirmations of faith, covenants, unlike confessions, had less to do with belief than with behavior and practice. Keach's covenant contained eight segments, in which members of a church agreed to "walk in Holiness," to "watch over each others" conversations and behavior, to pray for one another, to "bear one anothers Burdens," to be patient with "one anothers Weaknesses," to avoid divisions, to meet on "the Lord's Days," and to "Communicate to our Pastor or Minister."[9]

Covenants gave many English Baptist churches a strong sense of identity and community. These instruments were double-edged. While the church members agreed to care for one another, they also agreed to discipline those who failed to abide by the covenant. In short, covenant set the behavioral boundaries for the congregation individually and collectively.

A Believers' Church

Conversion

Seventeenth-century Baptist churches, whether Particular or General, required a profession of faith (conversion) of all who would receive baptism and church membership. Candidates for membership were asked to declare their experience of grace in the presence of the congregation. The true church was composed of believers only.

Benjamin Keach reported that candidates for baptism were asked to state "what God hath done for their Souls, of their Experiences of a Saving work of Grace upon their hearts."[10] Allowances were made for "bashfulness" whereby diffident persons were permitted to tell their story to the elder (pastor) and a small group of the members. If "full satisfaction" was not offered, the candidate was compelled to "be put by until Satisfaction is obtained." Consent of the congregational majority was essential for admission to church membership. Keach noted that "when the Majority are satisfied, and yet one or two Persons are not, the Church and Elder will do well to wait a little time, and endeavour to satisfy such Persons, especially if the Reasons of their dissent seem weighty."[11] Conversion had both individual and communal significance. Admission to membership rested in the ability of candidates to "give evidence" of a genuine experience of grace.

Baptism

Baptism followed profession of faith. In defending their practices, Baptists addressed questions of both authority and mode. John Spilsbury was one of the first to take on the issue of the proper administrator for baptism. In *Gods Ordinance, the Saints Priviledge* (1646), Spilsbury called "His ordinances" "memorials of Christs love unto all that believe in him, and look for him in his absence."[12]

Spilsbury defended the practice of reinstituting believer's baptism through an administrator who was not previously immersed. He insisted that where biblical norms had been neglected for centuries, it was acceptable for someone who had not received believer's baptism to begin the practice again for the church. He wrote, "We finde not Christ confining the dispensing of Baptisme in the hands of baptized persons, and excluding others: neither is there any example where ever any that did baptize, were examined whether they themselves were baptized. The Scriptures no where expresly hold out the Administrators to be baptized persons, the Apostle Paul onely excepted; for of none but him doth the holy Spirit anywhere speak expresly of their being baptized." He concluded, "By all which appeares that baptizedness is not essential to an Administrator, and therefore we ought not to stay without when Christ the Porter opens, and invites us in."[13]

Of belief, Spilsbury wrote, "By believing in Christ, I meane that believing that Jesus is the Christ, which John Speakes of in 1 john 5.1. That believing with all the heart, which Philip spake of in Acts 8.37. That believing with the heart unto righteousness, which Paul speaks of in Rom. 10.9-10."[14] Christ himself required that faith be "confessed" publicly, hence the need for baptism.

Spilsbury addressed the question of whether women might serve as administrators of baptism—a practice that may have occurred in some Baptist settings. He rejected the idea, and observed, "And for womens administering of Ordinances; Gods free love and true faith never admits or gives way unto any unlawfull or disorderly libertie…. God who is the God of order, hath in his Word of truth taught women what their dutie is: and namely in 1 Cor. 14.34,35. 1 Tim. 2.11,12. This rule forbids unto them the administering of ordinances."[15]

Concerning the administrator of baptism, the Particular Baptist Confession of Faith of 1646 affirmed, "The person designed by Christ to dispense baptism, the scripture holds forth to be a disciple; it being no where tied to a particular church officer, or person extraordinarily sent."[16]

Election

The doctrine of election was an important topic among Baptists, especially the Reformed-oriented Particular Baptist congregations. This accompanied questions of limited atonement, free will, predestination, and the nature of salvation. Spilsbury examined the doctrine in a treatise entitled *The Peculiar Interest of the Elect in Christ and His Saving Grace*. He asserted that Christ's death did not apply to all persons and maintained that it was offered only to the elect. He asserted, "Christ intended not by his death to save all men from their sinnes, but thus to save the Elect onely."

For Spilsbury, Arminianism was dangerous because it: (1) opposed the biblical teaching on predestination; (2) robbed "God of the glory of his speciall and singular love and mercy to his chosen ones"; (3) puffed up "believers with pride, persuading them that they have distinguished themselves from the rest of the world, and so saved themselves: for Christ for his part did no more for them, than for those that perish"; (4) robbed "the saints of assurance of perseverance, and so of assurance of salvation. For if men come to be believers by a common grace afforded to all, than they may also cease to be believers through that weaknesse and corruption that is in all"; (5) and held "forth God as making a shew of being equally loving to all, when indeed and in his purpose he is not so: and seeming most graciously to forgive the sinnes of all men, when yet he determines to punish the vessels of wrath eternally in hell for all their sinnes."[17] His Calvinism was at the center of his Baptist identity.

Other Baptists sought to navigate between Calvinism and Arminianism, particularly on the doctrine of election. Thomas Crosby suggested that the Fenstanton church and its pastor, Henry Denne, represented a "middle way, being neither properly Calvinist nor Arminian."[18] They supported the doctrine of original sin but denied the idea of Christ's limited atonement. Baptists agreed that salvation was essential to Christian profession but differed as to the process and candidates.

Baptismal Immersion

By the mid-seventeenth century, Baptists in England had accepted immersion (or "dipping") as the primary mode for believer's baptism. As noted previously, the initial baptismal rituals involved trine affusion—pouring water three times on the head of the professing Christian, in the name of the Father, the Son, and the Holy Spirit. In 1641, Edward Barber suggested that the proper New Testament mode of baptism was found in dipping, not affusion. The practice of sprinkling children he labeled "an invention of men, brought in neere three hundered yeares after Christ."[19]

Barber substituted the word "dipped" for the word translated as "baptism" in English Bibles. He rendered Matthew 28:19-20 as "dipping them in the Name of the Father, and of the Sone, and of the Holy Spirit." Barber concluded, "Thus it is cleare, that the Lord Christ commanded his Apostles, and servants of the Gospel, … to dip those that were taught and instructed in the mysteries of the Gospel."[20]

For Barber, "That Dipping whereof we speake, is Dipping, burying, or plunging a Beleever in Water." Through baptismal immersion, "God doth by this holy ordinance, assure, and manifest, that he hath washed us from all our sinnes, by the blood of Jesus Christ, Acts 22.16, and doth truly and visibly receive us into the Covenant of grace."[21] Immersion is an outward sign of an internal transformation made possible by the work of Christ.

Baptismal Debates

Despite their acceptance of immersion as the primary mode for believer's baptism, Baptists were not of one mind in their understanding of baptism and its function in the church. Perhaps the most famous debate among seventeenth-century Baptist communities involved John Bunyan (1628–1688), one of the best-known writers of the period. From his church in Bedford, Bunyan refused to make baptism in general, and baptismal immersion in particular, absolute prerequisites for church membership or admission to communion. For Bunyan, faith and Christian discipleship were the hallmarks of the true believer. Baptism was spiritually beneficial but not essential to full membership in Christ's church. He wrote, "That by the word of faith, and of good works, moral duties gospelized, we ought to judge of the fitness of members by, by which we ought also to receive them to fellowship."[22] He affirmed the importance but not the unequivocal necessity of baptism prior to admission to church membership. Bunyan's church thus admitted the nonimmersed, even the unbaptized, to membership and to the Lord's Table.

In a 1673 treatise entitled *Differences in Judgment about Water-Baptism; No Bar to Communion,* Bunyan commented, "That I deny the Ordinance of Baptism, or that I have placed one piece of an Argument against it, … is quite without colour of truth. All I say, is, That the Church of Christ hath not Warrent to keep out of their Communion the Christian that is discovered to be a visible Saint by the Word, the Christian that walketh according to his Light with God."[23] He concluded, "Because Water-Baptism hath nothing to do in a Church, as a Church; it neither bringeth us into the Church, nor is any part of our Worship when we come ther; how then can the Peace and Unity of the Church depend upon Water-Baptism? Besides, … It is the Unity of the Spirit, (not Water) that is here intended."[24]

Bunyan was severely criticized by various Baptists, especially those in London. William Kiffin charged that the Bedford preacher undermined the biblical doctrine of baptism itself. Kiffin affirmed that baptism and communion were nonnegotiables of the Christian experience. Such "prescriptions of Christ" could not "be altered, or varyed, in any tittle, upon any pretence whatsoever, God never having given any such Prerogative to mankind, as to be arbiters how he may be best and most decently worshiped."[25] The controversy abated somewhat as persecution descended and Bunyan was imprisoned for twelve years in Bedford jail for violation of the Clarendon Code. However, divisions over open versus closed communion and related membership policies characterized Baptist church life into the twenty-first century.

B. R. White questioned Bunyan's Baptist identity and commented, "Those with 'open membership' convictions have tended to be taken by historians not only as the norm but as therefore an integral part of the early Calvinistic Baptist body. Yet the fact is that the 'open membership' churches were in a minority during the seventeenth century."[26] White insisted that while these divisions did not preclude friendships among Baptists holding differing views of membership, they did eliminate formal "church fellowship," essentially creating two denominational subgroups of Particular Baptists.[27] Questions of baptism, its mode and meaning for church membership, have created controversy and disagreement among Baptists from the beginning.

Baptism and Infants: The General Baptists

Children created something of a theological dilemma for the early Baptists. Since infants were not candidates for baptism but were subject to a high mortality rate, Baptists were compelled to address their salvific state. From the beginning, General Baptists excluded children from church membership and baptism.[28] John Smyth dismissed the idea of the church as parish, since it was a company of covenanted believers, not a "mixed" group of believers and unbelievers alike. He rejected infant baptism because baptism in the New Testament was "associated with conversion and with initiation into the church."[29] Baptism required repentance, Smyth believed, and since infants could not repent, they could not receive the rite.

In England, Thomas Helwys wrote *A Short and Plain Proof That No Infants Are Condemned* in an apparent effort to address the spiritual state of unbaptized infants. In a study of these issues, Michael J. Walker wrote, "In considering infants Helwys brings together his idea of sin as a personal responsibility and his belief that the death of Christ was for all. He attacks those who would assign infants to hell before they know the difference between right and wrong. His argument is mainly directed against Calvinists who limited the effect of Christ's atonement."[30]

Henry Hagger, in *The Foundation of the Font Discovered* (1653), discussed the General Baptist belief in two deaths. The first death is mortality, which is common to all as a result of the Fall; the second death is punishment for failure to repent. Children receive the first death but not the second death.[31] Hagger wrote that although children "must dye for Adam's sin, yet Christ is become their resurrection, and they have no actual sin to be judged for."[32] The children of unbelievers and believers alike were under the grace of God, heavenbound should they die in infancy.

The Orthodox Creed of 1679 offered assurance that infants who died were saved, "whether born of believing parents or unbelieving parents ... by the grace of God, and merit of Christ their redeemer, and work of the Holy Ghost, and in being made members of the invisible church, shall enjoy life everlasting.... Ergo, we conclude, that opinion is false, which saith, that those little infants dying before baptism, are damned."[33] Christ's "pre-grace," said General Baptist Thomas Grantham (1634–1692), "sanctifies them [infants] in a manner known to us."[34] General Baptists thus advised that while all children would experience the "first death" (common mortality), because of the fall of Adam, they would not experience the "second death," because of their innocence and the power of prevenient grace.

Particular Baptists and Infants

Most Particular Baptists distinguished between elect and nonelect infants and adults. They denied "any 'fleshly privilege' to the infants of believers, claiming that the new covenant did not recognise 'fleshly seed,' the new covenant knowing none and owning none 'to be the seed, but such as are Christs.'"[35] They repudiated the analogy between circumcision and baptism that often was used by those who baptized infants. John Toombs, a Particular Baptist pastor, left the eternal destiny of those dying in infancy to the mercy of God. The truly elect were not limited to all the baptized or to those inside the visible church. Toombs suggested that infants born to Christian believers were "born in the bosom of the Church, of godly parents, who by prayers, instruction, example, will undoubtedly educate them in the true faith of Christ."[36] Certain infants were in relationship with God through election, and that relationship could apply to "the infants of believers, & unbelievers, of Turkes, & Indians."[37]

The Second London Confession (1689) dealt explicitly with the issue of infant salvation and declared, "Elect infants dying in infancy, are regenerated and saved by Christ through the Spirit."[38] Election and reprobation applied to all persons, infant or adult. Nonelect infants, by inference, were never chosen for salvation, even if they died before reaching adulthood.

Some seventeenth-century Baptists practiced the dedication of infants. Thomas Ewins, pastor of the Broadmead Baptist Church, accepted the use of "dry baptism" for infants and described one such case in which a woman in the congregation requested "that her children be presented to the lord by prayer." Ewins thus recommended the practice "to all sober Christians who are dissatisfied with their judgments and consciences about Infant baptism."[39]

Clearly, Baptists agreed that infant baptism was unscriptural. They could not agree on the eternal status of those who died in infancy.

Baptists and the Lord's Supper

The early General and Particular Baptist confessions affirmed the importance of both baptism and the Lord's Supper. The Short Confession of 1610 noted that there are "two sacraments appointed by Christ, in his holy church, the administration whereof he hath assigned to the ministry of teaching, namely, the Holy Baptism and the Holy Supper. These are outward visible handlings and tokens, setting before our eyes, on God's side, the inward spiritual handling which God, through Christ, ... setteth forth."[40] The document refers to the Lord's Supper graphically, if awkwardly, as "the alive-making bread, meat, and drink for our souls."[41]

Debates over the Lord's Supper were not easily resolved. John Smyth and the General Baptists who came after him promoted strict communion—sharing the Lord's Table only with other Baptists. These Baptists later went beyond even that view, rejecting at the communion table any who refused to accept the laying on of hands at baptism.[42] This was the case in the 1656 General Assembly. Members of the Kent Baptist Association in 1657 also adopted this practice, basing their views on conformity to the "Six Principles" taken from Hebrews 6:1-2.

Among the General Baptists, most communion services were closed to nonmembers, but those from other congregations could receive communion if they secured permission from their own church and carried a "testimonial" to the service they wished to visit. One such "testimonial," dated 1655, stated, "Dear and holy brethren, we commend unto you our beloved brother Thomas Disbrowe, he being a member of the church of our Lord Jesus Christ, received by us, according to the order of the gospel. Wherefore we beseech you to receive him in the Lord, as becometh saints, and to assist him in whatsoever business he shall stand in need of you; and we shall account it as done unto ourselves." The entire congregation retained power to exclude and receive members, but the elders were the ones who made the formal declarations of such cases.[43] Some congregations, such as the one at Fenstanton, prepared themselves for the Lord's Supper by sharing in a common meal, or "love feast." Other churches did not do so.[44]

Early Particular Baptists for the most part practiced closed communion. Within the first fifteen to twenty years of their history, however, they included both open and closed communion churches. E. P. Winter observed, "Particular Baptist churches might be of the 'Closed' Communion or 'Open' (alias 'Mixt') Communion types, or even have 'Closed' membership but with 'Open' Communion. Further … some erstwhile 'Open' membership churches became 'Closed' later, and vice versa."[45]

Strict communionists insisted that admission to the Lord's Supper was linked to baptism, and they restricted communion to those who had received the proper believer's baptism. Still other churches maintained closed membership but practiced open communion, permitting those Independents who had retained infant baptism to commune. Bunyan's church at Bedford did not distinguish between those who had received infant or believer's baptism. It was a "Mixt" congregation.[46] Church membership rather than baptism was the basis for admission to the Lord's Table. All these churches, whether open or closed communionist, required a confession of faith as prerequisite for membership.

Baptist Practices: A Seventeenth-Century Critique

Such practices and beliefs made seventeenth-century Baptists the target of frequent criticism. One document, *The Dippers Dipt, or, The Anabaptists Duck'd and Plung'd over Head and Eares*, at a Disputation at Southwark, was written by Anglican cleric Daniel Featley in 1646. He warned that among "Heretiques and Schismatiques," the Anabaptists should be "carefully looked unto, and severely punished, if not utterly exterminated and banished out of the Church and Kingdome."[47]

Featley suggested that the Baptists were dangerous in part because of their close link to "other damnable Heretiques, both ancient and Later." These included Millenarians, Marcionites, Novatians, Arminians, and Brownists. Also, they waged "audacious attempts upon Church and State" whereby they "expect somewhat more than a Toleration." Already the Baptist call for complete religious liberty was known in England. Featley then observed of the movement:

> They preach, and print, and practice their Hereticall impieties openly; they hold their Conventicles weekly in our chiefe Cities, and Suburbs thereof, and there prophesie by turnes; and … they build one another in the faith of their sect, to the ruine of their soules; they flock in great multitudes to their Jordans, and both Sexes enter into the River, and are dipt after their manner with a kinde of spell containing the heads of their erroneous tenets, and their engaging themselves in their schismaticall Covenants, and (if I may so speak) combination of separation. And as they defile our Rivers with their impure washings, and our Pulpits with their false prophecies and phanaticall enthusiasmes, so the Presses sweat and groan under the load of their blasphemies.[48]

In a related treatise, Featley ridiculed the intellectual acumen of his Baptist opponents. Much of his diatribe focused on the inability of the Baptists to comprehend complex theological issues, given their educational (and class) deficiencies. Featley declared with disdain, "If you will dispute in Divinity, you must be able to produce the Scriptures in the Original Languages. For no Translation is simply Authenticall, or the undoubted word of God…. The Bible Translated therefore is not the undoubted Word of God, but so Farre onely as it agreeth with the Originall, which (as I am informed) none of you understand."[49]

Daniel Featley was a formidable critic of Baptist practices. His treatise set forth the beliefs of the sect as a warning against the dangers of an uninformed interpretation of Scripture by those whom he thought unqualified for proper theological reflection.

Associational Relationships

The Formation of Associations

W. T. Whitley observed, "Baptists from the beginning sought to maintain sisterly intercourse between local churches; they never thought that one church was independent of others."[50] Baptist connectionalism developed early as small congregations joined together for common support and encouragement. These associational relationships offered fiercely autonomous churches an extended ecclesiastical connection. What might be called a "proto-association" was evident in London in 1644 when seven Particular Baptist congregations in London approved a common confession of faith. The London Confession of 1644 stated, "Although the particular Congregations be distinct and severall Bodies, every one as a compact and knit Citie in itself; yet are they all to walk by one and the same Rule." These churches were "by all meanes convenient to have the counsell and help one of another in all needfull affairs of the Church, as members of one body in the common faith under Christ their onely head."[51] The origin of such associations may be traced to British Independency, specifically in the Jacob-Lathrop-Jessey Church of Southwark, London.

Because of obstacles created by travel and distances, the early English Baptists often had several congregations meeting from a single church and spread throughout a given region. These branches joined together to enact discipline and share the Lord's Supper. They represented another early form of associationalism.[52]

A letter from "The Churches of Christ in Ireland" (Baptist), sent to England in 1653, lists a collection of churches that united together in exchanging letters and in pursuing goals of teaching and ministry.[53] The *Transactions of the Baptist Historical Society* concluded, "The Irish letter implies that the Association idea was already in the air, if indeed it had not taken material shape."[54]

Soon other connections developed among Baptists in England and Wales, and by October 1653, there were two distinct clusters of churches in England. One, in London, was composed of churches related to Jessey, Knollys, and Simpson. A second associational contingent was in the western provinces. Their intent seemed to be mutual encouragement, doctrinal agreement, and the commissioning of teachers. It was the western association of churches that issued the first Baptist Circular Letter in 1654, a form of associational communication that continued for over two centuries. For generations, circular letters were a method of exchanging information and raising doctrinal questions among the churches.

The Stuart Restoration and the resulting intolerance stifled associational relationships during the period 1660–1672, after which the Declaration of Indulgence increased the possibility religious toleration. By the time of the Act of Toleration in 1689, there were at least twelve associational bodies throughout Britain.[55] The western association of churches, particularly around the Baptist stronghold of Bristol, was extremely influential during this period.

Associational Meetings

Associational meetings followed a common pattern, with ministers often gathering at a local inn. Typically, the assemblage might open on Tuesday and continue until Thursday. Daily sermons were followed by business sessions. Letters from participating churches were read by their specific congregational representatives. A circular letter was prepared, read, and approved. Copies were distributed to the representatives to be read aloud in each of the churches. These letters reported on business, responded to doctrinal and practical queries, and examined specific theological concerns.

Associational cooperation was often intermittent, depending on the needs of the times and the state of the churches. The Fenstanton Baptist Church, near Cambridge, observed in the mid-seventeenth century that the association came together for the purpose of "attaining to, or retaining of, unity and order in the churches."[56]

Associational Origins

Theories about the origins of associations are not without controversy. William Lumpkin suggested that associational alignments among the early British Baptists paralleled similar "military and political organizations" of the period. "Before 1660," Lumpkin contended, "permanent Associations had become typical Baptist institutions."[57] Robert Torbet proposed, "The pattern of the more formal associational organization, as it was worked out, was provided by a military expedient with which Baptists had become familiar during the Civil Wars (1642–1649) between King and Parliament."[58] B. R. White challenged Torbet's thesis and asserted, "The scheme launched by Parliament in the winter of 1642–1643 had very little in common with the inter-congregational co-operation of the Baptists, apart from the rather remote parallel afforded by Parliament linking their supporters among the county gentry together at all."[59] Baptists, White noted, seldom utilized the term "association" during the 1640s and 1650s, preferring to describe their cooperative endeavors as the "General Meeting."[60] White concluded that the 1644 Confession of Faith, as accepted by representatives of numerous churches, exemplified the earliest configuration of "elders and messengers," from which the source of Baptist associations formed.[61] Whatever their specific origins, Baptist associations were gatherings beyond the local congregation for fellowship, mutual encouragement, doctrinal stability, and often disciplinary authority.

The English General Baptists were particularly strong in their connectionalism. General Baptist churches sometimes permitted the entire association to excommunicate persons from specific congregations—an act that cut the offender off from all churches in the association.[62] General Baptists also celebrated the Lord's Supper at associational gatherings—something Calvinistic Baptists would not do.

The Ordination of Ministers

From the beginning of their movement, Baptists recognized the need for an ordained ministry, but they were not uniform in their practices for "setting aside" appropriate candidates. As congregationalists, they generally acknowledged that the two basic officers of a New Testament church were pastors (elders) and deacons. Some, influenced by the presbyterian system, understood church leadership to be a fourfold office including pastors, teachers, elders, and deacons. A 1611 statement declared, "That the officers of every church or congregation are either Elders, who by their office do especially lead the flock concerning their souls ... or Deacons, men and women who by their office relieve the necessities of the poor and impotent brethren concerning their bodies." An early Particular Baptist Confession noted,

"Every church has power given them from Christ for their better well being, to choose to themselves meet persons into the office of Pastors, Teachers, Elders, Deacons."[63]

Some General Baptists believed that ordination applied only to ministry in a specific congregation. Thomas Helwys observed, "The officers of every church or congregation are tied by office only to that particular congregation whereof they are chosen." This is evidence of the Brownist, Separatist influence on the General Baptists and the idea of a covenant binding individuals to both God and the church.[64]

Helwys stressed the authority of the congregation in matters of the ordinances. He rejected the idea, present among the Mennonites, "that Elders must make Elders, and none but Elders must administer in the holie things." Rather, Helwys and his early band held that the power to celebrate the ordinances rested with the congregation, not exclusively with the clergy.[65] The authority of Christ was mediated through the covenanting community of believers, not through presbytery, synod, or episcopacy.

The Ordination Process

Seventeenth-century British Baptists often followed three stages leading to the appointment of ministers: (1) "election by the church" (General Baptist Confession [1678]); (2) approbation (approval) by the church, "that these officers are to be chosen by election and approbation of that church or congregation whereof they are members" (General Baptist Confession [1611]); and (3) ordination by the elders of the church.[66] From the beginning, Baptists recognized the importance of an ordained ministry and established procedures for shaping such offices.

The following procedure, although not necessarily normative, was developed by the Fenstanton Church for selecting officers from the congregation, as elders, teachers and deacons.

> That two companies should be sent forth from the congregation apart, the one from the other, to nominate persons.
>
> Secondly, that if the congregation should give their consent to the persons so nominated, that then they should testify the same by the holding up of the hand.
>
> Thirdly, that the persons thus chosen should be set before the elders of the church for their approbation.
>
> Fourthly, that if the persons chosen as aforesaid should be approved by the elders, that they should be ordained by the laying on of hands.[67]

When decisions were difficult, and the congregation divided over candidates, they might, as in the case of the Fenstanton church, cast lots to determine the proper leader. Such a process meant that "lots being made, prayer was made to the Lord that he would order and dispose of them, according to his own mind."[68] Early ordination services apparently utilized at least three basic elements: (1) prayer by the church for the candidate; (2) a charge or challenge to the minister; and (3) the laying on of hands. Candidates often were allowed to carry out the "ministry of preaching" but were not to be ordained until called to a specific congregation.[69] Financial support for ministers was also an important issue. The Particular Baptist Confession of 1644 noted, "The due maintenance of the officers aforesaid should be the free and voluntary communication of the church."[70] Yet the General Baptist confession of 1651 declared, "The servants of God or the Ministers of the Gospel ought to be content with necessary food and raiment and to labour with their hands that they may not be overchargeable."[71] Many ministers were required to support themselves as teachers, physicians, or tradespeople in order to make ends meet.

Ordination and the Administration of the Ordinances

Particular Baptists spoke of elders and deacons designated "with imposition of hands of the Eldership of the Church, if there be any before constituted therein."[72] Ordination was not necessarily a prerequisite for those who administered the sacraments. The Particular Baptist (London) Confession of 1644 labeled those who administered baptism to be the "considered disciple" or "preaching disciple," and noted, "it being no where tyed to a particular Church, Officer, or person extraordinarily sent, the Commission injoyning the administration, being given to them under no other consideration, but as considered Disciples."[73] This probably meant that baptism could be administered by an ordained preacher, and possibly by an unordained preacher, without need for a bishop or other church officers present.

Discussion of the participation of unordained persons in administration of communion led the Western Assembly of 1693 to determine that "no private brother (however gifted) if not solemnly called to ministerial office and separated thereto ought to administer the ordinance of baptism and the Last Supper.... A brother called to the office of elder by the suffrage of the church may administer all ordinances though he be not immediately ordained by the laying on of the hands of the elders." The General Baptists decided in 1689 that "distinct officers must have their distinct ordinances and the church has no way to delegate an office or power Ministerial but by Ordination."[74]

Messengers and Deaconesses

General and Particular Baptists alike maintained the office of "messenger" as a distinct ministerial function among their churches. Exactly when this practice began is unclear, but it seems to have grown out of the specific needs of the churches. In 1651, an effort to distinguish Baptists from the Fifth Monarchy movement included a reference to "many of the Messengers, Elders and Brethren belonging to severall of the Baptized Churches in this nation."[75] Minutes from a 1656 Baptist General Agreement signed by ten representatives indicate that "messengers and elders being both apt to teach is ye presbittery of the church and no other."[76] J. F. V. Nicholson observed, "It appears that throughout the decade 1650 to 1660 the term messenger was used by both General and Particular Baptists to denote anyone who was commissioned by one church to preach the Gospel and form new churches, or who was sent by one church to another to settle a dispute or discuss matters of common concern."[77] In areas of Kent and the Midlands, General Baptists understood messengers to be a clerical office distinct from that of elders.

The 1678 General Baptist Confession states that pastors or elders should be ordained by "a Bishop or Messenger God hath placed in the church he hath charge of."[78] The Fenstanton Church, in 1653, was one of the first to set aside "a messenger to divulge the gospel of Jesus Christ."[79] Messengers were understood to be "successors to the apostles," involved in itinerant ministry, overseeing ordination of pastors, and assisting "faithful Pastours or churches against usurpers."[80]

Thomas Grantham was one of the best-known General Baptist messengers. Often imprisoned for his views, Grantham was ordained to the messenger's office in 1666. Adam Taylor cites Grantham's own description in a book called *Dispute with Connould,* dated 1691. Grantham stated that he was "ordained messenger to oversee the churches in divers places that had need for help."[81]

By the eighteenth century, the term *messenger* was used to designate representatives, nominated by the local association, but approved by the general assembly and the local church. They were understood to be messengers of the baptized churches of a certain region. William Evershed's sermon "The Messenger's Mission" (1783) listed three duties of the messengers: (1) oversee order in the churches, visiting congregations in a specific region; (2) mediate in church disputes and abuses; and (3) participate in the ordination of elders. Thus, the General Baptists understood the messenger as a third order similar to that of apostle, or traveling preacher, in the New Testament.[82]

The idea, if not the actual practice, of selecting deaconesses in English Baptist congregations is apparent in several early Baptist documents. Such an office, found among the English Separatists, was described by John Smyth both before and after he instituted the Baptist congregation in Amsterdam. As early as 1607, while leader of the Gainsborough group of Separatist Puritans, Smyth discussed the office of deaconess as based on 1 Timothy 5:9. They were widows, over sixty years old, charged with ministering to the "bodily infirmities of the Saints."[83]

Thomas Helwys's earliest confession of faith listed women deacons with other officers, all elected by the membership. The article reads, "That the Officers off everie Church or congregation are either Elders, who by their office do especially feed the flock concerning their soules, Act. 20.28, Pet. 5.2, 3, or Deacons Men, and Women who by their office releave the necessities off the poore and impotent brethre[n] concerning their bodies, Acts. 6.1-4."[84] In the Helwys document, the women and men are both referred to as deacons. This appears to be the only such reference among the best-known English Baptist confessions of faith.[85]

While few English Baptist churches actually had females serving in the diaconate, the Broadmead Church in Bristol did. That congregation elected a deaconess in 1662, 1673, and 1679.[86] Selected by the church, these women were required to be over the age of sixty, to promise not to marry (see 1 Timothy 5:11), and to offer care and spiritual encouragement to the sick and the dying. They were to report specific needs to the elders and deacons. Women were permitted to be caregivers, but only within certain predetermined parameters that guarded against any hint of sexual indiscretion or exceptional ecclesiastical authority.

Baptist Churches and Discipline

The practices of the seventeenth-century Baptist congregations demonstrate areas of conformity and division inside and outside the local churches. For example, Baptist congregations did not hesitate to exercise discipline over their members. It was one of the identifying marks of the church within the Reformed tradition, in which the church was a community where the Word of God was preached, the sacraments rightly administered, and discipline carried out. Discipline was a community action aimed at leading recalcitrant members to repentance while safeguarding the moral and spiritual integrity of the church.

Generally, formal entry to membership in Baptist churches was by application. The applicant was required to recount a conversion experience and testify to a change of life and conduct. When members fell into sin, discipline preserved the purity of the church and the integrity of the gospel. Some scholars distinguish between preventive and corrective discipline in Baptist life. Preventive discipline was used to maintain orthodoxy and uniformity in ethics; corrective discipline offered a remedy for sins committed.[87]

Procedures for dealing with wayward members, as evidenced in a 1656 document from the General Assembly of General Baptists, illustrate common practices. The "first admonition" involved refusing the guilty party admission to worship. Shunning might also occur so that the sinner was "also not to be eaten with in common eating." If the individual continued to be "obstinate," then a second admonition was imparted. The rebellious person was "not to be looked upon as Brethren nor any ways belonging to the body so as the Church hath any more to do to looke after them." Exceptions were made, however. It was "agreed that in case of necessity as betwixt man & wife members may eat common food with P'sons that are incommunicable in other things." Often the offender was not allowed to receive the Lord's Supper until the specific charge was removed. After interviews with church leaders, a guilty verdict meant that offenders were officially excluded from "table of the Lord," "till they shall be satisffied of his reall & hearty repentance and give satisfaction to the church."[88] Serious offenses meant excommunication and a denial of full fellowship with the church. Repentance and confession brought reinstatement to the community. Discipline could be administered for things such as "fleshly lusts" and "ye sin of drunkenness & picking up hearlots in the streets."[89]

Sexual sins often were a cause for discipline against women. T. Dowley observed, "Whether this is because the women were more frequently guilty of sexual misdemeanors, or because looseness among male members was condoned or more easily overlooked, is impossible to say."[90] These accounts, written by men, suggest that women received discipline for sins in which men were also involved but for which men were not charged.

Absence from church meetings, general spiritual laxity, or attending non-Baptist services could lead to disciplinary action. One woman was disciplined at the Seventh-Day Mill Yard Church "for frequenting those places of worshipp where god is not worshipped according to his word."[91] Discipline could be administered for marriage outside the Baptist fold, especially if the spouse was Anglican. Doctrinal infidelity—denying the Trinity or the atonement, holding unorthodox biblical interpretations—also could lead to discipline from the church.[92]

Another example of seventeenth-century congregational discipline is found in the "Discipline Book" maintained by Robert Sneed during his tenure as copastor of the church first served by Hanserd Knollys. One entry from its 1689 minutes reads as follows:

Joseph Faircloth Being a member of the Church and an apprentice with a Haberdasher of Leeds [?] on London Bridge was charged with being gilty of a vaine wanton scandalous conversation with a woman that had an evil report for her light carriage who was wife to a cheesemonger in the Borrough of Southwark: For which He was admonished in the Church as also for his neglecting his master's business and being out late at night at unseasonable times with the woman aforesayd. But He appearing obstinate and impenitant and his offence or sin being greatly immorall to the reproach of his holy profession He was cast out of the Church and totally excluded from its communion.[93]

Discipline and excommunication revolved around the procedure set forth in Matthew 18 for dealing with disobedient members. While the specifics for confronting sinful members could vary, the primary cause of excommunication came from "failure to hear the church"—that is, the refusal of the member to receive the discipline and admonition of the congregation regarding a specific breach of conduct or belief. Thomas Helwys suggested that it was not the "committing of sin [that] doth cut off from the Church but refusing to hear the Church to reformation."[94]

Marriage outside the community of Baptist believers was also an offense that could cut one off from fellowship. Among General Baptists this had the effect of weakening the number of church members. The General Assembly of General Baptists in 1656 ruled that churches should accept such marriages after they were contracted and thereby permit members to remain in the church.[95]

Church discipline was an important element of seventeenth-century Baptist church life. It was also difficult to maintain. Congregational polity meant that churches could divide over disciplinary action on which the congregation could not agree. Likewise, discipline sometimes could give way to pettiness and selectivity in application.

Baptist Worship

General Baptist worship practices centered around prayers and preaching. A letter dating from around 1609 by Hughe and Anne Bromheade described the worship practices of Smyth's earliest congregation of Baptists:

> The order of the worshippe and government of oure church is .1. we begynne with A prayer, after reade some one or tow chapters of the bible gyve the sence thereof, and conferr Vpon the same; that done we lay aside ourebookes, and after a solemne prayer made by the .1. speaker, he propuundeth some text owt of the Scripture, and prophecieth owt of the same, by the space of one hower, or thre Quarters of an hower. After him standeth vp A .2. speaker and prophecieth owt of the said text the like tyme and space, some tyme more some tyme less.[96]

The "Morning exercise" began at eight and continued to noon. An afternoon session lasted from two to five or six "of the Clocke." The latter session concluded with a business meeting, with decisions determined by a majority vote of those present.

Baptist Hymnody

Even a brief survey of Baptist hymnody illustrates diversity in the worship life of the churches. From lining out the psalms to the singing of "man-made" hymns, Baptists debated the methods, the texts, and the theology of the hymns they sang. Hymns taught doctrine, nurtured spirituality, and united the faithful in a common liturgical endeavor. In seventeenth-century England, the standard Protestant practice was to sing the psalms as the only divinely inspired hymnody of the church. The psalms were sung, without accompaniment from musical instruments, as lined out by the presenter, who sang a phrase that was repeated back by the congregation. Gradually, certain hymns of human composition came to be used. Musical instruments were added much later.

Some suggest that the earliest hymns for children probably were written by Baptists, and many of the female hymn writers in Protestantism probably were Baptists.[97] One of the earliest, if not the first, of the Baptist women hymn writers was Anna Trapnell, a Fifth Monarchist who claimed immediate inspiration of the Spirit for her hymnody. She published a 1654 work of "prayers and spiritual songs" titled *The Cry of a Stone*. Another Baptist, Katherine Sutton, also published a volume of songs used as hymns, or solos, in Baptist meetings.[98] These materials were called "hymns"—a term that in the seventeenth century may have meant the adaptation of the psalms, a "devotional poem," or a basic song.

English Baptists came to accept the singing of hymns as well as the traditional psalm singing, but not without controversy. A leader in the effort to encourage hymn singing was Benjamin Keach (1640–1704), a Particular Baptist pastor at Southwark. In 1660, he became pastor of a General Baptist church in Aylesbury, and in 1664 he wrote a primer, *The Child's Delight: or, Instructions for Children and Youth*, for the instruction of children. For this, he was jailed for "writing, printing and publishing a schismatical book."[99] The book included poetry for teaching the Decalogue. It read, in part:

To School I'll go, and learn to do
whatever God doth say;
No God but he, that formed me,
I'll worship and obey.

> *My Parents too, I honour do,*
> *and them I will obey,*
> *In all things right, as in God's sight,*
> *and for them I will pray.*

Murder and kill, I never will,
nor malice in me bear
To he or she, although I see
my moral Foes they are.

> *Adultery, good Men defie;*
> *O 'tis a cursed evil:*
> *And such who to Whore-houses go,*
> *must perish with the Devil.*

I steal will not, that brings a blot,
that will not pass away.
The Thief also to Hell must go
in the most dismal day.

> *False witness bear, I will not dare,*
> *but will my Neighbour love;*
> *And harmless be continually,*
> *like to the pretty Dove.*

What others have I will not Crave,
but will in every thing
Of God's just Law stand still in Awe,
and honour to him bring.[100]

Keach published a collection of hymns, *Spiritual Melody*, in 1691, and a sequel, *Spiritual Songs*, in 1696. His lyrics exude earthiness, as evidenced in these couplets:

Our wounds do stink and are corrupt,
Hard Swellings we do see;
We want a little ointment, Lord,
Let us more humble be.

>*Repentance like a bucket is*
>*To pump the water out;*
>*For leaky is our ship, alas,*
>*Which makes us look about.*

Here meets them now that worm that gnaws
And plucks their bowels out;
The pit, too, on them shuts her jaws,
This dreadful is, no doubt.[101]

These hymns did not gain great popularity among English Baptists but were evidence of Baptist efforts to articulate a "people's theology."

Singing Hymns: A Baptist Debate

Hymn singing was not undertaken easily. In 1673, Keach prevailed upon his church to sing a hymn at the end of a communion service, citing appropriate biblical admonitions. Six years later, the congregation agreed to sing hymns on days of "public thanksgiving." It was another fourteen years before the church began to sing hymns consistently in worship.

Critics denied that congregational singing could be found in the New Testament. In a treatise entitled *The Controversy on Singing Brought to an End*, Baptist layman Isaac Marlow insisted that "there is no Example nor Command for such a practice in the worship of God under the Early Law ... nor in the first Gospel churches."[102] He contended that whatever singing did occur in the New Testament was a special gift of the Spirit, not comparable to any form of singing in contemporary churches.

Marlow also suggested that permitting women to sing in church was a clear violation of the biblical adages that compelled females to be silent. He wrote, "Seeing women are commanded not to teach nor to speak in the church but to learn in silence, and to be in silence; for the Apostle's words imply that for women not to learn in silence in the Church, but to break their silence there, ... is a usurpation of authority, and disobedience to the Law."[103]

Thomas Grantham was an articulate opponent of hymn singing. In his monumental *Christianimus Primitivus*, he observed that the church of his day had experienced "the encroachment of humane Innovations," of which hymn singing was a tragic illustration. Like other General Baptists, Grantham repudiated "promiscuous singing" in which Christians and non-Christians sang together in a service of worship.[104]

While most of the early General Baptists rejected hymn singing, Particular Baptists were divided on the topic. The controversy was so serious that in 1692 a committee was appointed to deal with the matter. It produced a condemnation of the attitudes of both sides and urged reconciliation. Divisions continued until both General and Particular Baptists accepted hymn singing as appropriate for public worship.[105]

Katherine Sutton, Baptist Hymn Writer

Katherine Sutton was one of the most prolific Baptist hymn writers of the seventeenth century. The title page to her hymnbook stated, "A Christian Womans Experiences of the Glorious Working of Gods Free Grace. Published for the Edification of others, by Katherine Sutton. Luk. 24.24, And they found it even so, as the Women had said....1663."[106] Hanserd Knollys's preface to Sutton's hymnbook indicates his belief that both prayer and hymn singing should be extemporaneous—that is, they should be unrehearsed and from the heart. Such an approach would have favored solos rather than congregational hymns in worship. Sutton's hymns probably were sung as solos by herself and by others.[107]

Sutton's own conversion followed the classic evangelical Calvinist pattern involving a sense of spiritual despair that extended over a two-year period. During this time, she wrote, "the God of comfort was pleased to withdraw and leave mee in a deserted condition."[108] With conversion came her decision to leave Anglicanism for the Baptists. In 1655, she reported that she was "indued with the gift of singing, in such a way and manner as I had not been acquainted with before," and received a revelation of several hymn-poems. Some of her poems are "Prophesyes," including:

> Shall light appear, and darkness done away:
> Shall sommers green be cloathed all in grey,
> Shall a bright morning set in shadowes dark,
> Oh! England, England, take heed thou dost not smart.[109]

Hymns and poetry were an acceptable way for Baptist women to have voice in the community of faith. The hymns and poetry reveal some of the first public efforts of Baptist women to offer theological reflection in and for the churches.

Baptist Poets

The contribution of early Baptists to the arts has received only limited attention from scholars. Poetry was a form of spiritual expression among seventeenth-century Baptist writers. Certain Baptists set out their thoughts in verse.

Some of Abraham Cheare's verses are included in a book published with the writings of Henry Jessey under the title *A Looking Glass for Children: Being a Narrative of God's Gracious Dealings with Some Little Children.*[110] Cheare (1626–1667/8?) was first imprisoned in 1661 for "encouraging religious assemblies" but was released after three months. He refused to take the Oath of Allegiance or any oath and was again imprisoned 1665. He then was exiled to the island of St. Nicholas, where he remained until his death. Cheare wrote of that experience in these verses:

> Nigh four years since, sent out from hence,
> To Exon Gaol was I,
> But special Grace in three months' space,
> Wrought bout my liberty.
> Till Bartholomew in sixty-two,
> That freedom did remain;

Then without bail to Exon Gaol,
I hurried was again,
Where having laid, as do the slain
'Mong dead men wholly free;
Full three years' space, my native place,
By leave I came to see.
And thought not then, I here again
A moneth's restraint should find,
Since to my Den, cast out from men,
I'm during life design'd.
But since my lines the Lord assigns
In such a lot to be,
I kiss the rod, confess my God
Deals faithfully with me.
My charged crime, in His due time,
He fully will decide,
And until then, forgiving men,
In peace with Him I bide.[111]

As might be expected, John Bunyan's literary gifts were evident in his response to a twelve-year imprisonment. His poetry, like his larger prose works *(Pilgrim's Progress* and *Grace Abounding to the Chief of Sinners)* offered a way of dealing with the realities of incarceration and deprivation. Bunyan's "Prison Meditations" from Bedford Gaol contain these verses:

I am (indeed) in Prison (now)
In Body, but my Mind
Is free to Study Christ, and how
Unto me He is kind.

>*For though men keep my outward man*
>*Within their Locks and Bars,*
>*Yet by the Faith of Christ I can*
>*Mount higher than the Stars.*

Their Fetters cannot spirits tame,
Nor tye up God from me;
My Faith and Hope they cannot lame,
Above them I shall be.

>*I here am very much refresh't*
>*To think when I was out,*
>*I preached Life, and Peace, and Rest*
>*To sinners round about.*

My business then was Souls to Save,
By preaching Grace and Faith,
Of which the comfort now I have
And have it shall to death.[112]

Baptists used poetry to assuage their spiritual and physical deprivations in the face of persecution and imprisonment. Art found its way into prison cells.

Concern for the Poor

There is some evidence of Baptist concern for the poor during the seventeenth century, as illustrated in a tract published by Thomas Lamb. Lamb's treatise *An Appeal to the Parliament Concerning the Poor, That There May Not Be a Beggar in England* (1660) urged leaders not to throw charity at the poor but to find ways to give them decent work. He implored proprietors to hire and train the impoverished and urged churches to provide such training to the indigent. He called for leaders to make known "the sad condition of the Poor," even when it was "trouble" to do so. He wrote, "They have such Multitudes of Beggars in this fruitful Kingdom, ... to hear them cry and not give, is not that trouble? To hear their cry, and give, is trouble also; not knowing whether it doth good or harm."[113]

"Poor relief" was a concern of most Baptist congregations. It was addressed by calls for public response, by special offerings, and by individual actions on the part of members.

The Instruction of Children

In an attempt to nurture children, Baptists published catechisms that introduced young people to the rudiments of Christian doctrine. One early catechism, *The Child's Delight: or, Instructions for Children and Youth,* was written by Benjamin Keach in 1664 as a primer to teach both reading and orthodoxy. Instruction provided moral admonitions in poetic form. The lessons began this way:

Learn to read, good Child, with Care,
    For what with Learning can compare?
It is a rare and precious thing,
    Which will both Grace and Vertue bring.
It yieldeth Joy, Delight, and Pleasure,
    With Riches too, the chiefest Treasure.[114]

The book included a catechism based on the traditional question/answer format. A section on the Lord's Supper also attacked Catholic doctrine:

Qu. What think you then of that Popish Doctrine of Transubstantiation?
Ans. I believe it is absurd, Blasphemous, and an Idolatrous Doctrine, to be abominated by all good Christians: For as it is against Scripture, so it is against Reason; Christ's body cannot be but in one place at once.[115]

Apparently, children were required to sort through the intricacies of "Real Presence" and other fine points of doctrine. Keach later published a larger, more extensive, catechism, which was widely used by Baptists well into the eighteenth century.

Baptist Beliefs: Seventeenth-Century Confessions of Faith

English Baptists summarized their beliefs in confessions of faith, outlines of doctrine used by churches and associations in defining orthodoxy and distinguishing Baptists from other Christian communions. While Baptists made extensive use of confessions, they often disagreed over the use of such documents and their relationship to Scripture, conscience, and congregational autonomy. William Lumpkin concluded, "No confession has ever permanently bound individuals, churches, associations, conventions, or unions among Baptists. Even when issued, the confessions have allowed for individual interpretation and perspective, so that each signatory was made to feel that the statements spoke for him."[116]

H. Wheeler Robinson maintained, "So far as the general substance and aim of these historic creeds [Apostles', Nicene, and others] are concerned, it may safely be asserted that Baptists are as loyal to them as are any of the evangelical Churches. Yet it is equally true that Baptists hold a very detached position in regard to creeds and formal confessions of faith as such."[117] Likewise, mere assent to the doctrines of any confession or creed was no substitute for personal regeneration as the basis of a believers' church. Nonetheless, when doctrinal disputes arose, Baptists were compelled to decide how to utilize confessions and deal with the schisms that might result.

The confessions written by seventeenth-century Baptists are particularly important because they informed the earliest doctrinal identity of the Baptist people and became guides for later confessional statements. Lumpkin noted that the Commonwealth Period (1650–1659) "was more productive of Confessions than any similar period in Baptist history."[118] These confessions demonstrate a doctrinal diversity covering a spectrum from Arminian to Calvinist. They set boundaries for specific Baptist groups. Those who differed were free to write their own statements.

Each confession included statements of general Christian orthodoxy and specific Baptist beliefs. They affirmed Trinitarian concepts of God, along with declarations on Christology, salvation, the sacraments (ordinances), Scripture, church polity, and the final judgment.

One of the earliest Baptist confessions, "A Declaration of Faith of English People Remaining at Amsterdam in Holland" (1611), no doubt written by Thomas Helwys, contained some twenty-seven articles written from an Arminian perspective. It declared, "GOD before the Foundation of the World hath Predestinated that all that beleeve in him shall-be saved, … and all that believe not shall be damned." It also acknowledged that believers may "fall away from the grace of GOD."[119]

The congregationalism of the group was expressed in no uncertain terms: "That as one congregation hath CHRIST, so hath all, 2. Cor. 10.7. And that the Word of GOD cometh not out from any one, neither to any one congregation in particular…. But unto every particular Church, as it doth vnto al the world Coll. i.5.6. And therefore no church ought to challeng any prerogative over any other."[120]

Like most of the early General Baptist confessions, this document commenced with a doctrine of God, not Scripture. Later, more Reformed-oriented confessions began with affirmations of Scripture.

In 1654, London General Baptists issued a confession known as "The True Gospel Faith," written both as a statement of their beliefs and as a means of distinguishing themselves from the Society of Friends, the Quakers. The document omitted reference to deacons, listing church officers as "Messengers, Pastors and Teachers."[121] It was the first Baptist confession to prescribe the laying on of hands for all the newly baptized—a practice promoted by various Baptist groups.[122]

Conflict with Quakerism was a factor in the decision of a Particular Baptist Association of churches in the western region of Somerset to produce a confession in 1656. Calvinist in its orientation, it is the only Baptist confession of the time to include a comment on the Jews alongside an article on the church's missionary role. It stated, "That it is the duty of us believing Gentiles, not to be ignorant of that blindness that yet lieth on Israel, that none of us may boast (Rom. 11:25), but to have bowels of love and compassion to them, praying for them (Rom. 10:1), expecting their calling and so much the rather, because their conversion will be to us life from the dead (Rom. 11:15)."[123]

In 1660, the General Assembly of General Baptists approved what became known as "The Standard Confession," "set forth by many of us, who are (falsely) called Ana-Baptists, to inform all Men (in these days of scandal and reproach) of our innocent Belief and Practice; for which we are not only resolved to suffer Persecution, to the loss of our Goods, but also Life itself, rather than to decline the same."[124]

The confession reflected controversial issues present in the fledgling Baptist communities. These included the eternal bliss of deceased infants (affirmed), the use of tithes (rejected), and the freedom of conscience (affirmed). Concerning conscience, the confession stated, "That it is the will, and mind of God (in these Gospel times) that all men should have the free liberty of their own Consciences in matters of Religion, or Worship, without the least oppression, or persecution, as simply upon that account."[125]

The conclusion of the document responds to what apparently were popular charges against Baptists in London, probably related to their involvement with the Fifth Monarchy movement and the use of armed resistance. It stated, "Moreover we do utterly, and from our very hearts, in the Lords fear, declare against all those wicked, and devilish reports, and reproaches, falsely cast upon us, as though some of us (in & about the City of London) had lately gotten knives, booked knives, & the like, & great store of Arms besides what was given forth by order of Parliament, intending to cut the throats of such as were contrary minded to us in matters of Religion."[126]

Perhaps the most important confession of the seventeenth-century Baptists was the so-called Second London Confession of Particular Baptists, published in 1689. It is one of the longest of the early confessions, with doctrinal statements mirroring the Calvinism of the period as set forth in the Westminster Confession of the 1640s. Its commitment to Reformed theology was precise and unapologetic, with attention to total depravity, the salvation of the elect, the particular atonement of Christ, and the perseverance of the saints. It declared, for example, that "neither are any other redeemed by Christ, or effectually called, justified, adopted, sanctified, and saved, but the Elect only."[127] As noted earlier, the confession recognizes the salvation of only elect infants, while acknowledging that all elect persons will be saved, even if they have not received the preached Word. The confession addressed the Baptist concern for the freedom of conscience, maintaining that "God alone is judge of the Conscience, and hath left it free from the Doctrines and Commandments of men which are in any thing contrary to his Word, or not contained in it."[128]

Articles on baptism and the Lord's Supper use the term "ordinances" rather than "sacraments" to describe the observance. The section on the Lord's Supper gives great attention to what the ordinance is not, with particular reference to the doctrine of Real Presence, or transubstantiation. Yet, consistent with Reformed theology, it accepts the idea of Christ's spiritual presence in the elements of bread and wine. It maintains, "Worthy receivers ... spiritually receive, and feed upon Christ crucified & all the benefits of his death: the Body and Blood of Christ, being then not corporally, or carnally, but spiritually present to the faith of Believers."[129]

These confessions reflect both the common ideals and the significant diversity of Baptist belief in the seventeenth century. Faith, baptism, the Lord's Supper, congregational polity, and freedom of conscience appear in one form or another in each of the documents. Basic Protestant orthodoxy abides throughout. Differences over the concepts of election, free will, perseverance, the laying on of hands, and in some cases, the salvation of infants show significant diversity.

Educational Institutions

From the beginning, Baptists have debated the benefits of formal education, particularly for clergy. While some of the early Baptist leaders (Henry Jessey and Hanserd Knollys) were educated at Oxford or Cambridge, many others received only limited educational training. Thomas Collier, a Baptist leader in western England, suggested in 1651, "It is the spirit of Antichrist that seeks after humane help [education] to supply the room or want of his Spirit of Christ and having gotten it they grow proud of it, are self conceited in it, make it their idol and dare reproach the Spirit and power of the Lord and His saints."[130] Some obviously felt that education was detrimental to faith and undermined the genuine piety of the minister.

Nonetheless, many Baptists insisted on an educated ministry and worked to establish schools. In 1675, London Baptist pastors called for a conference to develop "a plan for providing an orderly standing ministry who might give themselves to reading and study, and so become able ministers of the New Testament."[131] By 1679, Edward Terrill, member of Broadmead Baptist Church, Bristol, set aside property for supporting a minister who also would instruct younger ministers. This legacy funded the Bristol Academy, which officially got underway in 1720. Baptists, kept out of establishment colleges, moved slowly but surely to develop their own institutions.

Baptist Identity Takes Shape

Baptists in England came a long way in the seventeenth century. From the small groups of dissenters in Amsterdam and London, Baptists established churches and associations, wrote confessions of faith, and divided over open versus closed communion, Calvinism and Arminianism, Sunday and Sabbath worship, and other disputes. They experienced persecution, interacted with other dissenting sects, and demanded religious liberty from various monarchs. Amid diversity, they demonstrated a growing sense of unity and cooperation that would continue to evolve during the eighteenth century.

Notes

1.   B. R. White, "The Origins and Convictions of the First Calvinistic Baptists," *Baptist History and Heritage* 25 (October 1990): 43–44.

2. Paul S. Fiddes, "'Walking Together': The Place of Covenant Theology in Baptist Life Yesterday and Today," in *Pilgrim Pathways: Essays in Baptist History in Honour of B. R. White*, ed. William H. Brackney and Paul S. Fiddes (Macon, Ga.: Mercer University Press, 1999), 48.

3. Ibid., 53–55.

4. Karen Smith, "The Covenant Life of Some Eighteenth-Century Calvinistic Baptists in Hampshire and Wiltshire," in Brackney and Fiddes, eds., *Pilgrim Pathways*, 168.

5. Charles W. Deweese, *Baptist Church Covenants* (Nashville: Broadman, 1990), 26.

6. Ibid., 26–27. Knollys cited Acts 8:12, 35-39; 16:30-33; and 18:8 as evidence that covenants were no longer necessary.

7. Ibid., 27 (citing Benjamin Keach, *The Glory of a True Church, and Its Discipline Display'd* [London, 1697], 5).

8. Ibid., 30–31.

9. Ibid., 121 (citing Keach, *True Church*, 71–74).

10. E. P. Winter, "The Lord's Supper," *Baptist Quarterly* 17 (1957–58): 274 (citing Keach, *True Church*, 6-7).

11. Ibid.

12. John Spilsbury, *Gods Ordinance, the Saints Priviledge* (London: M. Simmons, 1646), 1.

13. Ibid., 10.

14. Ibid., 26.

15. Ibid., 29–30.

16. Thomas Crosby, *The History of the English Baptists*, 4 vols. (London, 1738–40), 1:21 (appendix).

17. John Spilsbury, *Gods Ordinance*, 80. The treatise on election is included in this larger tract on baptism.

18. Cecil M. Roper, "Henry Denne and the Fenstanton Baptists in England," *Baptist History and Heritage* 16 (October 1981): 33 (citing Crosby, *English Baptists*, 1:298).

19. Edward Barber, *A Small Treatise of Baptisme, or, Dipping* (London, 1641).

20. Ibid., 2–4. Barber is also one of the early Baptists to utilize the "Six Principles" taken from Hebrews 6:1-2 as a brief delineation of the basic faith and practice of the Baptists.

21. Ibid., 10–11.

22. John Bunyan, *The Whole Works of John Bunyan*, ed. George Offor, 3 vols. (London: Blackie & Sons, 1882), 2:607; see also Harry Lee Poe, "John Bunyan's Controversy with the Baptists," *Baptist History and Heritage* 23 (April 1988): 26.

23. John Bunyan, *Differences in Judgment about Water-Baptism; No Bar to Communion* (London, 1673), 3–4.

24. Ibid., 28.

25. William Kiffin, *A Sober Discourse of Right to Church-Communion* (London: G. Larkin, 1681) (cited in Sydnor L. Stealey, ed., *A Baptist Treasury* [New York: Crowell, 1958], 82).

26. B. R. White, *The English Baptists of the Seventeenth Century*, rev. ed. (Didcot, England: Baptist Historical Society, 1996), 11.

27. Ibid.

28. Michael J. Walker, "The Relation of Infants to Church, Baptism and Gospel in Seventeenth-Century Baptist Theology," *Baptist Quarterly* 21 (April 1966): 244.

29. Ibid., 245.

30. Ibid., 247.

31. Ibid.

32. Ibid., 248.

33. William L. Lumpkin, *Baptist Confessions of Faith* (Chicago: Judson Press, 1959), 330–31.

34. Ibid., 248–49.

35. Ibid., 254.

36. Ibid., 256.

37. Ibid., 260.

38. Ibid., 265.

39. Edward Terrill, *The Records of a Church of Christ in Bristol, 1640–1687*, ed. Roger Hayden (Bristol: Bristol Record Society, 1974), 53.

40. Lumpkin, *Baptist Confessions of Faith*, 109.

41. Ibid., 110.

42. Winter, "The Lord's Supper," 267.

43. Ibid., 268.

44. Roper, "Henry Denne," 33.

45. Winter, "The Lord's Supper," 272.

46. Ibid., 273.

47. Daniel Featley, *The Dippers Dipt, or, The Anabaptists Duck'd and Plung'd over Head and Eares, at a Disputation at Southwark* (London: Nicholas Bourne and Richard Royston, 1646), n.p.

48. Ibid. This lengthy passage is cited here because it provides an exceptional statement of basic Baptist views as described by a chief critic of the movement.

49. Daniel Featley, *A True Relation of What Passed at a Meeting in Southward, between D. Featley, and a Company of Anabaptists, October 17, 1642* (London, 1643), 1.

50. W. T. Whitley, *A History of British Baptists*, rev. ed. (London: Kingsgate Press, 1932), 86.

51. Lumpkin, *Baptist Confessions of Faith*, 168–69.

52. Hugh Wamble, "The Concept and Practice of Christian Fellowship: The Connectional and Inter-denominational Aspects Thereof, among Seventeenth-Century English Baptists" (Ph.D. diss., Southern Baptist Theological Seminary, 1955), 255–74.

53. "Association Life till 1815," *Transactions of the Baptist Historical Society* 5 (1916–17): 20.

54. Ibid.

55. Ibid., 24.

56. Roper, "Henry Denne," 37.

57. Lumpkin, *Baptist Confessions of Faith*, 72.

58. Robert G. Torbet, *A History of the Baptists*, 3rd ed. (Valley Forge, Pa.: Judson Press, 1973), 44.

59. White, *English Baptists*, 67.

60. Ibid.

61. Ibid., 68.

62. Winter, "The Lord's Supper," 269.

63. Roger Hayden, ed., *Baptist Union Documents, 1948–1977* (London: Baptist Historical Society, 1980), 27.

64. Ibid., 27.

65. G. Hugh Wamble, "Baptist Ordination Practices to 1845," *Baptist History and Heritage* 23 (July 1988): 16 (citing Thomas Helwys, *Advertisement and Admonition* [Amsterdam, 1611], 41).

66. Ibid., 35. John Smyth suggested that if no elders were present, the church could select appropriate male representatives.

67. Roper, "Henry Denne," 32 (citing Henry Denne, *Records of the Churches of Christ, Gathered at Fenstanton, Warboys, and Hexham, 1644–1720*, ed. Edward B. Underhill [London: Haddon Brothers, 1854], 187).

68. Ibid., 33.

69. Ibid., 37.

70. Ibid., 39.

71. Ibid.

72. Ibid., 62.

73. Wamble, "Baptist Ordination Practices," 17; see also Lumpkin, *Baptist Confessions of Faith*, 165.

74. Roper, "Henry Denne," 83.

75. J. F. V. Nicholson, "The Office of 'Messenger' amongst British Baptists in the Seventeenth and Eighteenth Centuries," *Baptist Quarterly* 17 (1957–58): 207 (citing *Minutes of the General Assembly of the General Baptist Churches in England*, vol. 1, ed. W. T. Whitley [London: Kingsgate Press, 1909], 1).

76. Ibid.

77. Ibid., 210–11.

78. Roper, "Henry Denne," 36.

79. Wamble, "Baptist Ordination Practices," 17.

80. Ibid. (citing Thomas Grantham, *The Successors of the Apostles* [London, 1674]).

81. Ibid., 211.

82. Ibid., 222.

83. *The Works of John Smyth*, 2 vols., ed. W. T. Whitley (Cambridge: Cambridge University Press, 1915): 1:259–60 (cited in Charles W. Deweese, "Deaconesses in Baptist History: A Preliminary Study," *Baptist History and Heritage* 12 [January 1977]: 53).

84. Lumpkin, *Baptist Confessions of Faith*, 121–22; also Deweese, "Deaconesses in Baptist History," 53.

85. Deweese, "Deaconesses in Baptist History," 43.

86. Ibid., 53.

87. T. Dowley, "Baptists and Discipline in the 17th Century," *Baptist Quarterly* (October 1971): 158.

88. Ibid., 159.

89. Ibid., 161.

90. Ibid.

91. Ibid., 162.

92. Ibid.

93. Robert Steed, "Baptist Church Discipline 1689–1699," *Baptist Quarterly* 1 (July 1922): 117.

94. Winter, "The Lord's Supper," 270 (citing Thomas Helwys, *The Declaration of Faith*, 17ff.).

95. Ibid., 270.

96. Champlin Burrage, *The Early English Dissenters in the Light of Recent Research (1550–1641)*, 2 vols. (Cambridge: Cambridge University Press, 1912), 2:177.

97. Hugh Martin, "The Baptist Contribution to Early English Hymnody," *Baptist Quarterly* 19 (January 1962): 195.

98. Ibid., 196.

99. Adam A. Reid, "Benjamin Keach, 1640," *Baptist Quarterly* 10 (1940–41): 67–78.

100. Benjamin Keach, *The Child's Delight: or, Instructions for Children and Youth* (London, 1664); also John C. Foster, "Early Baptist Writers of Verse," *Transactions of the Baptist Historical Society* 3 (1912–13): 98.

101. Reid, "Benjamin Keach, 1640," 77.

102. H. Leon McBeth, *A Sourcebook for Baptist Heritage* (Nashville: Broadman, 1990), 66.

103. Ibid., 67.

104. Ibid., 201.

105. Ibid., 207.

106. I. Mallard, "The Hymns of Katherine Sutton, *Baptist Quarterly* (January 1963): 24.

107. Ibid., 25.

108. Ibid., 26.

109. Ibid., 27.

110. Foster, "Early Baptist Writers," 96.

111. Ibid., 99.

112. Ibid., 105.

113. Thomas Lamb, "An Appeal to the Parliament Concerning the Poor, That There May Not Be a Beggar in England," *Baptist Quarterly* 1 (1922–23): 129–30.

114. Keach, *The Child's Delight*, 3.

115. Ibid., 39.

116. Lumpkin, *Baptist Confessions of Faith*, 17.

117. H. Wheeler Robinson, *The Life and Faith of the Baptists* (London: Methuen, 1927), 90.

118. Lumpkin, *Baptist Confessions of Faith*, 172.

119. Ibid., 118.

120. Ibid., 120.

121. Ibid., 194.

122. Ibid., 193.

123. Ibid., 213.

124. Ibid., 224.

125. Ibid., 232.

126. Ibid., 234.

127. Ibid., 255

128. Ibid., 280.

129. Ibid., 293.

130. Norman S. Moon, *Education for Ministry: Bristol Baptist College, 1679–1979* (Bristol: Bristol Baptist College, 1979), 2; and W. Morgan Patterson, "Changing Preparation for Changing Ministry," *Baptist History and Heritage* (January 1980): 15.

131. Patterson, "Changing Preparation," 14 (citing William Cathcart, ed., *The Baptist Encyclopaedia*, 2 vols. [Philadelphia: L. H. Everts, 1880], 1:135).

Chapter 4
Baptists in the United States: Beginnings

BAPTISTS BEGAN IN COLONIAL AMERICA AS A MARGINALIZED SECT OF RADICAL religionists, often exiled, jailed, or otherwise harassed by the prevailing religious establishments. Two centuries later, they had become one of the nation's largest denominations. Baptists shaped and were shaped by the American experience as were few other American religious groups. On issues of religious liberty, individualism, and democratic idealism, Baptists (at least some of them) often seemed to anticipate religious America. From a hesitant sectarian minority, Baptist groups created elaborate denominational systems and founded schools, publishing houses, missionary societies, and other benevolent organizations. Their theological diversity eventually extended from the Calvinism of the Primitive Baptists to the Arminianism of the Free Will Baptists, with innumerable doctrinal combinations in between. In certain regions, particularly the South, they grew from a persecuted minority to an enculturated, albeit de facto, religious establishment. Their actions often reflected a heritage of both dissent and cooperation in the American ecclesiastical order. Controversies as diverse as slavery, predestination, biblical inerrancy, and church architecture divided Baptists on the national, regional, and local levels.

In 1640, Baptists comprised approximately one-tenth of 1 percent of the colonial population. By 1760, they had risen to one-half of 1 percent, with one Baptist in every 180 colonial inhabitants.[1] By the twentieth century, Baptists had become the largest Protestant tradition in the United States, numbering more than 30 million members represented in over forty discernible groups.[2]

The development of Baptists in the colonies was not simply a result of their origins in England; it was, as William McLoughlin said, "essentially an indigenous, parallel movement to that in England and not an offshoot or extension of it."[3] He concluded that save for a kind of "general encouragement and example, the English Baptists provided little help or stimulus to their New England brethren."[4]

Both groups were impacted by ideas born of Puritanism in general and various Puritan subgroups—Separatism and Independency—in particular. Many of the earliest Baptists were restless spirits, moving in and out of assorted ecclesial communities in their search for a clearer revelation. They differed over polity and practice, dividing to found new churches, associations, and subdenominations. While Baptists eventually appeared throughout the colonies, their earliest congregations were established in New England.

The Puritan Ethos in New England

In 1620, 102 passengers arrived at Plymouth, Massachusetts, on the *Mayflower*. Forty-two of them were Separatists, part of the Scrooby/Gainsborough coalition, congregations that divided around the leadership of John Robinson (1575?–1625) and John Smyth. Although Robinson did not make the trip to America, his covenantal concept of the church no doubt influenced the governor, William Bradford (1590–1657), and the composition of the Mayflower Compact, by which the new colony organized itself. It declared:

> *In the name of God, Amen. We whose names are underwriten, the loyall subjects of our dread sovereign Lord, King James, ... do by these presents solemnly and mutually in the presence of God, and one of another, covenant and combine our selves togeather into a civill body politic, for our better ordering and preservation and furtherance of the ends aforesaid; and by virtue hereof to enacte, constitute, and frame such just and equall lawes, ordinances, acts, constitutions, and offices, from time to time, as shall be thought most meet and convenient for the general good of the Colonie, unto which we promise all due submission and obedience.*[5]

The Plymouth colony was the first but not the strongest of the early Massachusetts Puritan settlements. Disease, harsh climate, and other difficulties took their toll. Its Separatist commitments made Plymouth a haven for many dissenters.

The centrality of the church as a covenant community was a major concern of those non-separating Puritans who came to Massachusetts Bay (Boston and its environs) in the 1630s. These Puritans constituted an orthodox majority often at odds with sectarian groups, including Quakers, Seekers, Anabaptists, and Baptists. In *The Way of the Congregational Churches Cleared* (1648), Puritan leader John Cotton (1584–1652) asserted that the New England churches were "Not a Sect; for we professe the Orthodox Doctrine of Faith, the same with all Protestant Churches; and submit to the spirituall government of the same lawfull Guides, so farre as Christ and our own choyce hath set them over us."[6] This establishment mentality led to punitive actions against Baptists and other dissenters.

The Calvinist dogmas of the Massachusetts Standing Order (establishment) were informed by covenant theology and the necessity of a regenerate church membership. As nonseparating Puritans, they believed that the Church of England remained a true church, albeit badly corrupted and in need of reform. They insisted that New England was "a City on a Hill" that would point all the nations toward New Testament Christianity.

This reformation was defined by a covenant, the basis for the relationship between God and the elect. Such an agreement had individual and communal implications. As the Puritans understood it, God initiated a covenant with sinful persons by means of irresistible grace offered to the elect. Conversion—a personal experience of divine grace—was necessary for all who would claim Christian faith and membership in the church. The church was the community of the converted, an elect people bound by a covenant uniting believers with God and each other. Although insisting on a church composed only of believers, New England Puritans retained infant baptism as another sign of the covenant. They maintained that such a practice was the New Testament parallel to Jewish circumcision as given to Abraham "and his seed." The church was a community of "visible saints" who had professed faith in Christ and agreed to live according to a covenant in faith and practice.

Baptists in Colonial Culture

While Baptists strongly supported the idea of a regenerate church membership, they rejected the notion of infant baptism and required that the ordinance be administered only after an adult profession of faith. Puritans and Baptists also parted company over the relationship of church and state, religious liberty, and the nature of religious pluralism in the new colonies. New England Puritans generally believed that a religious establishment was necessary to protect the society from theological deviancy and moral anarchy. Although Massachusetts was not a theocracy, the Reformed Church and the colonial government were closely allied through a system of taxation, an established church, and certain legal sanctions against religious nonconformists. Baptist efforts on behalf of toleration and religious liberty often brought them into conflict with the Puritan establishment.

The Baptist movement in the colonies began with Roger Williams (1603?–1683) and John Clarke (1609–1676) in Rhode Island, a colony that offered religious liberty for its inhabitants. In Massachusetts, Baptists survived in spite of some serious harassment from the state. They thrived in the more tolerant middle colonies, particularly Pennsylvania and New Jersey. In the South, they faced an often hostile Anglican establishment, especially in Virginia. In the Carolinas, groups known as Regular and Separate Baptists divided and then reunited over revivalism, conversion, and the use of confessions of faith. Throughout the colonies, Baptists joined other dissenters in lobbying for religious liberty before and after the Revolutionary War. By the end of the seventeenth century, they were a small but solid part of the American religious landscape.

American sectarians had an important advantage over the British: space. The American land offered what seemed to be unlimited space where new communities could find sanctuary and create their own special environments. And some in the Standing Order were glad for them to go. In his treatise *The Simple Cobler of Aggawam in America,* published in 1647, Puritan Nathaniel Ward (1578–1652) declared, "All Familists, Antinomians, Anabaptists, and other Enthusiasts, shall have free Liberty to keep away from us, and such as will come to be gone as fast as they can, the sooner the better."[7] For many Puritans, the best way to be rid of dissenters was to exile them to the New England wilderness or ship them back to London. Roger Williams was one of those early exiles.

Roger Williams: A Restless Founder

To trace the beginnings of the Baptist movement in America is to examine the actions and ideas of Roger Williams, one of the most fascinating, if not eccentric, representatives of religious dissent in the colonies. Born in London, Williams was reared in the Anglican Church. He matriculated at Pembroke College, Cambridge, in 1624. By the time of his marriage to Mary Barnard in 1629, Williams's religious sentiments had turned toward Puritanism. As persecutions against dissenters increased under the ecclesiastical regime of Archbishop William Laud, Williams joined émigrés to the New World, departing in 1631.

After a brief time in Boston, he separated himself completely from the Church of England and moved to Salem as a teacher in its Separatist congregation. Roger and Mary

Williams then moved to Plymouth, where their first child was born in 1633. Soon after, they returned to Salem and Williams wrote his first book, *A Key to the Language of America*, a lexicon of the Narragansett dialect.[8]

The book contains native words and phrases with a corresponding English equivalent. Williams concluded each chapter with a poetic commentary on Native American life, often comparing it to corrupt European society, as evidenced in these couplets:

> *Boast not proud English, of thy birth & blood,*
> *Thy brother Indian is by birth as Good.*
> *Of one blood God made Him, and thee & All,*
> *As wise, as faire, as strong, as personall.[9]*

And, in one of his most famous rhymes:

> *When Indians heare the horrid filths,*
> *Of Irish, English Men,*
> *The horrid Oaths and Murthers late,*
> *Thus say these Indians then:*
> *We weare no Cloaths, have many Gods,*
> *And yet our sinnes are lesse:*
> *You are Barbarians, Pagans wild,*
> *Your Land's the Wildernesse.[10]*

By 1633, Williams's opinions had created controversy with the Massachusetts Puritan establishment. First, he suggested that the native peoples were the sole owners of the American land and should be justly compensated for it. Such an idea was not well received by representatives of the Massachusetts Bay Company, who claimed the land by virtue of a royal charter granted by the English crown. Governor John Winthrop responded to Williams's views in words that anticipated several centuries of conflict between immigrant and native peoples: "If we leave them [lands] sufficient for their use, we may lawfully take the rest, there being more than enough for them and us."[11]

Williams entered into debates over whether women should wear veils (he favored it), whether a cross should be on the English flag (he opposed it), and whether non-Christians should swear oaths (he called that blasphemy). His most controversial position, however, involved his insistence, as summarized by his nemesis John Cotton, "that the Civil Magistrate's power extends only to the Bodies and Goods, and outward state of men."[12] Williams maintained that God alone was judge of conscience, and the state could not assume religious authority by persecuting either the heretic or the atheist. He repudiated the idea of a national church allied with the secular state.

At that time, Williams was accused of preaching "the same course of rigid separation and anabaptistry which Mr John Smith at Amsterdam had done."[13] These ideas and Williams's refusal to keep his opinions to himself led to his official banishment from Massachusetts in the autumn of 1635. The charges declared that Williams "hath broached and divulged divers new and dangerous opinions against the authority of magistrates, as also writ letters of defamation both of the magistrates and churches here."[14] Isaac Backus (1724–1806), himself a defender of religious liberty, suggested that the basic reason for Williams's exile involved his denial of the "civil magistrate's right to govern in ecclesiastical affairs."[15] To avoid deportation back to England, Williams fled into the "howling wilderness" of New

England in January 1636. Of that experience, he later recalled, "I was sorely tossed for fourteen weeks, in a bitter winter season, not knowing what bread or bed did mean."[16] The Narragansetts rescued him, and later he purchased land from them to found Providence, named "in a Sense of God's merciful Providence to me in my distress."[17] Of that endeavor Williams wrote, "I having made covenant of peaceable neighborhood with all the sachems and natives round about us, and having, in a sense of God's merciful providence unto me in my distress, called the place Providence, I desired it might be for a shelter for persons distressed of conscience.... I communicated my said purchase unto my loving friends, ... who then desired to take shelter here with me."[18] Thus the colony of Rhode Island was born.

Roger Williams and the Rhode Island Colony

The Providence township was incorporated in 1638, and by 1640, additional articles of agreement included this declaration: "We agree, As formerly hath been the liberties of the Town, so Still to hold forth Liberty of Conscience."[19] By 1644, Williams had returned to England and secured a charter for the State of Rhode Island and Providence Plantations, a new colony with a "Free Charter."

A reputation for liberty soon drew other dissenters, among them Anne Hutchinson (1591–1643), banished from Massachusetts in 1638 for her claims of direct inspiration from the Holy Spirit, her rising spiritual authority over and against that of the male clergy, and her "enthusiastical" religious experience. Hutchinson's speculations regarding the inner workings of the Spirit alongside and apart from Scripture and ministerial authority created conflict with the Massachusetts clergy. Governor John Winthrop reported on her belief that "the Holy Ghost dwelt in a believer as he is in heaven; that a man is justified before he believes; and that faith is no cause of justification."[20] These views led to Hutchinson's excommunication from the Boston church and exile to Narragansett Bay in 1637. In 1643, the family moved to Long Island, where she and seven of her eight children were killed in conflicts with Native Americans.[21] Roger Williams assisted the Hutchinson family and a band of her followers in moving to Rhode Island. Although never Baptist in sentiments, Anne Hutchinson's presence in the new colony illustrated its openness to dissenters.

Although Hutchinson and Williams were perhaps the most infamous of the New England radicals during the first generation of Puritan settlements, Quakers and other dissenters also found their way to Rhode Island. Williams, no friend to the Society of Friends, debated its members at every turn. His anti-Quaker tract *George Fox, Digg'd Out of His Burrows* is a classic critique of the group. Nonetheless, he freely invited them to live in Rhode Island and enjoy freedom to form "meetings" and express their views.

The First Baptist Church in America

Although he remained a Baptist only briefly, Roger Williams participated in the founding of the first Baptist church in the New World, a communion organized at Providence. Debates continue as to the exact date for the founding of that congregation.[22] Even the mode of Williams's baptism is open to question. James Rushbrooke, for example, concluded that Williams was rebaptized, but not by immersion, since some ten years later he reported that "a new baptism and manner of dipping" had been put forth.[23]

It appears that Williams received baptism by affusion (pouring) from Ezekiel Holliman, a member of the new Baptist community. Williams then baptized Holliman and some twenty other individuals in the late 1630s.[24] Governor John Winthrop placed the date of Williams's baptism as March 1639, suggesting in his journal that Williams was drawn to "Anabaptistry" by the influence of a woman. He wrote, "At Providence things grew still worse; for a sister of Mrs. Hutchinson, the wife of one Scott, being infected by her to make open profession thereof, and accordingly was rebaptized by one Holyman, a poor man late of Salem. Then Mr. Williams rebaptized him and some ten more. They also denied the baptizing of infants, and would have no magistrates."[25]

With a "restless unsatisfiedness" in his soul, Williams remained with the Baptists for only about four months, concluding that in the cacophony of sects no person had authority to baptize or organize a church. He suggested that just as the Hebrews had declared a moratorium on temple sacrifices while the temple was in ruins, so his generation of Christians should relinquish all sacraments until a new act of divine intervention brought a fuller revelation of God's will. Robert Scott, a colonial Baptist turned Quaker, wrote, "I Walked with Him [Williams] in the Baptists' way about three or four months, in which time he broke from the society and declared at large the ground and reasons of it."[26] Awaiting such a revelation, Williams became a "seeker" anticipating the millennial return of Christ and the establishment of a new, divinely ordained authority.[27] In an apostate age, Williams believed, the "Apostolical Gifts and Abilities in the Men sent" and the genuine "spiritual power in the Senders" were missing. He wrote that in his day, no sign of true apostolic authority was "yet restored and extant."[28] Williams was succeeded as pastor by Thomas Olney, who retained the position until his death, in 1682.

The Providence church was a theologically "mixed congregation," with members sympathetic to both General and Particular Baptist doctrines. It was dominated by those of Particular (later known as Regular) Baptist persuasion.[29] By 1652, the General Six Principle (Arminian) Baptists gained control of the Providence church and a minority of Calvinist/Particular Baptists departed.[30]

Roger Williams and Religious Liberty

In spite of his exodus from the Baptist ranks, Williams's views on religious liberty had a powerful impact on Baptists. Many of Williams's opinions on religious freedom were set forth in his famous debate with John Cotton, Puritan divine and defender of the New England Standing Order. Their exchanges appeared in a series of treatises published over a period of several years. Williams wrote *The Bloudy Tenent of Persecution for Cause of Conscience Discussed* in 1644 in response to Puritan church-state issues. Cotton issued a rejoinder entitled *The Bloudy Tenent, Washed, and Made White in the Bloud of the Lamb,* published in 1647. Williams's response, *The Bloudy Tenent, yet More Bloudy: By Mr Cottons Endeavor to Wash It White in the Blood of the Lambe,* published in 1652.

In *The Bloudy Tenent,* Williams maintained that God alone, not the secular state, was the judge of conscience. He wrote, "That a civil sword, as woeful experience in all ages hath proved, is so far from bringing, or helping forward an opposite in religion to repentance, that magistrates sin grievously against the work of God, and blood of souls, by such proceedings."[31] Christ's own method, Williams believed, was to use "spiritual weapons" to "subdue the nations of the earth to the obedience of the gospel."[32] Anticipating the American religious future, Williams insisted that non-Christians could indeed be good citizens, and he inquired "whether or no such as may hold forth other worships or religions, Jews, Turks, or anti-christians, may not be peaceable and quiet subjects, loving and helpful neighbours, fair and just dealers, true and loyal to the civil government." "It is clear they may," he declared, "from reason and experience in many flourishing cities and kingdoms of the world."[33]

Civil states had jurisdiction over the "bodies and goods" of its subjects, but not over their "souls and religions."[34] The state was charged with maintaining order, protecting the populace, and maintaining justice, but it could not meddle in religion. Isaac Backus later observed that Rhode Island was the "first government upon earth, that gave equal liberty, civil and religious" to all people, anticipating the constitutional experience of the new nation.[35]

John Clarke and Newport

Newport became another Baptist center in the small colony of Rhode Island. Its leader, Dr. John Clarke, was born in Westhorpe, Suffolk County, England, and trained as a physician. He immigrated to Boston in 1637. Moving south to Rhode Island, he founded Portsmouth in 1638, assuming leadership of what was probably a Separatist congregation there. In 1639, with the help of Roger Williams and others, Clarke and a group of dissenters purchased land from Native Americans and founded Newport on Aquidneck Island in Narragansett Bay. There they constituted another church, which became discernibly Baptist by 1644.

Scholarly debates continue as to whether Providence or Newport had the first Baptist church. The original identity of the Newport church is difficult to assess because the earliest church records are missing. Some suggest that this church became Baptist sometime between 1641 and 1648.[36]

The first immersion practiced by Baptists in the American colonies probably was at Newport in 1648. Apparently, it was introduced in America by Mark Lucar, a member of Spilsbury's London Particular Baptist congregation who migrated to Newport in 1648. Immersion soon was accepted over affusion and became the normative mode among all Baptist communions.[37]

Although John Clarke was a Calvinist, the Newport church was a "mixed congregation" of Arminian and Calvinist, Particular and General Baptists. Divisions occurred when the Particulars gained control and the General Baptist contingent departed to found another congregation.[38]

Like Williams, Clarke was instrumental in securing a charter for the fledgling Rhode Island colony. He traveled to London in 1651, hoping to acquire the proper documents from what he thought to be a more friendly regime under the Protectorate of Oliver Cromwell. Negotiations on behalf of the colony kept Clarke in London for twelve years, through Cromwell's era and into the Stuart Restoration. The charter finally was granted on July 8, 1663, creating what some have called "the first secular state of modern times."[39] It stated that the citizens of Rhode Island "have freely declared, that it is much on their hearts (if they may be permitted), to hold forth a livelier experiment, that a most flourishing civil state may stand and best be maintained ... with a full liberty in religious concernements."[40]

At the heart of the charter was this assertion: "No person within said Colony, at any time hereafter, shall be in any wise molested, punished, disquieted, or called in question for any differences of opinion in matters of religion, ... but that all and any persons may, from time to time, and at all times hereafter, freely and fully have and enjoy his and their own judgments and consciences in matters of religious concernments throughout the tract of land hereafter mentioned."[41]

In 1652, Clarke published his own treatise on religious freedom, *Ill Newes from New-England; or, A Narrative of New-Englands Persecution, Wherein Is Declared That While Old England Is Becoming New, New-England Is Become Old.* It warned that just as England seemed to be moving toward greater religious toleration, New England was marked by growing intolerance. It also set forth elements of Clarke's Baptist views. He wrote, "I Testifie that Baptism, or dipping in Water, is one of the Commandements of this Lord Iesus Christ, and that a visible beleever, or Disciple of Christ Iesus ... is the only person that is to be Baptized, or dipped."[42]

Concerning conscience, Clarke wrote, "No such believer, or Servant of Christ Jesus hath any liberty, much less Authority, from his Lord, to smite his fellow servant, nor yet with outward force, or arme of flesh, to constrain, or restrain his Conscience, no nor yet his outward man for Conscience sake."[43] Baptism by immersion and concern for freedom of conscience clearly were marks of Baptist identity in the New World.

Mark Lucar (d. 1676), one of the original members of the Newport church, was an important link between British and American Baptists. He was part of the first Particular Baptist church founded in London and moved to America in time to participate in the establishment of the Newport church. Lucar was one of ten persons dismissed from the Lathrop congregation in London for insisting that Anglican churches were not true churches of Christ. By 1638, this group and other persons who were related to the Lathrop congregation accepted Baptist views. Lucar was one of those persons baptized by Richard Blunt after his return from the Netherlands in 1642 with the idea that "Baptism should be by dipping ye Body."[44]

Recent evidence suggests that he was in Newport before 1648, as in October of that year he was listed among the first twelve members of the Newport church. Some even speculate that he may have instructed John Clarke in the importance of baptism by immersion. Roger Williams's classic description of these practices mentions Lucar: "At Seekonk a great many have lately concurred with Mr. John Clarke and our Providence men about the point of a new Baptism and the manner of Dipping, and Mr. John Clarke hath been here lately (and Mr. Lucar), and hath dipped them."[45] William Whitsitt claimed that Lucar was perhaps the first Baptist to appear on the American continent.[46] While this is probably an overstatement, it is clear that Lucar forged some important bonds between the Particular Baptist communities in London and the fledgling Baptist churches in Rhode Island.

Baptists in New England

William McLoughlin suggested, perhaps with some exaggeration, that the Rhode Island Baptist experiment in religious liberty was "a magnificent failure" due to "the inability of Rhode Islanders to shape, by example or evangelism, the destiny of either New England or any of the other colonies."[47] In McLoughlin's view, Rhode Island was marginalized in the minds of most colonialists as a dumping ground for religious deviants and malcontents. He believed that the Baptists who remained in Massachusetts and endured the harassment of the Standing Order were the real champions of religious freedom.

In the end, however, Rhode Island anticipated religious America, and its pluralism promoted religious liberty for both heretic and atheist alike. In his *Ecclesiastical History of New-England,* Cotton Mather observed, "There never was held such a variety of religions together on so small a spot of ground." These, he said, included "Antinomians, Familists, Anabaptists, Antisabbatarians, Arminians, Socinians, Quakers, Ranters—everything in the world but Roman Catholics and real Christians."[48] In his history of the church in New England, Isaac Backus recalled the decision of the Massachusetts government to "outlaw" Baptists in 1644. The authorities gave numerous reasons for their actions. The law began as follows:

> Forasmuch as experience hath plentifully and often proved, that since the first rising of the Anabaptists, about one hundred years since, they have been the incendiaries of the commonwealths, and the infectors of persons in main matters of religion, and the troublers of churches in all places where they have been, and that they who have held the baptizing of infants unlawful, have usually held other errors or heresies together therewith, though they have (as other heretics use to do) concealed the same till they spied out a fit advantage and opportunity to vent them, by way of questions or scruple; and whereas ... some whereof (as others before them) denied the ordinance of magistracy, and the lawfulness of making war ... which opinions ... are like to be increased amongst us, and so must necessarily bring guilt upon us, infection and trouble to the churches, and hazard to the whole commonwealth.[49]

These laws required that persons who, among other things, denied infant baptism, taught others to reject it, and opposed the right of the state to make war should be arrested and, if convicted, banished from the colony.[50] They were applied to the case of John Clarke, Obadiah Holmes, and John Crandall, arrested in July 1651 for preaching and practicing their religion in the home of William Witter, a blind Baptist who lived in Lynn, Massachusetts. Clarke and Crandall paid their fines and were released, but Holmes refused to do so and was publicly whipped. Receiving thirty lashes, Holmes is said to have testified that he never "had such a spiritual manifestation of God's presence." When the beating was completed, he is said to have remarked, "You have struck me as with roses."[51] Holmes's experience was shared by other dissenters and became a symbol of the persecution carried out under Massachusetts's Governor Endicott.

Puritan leaders did not remain silent, however. Thomas Cobbet, pastor of the Congregational church at Lynn, attacked the Baptists for their "re-baptism" and their efforts to undermine an orderly, moral society.[52] Other Puritan divines warned that Baptist attempts to undermine church-state establishments would destroy the moral foundations of the society.[53]

John Cotton offered little sympathy for the persecuted Baptists. When Sir Richard Saltonstall lamented the Puritan establishment's efforts to "fine, whip, and imprison men for their consciences," Cotton responded that Obadiah Holmes could have escaped the lash if he had paid the fine.[54] He wrote, "As for his whipping, it was more voluntarily chosen by him than inflicted upon him."[55] Cotton suggested that the Baptists benefited from the food and clothing provided in prison, commenting, "I am sure Holmes had not been so well clad of many years before."[56] Baptist leader Isaac Backus concluded that the argument "of Mr Cotton shows the absurdities of his scheme of compulsion about religion."[57]

Obadiah Holmes

Obadiah Holmes (1607?–1682) was born in England, where he experienced conversion and took up the Puritan cause. He married Catherine Hyde in 1630, and in 1638 they joined the Great Migration to Boston, escaping the Laudian persecution. Settling at Salem he labored in one of the earliest glass factories in the colonies.[58] By 1643, he had moved to a new community called Rehoboth. Contact with Rhode Island Baptists led Holmes to accept immersion by 1650. Soon after, the Massachusetts establishment took action against him.

A member of the Newport church by 1652, Holmes became its pastor when John Clarke departed for England to secure the charter. This was the same year that the first African American Baptist, "Jack, a colored man," was baptized into the Newport church.[59]

In 1652, divisions developed in the Newport church regarding the application of the "Six Principles" derived from Hebrews 6:1-2. A group in the church demanded that the laying on of hands to the newly baptized be required for all church members (previously, it was considered optional.) A schism resulted, and by 1656, Newport's second Baptist church was formed by some twenty people who left the first Baptist church. That church then required all newly baptized persons to receive the laying on of hands.

This issue was significant for several reasons. First, it is an illustration of early Baptist biblicism—the attempt to maintain Scripture alone as the rule of belief and practice. Second, the Hebrews passage provided a basic statement of faith and practice taken directly from the Bible. Third, the practice of the laying on of hands to the newly baptized was an important symbol of the priestly status of all believers. It represented the coming of the Holy Spirit upon the Christian and the calling of all Christians to act as ministers in the world. The rite offered an implied egalitarianism in Baptist congregations regarding the roles of clergy and laity.

Baptists in Boston

Amid internal debates in the Newport Baptist church, Obadiah Holmes continued to travel throughout New England, even venturing to New York to preach and organize churches. Through his encouragement, the first Baptist church in Boston was organized in 1665, with Thomas Goold (or Gould, Gold) as pastor. Goold was a friend, perhaps even a disciple, of Henry Dunster, the first president of Harvard College (founded in 1636).

In 1653, Dunster initiated a public dialogue regarding the validity of infant baptism. He then refrained from having his newborn child baptized, insisting that in the New Testament, "the subjects of Baptisme were visible penitent believers, and they only by Vertue of any rule, example, or any other light in the new testament."[60] Forced to resign his office in 1654, Dunster moved to the Plymouth colony, where he died in 1659. Even after his resignation, charges were brought against him for resisting the baptism of his child, though the matter never came to court. Cotton Mather remarked that Dunster "had fallen into the briars of antipedobaptism."[61]

Dunster apparently never received believer's baptism himself, and his response to the baptism controversy had little impact on the Baptist organizations in New England. Nonetheless, for Harvard's first president to reject infant baptism meant that the Puritan establishment could not dismiss such views as prevalent only among a radical fringe.[62]

Thomas Goold and his wife refused to have their child baptized—a decision that marked them as Baptist sympathizers and led to an interrogation by representatives of the First Parish (Congregational) Church of Charlestown in 1658. At that gathering, Goold testified that the church had cut him off from communion, and he charged, in words reflecting the racial relationships of the day, that he "now had no more privilege than an Indian." This being the case, he no longer considered himself a church member.[63] The Charlestown church did not formally excommunicate Goold until 1665, when he was one of several dismissed for espousing Baptist views.

Goold then helped organize the First Baptist Church of Boston and became its first pastor. The congregation originally was comprised of seven members, some of whom came from William Kiffin's church in London. Others were from Congregational churches in New England.[64] The earliest gatherings were in Goold's home in 1663, but the church itself was not formally organized until June 1665.[65] Goold wrote of the new church, "God sent out of Old England some who were Baptists; we, consulting together what to do, sought the Lord to direct us, and taking counsel of other friends who dwelt among us, who were able and godly, they gave us counsel to congregate ourselves together; and so we did, being nine of us, to walk in the order of the gospel according to the rule of Christ, yet knowing that it was a breach of the law of this country."[66]

The church was organized with a confession of faith, each statement supported by extensive biblical citations. While the document stressed that only those who "received the word & are baptized" were appropriate members of the "visible church," it made no reference to the need for baptism by immersion and thus may have predated the normative use of the observance. The confession included statements on the Trinity, biblical authority, Christology, the role of magistrates, and the role of conscience. Of the latter issues, it noted, "We acknowledge majestracy to be an ordinance of god & to submitt ourselves to them in the lord not because of wrath only but also for consience sake."[67]

These developments led the Massachusetts religious establishment to take action against the little band of Baptists. The Charlestown constable was charged with investigating the group and compelling them to attend the church of the Standing Order (Congregational). Refusing to abandon their own services of worship, the Baptists were hauled into court in September 1665. There they presented their confession of faith as a means of clarifying their basic beliefs. The court was not satisfied and ordered them "to desist from their schismatical practices."[68]

In 1666, Thomas Goold, Thomas Osborne, and others of the group were charged with "Schismatticall opposition to the Churches of Christ heere settled" and imprisoned by Massachusetts authorities after they refused to pay their fines. Released, Goold and some others were imprisoned again in 1668. This occasion also involved a "public disputation" held in the meetinghouse of First Church, Boston, April 14–15, 1668.[69] David Benedict commented, "When the disputants met there was a long speech made by one of their opponents, showing what vile persons the Baptists were and how they acted against the churches and government here, and stood condemned by the Court. The Baptists desired liberty to speak, but they would not suffer them, but told them that they stood there as delinquents and ought not to have liberty to speak."[70]

William McLoughlin suggested that historians largely overlooked this important gathering and believed that the transcript showed that the Baptists took full advantage of their right to speak freely.[71] He noted that the transcript, though incomplete, "is the only document we have in which the founders of the first Baptist church in the Bay Colony defended their actions and principles at length."[72] The issue at the center of the debate was "Whether it be justifiable by the word of God for these persons and their company to depart from the communion of these churches, and to set up an assembly here in the way of Anabaptism, and whether such a practice is to be allowed by the government of this jurisdiction."[73]

The debate included this exchange between John Thrumble (1607–1687), a spokesperson for the Baptists (though not a member of a Baptist church), and Jonathan Mitchell (1624–1668), a Congregational minister in Cambridge.

Thrumble: We came for liberty of conscience as well as yourselves. You had not a patent for such a form: and you are not perfect. We are daily exhorted to be growing [in] grace and knowledge: and if you be not perfect: we are to look for light as well as you.

Mitchell: You say the patent give us liberty of conscience. Lo there is no such word as liberty of conscience. This people had made a sad bargain for themselves and their posterity if they had come hither for ... liberty.[74]

This debate and the many Puritan-Baptist confrontations in Massachusetts are important because they reflect divergent ways of understanding the church-state relationship. Puritans believed that religious equality for sectarians meant the loss of a common standard of morality and biblical interpretation, thereby opening the door to moral chaos and theological heresy and undermining the stability of both church and state. Baptists, on the other hand, often challenged the right of any establishment, religious or governmental, to determine orthodoxy for the majority or the minority. While not all were as radical as Roger Williams in demanding complete religious freedom for Christian, non-Christian, and unbeliever alike, they generally rejected the idea of any religious establishment.[75] While few, if any, anticipated American religious pluralism on the scale to which it developed, they did envision the egalitarian future of American religious institutions. In ways the early Baptists could not have anticipated, their ideas would ultimately be applied not simply to Christian sectarians and dissenters but to multiple religions brought by American immigrants.

Challenging the Establishment: The Half-Way Covenant

Even with the arrest and sometime imprisonment of their members, Baptists continued to challenge the religious hegemony of the Standing Order. With the Congregationalist approval of the renowned Half-Way Covenant and the controversy surrounding it, the Baptists in New England claimed vindication of their views. They saw the Covenant and its theological problems as evidence that the Puritan attempt to maintain a believers' church while retaining infant baptism was a theological and practical failure.

Like their Baptist antagonists, the Puritans who first arrived in New England, particularly the Massachusetts Bay Colony, were concerned to establish a visible church comprised only of Christian believers. They required that all persons attest to an experience of grace before they could claim membership in the congregation. Along with this emphasis on personal faith, however, they continued to baptize their infant children. They viewed infant baptism as a sign of the covenant, the New Testament counterpart of circumcision, offered to the "seed" of the elect. However, many of those baptized in infancy grew to adulthood without making the necessary confession of faith. When they sought baptism for their own new-borns, a theological dilemma arose: Did the covenant extend to the grandchildren of the elect? Should infant baptism be proffered to the children of the unconverted?

In 1662, a synod of some seventy delegates gathered at First Church, Boston, to deal with the dilemma. Fearing the loss of church discipline and moral order, the ministers agreed that unconverted adults who would "own the covenant" and promise to live ethically under the discipline of the church could have their children baptized. The unconverted and their children were not allowed to receive communion or vote in church business meetings until they could testify to conversion and receive full, not half-way, membership. The document stated, "The Members of Orthodox Churches, being sound in the Faith, and not scandalous in Life, and presenting due Testimony thereof; these occasionally coming from one Church to another, may have their Children baptized in the Church whither they come, by virtue of communion of Churches."[76] Baptists charged that the Puritans were simply perpetuating the worst of an untenable system, attempting to build a believers' church while retaining infant baptism; baptism should be administered only after the proper profession of faith.

The Puritans themselves were divided over the Covenant and its implications for the churches. Some utilized it extensively, while others ignored it altogether. Still others, such as Solomon Stoddard (1643–1729), prominent pastor of the Northampton church, went beyond it to admit the unconverted to communion as a "converting ordinance."[77] A generation later, Puritan preachers such as Jonathan Edwards and Gilbert Tennent denounced the Covenant, convinced that it undermined the mandate for a regenerate church membership. Baptists insisted that infant baptism was incompatible with the call for a believers' church.

Baptist Petitions

As the Half-Way Covenant took shape, and as persecution against the Baptists continued, some sixty-five non-Baptist citizens petitioned the colony for mercy for the Baptists, whom they described as "reputed godly and of a blameless conversation; and the things for which they seem to suffer seem not to be moral, unquestioned, scandalous evils, but matters of religion and conscience."[78] This entreaty, submitted in October 1668, reflected the development of a more moderate Puritan faction and the inability of the Puritan establishment to abolish dissent among Baptists and other sectarians in Massachusetts.[79]

Nonetheless, the General Court of Election ruled that Thomas Goold, William Turner, and John Farnum Sr., "obstinate and turbulent Anabaptists," who had constituted "a pretended church estate, ... to the great grief and offense of the godly orthodox" were to be exiled outside Boston.[80] It is unclear how successful the authorities were in enforcing this exile. Nonetheless, this was but one example of the continuing harassment of the Boston Baptists. During the period of the 1660s and 1670s, the imprisoned Baptists produced numerous documents attesting to their attempts to challenge the Standing Order and accept the retribution of the Massachusetts state. Thomas Goold died in 1675, and he was succeeded as pastor by John Russell Jr., son of another Massachusetts Baptist leader.

Persecution Continues

The Baptists were not the only ones to experience the punitive actions of the Puritan religious establishment. Quakers were particularly vulnerable. All New England was shaken in 1659 by the execution of Quaker preachers William Robinson and Marmaduke Stevenson, carried out under the regime of Governor John Endicott. This was particularly terrifying when Mary Dyer, the first woman executed in New England, was hung on Boston Common on June 1, 1660, for preaching Quaker views.[81]

A 1673 pamphlet published in London leveled spurious charges against certain Baptists, accusing them of having murdered a Boston cleric. The tract, written by a certain Mr. Baxter, was entitled *Baptiz'd in Bloud, or A Sad History of the Unparalleled Cruelty of the Anabaptists in New England*. It asked, "Dare any man affirm the Anabaptists to be Christians? For how can they be Christians who deny Christianity, deride Christ's Institution of Baptism, and scoffingly call it, *Baby sprinkling,* and in place thereof substitute their prophane *Booby dipping?*"[82]

Massachusetts officials boarded up the new meetinghouse of First Baptist Church, Boston, immediately after it was completed in 1679. The Baptists removed the barriers, only to have them replaced by order of the General Court.

Other churches soon appeared. John Miles, a leader in the Welsh Baptist church near Swansea, arrived in the colonies in 1662. Miles and seven other males (in reporting this, Isaac Backus does not list the females) formed a church near the Plymouth colony in 1663.[83] Amid fines and harassment from Massachusetts authorities, the town of Swansea was established in 1667. Backus claimed that the Swansea congregation was the fourth Baptist church instituted in America.[84]

Baptists in Maine

The first Baptist church in Maine was organized at Kittery by William Screven (1629–1713). In 1668, Screven migrated from England to Boston, where his dissenting views led to conflicts with the Standing Order and influenced his decision to move to the township of Kittery, Maine. Once there, he urged the British government to separate that province from the jurisdiction of Massachusetts because of Puritan opposition to religious freedom. The request was ignored, but Screven was marked as a religious troublemaker.

Although settled in Maine, Screven and his wife, Bridget Cutts, joined First Baptist Church, Boston, and apparently were rebaptized in 1681. The rebaptism was something of a mystery, as he had already received baptism by immersion while in England. Nonetheless, evidence of the previous event was scarce, and this may have been a way of assuring the fledgling community in Boston of the strength of his Baptist commitments.[85] The church also certified Screven's calling and his authority to preach and baptize new believers.

In 1682, Screven established the first Baptist church in Kittery, under sponsorship of the Baptist church in Boston. Records of the Boston church indicate that the Kittery congregation was formed "soe they might Injoy the precious ordinances of Christ which by reson of distance of habitason they butt seldome could injoy hae therefore thought meet to make Choice of us whose names are underwritten as Messengers to assist them in ye same."[86] The church members soon were persecuted by the Puritan establishment for, among other things, their opposition to infant baptism. Such abuse, Isaac Backus said, "scattered them, some to South Carolina, some to New Jersey, and some to Boston again, where they were useful afterwards."[87] The exile was not permanent, because Screven returned to Maine, held public office there, and never settled permanently in South Carolina.[88]

The Kittery church approved a covenant in 1682, perhaps the earliest church covenant used by Baptists in America. Just as a confession of faith set forth the doctrinal formulations of a specific Christian community, covenants promoted acceptable Christian behavior. This one led members to pledge to

> give up our selves to ye lord & to one another in Solem Covenant, wherein wee doe Covenant & promise to walk with god & with one another. In a dew and faithfull observance of all his most holy & blessed Commandmtts Ordinances Institutions or Appointments, Revealed to us in his sacred word of ye ould & new Testament and according to ye grace of god & light att present through his grace given us, or here after he shall please to discover & make knowne to us thro his holy Spiritt according to ye same blessed word all ye Dayes of our lives.[89]

In 1696, the congregation, still under Screven's leadership, moved to Charleston, South Carolina, where they soon formed the first Baptist church in the South. The earliest records of Screven's arrival in South Carolina date from December 7, 1696, and report on his having obtained a thousand acres of land.[90] Public documents indicate that the congregation (probably a combination of Particular and General Baptists) purchased land by 1699. By 1700–1701, they had constructed a meetinghouse, the lot for which was donated by one of the members. Nonetheless, the precise date of the Charleston church's origin is unclear.[91]

Screven served as pastor of the church until 1708. He urged members to select a new minister who would "be orthodox in the faith, and of blameless life, and does own the Confession put forth by our brethren in London."[92] The confession probably was the Second London Confession of Particular Baptists. This Calvinist orientation made Screven's church perhaps the earliest representative of the Regular Baptist tradition in the South.

Internal Controversies

Seventh Day Baptists

Colonial Baptists were not without their own internal controversies. They divided over a variety of issues that sometimes led to the creation of new Baptist communions. The First Baptist Church of Newport, Rhode Island, was the scene of divisions over the question of the Sabbath. In 1665, Stephen Mumford migrated from London to Newport, bringing with him certain beliefs of the Seventh Day Baptist meeting in Bell Lane, London. Soon, members of the Newport church were "keeping of the Lord's holy seventh day Sabbath." A woman named Tacey Hubbard accepted the practice in March 1665 and soon was followed by her husband, Samuel (1610–1692?), and some of their relatives, including son-in-law Joseph Clarke, the nephew of the Newport church founder. Obadiah Holmes opposed the movement, and a controversy ensued.[93]

The Sabbatarians remained within the Newport church until questions arose regarding their aggressive proselytizing efforts, their presence at communion, and the orthodoxy of their doctrine. Divisions were inevitable.

In 1671, Obadiah Holmes exacerbated the controversy with a sermon delineating the "offenses" of those who had deserted Christ for "Moses in the observation of days, seasons and such like."[94] Tensions increased, with heated exchanges of the influence of the Sabbatarian faction. In December 1671, a schism occurred involving five church members, including a man named Hiscox, three members of the Hubbard family, and Roger Baster.[95] This group formed the first Seventh Day Baptist church in America.

Baptists and Quakers

The Society of Friends (Quakers) also fostered divisions within the Baptist ranks, particularly in the beleaguered Newport congregation. The conflicts between Quakers and Baptists were ironic, given Baptist ideals on religious liberty. On one hand, the Baptists extended hospitality to Quakers in Rhode Island and made no effort to prosecute them; on the other hand, the Baptists believed certain Quaker ideas regarding the "inner light," Christology, and biblical interpretation to be heretical.

Quakers and Baptists took root among similar constituencies in seventeenth-century England. The Society of Friends began in the 1640s through the work of George Fox (1624–1691). Fox's subsequent visit to the America, along with the founding of the Quaker-based colony of Pennsylvania, made the Society a force to be reckoned with.

Quakers eschewed the sacraments of baptism and the Lord's Supper for the inward presence of Christ. They dispensed with the external rituals and symbols of traditional Christianity and preached an aggressive gospel that placed the inner light of Christ above all other "doctrines of men."

George Fox's visit to the colonies brought him to Newport in 1672, further extending Quaker influence.[96] About that time, Giles Slocum and other members of Newport's First Baptist Church turned to Quakerism, and once again schism struck the Newport congregation. In October 1673, Slocum and his family were excommunicated by the Baptists for their "error that the man Christ Jesus was not in heaven nor earth nor anywhere—that his body was entirely lost."[97] Quakerism continued to impact segments of the Baptist community well into the next century.

The Rogerenes

Quakerism and Sabbatarianism were factors in the formation of another group that, as Isaac Backus said, "came out from among the Baptists" during the seventeenth century. The group took the name Rogerenes, from its founder James Rogers (ca.1648–1721). In 1674, the baptism of Rogers and his sons, John and James, caused controversy among Puritans in Connecticut. In 1675, the Rogers family was received into First Baptist Church, Newport, "by prayer and laying on of hands." Shortly thereafter, James Rogers was imprisoned in

Hartford for his Baptist views. When Rogers and his followers began observing the Jewish Sabbath, some of them were arrested for "working on the first day of the week" (Sunday). Isaac Backus compared the Rogerenes to the Quakers because of their quietistic spirituality, but noted that they retained the outward observances of baptism and the Lord's Supper. They also refused "the use of means and medicines for their bodies."[98] Their "greatest zeal," he said, was their opposition to a "hireling ministry" (paid clergy) and Sunday worship.

While Rogers ultimately reinstated Sunday worship, he continued to insist that Christians were free to labor on any day. To make their point, Rogerenes took their hand labor into the meetinghouse, "the women knitting and the men whittling and making splits for baskets, and every now and then contradicting the preachers." Of these practices Backus commented, "This was seeking persecution, and they had plenty of it, insomuch that the New Englanders left some of them neither liberty, nor property, nor a whole skin."[99]

Like the Quakers, the Rogerenes rejected the use of spoken prayers and other traditional rituals in worship. After claiming the ability to work miracles, James Rogers asserted that he would not succumb to the Boston smallpox epidemic of 1721. However, he caught the disease and died.[100] Rogers wrote several treatises, including *An Epistle to the Churches of Christ Call'd Quakers* (1705) and *The Book of the Revelation of Jesus Christ* (1720).

The group's original church was in New London, Connecticut, where persecution against them included fines, imprisonment, and flogging. Another Rogerene church was organized in New Jersey around 1709, and a second New Jersey congregation was founded in 1734. The three churches never had more than a total of eighty members. The New Jersey churches declined by the early 1800s, and the Connecticut congregation disappeared from the scene by 1900.

The Rogerenes represented a sectarian group within a sectarian group. They believed that they had reconstituted the primitive church under the direct guidance of the Holy Spirit. They contributed to the continued divisions within the Baptist community.

Baptists and the New World

By the end of the seventeenth century, Baptists were present throughout the American colonies. They comprised a small, often persecuted sect with varying theological approaches to common distinctives. They established one colony, Rhode Island, which anticipated many significant aspects of American religious pluralism. Some of their number moved on to newer revelations amidst changing biblical interpretations. Numerically, the Baptists were a tiny minority, but their presence was noted, even in rural Virginia, where an act of the colonial Assembly, 1661–1662, declared:

> *Whereas, many schismatical persons, out of their averseness to the orthodox established religion, or out of the new fangled conceit of their own heretical inventions, do refuse to have their children baptized; Be it therefore enacted by the authority aforesaid, that all persons who in contempt of the divine sacrament of Baptism, shall refuse when he may carry their child to a lawful minister of that county to have them baptized, shall be amerced [fined] two thousand pounds of tobacco; half to the informer; half to the public.*[101]

A century would pass before Baptists and other dissenters would be delivered from such laws against religious minorities in the American colonies. Nonetheless, the Baptists had come to stay.

Notes

1. Robert G. Gardner, *Baptists of Early America: A Statistical History, 1639–1790* (Atlanta: Georgia Baptist Historical Society, 1983), 15.
2. Frank S. Mead, *Handbook of Denominations in the United States,* 9th ed. (Nashville: Abingdon Press, 1990), 34.
3. William G. McLoughlin, *Soul Liberty: The Baptists' Struggle in New England, 1630–1833* (Hanover, N.H.: University Press of New England, 1991), 17.
4. Ibid., 17.
5. H. Shelton Smith, Robert T. Handy, and Lefferts A. Loetscher, *American Christianity,* 2 vols. (New York: Scribner, 1960–63), 1:96.
6. Ibid., 103 (citing John Cotton, *The Way of the Congregational Churches Cleared* [London, 1648], part 1, 10–11).
7. Smith, Handy, and Loetscher, *American Christianity,* 1:127 (citing Nathaniel Ward, *The Simple Cobler of Aggawam in America* [New York: Scholars' Facsimiles & Reprints, 1937], 8–12).
8. Edwin S. Gaustad, *Liberty of Conscience: Roger Williams in America* (Grand Rapids: Eerdmans, 1991), 27–28.
9. Roger Williams, *A Key to the Language of America,* ed. John J. Teunissen and Evelyn J. Hinz (Detroit: Wayne State University Press, 1973), 133.
10. Ibid., 204.
11. Gaustad, *Liberty of Conscience,* 32.
12. Ibid., 39.
13. Isaac Backus, *Church History of New England from 1620 to 1804* (Philadelphia: American Baptist Publication Society, 1844), 43. Smyth's actions were known even in America.
14. Ibid., 38.
15. Ibid., 53.
16. Ibid., 39.
17. Gaustad, *Liberty of Conscience,* 46.
18. Isaac Backus, *A History of New England, with Particular Reference to the Baptists,* 2nd ed. (1871; reprint, 2 vols. in 1, New York: Arno Press, 1969), 1:75.
19. Gaustad, *Liberty of Conscience,* 49.
20. Smith, Handy, and Loetscher, *American Christianity,* 1:117 (citing James K. Hosmer, ed., *Winthrop's Journal: History of New England, 1630–1649,* vol. 1 [New York: Scribner, 1908]).
21. Smith, Handy, and Loetscher, *American Christianity,* 1:115.
22. Gaustad, *Liberty of Conscience,* 90. Gaustad, writing in 1991, placed the date at 1638. Also in 1991, William McLoughlin claimed 1639 as the original date (see *Soul Liberty,* 16, 19). Backus claimed that Williams's baptism and the founding of the church occurred in 1639 (see *Church History,* 50).
23. James H. Rushbrooke, "Roger Williams: Apostle of Soul Freedom," *Baptist Quarterly* 8 (1936–37): 22.
24. Obadiah Holmes, *Baptist Piety: The Last Will and Testimony of Obadiah Holmes,* ed. Edwin S. Gaustad (Valley Forge, Pa.: Judson Press, 1994), 17.
25. James K. Hosmer, ed., *Winthrop's Journal: History of New England, 1630–1649,* vol. 1 (New York: Scribner, 1908), 297. See also J. Stanley Lemons, *The First Baptist Church in America* (Providence: Charitable Baptist Society, 2001).
26. Rushbrooke, "Roger Williams," 22.
27. Backus, *Church History,* 50.
28. W. Clark Gilpin, *The Millenarian Piety of Roger Williams* (Chicago: University of Chicago Press, 1979), 149–50 (citing Roger Williams, *The Hireling Ministry None of Christs* [London, 1652]).
29. Gardner, *Baptists of Early America,* 32.
30. Ibid., 36.
31. Roger Williams, *The Bloudy Tenent of Persecution for Cause of Conscience Discussed,* ed. Edward B. Underhill (1644; reprint, London: Hanserd Knollys Society, 1848), 109.
32. Ibid., 111.
33. Ibid., 112–13.
34. Ibid., 218.
35. Backus, *Church History,* 69.
36. Smith, Handy, and Loetscher, *American Christianity,* 1:166.
37. Gaustad, *Liberty of Conscience,* 116.
38. Gardner, *Baptists of Early America,* 36.
39. Carl Bridenbaugh, *Fat Mutton and Liberty of Conscience Society in Rhode Island, 1636–1690* (Providence: Brown University Press, 1974), 5 (cited in Edwin S. Gaustad, "Baptists and the Making of a New Nation," in *Baptists and the American Experience,* ed. James E. Wood [Valley Forge, Pa.: Judson Press, 1976], 40).
40. Gaustad, "Making of a New Nation," 40.

41. O. K. Armstrong and Marjorie Armstrong, *The Baptists in America* (Garden City, N.Y.: Doubleday, 1979), 71.

42. Smith, Handy, and Loetscher, *American Christianity*, 1:167. See also John Clarke, *Ill Newes from New-England* (1652; reprint, New York, Arno Press, 1980).

43. Smith, Handy, and Loetscher, *American Christianity*, 1:168.

44. David J. Terry, "Mark Lucar: Particular Baptist Pioneer," *Baptist History and Heritage* (January 1990): 44.

45. Ibid., 46 (citing a letter from Roger Williams to John Winthrop, December 10, 1649, in *The Complete Writings of Roger Williams*, vol. 6 [New York: Russell and Russell, 1963], 188).

46. Ibid. (citing William Whitsitt, *A Question in Baptist History* [Louisville: Charles Deering, 1896], 149–51).

47. McLoughlin, *Soul Liberty*, 19.

48. Holmes, *Baptist Piety*, 21 (citing Cotton Mather, *Magnalia Christi Americana; or, The Ecclesiastical History of New-England* [1702; reprint, New York: Russell and Russell 1967], 2:520–21).

49. Backus, *Church History*, 52–53.

50. Ibid., 53.

51. Holmes, *Baptist Piety*, 29; see also Backus, *Church History*, 77.

52. Holmes, *Baptist Piety*, 36.

53. Ibid., 36.

54. Backus, *Church History*, 78.

55. Ibid., 80.

56. Ibid., 81.

57. Ibid.

58. Holmes, *Baptist Piety*, 10.

59. Ibid., 42.

60. Nathan Wood, *The History of the First Baptist Church of Boston* (Philadelphia: American Baptist Publication Society, 1899), 27.

61. Ibid., 28.

62. McLoughlin, *Soul Liberty*, 33.

63. Wood, *First Baptist Church of Boston*, 39 (citing minutes of First Parish Church).

64. Holmes, *Baptist Piety*, 47.

65. Wood, *First Baptist Church of Boston*, 55.

66. Ibid., 50.

67. Ibid., 66.

68. Ibid., 66.

69. William G. McLoughlin and Martha Whiting Davidson, eds., "The Baptist Debate of April 14–15, 1668" (reprinted from *Massachusetts Historical Society Proceedings*, 1964); reprinted in *Colonial Baptists: Massachusetts and Rhode Island* (New York: Arno Press, 1980). The full transcript was not completely deciphered until 1964.

70. Wood, *First Baptist Church of Boston*, 79 (citing David Benedict, *A General History of the Baptist Denomination* [New York: Colby, 1848], 384).

71. McLoughlin, *Soul Liberty*, 38.

72. Ibid., 38.

73. Ibid., 45.

74. Ibid., 71.

75. William McLoughlin suggested that after 1728, as Massachusetts began to exempt Baptists, Anglicans, and Quakers from tax support of Congregationalism, the Baptists "quietly agreed to the idea of an established church as long as they did not have to support it." See William McLoughlin, "Introduction: An Overview," in *Baptists in the Balance*, ed. Everett C. Goodwin (Valley Forge, Pa.: Judson Press, 1997), 65.

76. Smith, Handy, and Loetscher, *American Christianity*, 1:204.

77. Isaac Backus addresses the problems of the Half-Way Covenant in *A History New England, with Particular Reference to the Denomination of Christians Called Baptists*, 2 vols., 2nd ed. (Newton, Mass.: Backus Historical Society, 1871), 1: 468–69.

78. Holmes, *Baptist Piety*, 47.

79. McLoughlin, *Soul Liberty*, 43.

80. Wood, *First Baptist Church of Boston*, 81.

81. Backus, *Church History*, 91.

82. Wood, *First Baptist Church of Boston*, 111.

83. Backus, *Church History*, 93–94.

84. Ibid.

85. H. Leon McBeth, *The Baptist Heritage* (Nashville: Broadman, 1987), 144.

86. Robert A. Baker, *A Baptist Source Book, with Particular Reference to Southern Baptists* (Nashville: Broadman, 1966), 2 (citing church records of First Baptist Church, Boston, Massachusetts, 1682).

87. Backus, *Church History*, 123.

88. Robert G. Torbet, *A History of the Baptists*, 3rd ed. (Valley Forge, Pa.: Judson Press, 1973), 207.

89. McBeth, *The Baptist Heritage*, 144; Robert A. Baker and Paul J. Craven Jr., *Adventure in Faith: The First 300 Years of First Baptist Church*, Charleston, South Carolina (Nashville: Broadman, 1982), 60–61.

90. Torbet, *A History of the Baptists*, 207.
91. McBeth, *The Baptist Heritage*, 147; Torbet, *A History of the Baptists*, 207; Baker and Craven, *Adventure in Faith*, 76–78.
92. Armstrong and Armstrong, *The Baptists in America*, 82.
93. Holmes, *Baptist Piety*, 51–53.
94. Ibid., 54.
95. Ibid., 59–60.
96. Ibid., 60.
97. Ibid., 61.
98. Backus, *History of New England*, 1:381.
99. Ibid., 1:382 n.
100. Ibid., 381.
101. Baker, *A Baptist Source Book*, 7.

Chapter 5
English Baptists: The Eighteenth Century

THE RELIGIOUS ETHOS OF EIGHTEENTH-CENTURY ENGLAND TOOK SHAPE AS early as 1688 with the Glorious Revolution, which deposed the Catholic monarch James II and brought William and Mary from the Netherlands to the English throne. This revolution was "glorious" because it was "bloodless," a transfer of power achieved without civil war or armed rebellion, and because it established new liberties for the entire nation. The Act of Toleration, passed on May 24, 1689, retained the Anglican establishment but offered tolerance to nonconformist Protestants, ending their religious persecution. Dissenters were asked to swear or affirm loyalty to William and Mary, and to repudiate papal authority, transubstantiation, devotion to the saints, and the Mass, while accepting the doctrines of the Thirty-Nine Articles, Anglicanism's confession of faith. Like other nonconformists, Baptists continued to be treated as second-class citizens under a variety of sanctions set forth by the British religious and governmental establishments. While worship was permitted for Catholics and Protestant dissenters, members were forbidden to hold public office, matriculate at universities, or use consecrated burial grounds. They were allowed by special dispensation to worship in registered meetinghouses or conventicles. The state granted them toleration but not complete freedom of worship or citizenship. While not officially endorsed, Catholics were permitted to exercise private worship, and here and there a chapel was constructed.[1]

Baptists apparently made no formal statement or petition on the ascension of William and Mary to the throne. As a small religious community, they could but welcome their new freedom. Baptist congregations were small, most numbering no more than fifty to sixty members. The eighteenth century witnessed numerous developments in Baptist life relative to theological and spiritual enthusiasm, indifference, and controversy.

Some historians suggest that Baptists were impacted by a state of religious apathy evident in England during the early eighteenth century.[2] Others note that the rise of rationalism and the Enlightenment led certain General Baptists to challenge Trinitarianism, with an interest in Arianism and Unitarianism. Some Particular Baptists flirted with antinominianism—the belief that the elect were free from the law and not inhibited by traditional moral boundaries. Still others were caught up in the religious awakenings that swept the country as led by John and Charles Wesley, George Whitefield, and other evangelicals.[3]

The eighteenth century began with the reign of Queen Anne (1702–1714), the last of the Stuart-related monarchs. In spite of toleration laws, sanctions against nonconformists continued. For example, Baptists refused to participate in a practice that permitted nonconformists to serve in public office as long as they received communion in the Anglican Church. The practice was abolished in 1711. In 1714, the Schism Act was passed, limiting the prerogatives of nonconformist schools. Queen Anne died that year, and the Act was never enforced.[4]

English Baptists entered the eighteenth century divided into several distinct subgroups—Particular, General, and Seventh Day—each struggling for a place in the society and plagued by a series of internecine divisions. General Baptists administered the laying on of hands to the newly baptized and the anointing with oil to the sick. Some abstained from eating the blood of animals, in keeping with what they believed to be biblically correct dietary codes. Doctrinal debates covered a wide spectrum of beliefs and practices, including hymn singing, the deity of Christ, open church membership, and antinomianism. Some Baptist groups experienced significant numerical decline, while others grew in number.

In an attempt to cultivate fellowship, Particular Baptists in London often held their "Fraternals" in coffeehouses, which were fashionable gathering places of the day. The Hanover Coffee-House Club enlisted Particular and General Baptist ministers in fraternal conversation and charitable endeavors. They raised funds for French refugees and sought better relations between Baptists and Quakers. Controversies over baptism and communion within the General Baptist ranks led Particular Baptists to break away and form their own coffee-house fraternity by 1724.[5]

In 1717, the Particular Baptist Fund was established to encourage ministerial education and supplement ministerial compensation, but General Baptists were excluded from the enterprise. The Particulars reaffirmed their own Reformed heritage through formation of the Baptist Board, constituted in 1724. In 1726, the General Baptist Fund was established to provide ministerial support. The low salaries forced many Baptist pastors to maintain academies that provided boys with elementary education in the classics of literature, rhetoric, and languages.

Baptist Associations

Associational relationships among Baptists flourished during much of the eighteenth century. As noted previously, General Baptists maintained strong associational connections, while Particular Baptists placed greater emphasis on the autonomy of the local congregation.

Baptists continued to make use of three basic ministerial offices within the churches. Among General Baptists, these included messengers, pastors, and deacons. Messengers were traveling evangelist/overseers, while pastors and deacons functioned primarily within local congregations. Elected by associations of churches, messengers received ordination and the laying on of hands for the service of the churches that selected them.[6] Although these individuals were not viewed as bishops, they exercised churchly leadership beyond the local congregation. Messengers were ordained only by other messengers, in a kind of Baptist successionism.[7]

General Baptists linked associations into a larger body known as the General Assembly, organized on the basis of Hebrews 12:23: "to the general assembly and church of the firstborn, which are written in heaven, and to God the judge of all, and to the spirits of just men made perfect." The first such General Assembly was held in 1689. It was composed of messengers, pastors, deacons, and lay representatives of the churches.[8]

Beginning in 1689, Particular Baptists began an annual General Assembly in London and continued until 1692, when they divided into two regional groups, one based in London and the other in Bristol. The assemblies nurtured connectionalism but were torn by controversies over hymn singing, the nature of ministerial education, and other ecclesiastical debates.[9]

These associational meetings involved worship, business sessions, and the compilation and distribution of circular letters. Participation often was sporadic, depending on the times and the circumstances of the participating congregations.[10] Representatives were chosen by specific churches in a given region. Among General Baptists, associational representatives often were referred to as delegates, and later as messengers. Thus, by the eighteenth century, the term *messenger* was applied to associational ministers and associational representatives. The records of the Essex Association contain one of the few extant descriptions of the delegate's or messenger's task, found in the associational minutes of 1796. It reads, "That the messengers appointed by the churches shall bring an account, in writing, to the general meeting of the members of the Association, every year, of the number of persons added to their respective churches; of those who have been dismissed; and of the deceased in the preceding year; as also, of any important event that has taken place among them, and of the efforts made to propagate the Gospel around them."[11] Messengers might represent one association at the meeting of another associational body, prepare circular letters, and mediate in congregational disputes.[12]

During the early eighteenth century, some General Baptists nudged their churches toward increased fellowship with other Protestants. Benjamin Stinton (1677–1719), the son-in-law of the renowned Benjamin Keach, urged cooperation between General and Particular Baptists. Stinton collected historical materials that were used by his brother-in-law Thomas Crosby in *The History of the English Baptists* (1738–1740). W. T. Whitley suggested that Stinton's work "deliberately effaced all lines of distinction" between the General and Particular Baptists, "hoping to excite in each body a pride in the doings of both."[13] Clearly, there was interchange between the two Baptists communions, with ministers moving from one subgroup to another. Benjamin Keach, for example, began his ministry as a General Baptist but moved to the Particular Baptists when he became a staunch Calvinist. The Barbican Church, London, admitted both Particular and General Baptists to its membership.

Associational Communications

Associations aided churches in responding to controversy, and when disputes arose, congregations often proposed "queries" or "cases" to the associational body.[14] The Baptist Board meeting of November 9, 1724, included these questions: "Mr. Townsend propos'd three Questions Concerning marriage whether it was Lawful for a Man to Marry his Brothers Widdow by whom his Brother had Children? 2dly Whether tis Lawful for a Women to Marry with her fathers sisters Husband? 3dly Whether tis Lawful for a Man to marry two sisters when he had children by the first?" The Association ruled, "These Questions being considered they were Carried in the Negative."[15]

The records of the New Connection of General Baptists (1770) illustrate various theological and practical matters confronting eighteenth-century pastors and churches:

"April 15: 1777: Suppose a Christian House be broke and robed to the value of 12 or 14 pounds should they be encouraged to prosecute the thief. Answr. Did the law require no greater punishment than the nature of the crime deserves then we could encourage a prosecution: but as a person that is prosecuted for the above crime is liable to suffer death we look upon it that no person ought to be prosecuted for such a crime the law being too severe in its penalty for such offence."[16]

Associational Circular Letters

As noted previously, the use of circular letters was an important characteristic of English Baptist associational life. Circular letters often were theological treatises, useful in providing instruction for ministers and laity alike. They were a means of communication and theological education. A "Circular Letter from the Ministers and Messengers Assembled at Oulney [Olney], in Buckinghamshire," June 4 and 5, 1771, included a statement of "important Doctrines": "Three equal Persons in the Godhead; eternal and personal Election; the original Guilt and Depravity of Mankind; particular Redemption; free Justification by the imputed Righteousness of Christ; efficacious Grace in Regeneration; the Perseverance of the Saints in Grace unto Glory; and professing the primitive Order and Discipline of Churches."[17] It was addressed to specific "Baptized Churches of Christ" and offered a brief affirmation of the work of those congregations. An elaborate discussion of original sin reflected the Calvinistic orientation of these Particular Baptist churches. The letter was signed by the moderator, prominent Calvinist minister John Gill.

Eighteenth-Century Baptist Church Life

Baptist Marriages

Debates over marriage rites, partners, and fidelity characterized Baptist life in the eighteenth century. While the Anglican establishment refused to sanction nonconformist marriages, some Baptists debated the appropriateness of marrying "outside the faith." From 1754 to 1836, Lord Hardwicke's Marriage Act declared as "null and void" all marriages "except those of Jews and Quakers, which were not had under license, or after publication of banns, as well as marriages not solemnized in churches or chapels of ease."[18] The state refused to recognize marriages celebrated in dissenting chapels. Baptists supported laws for the public solemnization of marriages, but they were refused marriage in Anglican churches.[19] Those who did marry in the established church often were dismissed from Baptist churches.[20]

Thomas Grantham's *Truth and Peace; or The Last and Most Friendly Debate Concerning Infant Baptism* (1689) included a postscript on "Manner of Marriages among Baptised Believers." This General Baptist marriage covenant stated:

> *These are to testify to all men, that we … the day of the date hereof, entered into the covenant state of marriage, according to a solemn contract heretofore made between ourselves, and with the consent of such as are concerned in order thereunto; and we do now, in the presence of Allmighty God and the witnesses hereafter named, ratify the said contract and covenant-act of marriage this day verbally made: … from this day forward; to love each other as husband and wife,*

and faithfully perform all the duties to which we are bound by God's word until Lord by death shall separate us. In testimony whereof, law, and the good laws of the land, in the case provided, till we have hereunto set our hands.[21]

After the covenant was affirmed, witnesses signed the document. These Baptists restricted marriage to unions of church members only, discouraging marriage to non-Baptists.[22] Baptist identity led communities to insist that members marry inside the Baptist family.

Baptist Hymnody

During the eighteenth century, Baptists published several hymnals for use in the churches. Daniel Turner's *Divine Songs and Other Poems* was published in 1747. *Evangelical Hymns and Songs,* produced by Benjamin Wallin (1711–1782), appeared in 1750, and John Needham's edition of *Hymns Devotional and Moral* in 1768. One of the most important hymnals was the *Collection of Hymns Adapted for Public Worship* (1769), from editors Caleb Evans and John Ash. It included hymns by Watts, Wesley, and the Baptist hymn writer Anne Steele.[23]

Steele (1716–1778) was one of the most prolific and popular hymn writers of eighteenth-century Baptist life. Her *Poems* (1760) was primarily a collection of hymns. She compiled an anthology of hymns, published in 1769 and containing 312 hymns, 62 of which were written by Steele herself.

Hymnody was central to Baptist spirituality. Hymns gave voice to religious experience, nurtured corporate prayer, and provided theological instruction. They became an acceptable "voice" for women in the church, although not without controversy.

Baptist Spirituality: The Diary of Jane Attwater

Baptist spirituality and church life are described in the diary of Jane Attwater (1753–1789), a member of a literary group that revolved around the person and work of Anne Steele. The lengthy diary is important as a resource for into Baptist piety and practice in the eighteenth century as articulated and reflected upon by a Baptist woman. While not a daily account of events, it covers a period from 1767 to April 1834. Unmarried, Attwater lived alone or with relatives, attending church extensively and evaluating the sermons and services that she experienced.[24]

Of her baptism, in 1775, Attwater wrote, "Fearless & quite compos'd I descended into the Watery Tomb ... and my thoughts whilst in the water was set on the baptism of my Glorious Example Christ ... a calm serious joy seem'd to run thro' my very soul."[25]

Of her Baptist commitments, Attwater wrote, "I am happy being brought up in the Baptist denomination as from wt [with] one little Examination I have been inabled to make I think the Doctrines that those profess are really consistent with the word of God I wd [would] wish not to be of this persuasion by way of Tradition only but by way of choice not that I think that there is none good but those who adhere to just this particular way of thinking far from it."[26] Jane Attwater's diaries give evidence of Baptist ways and ideas as understood and evaluated by one woman "in the pew."

Ordination

Specific ordination requirements and rituals established in earlier eras continued, apparently with increasing uniformity. In the eighteenth century, British Baptists seem to have viewed ordination as a church event, by which the congregation delegated authority for preaching, administration of ordinances, and other pastoral concerns to persons whose gifts and callings they recognized. One New Connection Baptist pastor described the process and its meaning: "We are fully persuaded ... that all churches should choose their own officers; and that having done this, they have a right to request and invite such ministers as they think most proper, who are themselves ordained pastors, to set apart the persons they have chosen to the office to which they have chosen them."[27]

During this period, Baptists utilized "lay preachers," who often preached for years without ordination. They served in local and itinerant ministries.

English Baptist ministers belonged to a community of churches that remained a sectarian remnant in the nation as a whole. During the latter third of the eighteenth century, there were some two hundred Particular Baptist congregations throughout the country, and General Baptists, rapidly growing in the 1780s and 1790s, had about one hundred churches.[28]

Christological Controversies

As the circular letters illustrate, doctrinal divisions plagued British Baptist groups throughout most of the eighteenth century. General Baptists were especially susceptible to dissension regarding Arianism, a fourth-century movement that challenged the eternal preexistence of Jesus. It took its name from Arius, a presbyter in the church of Alexandria, who suggested that Jesus was a man, honored by God, and worthy of worship, but with an origin in time. By the 1790s, some Baptists turned to Socinianism, another ancient theory that stressed Jesus' humanity, minimized his divinity, and denied his preexistence. All this led certain Baptists to question the relation of the Father and the Son, the divinity of Christ, and the nature of the Trinity.

Particular Baptists experienced controversy over antinomianism—the belief that Christian believers were immune from the law. Antinomianism fostered the idea that Christ's death had completely abrogated the "old law," at least for those who were among the elect and lived under the "new law" of grace. Some believers, convinced of their election, asserted that they were free from the strictures of tradition and legalism.

Specific rifts among General Baptists occurred in the late 1690s surrounding the views of Matthew Caffyn (1628–1714). Caffyn originally denied the humanity of Christ, influenced by the Christology of sixteenth-century Radical Reformer Melchior Hoffman. Hoffmanite Christology was based on the belief that Jesus received no human attributes from his mother but passed through the virgin Mary "like water through a pipe."[29] Later on, he apparently denied the divinity of Christ, thereby forcing the General Assembly of General Baptists to bring charges of heresy against him.[30] Divisions over his acquittal created a schism in the General Baptist ranks from 1693–1731, when they reunited around doctrines derived from Hebrews 6:1-2.

This controversy highlighted the struggles of some Baptists to balance confessional orthodoxy with biblical authority. While some judged the Arians to have deviated from traditional Trinitarian doctrine, others were drawn to their biblical arguments for supporting such views. Sympathizers insisted that Trinitarian dogmas were not clearly evident in Scripture.

Such controversies illustrated the collision between Baptist orthodoxy and liberty of conscience. W. T. Whitley commented, "The question of Freedom of conscience became entangled with the question of Contending for the truth; and there was much bewilderment for awhile."[31] Baptists of the period were given to theological speculation that took them in various ideological directions. Schism was common.

Questions of ministerial orthodoxy may have led some Baptist ministers to begin using sermon manuscripts in the pulpit. Critics of the practice saw it as evidence of a departure from the spontaneity of Spirit-inspired preaching. The offending ministers responded that written sermons could be published and circulated to a broader audience. The use of sermon manuscripts may indicate the pastors' desire to have an exact text of what was stated from the pulpit in case they were accused of heresy.[32] Allegations of heresy were common enough that ministers felt the need to document their sermonic declarations.

Dan Taylor and the New Connection Baptists

Baptists, like other English Protestants, were influenced by the Wesleyan revivals and religious upheavals of the mid-eighteenth century. John Wesley (1703–1791), Charles Wesley (1707–1788), George Whitefield (1715–1770), and others were part of a religious renewal that had significant impact on British church and society in the latter half of the 1700s. Wesley, an Anglican cleric and missionary to the New World, experienced an assurance of salvation in the famous Moravian worship service at a meetinghouse on Aldersgate Street on May 24, 1738. His description of that evening became one of the hallmarks of Methodist history: "About a quarter before nine, while he was describing the change which God works in the heat through faith in Christ, I felt my heart strangely warmed. I felt I did trust Christ, Christ alone for salvation; and an assurance was given me that He had taken away my sins, even mine and saved me from the law of sin and death."[33]

Wesley's decision to engage in field preaching (outdoor services) and his energetic travels throughout England contributed to religious awakenings and the rise of Methodism. Small groups, or "societies," were founded within the Church of England, aimed at producing conversion, piety, and methodical responses to the pressing spiritual and physical needs of the day. Wesley's Arminian evangelicalism centered in a gospel of free grace and free will. His approach had significant influence on Baptists. Beginning in 1741, David Taylor, a servant to Selina Hastings, the Countess of Huntingdon, preached Wesleyan ideas in the Leicestershire region. He helped to form a church that by 1755 had accepted believer's baptism by immersion as normative.

This group remained relatively isolated until they encountered Dan Taylor (1738–1816), another convert of the Wesleyan awakenings.[34] A miner from Halifax, Yorkshire, he was an early devotee of Methodism until disputes over church discipline and a concern for the baptism of believers led him to the Baptists. One early account suggests that he was refused baptism by the Particular Baptists, who affirmed the genuineness of his conversion but rejected his belief "that the Lord Jesus tasted death for every man, and made a propitiation for the sins of the whole world."[35] Taylor was immersed by the General Baptists on February 16, 1763, in Gamston, Nottinghamshire. He returned to Yorkshire and founded the first General Baptist church in that region.

Dan Taylor eventually encountered David Taylor and his revivalistic churches. While these congregations practiced believer's baptism, they resisted membership in the local General Baptist association because of its indifference to the revivals. Through the influence of Dan Taylor, they became the first churches of the New Connection of General Baptist movement.

Frustrated with the antiquated methods, theological debates, and a weakened Christology of the General Baptists, Taylor and others determined to found a "New Connection" of General Baptist churches responsive to revivalism and traditional orthodoxy. The new denomination was officially established in London on June 6, 1770, as a means "to revive Experimental Religion or Primitive Christianity in Faith and Practice."[36] A confession of faith incorporating six articles was approved. They affirmed Arminian interpretations of human nature, the fall, Christ's atoning death ("for all the sins of all men"), repentance and faith, and immersion baptism.[37]

Gilbert Boyce (1712–1800), Taylor's General Baptist mentor, made an unsuccessful attempt to reconcile the two Baptist groups. General Baptists continued to demand that their members eat no "blood animals" and rejected the practice of congregational singing, both of which were permitted by the New Connection Baptists. Taylor himself repudiated the office of messenger and the laying on of hands to the newly baptized.[38]

New Connection churches, associations, and regional meetings were founded throughout the Midlands. Dan Taylor moved to London, where he continued to serve as a New Connection leader.[39] New Connection Baptists developed their own church life, encouraging members not to marry unbelievers and to avoid secret societies. They permitted hymn singing but refused to allow musical instruments in their churches.

Taylor declared, "I confess myself a Baptist for conscience sake." In a treatise on baptism, he offered the standard Baptist arguments, then observed, "No instance can be produced, in which, either by precept or example, the scriptures authorize the sprinkling of infants.... Now there is only ONE BAPTISM; and therefore, where the practice of sprinkling infants is adopted, Christian baptism, which is quite a different thing, is totally lost." He concluded, "To change a divine ordinance as represented in scripture, is a crime of great enormity."[40]

Taylor agreed that baptism did not wash away original sin or "make anyone 'a member of Christ.'" Yet baptism was commanded by Christ, whose own immersion served as the model. It was observed by the earliest Christians, was a means for professing faith in Christ, and was the "answer of a good conscience towards God 1 Pet 3.21."[41]

Taylor was convinced that each individual had the capacity to call upon Christ for salvation. He wrote, "When I say this salvation is free, I mean that it is freely imparted to the sinner, to every sinner who applies to Jesus for it in the way in which the gospel appoints, that is by faith ... without any merits, works, or deservings whatsoever."[42] The gospel was the source of election for all who chose to believe.

Taylor's concern for the baptism of adults did not cause him to neglect the nurture of children. He even wrote a catechism for instructing children in the faith. Like other catechisms, it provided an introduction to the essentials of Christian religion. The book begins with questions regarding Scripture, which include these:

> *Sect. Xi*
> *"The Certainty of eternal Misery to those who die unrecovered from their fallen and sinful State."*

Q. 1. Are all Men Sinners?

A. Yes; there is none righteous, no not one. Rom. iii.10.

Q. 2. Are you yourself in a sinful State?

A. Yes; I was shapen in Iniquity, and in Sin did my Mother conceive me. Psal. li.5.[43]

As with most Baptist catechisms and confessions of faith, statements included appropriate biblical texts in support.

New Connection Baptists brought new energy to English Baptists. While born of the Wesleyan revivals, they developed a powerful Baptist identity and ecclesiastical life.

Educational Efforts

Eighteenth-century Baptists established schools in order to provide their young people with a classical education. Calvinist John Fawcett was largely self-taught, and in addition to his work as pastor at Wainsgate in the west region of Yorkshire, he founded a school both to provide Baptists students with classical education and to support himself financially. The school had many students, including John Sutcliff (1752–1814), who became a Particular Baptist pastor and a leader in the Baptist missionary movement.[44]

Certainly, the most significant of these educational endeavors was the Bristol Academy, begun through the Broadmead Baptist Church. The oldest of the Baptist educational ventures, Bristol Academy was a seedbed for the evangelical Calvinism that shaped the Baptist missionary movement. Its tutors emphasized the training of pastoral ministers as well as those who would serve as missionaries abroad. Its early principal, Bernard Foskett, served in that post for thirty years. Ministers William Staughton and John Rippon, strong supporters of the mission endeavor, were educated at Bristol.[45] Efforts to provide funding for students led to the formation of the Bristol Education Society in 1770.

New Connection Baptists developed an academy in London in 1798. General Baptist John Evans, pastor of the Worship Street Baptist Church, Islington, also maintained an academy from 1795 to 1818. An advocate of Socinian views, he often was accused of promoting those beliefs among his students. Evans authored numerous books, among them a history called *A Brief Sketch of the Several Denominations* (1795), which surveyed contemporary religious communions.[46]

Calvinism: Debates and Divisions

Perhaps the most significant source of both unity and division among eighteenth-century Baptists was the influence and interpretation of Calvinism. While Particular Baptists asserted the benefits of Reformed theology over and against the Arminianism of the Wesleyan and General Baptist movements, they also divided over the nature of Calvinism itself. Much of the debate revolved around questions of divine sovereignty and the role of human beings in the salvific process. Did election and predestination mean that everything was determined before the foundation of the world? What was the role of free will in human salvation?

Strict Calvinism

Eighteenth-century Particular Baptists divided into numerous factions and subfactions. Strict, or High, Calvinism characterized much Particular Baptist theology during the eighteenth century. Some of these Baptists were supralapsarians, who believed that God had elected some persons for salvation and others for damnation before the foundation of the world. The fall of Adam and Eve was the divinely ordained means to facilitate the salvation of some and the damnation of others. Conversion was wholly the work of God, who needed no human means to accomplish salvation. Underwood observed that for these Calvinists, faith was "a consequence and not a condition of election."[47] Other High Baptists were sublapsarians, who suggested that God's choice of persons for salvation or damnation occurred after the Fall, as a result of the free, albeit evil, choice made by the first male and female.

John Skepp (d. 1721) and John Brine (1703–1765) were among those Baptist leaders who could be considered High Calvinists. Skepp's *Divine Energy; or, the Efficacious Operations of the Spirit of God upon the Soul of Man,* originally published in the 1720s, warned against theologically futile attempts to convince sinners to come to salvation. God alone was the agent of salvation, and only the infusion of divine grace could make salvation possible.[48] From his pastorate in Cripplegate, Brine resisted any action that might lead the unconverted to believe that they could choose salvation for themselves. His views were set forth in a treatise entitled *A Refutation of Arminian Principles Delivered in a Pamphlet Entitled, the Modern Question,* published in 1743.[49]

John Gill

Perhaps the most articulate advocate for this form of Calvinism was John Gill (1697–1771), prominent Baptist pastor and theologian. A native of Kettering, Gill received a classical education that included Latin and Greek. He later taught himself Hebrew. Baptized in 1716 in a Particular Baptist church, he soon began preaching, and in 1719 he was called as pastor of the Horsleydown Church, Southwark, a position he retained until his death fifty-two years later.[50]

His theological works include the *Body of Practical Divinity,* published in 1770, and the *Exposition of the Holy Scripture,* a nine-volume biblical commentary written between 1728 and 1767. Another book, *The Cause of God and Truth* (1735), was a widely read text on Calvinism.

Gill affirmed the doctrine of double predestination and suggested, "That there are universal offers of grace and salvation made to all men I utterly deny; nay, I deny they are made to any."[51] God was under no obligation to save any sinner; that any were elected was a gift of grace, and the fact that any person would be chosen for salvation represented a work of unmerited grace. Gill declared that election "is of particular persons; it does not merely respect events, characters, and actions; but the persons of men; as they are persons who are chosen in Christ."[52] He further observed, "We believe, that the work of regeneration, conversion, sanctification, and faith, is not an act of man's free-will and power, but of the might, efficacious and irresistible grace of God."[53] Like other strict Calvinists of the day, Gill restricted church membership to those who received immersion on profession of faith, and he offered the Lord's Supper only to those baptized by immersion.

Gill and other strict Calvinists often were criticized for undermining evangelism with their suggestion that "indiscriminate" preaching should be avoided because it drew the "unconvertible" into the church. Yet Gill was a caring pastor, ever concerned about the spiritual and physical needs of his flock. As one scholar commented, "A careful study of his sermons supports the view that he never knowingly discouraged presentation of the gospel to 'sinners.'"[54]

John Gill bequeathed a legacy of High Calvinism to English Baptists. The evangelical Calvinism of William Carey and Andrew Fuller represented a significant contrast to what was called "Gillism."

John Collett Ryland Sr.

Another of the Calvinistic Baptist leaders was John Collett Ryland Sr. (1723–1792). Ryland's strict Calvinism was evident in his alleged advice to the William Carey to "sit down" after the young Carey's famous sermon urging Baptists to embark on world missionary outreach. Ryland believed that God's sovereign will alone brought elected sinners to repentance. Missionary activity thus appeared to be a futile form of works righteousness. Ryland served as minister in Warwick and Northampton while supporting himself as a schoolteacher.[55]

By the late eighteenth century, many British Particular Baptists were frustrated with the numerical declines and spiritual lethargy evident in their churches. The scene was set for another interpretation of Calvinism—one that permitted the broader preaching of the gospel.

The Evangelical Calvinists

Evangelical Calvinists were those Baptists who believed that it was the duty of the redeemed to preach the gospel to "all nations." They understood that preaching would serve as a means to awaken the elect to salvation. In their concern to take the gospel to the world, the missionary movement began among Baptists.

Robert Hall Sr.

Evangelical Calvinism was evident in a sermon preached by Robert Hall Sr. (1728–1791) at the meeting of the Northampton Association in 1779. In it, Hall warned of the dangers of any theology (High Calvinism) that implicitly or explicitly kept sinners from repentance. Published as *Help to Zion's Travellers,* the sermon's circulation had a powerful impact on numerous Baptists, among them the young William Carey.[56]

Andrew Fuller

One of the most influential proponents of evangelical Calvinism was Andrew Fuller (1754–1815). As preacher, theologian, and denominational leader, Fuller bridged the eighteenth and nineteenth centuries, connecting numerous movements and events in English Baptist life.

Born February 6, 1754, in Cambridgeshire, Fuller experienced a conversion at the age of sixteen that reflected a process described by many eighteenth-century Calvinists. It began with a concern to know God within a profound sense of his own sinfulness. As the process intensified, Fuller sought help from the Bible and certain contemporary books, including John Bunyan's *Pilgrim's Progress.*[57] Seized by a deepening melancholy, he repudiated an earlier belief that he "could repent at any time."[58] In November 1769, an unbearable despair caused him to relinquish all hope of salvation. Gradually, he began to sense "a ray of hope mixed with determination, if I might, to cast my perishing soul upon the Lord Jesus Christ for salvation."[59] He then cast himself on Christ, noting, "If I perish, I perish." Ultimately, he concluded, "I knew experimentally what it was to be dead to the world by the cross of Christ, and to feel an habitual determination to devote my future life to God my Saviour, and from this time considered the vows of God as upon me."[60] On viewing an immersion conducted by the Baptists, he decided "that this was the primitive way of baptizing, and that every Christian was bound to attend to this institution of our blessed Lord."[61]

Baptized in his late teens, he joined a Baptist church and soon began preaching. In 1775, he received ordination and accepted a call to his first pastorate.[62] In 1776, he met John Sutcliff, John Ryland Jr., and Samuel Pearce—three friends who later joined with him in founding the Baptist Missionary Society. That same year, he married Sarah Gardiner. In 1782, Fuller became the pastor of the Baptist church at Kettering, a church he served for the next thirty-two years. Sarah Gardiner Fuller died in 1792. In 1794, he married Ann Coles, commenting in his memoirs, "Two days after our marriage we invited about a dozen of our serious friends to drink tea and spend the evening in prayer."[63]

Like other evangelical Calvinists of his time, Fuller was influenced by the writings of the American Congregationalist Jonathan Edwards (1703–1758). One of Edwards's early works, *A Faithful Narrative of the Surprising Work of God* (1737), was an account of the revival that occurred at his church in Northampton, Massachusetts. In it, Edwards suggested that revivals and their resulting conversions were truly a "surprising work" of God's sovereign will. Through a series of sermons on justification by faith, Edwards prepared the way for a revival that he hoped God would provide. He preached as if everyone could be saved, believing that God would use preaching to touch the hearts of the elect. He wrote that through preaching, the people "received thence a general satisfaction, with respect to the main thing in question, which they had been in trembling doubts and concern about; and their minds were engaged the more earnestly to seek that they might come to be accepted of God, and saved in the way of the gospel, which had been made evident to them to be the true and only way."[64] Edwards's approach to evangelism permitted Fuller and other Baptists to retain Calvinist principles while calling sinners to repentance.

Fuller rejected the efforts of Puritan pastor and theologian Richard Baxter (1615–1691) to promote "Universal Redemption," or the general atonement of Christ. Fuller noted, "I only contend for the *sufficiency* of the atonement, in itself considered, for the redemption and salvation of the whole world; and this affords a ground for a universal invitation to sinners to believe; which was maintained by Calvin, and all the old Calvinists."[65] From Fuller's perspective, Baxter wrote "as if the unconverted could do something towards their conversion, and as if grace were given to all, except those who forfeit it by wilful sin. But no such sentiment ever occupied my mind, or proceeded from my pen."[66] Fuller suggested that Jonathan Edwards's *Discourse on Justification* provided him with the "greatest instruction" on the topic.[67]

Andrew Fuller was the first secretary of the Baptist Missionary Society and a chief supporter of the Serampore mission in India. Fuller challenged the hyper-Calvinism of his day and its resistance to direct evangelistic efforts. In fact, his particular interpretation of Calvinism was sometimes labeled "Fullerism." He promoted a modified Calvinism with an emphasis on the responsibility of human beings to advance the gospel. He attacked "the immorality and absurdity of Deism," convinced that, like High Calvinism, it promoted indifference to the salvation of the world.[68] He wrote that the decision to send William Carey to India was "like a few men who were deliberating about the importance of penetrating into a deep mine which had never before been explored. We had no one to guide us, and while we were thus deliberating, Carey, as it were, said, 'Well I will go down, if you will hold the rope!' … There was great responsibility attached to us who began the business."[69]

Fuller traveled throughout Britain raising money for the mission and responding to those Baptists suspicious of missionary outreach. Doctrinal controversies were impossible to avoid. On one occasion, the Scottish Baptist church to which he was invited requested that he sign their confession of faith before he could deliver the sermon. Although he agreed with their doctrines, Fuller refused to sign the document, and the church withdrew its invitation. Retreating to a nearby congregation, he preached to a crowd of over four thousand people. The church that had rescinded its invitation later "repented" and forwarded an offering to the Mission Society.[70]

Fuller also responded to certain British politicians who charged that missionaries disrupted the peace of foreign regions by undermining native customs. In *Apology for the Late Christian Missions to India,* he insisted that conversion to Christianity could actually encourage a positive response to British rule from the indigenous peoples.[71] Although he urged Baptists "to be patriots, or lovers of our country," Fuller acknowledged that citizenship had its limits. Love of country was not an excuse for "clashes with universal benevolence." He wrote, "Such, I am ashamed to say, is that with which some have advocated the cause of *negro slavery.* It is necessary, forsooth, to the wealth of this country! No: if my country cannot prosper but at the expense of justice, humanity, and the happiness of mankind, let it be unprosperous!"[72]

Fuller called Baptists to resist all plots to overthrow the government or undermine its duly elected its leaders.[73] Christians, he believed, should eschew militarism, taking up arms only "as members of civil society, when called upon to do so for the defence of our country."[74] Nations could act in self-defense but not in aggression.

As theologian, pastor, and mission organizer, Andrew Fuller was a central figure in English Baptist life.

John Sutcliff

John Sutcliff (1752–1814) was another of the Baptist leaders who founded the Baptist Missionary Society. Educated at Bristol Academy, he served a lifelong pastorate at Olney. Sutcliff baptized William Carey and remained his adviser throughout his life. Influenced by Jonathan Edwards's call for "concerts of prayer" for a religious awakening, Sutcliff issued his own "Prayer Call" and urged English churches to pray "that sinners may be converted, the saints edified, the interest of religion revived, and the name of God glorified."[75]

John Rippon

Baptist hymn writer and preacher John Rippon was a strong supporter of the missionary cause. His first publication of *The Baptist Annual Register* (1793) informed Particular Baptists about the diverse activities of churches and societies and missionary enterprises. His missionary sentiments were expressed in verse form:

From East to West, from North to South,
Now be his name ador'd!
EUROPE, with all thy millions, shout
Hosannahs to thy Lord!
ASIA and AFRICA, resound
From shore to shore his fame;
And thou, AMERICA, in songs,
Redeeming love proclaim![76]

William Carey and the Mission Movement

The decision of British Baptists to send William Carey (1761–1834) to India mirrored the actions of various Protestant groups of the period. Of these events Brian Stanley commented, "To British eyes, the world beyond the troubled European continent remained largely unknown and threatening. In short, at the time of the French Revolution in 1789, British Baptists appeared to be an inward-looking sect in an insular nation in an unstable continent—hardly the most likely candidates for originating a movement which was to transform world history."[77] Baptists did not come easily to the endeavor.

Clearly, Britain's efforts to extend its empire, explore the world, and bring "civilization" to the masses shaped the decisions of Baptists and other Protestants to launch various missionary ventures. As noted previously, the works of Jonathan Edwards provided a theological underpinning for Calvinistic evangelicalism. Andrew Fuller's *The Gospel Worthy of All Acceptation* influenced the missionary enterprise "precisely because it enabled Particular Baptists to restore concepts of moral obligation and human responsibility to the very centre of their theology of salvation."[78] Missionaries were seen as vehicles of God's saving activity in history.

Certain Baptist schools became seedbeds of missionary enthusiasm. The Bristol Academy, in western England, became a center of missionary zeal.

While conversion was essential, the process might vary with the individual. Some claimed a dynamic experience of grace, punctuated by struggles with sin and the torments of hell. In 1791, Daniel Brunsdon, age fourteen, dreamt that he was in a field, and something, he said, "took hold of my shirt and shook me dead, or rather shook me into hell. I awoke in a very great agony of mind and spent some time in prayer. Indeed I was afraid to go to sleep lest I should die, for I knew I should go to hell if I did."[79] Others experienced what some called an "intellectual" conversion, which in the case of missionary William Grant took him through numerous philosophies—deism, Arianism, and atheism—and ended with "nothing like any conviction of sin." Grant's Latin studies with Joshua Marshman, another of the Serampore missionaries, convinced Grant of the veracity of the gospel, and he became a missionary.[80]

The Work of William Carey
The formation of the Baptist Missionary Society in 1792 is inseparable from the life and work of William Carey. Reared in the Church of England, Carey entered the Baptist ranks through English Independency. Immersed on October 5, 1783, he soon secured a pastorate at Moulton. By his own account, Carey's reading of Captain Cook's South Seas travels confirmed his

desire to consider missionary service.[81] He soon found others who shared his concerns, including John Ryland Jr., Andrew Fuller, John Sutcliff, and Samuel Pearce, who preached at Carey's ordination service in 1787.

A lifelong student of biblical languages, Carey did translation work that was widely recognized. His regimented study habits began early in his pastoral career. Mondays were given to the study of languages and the translation of texts. Tuesdays involved investigations into science, history, and writing. On Wednesdays he lectured in the mission school, and on Thursdays he visited members of the church. Friday through Sunday involved preparation for and participation in preaching and worship.[82]

Early in his pastorate at Moulton, Carey pressed his concern for missions. At a ministers' meeting in 1791, Sutcliff and Fuller preached sermons on the subject of the Christian mission. Carey insisted that they reach a decision on a mission society before the meeting adjourned. Although that action was not taken, the group did agree to let Carey print the sermons by Sutcliff and Fuller.[83]

At a gathering of the Northampton Association, Carey introduced a treatise entitled *An Enquiry into the Obligations of Christians to Use Means for the Conversion of the Heathens*—an apology for the church's worldwide mission that detailed population statistics from various continents and responded to the opponents of missionary ventures. He observed, "It has been objected that there are multitudes in our own nation, and within our immediate spheres of action, who are as ignorant as the South-Sea savages, and that therefore we have work enough at home, without going into other countries." He responded to that objection, "Our own countrymen have the means of grace, and may attend on the word preached if they choose it. They have the means of knowing the truth, and faithful ministers are placed in almost every part of the land." Those outside England, however, had "no Bible, no written language, (which many of them have not,) no ministers, no good civil government, nor any of those advantages which we have." He then called "for every possible exertion to introduce the Gospel among them."[84]

In 1792, Carey preached at the annual association meeting in Nottingham. His sermon became a classic in the annals of British missionary movements. Taken from Isaiah 54:2-3, the text read, "Enlarge the place of thy tent, and let them stretch forth the curtains of thine habitations: spare not, lengthen thy cords, and strengthen thy stakes; for thou shalt break forth on the right hand and on the left." He concluded with a phrase that became a missionary maxim: "Expect great things—attempt great things." One observer noted, "The effect of this discourse was considerable," and it produced a resolution "that a plan should be prepared against the next ministers' meeting at Kettering for forming a society for propagating the gospel among the heathen."[85]

Apparently, some felt that such efforts were not a vital part of the church's mission. But the momentum was in Carey's favor, and plans for a society continued. Andrew Fuller described the motivation for the new endeavor:

> The object of this society is to evangelize the poor, dark, idolatrous Heathen, by sending missionaries into different parts of the world where the glorious gospel of Christ is not at present published, to preach the glad tidings of salvation by the blood of the Lamb. Can it then be an object unworthy of the most ardent and persevering pursuit, to disseminate among them the humane and saving principles of

*the Christian Religion, in order to bring these uncivilized barbarians to yield obe-
dience to the Prince of Peace, and to found christian churches in places which now
exhibit nothing but scenes of desolation. Were these ignorant immortals but thoroughly instructed in the doctrines and precepts of christianity, their civilization
would naturally follow.*[86]

Others—Moravians, Methodists, and "brother George Liele, the Baptist Negro"—were
already in the field. Baptists should follow them.[87]

It was a complicated endeavor. Funds were nonexistent; would-be missionaries, inexpe-
rienced; and the difficulties of travel, extreme. As usual, many Baptists feared entrapment in
ecclesiastical alliances, and some fretted that "in forming a society there would be danger of
its falling under irreligious influence."[88]

Nonetheless, on October 2, 1792, a group of ministers met at Kettering, in the home of
Beeby Wallis, the widow of a Baptist deacon, to found "The Particular (or Calvinistic) Baptist Society for Propagating the Gospel among the Heathen." After a day of discussion and
prayer, "They then, in a most solemn manner, pledged themselves to God, and to one
another, to *make a trial* for introducing the gospel amongst the heathen."[89] The Baptist Missionary Society was organized, and a resolution was approved, stating, "Desirous of making an effort for the propagation of the gospel amongst the Heathen, agreeably to what is
recommended in brother Carey's late publication on that subject, we, whose names appear
in the subsequent subscription, do solemnly agree to act in society together for that purpose."[90] Membership was offered to those who would "subscribe ten pounds at once, or
ten shillings and six-pence annually."[91]

John Ryland Jr., Reynold Hogg, William Carey, John Sutcliff, and Andrew Fuller were
appointed an executive committee. Sutcliff, Carey, and Fuller were "empowered to act in
carrying into effect the purposes of the society."[92] Fuller was named secretary, and Hogg was
appointed treasurer. A self-perpetuating board of trustees was established to appoint ministers and church members of "like character."[93] John Rippon offered his support for the venture, but other London ministers refused to participate.[94]

On January 10, 1793, John Thomas and William Carey were appointed as the first missionaries. It was estimated that five hundred pounds would be needed to send them to India.
More than twice that amount was raised, and all of it was required when Carey decided to
take his family. The group set sail on June 13, 1793, and arrived in India on November 14.

The British East India Company refused to recognize or sponsor the new missionaries
because British authorities feared that missionary activity would cause religious controversy
in the territories. Their concerns were not without merit. In 1806, the Sepoy (native) troops
supported by the British rebelled—an action thought by many to be the result of issues raised
by missionary activity. Baptists and other mission-sending agencies were forced to resist the
East India Company's attempts to have them removed from British territories. Lacking
recognition from the East India Company, the missionaries accepted the protection of the
Danish India Company at Serampore.[95]

Carey, his wife, Dorothy, and their four children (one of whom was a newborn) set out
for Calcutta, accompanied by his sister-in-law, Katherine Plackett, and a missionary colleague, John Thomas. Funds soon were depleted, and Carey was compelled to find other
employment. Illness took its toll immediately. Carey and his party had multiple bouts with

fever. When her third son, five-year-old Peter, died from severe fevers, Dorothy Carey was overcome with grief and never recovered. Carey wrote, "My poor wife must be considered as insane and is the occasion of great sorrow." Her deteriorating mental and emotional state lingered until her death.[96]

Spiritual discouragements followed. Carey wrote in his journal, "This is indeed the valley of the shadow of death to me, except my soul is much more insensible than John Bunyan's Pilgrim. O what would I give for a kind sympathetic friend, such as I had in England, to whom I might open my heart. But I rejoice that I am here, notwithstanding, and God is here, who not only can have compassion, but is able to save to the uttermost."[97] In 1799, they were joined by Joshua Marshman (1768–1837) and his wife, Hannah (1767–1847), William Ward (1769–1823), Daniel Brunsdon (d. 1801), and William Grant (d. 1799).

The depth of Indian devotion to the Hindu religion surprised them, and conversions were a long time coming. It was not until December 1800 that two lone individuals, Krishna Pal and Gokul, accepted Christianity and received baptism. William Ward, who kept an extensive journal, offered his opinion of the Indian people and their culture. He wrote, "The Bengalese are naturally indolent. We are in a good deal of difficulty in this respect, and shall be more so if converts increase. If 100 persons were to come, more than 50 would, no doubt, be ignorant of every kind of business. For these people what can we do? They cannot be maintained in idleness, and they have not spirit to embark in anything new unless led like children."[98] Of the difficulties of converting the Hindus and Muslims, Ward commented, "I am ready to doubt whether Europeans will ever be extensively useful in converting souls by preaching in this country. God can do all things. Paul could become a Jew to win Jews, and a Gentile to win Gentiles; but, however needful, we cannot become Hindoos to win them, or Mussulmans [Muslims] to win Mussulmans."[99]

Men and women worked together in the missionary task, though their activities apparently were prescribed according to cultural norms. Hannah Marshman's school helped provide financial support for the mission. Ward observed of the work of the missionary women:

> Our sisters have in general a good deal to do. Br. C. directs the affairs of the family this month. Sister Grant helps him. In Bro. C.'s month she does as much or more in the family than any of our sisters. Looking over the servants, helping to clean the furniture, making tea, which is hard work in this country. Perhaps in an evening sometimes a sister has tea to make for 20 or 30 people. Sister Grant has the care of all the linen, &c., constantly, so that she is of considerable use to the Mission, though she has no husband, and cannot talk to the native women. Sister M.'s Labour for the Mission is the greatest.[100]

Death continued to take its toll, with ten individuals in the mission dying during 1811–1812. William Grant died soon after his arrival.[101] Ward wrote poignantly of Grant's last days: "Bro. Grant continued worse yesterday, and this morning he had a convulsive fit. At Half-past two o'clock he died very calmly.... I know not when any death so affected me. The infidelity of my heart says, surely if God meant to count the Hindoos to Christ, He would not cut off His instruments on the threshold of their work, after they have come 15,000 miles on such an errand!"[102]

In 1812, a fire at the mission destroyed many of Carey's manuscripts and printing implements. These setbacks created personal and theological dilemmas for the missionaries, who often wondered why God would lead them to foreign lands, only to have them die on arrival. But, as Brian Stanley observed, "Missionaries whose minds were thus captivated by the sovereignty of God possessed an extraordinary ability to transform discouragements into renewed incentives to faithfulness."[103]

Conflicts with the Missionary Society

Conflicts between the missionaries and the Baptist Missionary Society (BMS) were common. Missionaries were counseled to avoid political involvements in the societies they sought to evangelize, and Andrew Fuller often warned the missionaries to shun political entanglements. The mission board issued the following instructions to the departing missionaries: "Beware, both from a principle of conscience and from a regard to their own interest, and that of the mission, of intermeddling with any political concerns—to be obedient to the laws in all civil affairs—to respect magistrates, both supreme and subordinate, and teach the same things to others."[104]

In words that illustrate the prevailing attitude toward Indian culture, the board advised, "However gross might be the idolatries, and heathenish superstitions that might fall under their notice, they should sedulously avoid all rudeness, insult, or interruption, during the observance of such superstitions, observing no methods but those of Christ and his apostles, namely, the persevering use of scripture, reason, prayer, meekness, and love."[105]

John Fountain was one of the first missionaries specifically to receive Andrew Fuller's chastisement for political involvement. Fountain's political activities in India continued until his death eight years later. John Chamberlain, another of the missionaries to India, also was mixed up in politics, and he desired to begin a new mission station independent of Carey. Fuller wrote firmly, "The Society cannot think of supporting separate stations which should be at variance with each other, or with the station at Serampore. If you, or any brethren are so dissatisfied that you cannot comply with this, the sooner you or they return to England the better."[106]

Political involvement was not limited to the work in India. The missions committee attempted to send out two missionaries to the African country of Sierra Leone in 1795, but "through the indiscretion of one of them, and the ill health of the other, the undertaking failed."[107] The "indiscretion" involved Jacob Grigg, a missionary who encouraged the native peoples to resist British colonial rule. The society ordered him home and condemned his activities. Fuller wrote to Carey, "It is absolutely necessary that missionaries should confine themselves to their work, and not meddle in politicks."[108]

These and other difficulties with missionary personnel led Fuller to observe that he was less fearful of the financial problems than of the individuals sent out. He wrote, "It is not for want of money that we cannot send out more missionaries, but of suitable characters. That is a matter of importance…. We had better to wait than send unsuitable missionaries."[109]

Interdenominational Cooperation

The Baptists demonstrated a willingness to cooperate with other Protestants in the missionary work. One document observed, "But so far were we from having in view the exclusive promotion of our own peculiar principles, as Baptists, that we were determined from the beginning, if no opportunity appeared for sending out missionaries of our own, that we would assist other societies already in being amongst the Presbyterians and the Moravians."[110]

Once the BMS was established, the supporters willingly accepted funds from persons outside the Baptist fold. Brian Stanley commented, "The BMS was thus founded in a spirit of ecumenical idealism tempered by a liberal dose of denominational realism."[111] Cooperation did not mean intercommunion, however, and the Baptists continued to refuse the Lord's Supper to those who had not received immersion.

Carey and Biblical Translations

Carey was determined to translate the Bible into the languages of the people among whom he labored. By 1799, he had translated both testaments into Bengali. He obtained a printing press and printed some one thousand copies, including four volumes of the Hebrew Scriptures and a translation of the New Testament. An additional ten thousand copies of selected passages also were printed. As time passed, he worked toward further translations in Hindi, Orissa, Guzzeratte, Kernata, Telinga, Seeks, Burman, and Bengali.

In 1808, the Serampore (India) Mission issued its first "Memoir" concerning the translation of Bible. It was addressed to the BMS and to "fellow Christians in Britain and America." The document noted, "Nearly fourteen years have elapsed since the first and remote step was taken in this work, by Mr. Carey's immediate and assiduous application, on his arrival in India, first to the Bengalee and afterwards to the Sungskrit languages."[112] Decisions then were made to expand translation of texts to other languages. Carey wrote, "We were by no means, however, without our discouragements: the idea of three or four men succeeding in the acquisition of a number of languages, and the unspeakable responsibility attached to translating the word of God, with other difficulties, weighed so much with us, that we determined to conceal the fact of our having engaged in such a work till we had advanced so far as to convince ourselves and others of its practicability."[113]

Carey's concerns were not only for souls and translations but also for the physical world around them. When his son Jabez was appointed a missionary to the East Indies, Carey urged him to collect specimens of animal, insect, and plant life native to the region. He wrote, "I wish you to pay the minutest attention to the natural productions of the Islands and regularly to send me all you can. Fishes and large animals must be excepted, but these you must describe. You know how to send birds and insects.... And always send a new supply by every ship."[114]

Missionary Training

Training for the early missionaries was limited at best. Stuart Piggin commented that during its first two decades, the "BMS provided neither a systematic nor an extensive training for its missionaries."[115] A rudimentary training program was in place by 1798, when John Sutcliff offered instruction to two new missionaries. Later candidates received informal training, and then were sent to Bristol and Stepney academies. The Serampore trio continually complained that the educational level of the early missionaries was insufficient for the work required of them.

Baptists and the British Empire

The intricate relationships between the missionary enterprise and British colonialism confronted Baptists with many challenges. Although the British East India Company initially resisted Protestant efforts to missionize India, government agencies soon provided security for missionaries spread throughout the burgeoning British Empire. The missionaries recognized that they were protected, directly and indirectly, by the British presence in sometimes hostile countries. Robert Torbet noted, "The successful spread of British rule and protection to missionaries was hailed as a boon in Burma, South India, Assam, and Bengal-Orissa."[116] Missionaries often walked a thin line between a response to the culture in which they worked and the political realities of their native land.

English Baptists: Identity and Expansion

By the close of the eighteenth century, English Baptists had begun a worldwide missionary movement, with representatives sent out to a variety of foreign outposts. They solidified their identity as one of Britain's nonconformist communities, founding schools, expanding denominational connections, and organizing new churches. The Wesleyan awakenings influenced the beginnings of the New Connection Baptists and, concomitantly, the renewal ᵐinian theology. Evangelical Calvinism provided the theological justification for missic ors and accentuated duty to preach the gospel to the entire world. For many o' sion supporters, "civilization" accompanied salvation imported from the We

Notes

1. Williston Walker et al., *A History of the Christian Church*, 4th ed. (New York: Scribner, 1985),
2. Alfred C. Underwood, *A History of the English Baptists* (London: Baptist Union Publishing De
   W. T. Whitley, *A History of British Baptists* [London: Griffin, 1923], 163).
3. Raymond Brown, *The English Baptists of the Eighteenth Century* (London: Baptist Historic
4. Ibid., 53.
5. Underwood, *English Baptists*, 131–32; see also Joseph Ivimey, *A History of the English Baptists*, .
   3:133–135; Brown, *English Baptists*, 41.
6. Underwood, *English Baptists*, 120–21.
7. Ibid., 121.
8. Ibid.
9. Brown, *English Baptists*, 37–40.
10. "Associational Life till 1815," *Transactions of the Baptist Historical Society* 5 (1916–17): 26–27.
11. Cited in John Rippon, *The Baptist Annual Register* (London, 1797), no. 14, 485; see also John E. Steely, "Associational Messengers in Baptist History," *Baptist History and Heritage* 17 (April 1982): 8.
12. Steely, "Associational Messengers," 9–10. In the United States, certain Baptist groups—Southern Baptists, for example—preferred the designation "messenger" rather than "delegate," insisting that the former carried less official, and therefore less hierarchical, authority from or for the congregation. Such representatives could be chosen by the congregation, but their positions on issues were their own opinions, not necessarily those of the entire church that sent them. They could represent the church but not speak officially for it.
13. W. T. Whitley, *A History of British Baptists*, rev. ed. (London: Kingsgate Press, 1932), 180.
14. Steeley, "Associational Messengers," 6.
15. The Baptist Board, "Minutes from 1724," *Transactions of the Baptist Historical Society* 5 (1916–17): 100.
16. See "Minutes of the Monthly Conferences, Held by the Ministers and Officers of the Churches in Leicestershire, Which Were the Nucleus of the New Connexion of General Baptists," *Transactions of the Baptist Historical Society* 5 (1916–17): 119.
17. See "Marriages before 1754," *Transactions of the Baptist Historical Society* 1 (1908–9): 122.

18. "The Excellence and Utility of the Grace of Hope, Considered in a Circular Letter from the Baptist Minister and Messengers Assembled at Olney," June 4-6, 1782, 2.
19. Ibid., 123.
20. Ibid.
21. S. W. A. Moisey, "Marriage Covenants of the General Baptists," *Baptist Quarterly* 12 (1946–48): 203; see also Adam Taylor, *The History of the English General Baptists*, 2 vols. (London, 1818), 1:450.
22. Moisey, "Marriage Covenants," 206–7.
23. Brown, *English Baptists*, 92–93.
24. Majorie Reeves, "Jane Attwater's Diaries," in *Pilgrim Pathways: Essays in Baptist History in Honour of B. R. White*, ed. William H. Brackney and Paul S. Fiddes (Macon, Ga.: Mercer University Press, 1999), 207–9.
25. Ibid., 214.
26. Ibid., 215.
27. Dan Taylor, *A Charge and Sermon Delivered at the Ordination of the Rev. Mr. John Deacon* (London: J. Buckland, 1786), 26–27 (cited in John E. Steely, "Ministerial Certification in Southern Baptist History: Ordination," *Baptist History and Heritage* [January 1980]: 27).
28. Ivimey, *English Baptists*, 4:13.
29. Whitley, *British Baptists*, 172.
30. Underwood, *English Baptists*, 127.
31. Whitley, *British Baptists*, 173–74.
32. Brown, *English Baptists*, 59.
33. John Wesley, *The Journal of John Wesley* (Chicago: Moody Press, 1952), 63–64.
34. Underwood, *English Baptists*, 149–51.
35. Taylor, *English General Baptists*, 2:69–74.
36. Ibid., 2:139; see also H. Leon McBeth, *A Sourcebook for Baptist Heritage* (Nashville: Broadman, 1990), 107.
37. William L. Lumpkin, *Baptist Confessions of Faith* (Chicago: Judson Press, 1959), 304–44.
38. Underwood, *English Baptists*, 154.
39. Ibid., 156.
40. Dan Taylor, *A Compendious View of the Nature and Importance of Christian Baptism, for the Use of Plain Christians* (London, n.d.), 18–20.
41. Ibid., 21–23.
42. Dan Taylor, *The Christian Religion: An Exposition of Its Leading Principles, Practical Requirements, and Experimental Enjoyments* (London: J. Smith, 1844), 169–70.
43. Dan Taylor, *A Catechism, or, Instructions for Children and Youth, in the Fundamental Doctrines of Christianity* (Leeds: G. Wright and Son, n.d).
44. Brown, *English Baptists*, 82.
45. Ibid., 115.
46. Ibid., 100.
47. Underwood, *English Baptists*, 133.
48. H. Leon McBeth, *The Baptist Heritage* (Nashville: Broadman, 1987), 174–75.
49. Brown, *English Baptists*, 73–74.
50. O. C. Robison, "The Legacy of John Gill," *Baptist Quarterly* 24 (July 1971): 111.
51. Ibid., 119 (citing Gill, "The Doctrine of Predestination Stated and Set in the Scripture-Light in Opposition to Mr. Wesley's Predestination Calmly Considered with a Reply to the Exceptions of the Said Writer to the Doctrine of the Perseverance of the Saints," *Collection of Sermons and Tracts,*" Vol. 3, 1773, 269–70).
52. James E. Tull, *Shapers of Baptist Thought* (Valley Forge, Pa.: Judson Press, 1972), 81.
53. Ibid., 115.
54. Ibid., 117.
55. Underwood, *English Baptists*, 142–43.
56. McBeth, *The Baptist Heritage*, 180; Underwood, *English Baptists*, 160.
57. Andrew Gunton Fuller, *The Complete Works of the Rev. Andrew Fuller, with a Memoir of His Life*, 5 vols. (London: Holdsworth and Ball, 1831–32), 1:xi.
58. Ibid., xii.
59. Ibid., xv.
60. Ibid., xvi–xvii.
61. Ibid., xviii.
62. Ibid., xxiv.
63. Ibid., xcix.
64. Jonathan Edwards, *A Faithful Narrative of the Surprising Work of God, in Early American Christianity*, ed. Bill J. Leonard (Nashville: Broadman, 1983), 171.
65. Fuller, *Complete Works*, 2:552.
66. Ibid.
67. Gilbert Laws, "Andrew Fuller, 1754–1815," *Baptist Quarterly* 2 (1924–25): 76–89.
68. Ibid., 81.

69. Ibid., 82.
70. Ibid., 83.
71. E. F. Clipsham, "Andrew Fuller and the Baptist Mission," *Foundations* 10 (January–March 1967), 13.
72. Andrew Fuller, "Sermon IX," in Fuller, *Complete Works*, 4:122.
73. Ibid.
74. Ibid., 125.
75. Brown, *English Baptists*, 117.
76. Ibid., 118.
77. Brian Stanley, *The History of the Baptist Missionary Society, 1792–1992* (Edinburgh: Clark, 1992), 3.
78. Ibid., 5–6.
79. George Howells and Alfred C. Underwood, *The Story of Serampore and Its College* (Serampore, India: 1918), 62.
80. Ibid., 63–64.
81. Stanley, *Baptist Missionary Society*, 7–8.
82. F. Deaville Walker, *William Carey: Missionary Pioneer and Statesman* (Chicago: Moody Press, 1960), 62; W. Morgan Patterson, "Changing Preparation for Changing Ministry," *Baptist History and Heritage* 15 (January 1980): 15–16.
83. Baptist Missionary Society, *Brief Narrative of the Baptist Mission in India* (London: Button and Burdett, 1808), 6.
84. William Carey, *An Enquiry into the Obligations of Christians to Use Means for the Conversion of the Heathens* (Leicester: Ann Ireland, 1792), 13.
85. Baptist Missionary Society, *Baptist Mission in India*, 7.
86. Andrew Fuller, *An Account of the Particular Baptist Society, for Propagating the Gospel among the Heathen* (London: 1793), 1–2.
87. Ibid., 3.
88. Ibid., 8.
89. Ibid.
90. Ibid., 5.
91. Ibid.
92. Ibid., 6.
93. Baptist Missionary Society, *Baptist Mission in India*, 9.
94. Whitley, *British Baptists*, 248.
95. Stanley, *Baptist Missionary Society*, 24–26.
96. Timothy George, *Faithful Witness: The Life and Mission of William Carey* (Birmingham, Ala.: New Hope Publishers, 1991), 108.
97. Ibid, 109.
98. "Extracts from the Diaries of Rev. William Ward, of Serampore," *The Baptist Magazine* (May 1879): 213.
99. Ibid., 215.
100. Ibid., 213–14. Grant died soon after arriving in India, leaving his widow to carry on the mission work.
101. Ibid., 38.
102. "Diaries of Rev. William Ward," *The Baptist Magazine* (April 1879): 181.
103. Stanley, *Baptist Missionary Society*, 38.
104. Baptist Missionary Society, *Brief Narrative of the Baptist Mission in India*, 21.
105. Doyle Young, "Andrew Fuller and the Modern Missions Movement," *Baptist History and Heritage* 17 (October 1982): 21.
106. Letter from Andrew Fuller to John Chamberlain, May 18, 1809 (cited in Young, "Andrew Fuller," 20).
107. Andrew Fuller to John Chamberlain, May 18, 1809 (cited in Young, "Andrew Fuller," 20).
108. Letter from Andrew Fuller to William Carey, October 11, 1796 (cited in Young, "Andrew Fuller," 20).
109. Letter from Andrew Fuller to William Carey, August 6, 1796 (cited in Young, "Andrew Fuller," 21).
110. Baptist Missionary Society, *Baptist Mission in India*, 8.
111. Stanley, *Baptist Missionary Society*, 21.
112. Baptist Missionary Society, *Memoir Relative to the Translations of the Sacred Scriptures to the Baptist Missionary Society in England* (Dunstable, England: J. W. Morris, 1808), 3–4; see also "Memoir Relative to the Translations of the Sacred Scriptures," *Transactions of the Baptist Historical Society* 5 (1916–17): 44–64.
113. Baptist Missionary Society, *Memoir*, 5.
114. William Carey, "Instructions to a Missionary," *Transactions of the Baptist Historical Society* 1 (1908–9): 80–81.
115. Stuart Piggin, *Making Evangelical Missionaries, 1789–1858* (London: Sutton Courtenay Press, 1984), 159.
116. Quoted in Glenn T. Miller, "Baptist World Outreach and U. S. Foreign Affairs," in *Baptists and the American Experience*, ed. James E. Wood (Valley Forge, Pa.: Judson Press), 159.

Chapter 6
Baptists in the United States: The Eighteenth Century

BAPTISTS IN AMERICA ENTERED THE EIGHTEENTH CENTURY AS A SMALL BUT determined community, celebrating hard-won victories to secure their freedoms but struggling to maintain their identity in the face of external harassment and internal turmoil. During much of the century, they continued to encounter persecution, particularly in New England and in the South. They confronted issues of church and state, making persistent endeavors on behalf of freedom of religion. They demanded religious liberty, but their practices sometimes bespoke a concern for a "Christian commonwealth." Baptist organizational life took shape during the century, with new churches and associations forming throughout the colonies. Religious awakenings increased the number of conversions, rejuvenated churches, and fostered controversies. Baptists, like other religious Americans, took part in both the Revolutionary War and the westward migration. When the Revolution and break with Britain finally came in 1776, Baptists generally were among the strongest supporters of the patriot cause. With the birth of the new nation, they carried their battle for religious liberty to the Continental Congress and the formation of the Constitution and the Bill of Rights. Throughout the century, they struggled with their own internal controversies regarding theology, polity, and evangelism.

Colonial Baptists

As the eighteenth century commenced, the New England Puritan establishment continued to view Baptists as a sectarian rabble. As early as 1644, the General Assembly of Massachusetts enacted laws against them. One colonial documented noted, "Since the first arising of the Anabaptists about one hundred years since, they have been the incendiaries of the commonwealths, and the troublers of churches in all places where they have been."[1] In a treatise supporting infant baptism, Puritan patriarch Increase Mather (1639–1723) suggested that the sin of the Baptists was that of Jeroboam, who created priests of the lowest members of society. John Russell Jr., second pastor of First Baptist Church, Boston, responded, "Our evil in this respect, is our calling to office those who have not been bred up in colleges, and taught in other languages, but have been bred to other callings."[2]

While Baptists defended themselves against the charges leveled against them, persecution and other difficulties took their toll. Henry Vedder reported, "In 1700 there were only ten small churches [in New England] with not more than three hundred members."[3] Lynn E. May Jr. suggested that in 1700, there "were only about twenty [Baptist] churches in America." At the time of the signing of the Declaration of Independence, Baptists represented about 1 in 264 members of the population; by 1800, they would be 1 in 53.[4]

Baptists in the Middle Colonies

The middle colonies—New Amsterdam (New York), New Jersey, Delaware, and Pennsylvania—offered a very different environment for Baptists and other religious minorities. Generally, these colonies provided greater toleration to religious folk who settled there. The first immigrants came to New Amsterdam under the auspices of the Dutch West India Company in 1623. The appointment of Peter Minuit as governor, in 1626, fully established the colony. In 1664, the Dutch surrendered the colony to the English, with James Stuart, Duke of York and brother of the monarch Charles II, in control of New York.

Early in New Amsterdam's history the Dutch Reformed Church was the official religion, while Anglicanism became the established church with British possession of the colony. In New Jersey, British leaders Lord John Berkeley and Sir George Carteret set forth a statement of "Concessions and Agreements" in 1664, which acknowledged religious liberty while establishing the procedures for governing the colony. Certain regions of New Jersey were religiously diverse, with Puritans prominent in East Jersey and Quakers in West Jersey. From that Quaker enclave came John Woolman (1720–1772), one of the eighteenth century's most significant Quaker leaders.

Pennsylvania was, of course, the best-known Quaker colony. Founded by William Penn (1644–1718) with a grant from Charles II in 1681, Pennsylvania offered religious liberty, thereby attracting a variety of sectarian groups, including Baptists, Mennonites, Moravians, Dunkers, Rosicrucians, and Amish. Pennsylvania became a major center of Baptist activity in the middle colonies, with significant impact on Baptist life throughout America.

Baptists in New Jersey

Individual Baptists moved into New Jersey long before specific churches were established. For example, they were present in Middletown by 1665, but a congregation was not constituted until 1688.[5] The Baptist presence in New Jersey was a result of immigration from several regions. New Englanders came to East New Jersey, while many West New Jersey settlers came directly from Great Britain. Several members of the Middletown community came from Newport, Rhode Island, including Obadiah Holmes Jr. and Mark Lucar. The Middletown church was founded in 1688 and was followed a year later by a congregation at Piscataway. Thomas Killingsworth (d. 1710) was its founding minister. The Piscataway church became a notable congregation in the region. By 1690, Killingsworth helped to establish the Cohansey Baptist Church, and by 1740 there were Baptist churches in Bowentown, Cape May, and Hopewell.

Most churches were formed around a covenant in which members promised to maintain commitment to God and one another—as one document noted, "that he may be our God and we may be his people; through the everlasting covenant of his true grace."[6] Confessions of faith were not widely used in these early New Jersey churches, but the practice increased after the formal approval of the Philadelphia Confession in 1742. Divisions also occurred. For example, a group of some sixteen individuals followed Hezekiah Bonham out of the Piscataway Baptist Church in 1705 to found the first Seventh Day Baptist church in New Jersey.[7]

Baptists in New York

Morgan Edwards (1722–1795), one of the first Baptist historians in the colonies, suggested that Baptists were present in New York as early as 1669 but that they manifested no significant presence there until 1712, when Valentine Wightman (1681–1747) made several preaching forays into the colony. David Benedict reported that Wightman baptized five women "in the night, for fear of the mob."[8]

A second Baptist enclave was founded at Oyster Bay, Long Island, around 1700 by William Rhodes and Robert Feeks. Feeks became pastor of the church in 1724. By the mid 1700s, there were Baptists up the Hudson at Fishkill, and in the west in Oswego County. By 1762, a group of Baptists led by Jeremiah Dodge constituted a Regular Baptist church in New York City. This church called John Gano as pastor, and he held the position for twenty-six years. That congregation became a center of the Baptist community that expanded throughout the region. Gano (1727–1804) was a pivotal figure in eighteenth-century Baptist life. In New York he served as a trustee at King's College (Columbia) and a regent at New York University. In 1754, he became a traveling evangelist sponsored by the Philadelphia Baptist Association. A strong supporter of the patriot cause, he preached often to the troops.[9]

Baptists in Delaware

For many years, the only Baptist congregation in Delaware was the Welsh Tract Church, founded in 1703. This congregation was organized by a group of immigrants from Pembroke and Caermarthen counties in Wales. They arrived in Pennsylvania in 1701 and then secured land in Delaware. Led by Thomas Griffith (1645–1725), this church required the laying on of hands at baptism—an action that led them to break communion with Pennsylvania churches of Pennepack and Philadelphia (First Baptist Church). A reconciliation occurred in 1706 when, as Morgan Edwards reported, they "agreed that a member in either church might transiently commune with the other; that a member who desired to come under the 'laying-on-of-hands,' might have his liberty without offence; that the votaries of the right might preach or debate upon the subject with all freedom, consistent with brotherly love."[10]

Baptists in Pennsylvania

William Penn founded Pennsylvania in 1681 through a land grant from the English crown. This Quaker colony extended religious liberty to all groups and soon became a haven for dissenters. Baptists were particularly strong in Philadelphia and its environs. The Cold

Spring church was the first Pennsylvania Baptist congregation, founded by Thomas Dungan in 1684. After his death, in 1688, it struggled for survival and was gone by 1702. The Pennepack Baptist Church was founded by Elias Keach (1677–1701) in Philadelphia County. Keach was the son of British Baptist leader Benjamin Keach. Arriving in Pennsylvania in 1688, Keach wore a cleric's garb, and many supposed him to be a duly ordained elder. When asked to preach, he was consumed by remorse and confessed his charade. He subsequently claimed conversion, was baptized by Thomas Dungan, and became pastor of the Pennepack church. Keach returned to England in 1692 to become pastor of a church in London. The First Baptist Church of Philadelphia was founded in 1698 and maintained a dual relationship with the Pennepack congregation until 1746.

During the late 1600s, Baptists in Pennsylvania held "annual meetings" for worship, fellowship, and theological dialogue. The meetings often ended with the Lord's Supper. This rudimentary associationalism was formalized in 1707 when five Philadelphia-area churches—First Church, Lower Dublin, Piscataway (New Jersey), Middletown (New Jersey), and the Welsh Tract Church (Delaware)—founded the Philadelphia Association, the first enduring Baptist association in America.[11]

In 1742, the Philadelphia Association approved a confession of faith as a basic theological statement. Much of the Philadelphia Confession was taken from the Second London Confession of Particular Baptists (1689), with additional articles that permitted the laying on of hands and the singing of hymns.

The Confession noted that "singing the praises of God, is a holy Ordinance of Christ, … it being injoined on the churches of Christ to sing psalms, hymns, and spiritual songs."[12] It permitted the singing of both psalms and "man made" hymns in worship.

Concerning the laying on of hands, the Confession stated, "We believe that (Heb 5:12 and 6:1-2, Acts 8:17-18 and 19:6) laying on of hands (with prayer) upon baptized believers, as such, is an ordinance of Christ, and ought to be submitted unto by all such persons that are admitted to partake of the Lord's Supper."[13] The Philadelphia Confession and its Reformed theology provided a doctrinal foundation for innumerable Baptist churches in eighteenth- and nineteenth-century America.

The Philadelphia Association was a prototype of future associational and denominational organizations. It demonstrated the effort of early American Baptists to maintain local autonomy and congregational authority while joining in cooperative endeavors. It provided opportunity for fellowship, mutual encouragement, doctrinal debate, and a combination of resources beyond the local congregation. Walter B. Shurden suggested that although only ten Baptist associations were established before 1775, Baptists maintained a variety of connections that facilitated ministerial ordination, encouraged the founding of new churches, and addressed specific Baptist beliefs.[14] Associations formalized these practices and were the earliest form of Baptist denominationalism in the United States. By 1780, some thirteen Baptist associations existed in the American colonies.[15]

Pennsylvania: Keithian Baptists

The Baptist encounters with Quakers in Pennsylvania produced yet another schism related to the Keithian (or Quaker) Baptists. The movement began around 1691 when a Quaker named George Keith (1639–1716) initiated an attack on what he believed to be the doctrinal and disciplinary laxity of Pennsylvania Quakers. He minimized human "sufficiency" in conversion and insisted that God alone was the author of salvation. Keith subsequently joined the Anglicans, but four groups of Keithians near Philadelphia became Baptists. They retained Quaker ideals of passive resistance and simple worship.[16] These four churches probably had no more than fifty members and were relatively short-lived, but the Keithian movement reflected the theological connections between Baptists and Quakers.[17]

Philadelphia: Morgan Edwards

Morgan Edwards, the controversial pastor of First Baptist Church, Philadelphia, made a significant contribution to Baptist life in the eighteenth century. His collection of *Materials towards a History of the Baptists in Pennsylvania,* published in 1770, probably was the earliest history of Baptists in America. Thomas McKibbens wrote, "Edwards was actually more of a compiler than a historian, for his *Materials* consisted of nothing more than a listing of Baptist churches and their ministers with periodic anecdotes to keep the reader from becoming bored."[18]

In 1761, Edwards moved from Sussex, England, to become pastor of the First Baptist Church, Philadelphia. He gained a reputation as a preacher whose well-prepared sermons included extensive use of the biblical languages. By the time of his death, he had produced forty-two volumes of sermons. Theologically, Edwards was a Calvinist and a frequent critic of both General Baptist Arminianism and Presbyterian polity.[19]

Edwards encountered problems in 1771 when he was charged with "Immoral Conduct, and Disorderly Walk" for associating with "Drunkards, Frequenting Taverns, [and] Being often intoxicated."[20] Although he denied the accusations, Edwards was excommunicated for intoxication four years later. Readmission was granted him in 1778. Colonial Baptists apparently were less concerned that Edwards used alcohol than that he was intemperate. Tobacco was another issue, however. Of its use, Edwards wrote, "This weed makes the planters and the manufactures [sic] rich and swells the public revenue but must fail, as the raising of it hath already made a barren waste of a great part of the country."[21]

Baptists in the South

South Carolina

The founding of the Baptist church in Charleston, the first such congregation in the South, was noted previously. The colony itself was established in 1670, and individual Baptists arrived shortly thereafter. The earliest records of the First Baptist Church were lost in the Charleston Flood of 1752. However, documents from the late seventeenth century suggest that a Baptist church existed in Charleston by 1699.[22] Baptist leader William Screven arrived by 1696, and soon he was joined by members of his congregation from Kittery, Maine. The Kittery church was a congregation of some forty men and women, several of whom were members of Screven's own family.

Screven was a staunch Calvinist, but not all the members shared his views. The Charleston church apparently included individuals of both Particular and General Baptist sentiments. Other South Carolina Baptist churches began in the early eighteenth century.

Virginia

The first permanent settlement in Virginia was founded at Jamestown in 1607, but there was no Baptist church in that Anglican colony until 1714, when a congregation was formed in Prince George County. When the community was struck by an epidemic in 1742, the church disbanded and some of its members helped to establish the Kehukee Baptist Church.[23]

North Carolina

North Carolina became a colony in 1663, but no Baptist church was established there until 1727, when Paul Palmer (d. ca.1750) started a congregation in Chowan County. Palmer, a General Baptist, founded the colony's second Baptist church at Shiloah in 1729.[24] Robert Baker reported that by 1740 "Baptists had established 11 churches [in the South]."[25]

Communities and Congregations

Eighteenth-century Baptists responded to issues in their communities and their congregations in diverse ways. For example, Baptists in Swansea, Massachusetts, used their majority status to impose a tax on the entire community that was used to support the local Baptist congregation. During the years 1705–1717, these Baptists accepted the Puritan law that taxation could be used to support the majoritarian church in a given community. In approving this practice, Baptists in Swansea temporarily overlooked the long-standing Baptist opposition to taxation for religious establishments. In 1717, the Congregationalists regained a majority and reclaimed the tax funds for themselves.[26] While this was not in any sense normative, it illustrates that Baptists were not completely uniform in their response to issues of religious liberty.

Conflicts between Baptist clergy and congregations occurred throughout the eighteenth century. The experience of John Comer (1704–1734) illustrates this internal strife. Converted in 1721 after a bout with smallpox, Comer began study at Harvard but "as education was cheapest at New Haven," he transferred to Yale in 1723.[27] The death of a close friend "brought eternity so directly before him, as to spoil his plausible excuses for the neglect of [believer's] baptism."[28] He joined the First Baptist Church in Boston in 1725. Ordained a Baptist elder, Comer became a pastor of the First Baptist Church in Newport, Rhode Island, which at that time was a congregation of only seventeen members.[29] There he introduced "public singing" of hymns as well as the keeping of church records. Trouble arose when Comer supported the laying on of hands at baptism—a doctrine over which the tiny congregation was divided. Isaac Backus commented, "Therefore two of the most powerful members, who disliked his searching preaching, took this as a handle to crowd him out of their church."[30] These antagonists prevailed and Comer was dismissed from the pastorate in 1729.

Comer wrote of the experience, "The difficulty in my flock has been wounding, and sometimes almost confounding. But I see God's grace is sufficient for me. I am fully and clearly convinced that I should have fallen into many hurtful evils, if sovereign grace had not wonderfully prevented.... About this time I found my people so uncomfortable that we must divide from each other, which was exceeding grievous to me."[31]

Comer's life was plagued by tragedy. While serving as pastor of the Rehoboth church, he contracted consumption and died in 1734 when he was only thirty years of age.[32]

Religious Awakening

John Comer died about the time that a religious awakening descended upon New England and elsewhere in the colonies. The extent and significance of what is known as the First Great Awakening has been a matter of dispute among historians. Early accounts often cited its origins among certain Dutch Reformed churches in New Jersey as led by pastor Theodore Frelinghuysen (1691–ca.1747). Frelinghuysen's call for repentance and conversion for non-Christians and church members alike created a renewal of religious enthusiasm and a debate over the nature of salvation.

Presbyterian preacher Gilbert Tennent (1703–1764) was another of the early awakeners. Tennent belonged to a group of preachers trained in Log College, a school organized in Buck's County, Pennsylvania, by his father, William Tennent (1673–1746). Log College provided a classical education for these young evangelicals. Gilbert Tennent became pastor of several Presbyterian churches in the Raritan Valley of New Jersey, where signs of religious enthusiasm emerged.

Some historians view the phenomenon as a significant revival of religion that brought colonials into the churches, led to the founding of new schools (Princeton, Dartmouth), and fostered the development of new congregations throughout the colonies.[33] Others suggest that it was a "watershed" by which a disjointed nation experienced its first real sense of unity on the way to the Revolution.[34]

More recent analyses have challenged the traditional views, suggesting that this awakening, while present in certain churches and regions, was much more diverse and perhaps less pervasive. Jon Butler wrote, "The increases in religious pluralism provides an important clue to understanding the attempts at religious renewal in eighteenth century America. It was the breadth and diversity of these efforts—not their cohesion or their limitation to the 1740s—that solidified their significance." He concluded, "Although religious revival missed many colonies, it usually attracted notoriety and charges of political radicalism when it occurred."[35] Mark Noll acknowledged, "For the whole period 1730 to 1750 in Connecticut, about the same proportion of the population joined the churches through a profession of saving faith as had joined during the preceding thirty years."[36] Although church attendance seems to have declined throughout much of the eighteenth century, the First Great Awakening contributed to what Noll called a genuinely national experience.[37]

Central to the First Great Awakening was the revival that broke out at Northampton, Massachusetts, under the preaching of Jonathan Edwards (1703–1758). Edwards rejected the idea of halfway conversion in any form, and in 1734 he began a series of sermons calling for justification by faith alone for all who would claim membership in Christ's church. The congregation then experienced a "surprising work of God" in which at least three hundred individuals were converted, youth forsook their practices of "night walking" and "frolics" for moral and spiritual enthusiasm, and the spirit of renewal spread throughout the region.[38] This religious phenomenon seems to have been widespread, much of it aided by the "Grand Itinerant," George Whitefield, who traveled from Georgia to New England preaching for conversion and renewal.

From the eighteenth century forward, the First Great Awakening often was characterized

as a golden age of religious enthusiasm to be emulated anew by each contemporary generation. It became a powerful myth used by clergy and laity for encouraging religious devotion
in each generation. Baptist preachers often joined other evangelicals in calling for "another
Great Awakening" in their particular era that would mirror earlier periods of revival.[39]

Baptists and the Awakening

Baptists were not overtaken by the religious enthusiasm of the First Great Awakening as
quickly as those in certain Congregational and Presbyterian churches. In the 1740s they
were still a relatively small group, struggling to survive. There were only three churches in
Connecticut and eight in Massachusetts, five churches in New Jersey and six in Pennsylvania. Only one Regular Baptist congregation existed in Rhode Island, and the rest were designated as Seventh Day or Six Principle churches.[40]

Baptists may have been suspicious of the movement, as it began among religious communions that had persecuted them. Some were also skeptical of the "enthusiastical" outbursts sparked by the revivals.

This awakening ultimately found its way into Baptist life. Edwin Gaustad wrote that due
to the First Great Awakening, "whole churches and whole communities adopted Baptist
views and swelled Baptist ranks."[41] Indeed, Gaustad noted that the numerical growth of the
Baptists from 1750 to 1800 was so rapid that more established religionists feared that the
sectarians were getting out of hand.

One Massachusetts critic charged that Baptists promoted ignorance and undermined true
religion. He wrote, "Many people are so ignorant as to be charmed with sound [not] sense.
And to them, the want of knowledge in a teacher … may easily be made up, and overbal-
anced, by great zeal, an affecting tone of voice, and a perpetual motion of the tongue."[42] In
his early history of the Baptists, David Benedict noted that in Maine, "To prevent their
increase, every attempt was made, in almost every place, to prejudice the minds of the people against them. 'Ignorant fanatics,' 'bigoted baptists,' 'new lights,' 'close communionists,'
&c., were no uncommon epithets. Irony, slander, and reproaches were heaped upon
them…. When reviled they reviled not."[43]

The Separates

Perhaps the First Great Awakening's greatest impact on Baptists came from the so-called
Separates—revivalistic enthusiasts first evident among the Congregational and Presbyterian
churches. Many of these revival supporters came to believe that the churches of the Standing Order were indifferent, if not antagonistic, to the spiritual upheavals swirling around
them. They held meetings and even formed new congregations whose members often were
labeled "Separates" or "New Lights."

The Separates were a controversial lot. Isaac Backus observed that some were accused
of antinomianism, and he even noted that one group in 1746 claimed that "they had
passed the first resurrection, and were perfect and immortal; and one of them declared
that he was Christ."[44]

Another Baptist sect in Cumberland, Rhode Island, applied antinomian sentiments to
relationships between males and females. When Ebenezer Ward's daughter Molly was
deserted by her seafaring husband, Ward permitted her to take up with another man. Ward,

a Separatist, insisted that he did not believe there was any harm in it, "for they lay with the Bible between them."[45]

Backus pointed out that while Separatist churches dismissed these offending members, the churches of the Standing Order attacked Separatism for its questionable morality. Backus saw these practices as evidence that "hereby the least member might tyrannize over the whole church."[46]

The Separate Baptists

No doubt, Isaac Backus's strong defense of the Separatist movement sprang from the fact that many of its participants entered the Baptist ranks. Early in the First Great Awakening, Baptist and Congregational Separatists shared "the experiment of 'mixed [open] communion.'" He noted, "The Baptist and the Separate Congregational churches were bound together by the closest ties. The former left the latter from no ill feeling but with heartiest love, and this love continued, on both sides, after their separation."[47] Baptist and Separate divisions over infant baptism soon meant that "one by one, reluctantly, but at last universally, [the Baptists] abandoned the untenable ground."[48]

David Benedict reported that revival converts, known as "Separates," "were taught to throw aside tradition, and take THE WORD OF GOD ONLY as their guide in all matters of religious faith and practice. This was in perfect coincidence with all baptist teaching, and ... ultimately led thousands, among whom were many ministers, to embrace our views and enter our churches."[49]

Morgan Edwards recalled that New Light "ministers resemble those in tones of voice and actions of body; and the people in crying out under the ministry, falling-down as in fits, and awakening in extacies; and both ministers and people resemble those in regarding impulses, visions, and revelations."[50]

Although clearly orthodox, Separate Baptists refused to subscribe to formal confessions of faith and insisted that the Bible alone was the rule for faith and practice. Other "Regular" Baptists affirmed Calvinism but feared that revival enthusiasm undermined "decency and order" while promoting an unorthodox Arminianism.

Separate Baptist Congregations

Divisions between Separates and Regulars soon split Baptist churches. First Baptist Church, Boston, experienced a schism when a minority of its members got caught up in revival fervor. The majority accused pastor Jeremiah Condy of Arminianism for denying original sin, "intermixing" regeneration with "free-agency and cooperation," and "holding to falling from grace."[51] In 1743, the revivalists departed and formed Second Baptist Church, a Separatist congregation.

As they moved south, the Separates founded churches and associations, with particular strength in the central Appalachian region. New doctrines blossomed among some of the churches. For example, members of the South Kentucky Association advanced a doctrine of "Hell Redemption"—a belief that sinners endure a type of purgatory after death, until all are granted eternal bliss.[52]

Shubal Stearns and Daniel Marshall

The Separate Baptist movement entered the South with the families of Shubal Stearns (1706–1771) and Daniel Marshall (1706–1784), two Separatist Congregationalists who accepted Baptist views. A native of New England, Stearns was converted by the Separates and immersed and ordained by the Baptists in 1751. Marshall married Stearns's sister Sarah in 1747 and became a Baptist in 1751.

During the years 1752–1754, Daniel and Sarah Marshall were missionaries to the Mohawks. In 1755, the Marshalls and the Stearns left Virginia for North Carolina, where they settled at Sandy Creek in Guilford County. There they founded the Sandy Creek Baptist Church, with Shubal Stearns as pastor. That congregation became the parent church of more than forty other churches.

Morgan Edwards described Stearns this way: "Of learning he had but a small share, yet was pretty well acquainted with books. His voice was musical and strong, which he managed in such a manner as, one while, to make soft impressions on the heart, and fetch tears from the eyes in a mechanical way; and anon, to shake the very nerves and throw the animal system into tumults and perturbations. All the Separate ministers copy after him in tones of voice and actions of body; and some few exceed him."[53]

The Sandy Creek Church grew rapidly and soon increased from sixteen members to more than six hundred.[54] By the time of the Revolution, the church had fallen on hard times. Morgan Edwards observed that after "17 years it is reduced from 606 to 14 souls, and is in danger of being extinct." Such attrition, he believed, was due largely to British authoritarianism in the province of North Carolina.[55]

A church building, measuring thirty by twenty-six feet, was erected in 1762. Edwards noted, "Here ruling elders, eldresses, and deaconesses are allowed; also are the 9 Christian rites: baptism; Lord's Supper; love-feast; laying-on-of-hands; washing-feet; anointing the sick; right hand of fellowship; kiss of charity; devoting children."[56] Communion was celebrated weekly. David Benedict commented, "Nor did those who maintained the whole" of these practices "refuse communion with their brethren who neglected a part of them."[57]

Sandy Creek members founded other churches, among them the Abbott's Creek congregation, begun in 1758 by Daniel Marshall. That same year some of these new churches formed the Sandy Creek Baptist Association, the first in North Carolina. James Reed described the origins of the association: "At our first Association we continued together three or four days; great crowds of people attended, mostly through curiosity. The great power of God was among us; the preaching every day seemed to be attended with God's blessing. We carried on our Association with sweet decorum and fellowship to the end. Then we took our leave of one another with many solemn charges from our reverend old father, Shubael Stearns, to stand fast unto the end."[58]

In 1770, the Association divided into three: the Sandy Creek Association (North Carolina), the Congaree Association (South Carolina), and the General Association of Separate Baptists of Virginia.[59] General Baptists founded a church on the Chowan River in North Carolina in 1727, and in 1742 William Sojourner began the Kehukee Creek Church in Halifax County. By the 1750s, these churches reaffirmed Calvinist doctrine. In 1769, the Kehukee Baptist Association was founded on the basis of a Calvinist confession of faith.[60]

Separates and Regulars: Distinctive Characteristics

Separate and Regular Baptists differed in certain beliefs and practices. Regular Baptists were concerned for stability and order in worship and church polity. As Calvinists, their liturgical practices reflected those of other Reformed communions. Their worship services included the psalm singing, Scripture readings (often with comment), a lengthy pastoral prayer, and a sermon. Sermons typically were written out in manuscript with carefully reasoned theological arguments. Regular Baptists valued an educated clergy, and their ministers often studied in schools in New England or Britain.

In 1766, Regular Baptists in Virginia "armed off" from the Philadelphia Association to form the Ketocton Association. Regulars moved into Kentucky, Tennessee, and North Carolina, founding the Elkhorn Association in 1785—the first association west of the Alleghenies.[61] They continued in Appalachia and portions of the South throughout the twentieth century.

Separate Baptists were "hot gospellers" who cultivated greater spontaneity in worship, singing hymns, and preaching sermons characterized by emotional, exuberant rhetoric. While many of their preachers received educational training, others were suspicious that education might undermine the intensity of genuine faith. They called sinners to a dramatic conversion experience and insisted on a profession of faith for all who would request baptism and church membership. Some feared that associational relationships would undermine the autonomy of the local congregation. They often hesitated to utilize formal confessions of faith lest they subvert biblical authority.

In frontier North Carolina, the divisions between Separates and Regulars were obvious. One history of the Kehukee Baptist Association noted, "The Distinction between us and them was, that they were called *Separates,* and the Philadelphia, the Charleston, and the Kehukee Association, were called Regular Baptists."[62] In 1772, the Separates explained to the Kehukee Association the reasons why they held no communion with Regulars. First, "They complained of the Regulars not being strict enough in receiving experiences, when persons made application to their churches for baptism, in order to become church members." Second, "They refused communion with Regular Baptist churches, because they believed that faith in Christ Jesus was essential to qualify a person for baptism, yet many of the Regular churches had members in them who acknowledged they were baptized before they believed." Third, "The Separates found fault with the Regulars for their manner of dress, supposing they indulged their members in superfluity of apparel."[63] In October 1775, the Kehukee Regular Baptist Association split over differences between Regulars and Separates. A Separate Baptist association was established around the belief that communion should not be given to unbaptized persons.[64]

In describing the differences between Regulars and Separate, John Leland suggested that the northern churches called themselves Regular Baptists, while the southern churches designated themselves Separate Baptists. The Regulars, he said, used a confession of faith "first published in London, 1689, and afterwards adopted by the Baptist Association of Philadelphia, in 1742; but the Separates had none but the Bible." He observed, "The Regulars were orthodox Calvinists, and the work under them was solemn and rational; but the Separates were the most zealous, and the work among them was very noisy."[65] A union of Separate and Regular Baptists occurred in Virginia in 1787, and similar unions followed.

Separates in New England

The Separatist movement helped to shape some of the early Baptist associations in New England. The Warren Association, founded in 1767, probably was the first such Calvinistic Baptist association in the region. This group may have been influenced by the earlier Six Principle Calvinistic Baptist Association, which formed in the 1750s in Massachusetts, Rhode Island, and Connecticut.[66] William McLoughlin commented, "It represented the first spontaneous effort of the Separate Baptists to seek unity and order in the confusion following the breakup of the Separate movement after 1754."[67] The Six Principle Association was short-lived, but served as a prototype for others.

Isaac Backus

Isaac Backus (1724–1806), New England Congregationalist turned Baptist, personified significant elements of the Baptist community in the revival and Revolutionary eras. Backus's life and work mirrored significant developments in American life: the First Great Awakening, the break with the Standing Order, and the struggle for religious liberty. Born in Norwich, Connecticut, Backus was converted in 1741 following the death of his father. His description of the experience reflects classic Puritan morphology: "Sometimes I feared that I was given over to hardness of heart but blessed by God he did not leave me here but he laid open to me the fountain of Sin that was in my heart that I saw that all the Sins in the whole world were in me and on the 24 of August 1741 he brought the Commandment home…. Then he opened to my Soul the glorious way of Salvation by Christ and gave my Soul to Close therewith."[68]

Backus joined a group of New Lights who formed a Separate Congregational church in 1746.[69] He began preaching, thereby joining that "massive unleashing of an itinerant, vernacular, oral ministry [that] was one of the major democratizing forces of the pre-Revolutionary era."[70]

Backus served as a minister for fifty-eight years, and he authored some thirty-seven tracts on theology, along with a three-volume history of the Baptists. He supported himself as a farmer, eschewing the idea of a "hireling ministry." Although not ordained, Backus was a Separatist preacher from 1748 to 1756 at a church in Titicut, Massachusetts.[71]

In January 1756, Backus closed the Titicut church, received ordination, and founded the First Baptist Church in Middleborough, a closed-communion congregation. He was ordained in June of 1756 and remained pastor until his death, in 1806. He was successful in convincing other Old Baptist churches to accept the Separate position, and many New England Baptist churches followed suit.[72] By 1790, however, some thirty of the forty-six Separate Baptist churches in Massachusetts had returned to the Regular Baptist fold.[73]

The Warren Association

With its founding in 1767, the Warren Association became the first Baptist association in New England. James Manning, the president of Rhode Island College, wrote its first constitution, but Backus objected to the initial draft, suggesting, "The rights and liberties of particular churches are [not] sufficiently secured by what is said in your plan."[74] A compromise was achieved, and additional churches joined.

In 1780, the Warren Association claimed thirty-eight churches, most located in Massachusetts. In 1804, there were some thirteen such associations spread throughout New England, claiming 312 churches and a membership of over twenty-three thousand.[75] Baptist support for the Revolution, their democratic polity, and their evangelical fervor contributed to their growth and popularity.

Isaac Backus and Religious Liberty

Isaac Backus played a significant role in the public life of the Baptists, particularly as a champion of religious liberty. As an agent of the Warren Association, he promoted the cause of religious liberty both in the General Court of Massachusetts and the first Continental Congress in 1774. One of America's earliest lobbyists, he appealed to the Continental Congress on behalf of religious freedom. In response, the Congress approved the following resolution, signed by the president of the assembly, John Hancock. Dated December 9, 1774, the resolution acknowledged the Congress's "sincere wish" to extend "civil and religious liberty" to every denomination, "but being by no means vested with powers of civil government, whereby they can redress the grievances of any person whatever, they therefore recommend to the Baptist churches, that when a general assembly shall be convened in this colony, they lay the real grievances of said churches before the same, when and where their petition will most certainly meet with all that attention due to the memorial of a denomination of Christians, so well disposed to the public weal of their country."[76] Backus and other Baptists took their appeal back to the General Court of Massachusetts, but it was tabled, largely through the efforts of John Adams.

In 1790, Backus served as a delegate to the Boston convention called to ratify the Constitution. Backus himself did not live to see the triumph of disestablishment in Massachusetts. The practice endured until 1833, twenty-seven years after his death.

Backus insisted that the Baptists, not the contemporary Congregationalists, were the real heirs of the New England "errand into the wilderness." He maintained that "the first planters of New England requested no more than equal liberty of conscience"—the same principle advocated by Baptists.[77]

William McLoughlin maintained that unlike Roger Williams, Backus and his contemporaries believed that America was a Protestant nation. Backus anticipated "the day when Baptist ministers and evangelists would convert all Americans to antipedobaptism."[78] He opposed granting complete religious liberty to Roman Catholics, whom he viewed as enemies of democracy and freedom. McLoughlin concluded, "Backus and the Baptists of eighteenth-century New England thought primarily of religious liberty in terms of ending compulsory religious taxation, not in terms of a high wall of separation."[79] Backus supported the Constitution of Massachusetts, which required religious oaths of all officeholders. He affirmed efforts to regulate Sunday activities (blue laws) and to legislate against dancing, card playing, gambling, and theaters.[80]

Persecution: The Women's Role

In describing the struggle for liberty, Isaac Backus readily acknowledged the participation of women. In one account he reproduced a letter dated November 4, 1752, written by his mother, Elizabeth, "a private letter from a widow of fifty-four years old." Elizabeth Backus acknowledged her grief at the "trials" that her son confronted, and she wrote, "And now

I would tell you something of our trials. Your brother Samuel lay in prison twenty days. October 15, the collector came to our house, and took me away to prison about nine o'clock, in a dark rainy night. Brothers Hill and Sabin were brought there next night. We lay in prison thirteen days, and then were set at liberty, by what means I know not.... Though I was bound when I was cast into this furnace, yet was I loosed, and found Jesus in the midst of the furnace with me."[81] The two were imprisoned in Norwich for their failure to pay the required religious taxes.

Baptists in New England

Baptists in New England experienced slow but steady growth throughout the eighteenth century. In Maine, Baptist numbers increased through immigration and from the work of the New Light Baptist preacher Hezekiah Smith (1737–1805).[82] Pastor of the Baptist church in Haverhill, Massachusetts, from 1776 to his death in 1805, Smith traveled throughout New England and was instrumental in establishing churches in Maine and New Hampshire.

Separate Baptists thrived in Vermont, among them Jonas Galusha, a governor of the state. He and his son Elon were members of the congregation in Shaftsbury, the first Vermont Baptist church. Elon Galusha (d. 1856) was a well-known pastor who served several Baptist congregations in New York.

In Connecticut, the Six Principle Baptists formed a church at Groton in 1705 under the leadership of Valentine Wightman (1681–1747). It was the only Baptist congregation in the region for twenty years.[83]

Life in the Churches

Many of the early Baptist churches met in the homes of members. Meetinghouses finally were constructed, often years after the formation of the congregations they housed. During the colonial period, no musical instruments were used to accompany the singing. The Lord's Supper was celebrated monthly or quarterly, using bread and a common cup of wine, almost always presided over by an ordained minister.

Morgan Edwards published a handbook on church order—the first such book for Baptists in America—delineating some of the tasks of the ministers. Among them were these: "to convene the church; pray; read the Scriptures; preach; break bread; dismiss and bless the people; govern in conjunction with the ruling elders; take into the church; bind or retain sins; admonish; cast out of the church; loose or remit sin; lay on hands; baptize; visit; give example; anoint the sick; bury the dead; perform marriage; catechize; bless infants; defend the faith; assist at associations and other public meetings; &c."[84]

Sunday (or Saturday for some Baptists) was the primary occasion for public worship. Holy days such as Easter or Christmas were not observed, as they were considered to be "popish," with no biblical justification. Church discipline was tied to the church covenant in which members promised to live in accordance with the moral demands of the gospel and the church. Discipline was necessary to protect the moral and spiritual integrity of the congregation itself. Some Baptist preachers developed a homiletical style known as the "holy whine," described as "a very warm and pathetic address, accompanied by strong gestures, and a singular tone of voice (from which, perhaps, the *singing,* or *holy tone,* of some of their successors, originated). Being deeply affected themselves when preaching, corresponding affections were felt by their pious hearers, which was frequently expressed by tears, trembling, screams, and exclamations of grief and joy."[85]

Clearly, pastoral ministry extended beyond preaching and administration of the ordinances to significant life events. Baptist preachers also developed a distinctive pulpit style that contributed to specific congregational response.

Music and Hymnody

Baptists in America held varying views on the use of music in congregational worship. Debates over psalm singing and hymn singing continued throughout the eighteenth century. In 1716, the Welsh Tract Baptist Church in Pennsylvania adopted a British confession (1696) that contained a statement on singing. It noted that singing was a "holy Ordinance of Christ ... it being enjoined on the churches of Christ to sing psalms, hymns, and spiritual songs; and that the whole church in their public assemblies, as well as private christians, ought to ... sing God's praises according to the best light they have received."[86]

By the middle of the eighteenth century, many Baptist churches utilized Isaac Watts's *Hymns and Spiritual Songs,* published in England in 1707 and republished in Boston in 1739.[87] *Evangelical Hymns and Songs* (1762), compiled in England by Benjamin Wallin, was the earliest Baptist hymnal to be produced in America. A 1766 work, *Hymns and Spiritual Songs, Collected from the Works of Several Authors,* its editor now unknown, was the first hymnal both collected and published in America. *Hymns* included works by Isaac Watts, and among the spiritual songs were works written in America and sung to "popular folk tunes."[88]

The preface to Parkinson's *A Selection of Hymns and Spiritual Songs* (1809) contained this commentary on spiritual songs: "This kind of composition has, for several years past been greatly abused ... so barbarous in language, so unequal in numbers, and so defective in rhyme, as to excite disgust in all persons even of tolerable understanding in these things; what is infinitely worse, so extremely unsound in doctrine, that no discerning Christian can sing or hear them without pain."[89] Nonetheless, they continued to gain popularity in many Baptist congregations. Musical instruments would come later.

Baptist Subgroups

By the mid-1700s, numerous subgroups in colonial America claimed the name Baptist and were represented in various regions. They covered a wide spectrum of theology and practice.

Old Baptists
Old Baptists were antirevivalist, small in number, and conservative in theology. They incorporated numerous Baptist subgroups, including Six Principle, Five Principle, and

Seventh Day Baptists. The Six Principle Baptists promoted the laying on of hands for all who professed faith; the Five Principle Baptists refused to require the laying on of hands; and Seventh Day Baptists stressed Sabbath (Saturday) worship and other elements of the Hebrew covenant. Internally, these groups divided over Calvinist and Arminian theology.

German Seventh Day Baptists
German Seventh Day Baptists developed under the leadership of John Conrad Beissel (1690–1768) and other German immigrants. These Baptists, sometimes known as German Baptist Brethren or Dunkards, were formed by pietists who migrated to Pennsylvania. Beissel's group practiced communitarian living, with work and prayer observed in monasticlike regimen. Ultimately, they practiced celibacy and the community of goods. In 1732, they took the name of German Seventh Day Baptists and moved to Ephrata, Pennsylvania, where they developed a monasticlike atmosphere. An additional order of married couples and families was also permitted. Members wore white habits, maintained daily prayer, and supported themselves through farming and handcrafts.

These Sabbatarian monastics exercised significant influence among German immigrants in Pennsylvania, Virginia, and other nearby states. The community endured until 1934, although its long-term Baptist identity is questionable.[90]

Free Will Baptists
The New Light phenomenon impacted the formation of another Baptist group, the Free Will Baptists. Although Arminianism was present among the British General Baptists, in America their ideas and numbers often were overshadowed by the Calvinist Baptist majority. In 1727, Paul Palmer (1692–1763) of Perquimans County, North Carolina, began the movement with an emphasis on free will, free grace, and free salvation for all who believed. Churches were founded in North and South Carolina throughout the eighteenth century.

Benjamin Randall (1749–1808) was leader of the Free Will Baptists in the latter part of the eighteenth century. Converted in 1770, he received immersion in the Baptist church in Berwick, Maine, in 1776. A popular preacher, Randall, who held to Arminianism, soon created controversy among the Reformed Baptists. Ordained in 1779, he established a Free Will church in Durham, New Hampshire. Other churches soon joined the new movement.

Of his conversion, Randall wrote that he found in Christ "a universal love, universal atonement, a universal call to mankind, and was confident that none would ever perish but those who refused to obey it."[91] He insisted that Jesus Christ "tasted death for every man," not simply for a limited group of elect.[92] These sentiments were set forth in a covenant on "free salvation" written in 1782. Free Will Baptists were influenced by the theological writings of Henry Alline, the New Light awakener best known in Nova Scotia. Alline, though never a full-fledged Baptist, shaped Baptist life in the Maritimes and wrote treatises expounding the importance of "free grace."[93]

Free Will Baptists were the first Baptists in America to ordain women to public ministry. One early history of the movement suggested that by 1791 Free Will Baptists had recognized

Nancy Savage, a resident of New Hampshire, as a preaching minister. By the 1820s, numerous women were listed as preachers, including Almira Bullock, Hannah Fogg, Susan Humes, Judith Prescott, a Mrs. Quimby, Betsy Stuart, and Sarah Thornton.[94]

Clarissa Danforth and Martha Spaulding were among the nineteenth-century women preachers in Free Will Baptist life. Danforth was a New England evangelist, once described this way: "As a speaker, her language was ready and flowing, her gestures were few and appropriate, and her articulation so remarkably clear and full that she was distinctly heard in all parts of the largest house. Her meetings were everywhere fully attended and she would hold hundreds with fixed attention for an hour by the simplicity of her manner, the kindness of her spirit, the claims of her subject, and the novelty of her position."[95] The belief that God's free grace could claim all persons seems to have made Free Will Baptists more open to women as preachers.

Founding a Baptist College

Many eighteenth-century Baptists were concerned for ministerial education. In 1722, the Philadelphia Association encouraged ministerial candidates to accept the benevolence of British Baptist Thomas Hollis, a merchant and supporter of Harvard College who helped finance ministerial training among Baptists.[96]

Philadelphia cleric Isaac Eaton founded an academy at Hopewell, New Jersey, that later came under the sponsorship of the Philadelphia Association. Financial difficulties led to an appeal to British Baptists for books, office equipment, and funding. The academy endured for eleven years, producing graduates who became clergy, physicians, and lawyers. The desire to extend education beyond the "preparatory level" led many Baptists of the time to propose the establishment of a college.[97]

Discussion of educational needs led to a meeting between New England Baptists and representatives of the Philadelphia Baptist Association in 1760. The Philadelphia delegation included James Manning, Hezekiah Smith, Samuel Stillman, and John Davis. They joined with Isaac Backus and a group of the New Englanders considering the formation of a Baptist college.

Their decision to found a college led to a charter in 1764 and the opening of Rhode Island College in Warren in 1765. The school moved to Providence in 1770, and in 1805 the name was changed to Brown University to honor a gift of $5,000 from alumnus Nicholas Brown. James Manning (1738–1791) was the first president, and Isaac Backus served as a trustee for some thirty-four years. Until the 1930s, the charter of the college mandated that the president be a Baptist minister, and many of those individuals, notably Francis Wayland, made a significant impact on the Baptist and broader American communities. In 1774, the Charleston, Warren, and Philadelphia Associations agreed to a plan that asked every Baptist in their ranks to contribute sixpence each year to the work of the college.[98]

Not all Baptists welcomed the new college. Many were suspicious of formal education, associating it with the "corpse cold" clergy of the Standing Order. Some thought that it would create a special clergy class, thereby promoting a "hireling ministry."

Religious Liberty: Virginia

As noted previously, Baptist presence in Virginia began by 1729 with the founding of a General Baptist church in Isle of Wight County.[99] Between 1743 and 1756, three congregations associated with the Regular Baptists were founded in Berkeley and Loudon Counties.[100] Separatists came into the colony in waves. Daniel Marshall and Philip Mulkey crossed the border from North Carolina in 1760 to found the Dan River Baptist Church in Pittsylvania County. Marshall baptized Samuel Harris (b. 1724), a Virginia preacher whom David Benedict called "the head of the Separate Baptists in this state." Harris frequently was persecuted. Benedict reported that at Culpepper in 1765 Harris faced "violent opposition" from a mob with "whips, sticks, clubs and other rustic weapons."[101]

Other churches were founded in Staunton River and Black Water, Virginia, by 1761. Baptist preacher David Thomas came to Culpeper, Virginia, in 1765 but was run out of the region and into Orange County. In 1767, Harris, James Read, and Dutton Lane founded the Upper Spotsylvania Baptist Church, the center of the Separate Baptist movement in the area. Soon the Blue Run and Lower Spotsylvania churches were founded. These three churches called the brothers Elijah and Lewis Craig and John ("Swearing Jack") Waller, each of whom became a Baptist leader.[102] Elijah Craig (1743–1808) was baptized in 1765 and ordained in 1771 as pastor of the Blue Run Church. His lack of formal education, his fiery preaching style, and his refusal to receive a salary made Craig an exemplar of Separate Baptist ministry. In 1786, he moved to Kentucky, where he continued to preach, established a paper mill, and purportedly invented bourbon whiskey.[103]

Craig's brother, Lewis (1741–1824), was baptized in 1767 and ordained in 1770 as pastor of the Upper Spotsylvania Church. An outspoken opponent of religious establishments, Craig sometimes was imprisoned for his views. At one court hearing shortly after his conversion, Craig is said to have remarked, "I thank you, gentlemen, for the honour you did me. While I was wicked and injurious, you took no note of me, but now having altered my course of life and endeavoring to reform my neighbors, you concern yourself much about me."[104] In 1781, he led a portion of his Virginia congregation, known as the "traveling church," to Garrard County, Kentucky. In 1783, they moved to Fayette County, where they established the South Elkhorn Baptist Church, and, in 1785, the Elkhorn Baptist Association—the first association in Kentucky.

John ("Swearing Jack") Waller (1741–1802) was a gentleman from Spotsylvania County with a notorious past. Morgan Edwards offered this description of his early years: "Besides gaming, and vices usually attending it, Mr Waller was notorious for swearing, in so much that he was distinguished from the other Wallers by the name of Swearing Jack. Add to these, his fury towards the Baptists."[105] Converted under the influence of Lewis Craig, he was ordained in 1770 and thereafter was repeatedly imprisoned for refusing to secure a preaching license from the state. Waller's Baptist rhetoric led one Anglican minister to advise the authorities to "run the but end of the whip into Waller's mouth and so silence him."[106] He was a powerful Separate Baptist preacher.

Other Separate Baptist churches were constituted throughout Virginia in the 1760s. In the south, the Amelia Church was founded in 1769, and in the north, the Carter's Run Church in Fauquier County began the same year. The Ketockton Association—the first in the state and the fifth in America—was founded in 1766 by churches identified as Regular Baptists. In 1771, twelve Separate Baptist churches gathered in Orange, Virginia, and created the General Association of Separate Baptists. That association grew so rapidly that it divided into northern and southern districts by 1773.[107]

In 1787, the Separate and Regular Baptists reunited under the name United Baptists of Virginia. Regulars fretted that the Separates harbored an implicit Arminianism, while Separates feared that Regulars' concern for associationalism might undermine the autonomy of the local church.[108] The two groups approved a statement acknowledging that confessions of faith held "the essential truths of the gospel" but should not exert "a tyrannical power over the consciences of any," and therefore "we do not mean that every person is bound to the strict observance of every thing therein contained."[109]

Persecution against Baptists in Virginia was most intense during the period of 1768 to 1774. In 1773, for example, Patrick Henry paid the fines for Baptist preacher John Weatherford, who, along with John Tanner and Jeremiah Walker, was imprisoned in Chesterfield County. Other Baptists were arrested throughout Virginia that same year.

It was popularly assumed that Baptists, particularly the Separates, were disruptive to both society and majoritarian religion. They also were criticized for ignoring the law requiring licenses for dissenting clergy. Edwin Gaustad suggested that following the Revolution, Baptists "kept a steady pressure upon those lingering privileges ... which were still retained by the Episcopal Church."[110]

John Leland

What Isaac Backus was to Massachusetts, John Leland (1754–1841) was to Virginia—an articulate representative of Baptist concerns for religious liberty and freedom of conscience. Born in Grafton, Massachusetts, Leland was converted and baptized in 1774. Ordained to the ministry, he married Sally Devine of Hopkinton in 1775, and the couple moved to Virginia in 1777. Called to the Mount Poney Baptist Church, he soon confronted divisions over the laying on of hands at baptism. The Ketockton Association (Virginia) required the practice, while the Warren Association (Massachusetts) did not. He resigned his pastorate and moved to Orange, Virginia, where he continued to preach and work for religious liberty.

Leland and Religious Liberty in Virginia

Leland noted that even imprisonment could not silence Virginia Baptist preachers. He recalled, "They used to preach to the people through the grates: to prevent which, some ill-disposed men would be at the expense of erecting a high wall around the prison; others, would employ half drunken strolls to beat a drum and around the prison to prevent the people from hearing."[111]

Leland delineated numerous reasons for the Baptist dissent, all based on the freedom of the gospel and its implications for human rights. He stated, "No National church, can, in its organization, be the Gospel Church. A national church takes in the whole nation, and no more; whereas, the Gospel Church, takes in no nation, but those who fear God, and work righteousness in every nation."[112]

Like Roger Williams, Leland rejected the idea of the Christian nation and insisted, "The liberty I contend for, is more than toleration. The very idea of toleration, is despicable; it supposes that some have a pre-eminence above the rest, to grant indulgence; whereas, all should be equally free, Jews, Turks, Pagans and Christians. Test oaths, and established creeds, should be avoided as the worst of evils."[113] Leland also argued that Baptists were strong supporters of the state who held "it their duty to obey magistrates, to be subject to the law of the land, to pay their taxes, and pray for all in authority."[114]

Leland's understanding of religious liberty applied to believer and unbeliever alike. He wrote, "Whether, therefore, the Christian religion be true or false, it is not an article of legislation. In this case, Bible Christians, and Deists, have an equal plea against self-named Christians, who ... tyranize over the consciences of others, under the specious garb of religion and good order."[115]

Conscience, Leland believed, "is a court of judicature, erected in every breast, ... but has nothing to do with another man's conduct."[116] The concern for conscience influenced Leland's suspicion of confessions of faith—documents he feared would check any further pursuit after truth, confine the mind into a particular way of reasoning, and give rise to "frequent separations." While they might be "advantageous, the greatest care should be taken not to sacradize, or make a petty Bible of it."[117]

Leland's opposition to religious establishments was without compromise. He observed, "The fondness of magistrates to foster Christianity, has done it more harm than all the persecutions ever did. Persecution, like a lion, tears the saints to death, but leaves Christianity pure: state establishment of religion, like a bear, hugs the saints, but corrupts Christianity."[118]

Leland's concern for liberty led to his opposition to slavery. He asserted, "The whole scene of slavery is pregnant with enormous evils. On the master's side, pride, haughtiness, domination, cruelty, deceit and indolence; and on the side of the slave, ignorance, servility, fraud, perfidy and despair. If these, and many other evils, attend it, why not liberate them at once? Would to Heaven this were done!"[119] Leland was an early Baptist opponent of the slavery-based society.

Freedom was not easily secured for dissenters or slaves. Prior to disestablishment, Baptists in Virginia joined with other dissenting religious groups in defeating Patrick and James Henry's so-called general assessment bill, which would have made "the Christian Religion," as represented in all Christian communions the official religion of Virginia. It read, "The Christian Religion shall in all times coming be deemed and held to be the established Religion of this Commonwealth."[120]

Instead, Baptists gave strong support for the Act for Establishing Religious Freedom in Virginia, written by Thomas Jefferson. It stated, "That no man shall be compelled to frequent or support any religious worship, place or ministry whatsoever, nor shall he be enforced, restrained, molested, or burthened in his body or goods, nor shall he otherwise suffer on account of his religious opinions or belief; but that all men shall be free to profess, and by argument to maintain, their opinion in matters of religion, and that the same shall in no wise diminish, enlarge or affect their civil capacities."[121] Although some religious sanctions against dissenters remained, in 1794 the Virginia assembly repealed all religious laws except the Act for Establishing Religious Freedom, thus ending Virginia's state church.

Leland's friendship with James Madison figured in the struggle for religious freedom. There is some indication that he pressured Madison to support a bill of rights in behalf of religious liberty, and resisted the future president's bid for the Constitutional convention until some assurances were made.

After religious liberty came to Virginia, Leland returned to Massachusetts, where he spent the rest of his life as an itinerant preacher and even served in the Massachusetts legislature. With the ratification of the United States Constitution in 1789 and the approval of the Bill of Rights in 1791, Baptists' prolonged efforts in behalf of religious liberty were realized.

Baptists and the American Revolution

Though a numerical minority with serious questions about colonial establishments, Baptists were strong supporters of the American Revolution. Their struggle was against both the British government and the colonial Standing Order. Isaac Backus observed, "While the defence of the civil rights of America appeared a matter of great importance, our religious liberties were by no means neglected; and the contest concerning each kept a pretty even pace throughout the war."[122]

Preachers rose to the occasion. John Gano was one of numerous Baptist ministers who served as a chaplain in the Continental army. Not all Baptist congregations, however, supported the Revolution. New Jersey pastor David Jones was forced to leave his congregation at Upper Freehold Baptist Church because of his support of the patriot cause.[123] In a sermon called "Defensive War in a Just Cause Blameless," he declared, "A martial spirit from God has spread throughout the land. Surely, if this is not a heavy judgment, it is a presage of Success. We are fully persuaded that this spirit is not a judgment, because our cause is good, even in the sight of other States. To the Most High we can appeal and submit the event to his pleasure."[124]

In the South, Oliver Hart (1723–1795), pastor of First Baptist Church, Charleston, supported the Revolution and willingly offered spiritual counsel to the troops. When the British seized Charleston, Hart was forced to flee to New Jersey, where he became pastor of the Hopewell Baptist Church—a position he held until his death, in 1795.[125]

Another South Carolinian, Richard Furman (1755–1825), supported the patriot cause and used the occasion to lobby for religious liberty. He was one of several churchmen who encouraged the colony to abolish the Anglican establishment when the new state constitution was approved in the 1770s. Furman became pastor of First Baptist Church, Charleston, in 1787 and was one of the leading Baptists of the nineteenth century.

Backus listed five reasons why the Baptists supported the patriot cause. First, Baptists in America had more liberty than those in England. Second, their "worst treatment" in America came from the same people who opposed colonial freedom. Third, as Roger Williams had shown, governments are based on a compact, the violation of which may require resistance. Fourth, to concur with such a breach of compact would have been an untenable burden on Baptist consciences. Fifth, success in this effort might open the door to greater religious freedom. While most Baptists supported the war, Backus acknowledged, "It is not pretended that our denominating were all agreed, or had equal clearness in these points; but a majority of them were, more or less, influenced thereby."[126]

In 1774, when representatives of twelve of the thirteen colonies met in Philadelphia to develop a strategy for dealing with the British, Baptists sent an affirmation stating, "It has been said by a celebrated writer in politics that but two things were worth contending for,

Religion and Liberty. For the latter we are at present nobly exerting ourselves through all this extensive continent; and surely no one whose bosom feels the patriot glow in behalf of civil liberty can remain torpid to the more ennobling flame of Religious Freedom."[127]

By war's end, many Baptist church buildings had been severely damaged, with members killed or scattered and services disrupted. New Jersey pastor Abel Morgan noted in June 1778, "There was no meeting on this Lord's day, because of the enemy passing through our town the week past."[128]

Baptists' numerical growth was stymied by the war. In his statistical analysis of colonial Baptists, Robert Gardner observed, "Had Baptists grown at a regular rate between 1770 and 1790, the 1780 figure would have been 41,603 [members]—almost 56 percent more than the 26,748 which is recorded. Clearly the war was not conducive to prosperity." By 1790, however, the Baptists numbered some 68,067 members—a significant increase.[129]

Missionary Endeavors

The earliest missionary endeavors among American Baptists were intermittent at best. Walter Shurden suggested that the first associational missions involved simply sending ministers to regions and congregations that had no pastoral presence. He wrote, "The preeminent missionary concern of associations until the latter part of the eighteenth century was not so much to win new converts and build new churches as to strengthen individuals already converted and sustain churches already established."[130] While acknowledging that specific Baptist ministers were unashamedly evangelical, Shurden concluded that itinerant ministries were developed less from a precise evangelistic strategy than to provide ministers for frontier congregations.[131]

Century's End: Theological Controversies

Universalism

During the late eighteenth century, Baptists faced controversies inside and outside their churches. One of those was universalism, a movement that had many Baptist supporters.

Universalism's central affirmation was that "it is the purpose of God, through the grace revealed in our Lord Jesus Christ, to save every member of the human race from sin."[132] The first American Universalist church was founded in 1779 by Calvinist Methodist John Murray (1741–1815). The primary leader of the movement, however, was Baptist Hosea Ballou (1771–1852). Ballou published *Treatise on the Atonement,* in which he offered a biblical and evangelical basis for universalism. Preaching was necessary as a means of informing sinful people that they were all recipients of divine grace. Ballou denied the substitutionary theory of Christ's atonement and instead promoted the "moral influence" hypothesis that Christ died for all persons, but not in their place. His death was the source of power that enabled believers to live as Christ had lived. Many Baptists joined the movement. They included Arminians who believed that ultimately all persons would choose God's grace and Calvinists who presumed that election ultimately would include the entire race. In the end, grace truly was irresistible for every human being.[133] Universalism as both movement and ideology created extensive debate and division among the Baptists for the next two centuries.

Queries

Lesser controversies created questions and potential divisions as Baptists sought to deal with hard questions of faith and ethics. One response to controversies came in the form of "queries"—theological questions addressed by the minutes of the Sandy Creek Baptist Association.[134]

Query: Is ordination for itinerant ministry acceptable? Answer: Only under "extraordinary occasions." This meant that ordination for pastoral ministry only was the prevailing practice of the day.[135]

Query: Is foot washing an "ordinance of God," to be practiced until Christ's return? Answer: "That feet washing is a church ordinance, is the opinion of but very few, that it is a command of Christ to teach humility and equality, and to be observed by Christians in their social intercourse, is admitted. Baptism and the Lord's Supper are church ordinances, and require church authority for their administration. Feet washing is to be performed, not by a minister, or any other church officer, but 'by one another.'"[136] The association continued, "This command of the Savior has gone into disuse.... This, however, is no reason that it should not be performed by Christians, in their private and social relations."[137]

Likewise, questions arose as to the validity of ordinances (sacraments) administered by ministers of questionable character. Would immoral behavior on the part of the minister negate the ordinance? The association ruled, "If a minister acts without church authority, his ministerial acts are invalid. If he be clothed with valid church authority, his acts are valid, though he may be a bad man; that is, the validity of his official acts depends upon his being a member of the church, and clothed with ministerial authority."[138]

Associations were thus a forum for resolving or at least hearing disputes that continually arose and often divided local congregations. When churches needed help in resolving divisive questions, they turned to the association for advice.

Circular Letters

As in Britain, queries sometimes were part of circular letters sent out by associations in America. Such letters give evidence of the theological discussions and debates of the early American Baptists. They also were the predecessors of the Baptist periodicals and newspapers.[139] The earliest letters that Charles Deweese could find were from 1767, written by the Philadelphia Association. The letters "helped to solidify both the unity and the identity of Baptists around a general set of beliefs, even though variations in doctrinal interpretation were common."[140]

Concerning the ministry, a circular letter from the Kehukee Association suggested that a minister's primary training should be a "classical education" and that a minister must be a "man of erudition." The letter acknowledged that "many who have spent years in the schools to acquire a liberal education ... are ignorant of the true knowledge of God, and are unacquainted with the spiritual meaning of his word."[141] This discussion illustrates the tension Baptists experienced over formal education for ministers.

In 1789, the Charleston Association encouraged churches to utilize a council in the conduct of ordinations. One document observed, "It is advised, that the church call in the assistance of at least two, but rather three, of the ministers in union, who are the most generally esteemed in the churches for piety and abilities."[142]

Again, these documents reveal the connectional nature of interchurch relationships.

Deaconesses

Like some of their British counterparts, American Baptists utilized the office of deaconess to set aside women for particular ministries in the church. Although there are no references to the office evident among seventeenth-century Baptists, Morgan Edwards gave some description of the function of these women in certain eighteenth-century congregations. According to Edwards, they were present among a small number of Separate Baptist congregations in Virginia, North Carolina, and South Carolina. A few were found among the Particular Baptists in South Carolina.[143]

Edwards himself approved of the office, and he described its work as caring for the sick and the poor and providing ministries primarily "to those things wherefor men are less fit."[144] The Sandy Creek Church, formed in North Carolina in 1755, maintained the deaconess office—a practice that surely influenced other Separate Baptist churches to follow suit.

Baptists at the End of the Eighteenth Century

As the eighteenth century came to an end, Baptists seemed well equipped for the new era ahead. The nation had won independence that guaranteed religious liberty for all citizens. The Baptist vision of a free church in a free state had been secured. New Baptist subgroups emerged, and denominationalizing sentiments were slowly evolving, nourished by the burgeoning missionary zeal of the revivals. Within the next thirty years, this oft-persecuted minority would become one of the largest Protestant bodies in the United States.

Notes

1. Isaac Backus, *A History of New England, with Particular Reference to the Denomination of Christians Called Baptists,* 2 vols., 2nd ed. (Newton, Mass.: Backus Historical Society, 1871), 1:205.
2. Russell's narrative response to charges against Baptists is reproduced in Nathan Wood, *The History of the First Baptist Church of Boston* (Philadelphia: American Baptist Publication Society, 1899), 169–70.
3. Robert G. Torbet, *A History of the Baptists,* 3rd ed. (Valley Forge, Pa.: Judson Press, 1978), 208 (citing Henry Vedder, *A Short History of the Baptists,* rev. ed. [Philadelphia: American Baptist Publication Society], 302).
4. Lynn E. May Jr., "A Brief History of the Baptist Associations," *Quarterly Review* 37 (October–December 1976): 35.
5. Norman Maring, *Baptists in New Jersey: A Study in Transition* (Valley Forge, Pa.: Judson Press, 1964), 13.
6. Ibid, 19.
7. Ibid., 17.
8. David Benedict, *A General History of the Baptist Denomination in America* (New York: Colby, 1848), 541.
9. Bill J. Leonard, ed., *Dictionary of Baptists in America* (Downers Grove, Ill.: InterVarsity Press, 1994), 128.
10. David Benedict, *Baptist Denomination,* 627.
11. Maring, *Baptists in New Jersey,* 32.
12. William Lumpkin, *Baptist Confessions of Faith* (Chicago: Judson Press, 1959), 351.
13. Ibid.
14. Walter B. Shurden, *Associationalism among Baptists in America, 1707–1814* (New York: Arno Press, 1980), 10.
15. May, "Baptist Associations," 34–35.
16. Benedict, *Baptist Denomination,* 597–98.
17. Robert Gardner, *Baptists of Early America: A Statistical History, 1639–1790* (Atlanta: Georgia Baptist Historical Society, 1983), 51–52.

18. Thomas R McKibbens, "The Life, Writings, and Influence of Morgan Edwards," *Quarterly Review* (January–March 1976): 62.
19. Ibid., 59.
20. Ibid., 60–61.
21. Ibid., 65.
22. Robert A. Baker, *The Southern Baptist Convention and Its People* (Nashville: Broadman, 1972), 32.
23. Ibid., 38.
24. Ibid., 38–39.
25. Ibid., 39.
26. William McLoughlin, *Soul Liberty: The Baptists' Struggle in New England, 1630–1833* (Hanover, N.H.: University Press of New England, 1991), 93–99; Thomas W. Bicknell, *A History of Barrington, Rhode Island* (Providence: Snow & Farnham, 1898).
27. Isaac Backus, *Church History of New England from 1620 to 1804* (Philadelphia: American Baptist Publication Society, 1844), 144.
28. Ibid.
29. Isaac Backus, *A History of New England, with Particular Reference to the Baptists*, 2nd ed. (1871; reprint, 2 vols. in 1, New York: Arno Press, 1969), 2:18.
30. Backus, *Church History*, 145.
31. Backus, *History of New England*, 2:20–21.
32. Backus, *Church History*, 147.
33. O. K. Armstrong and Marjorie Armstrong, *The Baptists in America* (Garden City, N.Y.: Doubleday, 1979), 85–87; William Warren Sweet, *The Story of Religion in America* (New York: Harper & Row, 1950), 133–37.
34. Alan Heimert, "The Great Awakening as Watershed," in *Religion in American History: Interpretive Essays*, ed. John M. Mulder and John F. Wilson (Englewood Cliffs, N.J.: Prentice-Hall, 1978), 127–44.
35. Jon Butler, *Awash in a Sea of Faith: Christianizing the American People* (Cambridge: Harvard University Press, 1990), 177–78.
36. Mark A. Noll, *A History of Christianity in the United States and Canada* (Grand Rapids: Eerdmans, 1992), 97.
37. Ibid., 110.
38. Jonathan Edwards, "A Faithful Narrative of the Surprising Work of God," in *The Great Awakening: A Faithful Narrative*, ed. Clarence C. Goen (New Haven: Yale University Press, 1972), 144–211.
39. William McLoughlin, *Revivals, Awakenings, and Reform* (Chicago: University of Chicago Press, 1979).
40. Winthrop S. Hudson, "Baptists, the Pilgrim Fathers, and the American Revolution," in *Baptists and the American Experience*, ed. James E. Wood (Valley Forge, Pa.: Judson Press, 1976), 26.
41. Edwin S. Gaustad, "Baptists and the Making of a New Nation," in Wood, ed., *American Experience*, 42.
42. Ibid.
43. Benedict, *Baptist Denomination*, 510.
44. Backus, *History of New England*, 2:88.
45. Ibid., 2:89.
46. Backus, *Church History*, 90; William McLoughlin, *Soul Liberty*, 100–125.
47. Backus, *History of New England*, 2:115.
48. Ibid.
49. Benedict, *Baptist Denomination*, 392.
50. Morgan Edwards, "Materials towards a History of the Baptists in the Province of North-Carolina," vol. 4 (typescript, 1772), 17.
51. Benedict, *Baptist Denomination*, 393.
52. Howard Dorgan, "Old Time Baptists of Central Appalachia," in *Christianity in Appalachia: Profiles in Regional Pluralism*, ed. Bill J. Leonard (Knoxville: University of Tennessee Press, 1999), 120.
53. H. Shelton Smith, Robert T. Handy, and Lefferts A. Loetscher, *American Christianity*, 2 vols. (New York: Scribner, 1960–63), 1:365; also, Edwards, "Province of North-Carolina," 21–22.
54. Smith, Handy, and Loetscher, *American Christianity*, 1:361.
55. Edwards, "Province of North-Carolina," 17–18.
56. Ibid. This reference to "the 9 Christian rites" probably is from the later eighteenth century, not the founding.
57. Benedict, *Baptist Denomination*, 67.
58. Charles W. Deweese, "The Rise of the Separate Baptists in North Carolina," *Quarterly Review* (October–December 1976): 74.
59. Ibid., 75.
60. Ibid., 76.
61. Dorgan, "Old Time Baptists," 121.
62. Lemuel Burkitt and Jesse Read, *A Concise History of the Kehukee Baptist Association, from Its Original Rise Down to 1808*, rev. ed. (1850; reprint, New York: Arno Press, 1980), 41.
63. Ibid., 42.
64. Ibid., 44–45.
65. John Leland, *The Writings of John Leland*, ed. L. F. Greene (1845; reprint, New York: Arno Press, 1969), 105.

66. McLoughlin, *Soul Liberty,* 124–25. Another reference, from a sermon by Baptist minister-historian Charles Train, reported that such an association was organized in 1763.
67. Ibid., 125.
68. Isaac Backus, *The Diary of Isaac Backus,* 3 vols., ed. William McLoughlin (Providence: Brown University Press, 1979), 1:xvii.
69. Ibid., xviii.
70. Ibid., xix.
71. Ibid., xxiv.
72. Isaac Backus, *Isaac Backus on Church, State, and Calvinism: Pamphlets, 1754–1789,* ed. William McLoughlin (Cambridge: Belknap Press of Harvard University Press, 1968), 9–10.
73. H. Leon McBeth, *The Baptist Heritage* (Nashville: Broadman, 1987), 207.
74. William McLoughlin, "Introduction: An Overview," in *Baptists in the Balance,* ed. Everett C. Goodwin (Valley Forge, Pa.: Judson Press, 1997), 67.
75. Backus, *Diary,* 1: xxviii.
76. Armstrong and Armstrong, *The Baptists in America,* 99–100.
77. Hudson, "American Revolution," 29–30. Hudson cites *Backus's History of New England, with Particular Reference to the Denomination of Christians Called Baptists.*
78. McLoughlin, *Soul Liberty,* 259.
79. Ibid., 263.
80. Ibid., 268.
81. Backus, *Church History,* 175.
82. Benedict, *Baptist Denomination,* 402.
83. Ibid., 472.
84. Maring, *Baptists in New Jersey,* 22 (citing Morgan Edwards, *The Customs of Primitive Churches* [Philadelphia, 1768], 13).
85. George W. Purefoy, *History of the Sandy Creek Baptist Association, from Its Organization in A.D. 1758, to A.D. 1858* (1859; reprint, New York: Arno Press, 1980), 46–47.
86. William J. Reynolds, "Our Heritage of Baptist Hymnody in America," *Baptist History and Heritage* 11 (October 1976): 207; see also Lumpkin, *Baptist Confessions of Faith,* 351.
87. Reynolds, "Baptist Hymnody," 208.
88. Ibid., 208.
89. Ibid., 213.
90. Gardner, *Baptists of Early America,* 54–55.
91. George A. Rawlyk, *Ravished by the Spirit: Religious Revivals, Baptists, and Henry Alline* (Montreal: McGill-Queen's University Press, 1984), 44.
92. Ibid., 50.
93. Ibid., 53–66.
94. James R. Lynch, "Baptist Women in Ministry in 1920," *American Baptist Quarterly* 13 (December 1994): 305 (citing Isaac Dalton Stewart, *History of the Freewill Baptists for Half a Century* [Dover, N.H.: Freewill Baptist Printing Establishment, 1862]).
95. Lynch, "Baptist Women in Ministry in 1920," 306.
96. Robert G. Torbet, *A Social History of the Philadelphia Baptist Association: 1707–1940* (Philadelphia: Westbrook, 1944), 67.
97. Ibid., 67–68.
98. Ibid., 69.
99. Benedict, *Baptist Denomination,* 642.
100. Ibid., 643.
101. Ibid., 648.
102. Baker, *Southern Baptist Convention,* 53.
103. Leonard, ed., *Dictionary of Baptists,* 96.
104. Baker, *Southern Baptist Convention,* 64.
105. Morgan Edwards, "Materials towards History of the Baptists in the Province of Md," vol. 2 (typescript, 1772), 32–33.
106. Ibid., 34.
107. Baker, *Southern Baptist Convention,* 54.
108. Benedict, *Baptist Denomination,* 652.
109. Ibid.
110. Gaustad, "New Nation," 45.
111. Leland, *Writings,* 106–7.
112. Ibid., 107.
113. Ibid., 118.
114. Ibid., 120.
115. Ibid., 294.
116. Ibid.
117. Ibid.
118. Ibid., 149.
119. Ibid., 97.

120. Gaustad, "New Nation," 45.

121. Baker, *Southern Baptist Convention,* 70–71.

122. Hudson, "American Revolution," 32.

123. Maring, *Baptists in New Jersey,* 71.

124. Ibid., 72.

125. Armstrong and Armstrong, *The Baptists in America,* 105.

126. Backus, *History of New England,* 2:192.

127. Albert H. Newman, *A History of the Baptist Churches in the United States* (Philadelphia: American Baptist Publication Society, 1898), 107; Robert A. Baker, "Baptists and the American Revolution," *Baptist History and Heritage* 11 (July 1976): 157.

128. Maring, *Baptists in New Jersey,* 75.

129. Gardner, *Baptists of Early America,* 15.

130. Walter B. Shurden, "The Baptist Drive for a Missionary Consciousness: Associational Activities Before 1814," *Quarterly Review* 39 (April–June 1979): 60. This idea challenges earlier claims regarding missions and associations. See Albert L. Vail, *The Morning Hour of American Baptist Missions* (Philadelphia: American Baptist Publication Society, 1907), 21–61; Torbet, *Philadelphia Baptist Association,* 19; Robert A. Baker, *Relations between Northern and Southern Baptists,* 2nd ed. (1954; reprint, New York: Arno Press, 1980), 10.

131. Shurden, "Missionary Consciousness," 61.

132. Sydney Ahlstrom, *A Religious History of the American People* (New Haven: Yale University Press, 1972), 356–59, 482.

133. Ibid., 482–83.

134. Purefoy, *Sandy Creek Baptist Association,* 62.

135. Ibid., 76.

136. Ibid., 93.

137. Ibid.

138. Ibid., 122.

139. Charles W. Deweese, "The Role of Circular Letters in Baptist Associations in America, 1707–1799," *Quarterly Review* 36 October–December 1975): 51–52.

140. Ibid., 54.

141. Burkitt and Read, *Kehukee Baptist Association,* 81.

142. William H. Allison and William W. Barnes, *Baptist Ecclesiology: An Original Anthology,* ed. Edwin S. Gaustad (New York: Arno Press, 1980), 81.

143. Charles W. Deweese, "Deaconesses in Baptist History: A Preliminary Study," *Baptist History and Heritage* 12 (January 1977): 53–54.

144. Ibid., 54 (citing Edwards, *Customs of Primitive Churches,* 43).

Chapter 7
Baptists in Britain: The Nineteenth Century

NINETEENTH-CENTURY BRITAIN WAS DOMINATED BY INFLUENCES BORN OF THE development of industry, the growth of towns, and the expansion of the British Empire and the later Victorian period. As the century progressed, British Baptists solidified their organizational alignments, continued to develop missionary enterprises, founded schools, and confronted assorted controversies of theology and polity. The rotund figure of Charles Haddon Spurgeon loomed large from the pulpit of the Metropolitan Tabernacle and in the public square of English culture. Nonconformists, Baptists included, succeeded in securing the removal in 1828 of the seventeenth-century Test and Corporation Acts, which, though not seriously enforced during this period, were nonetheless a blight on the religious freedom of non-Anglicans.

Missionary activities, begun at the end of the eighteenth century, expanded as numerous individuals were sent forth under the auspices of the Baptist Missionary Society and other mission agencies. Missionary-explorer David Livingstone, although not a Baptist, was an important mentor for those who literally "surrendered their lives" to carry Christianity to Africa.

Baptist institutional identity also took shape during the nineteenth century. Some Baptists in Britain, long divided into varying theological and regional subgroups, moved toward increased cooperation and denominational organization.

The Baptist Union of Great Britain and Ireland

If the eighteenth century saw the organization of the Baptist Missionary Society in Britain, the nineteenth century witnessed the beginnings of the British Baptist Union. The formation of the missionary society was merely the first step toward larger denominational enterprises. In his history of nineteenth-century British Baptists, J. H. Y. Briggs suggested that missionary endeavors fostered new connections among congregations. He noted that through such efforts, "the form of church life became much more complex, the local church employing a rich diversity of agencies in its witness within its own community, acknowledging now the need to associate with others to promote gospel obedience nationally and internationally."[1]

The organization of a "General Union" occurred in 1813 among Particular Baptist churches and ministers from throughout the country. In 1811, Joseph Ivimey wrote an article called "Union Essential to Prosperity," in which he called for the formation of a formal union of Particular Baptists. Ivimey and John Rippon were leading advocates of a new organization. Union did not come easily, as Calvinistic Baptist churches had long resisted denominational connectionalism beyond the association. Nonetheless, an agreement was reached, and by 1815, the Union was begun, renamed the General Meeting of the Particular (or Calvinistic) Baptist Denomination. In 1832, it was reorganized as the Baptist Union, becoming in 1873 the Baptist Union of Great Britain and Ireland.[2] Founders of the Union hoped that it would promote "the cause of Christ in general; and the interests of the denomination in particular; with a primary view to the encouragement and support of the Baptist Mission (BMS)."[3] It began with forty-six charter members from among the Particular Baptist ministry.

James Hinton (1761–1823), one of the early leaders of the Union, noted in an 1812 address that such a gathering of Baptists should be grounded in "a harmony in Religious Principles" and doctrines around which they could agree. It should be "cemented by a holy delight in each other" as a celebration of community. It should also involve "some great and common objects of pursuit, and direct these our unremitted attention."[4] Such high expectations were short-lived. Early in its history, the Union generally was ignored by most Particular Baptists. Many churches were not even part of a regional association, and their denominational connection was limited to contributions to various benevolent and missionary societies.

Further efforts at extending participation reflected an attempt to be traditionally Baptist but avoid elaborate doctrinal formulations. The resolutions of the early Baptist Union included the following statement of "important doctrines": "'three equal persons in the Godhead'; eternal and personal election; original sin; particular redemption; free justification by the imputed righteousness of Christ; efficacious grace in regeneration; the final perseverance of real believers; the resurrection of the dead; the future judgement; the eternal happiness of the righteous, and the eternal misery of such as die in impenitence, with the congregational order of the churches inviolably."[5] This "creedal" declaration provided a brief doctrinal framework for unity. It was dropped in 1832 in order to include churches and ministers "who agree in the sentiments usually denominated evangelical."[6] This allowed for possible fellowship with non-Calvinist Baptists. New Connection Baptists were early participants in the Union and extended the boundaries of Baptist cooperation. Local autonomy, Baptist individualism, and a continuing hesitancy to participate in ecclesial alliances meant that cooperation was difficult to sustain. Ernest Payne wrote that the history of the Baptist Union "shows both the necessity and the difficulty of uniting churches of this character. Tensions and anomalies are inevitable."[7]

Another restructuring in 1863 saw increased support from Baptist churches and individuals. An agreement that formally brought the General Baptists into the Union was approved in 1891. During the late nineteenth and early twentieth centuries, the Union developed extensive work with mission societies and various Baptist boards.

By 1864, the Union faced the need for a reorganization of its institutional life. Its budget had declined significantly with fewer and fewer churches contributing to its support. In spite of financial difficulties, however, its relationship with multiple Baptist societies remained strong.[8]

British Baptist Societies

Denominational cooperation was enhanced by the participation of individuals and churches in a variety of Baptist missionary or benevolence societies. These organizations were often short-lived, appearing, disappearing, or merging with other groups. They included a Baptist Irish Society (1814) for evangelistic outreach; a ministers' Annuity Fund (1874); the Baptist Building Fund (1824); and the Baptist Total Abstinence Association (1874). Likewise, the alumni and friends of the Baptist colleges constituted a society of supporters for higher education.

Home missionary efforts influenced the formation in 1797 of the Baptist Society for the Encouragement and Support of Itinerant Preaching. During the nineteenth century, it became the Home Mission Society, and ultimately it was brought under the direction of the Baptist Union.

Early in its history, the Baptist Union depended on the members of the various societies for much of its support. For a time, the union rented space for its offices from the Baptist Missionary Society. Its annual assemblies were held in the society's headquarters in London's Moorgate section. As the Union gained influence, however, many of the societies turned to it for support and cooperation.[9]

Communion Controversies ... Again

No sooner was the Baptist Union underway than another controversy flared over the admission of nonimmersed persons to communion in Baptist churches. Robert Hall (1764–1831), minister of Harvey Lane Church, Leicester, published a treatise in 1815 entitled *On Terms of Communion with a Particular View to the Case of Baptists and Paedobaptists*. He urged Baptist churches to institute an open communion policy whereby all baptized Christians, even the nonimmersed, would be welcomed to the Lord's Table.

Particular Baptist ministers, including Joseph Ivimey, demanded closed communion only, and a lengthy debate ensued. Joseph Kinghorn (1766–1832), pastor of the Particular Baptist church at Norwich, published *Baptism a Term of Communion at the Lord's Supper*. Kinghorn believed that since infant baptism was invalid, the nonimmersed were not entitled to receive communion. He wrote, "It is not according to the law of Christ that persons not baptized should come to the Lord's table."[10] He criticized those churches that admitted pedobaptists to communion while refusing to admit them to church membership.

The baptismal controversy turned to schism when staunchly Calvinist Baptists left the Norfolk and Suffolk Association and established a new group known as Strict Baptists. They practiced closed communion and opposed "Fullerism," the evangelical Calvinism of Andrew Fuller and the Baptist Missionary Society.[11] They insisted that God alone was the agent of salvation and that missionary efforts were a form of works righteousness. Ernest

Payne, no friend of the movement, observed that the various Strict Baptist churches "lived an independent, isolated life, and when they tried to combine, soon found themselves involved in theological controversy."[12]

In 1846, the "Association of Strict Baptist Ministers and Churches in and about London" was organized with some ten to twelve churches participating. Another group, the "New Association of Particular Baptist Churches in London," was formed in 1849. In 1851, the name was changed to "The Association of Baptists Holding Particular Redemption and Practising Strict Communion."[13] Attempts to unite the two Strict Baptist groups were unsuccessful.

By 1860, most Baptist Union churches had accepted open communion. Toward the latter part of the century, the temperance movement prevailed upon most churches to substitute grape juice for wine in the communion service. Generally, churches observed communion monthly, but some pastors, including Charles Haddon Spurgeon, preferred a weekly celebration of the ordinance.

The Nature of the Ordinances

Debates over the nature of baptism continued throughout the nineteenth century. Although Baptists agreed that immersion was the normative mode, they were not always able to agree on its meaning. Was it sacramental? Did it convey grace? Was it essential to salvation? W. T. Whitley wrote, "Once admit that in baptism and the Lord's supper such grace is bestowed as can come in no other way, and soon a minister for these will be sought, and their observance will be exalted above preaching, ... while our Lord and the apostles would not baptize or serve tables but proclaimed salvation."[14]

Concerning both baptism and the Lord's Supper, Briggs concluded that the "ongoing emphasis" of nineteenth-century Baptists was "that the thing signified was necessarily more important than the sign which manifested it."[15] The prevailing opinion was that the outward and visible sign of immersion was not nearly as important as the inward and spiritual experience that it represented.

The Nature of the Church

Such individualism was evident in changing views of the nature of the church. Briggs suggested that many nineteenth-century Baptists eschewed traditional Puritan approaches to the church in favor of a more Enlightenment-based emphasis on voluntarism. Baptist leader Joseph Angus (d. 1902) utilized John Locke's description of the church as "a voluntary society of men, joining themselves together of their own accord, in order of the worshiping of God, in such a manner as they judge acceptable to him and effectual to the salvation of their souls."[16] Yet Angus was quick to assert that the voluntary principle did not mean "the authority of self-will" but "submission of the heart and of the life to Christ."[17] British Baptists continued to debate the relationship between the individual and the corporate elements of faith and practice throughout the twentieth century.

Baptists and Peace Societies

Nineteenth-century British Baptists participated in various movements for universal peace. The nondenominational Society for the Promotion of Permanent and Universal Peace (the Peace Society) was founded in 1816. Among its Baptist participants was George Pilkington (1785–1858), a former soldier who labeled military service "perfectly unlawful to the disciple of Christ." Denouncing war as "anti-Christian," Pilkington became an itinerant preacher, promoting peace and antislavery causes. He published a collection of "testimonies of ministers" that included essays from many Baptists who supported the cause of world peace.[18]

James Hargreaves was one of the Baptist peace advocates included in Pilkington's book. He joined the Peace Society in 1818 and served as its secretary for some twenty years. War, he maintained, was "a heathenish and savage custom of the most malignant, most desolating and most horrible character; the greatest curse and resulting from the grossest delusions, that ever affected a guilty world!"[19]

Preacher and social radical Arthur O'Neill also served as secretary of the Peace Society. In 1842, while addressing striking coal miners at the Cradley Heath Baptist Church, he was arrested, charged with sedition, and sentenced to a year in prison. Upon his release, he became a Baptist and organized a church. In addition to his peace sentiments, O'Neill opposed slavery, liquor, and capital punishment.[20]

Although apparently not a member of the Peace Society, Charles Haddon Spurgeon condemned militarism in general and the Crimean War in particular. In a well-known sermon, "War and the Spread of the Gospel," he declared, "And I do firmly hold that the slaughter of men, that bayonets, and swords and guns, have never yet been, and never can be promoters of the Gospel."[21]

Throughout the nineteenth century, several Baptist groups approved declarations against war. The Baptist Union assemblies of 1878 and 1886 made specific protests against war and its destruction of life and property. British Baptist associations and congregations often urged the government to resist war and armaments. For example, the Mill Yard Seventh Day Baptist Church issued a petition to Parliament in 1860 entreating the government "not to make any grant of public money for additional Fortifications, not to sanction any loans or create any annuities for such an unwise and wicked purpose."[22]

Educational Institutions

British Baptist concern for education was paradoxical. Many promoted education, while others remained suspicious of its benefits. Baptists organized schools, while often fretting that their young preachers would find education a door to Unitarianism or other liberal sentiments. As noted earlier, several Baptist schools were founded in the eighteenth century. Particular Baptists founded Bristol Academy, and General Baptists founded Midland College.

Horton Academy (later Rawdon College) was organized in 1804 by the Northern Education Society. William Steadman (1764–1837) was the first president of the institution. A well-known pastor and strong supporter of the Baptist Missionary Society, Steadman perceived that most Baptist ministers in the north of England "are illiterate, their talents small, their manners dull and uninteresting, their systems of divinity contracted, their maxims of church government rigid, and their exertions scarcely any at all."[23]

William Newman (1773–1835), the first principal of Stepney College, described the schedule for language study provided for its first three students:

> The bell rang at 6. Business at 7. Lecture on the article and the five declensions; reminded them, however, that my department is theological. Family worship at 8. Met them at 10. Rehearsal; heard them read the first psalm, parsing the words of the first verse. Dictated a few lines to be written on the slate to see their orthography, etc. They appear very attentive. Left them soon after 11. My soul is concerned for these young men who seem to be pious. O that I may be the instrument of much good to them. Met them at 2 p.m.; examined the five declensions.[24]

In 1834, Joseph Angus relinquished his position as secretary of the Baptist Missionary Society to join Stepney College, where he soon became principal. In 1855, the school moved to Regent's Park, London, and developed ties with the University of London. In 1928, the first Baptist students matriculated at its new location in Oxford.

By 1863, numerous Baptist-related educational institutions existed in Britain. These included Bristol College, Stepney College (later Regent's Park College, Oxford), Spurgeon's College, the Northern Baptist Education Society, and schools at Haverfordwest, Pontypool, and Llangollen (Wales).[25]

Nineteenth-century nonconformists worked diligently to secure entrance into British universities. Religious requirements for first degrees at Oxford and Cambridge were eliminated in 1871, making it easier for nonconformists to be admitted. This was not always a benefit to the noncomformist ranks, however, since many students from dissenting religious traditions turned to Anglicanism during their university years.[26]

Baptist Church Life

Much of British Baptist church life during the nineteenth century was characterized by a strong concern for preaching, exemplified in numerous popular pulpiteers whose sermons were widely published. These included Charles Haddon Spurgeon, Alexander Maclaren, Andrew Fuller, and John Clifford. Spurgeon, whose pulpit prowess was unrivaled, was Britain's most popular nineteenth-century preacher. Clifford was at once a preacher and a church leader who helped to shape and preserve the Baptist Union. Fuller's name was inseparable from the early Baptist missionary activity and the formation of the Baptist Missionary Society. Maclaren was a powerful preacher whose works were second only to Spurgeon's in circulation.

In general, church services were not liturgically elaborate but included hymns, prayers (a long pastoral prayer was common), and sermon. Congregational participation was minimal, and preaching was the central element of the services.

Hymnody was an important element of Baptist worship, with extensive use of John Rippon's *Selection of Hymns from the Best Authors*—a collection published in 1787. Rippon (1750–1836) was pastor of the Carter Lane Church, London. His "broad church" policies led him to address the first volume of the *Baptist Annual Register* (1790) to Baptists the world over, "with a desire of promoting an universal interchange of kind offices among them and in serious expectation that before many years elapse ... a deputation from all these climes will meet probably in London to consult the ecclesiastical good of the whole." Alfred Underwood suggested that these words sowed the seeds of what would become the Baptist World Alliance.[27]

During the nineteenth century, Baptists published numerous hymnbooks. Metropolitan Tabernacle produced *Our Own Hymnbook* in 1866. Particular Baptists published *A New Selection of Hymns* in 1828 and *Psalms and Hymns* in 1858. The New Connection Baptists published *Baptist Hymnal* in 1879. Wesleyan hymns, with their stress on the general atonement, were hesitantly added to many Baptist hymnals.

By the 1830s, British Baptist churches often altered their worship schedules from a second service on Sunday afternoon to a Sunday evening gathering. Supporters of the change insisted that in this way "an audience of a more miscellaneous kind was obtained, and the ministry insensibly assumed a more varied character. Subjects arising out of common life, or relating to public questions and prevalent social discussions, were handled in a manner calculated to interest the most careless persons, and to win their confidence in religious teachers."[28] Often, these services were labeled "lectures" as a way of attracting those who might not attend the Sunday morning sermon.

Ernest Payne claimed that during this period many Baptist churches became meeting places for various guilds and societies in their respective communities. These included Sunday schools, Bible classes, savings banks, female auxiliaries for instruction and evangelism, book societies, and other voluntary endeavors.[29]

The middle of the nineteenth century saw an increase in new Baptist congregations. W. T. Whitley suggested that the decade 1860–1870 led to the creation of London churches at a rate that "has never been equalled before or since."[30] Bloomsbury Baptist Church in central London began in 1848 and soon attracted large numbers of worshipers. The presence of a Baptist church in that location was an important symbol of Baptists' coming of age in nineteenth-century British life.

Ministerial calling and ordination again revealed the relationship between individual experience and congregational affirmation. Congregations in the nineteenth century seem to have played an increasingly important role in "calling out the called." The congregation of Upton Chapel issued a circular letter in 1806, which stated, "It is not sufficient that individual Members press after those things which may enable them to do good to others; the Churches must become nurseries to their gifts."[31]

Missionary Activities

The Baptist Missionary Society continued to send out workers, expanding their fields outside India. In May 1799, other British Baptist missionaries set out for India. These included the families of William Grant, Dan Brunsdon, and Joshua Marshman, along with William Ward, a single man. Grant died almost on arrival, and Brundson was dead by July 1801. In October, lacking permission from the British, they went to Serampore, a region near Calcutta under the control of the Danish East India Company. William Carey himself joined the group in January 1800. He, Marshman, and Ward were colleagues for over two decades, and came to be known as the "Serampore Trio."[32]

Joshua Marshman (1768–1837) was a preacher, teacher, and printer. His wife, Hannah Shepherd Marshman (1767–1847), lived longer than any of the other early missionaries. She gave birth to eight children, only four of whom lived to adulthood. She also ran the schools that made the mission financially viable. Without those funds, the mission might not have survived. The earliest were boarding schools for Europeans, but a school for Bengali boys was established in June 1800. Marshman revised his initial plans in 1816 in a work entitled *Hints Relative to Native Schools,* together with the *Outline of an Institution for Their Extension and Management.*

William Ward (1769–1823) was a printer who took responsibility for the publication of the various translations of Scripture prepared by Carey. John Mack (d. 1845), a close colleague of the Trio, arrived in India in 1821. He taught at Serampore College and succeeded Carey and Marshman as principal.[33]

In March 1812, a fire devastated the building where the missionaries printed their manuscripts. One observer noted, "The immense printing office, two hundred feet long and fifty broad, reduced to a mere shell. The yard covered with burst quires of paper, the loss in which article was immense. Carey walked with me over the smoking ruins. The tears stood in his eyes, 'in one short evening' said he 'the labours of years are ruined.'"[34]

The Serampore Trio complained that the educational level of the missionaries was insufficient, even among those who knew the classical and biblical languages.[35] Fires, deaths of missionaries, and other traumas created theological and logistical challenges for the missionaries—powerful reminders of their place in another society.

Serampore College

William Carey founded Serampore College in 1818, noting that its work would be to prepare "as large a body as possible of Christian natives of India for the work of Christian Pastors and Itinerants." Since England could never send enough missionaries, India would "never be turned from her grossness of idolatry to serve the true and living God unless the grace of God rest abundantly on converted natives to qualify them for Mission work."[36]

Its initial prospectus called for a "College for the instruction of Asiatic Christian and other Youth in Eastern Literature and European Science." While the founders desired that Christianity permeate the curriculum, their Baptist sentiments required them to promote liberty of conscience for all students. No Hindu or Muslim youth was required to participate in any religious service or observance that violated his or her conscience.[37] Howells and Underwood concluded, "Unlike their successors in 1883, they believed that the study of theology should be carried on in an open institution, in conjunction with a liberal course of arts and science."[38] Funding for the college did not come easily, and the services of faculty members were difficult to secure.

Debates with the Baptist Missionary Society

The relationship between the Society and its missionaries was stormy at times. Following the death of Andrew Fuller in 1815, new leaders were appointed, most of whom were unacquainted with the missionaries in India. In 1819, the BMS headquarters moved from Kettering to London—another sign of more formal organizational structure. By the 1820s, William Carey and his colleagues were involved in a debate with the BMS over control and authority. Questions arose as to whether a portion of the income secured in India should be controlled by the British board or the missionaries on the field. The younger appointees accepted the authority of the board more readily, separating themselves from the Serampore Trio and forming their own union based in Calcutta. In 1827, the Society and the Serampore Mission divided and remained so for a decade. The idea of BMS control of the mission prevailed, but only after the deaths of the three original missionaries.

Missions in Jamaica

The earliest British missionaries arrived in Jamaica in 1814 in the persons of John Rowe (1788–1816) and Sarah Rowe. They built on the work of two ex-slaves, Moses Baker and George Lisle. Others joined them, including the brothers Thomas and William Knibb, Thomas Burchell, and James Phillippo. While other missionaries came and went, William Knibb (1803–1845), Burchell (b. 1799), and Phillippo (b. 1798) remained a faithful trio of long-term BMS appointees in Jamaica. Some twenty-five individuals were sent out between 1814 and 1831.

Mission to Burma

The BMS sent James and Ann Chater, and Felix and Margaret Carey, as missionaries to Burma in 1807. The living conditions were so harsh that the men sent their spouses back to the mission in Serampore. Nonetheless, tragedy struck. Margaret Carey died in 1808, at the age of nineteen, leaving three children behind. Felix Carey remarried, but his second wife and their two children died in a shipwreck. The BMS ultimately relinquished control of the Burmese mission to American Baptists Ann and Adoniram Judson. During the nineteenth century, the Baptist Missionary Society began work in the East Indies, the West Indies, France, Italy, and Norway.

Baptists in China

The efforts of the BMS in China began in the 1860s with the appointment of Hendrik Kloekers and Charles Hall and their spouses to Shanghai. Charles Hall moved to Yantai (Chefoo) in Shandong (Shantung) province and attempted to make it the base for BMS work. By 1867, "ill health and overwork" compelled him and other Baptist missionaries there to resign. In 1869, a church of some thirty-five members was founded in the Yantai region by R. F. Laughton (d. 1870).

That same year, the board sent Timothy Richard (b. 1845), who within a few months of his arrival became the only BMS missionary in Yantai. He then moved to the industrial center of Chingzhou, where he provided aid during the harsh famine of 1876–1878 by helping to found five orphanages in the region. In 1877, he established a Baptist congregation in Taiyuan in the province of Shanxi. It became the central location for Richard's remaining mission work. He and his wife, Mary Martin, founded an orphanage in the city. He also made attempts to reach the Chinese upper classes.[39]

Richard's work was not without controversy. His desire to establish a college in China was rejected by the BMS board. Some of his younger British colleagues attacked his theology and methods, sending lengthy critiques back to the BMS.

Late in his career, Richard became editor of *The Tianjin Times*. His career was characterized by years of rancor with missionary colleagues and the BMS over questions of theology and missionary strategy. In 1891, he was named General Secretary for the Diffusion of Christian and General Knowledge. He remained a BMS missionary until his retirement in 1914.[40]

Africa

BMS work in Africa began in 1795 with appointment of James Rodway and Jacob Grigg to Sierra Leone. Their service was short-lived, however. South African missions from the BMS began in 1833 through the work of W. Davies and his spouse.

Baptist concern for western Africa—center of the slave trade—originated in Jamaica with former slaves who desired to see the gospel carried into their homelands. John Clarke and his wife originally were appointed to Jamaica, where they studied African culture and language. Clarke and Dr. George Kinghorn Prince went to Fernando Po, an island off the west coast of Africa, in 1841. They bought land and initiated religious services in the region.

Returning to Jamaica, Clarke and Prince sought additional support for missions in Africa. Other missionaries were sent, including Alfred Saker, who spent the rest of his life working in African missions. By 1845, Saker visited the Cameroons, where he worked to translate the Bible into the native Dualla language. He baptized the first convert in 1849.

Death and illness soon took their toll, and Saker was soon the only remaining member of the Cameroonian mission. He persevered in translating the Bible and in 1872 reported, "Four young men are now reading with me, two are already preachers, and the two other will, I hope, begin very soon."[41] In 1884, Germany took charge of the Cameroons, and shortly thereafter the British transferred control of the enterprise to the German Baptists.

British Baptist workers also went to the Congo, but again they faced difficulties in establishing stable communities. George Grenfell and Thomas Comber were well known as missionaries and explorers in the Congo region. Through their efforts, a mission station was established in San Salvador near the mouth of the Congo River.

During the 1870s, Grenfell, Comber, and their associates made numerous attempts to carry their message inland, all with limited success. Travel required transporting vast amounts of supplies and often reassembling or repairing river crafts along the way. Evangelization and exploration went hand in hand. Basil Amey noted that during the 1880s, "Grenfell charted 3400 miles of the Congo's waterways as he sought for areas where missionaries could be deployed."[42]

As in the other fields, conversions came slowly. The first baptism occurred in 1886, eight years after the mission was formed. A church was founded in 1887. Death claimed fifteen men and four women sent to the Congo in the first decade of the mission work. Nonetheless, Grenfell established new mission stations at Bolobo (1888), Upoto (1890), Monsembe (1890), and Yakusu (1896). The BMS mission in the Congo was perhaps their strongest in Africa.

The British Women's Missionary Movement

Women's missionary societies flourished in England and the United States. Many Baptist women insisted that Christian missions were essential in offering redemption and liberation for women shackled by "pagan" cultures and religions.

The initial "women's work with women" came from the wives of the Serampore Trio. William Carey called Hannah Marshman (d. 1847) "the equal of the three [male] missionaries of Christ and civilisation, whom she aided in the common home, in the schools, in the congregation, in Christian families, and even at the early time in purely Hindu circles."[43] Married female missionaries also opened schools for girls in Serampore and Calcutta.

Women in England were not blind to the work of Marshman's wife in assisting in the first Baptist missionary efforts in India. The "Form of Agreement" of the Serampore Brotherhood expressed the hope that women would participate in all mission work, since "a European sister may do much for the cause by promoting the holiness and stirring up the zeal of the native female converts."[44] Zenana missions provided occasions for women missionaries to work exclusively with women, thereby remaining within the "women's sphere" of Christian activity and outside male-dominated ministry. A zenana was the "women's court," or harem, in Indian society, but missionary women were permitted to enter.

The primary purpose of the zenana mission was to fund single women missionaries who would work with women in various mission settings. In 1867, two stations were opened in Calcutta and Delhi with female missionaries "Miss Robinson and Miss (E.) Page" and some "half-dozen Bible-women," local women trained to teach the Bible to their female counterparts.[45]

In Britain, mission-minded women insisted that the primary way to facilitate the conversion of males was through the conversion (and ultimate betterment) of the females. Women missionaries were necessary in order to convert Indian women. Nonetheless, conversion of males and females did not change the order of creation by which males were the "heads." The Form of Agreement continued, "Yet if man is the head of the family, woman is surely the heart, and in every land the missionaries have again and again found that the men are kept back from the confession of Christianity by the influence of the women, who cling to the bondage of priestcraft when the men are ready to throw it off."[46] Single women would accomplish these conversions through work in the zenanas.

Charles Bennett Lewis and his wife, missionaries to Calcutta, returned to England in 1865, and Mrs. Lewis (d. 1890; there seems to be no remaining record of her first name) wrote a pamphlet entitled *A Plea for Zenanas*. Appeals such as hers led to a gathering of twenty-five women at Baptist Mission House, London, on May 22, 1867. A. C. Underhill, secretary of the BMS, presided, and Mrs. C. B. Lewis spoke of the need for Christian work among women. The group agreed that (1) an association should be formed in connection with the BMS to aid its operations among the female population of the East; and (2) the funds contributed should especially be devoted to the support of women engaged in visiting the zenanas and of "Bible-women" in connection with the missionaries of the respective stations where the work was carried on.[47] The first year saw two stations open, Calcutta and Delhi, with two single women missionaries, Rachel Robinson (d. 1891) and E. Page (d. 1870). They were aided by six "Bible-women" translators.

The society originally was known as the "Ladies' Association for the Support of Zenana Work and Bible Women in India, in Connection with the Baptist Missionary Society." Mrs. Angus (d. 1893), wife of the principal of Regent's Park College, was foreign secretary of the society from 1869 to 1893. In 1897, the society was renamed the "Baptist Zenana Mission" (BZM). In 1917, Ceylon and the Congo were added to the program, and again the name was changed, this time to the "Women's Missionary Association of the Baptist Missionary Society," incorporating the Baptist Zenana Mission. Some British Baptist women's groups retained the name BZM into the twenty-first century.[48]

The zenana strategy involved Western missionary women as ministers to Indian women, engaging them in their familial and cultural settings. The women taught sewing, music, and other skills. Some even provided literacy instruction when invited to do so by their female hosts.

The British women did not hesitate to assess the treatment of women in Indian society. One document observed, "The evil system of early marriage, with all its attendant ills, the lack of fresh air and exercise, the absence of education and social life, the enforcement of life-long widowhood, and the oppression of dread and hopeless in their religion, have all combined to make the life of women in India a hard and trying experience."[49] Another commented, "These women need much shepherding and instruction after they are brought into church fellowship…. It should be the chief work of the missionaries of the future to cultivate Christian character, and develop the qualities of independence and leadership among the women of the church."[50]

The first women converts included three women who were baptized in 1869. During the first decade, ten mission stations for women were opened by the Zenana Society.

The first single women missionaries, Agnes Orr Kirkland and Lucy Shalders, were sent to China by the BMS in 1893. Shalders retired in 1901. Kirkland (d. 1940) remained in the field until 1926.

The women missionaries and the women who supported them believed that the divine call could come to females as powerfully as to males, though within certain prescribed parameters. One late-nineteenth-century missionary hymn specifically addressed the call of women to "foreign fields":

O Women-hearts, that keep the days of old
In living memory, can you stand back
When Christ calls?
Shall the Heavenly Master lack
The serving love, which is your life's fine gold?
Do you forget the Hand that placed the Crown
Of happy freedom on the Woman's head,
And took her from the dying and the dead,
Lifting the wounded soul, long trodden down?[51]

Missionary A. Deverill reported to the Society in 1878, "Heard yesterday of the sad and shocking death of one of my Zenana women, who destroyed her life by swallowing opium. Her husband's preference for another woman was the cause…. Oh, my heart is sad for her, and the question arises, had she understood from me the priceless love of Jesus? Oh, that I may be more faithful in the future to speak in season and out of season."[52]

Back in Britain: Divisions Continue

Divisions over theology, communion, missions, and polity created numerous crises for British Baptists. John Howard Hinton, British pastor and denominational leader, addressed such divisions in 1863. He described the many debates over Calvinism and Arminianism and over open versus closed communion. He delineated "six parties" evident among Baptists and concluded, "Denominational union among Baptists, has been slow in manifestation, and difficult of cultivation. We have long been a divided body, and we are so still; and if any progress at all has been made, it is questionable both that much remains to be done, and that the most recent efforts have met with little success.... The Baptist denomination, while in name one, is in fact many. If it were an evil spirit it might say, 'My name is Legion.'"[53] Such divisiveness even found its way into the ministries of England's most famous preacher, Charles Haddon Spurgeon, and the Baptist Union leader, John Clifford.

Charles Haddon Spurgeon

Charles Haddon Spurgeon (1834–1892) remains the best-known British Baptist preacher of the nineteenth century. His sermons drew multitudes to the Metropolitan Tabernacle, where he held forth to Sunday crowds of some ten thousand persons from 1861 until his death in 1892. Spurgeon's sermons remain popular to this day, published in multiple volumes throughout the world.

Born into a Congregationalist family on June 19, 1834, Spurgeon became a Baptist in 1850. He was soon preaching at a Cambridgeshire Baptist congregation with great success. In 1854, his reputation led to an invitation to become pastor of the prestigious New Park Street Chapel, London, then in decline. Baptist leaders Benjamin Keach and John Gill were numbered among its former pastors. Initially convinced that the congregation was mistaken in its choice, Spurgeon finally accepted their call with a statement characteristic of his sense of humility: "Remember my youth and inexperience, and pray that these may not hinder my usefulness. I trust also that the remembrance of these will lead you to forgive mistakes I may make, or unguarded words I may utter."[54] Its twelve-hundred-seat sanctuary soon was filled, and the church was forced to rent the much larger Exeter Hall in the Strand, where its forty-five hundred seats were almost immediately filled to capacity.[55] The church soon approved plans for a structure that would seat at least five thousand persons.

During the interim, Spurgeon scandalized many proper Londoners by holding services in the Surrey Music Hall, site of public entertainment spectacles. The crowds that came to hear him filled its twelve thousand seats. On October 19, 1856, a panic broke out in the Music Hall, contributing to the collapse of a balcony and the death of seven persons. Spurgeon was devastated, but he returned to the building and preached there to some ten thousand people each week until the completion of the Metropolitan Tabernacle in 1861. The Tabernacle's five-thousand-seat sanctuary became the center of Spurgeon's ministry until his death.

What drew the multitudes to Spurgeon's pulpit? The contents of his sermons reflected a traditional theology centered in an evangelical Calvinism that called sinners to a direct experience of grace through faith in Christ. In 1856, the *London Evening Star* reported of his preaching style, "When he has read his text, he does not fasten his eye on a manuscript and his hands to a cushion. As soon as he begins to speak, he begins to act—and that not as if declaiming on the stage, but as if conversing with you in the street. He seems to shake hands with all around, and put everyone at their ease."[56]

Spurgeon was a complex personality whose life and thought are not easily categorized. On the one hand, he seemed to be the pinnacle of Baptist orthodoxy, challenging the Baptist Union over theological liberalism and instigating the famous "Downgrade Controversy." On the other hand, he often seemed more concerned about converting individuals to Christ than about monitoring orthodoxy. When he felt that evangelism would be blunted by doctrinal negligence, he spoke out. He showed significant regard for Christian social action, based on his insistence that converted persons would then convert society.[57] Outspoken on many political issues of the time—alcohol abuse, slavery, poverty, education, and other causes—his responses often seemed somewhat naive and simplistic. He was sympathetic to the liberal Liberation Society and its defense of "political dissenters" in British life.[58] Intent on healing divisions created by class "warfare" in British, he even asserted, "Our confidence must be in our God, and under God, in ourselves; in our generous sympathy with one another; in the keeping of each rank in its own place."[59] At heart, Spurgeon was a conversionist, convinced that only through individual redemption could politics and society be transformed.

Spurgeon is one of the most widely published preachers of the Christian church, with almost four thousand of his sermons and two hundred books in print. The sermons were recorded by stenographers and edited by the preacher himself. In addition, he wrote numerous other works on church life and work, including the compilation of a catechism for children. Of that effort, he wrote, "I am persuaded that the use of a good Catechism in all our families will be a great safeguard against the increasing errors of the times, and therefore I have compiled this little manual from the Westminster Assembly's and Baptist Catechisms.... The words should be carefully learned by heart, for they will be understood better as the child advances in years."[60] Following the Westminster Catechism closely, it asked children to memorize doctrines. For example, in response to the question "What is justification?" the catechism states, "Justification is an act of God's free grace, wherein He pardoneth all our sins and accepteth us as righteous in His sight only for the righteousness of Christ imputed to us, and received by faith alone."[61]

Spurgeon was instrumental in the founding of Pastors' College in 1856. Later known as Spurgeon's College, it was intended as a training school for pastors and preachers who would "get to the hearts of the masses, to evangelize the poor."[62] Spurgeon was concerned that the school promote orthodoxy in the Calvinist tradition "within a broad context of scientific, philosophical and historical knowledge."[63] The school provided educational and ministerial instruction to working-class students. Spurgeon insisted that the school was a place where "rough and ready men could be drilled in the simple rudiments of education and so fitted for the work of preaching and discharge pastoral duties."[64] In 1880, the original two-year program was extended to three years. Soon it was preparing students to take London University examinations and extend their education further.

Charles Haddon Spurgeon had a significant impact on the public perception of Baptists in British society. His reputation, even in controversy, was unsurpassed in the religious life of nineteenth-century Britain. His sermons, books, theological concerns, and organizational activities shaped Baptist identity irrevocably.

John Clifford

Spurgeon's contemporary, another leader of nineteenth-century British Baptists, was John Clifford (1836–1923). His contributions included work as pastor, theologian, and denominational leader. Reared in the New Connection General Baptist chapel in Beeston, Nottinghamshire, Clifford was baptized at fifteen. He studied at Midland Baptist College, Leicester, and at University College, London. His pastorates were at Praed Street Baptist Church, London (1858–1877), and its successor, Westbourne Park Church, London (1877–1915). During his illustrious career, he served as editor of the *General Baptist Magazine,* as president of the Baptist Union, the National Council of Evangelical Free Churches, and the Baptist World Alliance, and in a variety of other positions.[65]

Clifford refused to differentiate between evangelism and social action as Christian responsibility. He called persons to conversion and urged Christians to respond to the social and political issues of their times. He insisted, "The business of a Christian Church is to find out the real needs of the people in the neighborhood in which it is placed and, as far as it can, supply all that will make for brightness and joy, for strength and service, for manhood and brotherhood. Now thousands of young men and women are in our locality, and we have a direct ministry to them and are responsible to God for discharging it."[66] Clifford's concern for social justice led him to oppose the Anglo-Boer War and the First World War. He was the champion of passive resistance to the Education Act of 1902, which gave advantages to Church of England schools at the expense of nonconformists.

The Downgrade Controversy

From his lofty pulpit, Spurgeon waded into controversies inside and outside the Baptist family. In 1864, he attacked what he believed to be the Anglican doctrine of baptismal regeneration. This also led him to break away from the British Evangelical Alliance. Divisions among Baptists as to Spurgeon's views led some to label him "the head of a denomination within a denomination."[67]

In 1865, Spurgeon and two other London Baptist pastors, William Brock (Bloomsbury Baptist Church) and William Landels (Regent's Park Chapel), founded a new London Baptist Association. *The Freeman* praised the expansiveness of the Association's intent, noting that "it was the ruling wish of all present was to give as little place as possible to differences of opinion, and rather to find the common basis on which they could practically agree."[68]

The greatest controversy of Spurgeon's life began in 1887 when a series of anonymous articles appeared in his periodical, *The Sword and the Trowel,* attacking the decline ("down grade") of nonconformist theology evident in the increasing presence of liberal ideas. One article, "The Down Grade," denounced these movements as detrimental to the Calvinist traditions of British Baptists.[69] Thus the "Downgrade Controversy" became the name for debates among Baptists over doctrine and practice. Later articles pointed to infidelity, Darwinism, and absence of evangelical zeal as evidence of the decline of Baptist spirituality and orthodoxy.

Spurgeon himself followed with another, more explosive series of articles. He charged, "A new religion has been initiated, which is no more like Christianity than chalk is cheese." It undermined the atonement, the authority of Scripture, the influence of the Spirit, and the resurrection of Christ.[70] Spurgeon refused to identify the liberals by name but insisted that they were present in Baptist life. Again, since no specific individuals were singled out, the charges cast aspersions on the work of a large segment of the Baptist ministerial community. He insisted that the Baptist Union could not continue to shelter this kind of unorthodoxy.

Baptist leaders, including John Clifford, responded to these charges, convinced that Spurgeon desired that all Baptists conform to his type of orthodoxy. Clifford urged Spurgeon to "trust us" in order to continue the work of God.[71]

Samuel Harris Booth was secretary of the Baptist Union, and Thomas Stockwell was editor of *The Baptist,* the conservative weekly periodical. Booth's attempts to keep the controversy from dividing British Baptists convinced Spurgeon that he was being "snubbed" and his concerns ignored. Spurgeon resigned from the Union on October 26, 1887. He used periodicals such as *The Sword and the Trowel* and *The Christian World* to circulate his views. In one article, he declared, "Fellowship with known and vital error is participation in sin."[72] Booth then urged the Union to make a public response to the controversy, while John Clifford and others urged Baptists to proceed with caution. Booth's efforts at developing a compromise kept many conservatives in the Union.[73]

In 1888, the Union appointed a committee to meet with Spurgeon. It was composed of Joseph Angus, John Clifford, Samuel Booth, and Alexander Maclaren. Their report to the Council of the Baptist Union led to the acceptance of Spurgeon's resignation. The Council also stated its recognition of "the gravity of the charges which Mr. Spurgeon has brought against the Union.… They consider that the public and general manner in which they have been made reflects on the whole body and exposes to suspicion brethren who love the truth as dearly as himself. And as Mr. Spurgeon declines to give the names of those to whom they apply, and the evidence supporting them … in the judgment of the council, [they] ought not to have been made."[74]

John Clifford opposed any suggestion that the Baptists needed a new creed. He charged that such statements were nothing more than "weapons of clerical absolution, tools of theological tyranny, padlocks on the Bible and foes of Christian brotherhood."[75] He wrote, "And for myself, I would elect a year in gaol rather than deliberately write against my brethren the terrible accusations in the 'Down Grade' articles, clench them by retiring from the Baptist Union, refuse to give either names or evidence, and leave my charges dangling on the side thread of one man's word."[76]

The Council approved a basic statement of beliefs that was not intended as a prerequisite for membership in the Union. The members of the London Baptist Association were deeply divided over the controversy and approved a doctrinal statement that they were willing to describe as a creed.[77] By 1888, the Downgrade Controversy had run its course, with no major split in the Baptist Union. Given Spurgeon's great popularity and public visibility, it was remarkable that the Union remained substantially intact. Nonetheless, there were serious fissures between Spurgeon's supporters and those who remained loyal to the Baptist Union. The seeds were sown for extended debates regarding the authority of Scripture, the role of confessions of faith, and the grounds for Baptist fellowship and cooperation.

Ecclesiology

Divisions over the nature of the church were evident among nineteenth-century British Baptists. Some promoted the traditional Puritan idea of the church as covenant community, whereby believers were united with God and one another. Others were drawn to the idea of the church as "a voluntary society," in which believers chose to unite for worship and fellowship.[78] Baptists were divided in their views of the church as a democratic congregation of believers or as a community of believers bound by the authority of Christ.

These divisions were personified in Andrew Fuller and John Clifford. Fuller affirmed congregationalism but suggested that the New Testament offered no complete system for church government. Rather, the New Testament communities formed a rudimentary polity upon which later Christians might build. While acknowledging New Testament guidance, Fuller gave room for adjustments in contemporary church life.[79] John Clifford, however, believed that churches were organizations that guided Christians toward the kingdom of God. He wrote, "The churches are Christ-appointed instruments for establishing the Kingdom of God and his righteousness, and for extending the gracious and redeeming power of God over the world."[80]

Nineteenth-century British Baptists also differed over the relationship between "doctrinal religion" and "experimental religion."[81] Did the church begin with the great dogmas of the faith, or with the personal religious experiences of individuals, who then became part of the community of faith? Obviously, both elements were essential, but the significance of each and their place in religious identity was a major concern of nineteenth-century British Baptist life.

Baptists in Scotland

Two efforts were made, in 1827 and 1835, to coordinate Baptist work in Scotland. The second resulted in the formation of the Baptist Union of Scotland in 1843 under the leadership of Francis Johnstone. Johnstone believed that the Union would encourage churches, establish a training school for ministers, create a fund for the construction of churches, sponsor the commissioning of itinerant preachers, and manage the printing of Sunday school materials. Some of these measures were developed, but not on a large scale.[82]

The Union itself went through numerous reorganizations. It was not until 1869 that a more permanent Baptist Union of Scotland was established. In that year, the Union set forth four basic goals: (1) to extend home missionary activity; (2) to offer financial support for struggling churches; (3) to encourage men to enter the ministry; and (4) to encourage Baptist identity and cooperation. Some of these programs were developed, but others, particularly educational efforts, met with limited success.[83]

British Baptists: Solid Denominationalism

As the nineteenth century came to a close, the British Baptist Union remained solidly intact. It weathered the fierce battles of the Downgrade Controversy with few losses. The Baptist Missionary Society created a world vision for fulfilling William Carey's mission imperative, and new missionaries were sent to other fields of service. Disputes over baptism and the Lord's Supper continued amid definitions of the nature of the church. Congregational polity prevailed even as a growing associational connectionalism linked churches in common fellowship and ministry. The once-beleaguered sect had become a denomination.

Notes

1. J. H. Y. Briggs, *The English Baptists of the Nineteenth Century* (Didcot, England: Baptist Historical Society, 1994), 18.
2. Ernest A. Payne, *The Baptist Union: A Short History* (London: Baptist Union of Great Britain and Ireland, 1959), 1.
3. Ibid., 21.
4. James Hinton, *The Baptist Magazine* (October 1812): 407–8. See also H. Leon McBeth, *A Sourcebook for Baptist Heritage* (Nashville: Broadman, 1990), 187.
5. Payne, *The Baptist Union*, 24.
6. Ibid., 3–4.
7. Ibid., 2.
8. Ibid., 91–93.
9. Ibid., 8–9, 66–67.
10. Alfred C. Underwood, *A History of the English Baptists* (London: Baptist Union Publishing Department, 1947), 171.
11. Ibid., 40–41.
12. Payne, *The Baptist Union*, 86.
13. Ibid., 86–87.
14. Ibid., 29 (citing W. T. Whitley, *Church, Ministry and Sacraments in the New Testament* [London: Kingsgate Press, 1903], 244).
15. Briggs, *English Baptists*, 63.
16. Ibid., 20.
17. Ibid., 21.
18. Paul R. Dekar, *For the Healing of the Nations: Baptist Peacemakers* (Macon, Ga.: Smyth & Helwys, 1993), 36–37 (citing *Testimonies of Ministers, of Various Denominations, Showing the Unlawfulness to Christians of all Wars, Offensive or Defensive* [London: G. Eccles, 1837]).
19. Ibid., 38.
20. Ibid., 39–40.
21. Ibid., 42–43.
22. Ibid., 43.
23. Underwood, *English Baptists*, 182.
24. Robert E. Cooper, *From Stepney to St. Giles': The Story of Regent's Park College, 1810–1960* (London: Carey Kingsgate Press, 1960), 37.
25. Payne, *The Baptist Union*, 94.
26. Briggs, *English Baptists*, 367–68.
27. Underwood, *English Baptists*, 78–79.
28. Payne, *The Baptist Union*, 76.
29. Ibid.
30. Ibid., 79.
31. Seymour J. Price, *Upton: The Story of One Hundred and Fifty Years 1785–1935* (London: Carey Press, 1935), 70; and Briggs, *English Baptists*, 73.
32. Basil Amey, *The Unfinished Story: A Study-Guide History of the Baptist Missionary Society* (London: Baptist Union of Great Britain, 1991), 18.
33. Ibid., 34.
34. Ibid., 25.
35. Stuart Piggin, *Making Evangelical Missionaries, 1789–1858* (London: Sutton Courtenay Press, 1984), 159.
36. George Howells and Alfred C. Underwood, *The Story of Serampore and Its College* (Serampore, India: 1918), 24.
37. Ibid., 25.
38. Ibid., 25.
39. Brian Stanley, *The History of the Baptist Missionary Society, 1792–1992* (Edinburgh: Clark, 1992), 178–85; Amey, *The Unfinished Story*, 65–66.
40. Amey, *The Unfinished Story*, 67; Stanley, *Baptist Missionary Society*, 189–96.
41. Amey, *The Unfinished Story*, 75.
42. Ibid., 83.
43. Baptist Missionary Society, *Jubilee 1867–1917: Fifty Years' Work among Women in the Far East* (London: Carey Press, 1917), 7.
44. Ibid., 8.
45. Ibid., 15.
46. Ibid.
47. Ibid., 14.
48. Ibid., 1.
49. Ibid., 3.
50. Ibid., 38.
51. Ibid., 39.
52. *Report of the Ladies' Association for the Support of Zenana Work and Bible Women in India, in Connection with the Baptist Missionary Society for 1877–78* (London, 1878), 55–56.

53. Payne, *The Baptist Union*, 85.
54. Charles Haddon Spurgeon, with Susannah Spurgeon and Joseph Harrald, *C. H. Spurgeon: The Early Years, 1834–1859* (London: Banner of Truth Trust, 1962), 87–88.
55. Albert R. Meredith, "Spurgeon and His Times: The Christian's Social Responsibility," *Quarterly Review* 35 (January–March 1975): 77–78.
56. Briggs, *English Baptists*, 32.
57. Meredith, "Spurgeon and His Times," 78–81.
58. Payne, *The Baptist Union*, 99.
59. Ibid., 78–81.
60. Charles Haddon Spurgeon, *A Catechism with Proof, Compiled by the Rev. C. H. Spurgeon* (London: Passmore & Alabaster, 1864), 13.
61. Ibid.
62. Briggs, *English Baptists*, 85.
63. Ibid.
64. Ibid., 89.
65. Dekar, *Healing of the Nations*, 61.
66. Ibid., 63.
67. Payne, *The Baptist Union*, 100.
68. Ibid., 101.
69. Nicholas D. Stepp, "The Downgrade Controversy: Following Jesus and Frequenting Theatres" (unpublished paper, Regent's Park College, Oxford, 2000), 20–21 (citing "The Down Grade," *The Sword and the Trowel* [March 1887]: 123). Stepp's excellent study utilized resources on the controversy not previously available.
70. Ibid., 23 (citing Charles Haddon Spurgeon, "Another Word Concerning the Down-Grade," *The Sword and the Trowel* [August 1887]: 397).
71. Ibid., 29.
72. Ibid., 31 (citing Charles Haddon Spurgeon, "The Down Grade," *The Christian World* [December 1, 1887]: 559).
73. The move of the Baptist Union from Baptist Church House, London, to a new facility at Didcot, near Oxford, led to the discovery of a box of materials pertaining to the Downgrade Controversy. See Mark Hopkins, "The Down Grade Controversy: New Evidence," *Baptist Quarterly* 35 (April 1994): 263.
74. Stepp, "The Downgrade Controversy," (citing "Rev. C. H. Spurgeon and the Baptist Union," *The Freeman* [20 January 1888]: 37).
75. Ibid., 40 (citing John Clifford, "Spurgeon's Appeal," *The Freeman* [8 February 1888]: 11).
76. Ibid. (citing Clifford, "Spurgeon's Appeal," 5).
77. Ibid., 43.
78. Briggs, *English Baptists*, 19–22.
79. Ibid., 16. See also Andrew Fuller, "Constitution of Apostolic Churches" (1810), in Andrew Gunton Fuller, *The Complete Works of the Rev. Andrew Fuller, with a Memoir of His Life*, 5 vols. (London: Holdsworth and Ball, 1831–32), 2:429.
80. Briggs, *English Baptists*, 23 (citing John Clifford, *The Free Churches of London: Their Faith and Their Future* [London: 1895], 13).
81. Ibid., 18.
82. H. Leon McBeth, *The Baptist Heritage* (Nashville: Broadman, 1987), 310.
83. Ibid., 311–12.

Chapter 8
Baptists in the United States: 1800–1845

BAPTISTS IN THE UNITED STATES CAME OF AGE IN THE NINETEENTH CENTURY. Once a persecuted minority of the colonial era, they became one of the new nation's largest denominations. Numerical growth led to the proliferation of Baptist subgroups born of conflicts and schism as well as regional, cultural, and theological differences. During this period, mission societies flourished, churches moved west, schools were established, and controversies raged, particularly over the question of human slavery. In 1790, there were 67,000 Baptists in the United States, with 61 percent in the South; by 1850, Baptists claimed 715,000 church members, with 59 percent in the South.[1]

As the nineteenth century got underway, America confronted the realities of nationhood. For the churches, religious liberty and the First Amendment meant that establishment gave way to voluntarism. Religious groups were compelled to secure "volunteers" who chose to participate in their particular brand of Christianity. National denominations developed as churches organized to establish colleges, mission boards, and publishing houses. So extensive was their influence that Sidney Mead labeled denominations the "shape of Protestantism" in the United States.[2] Denominationalism grew slowly but surely among Baptists, many of whom mistrusted bureaucracy and ecclesiastical hierarchies.

Baptists on the Frontier

The beginning of the nineteenth century brought significant migration to the frontier, the land west of the Allegheny Mountains. As noted previously, Baptists had migrated into frontier areas of the South—the Carolinas and Georgia—by the mid-1700s. As they moved west, they became part of another religious renewal, this one often referred to as the Second Great Awakening. The Awakening was associated with camp meetings that brought together Presbyterians, Methodists, Baptists, and other groups. Early camp meetings can be traced to the work of Presbyterian preachers such as James McGready (ca.1758–1817) and the "Sacramental" gatherings (meetings that concluded with the Lord's Supper) he instigated at his three frontier churches in Logan County, Kentucky. The meetings attracted large crowds and resulted in conversions and other expressions of "enthusiastical" religion.

Another Presbyterian preacher, Barton W. Stone (1772–1844), called a camp meeting at his log church at Cane Ridge, Bourbon County, Kentucky. Held in August 1801, the Cane Ridge camp meeting attracted an estimated crowd of from ten to twenty-five thousand people, including preachers of various denominations. Conversions were characterized by exuberant, emotional outbursts sometimes known as "exercises." As Stone described them, "The bodily agitations or exercises, attending the excitement in the beginning of this century, were various, and called by various names;—as, the falling exercise—the jerks—the dancing exercise—the barking exercise—the laughing and singing exercise, &c All classes, saints and sinners, the strong as well as the weak, were thus affected."[3]

Baptists participated in these assemblies, and their converts experienced many of the exercises. One Baptist leader maintained, "During the great revival that prevailed some three or four years previous to this date, and that still prevailed to some extent, falling down, jerking, laughing, and dancing, accompanied the religious exercises. These exercises prevailed to some extent among the Baptists, but more especially among the Methodists and Presbyterians."[4]

Frontier Competition

Competition among denominations evolved rapidly on the frontier. Churches that cooperated in the camp meetings soon competed openly for members. Methodist circuit rider, preacher, and raconteur Peter Cartwright (1785–1872) was quick to distinguish between the work of Methodists and that of Baptists on the frontier. In his autobiography, Cartwright recalled those days in the early nineteenth century:

> We preached in new settlements, and the Lord poured out his Spirit, and we had many convictions and many conversions. It was the order of the day, (though I am sorry to say it), that we were constantly followed by a certain set of proselyting Baptist preachers. These new and wicked settlements were seldom visited by these Baptist preachers until the Methodist preachers entered them; then, when a revival was gotten up, or the work of God revived, these Baptist preachers came rushing in, and they generally sung their sermons; and when they struck the long roll, or their sing-song mode of preaching, in substance it was "water!" "water!" "you must follow your blessed Lord down to the water!" ... Indeed, they made so much ado about baptism by immersion, that the uninformed would suppose that heaven was an island, and there was no way to get there but by diving or swimming.[5]

Peter Cartwright was an able opponent of the Baptists, often debating them and drawing converts from Baptist revivals into Methodist churches.

The Baptists responded to their critics, sometimes through their hymnody. One hymn from the frontier staked out the Baptist claim to be the one true New Testament church:

> Not at the Jordan River,
> But in that flowing stream,
> Stood John the Baptist preacher,
> When he baptized Him.
> John was a Baptist preacher,
> When he baptized the Lamb,
> So Jesus was a Baptist,
> And thus the Baptists came.[6]

Frontier Ministry

Congregational polity and local autonomy were well suited for frontier culture. Churches were constituted by constituents who required no approval from ecclesiastical tribunals. Many Baptist ministers were "farmer-preachers," individuals who lived in the community, worked the land throughout the week, and preached on Sunday. These grassroots ministers were often semiliterate or self-taught persons who exercised gifts of proclamation and ministry. Their bivocational occupations kept them close to the soil and to the people.[7]

Frontier Baptists soon developed procedures for recognizing and ordaining potential ministers. Debates continued over the education of ministers, clergy compensation, and the nature of ministerial authority—unending controversies in Baptist life. Ordination to ministry generally required a statement of conversion and "call" as verified by the congregation. One initiatory step involved "licensing," whereby a congregation formally vouched for an individual's calling and provided a kind of ministerial apprenticeship prior to ordination.

Licensed ministers and newly ordained preachers could also serve as "exhorters"—a particular assignment given to preach in the revivals. Exhorters were asked to "draw in the net" by entreating persons to receive salvation after the more seasoned preacher had offered the principal sermon. While some congregations permitted licensed ministers to conduct baptism and the Lord's Supper, most required full ordination as a prerequisite for administering the ordinances.

When the verification process was complete, an ordination could occur, often after the new minister received an official call from a specific congregation. An ordaining council (or presbytery) was constituted by local ministers, deacons, and associational representatives who evaluated the candidate's doctrinal soundness and spiritual maturity. The council made a recommendation that was voted on by the church. Candidates were required to describe their call, as illustrated in this statement from a nineteenth-century ordinand: "Tried evade it by excuses—had no gift for public speaking—my education was extremely limited—was wholly destitute of means to defray the expense of an education—and above all I lacked a natural ability.... At such seasons I was often much distressed and could find peace of mind only by yielding the point—casting myself wholly upon the Grace of Christ, with the determination, to do what seemed to be present duty to the extend my ability leaving the result with God."[8] The interaction between the church and the individual was an important element in discerning the veracity of the divine mandate for ministry.

Ordinations also could be revoked. In 1874, the Walnut Street Baptist Church, Louisville, Kentucky, revoked the ordination of a young man found guilty of public intoxication. The defrocked minister wrote to the church asking for reconsideration. He acknowledged that the charges against him were true. He was guilty, but only on two occasions: once after he conducted the funeral of his brother, and the second time after he was called as pastor of a Baptist church in Alabama.[9] The congregation did not relent, and the revocation stood.

Frontier Churches

Frontier congregations formed rapidly. Baptists continued to promote revivals, known as "protracted meetings," that began at a particular time and ended when the Spirit seemed to have run its course. These assemblies were scheduled around the farming cycle, with revivals in spring after planting and in fall before or after harvest. They became a staple of Baptist life in many regions of the country as a means of evangelizing sinners and renewing the spiritual life of the churches.

Church Order: The Documents

Churches often were organized around three types of documents: a covenant, a confession of faith, and rules of decorum. The covenant set forth the behavioral regulations to which members were subject. John Taylor (1752–1836) reported on the organization of the Buck Run Church in Kentucky in 1818 and its covenantal agreement "to fulfil the duty of brethren to each other."[10]

A confession of faith established the theological foundations of the church. Most congregations used existing confessions, such as the Second London or Philadelphia Confessions, or a combination of statements excerpted from several confessions and dealing with God, Scripture, faith, church, ordinances, salvation, final judgment, and other dogmas.

Rules of decorum dictated procedures for conducting the congregation's business, including election of officers and proper behavior during the meeting. The rules of the Buck Run Church stated, "There shall be no laughing, talking, or whispering in the time of a public speech, nor shall there be any ungenerous reflections on a brother who has spoken before."[11] Proper decorum required members to "move their membership" when taking up residence in a new location. As the Buck Run documents advised, "We consider it the duty of members, in removing their residence to distant bounds, to apply to the church for a letter of dismission, and join some other church, with speed or as soon as duty and prudence may dictate."[12] These documents were sources of order and stability, at least until members differed over their use or interpretation.

Frontier Baptisms

Baptisms were administered in creeks and rivers at every season of the year. John Taylor reports, "Sometimes two of us went into the water at once to baptize, and to prevent confusion, only one pronounced the ceremony, and that by the plural term, standing near together, and both getting ready, one would pronounce 'we baptize you in the name of the Father &c.'" He recalled that he "once baptized 26 myself, on a cold freezing day, the ice cut about six inches thick where the people stood, close on the edge of the icy grave."[13]

Baptisms were profoundly important rituals, with the congregation gathered all around, some shouting or crying when the candidate "went under." The community then reached out to the new converts, drying them off and welcoming them into the fellowship of the church.

Baptist Women and Frontier Churches

Women were at the center of frontier Baptist church life. In *Southern Cross: The Beginnings of the Bible Belt,* Christine Leigh Heyrman took a revisionist look at the impact of Southern evangelicalism on family values, the role of women, and ministerial identity. Among other things, Heyrman traced the changes in the perception of women in the revivalistic religious environments. Using journals and letters from both women and men, she contended that in the early days of the revivals, "Preachers not only regarded women's religious opinions as worthy of discussion but also endorsed their right to acquire the skills that would enable them to make independent judgments based on firsthand knowledge of the Bible."[14]

Baptists and other evangelical preachers gave great credibility to the "religious seriousness" of Christian women—a fact that served to draw women to the faith. In the early revivals, Baptists seemed willing to permit women to speak or "prophesy" in religious gatherings of both sexes—a practice that later would be abandoned. "Testifying" in "mixed gatherings" seems to have been more permissible for females than actual sermonizing.

These practices were encouraged by Baptist preachers such as John Taylor, who "celebrated his slave Letty, whose account of her conversion before his Kentucky church at the opening of the nineteenth century 'was more striking to the assembly present, than the loudest preachings.'"[15]

Critics viewed these activities as a violation of biblical mandates regarding women's silence in church. Many a "godless" husband was enraged by his wife's conversion and church affiliation. Yet preachers such as Taylor insisted that a wife's witness might ultimately lead to the husband's conversion. When Thomas Reese's wife received baptism, he concluded that she had "disregarded" and deserted him for religion. Reese stormed off, only to be overtaken by religious conviction. He subsequently was converted and received baptism.[16]

Fearing the loss of men to the church, ministers soon encouraged women to exercise their primary religious influence in the confines of the home rather than in the public arena. In the early days of the revivals, Baptist preachers sometimes secretly administered immersion to wives who feared to tell their husbands of their conversion. Later, the acquiescence of the husband became almost mandatory.

On one occasion, John Taylor accepted a woman who came for baptism, noting, "I reminded the church of her husband who sat near the door, the utility of his approbation, in her joining the church, he rose up before the question was asked of him and gave his consent."[17] Thus, frontier Baptists seem to have modified their response to women in an effort to appeal to men. These actions reflect the development of what some have termed the "woman's sphere"—prescribed boundaries in which women had great influence but beyond which they were not to venture. They could prepare communion but not serve it, feed the preacher but not preach themselves.

Baptist Subdenominations: Regulars and Separates

While divisions over doctrine and practice continued to occur within the Baptist ranks, there were also efforts at unity. The Separate and Regular Baptists, long divided over revival methods, worship, and the nature of ministry, sought greater union as early as the 1780s. In Kentucky, an alliance of Regulars and Separates formed in 1801 under the name United Baptists. The union was short-lived, ending in 1803 when the Elkhorn Association withdrew from the South Kentucky Association of Separate Baptists because the organization admitted a supposed Universalist to its membership.[18] After this split, Separate Baptists formed a Kentucky-based General Association of Separate Baptists in Christ. The South Kentucky Association and the Nolyn Association of Kentucky were the oldest and largest of the Separate Baptist associations.[19]

Separates in Kentucky rejected mission boards, a hired clergy, and the use of confessions of faith. They claimed that Baptists manifested the only genuine form of a New Testament church, and they placed great emphasis on individual interpretation of Scripture and doctrine. By the early twentieth century, they composed confessions of faith and required subscription to those documents as a testimony to orthodoxy in their ranks.[20] Many congregations practiced the washing of feet along with baptism and the Lord's Supper as ordinances of Christ.

Baptist Missions in America

Many nineteenth-century Baptists were convinced that theirs was a global task. Although this was not a new idea, it did create a new impetus to establish missionary societies and boards in a systematic effort to convert the "heathen." These early societies created the earliest national identity among Baptists. Millennialism and apocalyptic expectations shaped the missions movement. Many early revivalists, including Jonathan Edwards and Charles G. Finney (1792–1875), were postmillennialists. They believed that a millennium (a thousand years) of peace and spiritual enlightenment would precede the return of Jesus Christ. The church would expedite this golden age as religious revivals and mass conversions anticipated Christ's second coming. The conversion of the heathen would be one important indication that the millennium was at hand.[21]

Premillennialism—the belief that Jesus would return before the millennium as a divine intervention in an ever-deteriorating world—gained increasing popularity in the nineteenth century. Since the return of Christ was imminent, missionary activities and revivals were necessary to "snatch souls from the burning" before the final judgment.

Regional Missionary Societies

The earliest Baptist missionary organizations came from regional societies formed by associations and individuals. The Boston Female Society, founded by a group of eight Baptist and six Congregational women in October 1800, was one of the first women's missionary organizations in the United States. Its leader, Mary Webb (1779–1861), a person with certain physical disabilities, was an able spokesperson for the missionary cause. Initially concerned for missionary ventures on the frontier, the society later raised support for British Baptist missions in India.[22] It was comprised of women who were willing "to contribute their mite toward so noble a design as diffusion of the gospel light among the shades of darkness and superstition."[23]

The group distributed Bibles and other religious materials through the Congregational Massachusetts Missionary Society and soon funded its own appointees. Similar mission organizations were created by Baptists in each state between 1802 and 1820.[24]

Webb also helped form the Female Baptist Missionary Society in 1802. Members pledged one dollar a year to missionary support. Another agency known as the "Cent Society" asked only one penny a week from its members.[25]

The New York Missionary Society (1796) was the first American interdenominational organization, with work among the Chickasaws in Georgia and Tennessee. Baptists remained part of this organization until 1806, when they departed in a dispute over the baptismal mode administered to Native American converts.[26]

The Massachusetts Baptist Missionary Society, founded in 1802 and led by Thomas Baldwin, sent three missionaries to the American frontier the first year. The Society's purpose was "to furnish occasional preaching and to promote a knowledge of evangelistic truth, in the new settlements, within these Northern States, or farther, if circumstances should render it proper."[27] Probably the first home mission society begun by American Baptists was the Massachusetts Baptist Domestic Missionary Society, formed in 1802 with guidance from churches in the Warren Association of New England Baptists.[28]

In the South, Baptist Hepzibah Townsend founded the Wadmalaw and Edisto Female Mite Society in 1812, comprised of females in those two South Carolina villages. They supported mission work among the Catawbas.[29] The Virginia Baptist Foreign Mission Society, the first such regional organization in the South, was created in 1813. These women joined in "prayer concerts"—gatherings to pray for missions, revival, and church renewal. They frequently were opposed by men who charged that women should not be permitted to conduct religious services.[30]

A National Mission Society

The first national mission society was organized in 1810 by American Congregationalists. Known as the American Board of Commissioners for Foreign Missions, some of its earliest missionaries were Adoniram Judson (1788–1850), Ann Hasseltine Judson (1789–1826), and Luther Rice (1783–1836), a trio commissioned for India in 1812. Their decision to become Baptists led to the founding of a national mission society.

The First Baptist Missionaries

Adoniram Judson attended Andover Seminary at a time when many of its faculty were evangelical Calvinists committed to the missionary enterprise.[31] Ann Hasseltine attended Bradford Academy, founded in 1803 and one of the first institutions to provide formal education for women. While there, she read the works of Jonathan Edwards, Samuel Hopkins, and Joseph Bellamy—ministers intent on promoting revivals and morality in American society.

Of her own conversion, in 1806, she wrote, "I felt a disposition to commit myself unreservedly into his [God's] hands, and leave it with him to save me or cast me off."[32] It was said of her, "When reading Scripture, sermons, or other works, if she met with any sentiment or doctrine, which seemed dark and intricate, she would mark it, and beg the first clergyman who called at her father's, to elucidate and explain it."[33]

Hasseltine's decision to marry Judson and accompany him to India did not come easily. She wrote, "Yes, I think I would rather go to India, among the heathen, notwithstanding the almost insurmountable difficulties in the way, than to stay at home and enjoy the comforts and luxuries of life…. O, if he [God] will condescend to make me useful in promoting his kingdom, I care not where I perform his work, nor how hard it be."[34]

On board ship, they accepted Baptist views and, on September 6, 1812, received immersion at the hands of British Baptist missionaries. Judson's resignation, submitted to the American Board, stated, "The board will, undoubtedly, feel as unwilling to support a Baptist missionary as I feel to comply with their instructions, which particularly direct us to baptize 'credible believers with their households...'.' Whether the Baptist churches in America will be compassionate about my situation, I know not. I hope, therefore, that while my friends condemn what they deem a departure from the truth, they will at least pity me and pray for me."[35] India was no longer a viable mission station, so the Judsons moved to Burma, establishing residence in Rangoon and appealing to the Baptists for help.

Ann Hasseltine Judson fretted that her American friends would not understand her decision. She wrote to one, "Can you, my dear Nancy, still love me, still desire to hear from me, when I tell you I have become a Baptist? If I judge from my own feelings, I answer, you will, and that my differing from you in those things which do not affect our salvation will not diminish your affection for me, or make you unconcerned for my welfare."[36]

In her "cultural biography" of the Judson clan, Joan Jacobs Brumberg commented, "A conspicuous feature of the evangelicalism that absorbed New England and upstate New York in the period 1790 to 1850 was denominational mobility."[37] Persons changed affiliations in search of a clearer revelation and perhaps as "an institutional response to the geographic mobility that characterized the lives of so many in the antebellum period."[38] Luther Rice, the Judsons' missionary colleague, soon returned to the United States to encourage the Baptists there to support the Judsons. This action led to the formation of the first national Baptist mission society.

The Triennial Convention

The work of William Carey, along with the request of the Judsons, influenced the decision to begin a national society for Baptist missions. Rice's meeting with the Charleston Association in 1813 led to a recommendation "that a common united effort among the baptist churches in the United States to send the gospel among the Heathen, and Nations destitute of pure gospel light, is both laudable and expedient."[39]

In May 1814, delegates gathered in Philadelphia and formed the General Missionary Convention of the Baptist Denomination the United States. Known as the Triennial Convention because of its national meeting every three years, this body assumed support of the Judsons in Burma and established procedures for sending out other individuals. Its Constitution declared, "We the delegates from Missionary Societies, and other religious Bodies of the Baptist denomination, in various parts of the United States, met in Convention, in the City of Philadelphia, for the purpose of carrying into effect the benevolent Intentions of our Constituents, by organizing a plan for eliciting, combining, and directing the Energies of the whole Denomination in one sacred effort, for sending the glad tidings of Salvation to the Heathen, and to nations destitute of pure Gospel-light."[40] The willingness to use the word "denomination" to describe this new society was an important step for Baptists in the new nation. It brought together various associations, individuals and churches concerned about the foreign missionary task.

The constitution set the terms for the new organization: "That a triennial Convention shall, hereafter, be held, consisting of Delegates, not exceeding two in number, from each of the several Missionary Societies, and other religious bodies of the Baptist denomination, now existing, or which may hereafter be formed in the United States, and which shall each, regularly contribute to the Missionary Fund, a sum, amounting, at least, to one hundred Dollars, per annum."[41] Richard Furman, pastor of First Baptist Church, Charleston, South Carolina, was elected the first president of the body, and Boston's Thomas Baldwin (1753–1825) was chosen as secretary.

The Society in Baptist Organizational Life

Organizing a national Baptist missionary society was no easy task. Many feared that connectional alliances would undermine the autonomy of local congregations and contribute to the growth of a dreaded Baptist hierarchy. Previous ventures had not succeeded. As early as 1799, the Philadelphia Association had called for "a general conference, composed of one or more members from each Association, to be held every one, two, or three years, as may seem most subservient to the general interests of our Lord's kingdom."[42] This proposal was largely ignored because the objectives were not clearly defined, associations were forming state connections, and many Baptists remained suspicious of a national organization.[43]

- Societies were a compromise measure that permitted Baptists to form loosely knit agencies for pursuing specific ministries while avoiding elaborate bureaucracies. The Triennial Convention was itself a compromise between proponents of two divergent views of Baptist polity and organization. As Robert Baker commented, "The associational method of organization stressed denominationalism, while the society type magnified church independency and benevolence."[44]

Societies allowed local churches and individuals to select specific programs that they wished to support. Each society was responsible for raising its own funds. By contrast, the convention or associational system linked agencies more connectionally, with potential for collective funding from a common source.

Supporters insisted that societies were no threat to congregational autonomy. The Illinois Baptist Convention reported that societies "all disclaim, in the most express manner, all interference with the rights of churches" and concluded that Baptists had "the same authority to form such societies, as they have to form a society for any purpose."[45]

Initially, the Triennial Convention focused only on foreign mission endeavors. Additional societies for publishing, home missions, education, and evangelism soon were organized. There was limited connection among the various societies, each of which maintained its own programs and support. In this way, Baptists sought to avoid elaborate and centralized denominational structures.

Women's Missionary Societies

In 1834, David Abell, a Baptist missionary to China, issued an appeal for single women who would take the gospel to females otherwise unreachable with the Christian message. It went unheeded until 1861, when a Mrs. Doremus helped form the Woman's Union Missionary Society, an ecumenical organization of six denominations. Northern Baptist women organized the Woman's Baptist Foreign Missionary Society in Boston in 1871. That same year, in

Chicago, the Woman's Baptist Missionary Society of the West was founded. Within a decade, these two groups were supporting fifty-six American missionaries, ninety-eight "Bible women" (teacher-evangelists), and ninety-eight educational institutions.[46]

A Woman's Baptist Home Mission Society was established in 1877 in Chicago, and another formed in Boston in 1878. The Chicago-based society organized mission work among Native Americans, immigrants, and African Americans in places such as Selma, Alabama, Oklahoma Territory, and Minnesota.[47]

A Home Missionary Training School for women was begun in Chicago in 1881, aimed at training women for missionary service. That same year, the Atlanta Female Baptist Seminary was formed for African American women. Its name was changed to Spelman Female Baptist Seminary in 1884, and the school later became Spelman University.[48]

As early as 1868, Southern Baptist women held mission gatherings during the meetings of the Southern Baptist Convention (SBC). Women who accompanied their husbands to the annual SBC used those occasions to build relationships and develop mission strategy. Women's societies, organized in local churches throughout the South, established "Woman's Work" through programs coordinated by state-based Central Committees of Baptist women, the first one formed in 1876.[49] These efforts culminated in the founding of the Woman's Missionary Union, an auxiliary to the Southern Baptist Convention, in May 1888, aimed at "stimulating the missionary spirit and the grace of giving among the women and children of the churches and aiding in collecting funds for missionary purposes."[50] As an auxiliary, the Woman's Missionary Union created its own structure but functioned in cooperation with the Foreign Mission Board of the Southern Baptist Convention itself. Leaders assured men that they would not form a competing society. Lottie Moon, longtime missionary to China, wrote, "What we want is not power…. Power of appointment and of disbursing of funds should be left, as heretofore, in the hands of the Foreign Mission Board. Separate organization is undesirable, and would do harm; but organization in subordination to the Board is the imperative need of the hour."[51] Women's missionary work was thus an "auxiliary" to the "official" work led by men. It provided some of the most important funding and overall energy for the missionary enterprise among white Baptists in the South.

Baptist Periodicals

Religious periodicals were an early medium for communicating ideas and information. The first Baptist periodical in England was founded in 1790 as the *Baptist Annual Register,* with John Rippon, pastor of Horsley Down Church, London, as editor. In the United States, the first such journal was the *Massachusetts Baptist Missionary Magazine,* published by the Massachusetts Baptist Missionary Society in 1803. It became the official paper of the Triennial Convention in 1817 and later was renamed the *American Baptist Magazine.*[52] *The Watchman,* the first Baptist weekly, began in 1819. By the middle of the nineteenth century, Baptist periodicals were found throughout the country. Often, these papers combined with others in a seemingly unending series of mergers. For example, in Kentucky, the *Baptist Register,* founded in 1826, became the *Baptist Recorder.*

The Massachusetts Baptist Missionary Society, founded in 1802, began the *Massachusetts Baptist Missionary Magazine* in 1803. It circulated letters and other accounts of William Carey and the early Baptist Missionary Society work, while encouraging American

Baptists to respond to the task at hand. Carey himself wrote to William Rogers of Philadelphia, "I would strongly recommend to our Baptist brethren in America, the forming of a Mission Society.... The change of sentiment in brethren Judson and Rice, is a strong inducement for you so to do, and lays the churches in America under obligations different from any under which they lay before."[53]

Baptist missionary publications also increased information regarding the new work upon which the denomination and its churches had embarked. These included the *Massachusetts Baptist Missionary Magazine,* which was edited for fourteen years by Thomas Baldwin, pastor of Second Baptist Church, Boston, and which, as noted, became the *American Baptist Magazine.* Others included the *Latter Day Luminary* (1818), the *Christian Watchman* (1819), the *Columbian Star* (1822), and the *Religious Herald* (1828). These periodicals published sermons, financial appeals, and correspondence with missionaries. They represented a significant medium for disseminating information about missions, missionaries, and other ecclesial issues.[54]

The magazines also published accounts of missionary hardships. James Colman, missionary to Burma, wrote that God "has commanded his servants to go into all the world, and has engaged never to forsake them. Why then should difficulties appall me? ... Oh, that I might have the privilege of suffering for Christ in India." Colman died shortly after his arrival on the mission field.[55]

Baptist educator Francis Wayland saw missionary work as a means of redeeming the world "from the miseries of the Fall" and insisted, "Our indignation has kindled at hearing of men imortal as ourselves, bowing down and worshiping a wandering begar, or paying adoration to reptiles and to stones."[56] As Christianity had civilized Europe and America, so it would the rest of the world. James Colman speculated that if Christianity prevailed in Burma, "that wretched country would exhibit quite a different appearance."[57]

The Tract Society

Many of these articles were republished for circulation by the Baptist General Tract Society, founded February 25, 1824, in Washington, D.C. Its primary responsibility was the publication of educational materials on the Bible, doctrine, evangelism, and Christian instruction. The Society headquarters moved to Philadelphia in 1826 and made slow progress until 1840, when it became the American Baptist Publication and Sunday-School Society. In 1844, it was renamed the American Baptist Publication Society. This society provided books, tracts, and Sunday school materials for the Baptist constituency. The materials were sold by representatives known as "colporteurs." These traveling evangelists plied their wares in churches, on trains, and on the open road.

The Home Mission Society

In 1817, the Triennial Convention expanded its mission activities to include an educational institution and home mission work among Native Americans. John Mason Peck (1789–1858) and James E. Welch (1789–1876) were sent as missionaries to the Western Territory (Missouri). In April 1832, New York Baptists formed the Home Mission Society, authorized to carry out mission work throughout the United States. The first executive committee was charged with obtaining and disseminating information "respecting the actual moral condition of the country; particularly, as to that of the Valley of the Mississippi, and more especially within the Baptist denomination." The intent was to "excite the entire Baptist community to systematic, liberal and vigorous action ... [toward] the preaching of the gospel to every creature in our country."[58]

Home mission societies were encouraged to work with the new national society in raising funds and appointing candidates. Leaders apparently hoped that "the [fundraising] agent of each auxiliary would also be the agent of the parent society."[59] "Missionary agents"—itinerants who had no specific congregations—were distinguished from settled missionaries. Agents traveled extensively, aided "feeble churches" in securing pastors, developed "new fields of labour," preached widely, and submitted reports to the executive committee of the Society.[60] The report of 1836 detailed the work of Ebenezer Loomis, an Ohio missionary agent who in one year traveled 4,505 miles, preached 297 sermons, raised funds, "baptized several," and performed "other ministerial labour." The report showed that some ninety-six missionaries and agents had received appointment for all or a portion of the year.[61]

Jonathan Going (1786–1844) was named the first corresponding secretary. Going, a colleague of Peck, was committed to the cause of home missions. In 1837, he became president and professor at Granville Literary and Theological Institution in Ohio (now Denison University). The Society was based in New York, where it remained for more than a century. Like the Foreign Mission Society (General Convention), the Home Mission Society was a freestanding organization, charged with securing its own support. Its executive committee passed this resolution in 1836: "Resolved, That the Foreign Mission and Home Mission societies are so far from being rival institutions, they are twin sisters, and each an indispensable auxiliary to the other."[62]

The Home Mission Society permitted both individual and ecclesiastical memberships and contributions. The constitution stated, "Any person may become a member of this Society by contributing annually to its funds." It also noted, "Any Baptist Church, or Association, or State Convention, or Missionary Society, that contributes annually to the objects of this Society, shall be entitled to be represented by one or more delegates, in its annual meetings."[63] Other societies tended to limit delegates to individuals who made minimal contributions, not permitting membership from churches or associations.

Francis Wayland: The Dilemma of Denominationalism

The failure of Columbian College illustrated the difficulty of Baptist denominational cooperation. Why did these Baptists reject greater denominational connectionalism? Why were they so hesitant to link their societies and their funds in common endeavor?[68] Such hesitancy reflected a general mistrust of "hierarchical" alignments and a suspicion among some that formal education would weaken personal faith.[69]

The tensions over denominational connectionalism and congregational autonomy were personified in Baptist leader Francis Wayland (1796–1865). One of American Baptists' most prominent preachers and educators, he served as pastor of First Baptist Church, Boston, and then served as president of Brown University for twenty-eight years. An early advocate of denominational alignments, Wayland later rejected such arrangements, at least on a national scale, as detrimental to congregational and regional autonomy.

During the 1820s, under the pseudonym "Backus," he wrote a series of articles for the *American Baptist Magazine* in which he proposed a basic method for Baptist connectionalism. Wayland described the denominational linkage simply: "The model of our system of general and state governments will at once suggest itself to every American. The Associations in one state could easily send delegates to a state convention. This would embody all the information, and concentrate the energies of a state. These state conventions could send delegates to a general convention, and thus the whole denomination might be brought to concentrated and united action."[70] He made it clear that these affiliations would not involve "any creeds or articles to be imposed on ourselves, or our brethren. The Bible is our only standard, and it is a sufficient standard of faith and practice. But the fact is, we all understand the Bible alike, and we understand it in a manner somewhat different from any other denominations of Christians."[71] Baptist distinctiveness was itself a form of unity. This position, set forth early in Wayland's career, allowed for local, regional, and national relationships.

Wayland later repudiated the idea of an elaborate connectionalism as detrimental to congregational and individual freedom. Societies, he believed, were the only appropriate means of promoting cooperation. He wrote, "A missionary society is not a representative body, nor can any number of them speak the language of a whole denomination."[72] Society members came together "not as representatives of churches, for the churches have never sent them nor commissioned them; they come together on their own motion, merely as members of the Union, or of the Home Mission, or Bible, or any other Society."[73]

By 1859, Wayland had acknowledged the cumbersome nature of the society method, with its many duplications of programs and procedures. Rather than support greater centralization through a national denomination, however, he urged a return to direct local-church funding of mission work. Wayland's difficulties with denominationalism illustrate the Baptist struggle with affiliations beyond the local and regional levels.

Baptist State Conventions

State conventions were another form of regional Baptist organization. Many grew out of general committees of correspondence comprised of representatives from Baptist associations in a given geographic area. In 1812, a group of seven associations in North Carolina formed a general committee comprised of up to four messengers from each association. Its purpose was "to extend religious acquaintance, to encourage the preaching of the gospel and to diffuse useful knowledge."[74] These actions prepared the way for state convention organizations.

In 1821, South Carolina Baptists formed the first state convention in the United States, with Charleston pastor Richard Furman as president. While its members included representatives of Baptists from throughout the state, only three of seven associations participated. Soon, other state conventions were formed: Virginia, 1823; Georgia, 1827; Alabama, 1823; and North Carolina, 1830. Many of these regional efforts were minority movements in states divided over missions, education, and bureaucracy.

In 1826, the New York State Baptist Convention was founded through a union of the Hamilton Baptist Missionary Society (1808) and the Baptist Missionary Society of New York. Its specific purposes included these: (1) "to promote the preaching of the gospel and establishment and maintenance of Baptist churches in New York state"; (2) to encourage Baptist educational endeavors; (3) to establish denominational Sunday school programs; and (4) "to promote denominational acquaintance, fellowship and growth."[75]

State conventions fostered unity, identified Baptist principles, stressed the centrality of Scripture as the rule of faith, promoted cooperation among churches, and encouraged missionary endeavors.[76] Yet their existence sometimes caused concern among those who feared that such connectionalism would undermine the centrality of the local congregation. Francis Wayland ultimately viewed state bodies to be as problematic as national ones. He wrote in 1856, "When State Conventions were first proposed, it was by many believed … that through them we might establish a general Baptist organization.… I now rejoice exceedingly that the whole plan failed, and that it failed through the sturdy common sense of the masses of our brethren. The churches were from the first unwilling to confer this power on the Association."[77]

Christian Education

Baptists attended to education by founding schools and developing training programs in churches. They struggled with funding these endeavors and debated their purpose and methods.

A National College

As societies took shape, many Baptists urged the formation of a national Baptist educational institution. Some wanted to locate such a school in Philadelphia, while others preferred Washington, D.C. In 1820, the Triennial Convention developed plans for Columbian College, a school to be chartered in Washington in 1821. William Staughton (1770–1829), pastor of First Baptist Church, Philadelphia, and founder of the Philadelphia Theological Institute, was named principal of the school. Staughton hoped to unite missionary and educational work in Baptist benevolent activities. In an 1821 address he noted, "It is desirable that a public teacher be able to read the pages of inspiration in the languages in which they are written.… In the present age when missionaries are passing into almost every region of the earth, it is evident that to enable them with greater facility to acquire new languages, and to translate the Scriptures from the original text, a sound and extensive education is not only desirable, but necessary."[64]

Born in England, Staughton immigrated to the United States in 1793, and in 1805 he became pastor of First Baptist Church, Philadelphia. The church flourished during this period, assisting in the formation of the First African Baptist Church in Philadelphia, in 1809.

Staughton was active in the founding of the Triennial Convention and believed that the gospel offered both salvation and civilization to native peoples. In a 1798 address, he linked that process with Baptist missions to the Native Americans: "This [Philadelphia Missionary] Society while it is anxious that the heathen may hear the faithful saying that Christ came into the world to save sinners, is desirous of introducing amongst the Indians some of those arts which may lead the way to civilization.… The introduction of the loom, the forge, and the plough; of tame animals and useful metals is contemplated; that by the increase of civil information the wall of partition between Indians and the Unites States may be broken down, and the tomahawk and the bayonet become useless."[65] For these missionary-minded Baptists, education and civilization were the hallmarks of Christian evangelism.

Columbian College had two basic programs, one in classics and the other in theological studies. As its fund-raiser, Luther Rice raised money for the college and the mission enterprise.

These ambitious efforts taxed the limited resources of the Triennial Convention and its Baptist constituency. In 1826, Staughton and Rice supported efforts to link various agencies for education and missions, thereby creating a more connectional system between the churches and a national Baptist body. Rice's methods of administering funds soon were called into question, and the Convention moved to reconsider its relationship with the school.

Concerned that the college would require too many resources, delegates reaffirmed the Convention's purpose as a foreign mission society only. They relinquished all responsibility for educational institutions or home missions. The delegates reasserted their work as a society, noting, "The blending of these two concerns [missions and education] together must evidently injure the success of both of them in respect to all persons in both these classes. Either party would give more liberally towards his favourite object if it stood alone, and totally disconnected with the other." They concluded, "The history of this connection in the present case has abundantly demonstrated the evil of connecting these charities together. It has proved that each has been of very serious injury to the other."[66]

So serious was the injury between the two groups that the Convention voted to remove Rice from his position as its fund-raiser. State representation was rejected, and the existing organizational structure was maintained. Staughton and the faculty of Columbian College resigned, and the school closed down until 1828. His associate Ira Chase led a group in establishing the Newton Theological Institute (1825), the first Baptist seminary in the United States.[67]

Financial support was difficult to sustain, and Columbian College struggled from the very beginning. In 1852, the Maryland Baptist Union accepted some responsibility for the school's support, but no solid resources could be secured. Eventually, it was taken over by the United States government, and it became George Washington University. Baptists' formal association with the school ended in 1904.

Sabbath Schools

Baptists and other nineteenth-century Protestants utilized Sabbath schools to provide Christian education to the young. These schools began in England under the leadership of Robert Raikes (1735–1811) to provide literacy and religious instruction for underclass children. Schools were founded in the United States in Virginia in 1785 and in New York, New Jersey, and Massachusetts by the 1790s. In 1824, the American Sunday School Union was established to promote literacy through instruction in Bible study and catechisms, history, doctrine, and ethics, much of it aimed at fostering Christian conversion. The *Union Spelling Book* contained the following, intended to teach students punctuation and other lessons: "Did you hear of John Smith's death? Poor fellow! … You know he was drowned in his father's mill-pond. This comes from disobedience to parents. I saw the lad at Sunday-school a week or two ago. He was then (so far as I know) as well as usual. Alas! who of us can tell what a day may bring forth?"[78]

These early Sabbath schools were not the Sunday school Bible classes of a later era but educational efforts sponsored by churches. Norman Maring described the importance of these schools: "In a day when there were few free schools, the Sabbath schools served a useful purpose. Not only did they increase the rate of literacy, but they served also to give religious instruction."[79] As public education developed, churches turned to religious instruction for its own sake.

Sunday schools were not without controversy, especially when founded by women. When Ann Rhees attempted to begin a Sunday school in the First Baptist Church, Philadelphia, her pastor accepted her efforts but observed: "Well, my sisters, you can try it; blossoms are sweet and beautiful, even if they produce no fruit." A Baptist deacon in Massachusetts fretted that after establishing Sunday schools, "These women will be in the pulpit next!"[80] In time he would prove to be right.

Ministerial Education

State conventions were instrumental in the formation of Baptist-related colleges. Efforts to promote Baptist higher education accelerated in the 1830s and 1840s. Donald Mathews observed, "By the 1830s Methodists and Baptists were energetically establishing educational societies throughout the South in an attempt to broaden the scope and constituency of Evangelical education." He acknowledged that although certain Protestant "academies" were also formed during this time, "they did not represent Evangelical aspirations and ambitions so well as the fragile 'denominational' colleges which began to spring up in the 1820s and 1830s."[81] In the North, these colleges included Franklin College (Indiana, 1834), Lewisburg University (Pennsylvania, 1846 [later Bucknell]), Hamilton Literary and Theological Institution (New York, 1819 [later Colgate]). Southern schools included Georgetown College (Kentucky, 1829), Wake Forest College (North Carolina, 1834), Richmond College (Virginia, 1840), Mercer University (Georgia, 1837), and Howard College (Alabama, 1841 [later Samford]). Most of these colleges were founded to provide educational opportunities for Baptist ministers.

As other denominations began to develop seminaries for further ministerial training, Baptists responded. Andover Seminary was established in 1807 by Congregationalist conservatives who opposed Harvard's move toward Unitarianism. In 1825, Massachusetts Baptists organized Newton Theological Institution with Ira Chase, former professor of languages and biblical criticism at Columbian College, as professor of biblical theology.

Not all Baptists were pleased with this effort to establish educational institutions. Some rejected formal education outright, while others feared it would subvert both faith and piety. The "Black Rock Address," approved by a group of Old School (Primitive) Baptists in 1832, was sharply critical of Baptist-sponsored higher education for several reasons. First, while they affirmed their concern for education, these staunchly Calvinistic Baptists were opposed to the idea of "sectarian colleges"—Baptist, Presbyterian, and others—as that implied that "our distinct views of church government, of gospel doctrine and gospel ordinances, are connected with human sciences, a principle which we cannot admit."[82] Second, they objected to the idea of a faculty member in "divinity," since that implied that God's revelation was "a human science on a footing with mathematics, philosophy, law, &c." Third, they rejected the idea that persons "called of the Lord to preach his gospel" should go to school to learn how to proclaim God's Word. They insisted that God called "no man to preach his gospel, till he has made him experimentally acquainted with that gospel, and endowed him with the proper measure of gifts suiting the field he designs him to occupy."[83]

In spite of these criticisms, Baptists continued to form educational institutions. The schools served many purposes, providing Christian higher learning in a Baptist context and offering Baptist youth the possibility of a better economic future. Generations of Baptist young people attended such schools, many returning to their communities as active church members and citizens. Conflicts over the nature of Baptist-related higher education continued throughout the nineteenth and twentieth centuries.

Missionary Tales: Developing a Mythology

The early mission societies were created with more zeal than certitude as to the task at hand. Few understood the complexity of funding and maintaining missionary activity in a non-European culture. Conflicts developed with the colonial governments from Europe as readily as with native peoples. Travel was difficult, and the missionary mortality rate, particularly for women and children, was astonishingly high. Like their British Baptist counterparts, the Americans were forced to deal with the reality of death. When Harriet Newell, a Congregational missionary who accompanied the Judsons to India, died in 1812, Ann Hasseltine Judson wrote, "Harriet is dead. Harriet, my dear friend, my earliest associate in the Mission, is no more. O death, thou destroyer of domestic felicity, could not this wide world afford victims sufficient to satisfy their cravings, without entering the family of a solitary few, whose comfort and happiness depended much on the society of each other?" Judson concluded that she and her husband had "not one remaining friend in this part of the world."[84]

Baptist missionaries and their work in home and foreign settings became important resources for motivating others to service and spiritual experience. Missionaries took on a mythic quality, and the stories of their exploits were published widely. These sources found their way into the lore of the pulpit and the home. No family represented that missionary model of piety and service more than the Judsons of Burma.

The Judsons

Adoniram Judson and the three women to whom he was married were exemplars of missionary sacrifice and devotion. In their work as translators, teachers, organizers, and evangelists, they modeled a selfless dedication that encouraged generations of later mission volunteers.

Their saga was the stuff of legend. Converted during the Second Great Awakening, they went to India as Congregationalists, became Baptists, and initiated mission work in Burma. With Ann Judson's assistance, Adoniram began translating portions of the Bible into Burmese. She learned Siamese (Thai), and by 1891 she had translated the first texts into that language. Their troubles with the Burmese government led to Adoniram Judson's imprisonment in the town of Ava in 1824. Ann Judson bribed the guards, smuggled food and medicine to her husband, and lobbied authorities for his release.[85]

Adoniram was freed in 1826, but Ann died the same year, followed in death by their infant daughter, Maria. Judson, absent at Ann's death, composed the following poem to the memory of wife and daughter:

> And when I came, and saw her not
> In all the place around,
> They pointed out a grassy spot,
> Where she lay under ground.
> And soon another loved one fled,
> And sought her mother's side;
> In vain I stayed her drooping head;
> She panted, gasped, and died.[86]

To his own mother, he wrote of Ann, "True, she has been taken from a sphere in which she was singularly qualified, by her natural disposition, her winning manners, her devoted zeal, and her perfect acquaintance with the language, to be extensively service-able to the cause of Christ; ... but infinite wisdom and love have presided, as ever, in this most afflicting dispensation."[87]

Judson soon was remarried, this time to Sarah Hall Boardman, the widow of missionary George Boardman (d. 1827). Sarah Boardman Judson translated the Bible, taught women of the Karen tribe, and served as administrator of schools, all while caring for her son by Boardman and bearing seven children in eight years with Adoniram Judson. They included Abby (1837), Adoniram (1838), Elnathan (1839), Henry (1842), Henry Hall (1842), Charles (1843), and Edward (1844). Sarah Boardman Judson died in 1845, and Judson took his family back to the United States, where he married Emily Chubbuck (1817–1854), a writer of "women's fiction." They returned to Burma in 1846. One child, Emily Francis, was born of that union in 1846. Adoniram Judson died in 1850, and Emily Chubbuck Judson died four years later, aged thirty-seven. Their daughter was only eight years old when she became an orphan.

The Judson's situation was not unique among nineteenth-century missionary families. All, especially women and children, were ever at the mercy of illness and disease. As with their British counterparts, the theological implications of these realities were not lost on the American missionaries. It elicited reflection on the nature of the divine call and the missionary imperative.

Ann Judson's response to the death of her firstborn son in 1816 reveals something of the theological struggle she confronted. She went daily to a spot near his grave to honor and mourn her lost child. Of his death, she observed, "Deprived, as we were, of every source of enjoyment of a temporal nature, our every affection was entangled by this darling object. When our heavenly Father saw we had converted the precious gift into an idol, he removed it from us, and thereby taught us the necessity of placing our supreme affections on Him." She insisted that God had "removed" her son from this world "to show us that we need no other source of enjoyment but God himself. Do not think, though I write thus, that I repine at the dealings of Providence, or would wish them to be otherwise than they are. No ... God is the same when he afflicts, as when he is merciful."[88]

Why did these missionaries choose such a way of life and death? Writing in the 1920s, O. W. Ellsbree suggested that much missionary enthusiasm was drawn from the Great Awakening and the influence of Edwardsian theologians such as Samuel Hopkins. Hopkins

(1721–1803) believed that one must be willing to be damned for the greater glory of God. He called this idea of total submission to God's sovereign will "disinterested benevolence," a complete loss of the self. This sense of duty to the divine command was a major factor in the decision of the Judsons and others to go out as missionaries. Dana Robert noted, "The high rate of death of the early foreign missionaries needed explanation to detractors of the movement as more than a wanton waste of life. But in the early years of foreign missions, expectations that a missionary commitment was for 'life' made death on the field preferable to a return, even to preserve one's health."[89] Whatever the motive, the nineteenth-century missionaries were forced to confront the immediacy of disease and death for themselves and their families. Few were spared in the difficult environments of missionary service.

Women and Missions

Ann Hasseltine Judson was one of many women, married and single, who were in the vanguard of the earliest Baptist missionary efforts. The appointment of single women challenged traditional interpretations of a female's place in the church. Adoniram Judson apparently requested a "shipload" of them, but Baptists in America were hesitant. In a study of these dynamics, Helen Falls observed, "In effect, they were told that if God wanted them on the mission field, he would send them husbands."[90] In time, single women were appointed, especially for work with women and children. Gradually, a "women's work with women" program evolved in many mission societies and became the sphere wherein females served as teachers, founded schools, and provided other instructional opportunities.

In 1814, Charlotte H. White, a widow, became the first unmarried woman to apply to the Triennial Convention for appointment as a missionary to Calcutta. She provided her own funding and lived with her sister and brother-in-law, who served in India. White said, "Hitherto I have been excluded from rendering any service to the mission; but I now rejoice that God has opened a way, and directed my mind to missionary exertions.... Having found no period of life exempt from trials, I do not expect to leave them on leaving my native land, but rather to add to their weight and number."[91] When White was appointed, the Society set the boundaries for her work: "While it must be accepted as the duty of single ladies to be helpful in all departments of the work, it ought to be expected of them that they will carefully abstain from any interference with matters not specially committed to their hands."[92]

Eleanor Macomber was the first single female to be funded directly by the Mission Board. She was sent to Burma in 1832 as an evangelist and church organizer.[93] Southern Baptists' first single female missionary was Harriet A. Baker, sent out from Virginia as a missionary to Canton, China, in 1849, just four years after the Convention was formed. Health considerations forced her resignation in 1853, and it was not until 1872 that Lula Whilden and Edmonia Harris Moon, single women, were sent out. Edmonia Moon was followed by her sister, Charlotte Digges (Lottie) Moon (1840–1912), perhaps the best-known missionary in Southern Baptist history. Edmonia Moon was supported with $400 per year by the Woman's Missionary Society of Richmond, Virginia. Lottie Moon received support from Baptist women in Georgia.[94]

Some women experienced the call after reading stories of the first generation of missionaries. Emily Chubbuck recalled reading an edition of the *Baptist Register* that included an account of Ann Hasseltine Judson: "My eyes fell on the words: 'Little Maria lies by the side of her fond Mother' [Ann H. Judson]. I had read about the missionaries, and my sister had told me respecting them; I knew, therefore, that the letter was from Mr. Judson and that his little daughter was dead. How I pitied his loneliness! And then a new train of thought sprung up, and my mind expanded to a New Land of Glory.... Yes, I will be a missionary."[95]

Why did the Baptists and other evangelicals insist on sending missionary families into such physically hostile environments? Brumberg suggested that it was the belief that "Christian familial and social patterns could not be taught to heathens unless there were present, on the scene 'missionaries, who are married to well educated and pious females, who have formed all their habits and modes of thinking in a Christian country.'"[96]

In spite of women's concern for missions, their efforts to form their own missionary societies were not without controversy. When the disabled Mary Webb (1779–1861) led in founding the Baptist-related Boston Female Society for Missionary Purposes in 1801, she anticipated the criticism that women were stepping outside their sphere. She wrote, "Our object is not to render ourselves important, but, useful. We have no wish to go out of our province, nor do we undertake to become teachers in Israel; it is our pleasure to see our brethren go before, and we are content to be permitted 'to glean after the reapers.'"[97]

Isabel Crawford, another mission leader, was born May 26, 1865, to a British Baptist family that had migrated to Canada. Her father, John Crawford (1819–1892), was a church historian and biblical studies professor at Woodstock Institute in Canada. Determined to be a missionary, she took a two-year study program at Missionary Training School in Chicago. The school was run by Mary G. Burdette, corresponding secretary for the Women's American Baptist Home Mission Society. Its thirteen professors taught theological and biblical studies along with curriculum in medicine and educational methodology.[98]

Students did mission service in the inner city of Chicago, working with prostitutes, alcoholics, and the homeless. Concern for the plight of the poor and the indifference of the rich led Crawford to continue her urban endeavors. She kept a diary of her experiences and wrote after attending the Chicago World's Fair in 1893, "The American people are more religious than they get credit for, and the American women are going to stand alongside of the men in everything."[99] Crawford insisted on equal rights for women and thought that women had a particular mission to fulfill, albeit one different from that of men. She asserted that women were more compassionate and less materialistic than men and believed that the poor would listen to the message of Christianity if presented by women, who, unlike men, were not the exploiters of the downtrodden.[100] In 1893, upon graduating from the missionary training school, she and Hattie Everts were sent to work with the Kiowas of Elk Creek, Oklahoma Territory.

Sallie Paine Peck (1789–1856) was a home missionary who traveled with her husband, John Mason Peck, while bearing and caring for children along the way. Of their marriage, in 1809, John Peck wrote, "We knew nothing of the sickly, sentimental, mixed emotion called love, so faithfully and foolishly portrayed in the novelettes and periodicals of this age."[101] Of their arrival in St. Louis in 1817, after a four-month journey from the East, Sallie Peck said, "I am now seven months pregnant, and I am apprehensive about the arrival of another child as medical services are mostly unknown here on the frontier." The Pecks and their three other children took up residence in "a small one-room accommodation that is about twelve by fifteen feet."[102]

Apparently, faith did not come easily for Sallie Peck. Her husband recalled, "She had always had doubts about her interest in Christ and many misgivings lest she would rest on a false foundation; but since her illness she had gained clearer views of the all-perfect righteousness of Christ, and all doubts were gone." Sallie Peck died of fever on October 24, 1856.

Since the rate of female mortality was high, their death experiences provided "lessons" that were described in sermons and articles. Many Baptist missionary magazines contained obituaries or "memorials" praising godly women on the occasion of their deaths. Essays traced the conversion and piety of the women, with particular attention to their insights about death. One obituary described the dying of Mrs. Benjamin Thaw (her given name was not provided). It commented, "The house of God, notwithstanding, was her delight. She was ever seen occupying her place, and in so doing presenting an example worthy of universal imitation. Her countenance bespoke the habitual solemnity of her mind on spiritual subjects."[103]

Missionary concerns led to an attempt in 1882 to permit women to have participatory roles in the Southern Baptist Convention. A recommendation was made that the Home and Foreign Mission Boards appoint "some competent woman as Superintendent of the State Central Committees, whose duty shall be to collect and disseminate information and in other ways to stimulate and strengthen woman's work for woman in all lands." The proposal failed, as some thought that it created "a difficult and delicate problem."[104] Apparently, men worried that bringing women into the inner workings of the mission boards would appear to sanction the suffrage movement and other women's rights efforts.

Home Mission Missionary Work: The Native Americans

By the mid-1830s, some one hundred Baptist home missionaries were at work in fourteen states. Of his calling to evangelize, John Mason Peck wrote in 1816, "Ever since I have thought upon the subject of missions, I have had my eye upon the people west of the Mississippi, particularly the Indian nations.... I have often thought that if it was my lot to labor among the heathen, the Louisiana-purchase, of all parts of the world, would be my choice."[105]

Native Americans were a matter of curiosity, mystery, and certain evangelical concern for American Protestants from the early colonial settlements. In 1674, the first Native American Baptist, a man named Japheth, was baptized by the Seventh Day Baptist church in Newport, Rhode Island. Between 1705 and 1790, records suggest, some twenty-seven Native Americans were part of several Baptist groups, including General Six Principle Baptists, Seventh Day Baptists, Separate Baptists, and General Baptists. Three were members of white churches. Some nine congregations whose members were exclusively Native Americans were founded without the help of white missionaries.[106] The work was difficult, however, and by 1790, there were no more than 159 Native American Baptists. While some associations and missionary agencies supported Native American missions, few Baptists worked with these peoples until the nineteenth century.[107]

By 1802, the Charleston Association (South Carolina) initiated missionary efforts among the Catawbas. In 1817, Isaac McCoy (1784–1846) was appointed by the Triennial

Convention as a missionary among the Native Americans of Indiana and Michigan. He helped found the first Native American Baptist church in Oklahoma in 1832.[108]

McCoy's strategy included an idea for a single Native American nation—a concept born of his efforts as an agent of the programs of government "removal" directed toward certain tribes. William Brackney maintained that McCoy "was for his era the chief white advocate of Native American rights and identity."[109]

Missionary appointments ranged from as few as five in 1817 to as many as seventy-one in 1845, spread throughout the country from New York to Oklahoma.[110] Baptist missionaries established forty-eight mission schools during the mid-nineteenth century. These schools claimed an enrollment of approximately 230 persons per school.[111]

The General Convention sent Humphrey Posey, Evan Jones, and Thomas Roberts to the Cherokees at the Valley Towns station in Georgia during the 1820s. Cherokee leaders responded favorably to the effort, convinced that their children should receive mission school education. As one tribal leader told the Baptists, "We want our children to learn English so the white man cannot cheat us."[112]

Thomas Roberts challenged Anglo-Saxon caricatures of Cherokee children when he noted that they "are kind, obedient, and industrious" and that their "mental powers appear to be in no respect inferior to those of whites."[113] Nonetheless, Roberts used Anglo children as his standard for comparison with Native American youth: "Though their skin is red or dark, I assure you, their mental powers are white—few white children can keep pace with them in learning."[114]

Support from neighboring whites was less than enthusiastic. One missionary observed, "The White people are constantly opposing every effort to instruct the poor benighted Indians. The great objection urged by most people in these parts is the enmity of the old wars in which some of their friends have been killed by them [Native Americans]."[115]

As with other tribal missions, work among the Cherokees went slowly. Basic communication was a particular problem. Baptist Evan Jones was said to be fluent in Welsh, Latin, Greek, and Hebrew, but it took him almost ten years to learn Cherokee sufficiently enough to preach in the language. Christian concepts such as original sin and the atonement were not easily explained. Jones described one Cherokee who knew English but "seemed quite ignorant of the depravity of [human] nature, though he has often heard the gospel." He commented that Cherokees "seem to have no other fear of death than that which arises from the apprehension of the bodily pain with which it may be accompanied."[116] Thomas Roberts remarked, "The misfortune is they do not understand English and we have no good interpreter."[117]

Symbols and rituals did create some affinity, however. William McLoughlin suggested that baptismal immersion elicited a positive response from the Cherokees, who connected it with the tribal rite of passage known as "going down to the water."[118]

In 1838, when many Cherokees were forcibly removed to Oklahoma on the famous "Trail of Tears," the exiled included several Native American Baptist preachers, among them John Wyckliff, Beaver Carrier, Alexander M'Grey, and Jesse Bushyhead. Bushyhead (1804–1844) was a Cherokee Baptist who helped form churches in Oklahoma. Educated by Presbyterians, Bushyhead became a Baptist under the influence of missionary Evan Jones. He worked as a translator and founded the first Cherokee Baptist

Church at Amohee, Tennessee. He served as chief justice of the Cherokee Supreme Court and as missionary for the Baptist Home Mission Board.[119]

Not all of the Cherokees departed the eastern United States during the Trail of Tears. Many hid in the mountains and remained on their ancient land. In 1840, Alford Corn, a Cherokee Baptist preacher, began a mission to his tribe in the Carolinas. This led to his appointment by the Southern Baptist Domestic Mission Board in 1858. The effort influenced the founding of the Swain Indian Baptist Association of North Carolina in 1881. By 1841, there were some six hundred Cherokee Baptists, and by the 1860s, there were fifteen hundred.

Northern Baptists were fortunate to secure help from Almon C. Bacone, a Native American educated at Rochester University. Sent to Oklahoma territory in 1878, he founded a school that became Bacone Junior College, a coeducational school for Native American and Anglo students. The school, located in Tahlequah, became Bacone College in 1910. Northern Baptists utilized schools and children's homes in establishing missions with native tribes.

Work with the Creeks led to the formation of the American Indian Missionary Association in Kentucky in 1842. In 1855, the Association merged with the Southern Baptist Convention, and Henry Frieland Buckner and ten Creeks were appointed to work among the tribe. By 1875, they reported fifty churches and some two thousand Creek Christians.[120]

In 1877, a group of Native American preachers, including John Jumper, chief of the Seminoles, preached to a large group of Plains natives near Fort Sill, Oklahoma. Several were baptized, including Soda Arko, chief of the Wichitas, and a church was founded in June 1877. Soon churches were established among the Cheyennes and Arapahos. This work was carried out by Anglo and Native American preachers.[121]

Many Baptists believed that the salvation of native peoples would facilitate their "civilization." An 1818 statement by the Triennial Convention Mission Board suggested, "Our British brethren in India have found, by the experience of more than twenty years, that 'civilization and salvation go hand in hand.' And if this be true respecting a people in some degree enlightened, it obtains with a ten-fold consideration, when applied to the aborigines of our own country, destitute of a written language, and every art of cultivated life."[122] Baptists themselves divided over the concern for souls and the desire to overcome native culture.

Nineteenth-Century Baptist Controversies

Controversies among nineteenth-century Baptists were deep and divisive. New churches and denominations were born as individuals divided over issues as varied as missions and musical instruments, Restorationism and human slavery.

Controversy: Daniel Parker and Antimissionary Baptists

The missionary movement raised significant theological and organizational questions. Calvinistic Baptists insisted that God alone was the agent of salvation, offered irresistibly to the elect. Missionary efforts, therefore, were little more than human interference in ministrations known only to God. Mission societies were unacceptable because they lacked biblical precedent. Daniel Parker (1781–1844) was an articulate spokesperson for the antimission cause. Born in Virginia and raised in Georgia, Parker was baptized in 1802 and ordained in Tennessee in 1806. After moving to Crawford County, Illinois, in 1817, Parker published a series of works that challenged the theological rationale for the missionary movement. As a result, numerous Baptist associations in Indiana, Kentucky, and Illinois divided over Parker's antimission and "two seed" theology.

In *Views on the Two Seeds Taken from Genesis,* published in 1826, Parker espoused the doctrine of "two seeds," a belief that at birth all persons received the seeds of salvation or damnation. Citing Genesis 3:15, Parker claimed that the "Serpent's seed" existed in the "Non-Elect, which were not created in Adam, the original stock, but were brought into the world as the product of sin, by way of a curse on the woman, who, by reason of sin, was made susceptible of the seed of the Serpent, through the means of her husband, who had partook with her in the transgression."[123] He concluded, "It is evident that there are the two seeds, one of the Serpent, the other of the woman; and they appear plain in Cain and Abel, and in their offerings."[124] Election and predestination were irrevocably determined at conception, "in our mother's womb." God alone granted salvation, from "before the foundation of the world." Missionary efforts not only were unnecessary, but also were a futile attempt by sinful human beings to claim divine prerogative. Missionary ventures were evidence of hubris, not human compassion.

Parker's actual response to the founding of missionary societies is a bit unclear. On the one hand, he seemed to be opposed to all missionary endeavors, convinced that the irresistible grace of God ultimately would seek out all the elect; on the other hand, his arguments seem to be directed at missionary societies, for whose existence he could find no New Testament support.

From 1829 to 1831, Parker circulated his views through a journal entitled *The Church Advocate.* In 1834, Parker moved to Texas, taking with him the entire congregation of the Pilgrim Predestinarian Regular Baptist Church, of which he was pastor.

Parker's critics charged that he had misread the New Testament completely. John Mason Peck called him "one of those singular and extraordinary beings whom divine Providence permits to arise as a scourge to His church, and a stumbling-block in the way of religious effort."[125]

Parker was joined in his opposition to certain mission endeavors by the frontier preacher John Taylor, who outlined his views in *Thoughts on Missions,* published in 1819. In the East, the opposition to missions came from persons who called themselves "Old School" or "Primitive" Baptists. These groups maintained that mission and revival activities were departures from traditional Baptist doctrine and practice.

In one sense, these debates simply reflect the theological boundaries that separated traditional Calvinists from evangelical Calvinists and led to the development of new Baptist subgroups that promoted those distinctive views. Some view the controversies as an accommodation made by Baptists to the cultural experience of the American frontier and the impact of democratic idealism.[126] Others insist that the antimission movement was merely an amalgamation of "religious individualism, primitivism, and pessimism."[127] Norman Maring remarked that although "Old School Baptists were correct in regarding the new [missionary] movements as modifications of Baptist theology," these mission opponents were not necessarily the paragons of "true" Baptist dogma. Rather, "As is often true of movements which are in reaction against something, there was a stress upon certain elements of Baptist thought and life which lacked balance. Therefore, the Old School group might be regarded more as a caricature of eighteenth-century American Baptists than as a replica."[128]

As noted previously, the so-called "Black Rock Address" set forth by a group of Old School Baptists in Maryland in 1832 was an important statement of opposition to missionary activity. The document condemned missionary societies, tract societies, Bible societies, Sunday schools, "Colleges and Theological Schools," and "four-day or protracted [revival] meetings."[129]

As the Old School Baptists saw it, there was no scriptural basis for such activities, which represented certain "arrogant pretensions" that "regeneration is produced by impressions made upon the natural mind by means of religious sentiments instilled into it."[130] The Black Rock statement concluded with the affirmation that "regeneration, we believe, is exclusively the work of the Holy Ghost, performed by his divine power, at his own sovereign pleasure, according to the provisions of the everlasting covenant."[131]

These differences created long-standing divisions between missionary and nonmissionary Baptists in the United States. The Black Rock statement reflected the schismatic nature of these disagreements by referring to its signers as "Old School" Baptists, over against "New School" societies. Old School Baptists later would be known as Primitive Baptists, Regular Old School Baptists, or Hardshell Baptists.[132] This last term meant that they were stubbornly set in their ways.

Controversy: Restorationism

Baptist "primitivism" was challenged by another movement, portions of which grew directly out of the Baptist ranks. "Restorationism," as it came to be called, centered in the belief that the true church of Jesus Christ had been lost through corrupt doctrine and alliances with the state. Restorationists believed that they had reconstructed apostolic Christianity directly from the New Testament. Restorationist ideals were evident in the work of Barton Warren Stone, Thomas Campbell (1763–1854), and Alexander Campbell (1788–1866).

Frustrated with sectarian division over missions, predestination, and limited atonement, Stone and a group of "New Lights" drafted the "Last Will and Testament of the Springfield Presbytery" in 1804. It called for the abolition of all denominational names in favor of a community of "Christians only." It affirmed New Testament authority, free will, and the general atonement. By 1807, they had accepted baptismal immersion for the remission of sins. Many Baptists joined them.

Thomas Campbell and his son Alexander echoed and extended many of Stone's Restorationist ideas. After moving to Pennsylvania in 1807 as part of the Seceder Presbyterian movement, Thomas Campbell advocated the restoration of New Testament Christianity. Alexander, an articulate preacher and polemicist, arrived in 1809, and the family soon found their way into the Baptist ranks. During the years 1815–1830, they were active participants in the Redstone (Baptist) Association in Pennsylvania and the Mahoning Association in Ohio. Alexander Campbell published several journals that set forth his Restorationist views. These included *The Christian Baptist* (1823–1829) and *The Millennial Harbinger* (1830–1863). Campbell had much in common with the Baptists. He emphasized believer's baptism, the New Testament as the primary authority for doctrine and practice, congregational autonomy, and the priesthood of the laity. Affirming "no creed but Christ," he eschewed denominational entanglements, mission boards, and the use of the title "Reverend" for church ministers. He understood conversion as a simple mental assent to Jesus as the Messiah, baptism as inseparable from faith, and the Lord's Supper as a weekly ordinance of the church. Restorationism, or "Campbellism," as it was sometimes known, divided many Baptist churches. Some congregations were split so severely that they were forced to ask the courts to determine the rightful owners of church properties. A schism in First Baptist Church, Louisville, Kentucky, occurred when a majority of the members accepted Restorationist views, and "on Thursday before the first Lord's Day in September, 1825, rejected its covenant and confession [the Philadelphia Confession] as human instruments of union, and recognized the New Testament as its foundation and only rule."[133] Several ministers and a majority of members in Louisville's First and Second Baptist Churches united to form a new Christian congregation.

The Baptist minority called itself the Old Baptist Church, Church of Christ. By 1833, the Restorationist members were labeling themselves the "Congregation of Disciples" as a way of repudiating denominational labels. A formal schism occurred in 1835, with the "Christians" gaining the property.[134] Hundreds of Baptist churches experienced similar schisms as a result of the Restorationist movement.

Controversy: Old Landmarkism

Baptists did not leave the Restorationists unanswered. They turned to an ideology that traced Baptists in an unbroken line directly to the New Testament church and enabled Baptist churches to claim a unique historical authenticity. Successionist George Orchard wrote, "It is a history especially needed by Baptists, to assist them in replying to the taunting interrogations of Paedobaptists."[135] For Orchard, Baptists were "the only Christian community which has stood since the times of the Apostles; and ... preserved pure the doctrines of the gospel through all ages."[136]

Taking its name from Proverbs 22:28, "Do not remove the ancient landmarks that your fathers set up," Landmarkists argued that "all Christian communities during the first three centuries were of the Baptist denomination, in constitution and practice."[137] Baptist churches existed in an unbroken line from Jesus' baptism at the hands of John in the Jordan River. Landmarkists rejected apostolic succession for a series of apostolic churches, sustained by crypto-Baptist congregations since the New Testament era. Since they antedated the Reformation, they were not really Protestant.

The term "Landmark" was first used in an essay published in 1854 by James M. Pendleton (1811–1891), pastor of First Baptist Church, Bowling Green, Kentucky. Pendleton addressed the question "Ought Baptists to recognize Pedo-baptist [infant baptizer] preachers as gospel ministers?" The book, written at the request of James R. Graves of Nashville, Tennessee, was titled *An Old Landmark Reset,* and was the first of numerous works composed by Pendleton, Graves, Amos Dayton (1813–1865), and other Landmarkists.

In *Old Landmarkism: What Is It?* James Graves (1820–1893) delineated the "marks" of the true (Baptist) church. He believed: (1) "The church and kingdom of Christ is a Divine institution." Christ's kingdom is synonymous with the local congregation.[138] (2) There is no invisible church, that mysterious communion of the saints, but "the only church that is revealed to us is a visible church."[139] (3) "The locality of Christ's church, and therefore kingdom, is this earth; all the subjects of His kingdom are here; all the work of His church is here." The church exists only in this world, not in the next.[140] (4) The church is only "a local organization, a single congregation." Only a local church—the only true interpretation of the New Testament word *ekklesia*—has authority to administer the ordinances.[141] (5) "The membership [of the church] are all professedly regenerate in heart before baptized into it."[142] (6) Baptism is "an act by which we profess the saving faith we possess."[143] (7) The Lord's Supper is a "simple memorial of Christ's work and love for us."[144]

Graves concluded that in the true church, "THE PEOPLE—THE WHOLE PEOPLE— in each community choose their own officers, receive and expel members, conduct all business as a body politic, decide on all questions of discipline, and observe all the institutions of Christ."[145]

Since non-Baptist churches lacked the marks of the true church, they could be referred to only as societies. While they might include true Christians, they were not ecclesiastically valid institutions, and their ministers could not lead Baptist worship services.

They also denied the veracity of immersion administered in non-Baptist churches—a practice labeled "alien immersion." All persons so baptized were compelled to receive reimmersion upon joining a Landmark Baptist church. Landmarkists promoted closed communion, and refused to administer the Lord's Supper to anyone who was not a member of the specific congregation in which it was celebrated.

Landmarkists published their views widely. Amos Cooper Dayton's Landmark polemic took the form of a novel entitled *Theodosia Ernest*, published in 1857. It tells of the quest of a woman named Theodosia to discover the true New Testament church. Popular among many church folk, the novel remains a poignant symbol of the fictional nature of the Landmark movement itself. The use of a female character to impart theological insights is also a significant element of the book.

Landmark ideas and practices impacted large segments of the Baptist community, especially in the South. Taken abroad by Baptist missionaries, they had varying influence upon Baptists internationally. Landmarkism and its residual influences weighed heavily on significant elements of Baptist life well into the twentieth century, particularly regarding the question of rebaptism for Protestants seeking membership in Baptist churches. Landmarkism provided a systematic history and theology that Baptists could use in teaching the faithful and debating their opponents. It was an effective, although "made up" history, creating a legacy that shaped elements of Baptist polity and theology long after the original movement had passed off the scene.

Amid its biblical and theological conservatism, Landmarkism reflected a solid democratic idealism. Graves, Pendleton, and others advocated radical freedom of the Christian in the liberty of a free state. They were outspoken opponents of establishments, secular or religious, that would undermine the freedom of conscience and religious liberty. In its aggressive emphasis on the autonomy of the local congregation, Landmarkism reflected democratic sentiments of post-Revolutionary American life.

Many historians have overlooked Graves's own political views and his surprisingly optimistic attitude toward American democracy and progress. In a brief book called *The Watchman's Reply* (1853), Graves associated Baptists with the oft-persecuted "poor" and "oppressed" peoples of the world. He predicted that the outbreak of "popular revolutions" throughout the world would demonstrate the triumph of Christian and democratic principles over "tyranny and caste."[146] Democracy and freedom were purchased with the blood of the Revolutionary War and with "the precious blood of Him who died on Calvary."[147]

Landmarkism was a powerful influence on many Baptist communions. Its existence testifies to the complex nature of Baptist history and to the creative efforts to reduce that heritage into a manageable historiography suitable for popular consumption.

Controversy: Musical Instruments

The early Baptists, like many of their Protestant counterparts, did not utilize musical instruments in worship. Indeed, there was considerable debate among some as to the use of any congregational singing or simply psalm singing in worship. With time, however, Baptists in America began to use certain musical accompaniments for congregational singing. Near the beginning of the century, the First Baptist churches in Newport and Providence, Rhode Island, began using the bass violoncello in their worship services, primarily as an accompaniment to their choirs. Choirs also appeared in Baptist churches during this period.[148]

The first church organ to be used by Baptists probably was in the church at Pawtucket, Rhode Island, around 1819. Originally, it was intended only for the local Mozart Society, but eventually was included in church services. The Clarendon Street Church, Boston, probably was the second congregation to install an organ in 1828.[149] In the South, First Baptist Church of Charleston, South Carolina, also secured an organ during this period, probably by 1831.[150]

The National Controversy: Slavery

Clearly, the issue of human slavery and the institutions surrounding it was the most divisive issue for Baptists and for the entire American nation. Debates over slavery precipitated schism between Baptists north and south in 1845—an act that anticipated the division of the nation at large.[151]

As Baptists expanded their influence, they were something of a "people's church," drawing constituency from the poor and lower classes, who were less likely to own slaves or to be involved in the slave economy. This meant that many Baptists opposed slavery in principle and insisted that it should be abolished as soon as pragmatically possible. They urged the evangelization of slaves and called upon masters to observe scriptural admonitions regarding "Christian" treatment of those in bondage. Yet they recognized that the debates over slavery were a threat to their fragile unity. Denominationalists often refrained from public discussion of the subject and promoted compromise measures that would evade potential schism.

In 1790, Baptists in the United States numbered some sixty-five thousand, with approximately twenty thousand in Virginia and eighteen thousand throughout other regions of the South.[152] Many Baptists joined other denominations in condemning the idea of slavery and calling for its ultimate elimination. In 1785, the Baptist General Committee of Virginia declared slavery to be "contrary to the word of God." Five years later, however, a committee charged with addressing the issue was too divided to present a report, passing the responsibility on to patriarch John Leland, a preacher with strong antislavery sentiments. Leland's document declared slavery to be "a violent deprivation of the rights of nature, and inconsistent with a republican government."[153] It urged the extirpation of "the horrible evil from the land." The statement was approved by the General Committee, but it was not well received by associations in the state.

David Barrow (d. 1819) was another Virginian vehemently opposed to human bondage. He moved to Kentucky as pastor of Mount Sterling Baptist Church. After unsuccessful efforts to get associations to take a strong stand against slavery, Barrow led Mount Sterling and eight other churches in 1807 to form a new union called the "Baptized Licking-Locust Association, Friends of Humanity." This thoroughly abolitionist body refused all fellowship with slaveholders and with churches or associations that accepted them. At its height in 1812, the Association included some twelve churches. Thereafter it experienced a steady decline, until it disappeared in 1820. Association resolutions denounced the "abhorrence" of the slave system and declared, "There are professors of Christianity in Kentucky, who plead for it as an institution of the God of mercy; and it is truly disgusting to see what pains they take to drag the holy scriptures of truth, into the service of this heaven daring iniquity."[154] Nonetheless, support for abolitionism was growing among Baptists and other Protestants. When the New England Anti-Slavery Society held its meeting in 1835, over two-thirds of the delegates were Baptist or Methodist ministers.[155]

Abolitionist sentiments were not extensive in the Deep South, where evangelization of slaves and continuation of slavery were dominant social attitudes, often supported with religious underpinnings. Some 90 percent of the churches in Georgia were either Baptist or Methodist, as were probably 80 percent in all the other Southern states.[156] When eleven states left the Union, it was estimated that 45 percent of the Southern churches were Methodist, 37 percent Baptist, and 12 percent Presbyterian—a total of 94 percent of the religious communions in the South.[157]

By the 1830s, polarization over slavery had increased dramatically. With the invention of the cotton gin, slavery had become an economic "necessity" in many of the Southern states. Slave revolts by Denmark Vesey (ca. 1767–1822) in South Carolina in 1822 and Nat Turner (1800–1831) in Virginia in 1831 increased Southern apprehensions and led to intensified monitoring of slaves. Even religious gatherings were forbidden without careful supervision. The rise of a more militant abolitionism, whose supporters demanded immediate manumission, led proslavery Christians to develop more elaborate defenses.

In 1833, the American Anti-Slavery Society began in Philadelphia under the leadership of William Lloyd Garrison (1805–1879) and the wealthy Tappan brothers, Arthur (1786–1865) and Lewis (1788–1873). Its outspoken advocacy of immediate emancipation, circulated through the *Public Liberator,* encouraged the formation of similar abolitionist bodies.

In an address to the South Carolina legislature in 1822, Richard Furman, pastor and slaveholder, enunciated one of the South's most popular "biblical" defenses of slavery. Furman insisted, "The right of holding slaves is clearly established in the Holy Scriptures, both by precept and example." He reasoned, "Had the holding of slaves been a moral evil, it cannot be supposed, that the inspired Apostles, who feared not the faces of men, and were ready to lay down their lives in the case of their God, would have tolerated it for a moment, in the Christian Church."[158] Furman concluded, "In proving this subject justifiable by Scriptural authority, its morality is also provided; for the Divine Law never sanctions immoral actions."[159]

That the pastor of such a prestigious congregation and the first president of the Triennial Convention should express these views further escalated the division of opinions inside the Baptist community. Southerners defended their "Peculiar Institution," while abolitionists called for immediate emancipation. By 1841, as many as 180 of Maine's 214 Baptist ministers were fully committed abolitionists.[160]

Most of the early leaders of what became the Southern Baptist Convention maintained proslavery sentiments. These included James P. Boyce, John L. Dagg, R. B. C. Howell, Jeremiah B. Jeter, Basil Manly Sr., Basil Manly Jr., Isaac T. Tichenor, Henry Allen Tupper, and P. H. Mell.[161] Mell commented, "In every respect, the condition of the slave, in these United States of America, is better than that occupied by his brethren in any part of the world, now, or during any past age."[162] In spite of this, few Baptists in the South were slaveholders.

Not all Baptists in the North subscribed to the abolitionist agenda. Some saw in the polarization over slavery the ultimate division of the Triennial Convention and its missionary activity.

Northerner Francis Wayland sought to protect the Triennial Convention from an abolitionist takeover. He and slavery advocate Richard Fuller (1804–1876) exchanged letters regarding the slavery issue and Baptist responses to it. Fuller, vice president of the Board of Managers of the General Convention, argued that slavery was acceptable to New Testament Christians. Wayland offered a firm but moderate response, warning against the divisiveness created by both the abolitionists and the defenders of slavery. He suggested that while the New Testament permitted slavery, the gospel contained principles that would lead to its ultimate extinction.

Fuller responded that slavery contributed to the conversion of persons who otherwise would have been lost to the Christian gospel, and thus lost for eternity. He acknowledged a personal concern for the spiritual welfare of his slaves and the need to bring them to conversion. Fuller concluded, "Will my brother, or any man at the North, undertake to remove them [slaves] and give me bond and security that their condition shall be improved? If so ... I will then make a proposition which shall at once ... determine who is the friend of the slave, and who is willing to make sacrifices for his good."[163]

Wayland denied the appropriateness of slavery, based on the Enlightenment idea of human freedom. He affirmed that all human beings were "created with an equal right to employ their faculties, of body or of mind, in such a manner as will promote their happiness, either here or hereafter."[164]

Disturbed by these moderate efforts inside the Triennial Convention, abolitionist Baptists organized the American Baptist Anti-Slavery Convention in April 1840, with Elon Galusha (d. 1856), vice president of the Board of Foreign Missions, as president. The organization quickly barred all fellowship with slaveholders and their churches, declaring, "We cannot, at the Lord's table, cordially take that as a brother's hand, which plies the scourge on woman's naked flesh."[165] Members called for separation from any denomination or society that implicitly or explicitly supported slavery.

Such language infuriated Southern Baptists, who saw their ethics and their Christianity called into question. Divisions deepened as the rhetoric became more heated. In 1840, the Mission Board again sought to maintain moderation by circulating an "address" that insisted that the work of missions and evangelism was its primary purpose, implying that slavery was a topic beyond its distinct purpose.[166] This effort at neutrality angered abolitionists and slaveholders alike, since it seemed to produce equivocation on a matter about which both sides wanted a precise response.

The 1841 meeting of the Triennial Convention appeared to go in the proslavery direction. Several antislavery officers, such as Elon Galusha, were replaced by Southerners. William B. Johnson of South Carolina, a slaveholder, was elected president, and the Board passed a new statement asserting that "no new test unauthorized by the Scriptures and by the established usage" of the churches would be permitted to disturb the unity of the missionary endeavor.[167]

In 1843, the American Baptist Free Mission Society was formed as an agency committed to appointing only nonslaveholding missionaries. Southerners applauded this rift, hoping that the antislavery forces would completely depart the Triennial Convention. Many Northern moderates feared that the loss of their abolitionist colleagues would leave them in a denomination controlled by Southerners.

Staunch Baptist abolitionists formed the American Baptist Free Mission Society (sometimes called the American and Foreign Baptist Missionary Society) in 1843. The members refused to participate in any "religious societies that are supported in common with slaveholders."[168] Its rabid abolitionist, anti-alcohol, and anti-Masonic agendas also meant that the society remained a remnant, representing no more than one-sixteenth of Baptists in the North and finding almost no support in the South.[169] The Society committed itself to "the overthrow and utter extinction of slavery." Its constitution demanded that members not only repudiate slavery but also "believe that slavery, under all circumstances, is sin, and treat it accordingly."[170]

In 1841, the Executive Committee of the American Baptist Home Mission Society issued a circular letter that repudiated efforts to make slaveholding an issue in missionary appointment. It concluded, "As patriots, we must cherish religious union as one among the strongest, although not the most prominent, of the bonds that hold together the Union of these States."[171] These efforts to link denominational and national unity led Clarence Goen to conclude that the divisions of the three great Protestant churches—Baptist, Methodist, and Presbyterian—anticipated the dissolution of the Union itself.[172]

The scene was set for yet another challenge to Board policy. In 1844, rumors circulated that the Home Mission Society might move to refuse any appointment of slaveholding missionaries. In anticipation of such an action, Georgia Baptists submitted the name of a known slaveholder, James Reeve, as missionary to Native Americans in that state. The Board, meeting in October 1844, voted seven to five against the appointment of Reeve, insisting that Georgia Baptists had inappropriately introduced slavery into the requirements for missionary service. The report concluded that since "it is not expedient to introduce the subjects of slavery or anti-slavery into our deliberations," they were rejecting Reeve's application.[173]

In November 1844, the Alabama State Baptist Convention passed a resolution demanding that the Triennial Convention acknowledge the right of slaveholders to secure missionary appointment. The Board representatives responded to the resolution in December 1844. Although not releasing its statement until later, the Board rejected the Alabama request and insisted that missionary candidates who refused to relinquish their slaves would not be appointed. It concluded, "One thing is certain: we can never be a party to any arrangement which would imply approbation of slavery."[174] These divisions over the appointment of slaveholding missionaries led Baptists in the South to hold meetings that would lead to the formation of a new denomination.

The Southern Baptist Convention

Convinced that the mission board had been co-opted by abolitionists and that Southerners were no longer candidates for missionary appointment, a group gathered in First Baptist Church, Augusta, Georgia, on May 8, 1845, and established the Southern Baptist Convention. With no reference to slavery, the new denomination was founded, as the constitution suggested, "for the purpose of carrying into effect the benevolent intention of our constituents, by organizing a plan for eliciting, combining, and directing the energies of the whole denomination in one sacred effort, for the propagation of the Gospel."[175] Denied their right to hold their positions on slavery and fulfill their understanding of the missionary imperative, the Southerners began a new movement that was at once united around evangelical zeal and Southern cultural mores.

Southern Baptists immediately established a more connectional organization, a convention, in which specific agencies were less separate and autonomous, with a more unified approach to programs, communication, and, ultimately, funding. This was largely due to the work of individuals such as William B. Johnson (1782–1862), former president of the Triennial Convention and first president of the Southern Baptist Convention. Johnson suggested that the schism would have positive effects by producing two mission organizations and expanding the number of missionaries. He proposed an organization based on the idea of "one Convention, embodying the whole Denomination, together with separate and distinct Boards, for each object of benevolent enterprise, located at different places, and all amenable to the Convention."[176] The phrase "all amenable to the Convention" meant that the new denomination would begin on a more connectional base than had previous Baptist groups in America. While agencies were connected through the convention, a society method of funding was retained. Membership and representation could come from individuals, churches, associations, and state conventions.

The question of human slavery was at the heart of the schism. An editorial in the *Virginia Religious Herald* contended that Southerners separated from "the Boston Board," "not because we reside at the South, but because they have adopted an unconstitutional and unscriptural principle to govern their future course. The principle is this—That holding slaves is, under all circumstances, incompatible with the office of the Christian ministry. On this point we take issue with them; and verily believe, that, when the mists of prejudice shall have been scattered, we shall stand justified in the eyes of the world."[177]

Some Southern Baptist historians placed slavery in the broader context of "sectionalism," a claim that tended to minimize the denomination's support of the South's "Peculiar Institution."[178] Others viewed slavery as the deciding factor in the creation of a denomination born of "schism and racism."[179]

A Response to Controversy: Baptist Confessions of Faith

Amid divisive controversies and the formation of new denominations, Baptists looked to confessions of faith to provide a framework for unity and doctrinal stability. Two confessions, the New Hampshire Confession of Faith and a Free Will Baptist Confession of Faith, illustrate the effort to articulate common dogmas. The New Hampshire Confession represents a more modified Calvinism, while the Free Will Confession demonstrates a specific kind of Arminianism evident in American Baptist life.

The New Hampshire Confession: Modified Calvinism

The New Hampshire Confession became one of the most popular statements of Baptist faith used by churches and denominational organizations well into the twentieth century. It was written at a time when certain Baptists struggled to modify elements of Calvinism, and it became an effective response to controversies involving Arminianism, Landmarkism, and the antimission movement.

The need for a confession developed in part because Free Will Baptists were disseminating their Arminianism throughout New Hampshire by the late 1700s.[180] It made a case for preaching the gospel to the entire world in order that all might hear and (potentially) respond to the Word of God. Further, the modification of Calvinist doctrines of predestination and election reflected the growing democratic idealism of the American experience and the belief that individuals could have a say in their political and spiritual future.

The idea for the Confession began in 1830 when the Baptist Convention of New Hampshire established a committee to construct "such a Declaration of Faith and Practice, together with a Covenant, as may be thought agreeable and consistent with the views of all our churches in the State."[181] A final draft was approved by the Board in 1833, but it was never officially approved by the Convention itself. All copies of the original have been lost, and the Confession was revised later by numerous individuals, churches, and organizations.

The document gained prominence and popularity when it was published by John Newton Brown (who added articles on "Sanctification" and "Repentance and Faith") in *The Baptist Church Manual*. It was republished in 1867 as a *Church Manual*, compiled by Landmarkist James Pendleton.

The statement on "the Scriptures" asserted that "the Holy Bible was written by men divinely inspired, and is a perfect treasure of heavenly instruction; that it has God for its author, salvation for its end, and truth, without any mixture of error, for its matter."[182] Although the phrase "truth, without any mixture of error" became a popular definition of biblical authority, its exact meaning has been debated extensively, especially in terms of the doctrine of biblical inerrancy.

A section on "the Freeness of Salvation" opened the door to the idea that all persons, not simply a predetermined elect, might receive salvation. It reads, "That the blessings of salvation are made free to all by the Gospel; that it is the immediate duty of all to accept them by a cordial [penitent] and obedient faith; and that nothing prevents the salvation of the greatest sinner on earth except his own ... voluntary refusal to submit to the Lord Jesus Christ."[183] This represents something of a departure from the doctrine of election taught in the Philadelphia Confession of Faith. Indeed, the New Hampshire Confession defines election as "the gracious purpose of God, according to which he [graciously] regenerates, sanctifies, and saves sinners; that being perfectly consistent with the free agency in man."[184] The document retains a staunchly Calvinist understanding of "the Perseverance of Saints," noting, "That such only are real believers as endure unto the end."

A "Gospel Church" is defined thus: "A visible Church of Christ is a congregation of baptized believers, associated by covenant in the faith and fellowship of the Gospel."[185] The church observes baptism as showing forth in "a solemn and beautiful emblem, our faith in a crucified, buried, and risen Saviour, with its purifying power." Likewise, through the Lord's Supper, church members "by the [sacred] use of bread and wine, are to commemorate together the dying love of Christ."[186]

By the middle of the nineteenth century, the unofficial New Hampshire Confession took its place along with the Philadelphia Confession as one of the major theological statements used among Baptists in America. Churches were organized around its theological formulations, Baptist associations and conventions used it to define terms of fellowship, and schools employed it to establish doctrinal boundaries for teachers. Its modified Calvinist dogmas served as a helpful outline for many evangelical, revivalistic Baptist groups. The New Hampshire Confession served as the guide for Southern Baptists' first confession, the Baptist Faith and Message, initially approved in 1925.

A Free Will Baptist Confession of Faith

The New Hampshire Confession was not the only doctrinal statement composed by nineteenth-century Baptists. Free Will Baptists, begun by Benjamin Randall, adopted their first Confession of Faith in 1834. Commissioned by the General Conference, the Confession received the Conference's official approval seven years later.

The Free Will Baptists in the North merged with the Northern Baptist Convention in 1911. Free Will Baptists in the South formed several different groups or conferences, dividing over foot washing and other doctrines and practices. In 1935, the Cooperative General Association and the Eastern General Conference were united into the National Association of Free Will Baptists. A revised Confession of Faith was approved in 1948.

The early Confession affirmed the general atonement, the salvation of infants, and the idea that "the call of the Gospel is co-extensive with the atonement to all men."[187] Salvation involves both an act of God and the cooperation of the sinner. "The power to believe is the gift of God, but believing is an act of the creature, which is required as a condition of pardon, and without which the sinner cannot obtain salvation."[188] The document acknowledged that although "there are strong grounds to hope that the truly regenerate will persevere unto the end, and be saved, ... their future obedience and final salvation are neither determined nor certain, since through infirmity and manifold temptations they are in danger of falling."[189] It also contained articles supporting "tithing" as the primary biblical source of church funds, and "ordinances," including baptism, the Lord's Supper, and the washing of feet. This last practice was described as "a sacred ordinance, which teaches humility," and as "the duty and happy prerogative of every believer" to practice.[190]

Doctrinal statements such as the Free Will Baptist Confession, the New Hampshire Confession, and the Philadelphia Confession reflect the similarities and differences of Baptist groups in the United States. They demonstrate the breadth of Baptist doctrinal opinions across a wide theological spectrum.

American Baptists at Midcentury

By the middle of the nineteenth century, Baptists represented a powerful spiritual and political force in the United States. They had produced numerous subgroups, with theological orientations from Calvinist to Arminian. Some were deeply committed to the missionary imperative, while others eschewed it entirely. However hesitantly, many Baptists participated in the formation of denominational programs and structures alongside and beyond their local congregations. Baptist women, kept out of official church leadership, provided significant guidance for Baptist entities from the local church to the foreign mission field. Although Baptist churches included many African American members, those same communities of faith divided over the nature of slavery and its place in the Bible and the nation. The schism that struck the Baptist community in 1845 was a prelude to divisions that soon would descend on the entire country.

Notes

1. Gregory A. Wills, *Democratic Religion: Freedom, Authority, and Church Discipline in the Baptist South, 1785–1900* (New York: Oxford University Press, 1997), 8.
2. Sidney Mead, *The Lively Experiment: The Shaping of Christianity in America* (New York: Harper & Row, 1963).
3. Ibid., 40.
4. George W. Purefoy, *A History of the Sandy Creek Baptist Association, from Its Organization in A.D. 1759, to 1858* (1859; reprint, New York: Arno Press, 1980), 75.
5. Peter Cartwright, *The Autobiography of Peter Cartwright* (New York: Phillips and Hunt, 1856), 133–34.
6. William Warren Sweet, *Religion in the Development of American Culture, 1765–1840* (New York: Charles Scribner's Sons, 1952), 158.
7. Ibid., 111.
8. Bill J. Leonard, ed., *Early American Christianity* (Nashville: Broadman, 1983), 123.
9. Minutes of the Walnut Street Baptist Church, Louisville, Kentucky, 1874.
10. John Taylor, *A History of Ten Churches* (Frankfort, Ky.: J. H. Holeman, 1823), 37.
11. Ibid., 141.
12. Ibid., 142.
13. Ibid., 69.
14. Christine Leigh Heyrman, *Southern Cross: The Beginnings of the Bible Belt* (New York: Knopf, 1997), 162. Heyrman also suggests that such spiritual insight was not necessarily extended by white preachers to African American women (165).
15. Ibid., 166.
16. Ibid., 179.
17. Ibid., 201.
18. James Owen Renault, "The Changing Patterns of Separate Baptist Religious Life, 1803–1977," *Baptist History and Heritage* (October 1979): 16.
19. Ibid., 16–17.
20. Ibid., 20.
21. Glenn T. Miller, "Baptist World Outreach and U.S. Foreign Affairs," in *Baptists and the American Experience*, ed. James E. Wood (Valley Forge, Pa.: Judson Press, 1976), 156.
22. Helen Emery Falls, "Baptist Women in Missions Support in the Nineteenth Century," *Baptist History and Heritage* (January 1977): 26.
23. Ibid. (citing R. Pierce Beaver, *All Loves Excelling: American Protestant Women in World Mission* [Grand Rapids: Eerdmans, 1968], 14).
24. William H. Brackney, *The Baptists* (New York: Greenwood Press, 1988), 280.
25. Falls, "Baptist Women," 27.
26. Walter B. Shurden, "The Baptist Drive for a Missionary Consciousness: Associational Activities before 1814," *Quarterly Review* (April–June 1979): 63.

27. Roger Hayden, "Kettering 1792 and Philadelphia 1814," *Baptist Quarterly* (January 1965): 5.
28. Shurden, "Missionary Consciousness," 64.
29. Ibid., 28.
30. Ibid., 28–29.
31. Ibid., 27.
32. Dana L. Robert, *American Women in Mission: A Social History of Their Thought and Practice* (Macon, Ga.: Mercer University Press, 1996), 7 (citing James D. Knowles, *Memoir of Mrs. Ann H. Judson, Late Missionary to Burmah: Including a History of the American Baptist Mission in the Burman Empire,* 4th ed. [Boston: Lincoln & Edmands, 1831], 19–20).
33. Ibid., 8 (citing Knowles, *Ann H. Judson,* 19–20).
34. Ibid., 19 (citing Knowles, *Ann H. Judson,* 19–20).
35. Francis Wayland, *A Memoir of the Life and Labors of the Rev. Adoniram Judson, D.D.,* 2 vols. (Boston: Phillips, Sampson, 1853), 1:110.
36. H. Leon McBeth, *A Sourcebook for Baptist Heritage* (Nashville: Broadman, 1990), 207.
37. Joan Jacobs Brumberg, *Mission for Life: The Story of the Family of Adoniram Judson, the Dramatic Events of the First American Foreign Mission, and the Course of Evangelical Religion in the Nineteenth Century* (New York: Free Press, 1980), 5.
38. Ibid.
39. Shurden, "Missionary Consciousness," 66 (citing minutes of the Charleston Association, 1813).
40. William H. Brackney, *Baptist Life and Thought: 1600–1980* (Valley Forge, Pa.: Judson Press, 1983), 170 (citing minutes of the General Missionary Convention, May 21, 1814).
41. Ibid., 170.
42. Walter B. Shurden, "The Baptist Drive for Denominational Unity: Associational Activities before 1814," *Quarterly Review* 40 (October–December 1979): 53 (citing A. D. Gillette, *Minutes of the Philadelphia Baptist Association* [Philadelphia: American Baptist Publication Society, 1851], 343).
43. Ibid.
44. Robert Baker, *The Southern Baptist Convention and Its People* (Nashville: Broadman, 1972), 108.
45. "Proceedings of the Baptist Convention of Illinois, October 9–12, 1834," *American Baptist Quarterly* (September 1984): 255.
46. Falls, "Baptist Women," 32.
47. Ibid., 32–33.
48. Ibid., 33.
49. H. Leon McBeth, "The Role of Women in Southern Baptist History," *Baptist History and Heritage* 12 (January 1977): 5.
50. Falls, "Baptist Women," 35.
51. McBeth, "Role of Women," 6.
52. Albert H. Newman, ed., *A Century of Baptist Achievement* (Philadelphia: American Baptist Publication Society, 1901), 250.
53. *Massachusetts Baptist Missionary Magazine* 3 (1813): 290. See also James A. Patterson, "Motives in the Development of Foreign Missions among American Baptists 1810–1826," *Foundations* 19 (October–December 1976): 300.
54. Miller, "Baptist World Outreach," 158.
55. *Massachusetts Baptist Missionary Magazine,* 304.
56. Ibid., 308.
57. Ibid., 312.
58. *Proceedings of the Convention Held in the City of New York on the 27th of April, 1832, for the Formation of the American Baptist Home Mission Society* (New York, 1831), 6.
59. Ibid., 12.
60. *The Fourth Report of the Executive Committee of the American Baptist Home Mission Society* (New York: 1836), 18.
61. Ibid, 18–19.
62. Charles White, *A Century of Faith* (Philadelphia: Judson Press, 1932), 45.
63. Robert A. Baker, *A Baptist Source Book, with Particular Reference to Southern Baptists* (Nashville: Broadman, 1966), 62–75; also Clarence C. Goen, *Broken Churches, Broken Nation: Denominational Schisms and the Coming of the American Civil War* (Macon, Ga.: Mercer University Press, 1985), 60.
64. Roger Hayden, "Bristol Baptist College and America," *Baptist History and Heritage* (October 1979): 32–33. The original source of these remarks is not indicated.
65. Ibid., 32. The original source of this quotation is not given.
66. Brackney, *Baptist Life and Thought,* 177–79 (citing *American Baptist Magazine* [July 1826]: 208–9).
67. Hayden, "Bristol Baptist College," 29.
68. Winthrop Hudson suggested that Francis Wayland and other New England Baptists gained control of the Triennial Convention and discouraged regional connections; see Hudson, "Stumbling into Disorder," *Foundations* 1 (April 1958): 45–60. Robert Torbet asserted that the denomination was not yet mature enough for a national identity and needed time to develop regional alliances; see Torbet, *A History of the Baptists,* 3rd ed. (Valley Forge: Judson Press, 1973,) 310.
69. Hayden, "Bristol Baptist College," 32.
70. McBeth, *Sourcebook,* 216 (citing *American Baptist Magazine* and *Missionary Intelligencer* [May 1824]: 324–28).
71. Ibid., 215.
72. Baker, *Southern Baptist Convention,* 111.

73. McBeth, *Sourcebook,* 220 (citing Francis Wayland, *Notes on the Principles and Practices of Baptist Churches* [New York: Sheldon, Blakeman, 1857], 177–95).

74. Shurden, "Denominational Unity," 51 (citing "Constitution of the North Carolina General Meeting of Correspondence," *The Wake Forest Student* [October 1905]: 55–60).

75. Newman, *Baptist Achievement,* 309.

76. Ibid., 314.

77. Wayland, *Principles and Practices,* 183–84. See also James E. Carter, "Dealing with Doctrinal Conflict in Associational History, " *Baptist History and Heritage* (April 1982): 37.

78. Norman Maring, *Baptists in New Jersey* (Valley Forge, Pa.: Judson Press, 1964), 117 (citing *The Union Spelling Book* [Philadelphia: American Sunday School Union, 1838], 115).

79. Ibid., 117.

80. Nancy Hardesty, *Great Women of Faith: The Strength and Influence of Christian Women* (Grand Rapids, Mich.: Baker, 1980), 73.

81. Donald G. Mathews, *Religion in the Old South* (Chicago: University of Chicago Press, 1977), 88; and Bill J. Leonard, "What Can the Baptist Tradition Contribute to Christian Higher Education?" in *Models for Christian Higher Education,* ed. Richard Hughes and William Adrian (Grand Rapids, Mich.: Eerdmans, 1997), 367–82.

82. McBeth, *Sourcebook,* 238.

83. Ibid.

84. Brumberg, *Mission for Life,* 48 (citing Knowles, *Ann H. Judson,* 91).

85. Brumberg, *Mission for Life,* 96–103, has an excellent description of these ordeals.

86. Wayland, *Adoniram Judson,* 1:476.

87. Ibid., 1:423.

88. Ann H. Judson, *A Particular Relation of the American Baptist Mission to the Burman Empire* (Washington City: John S. Meehan, 1823), 62–63.

89. Robert, *American Women in Mission,* 49.

90. Falls, "Baptist Women," 30.

91. McBeth, *Sourcebook,* 211 (citing *Second Annual Report of the Baptist Board of Foreign Missions* [Philadelphia, 1816], 112).

92. Falls, "Baptist Women," 31.

93. Ibid.

94. Ibid., 33.

95. Brumberg, *Mission for Life,* 70.

96. Ibid., 80.

97. H. Leon McBeth, *The Baptist Heritage* (Nashville: Broadman, 1987), 205.

98. Salvatore Mondello, "Isabel Crawford, the Making of a Missionary: Part 1," *Foundations* 21 (October–December 1978): 325–27.

99. Ibid., 334.

100. Ibid.

101. McBeth, *Sourcebook,* 227 (citing Rufus Babcock, ed., *Forty Years of Pioneer Life: Memoir of John Mason Peck, D.D.* [Carbondale: Southern Illinois University Press, 1965], 48–49).

102. R. Virgil Santee, "Sallie Paine Peck," *American Baptist Quarterly* (September 1984): 226.

103. *Massachusetts Baptist Missionary Magazine* (September 1811): 83. For other memorials, see *Massachusetts Baptist Missionary Magazine* (May 1813): 308–16.

104. McBeth, "Role of Women," 7.

105. McBeth, *Sourcebook,* 226.

106. Robert G. Gardner, "Baptists and the Indians of North America, 1674–1845," *Baptist History and Heritage* (July 1983): 21.

107. Ibid., 23.

108. Frank H. Woyke, "Other Ethnic Baptists," in Wood, ed., *American Experience,* 326.

109. Brackney, *The Baptists,* 223.

110. Gardner, "Baptists and the Indians," 23.

111. Ibid., 25.

112. William McLoughlin, *Cherokees and Missionaries, 1789–1839* (New Haven: Yale University Press, 1984), 155.

113. Ibid.

114. Ibid.

115. Ibid.

116. Ibid., 157.

117. Ibid., 156.

118. Ibid.

119. Russell Begaye, "The Story of Indian Southern Baptists," *Baptist History and Heritage* 18 (July 1983): 30; Bill J. Leonard, ed. *Dictionary of Baptists in America* (Downers Grove, Ill.: InterVarsity Press, 1994), 68–69.

120. Begaye, "Indian Southern Baptists," 31.

121. Ibid., 32.

122. *American Baptist Magazine and Missionary Intelligencer* (1818): 445.

123. Daniel Parker, *Views on the Two Seeds Taken from Genesis* (Vandalia, Ill.: Robert Blackwell, 1826), 7.

124. Ibid., 8.

125. Frank M. Masters, *A History of Baptists in Kentucky* (Louisville: Kentucky Baptist Historical Society, 1953), 196–97.

126. William Warren Sweet, *The Baptists, 1783–1830*, vol. 1 of *Religion on the American Frontier* (Chicago: University of Chicago Press, 1931), 72–76.

127. Maring, *Baptists in New Jersey*, 131 (citing Byron C. Lambert, "The Rise of Anti-Mission Baptists: Sources and Leaders, 1800–1840" [Ph.D. diss., University of Chicago, 1957], iv–viii, 405–12).

128. Ibid.

129. B. L. Beebe, comp., *The Feast of Fat Things* (Middletown, N.Y.: G. Beebe's Son, n.d.), 3–4. See also W. J. Berry, comp., *The Kehukee Declaration and Black Rock Address* (Elon, N.C.: Primitive Publications, n.d.), 24–41.

130. Ibid., 9.

131. Ibid., 21–22.

132. Terms for the so-called hyper-Calvinist, or Old School, Baptists evolve over time and are often difficult to track precisely. Many appear in W. P. Throgmorton, *The Throgmorton-Potter Debate* (St. Louis: Nixon-Jones, 1888).

133. Bradley T. Kimbrough, *The History of the Walnut Street Baptist Church, Louisville, Kentucky* (Louisville: Press of Western Recorder, 1949), 13–14.

134. Bill J. Leonard, *Community in Diversity: A History of Walnut Street Baptist Church, 1815–1990* (Louisville: Simons-Neely, 1990), 24–25.

135. George H. Orchard, *A Concise History of Foreign Baptists* (Nashville: Graves, Marks, & Rutland, 1859), xii.

136. Ibid., xviii.

137. Ibid., xiv.

138. James R. Graves, *Old Landmarkism: What Is It?* (Memphis: Baptist Book House, 1880), 26.

139. Ibid., 27.

140. Ibid., 28.

141. Ibid., 32.

142. Ibid., 41.

143. Ibid., 61.

144. Ibid., 68.

145. James M. Pendleton, *Distinctive Principles of Baptists* (Philadelphia: American Baptist Publication Society, 1882), 168.

146. James R. Graves, *The Watchman's Reply* (Nashville: Graves and Shankland, 1853), 11.

147. Ibid., 15.

148. David Music, "The Introduction of Musical Instruments into Baptist Churches in America," *Quarterly Review* 40 (October–December 1979): 57–60.

149. Ibid., 59–60.

150. Ibid., 60.

151. Goen, *Broken Churches, Broken Nation*.

152. H. Shelton Smith, *In His Image, but ... : Racism in Southern Religion, 1780–1910* (Durham, N.C.: Duke University Press, 1972), 47.

153. Ibid., 48 (citing minutes of the Virginia Baptist General Committee, 1790).

154. Ibid., 50–51.

155. Robert A. Baker, *Relations between Northern and Southern Baptists*, 2nd ed. (1954; reprint, New York: Arno Press, 1980), 43.

156. Edwin S. Gaustad, *Historical Atlas of Religion in America*, rev. ed. (San Francisco: Harper & Row, 1976), 58.

157. Ibid., 54.

158. Richard Furman, "An Exposition" (Charleston, December 24, 1822), in Leonard, ed. *Early American Christianity*, 381–82.

159. Ibid., 383.

160. Smith, *In His Image*, 115.

161. Larry E. Tise, *Proslavery: A History of the Defense of Slavery in America, 1701–1840* (Athens: University of Georgia Press, 1987), 363–66.

162. Smith, *In His Image*, 143.

163. James H. Cuthbert, *Life of Richard Fuller, D.D.* (New York: Sheldon, 1879), 155–57.

164. Francis Wayland, *Elements of Moral Science*, 4th ed. (Boston: Gould, Kendall, and Lincoln, 1848), 203 (cited in Smith, *In His Image*, 138–39).

165. Ibid., 119.

166. "Address," *Baptist Missionary Magazine* 20 (December 1840): 281–84.

167. Smith, *In His Image*, 121.

168. Baker, *Baptist Source Book*, 94.

169. F. Calvin Parker, *Jonathan Goble of Japan: Marine, Missionary, Maverick* (Lanham, Md.: University Press of America, 1990), 79.

170. Ibid., 80.

171. Goen, *Broken Churches, Broken Nation*, 93.

172. Ibid., 93–98.

173. McBeth, *Sourcebook*, 257 (citing *Minutes of the Meetings of the American Baptist Home Mission Society and of Its Executive Committee*, book 2 [October 7, 1844]: 303).

174. Ibid. (citing *Minutes of the Meetings,* 303).

175. Baker, *Baptist Source Book,* 116.

176. Ibid., 114.

177. Brackney, *Baptist Life and Thought,* 232 (citing *The Religious Herald,* April 10, 1845).

178. Baker, *Southern Baptist Convention,* 153–59; William W. Barnes, *A History of the Southern Baptist Convention, 1845–1953* (Nashville: Broadman, 1954), 18–19.

179. McBeth, *The Baptist Heritage,* 381–91; Jesse C. Fletcher, *The Southern Baptist Convention: A Sesquicentennial History* (Nashville: Broadman & Holman, 1994), 39–40; Bill J. Leonard, *God's Last and Only Hope: The Fragmentation of the Southern Baptist Convention* (Grand Rapids, Mich.: Eerdmans, 1990).

180. William Lumpkin, *Baptist Confessions of Faith* (Chicago: Judson Press, 1959), 360.

181. Ibid.

182. Ibid., 361–62.

183. Ibid., 363.

184. Ibid., 364.

185. Ibid., 365.

186. Ibid., 366.

187. Ibid., 373.

188. Ibid.

189. Ibid. 374.

190. Ibid., 375–76.

Chapter 9
Baptists in the United States: 1845–1900

THE SECOND HALF OF THE NINETEENTH CENTURY WAS A TIME OF BOTH TRAUMA and promise in American religious and social life. The Civil War created an almost unbearable national crisis evident in loss of life, devastation of property, and divisions that endured well into the twentieth century and beyond. The war's aftermath witnessed the increasing industrialization of the North, the long road to "Reconstruction" in the South, and the subsequent westward expansion of the nation.

Also during this period, Baptist denominationalism continued to develop, often around regional and ethnic distinctions. Baptist denominations, churches, and individuals were caught up in many of the great crises and controversies of the times. The schism of 1845 led to new organizations and identities, North and South, inside and outside the old Triennial Convention. Other Baptist groups also took shape during the period.

Baptists and the Civil War

Prelude: The Mexican War
The Civil War was not the first armed conflict to divide Baptists in America. The Mexican War created divisions among Baptists, particularly over the question of slavery and its role in the admission of new states to the Union. The war began in 1846, less than a year after the schism over slavery. Morgan J. Rhees, pastor of Second Baptist Church, Wilmington, Delaware, reflected the views of many northern Baptists when he declared, "I believe that God has a controversy with this nation because ... of the oppression of the Indian and the African ... to which we are now adding blood guiltiness in war [with Mexico]. That vengeance may be averted ... I firmly believe, but if it is, it must be by the preserving and purifying influence of the Gospel of Christ."[1]

In its 1848 report, the American Baptist Home Mission Society (ABHMS) observed that the war with Mexico had "been productive of much moral evil, especially in the western states. The military spirit has diffused itself widely among all classes of community, reaching even the churches, and inducing many of their members to gird themselves for bloody conflict with their fellow men."[2]

While some Southern Baptists supported the Mexican War, others opted to "leave it to Caesar." This hesitancy about war largely vanished with the beginning of the siege of Fort Sumter.[3] Prior to the Civil War, certain Baptist leaders promoted peace efforts aimed at avoiding civil conflict at home or abroad. Francis Wayland served as president of the American Peace Society from 1859 to 1861. Wayland told the Boston Baptist Foreign Missionary Society in 1823, "Our object is to purify the whole earth from abominations [slavery, widow-burning]. Our object will not have been accomplished till the tomahawk shall be buried forever, and the tree of peace spread its broad branches from the Atlantick to the Pacifick."[4]

Confrontations over slavery created a dilemma for the American Peace Society, and most of its members reluctantly accepted the war as a means to exterminate the greater evil of slavery. Wayland acknowledged that war might be a form of divine judgment and noted, "The Judge of the whole earth will do justice. He hears the cry of the oppressed, and he will in the end terribly deliver them."[5]

The Civil War: The Early Years

With the outbreak of Civil War, Baptists North and South enlisted, ministers became chaplains, and denominational groups rallied in support of their respective nations. In 1861, the Southern Baptist Convention (SBC) approved ten resolutions that championed the Southern position. One declared, "That we most cordially approve of the formation of the Government of the Confederate States of America, and admire and applaud the noble course of that Government up to this present time."[6] In 1863, SBC resolutions condemned the United States government for "the war which has been forced upon us" and expressed opposition "to a reunion with the United States on any terms whatever." They acknowledged "the hand of God in the preservation of our victories with which he has crowned our arms."[7] In the North, the newly renamed American Baptist Missionary Union offered a resolution in 1861 stating that "what was bought at Bunker Hill, Valley Forge, and Yorktown, was not, with our One consent, sold at Montgomery; that we dispute the legality of the bargain, and, on the strength of the Lord God of our fathers, shall hope to contest, through this generation, if need be, the feasibility of the transfer."[8] They also called for a pastoral response to the needs of their troops.

Colporteurs and Chaplains

As the war escalated, Baptists and other Southern Protestants commissioned bands of colporteurs who distributed Bibles and other religious literature among soldiers. In his study of "religion in Lee's Army," written after the war, Baptist chaplain J. William Jones observed, "Earliest in the important work of colportage was the Baptist Church, one of the most powerful denominations in the South." He cited the actions of the General Association of the Baptist Churches in Virginia, which began work among the troops by May 1861.[9] The Publication Board called for "colportage effort among the soldiers" because "these are exposed to peculiar temptations, and in no way can we better aid them in resisting these than by affording them good books."[10] Along with the "plan of salvation," Southern tractarians addressed topics such as "Profane Swearing," "Gambler's Balance Sheet," and "Lincoln and Liquor." The South's most popular tract, however, was "A Mother's Parting Words to Her Soldier Boy," a treatise that reportedly contributed to numerous deathbed conversions.[11]

Southern Baptist chaplains also were on the scene. The *Louisville Courier* reported from Virginia, "Our fighting chaplain, Rev. H. A. Tupper, of the Ninth Georgia, a chaplain in the Confederate army and a Baptist minister at home, a lover and defender of civil and religious liberty everywhere, preached us a very able discourse from the advice of Eli to Joshua: 'Be ye men of good courage.' It was no war philippic, but an earnest, heartfelt, Christian discourse."[12]

Wartime Competition

Denominational competition persisted even in wartime. Baptist chaplain William Jones was accused of "his own peculiar [Baptist] doctrines" and of reading "to the crowd of all them Baptist Scriptures." To this a Presbyterian chaplain responded, "Why, I do not admit that those are 'Baptist Scriptures.'"[13] The call for chaplains continued throughout the war, with the SBC in 1863 offering a resolution that "the providence of God calls loudly on His people to make prompt and vigorous efforts to secure the services of chaplains, and to send forth missionaries and colporteurs into the field."[14]

Many Baptists opposed paying chaplains with public funds. In 1864, Georgia Baptists passed a resolution suggesting that "this Convention does not approve of the principle of appointing chaplains for the army to be paid out of the public treasury."[15] As the Northern armies gained Southern territory, representatives of the Northern Missionary Society were given jurisdiction over Baptist churches in the region. In 1864, the War Department issued an order directing military units "to place at the disposal of the American Baptist Home Mission Society all houses of worship belonging to the Baptist Churches South, in which a loyal minister of said church does not now officiate." The directive noted that "no doubt is entertained" as to the loyalty of the Board's representatives. Southern Baptists were not pleased with the participation of the Mission Society in such endeavors. The Northerners answered that they were protecting Baptist meetinghouses from confiscation by the military.[16] After the war, the Northern Home Missionary Society directed its energies toward the evangelization and education of newly freed men and women.

At War's End

With the South's surrender, some Northern Baptists demanded both repentance and retribution from the South. The General Conference of Free Will Baptists, meeting in October 1868, adopted a statement that hallowed "the memory of our patriot dead, ... believing as we do that men never died in a holier cause." The resolution also declared, "That the rebellion of 1861 should be branded by our government as a high crime against God, liberty and humanity" and warned, "That any church or political party that affiliates with the unrepentant rebels in ecclesiastical or political action, is deserving of the same contempt as that in which we hold the rebels themselves."[17]

Francis Wayland, angry with Southern recalcitrance, maintained, "The temper of the South in this war has been as bad as it can be, and in the professors of religion worse of all. If they were hungry, I would feed them; if thirsty, I would give them drink; if sick or in prison, I would visit them; but beyond this I eschew them. Selah."[18] Although the nation was reunited, Southern Baptists resisted reunification with Baptists in the North. A postwar resolution stated, "Resolved, 1st. That the Southern Baptist Convention is a permanent institution.... The necessity of sustaining it is more imperative now than at any former time."[19]

The war's end brought a rebirth of Baptist pacifism. George Dana Boardman (b. 1828), pastor of First Baptist Church, Philadelphia, acknowledged that like the Revolutionary War and certain biblical conflicts, the Civil War was "relatively right." However, he rejected all future wars as "absolutely wrong." Boardman contended, "All war in this closing part of the nineteenth century of Christ's grace is inhuman and unchristian."[20] Other Baptists also made known their pacifist sentiments.

The American Baptist Missionary Union

In 1846, the General Convention of the Baptist Denomination in the United States for Foreign Missions was reorganized and renamed the American Baptist Missionary Union. The new Union's "single object" was to "diffuse the knowledge of the religion of Jesus Christ, by means of missions, throughout the world."[21] Initially, only "life members" were accepted. These included persons who were present at the first meeting and others who made a contribution "at one time, of not less than one hundred dollars."[22] Meetings were held annually, and all members were invited to attend. The American Baptist Missionary Union remained a society focused only on foreign missions. In 1910, the name was changed to the American Baptist Foreign Mission Society.[23]

Both the Home Mission Society and the Publication Society revised their charters after the break with the Southerners. The American Baptist Home Mission Society retained its original name, while the American Baptist Publication and Sunday School Society became the American Baptist Publication Society. The purpose of the latter organization was "to promote evangelical religion by means of the Bible, the Printing-press, Colportage, Sunday Schools, and other appropriate ways."[24] In April 1845, the Home Mission Society, anticipating a schism with the South "owing to the strong views of Churches and individuals against the appointment of Slaveholders to serve the Society," recommended that the Northern churches retain the original charter, as incorporated in the North. The Executive Committee of the Society was encouraged "to adjust, upon amicable, honorable and liberal principles, whatever claims may be presented by brethren who shall feel, upon the separation, unable further to co-operate with the Society."[25]

The Home Mission Society voted in 1862 to provide means "for the occupation by our missionaries of such southern fields as in the Providence of God may be opened to our operations."[26] This meant that the Northerners would minister "to free and bond throughout the whole southern section of our country, so fast and so far as the progress of our arms, and the restoration of order and law shall open the way."[27] The presence of Northern Baptist workers in the South enhanced mission work and extended the divisions.

Women's Missionary Societies

Long active in the missionary cause, Baptist women formed societies and auxiliaries after the Civil War. Most were based on the earlier strategy of "woman's work for woman." As Dana Robert noted, the basic goal was "to evangelize women and so to bring them to salvation." Yet it also was "intertwined with civilization, with being elevated by Christianity into social equality with western women and into positions of respect in their own societies."[28] To accomplish this end, a female missionary task force was necessary. Baptist agencies began an effort to send more women, married and single, to the field.

The idea of "woman's work for woman" was evident in the charter of the Woman's Baptist Missionary Society, founded in 1874 "for the purpose of the Christianization of women in foreign lands."[29] In 1883, it became the Woman's Baptist Foreign Missionary Society, aimed at "the elevation and Christianization of women and children in foreign lands."[30] It intended to engage Baptist women "in sending out and supporting women missionaries to do evangelistic, educational and medical work on the foreign fields; in developing and employing native Christian teachers and Bible women, physicians and nurses, and in erecting such buildings ... necessary for the prosecution of the work."[31] The Society sponsored women who would preach and teach the gospel to children and women and enlist the services of indigenous "Bible women" to work among their own people.

Women participated in the founding of home missions societies. Among the first was the Woman's Baptist Home Mission Society of Michigan, founded in 1873. It aimed at evangelizing "the freed men and other needy people of this country." In February 1877, the Women's Baptist Mission Society was founded in Chicago. The Woman's American Baptist Home Mission Society, Boston, began in the same year. Its purpose was "the evangelization of women among the freed people, the Indians, the heathen immigrants, and the new settlements of the West." These three groups carried out separate ministries for over thirty years, until 1909, when they united in the Woman's American Baptist Home Mission Society.

In 1877, the Chicago-based Society commissioned Joanna P. Moore, a woman already working among freed blacks. Sent to postwar New Orleans, she was joined in 1878 by Jennie Peck, Helen Jackson, Agnes Wilson, and Sarah Butler. They aided African American women in developing Sunday schools and other educational programs. An appeal from two African American pastors in Alabama led the Society to appoint Ela Knapp and Anna L. Boorman in the early 1890s. They spent thirty-five years developing educational programs, Bible classes, and women and children's programs. Their extensive association with the black community made them an object of controversy in the segregated South.[33]

In response to alcohol abuse among indigent families, the missionary women organized "Bands of Hope," which promoted temperance (abstinence). They taught children to sing, "Pure cold water, that's the drink for me, For I'm a young abstainer, from drinking customs free."[34] The Woman's ABHMS established schools to serve particular populations, especially in the South. By 1881, they were the sole supporters of the Mather Industrial School, established in 1867 in Beaufort, South Carolina, by Rachel Crane Mather, a Boston Baptist teacher. In 1881, the Society also established Spelman College in Atlanta for the purpose of teaching African American young women. These are but two of a number of educational and training schools that the Society helped to support. More than thirty such schools were formed by the Women's Society in the late nineteenth and early twentieth centuries. They organized an array of "friendship houses" as community centers for women, children, and families in locations inside and outside the United States.[35]

The Woman's American Baptist Home Mission Society (Chicago) was founded to "aid in Christianizing North America by means of evangelistic and educational work in homes, through schools, by cooperation with churches, and by such other means as may be deemed desirable."[36] Among the many activities of the Woman's Society was the preparation of "missionary boxes" to be sent to missionaries and their families. Items included "plain, substantial wearing apparel, bedding, stationery, theological books and Sabbath school books," as well as "any light articles which are useful in families, as knives and forks, spoons, scissors, needles, pins, thimbles, thread, yarn, etc."[37]

In 1881, the Woman's ABHMS organized the Baptist Missionary Training School in Chicago. The training school was the "first school in the world established for the definite training of women for missionary service, pioneer and pattern for later similar institutions."[38] The program lasted three to six months and offered instruction in biblical studies, rudimentary medical care, and "domestic" affairs. By 1883, the program was extended to ten months. In 1924, an affiliation was developed between the women's training school and Berkeley Baptist Divinity School in California. It offered a two-year master's degree to women who had a bachelor's degree. Women with no college training could take a four-year program toward a bachelor of theology.[39]

Missionary Appointments

Following the division of 1845, the mission boards, North and South, continued to appoint missionaries. One of the more colorful and controversial missionaries to be sent out before the Civil War was Jonathan Goble (1827–1896), who, along with his wife, Eliza, and their daughter, Dorinda, was sent to Japan by the American Baptist Free Mission Society, an antislavery group. Although appointed in 1859, Goble was compelled to subscribe his own support as the Baptists' first missionary in Japan.[40]

The family arrived in Japan in April 1860. Goble worked as a cobbler—a trade that he actually introduced into Japanese culture. During their first term, 1860–1871, Goble worked to translate the Gospels and the book of Acts into Japanese. A second term began in 1873, with Goble serving as an appointee of the American Baptist Missionary Union. That agency dropped him after a year, largely because of his outbursts of temper that produced physical assaults on Japanese converts. He continued missionary work as a colporteur for the American Bible Society and ultimately returned to the United States, where he died destitute in 1896.[41]

Southern Baptists' first missionaries to China included R. H. Graves, Matthew Yates, and T. P. Crawford. Crawford (1821–1902) was a genuine eccentric who took on Chinese dress and made a fortune in real estate speculation. Ultimately, he left the board and promoted Landmark views. Like other mission endeavors, those of the Southern Baptists were not immune to tragedy and death. J. L. Holmes was murdered by Chinese rebels; Robert Gaillard died in a Canton typhoon; and R. H. Graves's spouse died in China.[42] H. A. Tupper, who became executive secretary of the SBC Foreign Mission Board in 1872, commissioned postwar missionaries, including Edmonia Moon, the first single woman dispatched to China. Having had little or no training or preparation, Moon returned home worn out from the ordeal. As noted previously, her sister, Lottie, followed her to China and thrived there, becoming a missionary icon.

Baptists North and South: Divisions Continue

Southerners continued to complain about the work of the Northern Missionary Society in their regions, and many state conventions eschewed cooperation with Northern Baptist work. J. S. Backus, secretary to the Northern Society, insisted that the Confederacy and the SBC itself were anomalies that no longer could claim control over certain regional boundaries. He declared, "And now if it is politically and morally wrong to support 'the Southern Confederacy,' how can it be religiously right to support 'the southern Baptist Convention'? If the Government is to be one, why should not the Baptist denomination be one?"[43] While such statements were not well received by Southern Baptists, Baptists in the North continued to press for a reunion of the two denominations. During the 1870s, some Southern Baptist leaders, such as Richard Fuller, also voiced their hope for some reunion. During the period 1864–1888, the Home Missionary Society made numerous overtures for reunion, only to have them rejected by the Southerners.[44]

Following the war, the Home Missionary Society proposed a return to earlier auxiliary relationships with state Baptist conventions in the South. During the 1880s, state conventions in Texas and Arkansas began formal relationships with the Society. Georgia and Mississippi maintained partial connections, while other state conventions cooperated more informally. By 1883, the Baptist General Convention of Texas had developed a dual alignment with both the Home Mission Society (Northern) and the Southern Baptist Convention. The state convention, desperate for funds following the war, needed the $3,000 provided annually by the Mission Society. (Texans matched those funds through their own convention.) This relationship endured until 1886, when the Texas convention limited its affiliation entirely to the SBC.[45]

Robert A. Baker suggested that the decision of the Southerners to organize a connectional-based convention system rather than the older society structure contributed to the continuing divisions between Baptists, North and South. He wrote, "Had the south simply formed separate benevolent societies for each type of activity, it would have been possible for the various societies, conceived as they were, to work side by side in comparative harmony. It is doubtful that a denominational rigidity would have developed." The differences in polity worked against cooperation and reunion. Likewise, the war and its aftermath produced "a distinctive geographical area in a cultural, social, and economic atmosphere" that created "a territorial consciousness" for the new Southern denomination.[46]

As the nineteenth century drew to a close, Southern Baptists continued to complain about the presence of the Northern Mission Society in southern and southwestern regions. In 1882, E. T. Winkler of the Southern Home Mission Board observed that the Northern Society had 120 missionaries in the South—at least three times those supported by the SBC. Northerners contributed some $84,000 annually, while Southerners gave only $29,000 to comparable mission activity in the region. He also remarked, "Every one of the border States of the South is occupied by the Home Mission Society; and most of our older States are in co-operative alliance with the American Baptist Publication Society in colportage and Sunday School work."[47]

The scene was set for negotiations over these actions. At the Fortress Monroe (Virginia) Conference in 1894, Northerners and Southerners agreed to a plan for coordinating their missionary activities in the United States. In essence, the two groups agreed to continue their work in behalf of African Americans, but for reasons of space, finances, and polity, the Northern Home Mission Society would gradually decrease its activities in the South. They agreed that the SBC Home Mission Board would work to raise funds for "schools among the colored people" then under the support of the American Baptist Home Mission Society. While the schools remained under the supervision of the American Baptist Mission Society, advisory committees of Southern Baptists would be appointed for each of the schools. The representatives agreed that duplication of mission work "in the same locality" and "all antagonisms" would be avoided. New mission work would be directed "to localities not already occupied by the other."[48] Changes in Baptist organizational and regional life soon challenged the Fortress Monroe proposals.

Southern Baptists Deal with Defeat

The defeat in the Civil War brought spiritual, financial, and ideological devastation to the South. Churches were burned and destroyed, and financial resources were depleted.

Many Baptists were forced to come to terms with the South's defeat and its implications for their interpretation of the Bible. Some Southern Baptists simply could not believe that their biblical interpretations of slavery were mistaken. A Virginia editor insisted that God could never have permitted the South to suffer in order "that an inferior race might be released from nominal bondage and endowed with a freedom which, to them, is but another name for licentiousness, and which must end in complete extermination."[49] Others concluded that God permitted the South's defeat not because slavery was wrong but because Southerners failed to evangelize slaves adequately.[50]

In the search for ways to cope with defeat, Southern Baptists and other Southern Protestants looked to the "religion of the Lost Cause"—the idealization of the South's culture and religion. Defeated politically, the South turned to the cultural superiority of its mythic past. As Charles Reagan Wilson commented, "The Lost Cause was therefore the story of the linking of two profound human forces, religion and history."[51] Southern churches and their ministers exalted the heroism and values of the martyred Southern leaders, who had redeemed the region through a "baptism in blood." Wilson observed that Protestant ministers "used the Lost Cause to warn Southerners of their decline from past virtue, to promote moral reform, to encourage conversion to Christianity, and to educate the young in Southern traditions; in the fullness of time, they related it to American values."[52]

Churches also were forced to confront the devastation of the Southern economy. In an attempt to complete a new building, First Baptist Church, Wilmington, North Carolina, appealed for assistance beyond its membership. A solicitation letter read, "The general derangement of public affairs, consequent upon war, not only prevented any further progress upon the building, but has caused us to suffer a heavy loss, both in materials and money. While we are making every effort within ourselves to carry on the work, our present necessities require aid from abroad. Will you be so kind as to enclose ONE DOLLAR for this object?"[53] The building was completed with help from former Northern adversaries. Southern Baptists would accept Yankee money but not reunion.

Appalachian Baptist Communions

The SBC did not incorporate all Baptist groups in the South. The Baptist presence in the central Appalachian region is evident in numerous subdenominations that often refer to themselves as "old-timey" Baptists. These include Regular, Separate, Union, Primitive, and Old Regular Baptists. Howard Dorgan identified certain common characteristics shared by these Baptist communions, including (1) chanted songs sung a cappella, often accompanied by shouting and hugging; (2) foot washing and "living water" (outdoor) baptisms; (3) "governance rules that preserve Pauline gender mandates" and articles of decorum used by colonial Baptists; (4) sanctions against divorce and "double marriage" (remarriage while a divorced spouse is still living); and (5) similarity of preaching styles and other liturgical practices.[54]

Separate Baptists

Separate Baptists are Calvinists who date their origins from the First Great Awakening and the work of Shubal Stearns and Daniel Marshall. They include the South Kentucky Association of Separate Baptists and other participants in the General Association of Separate Baptists in Christ. Unlike many other Appalachian Baptist groups, Separate Baptists permit women to lead in worship and preach but do not ordain women to the ministry.[55]

Regular Baptists

Regular Baptists trace their roots to the 1760s and the founding of the Ketockton Association from the Philadelphia Association. Many Regulars moved into the Shenandoah Valley, spreading to Tennessee, North Carolina, and Kentucky. By the end of the twentieth century, Regular Baptist churches were evident in Allegheny, Ashe, Avery, Wilkes, and Yadkin Counties in North Carolina, and in the Virginia counties of Grayson and Smyth. The Little River Association of Regular Baptists included three congregations in North Carolina, one in Virginia, and one in Maryland. The Mountain Union Association of Regular Baptists included two North Carolina churches, two Maryland churches, and one communion in Pennsylvania. The Original Mountain Union Association of Regular Baptists claimed nine congregations in North Carolina and one in Virginia.[56]

Union Baptists

Several Union Baptist congregations developed in the 1860s as a result of schisms among the Regular Baptist churches. The name "Union" signified their support for the Northern cause in the Civil War. Nonetheless, Dorgan's studies have led him to classify them along with the Regulars, not as a separate subdenomination.[57]

Old Regular Baptists

Dorgan calls the Old Regular Baptists the "most traditional of the Central Appalachian Old-Time Baptist groups." He and Deborah McCauley document the beliefs and activities of the group in lined-out hymns, outdoor immersions, extemporaneous sermons, male-dominated leadership, Calvinistic theology, and dress codes. For these Baptists, conversion and baptism often come late in life. The normal baptismal age is near thirty, and persons are urged to "wait" on the drawings of the Spirit on the elect.[58]

Old Regulars claim some seventeen associations, with approximately fifteen thousand members and another fifteen thousand or so "attending nonmembers."[59] A poem by Sister Beulah Jones Patrick, written around 1987, set forth the basic beliefs and practices of the Old Regular Baptists as described by an insider:

We may ask you to go to church;
We will not beg you in.
We believe you will follow
When Jesus forgives you for your sins.
We have no guitars in our church,
No piano or tambourine.
All we have are saints of God,
And our music is when they sing.
Our songs may be a little slow,
And some of us may cry.
We may stop and hug your neck and
Shake your hand as we pass by.
We may not be very educated.
Some of us may not read.
But our preachers can paint a picture
That a child can plainly see.
You won't see much make-up on
Our sister's face,
For she has a "new look now"
She's cleaned ... by His saving grace.
If you wonder who I am,
Why this way I do feel,
I'm an Old Regular Baptist,
Who's been raised in these old hills.[60]

Like other of these subdenominations, the Old Regular Baptists continue to perform baptisms out-of-doors and take the Lord's Supper in conjunction with the washing of feet. Their church buildings are simply worship centers, often located in rural, mountainous areas.

Primitive Baptists

Primitive Baptists are perhaps the best known of the Appalachian Baptist groups, with numerous congregations inside and outside the region. Although they share Calvinistic theology with Old Regulars and others, Primitive Baptists generally affirm the Fulton Confession of Faith (1900). It draws on the First and Second London Confessions, with additional statements on biblical inerrancy, baptismal immersion, closed communion, and the rejection of divorce and remarriage.[61] As noted previously, Primitive Baptists eschew Sunday schools, missionary activities, revival services, and direct evangelism, insisting that God alone will draw the elect to salvation.

Primitive Baptists may be divided into at least four subgroups, including (1) Single-Predestinarians, who accept election of the redeemed, but reject God's "predestination of all things," including the damnation of the lost; (2) Double-Predestinarians, who believe that God predestines all things, choosing some persons for salvation and others for damnation before the foundation of the world; (3) some Primitive Baptists who have modified earlier practices to include Sunday schools, paid clergy, evangelical witness to the all the unredeemed, and instrumental music in church; and (4) Primitive Baptist Universalists (not recognized by other Primitives), who believe that all persons will ultimately be redeemed, after being purged of sin in this life.[62]

Primitive Baptist Universalists, sometimes incorrectly labeled "No-hellers," are a little-known subgroup with four associations in Tennessee, Kentucky, Virginia, and West Virginia. These Primitives insist that "Christ tasted death for all," and that in the resurrection all will share eternity in heaven. As Adam's death brought sinfulness and retribution to all humanity, so Christ's death brought salvation for all.[63] Primitive Baptists have spread to the Midwest and the Southwest. They are the largest of the Appalachian Baptist subdenominations.

Swedish Baptists in the United States

The Triennial Convention and the two denominational groups that came out of it were not the only Baptist communions to undergo change and development during the nineteenth century. New Baptist groups were formed as immigrants poured in from Europe. Swedish Baptists were one of the first immigrant Baptist bodies to take shape.

The first Baptist church in Sweden was organized September 21, 1848, by Frederic Olaus Nilsson (1809–1881). Converted when he was twenty-five, Nilsson was baptized by J. G. Oncken in 1847, the year before he founded Sweden's first Baptist congregation. His Baptist views were declared heretical in April 1850, and the civil authorities banished him from the country. Forced from his native land, Nilsson and his wife, Ulrika Sophia Olsson, went to Denmark, and then to America, settling near Minneapolis, in a community he dubbed Scandia. He bought land, writing in 1857, "I proved up and paid for my land. It comprises 160 acres ... $1.25 and acre, or $200, of which $5 was for 'proving up' and $2 for I know not what.... Praise be unto the Lord who has privileged me to own a little earthly home at the age of 48 years."[64] In Minnesota he helped to found numerous Baptist churches. Nilsson was given a pardon by the king of Sweden in 1860, and he returned to his native land, where he ministered until 1868, at which point he went back to America.

The Baptist churches in Sweden and the United States were influenced by evangelical movements in Scandinavia, including Christian pietism, or *Lasare*. Pietism emphasized the necessity of the new birth, meditation, and the importance of sanctification, or going on in grace. These sentiments were evident in a Baptist group in the Swedish town of Orsa. State persecution led them to escape to the United States, where they settled in Minnesota.[65] Conflicts with Lutheran communities in Minnesota were common.

Anders Wiberg (1816–1887), a former Lutheran minister, was an early leader of Swedish Baptists in America. Immersed as a Baptist in 1852, he later wrote *Det Kristliga Dopel, Framstalt i Bibelns Egan Ord, or, Christian Baptism Stated in the Very Words of the Bible*. His zeal for Baptist views often brought him into conflict with Lutherans in both Sweden and the United States.[66]

In 1852, Wiberg and Gustaf Palmquist founded the first Swedish Baptist church in the United States, at Rock Island, Illinois. By 1871, Swedish Baptists claimed some fifteen hundred members located in seven states. By 1902, the group numbered twenty-two thousand adherents in 324 churches.[67]

Like their Lutheran counterparts, Swedish Baptists were an immigrant people who retained a strong ethnic identity well into the twentieth century. Their worship services were conducted in their native tongue, and they often were perceived to be outsiders, not only in the broader American culture, but also in the Lutheran-dominated immigrant communities of the upper Midwest. Swedish Baptists, like other immigrants, often were accused of "un-American" activities in their retention of Old World languages and customs.

When John Alexis Edgren (1839–1908) founded the Swedish Baptist Seminary, Chicago, the Baptist editor of *The Examiner* criticized his decision to retain Swedish in the classrooms. The article noted, "It is understood that the new institution is to perpetuate the use of foreign languages and separate church organizations for foreign born people in this country." The writer recommended, "This seminary should be opposed by every man who desires to be at once a loyal Baptist and a loyal citizen of the Republic."[68]

Edgren was undeterred. Educated at Princeton as well as at Baptist schools in New York and Chicago, he was determined to provide theological training for Swedish Baptist ministers. The school began in 1881 with only one student. Edgren was forced to resign for health reasons in 1887.

In 1908, when the Swedish Baptist Seminary became part of the University of Chicago Divinity School, its dean, Shailer Mathews, inquired of the Swedish Baptist Conference how much longer instruction should continue in Swedish. The response, published in 1909, indicated that only six of 357 churches used English, and those six permitted it only in Sunday evening worship services.[69] The Swedish Baptist hymnbook *Nya Psalmisten,* or *New Psalmody,* was also used by American Swedish churches.

In their effort to convert the growing number of Swedish immigrants, the American Baptist Home Mission Society supported the work of leaders, including Wiberg and Nilsson, in the United States and Sweden. In 1879, Swedish Baptists joined two other Scandinavian groups, the Danes and the Norwegians, to form the Scandinavian Baptist General Conference in America. That union did not long endure, and the Scandinavian Conference soon became the Swedish Baptist General Conference. By the second year, efforts were made to send a missionary to the Swedes settling in the West. The American Baptist Home Mission Society provided $400 toward the salary of $800 per year.[70] Attempts to evangelize Swedish immigrants were a major emphasis of the General Conference Baptists until the period following the Second World War.

Norwegian and Danish Baptists in the United States

The first Norwegian Baptist church was organized in LaSalle County, Illinois. Its leader was Hans Valder (1813–1899), a Norwegian Lutheran who came to America in 1837, settling first in New York and then in Chicago. In 1841, he became a "personal Christian," and he joined the Baptists a year later. In 1844, he was ordained "to work among the Norwegians." Since Baptists did not begin in Norway until 1857, this made Valder the first Norwegian Baptist minister anywhere.[71]

Valder organized the first Norwegian Baptist church in America, at Indian Creek, Illinois, in January 1848. He soon was named its pastor. In letters written to the American Baptist Home Mission Society in 1848, he discussed the difficulties of the fledgling church, and opposition from "Norwegians and Americans" in the region. Lutherans labeled him a "rebaptizer" and linked him with Martin Luther's scathing denunciation of Anabaptists. Valder remarked, "They thought they had good authority for abusing a poor Baptist and calling him a heretic." Valder asked the Society for help and said, "If the Baptist denomination can aid us a little in supporting a minister to labor among us, the cause of Christ may yet prosper and sinners be converted unto God."[72] The ABHMS responded positively, and Valder became the first Scandinavian missionary appointed by the Society. Valder later relinquished his Baptist pastorate and moved into local politics.[73]

In Wisconsin, Danish and Norwegian Baptists joined in cooperative efforts by the 1860s. Jorgensen Hague cited one Baptist who wrote, "The Danes came usually as individuals into the Baptist church through baptism, but the Norwegians came in groups. Sometimes I baptized most of the members of a church in one day and organized the church later by instructing them and by assisting them to choose elders."[74]

The first Danish "Baptism church" was organized on February 14, 1864, in Chicago. Norwegians also joined the church, but soon they established their own congregations.

In 1877, the First Norwegian Baptist church was founded in Chicago. Its aim was to convert Norwegian immigrants to Christian and Baptist faith. Church records noted, "The question of nationality and of language and the inactivity of the Norwegian Baptists were causes why more of the countrymen were not converted." Leaders observed, "According to Romans 9:1-4, it is natural to have most love for one's own nationality."[75]

Theologically, these Scandinavian churches faced controversies over the meaning of baptism and the role of women. They were evident in the Danish-Norwegian Baptist Conference in the North-Western States, founded in 1864. On the question "Can sisters take part in the public service?" the Conference responded, "We believe the sisters may pray and thank God, just as well as the brothers. But they must not preach or teach. They ought not to take part in quarrels, but they may vote in the churches just as the brothers."[76]

In 1866, delegates to the Conference voted that the body had authority "to pass judgment" regarding cases brought before the churches. Some claimed that the Conference had the authority to ordain ministers, but that idea was rejected by the majority. In 1877, the Conference ruled that it was not "a legislative body that can dictate to the churches." Rather, it was "an advisory body" that "does not discuss local church matters." The Conference was to "unite the works in the Kingdom of God, so they may labor in harmony," "work for unity among the churches … to try to bring the gospel to our fellow-men," and "labor for a higher spiritual life and for a spiritual revival in the churches where the Conference meets."[77]

Seventh Day Baptists: A General Conference Organized

A concern for missionary outreach led to the founding of a national assembly of Seventh Day Baptists in September 1802. The new organization sought to unite churches in common endeavor, delineate doctrine, foster education, and promote specific programs of ministry.[78] The Sabbatarian General Conference was officially established in the constitution of 1805. In 1817, the name was changed to Seventh Day Baptist General Conference. Membership was extended to specific churches whose members accepted both the Sabbath and baptism by immersion. A confession of faith was approved in the 1830s, but it was used as a source of theological demarcation, not as "a test for orthodoxy." One commentary concluded, "this Expose is not adopted as having any binding force in itself, but simply as an exhibition of the views generally held by the denomination."[79]

The denomination soon adopted educational programs to extend Sabbatarian identity to succeeding generations. Societies for missions, publication, and education also were established. The General Conference fostered a broader denominational, connectional consciousness among the Seventh Day Baptists.

The earliest Seventh Day Baptist associations were founded in 1834. The Eastern Association included churches in Rhode Island, New Jersey, and Connecticut. The Central Association linked churches in New York State. A Western Association was organized by churches in western New York and northern Pennsylvania. The Southeastern Association included Virginia, Pennsylvania, and Ohio. The Northwestern Association involved portions of Ohio, Kentucky, Tennessee, Wisconsin, and various states in the West. The Southwestern Association linked Texas, Mississippi, Missouri, and Arkansas, while a Pacific Coast Association was formed in the early 1900s. The associations maintained a fraternal connection with the General Conference.

Organizationally, Seventh Day Baptists utilized both societal and associational connections. Don Sanford observed that for Seventh Day Baptists, an association "refers to the organization of churches having a common interest for mutual benefit," while "a society is composed of individuals banded together by specific interests."[80]

The General Conference fostered denominational or associational relationships but utilized societies for collective activity in missions, education, and publication. The missionary society controlled its own membership, finances, and programs, but it was "thought not advisable for any one society to send out any missionaries, even at their own expense, unless by first obtaining the approbation of the General Conference for the person sent out."[81]

The Seventh Day Baptist Missionary Society appointed its first missionaries in 1819, commissioning William Satterlee, Amos R. Wells, and William B. Maxson for service at home. In 1824, the Seventh Day Baptist General Board of Missions was established, and the American Seventh Day Baptist Missionary Society was founded in 1828.

In 1849, the General Conference approved a resolution stating that "our young men proposing to enter the gospel ministry ought, whenever it is at all practicable, to go through the regular collegiate course of instruction, or its equivalent, previous to ordination."[82] The Seventh Day Baptist Education Society was founded in 1855, and it raised funds that enabled Alfred Academy (1843) to become a university in 1857.

Seventh Day Baptists were early opponents of both slavery and liquor. In 1836, the General Conference issued a circular letter with strong resolutions against "human slavery" and "the use of ardent spirits, wines and fermented liquors as a beverage."[83]

During the decade 1851–1861, the General Conference issued resolutions denouncing the Fugitive Slave Law, civil war, and Christian efforts to compromise on slavery. When the

Civil War broke out, the Conference affirmed its loyalty to the Union.[84] In 1838, an "American Seventh-day Baptist Society, for the promotion of Christianity among the Jews" was formed. William B. Maxson was appointed a missionary to the Jews and began work among Jews in New York City. There was little success with this endeavor, though varied contacts with Jews were made.[85]

The 1841 meeting of the American Seventh Day Baptist Missionary Society met in Alfred, New York, and voted, "That this society will, with the blessing of God, employ one or more ministering brethren during the coming year to travel through our societies and the regions where our brethren have made settlements, to preach the gospel and solicit funds in aid of the society's object."[86]

These early missionaries were on the home front. Foreign mission work began in 1845, when Solomon Carpenter and Lucy Clarke Carpenter were trained for work in Abyssinia. This assignment was later deemed to be too difficult, and the two were sent to China. Nathan Wardner and his wife (name not given) were sent out with the Carpenters in 1847.[87]

The 1887 meeting of the Seventh Day Baptist Missionary Society reported foreign mission work in China and Holland, with home missionaries spread throughout the nation. The general fund of the Society reported an amount of over $11,000 in the mission fund. The Woman's Board of the denomination was organized in 1884, and Susie Burdick was appointed in 1889.

By the turn of the century, the work in China included three missionaries, two native preachers, two native teachers, one "Bible woman," and several helpers. The mission to the Jews continued with two workers and "no baptisms but several adherents."[88]

Benoni Stinson and the General Baptists

A revival of interest in Arminian Baptist views was promoted by Benoni Stinson (1798–1869) and another group of General Baptists. Converted in 1820, Stinson soon was ordained by the United Baptist Church in Wayne County, Kentucky. United Baptists often included both Arminians and Calvinists, who cooperated by agreeing that "the preaching that Christ died for every man should be no bar to fellowship."[89] This harmony did not extend to Indiana, where Stinson's belief in Christ's general atonement led Calvinists to brand him a heretic.

These conflicts led Stinson and others to found the Liberty Church of Christ in 1823. As pastor, Stinson prepared a confession of faith that affirmed biblical authority, human depravity, perseverance of the saints, eternal rewards and punishments, and immersion baptism as requisite for the Lord's Supper. It concluded with an Arminian declaration: "We believe that Jesus Christ, by the grace of God, tasted death for every man, but that no one can receive his divine benefits but by repentance toward God and faith in our Lord, Jesus Christ."[90] The phrase "Christ tasted death for every man" became a watchword for the new church and a revitalized Baptist Arminianism. It meant that Christ's death was potentially efficacious for all persons and was actualized by repentance and faith. Some who joined the Liberty Church were "excommunicated," or at least not "lettered" (refused a letter of dismissal) by their home congregations.

The Liberty Association of General Baptists was founded in October 1824, comprised of the Liberty Church and three other congregations. The organizing documents included a constitution, articles of faith, and rules of decorum.[91] In 1829, Stinson and others composed a circular letter that defended their approach to Baptist doctrine.

While these General Baptists originally practiced closed communion, they soon opened it to certain "pedobaptists" who had received baptism as infants. Stinson wrote, "Although we may not think our pedobaptist brother has been properly baptized, still he believes it, and we are therefore willing for him to examine himself on this point, and come to the Sacrament on his own faith."[92] Soon, churches and associations were organized in Indiana, Kentucky, and Illinois. By 1860, six General Baptist associations had churches totaling some thirty-four hundred members. A decade later, the number of associations had doubled, and membership in the churches was placed at 9,642.[93]

Non-Arminians were quick to attack the new communion. In 1861, the *Tennessee Baptist* declared of "this new sect" that it "holds and teaches neither the faith or the order of a church of Christ, and therefore is not entitled to the least recognition or fellowship from us." In fact, the paper asserted, "That new society has no more authority to baptize than a temperance society, or Masonic lodge."[94] Nonetheless, General Baptists insisted on free will, free salvation, and open communion for all professing Christians. They frequently debated Calvinist Baptists over these dogmas.

In 1870, the General Association of General Baptists was formed, with headquarters in Poplar Bluff, Missouri. A Home Missions Board was founded a few years later to "aid in extending the Gospel and the influence of the General Baptist denomination."[95] A periodical, *The General Baptist Messenger,* was begun in 1885. A Foreign Mission Board was founded in 1889, and it initiated missionary work in India in cooperation with the British General Baptists. The Oakland Institute (later Oakland City College) was founded in Oakland City, Indiana, in 1866.[96] General Baptists grew slowly but steadily in Indiana and in other parts of the Midwest.

Italian Baptists

Baptists began efforts to "evangelize" Catholic immigrants soon after the Civil War, and in 1896, Italian Baptist immigrants founded the First Italian Baptist Church, in Buffalo, New York.[97] Italian Baptist missionaries preached in the Bronx and other urban areas in an attempt to draw Italians into storefront churches. The first national association of Italian Baptists was established in New York in 1899. Four years later, a periodical, *Il Messaggiero,* was instituted. After several name changes, it became the *New Aurora.*[98]

In 1904, the American Baptist Home Mission Society appointed Antonio Mangano (b. 1869) as general missionary charged with coordinating evangelism among Italians. Converted to the Baptists in 1888, Mangano held degrees from Brown University and Union Theological Seminary. He founded churches and ministries among Italian immigrants. By 1928, Protestant Italian Americans numbered only some fifteen thousand persons. In 1924, there were only about three thousand Italian Baptists in the United States.[99]

William Miller and the Millerite Movement

The millennialism of the Baptist preacher William Miller (1782–1849) had significant impact on Baptists and other American Protestants. Miller developed elaborate mathematical calculations based on a literalist reading of "prophecies" in both Testaments and concluded that Christ would return sometime between March 1843 and March 1844. Miller traveled throughout the East proclaiming his views and publishing them widely. The Millerite (later Adventist) phenomenon became a powerful popular movement, drawing the faithful and the curious to revivals where Miller urged repentance before it was too late. When the "First Great Disappointment" occurred in 1844, a Millerite named Samuel Snow claimed to have received a new revelation of Christ's return on October 22, 1844. As the date approached, Miller reluctantly acquiesced to the prediction. The passing of that date led to the "Second Great Disappointment" and the end of the Millerite phase of the movement. Miller returned to his farm, where he died in 1849. While many fell away, others, including Hiram Edson and Ellen White, reshaped Millerite beliefs into the Seventh Day Adventist movement—one segment of various Adventist communions.

The Millerite program attracted numerous Baptists, among them Elon Galusha (d. 1856), a prominent Baptist in New York. Miller lectured at Galusha's church in Lockport, New York, and the Baptist pastor soon accepted Miller's calculations. Although he was hesitant to promote specific dates, Galusha's support gave the Millerites significant credibility among Baptists in New York. In the aftermath of Millerite "disappointments," Galusha returned to the Baptists, sobered but unrepentant for his millennial beliefs.[100]

Northern Baptist Organizations

Baptist growth continued following the Civil War. The 1868 *American Baptist Almanac* claimed 1,157,221 Baptists in the United States.[101] In the North, certain societies were reorganized and renamed. The American Baptist Education Commission was begun in 1868 to address educational needs of the churches. It was absorbed by the American Baptist Education Society, founded in 1888. The Society encouraged higher education among Baptists, the formation of Baptist colleges and secondary schools in each state, and Baptist support for higher education. Its work influenced the formation of the University of Chicago. In 1912, it became a society of the Northern Baptist Convention.[102]

The postwar programs of the American Baptist Missionary Union included the establishment of the Livingstone Interior Mission in Africa in 1874. The agency also developed additional work in India and China. One of its most important supporters was Boston preacher Adoniram Judson Gordon (1836–1895), who became the Union's president in 1871 and served for twenty-three years. It became the American Baptist Foreign Mission Society in 1910.

The American Baptist Home Mission Society continued its work after the Civil War, with programs to Native Americans, immigrants in the urban North, and new churches in the West. Following the war, the society encountered significant controversy with Southern Baptists regarding continued work in the South. H. L. Morehouse (1834–1917), the organization's corresponding secretary, insisted that its ministries continue with Native Americans,

African Americans, and immigrants. Morehouse served as an appointee of the Home Mission Society and was a leader in founding the Education Society. Morehouse's service to home missions, particularly among African Americans, led the trustees of Atlanta Baptist College to rename the school Morehouse College in 1913.

The Board's 1879 minutes contained a resolution commending the president of the United States for "warning off unauthorized settlers who have encroached on the [Indian] Territory" and encouraged the chief executive to continue policies that "protect the Indians in the enjoyment of their rightful possessions."[103]

In 1845, the American Baptist Publication and Sunday School Society was renamed the American Baptist Publication Society. Well-known home missionary John Mason Peck served as corresponding secretary. Book editor J. Newton Brown encouraged the publication of various church manuals that included Brown's church covenant and the Philadelphia Confession of Faith—documents used widely by nineteenth- and twentieth-century Baptist churches. The Society published the earliest American Baptist hymnal. In 1853, it formed a department of history that became the American Baptist Historical Society—an organization charged with preserving and promoting the denomination's heritage.

The Society continued to send out colporteurs who distributed tracts and other religious materials. Corresponding Secretary Benjamin Griffith began work in 1857 and led in the formation of *The National Baptist* periodical and multilingual publications for use among immigrant peoples.[104]

In 1879, the Publication Society defined its functions as promoting "evangelical religion by means of the Bible, the printing press, colportage, and the Sunday-school." Between 1824 and 1879, the Society circulated more than "ninety millions of copies of religious publications."[105]

The Society led in establishing the Baptist Young People's Union of America (BYPU) in 1891. It grew out of earlier Christian youth movements, such as the Young Men's Christian Association. The BYPU became a model for similar youth organizations formed in other Baptist and Protestant bodies.[106]

Southern Baptist Organizations

The organization of the Southern Baptist Convention demonstrates the impact of American denominational influences on a highly regionalized religious community. The links between Southern culture and Southern Baptist denominational consciousness were deep, if not inseparable. Convention leaders worked to create boards, programs, and policies that united diverse churches from Virginia to Texas around a sense of "Southern Baptistness." Boards and agencies were located throughout the South: the Foreign Mission Board (Richmond, Virginia), the Home Mission Board (Atlanta), and ultimately, the Publication Society, later the Sunday School Board (Birmingham, Alabama).

Leaders such as Basil Manly Jr. (1825–1892) pressed churches to develop Sunday school programs (few Southern churches had them in the mid-nineteenth century) and promoted the Publication Society as a vehicle for providing teaching materials. Early institutional efforts were not successful. Four attempts to form a publication board ended in failure. It was not until 1891, and the founding of the Southern Baptist Sunday School Board under the leadership of James Marion Frost (1848–1916), that a viable publication agency was established.

A Board of Domestic Missions was founded in 1845 with the formation of the new denomination. It soon became known as the Home Mission Board. The Board struggled over issues of funding and direction for several years after it began. Conflicts with Northern Baptists over the proper "territory" for the two denominations were not easily resolved. I. T. Tichenor (1825–1902), who became executive secretary in 1882, moved the agency from the tiny town of Marion, Alabama, to Atlanta, Georgia, and secured its future. Its early ministries included work with Native Americans and freed slaves. Also, new churches were founded. Tichenor confronted the Northern Baptists over their work in the South. He also proposed work in education, hospital ministry, orphanages, and of course, evangelism.[107] Always there was the problem of the lack of funds and the will of churches to contribute to a denominational agency. Among other things, Tichenor founded a department that offered advice on construction of churches, began Home Mission Board efforts in Cuba, helped form institutes for educating African Americans, and established mountain mission schools in Appalachia.[108] By 1899, Tichenor's last year at the Board, the organization had achieved a more secure financial base.

Ministerial Education

Education for ministers was a pressing issue for the new convention. In 1859, the Southern Baptist Theological Seminary was founded on the campus of Furman University in Greenville, South Carolina. Its founding faculty included James Petigrew Boyce (1827–1888), John R. Broadus (1827–1895), William Williams (1821–1877), and William Whitsitt (1841–1911). Boyce, the first president, saw the endeavor as a new paradigm in theological education that would train Baptist ministers who had limited educational background and would offer graduate education for those who would serve as professors in Baptist colleges in the South. While some took classical languages (Hebrew, Greek, Latin), "an English course of study for those who have only been able to attain a plain English education" would be provided. Also, emphasis was given to "instruction in the nature of Pastoral duties."[109] After the Civil War, the seminary was decimated and began again with a blind Confederate veteran as its sole student. In 1877, the school was moved to Louisville, Kentucky, a city less devastated by the war. Throughout much of its history, the seminary experienced numerous controversies, internal and external, regarding the views of faculty, faculty-administration conflicts, and the general debate in the SBC regarding the nature of theological education.

The Whitsitt Controversy

One of the most dramatic controversies involved William H. Whitsitt, professor of church history and president of the seminary (1895–1899). During the 1890s, Whitsitt published the results of his research into baptismal practices among seventeenth-century British Baptists. Using the "Kiffin Manuscript" and other materials, he concluded that Baptists did not institute baptismal immersion until 1641. His conclusions challenged the prevailing Landmark historiography that Baptist churches were in unbroken succession from Jesus' own baptism. Whitsitt first published his findings in a brief encyclopedia article and then, in 1896, in the book *A Question in Baptist History*.

Texan B. H. Carroll (1843–1914), a seminary trustee, challenged Whitsitt's views and his presidency. The trustees initially voted to support Whitsitt, but when Carroll and others urged the SBC to cut off funds to the school, Whitsitt resigned and became a professor at the University of Richmond. While the controversy proved the power of the Landmark ideology and the vulnerability of educational institutions to the populism of the denominational constituency, Whitsitt's views ultimately were vindicated.

Church Order: Baptist Manuals

Nineteenth-century Baptist life was characterized by the wide use of "church manuals"—volumes that provided guidance for the organizational life of the churches. Their extensive circulation reflected the need for resources concerning institutional structure of local churches and the need for manuals that offered a systematic approach to basic ecclesiastical order. These included William Crowell's *The Church Member's Manual* (1845), Edward T. Hiscox's *The Baptist Church Directory* (1859), and J. M. Pendleton's *Church Manual* (1867). By 1946, Pendleton's manual had sold at least 150,000 copies.[110]

Hiscox's work later was entitled *Principles and Practices for Baptist Churches* and was republished well into the twentieth century. Like other volumes of its kind, it provided basic introductions to Baptist history, doctrine, and practice, offering instructions for churches and individuals in the ways that Baptist churches believed and functioned. For example, Hiscox delineated three ways in which persons united with Baptist churches. These included admission by baptism upon profession of faith, by letter, or by experience. The letter from the church where the individual was a member "certifies to his good Christian character and regular standing, and commends him to the confidence of, and membership in, the other church." Once the individual's commitments were confirmed, a "vote of the Church" was necessary for formal admission to membership.[111] Union with a church by experience (later known as statement of faith) was applied to those candidates who "have been baptized, but by some means have lost their membership."[112]

The Lord's Supper, Hiscox noted, was observed quarterly, bimonthly, or monthly in Baptist churches. In many congregations, the "hand of fellowship" was offered to new members on communion Sunday. He acknowledged that some objected to "individual communion cups" and "the practice of holding the bread till all are served." Apparently, some feared that these formalities would "exalt the form over the spirit and make the service ritual rather than spiritual."[113] While some churches continued to use wine in communion, others, influenced by the temperance movement, turned to unfermented grape juice.

Baptist Revivals

The post-Civil War era witnessed the rise of a variety of urban evangelistic "campaigns," personified in the prominent Northern evangelist Dwight Lyman Moody (1837–1899) and extending into the Baptist community. Moody and others united urban churches and denominations in an effort to reach the unchurched. Budgets were subscribed from wealthy business leaders so that no offerings were necessary. Meetings were held in public halls to attract those who eschewed formal church attendance. Special meetings for target groups—men, "fallen women," children, African Americans—also were held. Music was boisterous and exuberant, often with special hymnals for choirs and congregations. Moody's famous associate Ira Sankey (1840–1908) set the standard for such music, accompanying the singing from a reed organ and editing hymnbooks for revival use. Campaigns were carried out over several weeks to maximize the impact on the city.

Jacob Knapp and Jabez Swan were prominent Baptist evangelists who preached revivals across the Northeast. Reared an Episcopalian, Knapp (1799–1874) was baptized into the Masonville Baptist Church in New York State in 1819. Educated at the Hamilton Literary and Theological Institute, he became pastor of a Baptist church in Watertown, New York. Jabez Swan studied at Hamilton Literary and Theological Institute, and received ordination in 1827. He held pastorates in Baptist churches in Stonington, Connecticut (1827–1830), and Norwich, New York (1830–1838). He preached in revivals throughout Connecticut and portions of New York and soon was designated "the chief protracted meeting [revival] engineer of the Chenango Valley."[114]

Knapp and Swan conducted revival campaigns in New York, Philadelphia, and Boston. They called sinners to immediate conversion in ways that challenged the dominant Calvinism of the times. One Reformed Baptist told Knapp, "When God wanted to convict or convert a sinner he knew where to find him and how to do it without the intervention of human effort, and in his own 'good time' he would, in his own way, bring his elect into the fold."[115] Swan observed, "A general impression among the Baptists prevailed, that there were set times for God to work in pouring salvation upon communities and that any attempt at awaking and trying to break up fallow ground was getting ahead of God."[116]

As a Baptist, Swan insisted on immersion "in the liquid grave." He often took converts directly to a river or stream for immediate immersions at all hours of the day or night.[117] He denounced slavery, liquor, Mormons, Masons, Unitarians, Deists, Universalists (a "fire insurance company"), and Roman Catholics.

Knapp attacked similar enemies and claimed to have baptized as many as sixty people in thirty minutes. His earthiness bordered on vulgarity, and his public attacks on specific individuals created near riots in Boston and New Haven.[118] His fundraising methods likewise were controversial. William McLoughlin suggested, "Knapp's chief claim to fame in the history of modern revivalism was that he was the first new measure evangelist to be publicly accused of making money from his preaching."[119] Knapp represented a new generation of revivalists who used a variety of entrepreneurial methods to bring persons to salvation.

Baptists and the Social Gospel

The industrial explosion of the post-Civil War era created significant challenges for American churches. Many welcomed the economic and material benefits of the age and developed theologies to support them. Others questioned the growth of industries that gave wealth to the few while exploiting the many. *The Gospel of Wealth,* written in 1889 by industrialist Andrew Carnegie (1835–1919), used Calvinism to support the claim that God had ordained some to make large amounts of money and had given them responsibility for distributing some of it to the less fortunate.[120] Since few people knew how to use money wisely, it was best that they not have it. The rich were to live modestly and give monies to benefit the less fortunate.

Baptists were not immune to these ideas. Russell Conwell (1843–1925), pastor of Temple Baptist Church, Philadelphia, was well known for his sermon "Acres of Diamonds"— his own version of the "gospel of wealth." In it he declared, "Every good man ought to be rich. Every good man would be rich if he has as much common sense as goodness. I say, Get rich, get rich! But get money honestly or it will be a withering curse."[121] Conwell warned that since poverty itself could be punishment for sin, Christians should be cautious in helping the poor lest they interfere with God's judgment. He insisted that the accumulation of wealth was a Christian duty.[122] Conwell's remarks were widely circulated throughout Baptist and other Protestant churches of the period.

Others were not convinced. Baptist Walter Rauschenbusch (1861–1918) reacted negatively to these positive assessments of materialism, laissez-faire capitalism, and the excesses of the Industrial Age. Rauschenbusch was one of the chief representatives of what came to be known as the "Social Gospel" movement—an effort to take seriously the corporate nature of sin and the need to Christianize the social order itself.

Born in 1861 in Rochester, New York, Rauschenbusch was the son of German immigrants. His father, August Rauschenbusch, departed Lutheranism for the Baptists before immigrating to America in 1854. Walter Rauschenbusch was educated at Rochester Seminary, shaped by a childhood religious conversion and a decision to become a minister. After seminary graduation, he became pastor of Second German Baptist Church in New York, located on the edge of the infamous Hell's Kitchen. There he confronted firsthand the results of poverty and exploitation rampant in the urban setting. In 1897, Rauschenbusch accepted a teaching position in the German department at Rochester Theological Seminary, and he was named professor of church history five years later. The school served as a base for his teaching and writings for the rest of his life. In 1888, he lost much of his hearing, and as one scholar remarked, "Deafness, however, was less of a handicap to a 'professor,' and may have been prerequisite for his final evolution into a 'prophet.'"[123] His first book on the social imperative of Christianity was published in 1907: *Christianity and the Social Crisis*. Other works followed, including *Christianizing the Social Order* (1912) and *A Theology for the Social Gospel* (1917).

For Rauschenbusch, Christianity had both personal and communal implications. Sin was both individual and corporate, and the church was compelled to address the implications of evil in every realm. The responsibility for sin was not limited to the persons who through alcohol or drug abuse wreaked havoc on family or society; it also belonged to the institutions that created environments that contributed to such personal abuses. He maintained "that the essential purpose of Christianity was to transform human society into the kingdom of God by regenerating all human relations and reconstituting them in accordance with the will of God."[124] Like other Social Gospelers, Rauschenbusch distinguished between the church as "a fellowship for worship" and the rule of God as "a fellowship of righteousness."[125] In *A Theology for the Social Gospel*, he issued this classic definition: "The Kingdom of God is humanity organized according to the will of God." It brought society in conformity to the ethics of Jesus.[126]

Rauschenbusch's views were shaped by various Baptist subgroups that organized to address the changing social situation. One of these was the Baptist Congress for the Discussion of

Current Questions—an informal gathering that began in 1882. It provided occasions for discussion of a wide variety of theological and social questions by young ministers, many of whom became strong supporters of the Social Gospel movement. At its meeting in 1898, Rauschenbush urged the group to support the legitimacy of strikes and "strengthen public opinion in its demand for justice and humanity."[127]

Rauschenbusch and other Baptist preachers, including Nathaniel Schmidt, Leighton Williams, and Samuel Zane Batten, organized the Brotherhood of the Kingdom in 1892. It brought young ministers together to present papers aimed at promoting the belief that "the Spirit of God is moving men in our generation toward a better understanding of the idea of the Kingdom of God on earth." The ministers pledged to live by the ethics of Jesus and to "lay special stress on the social aims of Christianity."[128]

The reform group believed that religious imperatives could be united with social progress until human society conformed to the kingdom of God.[129] Of the Brotherhood's intentions, Rauschenbusch wrote, "We stood for the pre-eminence of the Kingdom of God in Christian Thought, and thereby—perhaps more than we realized—tended to substitute a power, more ethical, more synoptic, of a more Christian type of doctrine for the old 'scheme' of salvation, and all theology is drifting that way."[130] Resolutions supported striking coal miners and other labor groups.[131] Charles Hopkins linked the Brotherhood with the idealism of the early Franciscans and their effort to reform both church and society. He called the movement "perhaps the most important social-gospel society in a period remarkable for organizations."[132]

In the South, Charles S. Gardner (1859–1948), professor of homiletics and sociology at Southern Baptist Seminary, also directed attention toward the social implications of the gospel. He challenged a capitalism that he believed contributed to the existence of slums, exploitation of workers, crime, and alcoholism. Gardner's evangelicalism was evident in his concern that persons be brought to an experience with Jesus Christ—the primary means of bringing in the kingdom of God.[133]

Many local churches established social outreach programs. Calvary Baptist Church, Providence, Rhode Island, formed Calvary Baptist Institute in 1898 "to promote the physical, mental, social and moral interests of all its members and patrons."[134] C. Allyn Russell observed that the Institute's significance was "in the pioneering service which it performed in endeavoring to meet the total needs of people as well as ministering to those beyond the immediate membership of the congregation."[135]

Attention to social Christianity increased in many Baptist congregations in the late nineteenth century. Efforts were made to reach the masses with both evangelism and social action. During this period, many Baptist and other Protestant churches relinquished "pew rents" as a means of financial support, fearing that such practices excluded, implicitly or explicitly, those who could not pay.

Baptists and Racial Issues

Baptists in the South struggled with race and its role in the churches. Jeremiah Jeter (1802–1880), editor of the *Virginia Religious Herald,* opposed direct correspondence between the General Association of Baptists in Virginia (Anglo) and the Virginia Baptist

State Convention (African American). He wrote, "God has made two races widely different; not only in complexion, but in their instincts and social qualities. We take it for granted that it was not the purpose of the creator that they should be blended." Jeter concluded, "Religious and social intercourse are closely, if not inseparably connected. Suppose we admit colored delegates to seats in our association, we must of course, allow them to sit where they choose, in juxtaposition with our wives and daughters, and the privilege granted to them must be equally granted to their associates."[136]

The members of the Virginia Baptist State Convention responded in a resolution of 1872, "That we will make no further efforts for correspondence with said [white Baptist] association, but shall proceed separate and alone of them in our work of evangelization, in the even tenor of our way—trusting in God who has no respect to every nation is accepting of Him—considering that said proffers of friendship are hypocritical, and that we have shown ourselves to be destitute of prejudice to our white brethren."[137]

Other voices prevailed, and in 1879, the General Association of Baptists in Virginia approved a resolution opening their meetings to guest delegates from "our brethren of the Colored churches." It declared, "We recommend the appointment on the part of this Association of five delegates to the Colored Baptist Convention of the State and that this Association invite such Colored Baptist Convention to send delegates to it."[138]

These tensions between African American and Anglo-Saxon Baptists in the South continued well into the twentieth century. Sometimes there was cooperation; sometimes, distance and exclusion.

Baptists and Immigration

Social Gospel progressivism did not overcome the suspicions of many Baptists regarding the dangers of immigration and "foreign" elements who brought their religions, particularly Catholicism, with them. In an important work on the subject, Lawrence B. Davis noted that Baptists, like other nineteenth-century Protestants, desired to create a "Christian civilization." He concluded, "When immigration threatened the prospect of an all-embracing Protestantism, the Baptist reaction bespoke the fears of thousands of Americans."[139]

In California, Baptists attempted to convert Chinese immigrants and opened preaching stations in Oregon as early as 1874. By the 1880s, however, some Baptists recommended limitations on Chinese immigrants. San Diego Baptist pastor Oliver Gates urged continued evangelization. He wrote, "Do not expect to gain them to your faith by disparaging their false religious knowledge or by berating their bad morals. Do not put before them creeds and confessions." He suggested that the New Testament be used to teach English to the Chinese and thereby introduce them "to a knowledge of Jesus."[140] Nonetheless, by the late 1880s, many Baptists viewed immigrants as undesirable elements in the society.

Some Baptist leaders believed that immigration enhanced the Anglo calling to take Christianity and democracy to the world. Hubert C. Woods, a superintendent of the Home Missions Society, declared, "In the gathering of all nations and races upon our shores, do we not witness the providential preparation for a second Pentecost that shall usher in the millennial glory? All these facts lead us to the conclusion that under God and by his appointment 'America holds the future.'"[141]

Catholic immigration reinforced opposition to "Romanism" by many Baptists, who called it a false religion that was antidemocratic, culture dominant, and an enemy of public education.[142] As Catholics increased in numbers, so did Baptists' concerns that Catholic agendas would unduly influence American life.

Baptists and Education

At the end of the century, Baptists claimed some thirty-six colleges and universities in the United States, with a student population of twelve thousand. They also had seven seminaries, with eleven hundred students. There were twenty-nine women's colleges, numbering four thousand students. Baptists established some twenty-three colleges between 1850 and 1860 and formed others after the Civil War. Among Baptists in the North, colleges included William Jewell (1849) and the Baptist Female College of Columbia (1856), both founded by the General Association of Missouri Baptists. Baptists helped to establish the old University of Chicago in 1857. John C. Burroughs, pastor of Chicago's First Baptist Church, was named the first president. Financial difficulties required its reorganization in 1890 with funding from Baptist layman John D. Rockefeller Jr. The new university's president, William Rainey Harper, shaped the university significantly by improving its undergraduate and graduate programs. Harper also merged the school with the Baptist Union Theological Seminary in Morgan Park (where he was a professor) to create the Divinity School of the University of Chicago.[143]

In the Southwest, an academy was founded in Waco, Texas, as early as 1856, and it became Baylor University in 1886. A department of Bible at Baylor, headed by B. H. Carroll, ultimately moved to Fort Worth in 1908 to become Southwestern Baptist Theological Seminary. About fifteen Baptist-related colleges were established in Texas in the 1890s, many of which disappeared for lack of financial success.[144]

William Hooper, president of Wake Forest College (North Carolina), articulated the rationale for Baptist-oriented education. First, he insisted that such efforts "may raise our people & our ministry to a point from which our successors may raise them to still greater elevation." Second, Baptists knew that such schools would help prepare denominational leaders, clergy and laity alike. Third, higher education offered Baptists an occasion for improving their lot socially and economically in American society. Finally, their schools helped to foster Christian and Baptist ideals and identity for succeeding generations of youth.[145]

These schools struggled financially throughout much of their early history. They also educated generations of Baptist leaders, both laity and clergy.

Baptists and the Temperance Movement

Prior to the nineteenth century, Baptists generally did not oppose the use of alcohol in all circumstances. Although seventeenth- and eighteenth-century Baptists eschewed the use of strong drink and drinking to excess, the moderate use of beer and wine generally was accepted. Wine also was used in communion, and total abstinence was not widely advocated.[146] Liquor was a common beverage at social events, including weddings, funerals, and often ordinations. As the use of alcohol continued to rise, the social effects of abuse became increasingly evident. By the late eighteenth century, Baptist groups approved more specific statements on the need to curb the excesses of liquor. Baptists, however, were not prominent in most of the early temperance societies, which sprang up in the early 1800s. During the 1830s, the Philadelphia Association called for total abstinence from alcohol, and many Baptists divided over the admission of nonabstainers to church membership.[147]

Following the Civil War, concern for temperance again gained momentum. Many temperance advocates saw the victory over slavery as evidence that the "liquor traffic" also could be defeated. The Women's Christian Temperance Union was founded in the 1870s, and many Baptist women joined it. The Prohibition Party was rejuvenated in 1881, and it developed a national agenda. Joshua Levering (1845–1935), a leading Baptist layman, was nominated for president of the United States on the Prohibition ticket in the election of 1896. A native of Baltimore, Levering was a frequent contributor to Baptist institutions of higher learning and a longtime trustee of the Southern Baptist Foreign Mission Board. The Baptist Ministers' Conference of Philadelphia requested that the Pennsylvania State Legislature exempt churches from proposed laws that would prohibit the production and sale of wine, thus allowing for its continued use in the Lord's Supper.[148] Over time, Baptists generally came to support total abstinence as the Christian duty of church members. Some churches disciplined members who drank or worked in establishments where liquor was sold.

Baptist Women

During the late nineteenth century, Baptist women continued to work in churches, denominations, and mission societies. Baptist males continued to set parameters for the "women's sphere."

Among Baptist leaders in the North, Helen Barrett Montgomery (1861–1934) not only served as president of the Woman's American Baptist Foreign Mission Society, but also moved into a variety of ecclesial and political settings. The first woman to serve on the school board of Rochester, New York, she was a longtime proponent of female suffrage. Montgomery helped to establish the first ecumenical women's World Day of Prayer in 1919, and her *Centenary Translation of the New Testament* was published in 1924. She was an articulate representative of women's leadership.

In the South, during the latter part of the nineteenth century, occasional articles appeared on the place of women in church and society. An article dealing with "Female Education," published in the *Kentucky Western Recorder,* repudiated any idea of coeducation, noting the "erroneous opinion that the mental powers of the sexes are equal." Rather, the author suggested, women's intellectual abilities, like their bodies, are weaker than those of males— a reality compensated for by their beauty.[149]

Writing in 1892, the editor of the *Biblical Recorder* denounced the idea (present in the North and in the South) that women could serve as "public lecturers, or speakers before mixed assemblies, or as ordained preachers of the gospel." He concluded, "Once for all, let it be known everywhere that our people South, as a rule are unalterably opposed to this thing." He insisted that Baptist church facilities should not be opened to women speakers, no matter what the cause.[150] Thus, even temperance meetings where women spoke publicly to males and females would be unacceptable. The editor rejected practices by the Baptist Young People's Union wherein young males and females spoke in programs together. He recommended that this custom, begun in the North, be disallowed among Baptists in the South.

Some Southern Baptist males continued to fret over the appointment of women to the mission fields, fearing that they would somehow preach to males and thus violate the Scripture. Some women challenged such ideas, and others, even in the South, retained their family names after marriage, were willing to divorce abusive husbands, and sought to be equal partners in family decision making.[151]

In 1885, the question of admitting women as messengers to the Southern Baptist Convention arose when the Arkansas delegation brought two women, Mrs. Early and Mrs. Eagle. So great was the outcry from males that the constitution of the denomination was changed to read "brethren" rather than the original "messengers." Opponents worried aloud that such approval would lead to a flood of women into the annual convention, perhaps even "occupying the president's chair."[152] Commenting on these actions, H. Leon McBeth wrote, "For almost twenty years the women who attended Southern Baptist Convention sessions at all sat in the balconies."[153] It was not until 1918 that the role of messenger was made available to Southern Baptist women.

Many Baptist associations in the South resisted efforts to permit women to speak in "mixed" public gatherings. During the 1880s, the Kehukee Association (North Carolina) allowed women to speak publicly in matters of church discipline, but this seems to have been an exception for the times. Indeed, few nineteenth-century Baptist churches permitted women to vote in disciplinary cases, even when other women were being disciplined.[154] Gregory Wills observed that throughout the nineteenth century, women "were almost one and a half times more likely to suffer excommunication than males."[155]

Baptists in the Nineteenth Century

The nineteenth century was a formative period for Baptists in the United States. During that time, Baptist denominationalism took shape, not only between the dominant Anglo-Saxon groups, North and South, but also among immigrant communities, African American constituencies, and various subdenominations from Free Will Baptists to Primitive Baptists. The Civil War, the Industrial Revolution, and the collapse of the slave society and the beginnings of segregation all offered tremendous challenges to Baptist churches and denominations throughout the country. Nonetheless, the struggling minority had become a significant majority among American Protestants. The nineteenth century extended Baptist numbers, influence, and controversy.

Notes

1. Morgan J. Rhees, *Our Privileges, the Measure of Our Responsibility: Substance of a Discourse Preached on the Day Appointed for Public Thanksgiving* (Wilmington, Del: Porter and Naff, 1846), 4, 9, 11, 13, 14. See also Victor B. Howard,

"The Baptists and Peace Sentiments during the Mexican War," *Quarterly Review* 38 (April–June 1978): 68–84.

2. *Sixteenth Report of the American Baptist Home Mission Society* (1848), 14.

3. Howard, "Baptists and Peace Sentiments," 74.

4. Paul R. Dekar, *For the Healing of the Nations: Baptist Peacemakers* (Macon: Ga.: Smyth & Helwys, 1993), 51.

5. Ibid., 54.

6. *Proceedings of the Southern Baptist Convention* (1861), 63–64.

7. *Proceedings of the Southern Baptist Convention* (1863), 54–55.

8. *Minutes of the American Baptist Missionary Union* (May 29, 1861) (cited in Clarence C. Goen, *Broken Churches, Broken Nation: Denominational Schisms and the Coming of the American Civil War* [Macon, Ga.: Mercer University Press, 1985], 176).

9. J. William Jones, *Christ in the Camp, or, Religion in the Confederate Army* (1887; reprint, Harrisonburg, Va.: Sprinkle Publications, 1986), 156.

10. Ibid., 156–57.

11. C. Clinton Prim Jr., "Colporteurs: Propagandists and Revivalists in the Confederate Army," *American Baptist Quarterly* 2 (September 1983): 233–34.

12. Jones, *Christ in the Camp*, 35.

13. Ibid., 224.

14. Ibid., 393.

15. *Minutes of the Georgia Baptist Convention* (1864), 11. See also Rufus Spain, *At Ease in Zion: Social History of Southern Baptists, 1865–1900* (Nashville: Vanderbilt University Press, 1967), 33.

16. Robert A. Baker, *A Baptist Source Book, with Particular Reference to Southern Baptists* (Nashville: Broadman, 1966), 126.

17. A. D. Williams, *Benoni Stinson and the General Baptists* (Owensville, Ind.: General Baptist Publishing House, 1892), 157.

18. C. Allyn Russell, "Rhode Island Baptists, 1825–1931," *Foundations* 14 (January-March 1971): 39.

19. *Proceedings of the Southern Baptist Convention* (1866), 25.

20. Janet Kerr Morchaine, "George Dana Boardman: Propagandist for Peace," *Foundations* 9 (April-June 1966): 147.

21. Charter of the American Baptist Missionary Convention (published in *Annual of the Northern Baptist Convention* [1921], 369).

22. William H. Brackney, ed., *Baptist Life and Thought, 1600–1980* (Valley Forge, Pa.: Judson Press, 1983), 235–36.

23. Charter 99 of the Laws of Massachusetts (1910) (cited in *Annual of the Northern Baptist Convention* [1921], 371).

24. Act of Incorporation of the American Baptist Publication Society (cited in *Annual of the Northern Baptist Convention* [1921], 400–429).

25. *Thirteenth Report of the American Baptist Home Mission Society* (1845), 7.

26. H. Leon McBeth, *A Sourcebook for Baptist Heritage* (Nashville: Broadman, 1990), 271.

27. Ibid.

28. Dana Robert, *American Women in Mission: A Social History of Their Thought and Practice* (Macon, Ga.: Mercer University Press, 1996), 130.

29. Certificate of Incorporation of the Woman's Baptist Missionary Society (cited in *Annual of the Northern Baptist Convention* [1921], 391).

30. Ibid., 392–93.

31. Ibid., 393.

32. Bertha Grimmell Judd, *Fifty Golden Years: The First Half Century of the Woman's American Baptist Home Mission Society, 1877–1927* (Rochester, N.Y.: Du Bois Press, 1927), 7–8.

33. Ibid., 13.

34. Ibid., 86.

35. Ibid., 208–34.

36. Certificate of Incorporation of the Woman's American Baptist Home Mission Society (cited in *Annual of the Northern Baptist Convention* [1921], 400–417).

37. *American Baptist Home Mission Record* (May 1847), 4.

38. Judd, *Fifty Golden Years*, 127.

39. Ibid., 153.

40. R. Calvin Parker, *Jonathan Goble of Japan: Marine, Missionary, Maverick* (Lanham, Md.: University Press of America, 1990), 80–83.

41. Bill J. Leonard, ed., *Dictionary of Baptists in America* (Downers Grove, Ill.: InterVarsity Press, 1994), 132.

42. Jesse C. Fletcher, *The Southern Baptist Convention: A Sesquicentennial History* (Nashville: Broadman & Holman, 1994), 84.

43. Robert A. Baker, *Relations Between Northern and Southern Baptists*, 2nd ed. (1954; reprint, New York: Arno Press, 1980), 95.

44. Ibid., 105, 154–55.

45. Ibid., 135–36.

46. Ibid., 145–46.

47. Ibid., 161.

48. McBeth, *Sourcebook*, 290–91.

49. Spain, *At Ease in Zion*, 18–19 (citing *Religious Herald* [February 22, 1866], 1).

50. Ibid., 19.

51. Charles Reagan Wilson, *Baptized in Blood: The Religion of the Lost Cause, 1865–1920* (Athens: University of Georgia Press, 1980), 1.

52. Ibid., 11.
53. Form letter (1866), archives of First Baptist Church, Wilmington, North Carolina.
54. Howard Dorgan, "Old Time Baptists of Central Appalachia," in *Appalachian Christianity: Profiles in Regional Pluralism*, ed. Bill J. Leonard (Knoxville: University of Tennessee Press, 1999), 117–18.
55. Ibid., 120
56. Ibid., 120–21.
57. Ibid., 121. This is a departure from the position he took in an earlier, larger work, *Giving Glory to God in Appalachia: Worship Practices of Six Baptist Subdenominations* (Knoxville: University of Tennessee Press, 1987), 32–36.
58. Dorgan, "Old Time Baptists," 124. See also Howard Dorgan, *The Old Regular Baptists of Central Appalachia* (Knoxville: University of Tennessee Press, 1989); Deborah Vansau McCauley, *Appalachian Mountain Religion: A History* (Chicago: University of Illinois Press, 1995).
59. Dorgan, "Old Time Baptists," 125.
60. Cited in Dorgan, *Old Regular Baptists,* 27–28.
61. Dorgan, "Old Time Baptists," 129.
62. Ibid., 129–32.
63. For an in-depth study of these fascinating Baptists, see Howard Dorgan, *In the Hands of a Happy God: Primitive Baptist Universalists of Central Appalachia* (Knoxville: University of Tennessee Press, 1997).
64. Virgil A. Olson, "Neither Jew nor Greek: A Study of an Ethnic Baptist Group, the Swedish Baptists, 1850–1950," *Baptist History and Heritage* 25 (January 1990): 32.
65. Ibid., 34–35.
66. William H. Brackney, *The Baptists* (New York: Greenwood Press, 1988), 281–82.
67. Leonard, ed., *Dictionary of Baptists,* 47.
68. Ibid., 37 (citing *The Examiner* [September 4, 1884]).
69. Ibid., 38.
70. Ibid., 40.
71. Peder Stiansen, *History of the Norwegian Baptists in America* (Wheaton, Ill.: Norwegian Baptist Convention of America and American Baptist Publication Society, 1939), 22–23.
72. Ibid., 24–25.
73. Ibid., 27.
74. Ibid., 36.
75. Ibid., 77.
76. Ibid., 89.
77. Ibid., 93.
78. Don A. Sanford, *A Choosing People: The History of Seventh Day Baptists* (Nashville: Broadman, 1992), 149–50.
79. Ibid. 152.
80. Ibid., 170–71.
81. Ibid., 173.
82. Albert N. Rogers, "Ministerial Training and Seventh Day Baptists," *Foundations* 16 (January–March 1973): 57.
83. Seventh Day Baptist General Conference, *Seventh Day Baptists in Europe and America,* 2 vols. (1910; reprint, New York: Arno Press, 1980), 1:181.
84. Ibid., 189–91.
85. Ibid., 338–40.
86. Ibid., 341.
87. Ibid., 346–48.
88. Ibid., 384.
89. Williams, *Benoni Stinson,* 16.
90. Ibid., 42.
91. Ibid., 51–52.
92. Ibid., 66.
93. Ibid., 78–80.
94. Ibid., 22. See also *Tennessee Baptist* (March 7, 1861).
95. Ibid., 211.
96. Ibid., 239–41.
97. Salvatore Mondello, "Baptist Churches and Italian-Americans," *Foundations* 16 (July–September 1973): 225.
98. Ibid., 227.
99. Ibid., 229–31.
100. David L. Rowe, "Elon Galusha and the Millerite Movement," *Foundations* 18 (July–September 1975): 252–59.
101. Brackney, ed., *Baptist Life and Thought,* 246.
102. Leonard, ed., *Dictionary of Baptists,* 22.
103. Brackney, ed., *Baptist Life and Thought,* 304.
104. Leonard, ed., *Dictionary of Baptists,* 25–26.
105. Brackney, ed., *Baptist Life and Thought,* 310–11.
106. Leonard, ed., *Dictionary of Baptists,* 53.

107. Robert A. Baker, *The Southern Baptist Convention and Its People* (Nashville: Broadman, 1972), 263.

108. Ibid., 264.

109. William A. Mueller, *A History of Southern Baptist Theological Seminary* (Nashville: Broadman, 1959), 26.

110. Michael A. Smith, "Baptist Deacons in the Nineteenth Century," *Quarterly Review* (October–December 1982): 69–71.

111. Edward T. Hiscox, *Principles and Practices for Baptist Churches* (1894; reprint, Grand Rapids, Mich.: Kregel, 1980), 75.

112. Ibid., 76.

113. Ibid., 139–41.

114. William G. McLoughlin, *Modern Revivalism: Charles Grandison Finney to Billy Graham* (New York: Ronald Press, 1959), 136–37.

115. Ibid., 136.

116. Ibid.

117. Ibid., 138.

118. Ibid., 141.

119. Ibid., 142.

120. Carnegie's essay originally was published as "Wealth," *North American Review* 148 (1889): 653–64.

121. Russell H. Conwell, *Acres of Diamonds* (Philadelphia: Columbian Advertising and Distributing Co., 1892), 19.

122. Clyde K. Nelson, "Russell H. Conwell and the 'Gospel of Wealth,'" *Foundations* 5 (January 1962), 39–51.

123. Robert Cross, foreword to Walter Rauschenbusch, *Christianity and the Social Crisis,* ed. Robert Cross (New York: Harper & Row, 1964), xii.

124. Ibid., xxiii.

125. H. Shelton Smith, Robert Handy, and Lefferts A. Loetscher, *American Christianity,* 2 vols. (New York: Scribner, 1960–63), 2: 404.

126. Ibid., 2:406.

127. Charles Howard Hopkins, *The Rise of the Social Gospel in American Protestantism, 1865–1915* (New Haven: Yale University Press, 1940), 150.

128. Ronald C. White Jr. and C. Howard Hopkins, *The Social Gospel: Religion and Reform in Changing America* (Philadelphia: Temple University Press, 1976), 73.

129. Ibid., 75.

130. Cited in James E. Tull, *Shapers of Baptist Thought* (Valley Forge, Pa.: Judson Press, 1972), 204.

131. Hopkins, *Social Gospel,* 133.

132. Ibid., 131.

133. Glenn T. Miller, "Baptist Businessmen in Historical Perspective," *Baptist History and Heritage* 13 (January 1978): 61.

134. Russell, "Rhode Island Baptists," 35.

135. Ibid., 36.

136. *Religious Herald* (September 7, 1871) (cited in Ralph Reavis, "The Development of Black Baptists in Virginia, 1867–1882," in *Baptists in the Balance,* ed. Everett C. Goodwin [Valley Forge, Pa.: Judson Press, 1997], 339).

137. Virginia Baptist State Convention, *Proceedings of Fifth Annual Session* (1872), 14 (cited in Reavis, "Black Baptists in Virginia," 339).

138. Reavis, "Black Baptists in Virginia," 340.

139. Lawrence B. Davis, *Immigrants, Baptists, and the Protestant Mind in America* (Urbana: University of Illinois Press, 1973), 2.

140. Ibid., 26.

141. Ibid., 50.

142. Ibid., 52–59.

143. Robert G. Torbet, *A History of the Baptists,* 3rd ed. (Valley Forge, Pa.: Judson Press, 1973), 320–21.

144. Ibid., 324.

145. Donald G. Mathews, *Religion in the Old South* (Chicago: University of Chicago Press, 1977), 92–93; Bill J. Leonard, "What Can the Baptist Tradition Contribute to Christian Higher Education?" in *Models For Christian Higher Education,* ed. Richard T. Hughes and William B. Adrian (Grand Rapids, Mich.: Eerdmans, 1997), 367–82.

146. Mathews, *Old South,* 77.

147. Ibid., 78–81.

148. Ibid., 139.

149. H. Leon McBeth, "The Role of Women in Southern Baptist History," *Baptist History and Heritage* 12 (January 1977): 9 (citing A. McDowell, "Female Education," *Biblical Recorder* [August 26, 1868]).

150. Ibid. (citing *Biblical Recorder* [February 10, 1892]).

151. Ibid., 11.

152. Ibid. (citing *Tennessee Baptist* [May 14, 1885]: 6).

153. Ibid., 14.

154. Norman H. Letsinger, "The Status of Women in the Southern Baptist Convention in Historical Perspective," *Baptist History and Heritage* 12 (January 1977): 39.

155. Gregory A. Wills, *Democratic Religion: Freedom, Authority and Church Discipline in the Baptist South, 1785–1900* (New York: Oxford University Press, 1997), 55.

Chapter 10
Baptists in the Americas and the Caribbean

Baptists in Canada

IN *A HISTORY OF CHRISTIANITY IN THE UNITED STATES AND CANADA*, MARK
Noll noted, "Christian developments in nineteenth-century Canada bear striking similarities
to what was happening at the same time in the Unites States. Like the faithful in the American Republic, Canadian believers mobilized to preach the gospel in new settlements spread
over a vast frontier. Canadians also linked the progress of Christianity with the advance of
civilization. And they succeeded in bequeathing a Christian tone to the institutions, habits,
and morals of public life."[1] Noll acknowledged numerous differences between the two
countries, including Canada's continuing ties to Britain, its large Catholic population, and
its strong French culture.[2]

The modern Canadian state originated in 1867 with a federation formed by Quebec,
Ontario, Nova Scotia, and New Brunswick. The composition of diverse regions into one
"Dominion" was influenced by the British willingness to permit greater autonomy, the self-
interest of each constituency, and a strong desire to resist being drawn into an "American
empire" dominated by the United States.[3] Additional provinces were added between 1871
and 1949 and included British Columbia, Prince Edward Island, Manitoba, Alberta,
Saskatchewan, and Newfoundland. Though significant groups of indigenous peoples are
present throughout the country, much of the Canadian population, like that of the United
States, is comprised largely of immigrants. Its 2001 population was over 31 million, with
extensive ethnic and linguistic diversity.

Baptist life in Canada reflects the regionalism of the vast country. Mission and ministry
are distinct in the maritime provinces of Nova Scotia, New Brunswick, and Prince Edward
Island, in the central provinces of Quebec and Ontario, and in the western provinces stretch-
ing from Manitoba to British Columbia.

Baptist Beginnings in Canada
The first reference to a Baptist presence in Canada appeared in a 1753 report from Anglican missionary Jean Baptiste Moreau, who observed that "Lutherans, Calvinists, Presbyterians, and Anabaptists" had come from England or New England.[4] The earliest Baptist

churches apparently were the result of immigration from the New England colonies. Ebenezer Moulton, a Baptist dissenter from Massachusetts, ventured to Nova Scotia in 1760. While pastor of the Baptist church in Brimfield, Massachusetts, he challenged laws requiring payment of church taxes to the Congregational establishment. Persecution from the Standing Order and the bankruptcy of his "merchandizing" business led him to Canada after the Seven Years War (1756–1763). He worked in Nova Scotia until returning to Massachusetts in 1771. Moulton apparently organized a short-lived congregation in the regions of Horton and Cornwallis comprised of persons whom he immersed and others who had received baptism as infants.[5]

Another congregation of Six Principle Baptists appeared briefly in Sackville on the Bay of Fundy. It probably was formed around 1763 by a group of émigrés led by Pastor Nathan Mason from Swansea, Maine. Although the church was soon disbanded, some Baptists remained in the region.[6]

A Separate Baptist church was formed in Sackville in 1767 and seems to have endured until the years 1771–1777. It developed from what Isaac Backus called "a considerable season of conviction and conversion" in these colonial territories.[7] Baptist Job Seamans's unfinished memoir says of the church, "As we had no meeting-house, we met, as usual in a private house," or at "the water-side."[8] A more permanent congregation was gathered in Sackville in 1799.

The persecution of eighteenth-century Baptists and other dissenters in New England led many to migrate to the Maritimes. These individuals often were supporters of the revivalistic New Light movement. Daniel Dimock (d. 1804) was a New Light Separatist from Connecticut who received believer's immersion from Baptist ministers emigrating from New England. In 1775, Dimock, a lay Baptist preacher, baptized his father, Shubael (d. 1781), in the Kennetcook River. Dimock's son Joseph became a leader among the next generation of Maritime Baptists.[9]

In 1713, Acadia, a large landmass including Nova Scotia, was ceded to the British as part of the Treaty of Utrecht. Disputes with the French over the territory continued, but in 1749 British governor Lawrence expelled the French-speaking Acadians and solidified British control. By the 1760s, British "planters," many from the American colonies, had settled in the region. Most of the New Englanders were members of the Congregational establishment, some with New Light revivalist sentiments. Among them was the New Light evangelist Henry Alline.

Henry Alline and the New Light Revivals

Although never actually a Baptist, Henry Alline (1748–1784) was one of the best known of the revivalists of the period. His New Light movement had significant impact on the formation of Baptist identity in the Maritimes. D. G. Bell observed, "In the New Brunswick context, where the tradition flourished longest, there was a perceptible cultural transmission from Allinite to Newlight Baptist to the Free Christian Baptist conference (1832) with its two purist schisms (the Primitive Baptists and the Reformed Baptists) and its remnant of Free Baptists who refused to follow the Free Christian Baptists into the United Baptist reunion of 1906."[10]

Born in Newport, Rhode Island, Alline moved his family to Falmouth, Nova Scotia, in 1760. From early childhood he was concerned "to please God, or to get reconciled to

Him."[11] Of his conversion in 1775, he wrote, "My whole soul, that a few minutes ago was groaning under mountains of death, wading streams of sorrow, racked with distressing fears, and crying to an unknown God for help, was now filled with an immortal love, soaring on the wings of faith." In less than an hour he accepted a call to "labour in the ministry and ... preach the gospel."[12] Alline's public ministry was relatively brief, lasting from April 1776 to his death, at age thirty-five, in February 1784. Yet his work had a profound effect on the religious life of evangelical Protestants, especially Baptists, in Nova Scotia.

Drawn to the conversionism of the New Light movement, Alline began an itinerant ministry throughout English-speaking Nova Scotia from which new congregations were formed. In 1778, he helped to establish the first Baptist church to be formally organized in Canada. Founded at Horton (Wolfville), the church set aside its initial officers thus: "Benjamin Kinsman laid his hand on the head of Mr. Pierson, and gave him the charge to be a faithful pastor. After this, Mr. Pierson laid his hands on Mr. Kinsman's head and set him apart to the office of deacon."[13] Alline was present and preached at the gathering. In 1779, he received ordination at the hands of representatives of three churches, two of them Congregational, the other Baptist. Alline traveled throughout Nova Scotia, organizing as many as six churches. He wrote poetry and hymnody, including *Two Mites on Some of the Most Important and Much Disputed Points of Divinity* (1781) and *The Anti-Traditionalist* (1783).

In spite of his links with the Baptists, Alline apparently viewed immersion as only one mode for baptism and preferred to speak of the inner baptism "of the spirit of Christ." His views were expressed in this bit of verse:

'Tis not a zeal for modes and forms
That spreads the gospel-truths abroad;
But he whose inward man reforms,
And loves the saints, and loves the Lord.[14]

He urged the new churches to accept converted persons whatever their mode of baptism, and he invited all true Christians to come freely to the Lord's Table. Some Canadian Baptists found these admonitions difficult to accept.

Alline returned to New England in 1783 and died of consumption the following year. Many compared him to the "Grand Itinerant," George Whitefield. With few exceptions, New Lights in Nova Scotia divided between Allinites and Wesleyan Methodists.[15] Some Allinites became associated with the "New Dispensation," persons convinced that the old laws no longer applied and they were free from certain moral and communal restraints. Their antinomianism led to various ethical and doctrinal scandals—actions that discredited the movement. Baptists were another subgroup within the Allinite New Light faction, evident by the 1790s. The splintering of the Allinites is itself an important part of the evangelical story in Nova Scotia.

Certain Allinites received immersion but did not join Baptist churches or require immersion of everyone. Thomas Chipman (b. 1756) and Joseph Dimock were converted, immersed, and began preaching in the 1780s and 1790s, but they refused to make immersion a prerequisite for church membership. Nonetheless, Chipman was ordained a Baptist minister in 1782. Henry Alline participated in the service held in an Annapolis church comprised of both Congregationalists and Baptists.[16]

Baptist New Lights grew steadily. In the 1790s, Joseph Crandall, a New Light preacher discredited in the New Dispensation movement, turned to the Baptists. In 1800, Anglican

Bishop Charles Inglis observed that initially New Lights baptized infants, "but by a recent illumination, they have adopted the Anabaptist scheme, by which their number has been much increased and their zeal inflamed."[17] Why the move to immersion and the Baptist views? Bell suggested that it may have been a way to provide an obvious break with the beliefs of the discredited New Dispensation. He noted, "Baptism by immersion was just the latest phase of a whole generation of religious novelties that had begun with Alline himself."[18] Immersion was a distinguishing mark for those who already accepted the idea of a believers' church, radical conversion, and congregational polity. It was an outward and visible sign that set believers apart in a public way.

Alline's ideas on free will and free grace, along with his response to Calvinism, made him an important influence on the Free Will Baptists. There is no question that Alline's theology was known to Benjamin Randall, the founder of the Free Will Baptists. They were among the first to publish Alline's theological works and hymns.[19]

In his study of Henry Alline, George Rawlyk observed that the Free Will Baptists "found in Alline a dynamic 'New Light' pietism and mysticism and language which linked their movement to a Whitefieldian past and also to a nineteenth-century evangelical outlook with its special emphasis on individualism, optimism, and sense of mission."[20] Alline made a significant contribution to a variety of Baptist groups.

By the 1790s, Baptists in Nova Scotia were at the center of another religious awakening. Conversions led to immersions, as Anglican Bishop Charles Inglis observed: "A rage for dipping or total immersion prevails all over the western counties of the Province, and is frequently performed in a very indelicate manner before vast collections of people. Several hundreds have already been baptized, and this plunging they deem to be absolutely necessary to the conversion of their souls."[21] Many of the participants were Baptists influenced by the earlier Allinite movement. Rawlyk maintained that by the late eighteenth century Nova Scotia Baptists had moved away from Alline's more open attitude toward baptism and communion. He suggested that soon, "Alline's 'non-essential' adult baptism had become a Baptist, closed-communion 'essential.'"[22]

New Light Baptist Associations

New Light believers founded a Congregational and Baptist Association in 1798. In 1800, it became a solely Baptist body, expelled John Payzant, the nonimmersed minister, and entered into a relationship with the Danbury Association in New England. Although retaining strong New Light sentiments, Maritime Baptists were approaching a new organizational phase.[23]

The Association of Baptist Churches in Nova Scotia was formed in 1800, but soon it divided over issues of open or closed communion. In 1809, the Association dismissed the churches that practiced open communion. This was a repudiation of earlier Allinite sentiments for open communion among all born-again believers.[24] Over a third of the membership was expelled, and divisions permeated the churches. In Onslow, for example, the Allinite church voted in 1809 to approve closed communion. The records noted that "in a Clamorous manner," the majority "declared themselves a Baptist [closed communion] Church not having taken any regular steps of Organization to make them so, the Rev'd m'r Cleavland being by appearance their leader and very active for the purpose of having the members which are not Baptized [immersed] to be separated from the Church."[25] Isaac Case wrote to the Massachusetts Baptist Missionary Society in 1812 regarding his evangelistic efforts in Nova Scotia and New Brunswick Association. He counted seventeen churches and thirteen ordained ministers and noted, "They were first gathered upon the open communion plan, and remained so until, I think, two years ago last June; when, having gained further light into the apostolic doctrine and practice, they came upon gospel ground."[26] This division within the Maritime Baptist bodies was not healed until the reunion movement of 1906.[27]

These changes, some believe, were an attempt to bring the Nova Scotia Association "into harmony with the New England Baptist associations." Thus, during the early nineteenth century, "Maritime Baptist leaders were drawn deeply into the American orbit."[28]

Open communion created further divisions among Free Baptists, Free Will Baptists, and Free Christian Baptists. This last group, closely connected to the Allinite New Lights, was given to mystical religion, antisacramentalism, and opposition to religious formalism. These Baptists were particularly strong in New Brunswick.[29]

In 1814, Baptists formed a mission society and, soon after, a Baptist missionary magazine. In 1821, the Association was divided into the Nova Scotia Baptist Association and a similar one in New Brunswick.[30] The 1827 census in Nova Scotia listed a population of 123,630. This included approximately 28,655 Anglicans, 37,647 Presbyterians, 20,401 Roman Catholics, and 19,790 Baptists. This suggests that Baptists comprised some 16 percent of the population. By the middle of the nineteenth century, Baptists had become the largest Protestant communion in New Brunswick.[31]

James Manning: New Light Evangelist

James Manning (d. 1818), an itinerant New Light preacher, traveled throughout the Maritimes and recorded his exploits in a journal that offers insight into the church life, spirituality, and hardships of the era. His own spiritual experiences sometimes were characterized as "breakdowns" and were described by one observer thus: "He eats but little & wishes to talk less. Stupidity or a painful anxiety of mind are his constant companions. He still declares himself unfit company for either Saint or Sinner, the one is a burthen, the other a grief to him."[32]

Manning's journal details his work among the Baptists in this account from Sunday, September 6, 1801: "Repard [repaired] to the water ... and tow [two] Came and told there Exspearance/ oh it was Easy to pray and easy to sing/ it was a happy time/ ... they Sang from the water to they House and there I think the Supper was administe[red] oh what a Glowry appeard in the Holy ordenances."[33] Manning preached widely and was instrumental in spreading Baptist views. His conversionist views led him to encourage revivals.

Educational Institutions

Canadian Baptists founded the Nova Scotia Education Society in 1828. Horton (Wolfville) Academy was established in 1829, and in 1841, with some support from public funds, it became Acadia College, graduating its first class in 1843. A department of theology was formed in 1844 with an endowment from British Baptists, matched by Baptists of the Maritimes. E. A. Crawley, formerly a lawyer and pastor of the Granville Street Church, Halifax, was chosen as head of the theology department, and he taught Hebrew, homiletics, and theology. The department graduated three students by 1846 and then none until 1849.[34]

In 1833, a theological college was established in Montreal to provide training for ministers. Its constituency was primarily open-communionists from the Ottawa Valley and the Montreal region. Closed-communionists, particularly in the West, were hesitant to support such an endeavor and were even more reticent when the school began a broader liberal arts program to "educate a few youths, thirteen and upwards in English, German, Latin and Oriental Languages as well as mathematics, Logic and Philosophy."[35] Financial difficulties, divisions among the Baptists, and other problems led to the closing of the Montreal College in 1949.

In 1836, another Baptist seminary was founded in Fredericton, New Brunswick, the first such Canadian school to allow both men and women to receive training. Its open admissions policy brought students from various denominational traditions and social contexts. More than half of the seventy students in the first class were non-Baptists. The first principals of the male and female departments were Rev. and Mrs. F. W. Miles.[36] The school endured until 1873, when it closed due to a series of financial deficits.

Ontario's first Baptist-related college was Woodstock College, founded in 1860. In 1881, the school's theological department was moved to Toronto to facilitate founding the Toronto Baptist College. The founders hoped that it would become a centralized school, drawing students from throughout Canada. Wealthy Baptist layman William McMaster (1811–1887) helped to fund construction of a building. In 1887, Woodstock College was moved to Toronto, and the school was renamed McMaster University. It remained in Toronto until 1931, when it was moved to Hamilton.[37]

In western Canada, Brandon College was founded in 1899, with A. P. McDiarmid as president. Its intent, Walter Ellis suggested, was "to socialize students who, mellowed by culture, refinement, social convention and ivy-covered institutions, would create an environment [in the West] where sectarianism would diminish and ecumenical cooperation and progress would flourish."[38]

Free Will Baptists

Free Will Baptists were present in Canada by the 1830s. Like other Arminians, they stressed Christ's general atonement, freedom of the will, and human choice in salvation. They practiced open communion and favored financial support for ministers through congregational offerings. Free Will Baptist leaders included Asa McGray (b. 1780), who founded the first Free Baptist Church in Nova Scotia in 1821. McGray also helped established a union of Free Baptist churches in 1834. In 1837, some degree of unity was achieved between these Baptists and a group known as Christians or Christian Baptists. They agreed to call themselves Free Christian Baptists and acknowledged, "We consider it an undoubted privilege to choose that name which best expresses our faith; and as we believe in and practise baptism by immersion, we must be Baptists, and if we are disciples of Christ, which we profess to be, we must be Christians; but as no form or rite can of themselves make us Christians, we must be made free by the Son of God, and if made free by the Son, we must be Free Christian Baptists."[39] Groups of Free Will Baptists and Free Christian Baptists continued until 1867, when a merger was completed and they became known as Free Baptists. One of the early leaders of this movement was Ezekiel McLeod (1812–1867), who served as pastor of numerous Free Baptist churches in New Brunswick. He established *The Religious Intelligencer* in 1853.

The Baptist Convention of Nova Scotia, New Brunswick, and Prince Edward Island was organized in 1846. Baptist support for temperance, Sabbath keeping, and personal conversion made them an important nineteenth-century religious group.[40] By the 1840s, Baptist communions in the Maritimes included the Baptist Convention of Nova Scotia, Regular (Calvinistic) Baptists, and Free Christian Baptist Conferences.

German Baptists

August Rauschenbusch, father of Social Gospel leader Walter Rauschenbusch, was instrumental in the formation of German Baptist work in Canada. Arriving in Canada in 1848 as a Lutheran minister, Rauschenbusch accepted Baptist views in 1851, received immersion, and aided in establishing the Bridgeport German Baptist Church in Waterloo County, Ontario. That same year, he served as Canadian representative to the first general conference of the German Baptists of North America in Philadelphia.[41]

Relationships between German Baptists in Canada and the United States often were tenuous, and the Canadians created an independent missionary society in 1876. The relationship was restored in 1883 with the founding of the General Missionary Society of German Baptists. An 1886 article in the *Northwest Baptist* declared, "The Germans are coming in large numbers and the Baptists are the only body who has a ministry among them."[42]

F. A. Petereit came from Germany to North America and settled in western Canada with support from German Baptists in the United States and Canada. He organized a German Baptist church in 1886 at New Toulcha and was instrumental in the founding other churches in Saskatchewan, Manitoba, Winnipeg, and Alberta in the 1880s and 1890s. By the late nineteenth century, German Baptists in Canada had developed close relations with their counterparts in the United States. In 1900, the two groups developed a denominational organization that divided portions of the United States and Canada into *Vereinigungen* (associations) linked by seven annual *Konferenzen*. The General Conference carried out ministerial training, missionary activity, and publication work. In 1900, there were some 22,824 German Baptists in North America.[43]

In 1909, the Baptist College at Brandon invited German Baptists to support a professor who would provide specific programs for German ministerial students. The Germans rejected the offer, preferring instead to continue their singular relationship with Rochester Seminary, still an ethnically German school. They maintained, "Our German pastors must have their training in a German school." This was only one of several issues that pushed the Northern Conference German Baptists toward their counterparts in North America and away from Canadian (non-German) Baptists.[44]

By the late twentieth century, Canadian German Baptists claimed over fifteen thousand members. A master of divinity program was begun in the North American Baptist College, Edmonton, for studies in ministry, lay programs, religious education, and music.[45]

Maritime Baptist Missions

Baptists in the Maritimes took their first offering for foreign missions in 1814 at the Association meeting in Chester. The gathering gave significant attention to home missionary activities in the region. As a result, missionaries Joseph Crandall and James Munro were sent east of Halifax the following year. By 1818, funds were being received by the Association from the Female Mite Society of the City of Saint John—the first such endeavor among Canadian Baptists. Other such societies soon followed.[46]

Home missionary work supported by the Nova Scotia Association took Baptist Charles Tupper to Prince Edward Island in 1825. Tupper and other missionaries founded numerous churches on the island. Tupper himself became pastor of the church at Bedeque and Tryon in 1833.[47]

Maritime Baptists established the *Baptist Missionary Magazine* in 1827—the earliest publication by Baptists in British North America. It provided information regarding the Carey mission in India and appealed for funds from Canadian Baptists for the foreign missionary enterprise. Richard Burpee, a graduate of Acadia College, was the first to be sent out in a joint affiliation with the American Baptist Missionary Union and the Maritime Baptists. He and his wife went to Burma in 1845, returning to Canada in 1850 for reasons of health. He died of tuberculosis in 1853.[48]

Arthur R. R. Crawley (d. 1876) was sent to Burma in 1853 through a joint appointment from the American Baptist Foreign Mission Board and the Foreign Missions Board of the Baptist Convention of the Maritime Provinces. By 1869, Maritime Baptists were funding twenty-eight missionaries whose appointments were made in conjunction with American Baptists. In 1867, Minnie DeWolfe became the first single woman to be sent by Canadians as a foreign missionary. Arriving in Burma in 1868, she served under the auspices of the American Baptist Missionary Union, with funding provided entirely by Maritime Baptists. Because of health difficulties, DeWolfe remained in Burma no more than five years.[49]

Home mission work developed association by association. A mission to the Micmac tribe of the Maritime region led Baptists to appoint Silas Tertius Rand (1810–1889) in 1849. With other Protestant missionaries, he participated in the founding of the Micmac Missionary Society in 1850. In this interdenominational program, Rand was concerned primarily with Christianizing the native Canadians rather than making Baptists of them. Settling at Hantsport, Nova Scotia, in 1853, he was engaged in mission work until his death in 1889. Much of his time was spent translating the Bible into the languages of the tribes. During the latter years, he abandoned direct fundraising from churches and societies and maintained a "faith mission" whereby he depended on divine providence to inspire persons to contribute to his support.[50]

Rand continually voiced concern over the treatment of native peoples by white Protestants who demonstrated, in his words, "abominable and unreasonable ideas of caste." He acknowledged the difficulties involved in leading some Micmacs to accept Christianity and in turning others from Catholicism to Protestantism. He lamented, "I have been so dissatisfied with the Protestant church generally, that I have had no heart to urge the Indians, even if I believed them converted, to leave their [Catholic] church and join ours."[51] Rand was a master linguist and a composer of hymns and poetry.

Local associations carried on mission work in the Maritimes until 1872, when the Home Missions Union in Nova Scotia was established. That same year, the Prince Edward Island Baptist Home Mission Society joined the Union. Efforts were made to consolidate limited funds and overlapping programs. In 1873, the Canadian Baptist Missionary Society was begun, uniting mission work among Baptists in Ontario, Quebec, and the Maritimes.[52]

Sunday schools began among Canadian Baptists in the 1820s. An 1832 resolution by the

Nova Scotia Association "recommended that particular attention be paid to the encouragement of Sabbath Schools throughout the churches"—sentiments echoed the next year by the New Brunswick Association. Nova Scotia Sunday school unions began in the 1830s, failed, and were reorganized in the 1860s.[53]

Temperance societies appeared among Canadian Baptists as early as 1829. Although moderate drinking was often tolerated, drunkenness was cause for dismissal from the church. By the 1830s, Canadian Baptists were promoting total abstinence through "pledges" never to touch alcohol. At Wilmot in 1829, eight Baptist subscribers declared that they would reject "the use of intoxicating liquor as a beverage ... except when prescribed by a physician as a medicine in case of sickness."[54] Such pledges frequently were included in revival meetings where preachers called sinners to conversion and total abstinence.

A Baptist Convention in Nova Scotia

In September 1846, the Baptist Convention of Nova Scotia, New Brunswick, and Prince Edward Island was formed in St. John. Leaders such as E. A. Crawley of Acadia College and Charles Tupper, a prominent pastor, supported an effort to bring regional associations together in a broader convention relationship. The Convention's constitution set forth the objectives of the new body: "To advance the interests of the Baptist denomination, and the cause of God, generally; to maintain the religious and charitable institutions hereinafter mentioned; to procure correct information relative to the Baptist body and to advise and carry such measures as may, with the Divine blessing, tend to advance the interests of the Baptists denomination and the cause of God, generally."[55] The charitable institutions included missions and educational societies along with financial support for ministers. The Convention sought to coordinate the work of its three associations and thereby avoid duplication of missions and ministries.

Maritime Baptists continued to pursue the possibility of union until the United Baptist Convention of the Maritime Provinces was founded on October 10, 1905. Its "Basis of Union" reflected the continued tension between local church autonomy and associational cooperation. One portion of the document noted, "The voluntary principle underlies the whole church polity of the New Testament. Each church is independent, but the churches are interdependent. All the power the more general bodies have over the less general and individual churches is to advise and to enforce ... with the strongest moral motives."[56]

The concern for local autonomy was one way of dealing with the inevitable division over open versus closed communion. The document cited Matthew 26:26-30 as evidence for permitting congregations to establish their own policies for admission to the Lord's Table.[57]

In 1906, Free Baptists of Nova Scotia merged with the United Baptist Convention of the Maritime Provinces. At that time, the group then claimed a membership of 64,189 from 569 congregations.[58]

The Canadas

For many years, Baptist strength in Canada was situated primarily in the Maritimes. By the latter part of the nineteenth century, Baptists comprised about 6 percent of the Canadian population. Churches were founded in Ontario and Manitoba, but national associations emerged slowly. The Maritime Convention accepted seventeen African churches into its fellowship in

1884. The Regular and Free Will Baptists combined membership in 1906–1907 to form the Maritime United Baptists.[59]

Upper Canada (modern-day Ontario) was home to numerous Baptist groups. These included Regular Baptists from the United States, Strict or Ultra-Calvinist Baptists from England, Scotch Baptists, and Free Will Baptists. A Baptist presence may have developed in the Canadas as early as 1776, but, as Morgan Edwards reported, it certainly was evident by 1789.[60] Canadian Regular Baptists tended to follow the Philadelphia Confession as their basic doctrinal statement.

Free Communion, Free Will, and Free Baptists were names used for Arminian Baptist groups in the United States and Canada. Free Communion Baptists began as early as 1783 in western New York. In 1841, a union of Free Will and Free Communion Baptists occurred among those churches in the United States. Free Will Baptist churches first appeared in 1802. The Free Communion Baptist Conference of Canada began in 1829.[61] Although these early Canadian Free Communion and Free Will Baptists created no formal union, they readily acknowledged their similarities. Of their differences, an 1829 document noted that Free Will Baptists believed that "a saint" in "reprobation" "may lose that grace and that character that constitute him such, and thus finally perish." Free Communion Baptists maintained "the reverse" and utilized a few "written articles of faith." Free Will Baptists, however, accepted "no standard but the Bible."[62]

Throughout much of the nineteenth century, Canadian Strict/Regular and "Evangelical" Baptists divided over issues such as open versus closed communion and the nature of the church. Evangelicals were more mission-oriented in their ecclesiology, while Regulars reflected the impact of Old Landmarkism.[63] The Strict/Regular Baptists organized mission societies, including the Baptist Missionary Convention of Upper Canada, 1833–1836. These Baptists were influenced by the American Baptist Home Mission Society (ABHMS), while Evangelical Baptists gravitated toward the Baptist Missionary Society in England.[64]

Baptiste Liberaux

Concerns by Ottawa Protestants to pursue the conversion of French Catholics led to an appeal for aid from European Protestant churches. In 1834, Henri Oliver, a native of Switzerland, went to Montreal, where he received immersion. Before returning to Europe in 1835, Oliver was joined by Louis Roussy and Henrietta Feller. These individuals called themselves "Baptiste Liberaux" (Free Baptists). They emphasized local church autonomy and the church's missionary imperative. Anxious to liberate Canadians from the "yoke" of Catholicism, they constituted the Grande Ligne Mission, located on a road known as La Grande Ligne in the Richelieu Valley.[65]

Some members of the group were immersionists and others were not. Because of this division, the Mission's early relationship with the Canada Baptist Missionary Society was dissolved from 1839 to 1845, when the groups were reunited. The two organizations became part of the Canada Baptist Union, founded in 1843 to enhance Baptist influence in Canada and to avoid the "detached and insulated position" of early Canadian Baptists.[66]

In 1850, the Mission was reorganized under the name Evangelical Society of Grande Ligne, with support from the American Baptist Home Mission Society. This relationship ended during the Civil War. Further divisions occurred inside the group over issues of open communion and regional mission responsibilities. In 1970, the society was reorganized as the Union d'Églises Baptistes Françaises au Canada.[67]

Toward a Union

The Regular Baptist Union of Canada began in 1848, founded by various associations of Regular Baptists. Organizers made it clear that this was not "The Baptist Church of Canada," and they rejected the idea of "a visible church composing all Christians of a denomination of a land."[68] In 1855, the Canada Baptist Union—an organization founded in 1836 but at that time dormant—was resurrected, with members declaring their Christian orthodoxy and missionary zeal. Phillip Griffin-Allwood noted that while the Union did not have great strength, it served as "a denominational home" for certain Evangelical Baptists "excluded from fellowship with the Strict/Regular Baptists."[69]

During the nineteenth century, a variety of regional conventions emerged in Canadian Baptist life. Unions were difficult to sustain because, among other things, disagreement continued over open versus closed communion. Even the Spurgeon family was brought into the controversy. When the brother of Charles H. Spurgeon was invited to preach at an Ontario Regular Baptist church, the Canadian Baptists warned that the invitation should be withdrawn because he accepted open communion. Charles Spurgeon wrote in support of his brother, "He is as good and staunch a Baptist as you are, though like myself he is not a strict communionist."[70]

Union efforts continued, and the Baptist Union of Canada was formed by an act of the Dominion Parliament in 1879. Griffin-Allwood commented that it was 1888 when the various mission activities of the Baptists of Ontario and Quebec were "finally brought together in transcongregational entity after decades of division."[71]

Western Canada

In western Canada, Baptists were late arrivals, with the first churches founded after Baptist leader Alexander MacDonald settled in the region in 1883. Work soon developed in Winnipeg, Brandon, Edmonton, and Calgary. These early Baptist churches reflected the influence of Reformed theology as set forth in the Philadelphia Confession of Faith.[72] Many Baptists in the region offered their support for liberal politics and certain aspects of the Social Gospel. Political liberals such as J. C. Bowen, lieutenant governor of Alberta, and W. J. Estey, justice of the Supreme Court, were Baptists from the Canadian West.[73]

Western Canada was the scene of two diverse social movements, the leftist Cooperative Commonwealth Federation (CCF) and the rightist Social Credit Movement, both organized in the early twentieth century. Baptists were involved in these movements and divided over their respective ideologies.[74]

Western Canadians, Baptists included, did not readily cooperate with other regions of the country. The Baptist Union of Western Canada was formed in 1907, and by 1911 it was participating with other Canadian Baptist unions in formation of the Canadian Baptist Foreign Mission Board.[75]

Immigration in the latter half of the nineteenth century brought numerous ethnic groups into Canada, especially from Germany and Scandinavia. Baptists established churches among these ethnic communities, often with the help of numerous Baptist immigrants. Evangelism often was done through "mission halls" that provided meals, educational programs, festivals, medical treatment, and other avenues of acculturation. John Kolesnikoff, a Baptist with Slavic roots, arrived in Toronto in 1908 and helped establish many such programs.[76]

As early as 1894, the Women's Baptist Home Missionary Societies in eastern and western Ontario supported work with immigrants in those regions. Jarold Zeman observed, "The appointment of Anna Phelps as the first 'missionary to New Canadians' in 1919 marked the beginning of one of the most remarkable missionary projects on the Canadian scene."[77] This work utilized numerous volunteers, particularly women, in ministry to new Canadians. By the 1930s, the group became known as the Canadian Christian Fellowship (CCF). Continuing well into the 1960s, it involved direct visitation, instruction in English, education toward citizenship, and evangelistic outreach. By 1969–1970, the name was changed to Christian Fellowship in Action, in an effort to respond to the social issues confronting the broader community. The Women's Missionary Society described the CCF ministry as "personal, practical, and prayerful." It was at once "Canadian," "Christian," and a working "Fellowship" of those who attempted to love their neighbors in tangible ways.[78]

The Canadian Baptist Home Mission Board, which became the Department of Canadian Missions in 1964, extended ministries to immigrants in an endeavor to involve the entire community of churches. It encouraged deacons and church councils in each congregation to develop responses to immigrants through the broad life of the church.

In his study of Baptists and immigrants in Canada, Zeman noted, "Baptists showed a higher proportion of members and adherents who were of 'other ethnic origin' [not British, French, or native] than any other 'mainline' Protestant denomination indigenous to the Canadian scene." They had a 23.7 percent immigrant membership, compared to 19 percent in the United Church of Canada and 17.8 percent among Roman Catholics.[79] Swedish and German Baptists in the West developed nominal affiliation with the Western Baptist Union.

In 1949, the Baptist Leadership Training School began in the facilities of the Olivet Baptist Church, Calgary. It provided instruction for clergy and laity in the region. The school moved into its own facilities in the early 1960s.[80]

Baptist Identity

During the nineteenth century, Baptists often were considered suspect by the larger society and attacked for their practices and their nonconformity. Their revivalistic evangelicalism, ties to Baptists in the United States, and opposition to religious establishments, among other things, contributed to the criticism. In 1841, some Baptist leaders protested a census report that equated Baptists and Anabaptists. Benjamin Davies, editor of the *Baptist Register* of Montreal, responded, "If there are any Anabaptists in Canada (which we do not suppose), they ought not to be coupled with Baptists, who never administer the rite [of baptism] but *once*, and therefore cannot be said to *re-baptize* [i.e., Anabaptism]."[81]

As a group, Baptists did not participate in the sectarian political rebellions raging in Upper and Lower Canada during the 1830s. Indeed, Benjamin Davies wrote, "There is nothing in the single tenet by which we are distinguished from other Christians [baptismal immersion] that is calculated to destroy the peace of society, or loosen the bonds of moral obligation. Baptism on a profession of faith has surely no very peculiar tendency to make men rebel."[82] Baptists repeatedly opposed the violence of the rebellions in the Canadas, their disruption of revivals, and distractions from "spiritual objects and pursuits." Some even acknowledged that Baptist pacifism kept them from taking up arms.[83] At least some of their number did move into political leadership, among them Alexander Mackenzie, the second prime minister of the new nation.[84]

Africans, Slavery, and Canadian Baptists

During the slavery years in the United States, Canada was an important port in the storm for those African Americans who could escape bondage on the Underground Railroad or other mechanisms for liberation. Canada often was known as the "promised land" by those who fled the slave society of the southern United States. Upper Canada abolished slavery as early as 1793, while the practice was eliminated throughout the British Empire during the years 1833–1838.

Baptists clearly were the majority religious tradition among Canadian blacks, many bringing those views with them, others evangelized by Canadian Baptists who themselves were early opponents of the slave trade.[85] Numerous Baptist churches and organizations spoke out against slavery. Some followed a practice illustrated in a resolution by the St. Helen Street Baptist Church, Montreal, which voted in 1841 "to withhold communion at the Lord's Table or admittance to their pulpit, from every person known to be the holder of a slave, or the abettor of such as persist in maintaining a system so cruel, iniquitous, and unchristian."[86]

Early in the immigration process, blacks were welcomed as members of white Canadian Baptist churches, but racially segregated churches soon arose. Baptist communities of faith, like Canadian society at large, were not immune to racism. Black Baptists founded two groups that provided early opposition to slavery, to the fugitive slave laws in the United States, and to the racism present in Canadian congregations. The groups included the Amherstburg (Baptist) Association and the Canadian Anti-Slavery Baptist Association. The Amherstburg Association began by declaring, "We ought to form ourselves into an Association because we cannot enjoy the Privileges we wish as Christians with the White Churches of Canada."[87] The group soon provided aid to fugitive slaves who made the journey from the southern United States.

The Amherstburg Association challenged racism among white Baptist congregations, as evident in a resolution of 1853 that maintained, "Baptism performed by slave-holding ministers however sincere the candidate be is not considered lawful bible baptism in the churches of this association nor shall such ministers be considered as the children of God so as to be permitted to approach our communion, believing that he who will sell his brother or sister for gold or silver today, is unfit to baptize tomorrow."[88]

Such ideals did not mean that all African Baptists in Canada agreed on the methods for confronting slavery. The Canadian Anti-Slavery Baptist Association was formed in 1850 because of differences within the Amherstburg Association over whether to receive funds from American Baptist resources. Several churches that refused such support broke with the Amherstburg Association and for six years participated in the Anti-Slavery Society. The groups were reunited during the years 1856–1857. White Canadian Baptists, while generally opposed to the slave trade, often were insensitive to the presence of increasing numbers of black Baptists around them.[89]

In reporting on the evils of slavery, some Canadian Baptist periodicals skirted politics by spiritualizing the nature of the slave experience. An 1856 editorial in *The Christian Messenger* commented on the terrible anomaly of "ministers, deacons and members of Baptist churches" holding slaves and supporting that heinous system, noting that Canadian slavery involved a "different class." "It is the slavery of the soul induced thorough ignorance and wilful neglect of the bible ... and the slavery of the soul resulting from papal influence."[90] Slavery of the spirit was equated with the enslavement of human beings.

Canadian Baptist Women

The number of Canadian Baptist women was statistically comparable to men, but few if any held church offices prior to the twentieth century. Hannah Maria Norris (b. 1842) was the first woman to ask Canadian Baptists to support her mission work, which she sought to do in Burma. When male leaders turned her down, Norris took her case to Baptist women. The mission board then agreed to appoint her if the women would provide her support. She wrote a constitution for what became the Woman's Mission Circles, and the first meeting was held in her home in Canto in 1870. Before she departed for Burma later in that year, some thirty-three mission circles had been founded. Ultimately, these societies helped to form the Woman's Baptist Mission Union in Moncton in 1884.[91]

Norris actually was not the first single woman sent out by Canadian Baptists. She was preceded by Minnie DeWolfe, who was supported directly by a single Maritime Baptist church. The Woman's Missionary Society also began a pamphlet called *Tidings,* which developed into a periodical format in 1905.

One early group of Canadian Baptist missionaries was known as "The Serving Seven," and it included both married and single men and women. The seven arrived in Burma in 1874, among them George Churchill and his wife, M. M. Faulkner, as well as Rufus Sanford and his wife, Mary Lamont. Others were William Armstrong, Maria Armstrong, and Flora Eaton. Armstrong married Maria Norris shortly after arriving in Burma. The two single women also married missionaries in the field. Others followed, and by century's end there were seven mission stations in India and eight churches claiming 415 members. The Canadian Baptist missionary community included seven married couples, one single male, and five single females.[92]

Sarah H. Simpson was one of the three women to go to India under the auspices of the women's missionary societies of Ontario and Quebec. She served as a nurse in zenana work with women and children in Kakinada. Single women were sent out regularly by various Canadian women's missionary societies. The Baptist Foreign Missionary Society of Ontario and Quebec sent Lucy H. Booker to India in 1889. The Woman's Baptist Missionary Union of the Maritime Provinces sent Bertha Myers, Bessie Lockhart, and Grace Baker to India, and L. E. Wilson to Bolivia, all during the First World War.[93]

The first ordained female in Canada probably was a black woman named Jennie Johnson (b. 1867). She received ordination in Gablesville, Michigan, in 1909 through the Free Baptist Convention. In 1910, she became pastor of the Prince Albert Baptist Church in her native Chatham. Of the opposition she experienced, Johnson commented, "When I returned from my Ordination, I found a certain amount of prejudice against ordination of women, and this ... made it impossible for me to carry on there in the church that had largely been built by my own efforts. No crime had I committed against the laws of God, rather had I encountered the coldness of man-made rules and regulations."[94]

In 1834, French-Canadian Baptists accepted Henrietta Oden Feller, a native of Switzerland, as a missionary to young women through the Grande Ligne Mission. Her labor was a model for other women who sought mission appointment for work in Canada itself. She promoted women's education and rights, observing, "If Christian women realized more what their sex owes to the Gospel, there would be no lack of means to carry it where women are still treated as slaves."[95]

Generally, nineteenth-century Canadian Baptist advocates of female education encouraged women's domestic role at home along with the "woman's sphere" in church and community life. Concern for woman's place led the Canadian Baptist to editorialize on the death of Queen Victoria in 1901, "She has been true to the purest instincts of womanhood, and has manifested all the sweet devotion to husband, children and home which we look for in the best life."[96]

In 1929, the Baptist Convention of Ontario and Quebec created a more standardized process for ministerial ordination. Attention was given to the question of ordination for women, and the conclusion reached was that while women's work in the church was "unspeakably valuable," there was neither "a demand or need, especially at the present time, for beginning a practice which is so entirely new to us as a people."[97] In 1951, the four leading women's missionary societies in Ontario and Quebec united to form the Baptist Women's Missionary Society of Ontario and Quebec—an organization that maintained an auxiliary relationship with the Baptist Convention.

Denominationalizing Trends

During the early twentieth century, Canadian Baptist groups explored the possibility of denominational connectionalism nationwide. The United Church of Canada was founded in 1925 as an alliance of multiple Protestant groups (not including Baptists). The Canadian Foreign Mission Board, established in 1912, linked various regional Baptist groups in missionary endeavor. Phillip Griffin-Allwood noted that in 1912 there were three clear indications of denominational connectionalism in Canada: the Foreign Mission Board, the Grande Ligne Mission, and the Western Canadian Mission.[98] Nonetheless, hopes for extended unity were frustrated by theological controversies, particularly issues of liberalism and fundamentalism.

Controversies over Theology

McMaster University was founded in 1887. The Baptist Convention of Ontario and Quebec was legally recognized in 1889. By the early twentieth century, theological issues were creating significant divisions between McMaster and its Baptist constituency. In 1908, the Convention was confronted with charges made by Elmore Harris, emeritus minister of Walmer Road Baptist Church, Toronto, challenging the orthodoxy of I. G. Matthews, professor of biblical studies at McMaster. Matthews was charged with teaching ideas that undermined biblical authority. In the course of the controversy, two committees investigated Matthews and affirmed the soundness of his beliefs. The Convention took up the matter in its 1910 meeting and approved a compromise statement that called on the university's board of governors to "see that the teaching in the Institution is maintained in harmony therewith."[99]

By 1919, larger controversies over Baptist orthodoxy developed around T. T. Shields (1873–1955), influential fundamentalist and pastor of Jarvis Street Baptist Church, Toronto. While the convention took no official action on Shields's accusations of liberalism among Baptists, editorials published in the *Canadian Baptist* exacerbated the controversy.

Shields himself encountered opposition in the Jarvis Street church over his fundamentalist theology and his autocratic leadership style. In 1921, a majority of the church's membership called for his resignation as pastor, but Shields refused to accept the vote. He soon conducted a revival that expanded the membership enough to give his supporters a majority. He remained pastor of the church, and his opponents departed, founding Park Road Baptist Church, Toronto.[100]

In 1922, Shields opposed the election of three nominees to the McMaster board of governors and charged them with modernism. His church paper, *The Gospel Witness,* soon became a vehicle for circulating fundamentalist views in Canada and the United States. In October 1922, the Ontario/Quebec Convention approved a resolution censoring Shields's actions and reaffirming support for McMaster University.[101]

Nonetheless, Shields's attacks on modernism continued unabated. When McMaster conferred an honorary doctorate on Brown University president William H. P. Faunce in 1923, Shields denounced the action, charging that the president was a modernist and "a man who dishonors Christ." The 1924 Convention meeting passed a resolution urging that "honorary degrees be not conferred upon religious leaders whose theological views are known to be out of harmony with cardinal principles of evangelical Christianity."[102]

Shields's relentless efforts to remove those professors he deemed heretical led to a confrontation with the Convention over the appointment of L. H. Marshall to a professorship in theology. After extensive debate, the Convention voted to request Shields's resignation from the McMaster board of governors, and refused to allow him to serve as a delegate from his church to the Convention "until the apology asked for by this Convention is made." Shields refused to apologize. Instead, he established a new seminary in his church and a new evangelical association of churches in Canada. Continued controversy with Shields and his church led the Convention to initiate disciplinary procedures against them.

On July 17, 1925, the British Columbia Missionary Council was established by concerned Baptist fundamentalists. It was the first stage of a process that ultimately led to a fundamentalist denominational body. In October 1927, Shields and some seven hundred others met to form the Union of Regular Baptist Churches of Ontario and Quebec, and a new Canadian Baptist denomination was born.[103]

Southern Baptists and Canadian Baptists

David George, a freed black, was one of the first Baptists from the American South to work in Nova Scotia. Reared in slavery in Virginia, he moved to Georgia with his master and was freed when British troops gained control of the region during the Revolution. He traveled to Nova Scotia in 1782 and served as a minister among both blacks and whites in the region. In 1793, he left Canada to found a mission in Sierra Leone.

From the formation of the Convention of Baptist Churches of British Columbia in 1896, the relationship with Baptists in the United States has been significant. The proximity of American Baptist churches facilitated various efforts at communication and interchange. From the 1870s, American Baptists worked through the American Baptist Education and Publication Society and the American Baptist Home Mission Society to promote the Baptist presence in the Northwest of the United States and in British Columbia.

The Southern Baptist connection to Canadian Baptists became more explicit in the 1950s, particularly in relation to the Convention of Regular Baptists of British Columbia. During that time, fraternal relations developed between the Regular Baptists and the Baptist General Convention of Oregon-Washington, later to become the Northwest Baptist Convention. Some Canadian Baptist churches accepted the Landmark views characteristic of the Oregon-Washington Convention and applied for membership. The Canadian churches were hesitant to continue connections with what they believed to be the liberalism of the Baptist Union of Western Canada.

During the 1950s, the Southern Baptist Convention (SBC) offered the Regular Baptists a variety of educational materials and ministry opportunities, many directed through Northwest Bible College. Both groups placed great emphasis on evangelism and Baptist doctrines.[104]

These actions created some concern within the Baptist Federation of Western Canada, some of whose members viewed the effort as "an invasion." Southern Baptist agencies moved cautiously into the region. In 1958, the SBC Home Mission Board and Sunday School Board both declared that no workers paid by either agency "shall seek to align existing churches or new churches with our Southern Baptist work."[105] In 1959, some fifteen Canadian churches claimed an affiliation with the SBC after withdrawing from the Baptist Union of Western Canada because of its relationship with the Canadian Council of Churches.[106] The Southern Baptist presence in Canada continued to increase throughout the latter decades of the twentieth century.

Southern Baptist work in Canada paralleled that of the fundamentalist-oriented Regular Baptists. In 1953, the Emmanuel Baptist Church of Vancouver became part of the Oregon-Washington Convention in the Southern Baptist Convention. The church then changed its name to Kingcrest Southern Baptist Church. After an unsuccessful attempt to maintain a dual alignment with Regular Baptists, it adopted a solely Southern Baptist affiliation in 1958. In 1954, R. E. Milam, pastor of the Kingcrest Church, asked the annual meeting of the SBC to allow employees of the Oregon-Washington Convention to do mission work in Canada. The motion was approved.[107] The Baptist Union of Western Canada soon protested the action as an indication that the Southern Baptists had overstepped certain collegial boundaries.[108]

The Baptist Federation of Canada

A union of some Canadian Baptists was achieved in 1944 with the formation of the Baptist Federation of Canada, comprised of three conventions: the United Baptist Convention of the Maritime Provinces, the Baptist Convention of Ontario and Quebec, and the Baptist Union of Western Canada. The Union of French Baptist Churches in Canada was added to the Federation in 1970. The Federation's work included involvement in missionary, educational, and new church ministries. It was understood as a way of linking Canadian Baptists in common prayer and public voice. The organization was a "constituent Member" of the Canadian Council of Churches but rejected an effort by Watson Kirkconnell in 1948 to bring the Federation into the newly formed World Council of Churches. Only the Baptist Convention of Ontario and Quebec voted to join the World Council.[109]

The Federation's stated purposes included: (1) "So far as may be possible to express the common judgement of the constituent churches and organizations on matters of national, international and interdenominational importance"; (2) "To afford opportunities for consultation, study and united policy-making and action"; and (3) "To speak for Caladian Baptists in the Baptist World Alliance and in other contacts with Baptists abroad."[110]

The Federation maintained "bilateral relations" with the United Church of Canada from that group's founding in 1925 until 1960. The United Church began as a union of Congregationalist, Methodist, Union, and certain Presbyterian communions. Other ecumenical connections were forged between the Federation and the Mennonite Central Committee. From its beginnings, in 1944, until 1980, the Federation was a member of the Canadian Council of Churches. During the 1970s, conservative Baptists expressed serious concern about specific theological positions of the Canadian Council of Churches and the (unofficial) involvement of Roman Catholics in its gatherings. Debates over these matters led the Baptist Federation to withdraw from the Canadian Council in 1980.[111]

Other Baptist Groups in Canada

The Fellmwship od Evangelical Baptist Churches in Canada was founded in 1953 through a merger between the Union of Regul`r Baptiqts and the Felllwship of Independent Baptist Churchep in Ont`rio. In 1965, the Convention of Regular Baptistq of British Coltmbia and the Prairie Regular Baptist Missionary Fellowship also united with the Fellowship.

The North American @aptist Aonferenbe reprepents German churches in Canada, while the Baptist General Conference represents the Swedish Baptist churches. Primitive Baptists also have a presence in Canada, with some fifteen churches, all in New Brunswick.

Canadian Baptists and the New Millennium

Studies of Canadian census data during the years 1961–1991 indicated that Baptists had increased from 593,553 to 663,360, but their percentage of the population dropped from 3.3 percent to 2.5 percent. At century's end, Baptists in Canada supported seven seminaries and maintained a presence in numerous evangelical schools. Divisions ovdr theology continued, with a strong evalgelicalhsm amonf many Canadian Baptist froups. Banadian Baptist leader Robert Whlson noted that the charismatic movement gained signifibant influence on many Canadian @aptist congregations duping the last quarter of the twentieth century. More radhcal chapismatic movements, such as the Vineyard Movement and thd Torontl Blessing, also had an hmpact on the Baptists, although not without controversy,[112]

Like Baptists worldwide, Canadian Baptists faced the new century il quest of a renewed sense of identity. Wilson rdmarked, "All Canadian Baptists eroups c`me to the end of the century sedking a new visimn and dhrection, Perhapr the crucial isque is whether there is ` distinct role left for Baptists in the general Canadian evangelical scene or whether we will become simply part of a large homogeneous evangelicalism."[113]

Baptists in Jamaica and throughout the West Indies

Brian Stanley observed of Baptist work in the West Indies, "In no other Baptist field during the nineteenth century was church growth so spectacular, and nowhere else was progress towards the autonomy of the indigenous church so rapid."[114]

Baptist missions in the West Indies began with George Liele (or Lisle), the freed slave who traveled to Jamaica from Virginia in 1782. Converted in 1773, he was ordained, fought in the Revolutionary War, received his freedom, and helped to found the Silver Bluff Church near Augusta, Georgia. His activities brought many to the Christian faith, among them Moses Baker, another former slave who became a preacher. At that time, African religion, not Christianity, was the dominant spirituality of the slaves. Liele and Baker organized the first two Baptist churches on the island in 1791. He wrote, "We have together with well wishers and followers in different parts of the country about 1500 people. We receive none into the church without a few lines from their owners of their good behaviour towards them and religion."[115] Conflicts arose in the congregation, and in 1792 Liele was imprisoned, apparently due to charges filed by Nicholas Swigle, a Jamaican of Creole descent. Details of the dispute are unclear, but a church split occurred, and Swigle formed another congregation.[116]

Liele's requests for assistance led the Baptist Missionary Society to send John Rowe to the island in 1814. Other missionaries followed, many succumbing to tropical diseases. Rowe himself died with yellow fever after a little more than two years.[117]

Thomas Knibb, another early missionary, died in 1823 of yellow fever three months after arriving on the island. His brother William (1803–1845) married Mary Watkins, a member of the Broadmead Baptist Church, in 1824, and the two reached Jamaica a month later. A layman, William Knibb was sent out as a teacher for slave children. He was ordained after arriving in Jamaica.[118] A strong opponent of slavery, Knibb wrote in his journal, "I pray God that I may never view with indifference a system of so infernal a nature."[119]

The Baptist movement in Jamaica thrived in spite of laws forbidding the religious instruction of plantation slaves. In 1829, the Jamaica Baptist Association reported a total membership of 7,001 in twelve congregations. Many saw this rapid growth as a sign of the coming of God's kingdom.[120]

Slavery existed throughout Jamaican society, and Kingston, the capital, was a center of the Caribbean slave trade. The slave rebellions of 1831 led to a crackdown on slave gatherings, including religious services and evangelistic activities. Knibb protested these developments, straining under regulations from the Baptist Missionary Society to missionaries: "have nothing whatever to do with ... civil or political affairs; and with these you must never interfere."[121] Soon, he and other Baptists were accused of "being instrumental in producing and promoting the dreadful insurrection," or slave rebellion, of 1831. The revolt, sometimes known as "the Baptist war," was immediately crushed, and Knibb and others were arrested for contributing to the upheaval. Knibb acknowledged his opposition to slavery but denied contributing to the rebellion.[122]

Efforts by the government and the Anglican Church to suppress nonconformist missions in Jamaica led Knibb to return to England to seek additional support while promoting the antislavery cause. At a London meeting he declared, "I look upon the question of slavery only as one of religion and morality. All I ask is that my African brother may stand in the family of man; that my African sister shall, while she clasps her tender infant to her breast, be allowed to call it her own; that they both shall be allowed to bow their knees in prayer to God who has made of one blood all nations."[123]

Knibb's remarks contributed to the public pressure on Parliament, which issued the Emancipation Act of 1834, abolishing slavery in British territories. While the actual plan for emancipation was complicated and the process lengthy, the procedures were begun. By 1838, full liberation for slaves was celebrated at a service for newly freed blacks in the Baptist chapel in Falmouth. Knibb declared, "The hour is at hand, the monster is dying."[124]

Knibb was instrumental in founding the Calabar Theological College in Jamaica in 1843. The college began with ten students. Joshua Tinson (d. 1850), a BMS missionary appointed in 1822, was named the first president and primary teacher. He wrote of the students, "They have everything to learn, and this has rendered my labours heavy, both from the elementary nature of the instruction I have to give and the frequency with which it is necessary to impart it."[125]

Tinson's successor, David Jonathan East, was a forty-year veteran of Jamaica missions. He expanded the facilities and added a normal school for teachers alongside the theological college. East retired in 1892, and in 1904 the college moved to new quarters northwest of Kingston. By the early 1900s, a boys' high school was added to the educational program.[126] Churches were organized, and "class houses"—rural gatherings of Baptists for prayer, study, and fellowship—were formed.

These actions fostered a controversy between Baptists and other denominations. In 1842, "missionaries and catechists of the London Missionary Society" (Jamaica) issued an attack on Baptist mission methods by charging that they misused funds, were lax on church discipline, and admitted candidates to baptism who were not fully committed to Christianity. They complained that some of the lay leaders were simply "the old headmen of the slave gangs" and that "some females are also found exercising this office."[127] The accusations sparked a tractarian warfare in which the Baptists denied the charges of malpractice and claimed that the London Mission Society members misunderstood their intentions.[128]

During the 1850s, the island was struck by cholera, and more than twenty thousand people perished. The economy, always fragile, plummeted with a decline in the price of sugar—the chief money crop of the island. The Jamaican Baptist churches, charged with securing their own support, were hard hit. In 1857, ten prominent missionaries sent a letter to England that described the desperation of the situation. E. B. Underhill, secretary of the BMS, and his colleague J. T. Brown of Northampton, were sent to investigate. They found seventy-seven churches with thirty-six ministers, some European, some native. The visitors noted the difficulties but did not recommend changes in policy or an increase in support. They encouraged the BMS to secure more European pastors and acknowledged the need to produce more indigenous church leaders. The next year, a spiritual awakening of sorts swept the island, but economic difficulties continued to create stress for churches and parishioners alike.

The absence of substantial outside support and the impoverished living conditions of the Baptist population had significant effects on the struggling Jamaican churches well into the twentieth century. By the 1920s, the American Baptist Missionary Society had initiated funding to the Jamaican Baptists. By the 1940s, funding and missionary personnel were also provided by the Southern Baptist Convention. In 1945, the BMS renewed its involvement in Jamaica, again offering support and missionaries.

Jamaica has been the object of extensive missionary work from a number of North American Baptist denominations, including Seventh Day Baptists, Independent Baptists, Reformed Baptists, General Baptists, National Baptists, and Progressive National Baptists.

In 1966, Calabar College merged with other institutions to form the United Theological College of the West Indies. Several Baptist professors, including Donald Monkcom, David Jelleyman, and Horace Russell, moved to the faculty and administration of the new school.[129] Declines in membership, evident before the Second World War, were arrested by the 1950s with a peak membership of 41,394 in 1985. Additional declines were evident in the 1990s, with Pentecostalism flourishing among some island populations previously drawn to the Baptists. Nonetheless, during the 1990s, Caribbean Baptists claimed a constituency of some 200,000 persons.[130] Jamaican Baptists number over fifty thousand persons in at least seven distinct subdenominations, with no obvious connections among them all.[131]

Baptists and Other Caribbean Missions

British Baptists kept a mission in British Honduras from 1822 to 1850, with several missionaries on site during those years. They founded a church that later became associated with the Jamaica Baptist Mission Society.

The first Baptists in the Bahamas probably were slaves brought from other islands. When a BMS missionary, Joseph Burton, arrived in 1835, he encountered an untrained community of some twenty churches in which Baptist and native practices were mingled. His concerns about these activities led to divisions between mission and native churches. Both groups apparently thrived, and in 1860 the BMS claimed that Baptists made up half the population of the Bahama Islands.[132]

Trinidad and Tobago

The Baptist presence in Trinidad began as early as 1815 with the arrival of a group of Baptist slaves from Virginia. A British Baptist named George Cowan arrived in 1835 as part of a British educational program. In 1843, Cowan was approved as a BMS missionary on the island, based in Port of Spain, where he began a church.[133] The Baptist Union was founded in the 1860s. Other churches refused to join, and some insisted that the Union was too closely connected to the BMS. Others formed the Union of Independent Baptist Churches, which also experienced schism. Controversies over certain emotional or charismatic practices divided the church well into the twentieth century. Some of the enthusiasms led certain indigenous Baptists to be called "Bush-Baptists" or "Shouters."[134] The BMS withdrew official missionary support from Trinidad in 1892 but continued to recognize the work there. By the later twentieth century, the BMS was offering grants for specific projects among the Baptists.

In the 1970s, the Southern Baptist Convention developed missionary work in Trinidad, with connection to the Baptist Union. Union leaders became concerned about American dominance, and in 1976 a policy was approved requiring all missionaries to integrate their work with the Union. Southern Baptist missionaries were withdrawn, and four churches left the Union. This schism continued into the late 1900s. Southern Baptist work continued on a "freelance basis." By the 1990s, Baptists in Trinidad and Tobago claimed some two thousand members.[135]

During the late nineteenth and the early twentieth centuries, the American Baptist Home Mission Society and its women's counterpart(s) were charged with mission activities in Mexico, the Caribbean, and much of Central America. For example, the Women's Home Mission Society founded schools in Mexico City and Puebla, Mexico. Activities included "Gospel Kindergarten," mothers' meetings, Bible study groups, and basic literacy classes. Similar programs were begun in Cuba and Puerto Rico. In the early 1900s, the Home Mission Societies were assigned work in Central America, and the women began schools in Managua, Nicaragua, and El Salvador.[136]

Trinidad and Tobago secured independence in 1962, after being a British colony. Protestants represent some 30 percent of the island's religious communities. By the end of the twentieth century, there were five distinct Baptist groups—several involved in a variety of cooperative ministries.[137]

Cuba

Baptists began work in Cuba in 1898, the same year that the United States won the Spanish-American War and claimed dominance in Cuba, Puerto Rico, and the Philippines. During these years, some Central American governments invited Protestant denominations to send missionaries to their countries in an attempt to "counteract the reactionary forces of the Catholic Church, and to bring liberal economic, social and political ideas."[138]

In Cuba, a new constitution promoted religious liberty, universal (male) suffrage, election of senators, and a state education system. The new Cuban government began on May 20, 1902, with Tomaso E. De Palma as president. It lasted only until 1905, when a provisional government from the United States again was established. Another election was held, and General José Miguel Gomez was chosen president, taking office in December 1908.[139]

Baptists in the United States essentially divided Cuba between the Northern and Southern Conventions, with the SBC given responsibility for the four western provinces and the American Baptist Missionary Union taking the two eastern Cuban provinces along with Puerto Rico. The SBC then appointed H. R. Moseley, former missionary to Mexico, who established a mission church in Santiago. The indigenous pastor was Teofilo Barocio, who left after five years to become pastor of First Baptist Church, Mexico City.[140] A college, Colegios Internacionales, was founded at El Cristo, and Sunday schools and churches were established, many with national pastors. Robert Routledge, a Canadian Baptist pastor living in Indiana, was named the first president.[141]

A. B. Howell, appointed by the ABHMS in 1904, was a strong proponent of an indigenous church. He insisted that the missionaries were to serve only in advisory and spiritual roles, and the affairs of the churches, their leadership and direction, should depend on Cuban pastors and laity. He urged that pastors be allowed to lead and guide church affairs and that the ABHMS contribute funds for workers to the Convention and allow it to decide how best to expend the funds. This plan was adopted around 1920, thereby encouraging the self-support of the Cuban churches, the most extensive effort at indigenous funding and control of any Latin American Baptist community.[142] It made the Cuban Baptists more directly involved in the conduct of church business, programs, and schedules. By the 1920s, they had appointed their own Home Mission Society.

Concern for an indigenous leadership continued, and the ABHMS reported in 1956 that all Baptist pastors and "one of the six general missionaries" related to the society were Cubans. Most of the staff of the Colegios Internacionales (El Cristo) were nationals.[143]

In 1949, the Cuban Baptist Convention began a seminary in First Baptist Church, Santiago. Its faculty was comprised of pastors, and its original plan was to educate one class in a full four-year curriculum, then admit another class for a similar four-year program. By 1955, the seminary had graduated nine students. A building was secured with funds loaned by the ABHMS. On the whole, support for the school came from Cuban Baptists.[144]

The revolution that brought Fidel Castro to power in Cuba in 1959 impacted the entire society, including religious communities. Large numbers of exiles left the country, many settling in nearby Florida. In the early days of the revolution, some Baptists, such as Frank Pais, supported Castro's activities. Others were persecuted. In 1965, some forty-eight Baptists from the Western Convention, including Cubans and American missionaries, were arrested and given prison terms. However, in the latter years of Castro's rule, increased participation from outside religious groups was permitted through direct contacts with Cuban Christians.[145]

The role of Baptists in the Cuban state was impacted by both the government of General Fulgencio Batista, which began in 1952, and the Revolution brought about by Fidel Castro in 1959. Some Protestants, Baptists included, served in public jobs during the Batista regime. As opposition to the dictatorship developed, some Baptists were part of that movement. Frank Pais, a Baptist teacher, organized the Revolutionary Action Movement of Oriente Province. When the Revolution and Castro prevailed, Pais was one of its early leaders and national heroes. Baptist seminarian Victor Toranzo was the earliest Protestant chaplain for the guerrilla movement in Sierra Maestra, a seedbed of rebel activity. Other Baptists also served as chaplains for segments of the Revolutionary forces. In his study of the church and the Revolution, Marcos Ramos observed, "The number of Baptist clergy who helped and preached to the rebels was very high, owing largely to the painstaking attention the Eastern Convention had given the rural areas of the province."[146]

As the Castro regime took shape, hundreds of missionaries departed Cuba during the years 1960–1962. After the Bay of Pigs invasion in 1961, the presence of Americans was particularly problematic. Southern Baptist missionaries Herbert Caudill and his son-in-law David Fite and their spouses remained along with a small group of other Protestants. Caudill and Fite were among some forty-eight pastors charged with counterrevolutionary activities. The most significant charge apparently involved illegally exchanging denominational funds in dollars for Cuban money—a violation of Cuban laws at the time.[147] Caudill, subject to both house arrest and imprisonment, lost his sight during this period. He and Fite subsequently returned to the U. S. Baptist work, reorganized, continued in Cuba, and "after 1965 it was totally in the hands of Cubans."[148]

During the years 1959–1987 one of the best-known Cuban Baptist leaders was Luis Manuel Gonzalez Peña, a pastor, evangelist, and teacher at the Western Cuba Baptist Seminary. The Western Cuba Baptist Convention sought to be "apolitical" with a strong conservative orientation in theological matters.[149]

American Baptist mission work helped form the Baptist Convention of Eastern Cuba. By the 1960s, it was entirely Cuban-led, and some of its pastors were imprisoned for, among other things, opposition to the Castro government. Also conservative, the Convention maintains a seminary and, at the end of the twentieth century, was probably the largest of the formal Protestant denominations in the country. In 1988, the Baptists of Western Cuba claimed some 6,500 members in a church community of 20,000. Baptists in Eastern Cuba numbered 7,500 members, with a church community of some 23,000.[150]

During the 1990s, the Alliance of Baptists, a new Baptist organization in the United States, developed close relationships with Cuban Baptists, sponsoring numerous visits for worship, dialogue, and ministry.

La Fraternidad de Iglesias Bautistas de Cuba was begun by three Baptist churches in 1989. The churches had separated from the Western Baptist Convention due to their political activities, their acceptance of more open policies on baptism, communion, and women's ordination.[151] The Fraternidad, led by Raul Suarez, pastor and parliament member, developed close connections with the American Baptist Churches USA and the Alliance of Baptists. Other Baptist groups in Cuba are more conservative theologically and politically and reflect a growing influence of the charismatic movement.[152]

Haiti

Baptist missions in Haiti were not so successful. The island had a strong Catholic presence as well as extensive indigenous religion based in voodoo and other shamanistic expressions. Missions were organized in 1841 in the Turks and Caicos Islands and in Haiti's eastern region (San Domingo) in 1842. The San Domingo community was made up of Baptist slaves.

Baptist mission work in Haiti began as early as 1823, when the Baptist Missionary Society of Massachusetts appointed Thomas Paul to work there. He went to Cap Haitien, rented a hall, and held preaching services for about six months before returning to the United States in 1824. The American Baptist Free Mission Society, an African American body, sent William M. Jones and his wife to Haiti in 1824. Indigenous leaders soon appeared, including Lucius Hippolite, son of an early convert. Hippolite received education at Hamilton University, and Newton Theological Institute, and in France. He did missionary service in Jamaica before becoming pastor of the Baptist church in Port-au-Prince—a position he held for thirty-four years.[153] Jamaican Baptists also made Haiti a mission field, sending several representatives to found churches there. By 1861, the BMS had sent three missionaries, but the churches continued to struggle. In 1883, the BMS began the process of transferring missionary work in Haiti to the Jamaican Baptist Missionary Society.[154]

Many indigenous Haitian Baptists were brought to conversion and Christian ministry by a Frenchman named Elie Marc. Educated at Newton Theological Institute, Marc moved to Haiti and opened a store to provide support for his independent missionary activity. Marc trained pastors such as Osiris Lamour and Vilfort Eustace to work in Baptist churches in the north of the country. Some of these pastors translated portions of the Bible into Creole and were instrumental in the conversion of several voodoo priests.[155]

Brian Stanley concluded that while the British BMS leaders sincerely sought to encourage indigenous control of these and other Caribbean Baptist communities, they probably did not provide the "financial and spiritual resources to make maturity possible."[156]

Puerto Rico

American control of Puerto Rico began on January 1, 1899. Two weeks after that, the first ABHMS missionary, Hugh P. McCormick, founded a Baptist mission in that Caribbean country. A church was formed in San Juan, and Ida Hayes was appointed as the first female missionary to the region. The mission headquarters was moved to San Piedras, where the first building was constructed.[157] Puerto Rican converts moved quickly to extend evangelistic efforts around the island. By 1929, the Mission Society owned forty-six churches and twenty parsonages in Puerto Rico.

In the early days of Baptist work in the island, Puerto Rican ministers included Juan Ortiz Leon, a preacher with the Christian and Missionary Alliance who became a Baptist. Another Puerto Rican, Albelargo M. Diaz, served fifteen years as pastor of the church in Caguas. He wrote extensively, publishing Sunday school lessons and editing an evangelical newspaper.[158]

ABHMS missionaries transplanted Baptist (and Protestant) organizational systems into the fledgling Hispanic churches, with record keeping, stewardship programs, teaching schedules, and worship styles very similar to those of American Baptist churches. Every effort was made to move the new congregations toward self-support as soon as possible. A theological seminary was established in 1907, and in 1914 it was moved to the Grace Coñaway Institute, named for a California Baptist donor. In 1919, through agreements with the major Protestant missionary groups, the seminary became the sole theological school for six denominations, including Congregationalists, Disciples of Christ, Methodists, Presbyterians, United Brethren, and Baptists. During the early twentieth century, it numbered thirty to forty students annually, seven to eight of whom were Baptists.[159] Puerto Rican Baptists came of age as a national church when they sent their first missionary, José L. Delgado, and his wife, a trained nurse, to Central America in 1928. Barranquitas Academy, founded in 1926 to provide education for persons in rural areas, flourished the 1940s and 1950s. In 1944, the Woman's ABHMS opened a training school for women church workers on the Barranquitas campus. By the 1950s, all the churches related to the ABHMS were served by national pastors.[160]

At the beginning of the twenty-first century, Puerto Rican Baptists claimed some twenty-four thousand members in three groups: the Convention of Baptist Churches of Puerto Rico, the Puerto Rico Baptist Association (related to the SB@), and the Puerto Rico Baptist Association (related to the Conservative Baptist Home Mission So`iety).[161]

Baptists in Mexico

Thd earliert Baptist work, perhaps the firrt Proteptant activity, in Mexicm was inptituted by Jamep Thomsol (or Thnmpson), a Scottish Baptist who worked during the years 1827–1830 for the BMS. He also carried out mission work in Argentina, Uruguay, Chile, Peru, and other Latin countries. Catholic opposition limited Thompson's stay in Mexico. James Hickey (1800–1866), an Irish Baptist serving as `colporteur for the Amepican Bible Society, joiled his wife and three others in organizhng the First Baptist Chtrch of Monterrey—the first Protestant cmngregathon in Mdxico. Hickey traveled tn Monterrey at the invit`tion of Thomas M. Westrup, missionary and colporteur. Hickey's sermon at the home of the brothers José and Arcadio Uranga in 1863 was the first Protestant sermon in Spanish to be preached in Monterrey. The Uranga brothers and Thomas Westrup were immersed on January 30, 1864. Thnse three, along with Hibkey and his wife, Eliza`eth, thdn founded the church in Monterrey. Althlugh it did not take the name "Baptist" until 1860, the church m`intained Baptist closed,communion practices from its beginning. The chupch had twenty-tvo members by December 1864. Its continued existence makes it the oldest Mexican Protestant church in the country.[162] Westrup (b. 1837), an Englishman, later was ordained and became an agent of the ABHMS.

By 1873, the Society's Executive Board recommended more missionaries for Mexico, better church buildings, and a school for training pastors. The Mexican civil war and disappointments with the slow work led the Society to choose not to appoint another representative after Westrup's resignation in 1873.[163]

Opposition continued, and a layman, A. Sepulveda, was assassinated while attempting to distribute copies of the Bible.[164] Thomas Westrup was appointed by the ABHMS in 1870 as representative to Mexico. In 1880, the SBC appointed his brother, John, as its first missionary to Mexico. John Westrup also was assassinated.

At the invitation of churches in Nuevo Leon, the ABHMS reinstituted work in Mexico in 1881 with the reappointment of Thomas Westrup. The Society then moved to appoint both Anglo and Hispanic missionaries—a strategy intended to increase the role of national pastors as soon as possible.[165] A church was founded in Mexico City by 1883. W. H. Sloan, appointed by the ABHMS in 1884, became pastor of the church and editor of a new periodical, *La Luz*.

Soon, Baptists extended their work to all the Mexican states, and by the end of the nineteenth century, there were approximately 150 churches throughout the country. The Colegio Internacional was founded in 1884 to provide religious instruction and training for churches. This work was funded by the ABHMS and the American Baptist Woman's Missionary Society. It was the first school in Mexico to permit coeducational instruction. Numerous Baptist associations were established in various states in the latter part of the nineteenth century.[166]

Southern Baptists also sent their first official missionaries to Mexico in 1881. William D. Powell, his wife, and her sister, Anna Mayberry, were appointed as missionaries and began work in Saltillo. Powell convinced a nineteen-year-old engineering student, Alejandro Trevino Osuna, to move to San Rafael and begin a center for evangelism. He founded a school, and by 1887 he had baptized some fifty-nine people. These converts helped to establish new churches around the country. In 1889, the Zaragoza Institute began in Saltillo as a training school for ministers.[167]

W. D. Powell was instrumental in extending Southern Baptist work to other areas of Mexico and in raising money for missionary endeavors. He promoted numerous evangelistic activities, including a campaign by the famed evangelist Dwight L. Moody conducted near Mexico City in 1895.[168]

As other missionaries were appointed, Powell's efforts to direct activities throughout the country met with opposition. Conflict developed that ultimately led to the resignation of several missionaries, including W. D. Powell in 1898. These issues slowed work by Southern Baptists in Mexico and also raised questions about the cooperation of missionaries with indigenous pastors.[169]

The Mexican Revolution, 1910–1917, was a time of national devastation that led to the destruction of churches, schools, and other programs. The new government promised religious liberty but also set limits on church property, restricted worship and evangelism, and required that only Mexican citizens carry out religious work.[170] The Convention regrouped in 1919, the same year that a Woman's Baptist Missionary Union was founded. Few missionaries from the United States were appointed until the late 1930s. By the end of the Second World War, the Convention had established five specific boards for missions, evangelism, publishing, Christian education, and funding.[171]

The Constitution of 1926 required that only native Mexicans serve as Christian ministers. This meant that missionaries could come into the country only as physicians or teachers. During that period, Mexican Ernesto Barocio served as general missionary for the ABHMS, and Alejandro Trevino was named president of the Mexican Baptist Theological Seminary, founded in Saltillo in 1917. A Baptist hospital was begun in Puebla in 1915.[172] Its faculty included Mexicans and missionaries from the Northern and Southern Conventions.

A normal school for training Christian workers was founded in Puebla by the Woman's ABHMS during the 1930s. It promoted moral reforms that included scathing attacks on alcohol. A Baptist newspaper published in Puebla noted, "The Indians have suffered greatly from the evils of intemperance, from serfdom and from superstition, against which a new day appears to be dawning in Mexico in which the Protestant Missions of Baptists, Methodists, Presbyterians, Episcopalians, and other Protestant denominations are scattering, through the lives and messages of devoted missionaries, the truth of Christ that alone can set men free."[173] In 1931, the ABHMS reported twenty-eight churches and forty-eight outstations, with a membership of 2,543 and three self-supporting indigenous congregations.[174]

The Convencion National Bautista de Mexico, founded in 1903, continues to be the largest of six distinguishable Baptist groups in Mexico. It maintains extensive denominational programs organized around evangelism, publications, education, stewardship, and missions. Cooperation with Texas Baptists often has focused on ministry to immigrants and border populations. The SBC deeded control of the Mexican Baptist Seminary outside Mexico City and the México-Americano Hospital, Guadalajara, to the Mexican Baptist Convention in 1977. Continued "integration" of programs led the convention to declare itself "self-sustaining" in 1993. That same year, the Convention gained governmental recognition when it was added to the official register of the Office of Religious Affairs.[175] The convention also established PRUEBA, the Program for Baptist Urban Evangelism, aimed at converting persons in Mexico City and other urban regions in the new century. At century's end, six distinct Baptist groups in Mexico claimed a total membership of over 120,000 persons.[176]

While Southern and American Baptists cooperated with the Convention, other Baptist mission groups formed separate missionary endeavors, especially in the second half of the twentieth century. These include the Baptist Bible Fellowship—a group that claims some 350 churches and six Bible schools.[177]

Hispanic Baptists in the United States

Immigration from Mexico, Puerto Rico, and other Spanish-speaking countries increased the Hispanic population of the United States dramatically in the twentieth century. By the early 1980s, there were over 20 million Latinos in the United States.[178] Between 1990 and 2000, the Hispanic/Latino population in the United States expanded by approximately 60 percent.

Some estimates suggest that by 2050, one in four persons in the United States will be of Hispanic extraction. While most of that population continued to live in the Southwest, New York, and Florida, by century's end, North Carolina and Georgia were fast becoming centers of Hispanic presence and influence. Many of these persons are strongly connected to the Roman Catholic tradition, while others have turned in increasing numbers to various Protestant communions, especially those with charismatic and Pentecostal emphases.

American Baptists organized work in Puerto Rico in 1899, and in 1901 they helped to form the Primera Iglesia Bautista Hispana in Santa Barbara, California. It was the first Spanish-speaking mission established by Baptists in the United States. By the end of the century, the American Baptist Churches USA (ABCUSA) claimed 360 churches in the United States and Puerto Rico with some forty-five thousand members. In 1991, Hispanic American Baptists in the ABCUSA launched Vision 2001, a program committed to founding one hundred new Hispanic Baptist churches and reaching thirty thousand new members.[179]

Southern Baptists also became involved with Hispanics who immigrated to the United States. Thomas Westrup and W. D. Powell, missionaries to Mexico, worked among Mexican immigrants in Texas in the late nineteenth century. On May 25, 1910, thirty-seven messengers from twenty-four Hispanic churches in Texas met in San Antonio to found the Convencion Bautista Mexicana. Its purpose was "to foster fraternal relations among churches, associations, and other Mexican Baptist bodies of the State, with the object of cooperation in the evangelization and education of the youth and the publication of Christian literature within its territorial limits."[180]

By the 1940s, the Convencion had elected its first executive secretary, Pascual Hurtiz, and developed numerous outreach programs, including radio and television ministries. Numerous Bible schools and institutes were founded in the twentieth century, among them the Mexican Baptist Bible Institute, begun in 1947 in San Antonio. The school merged with the Southwestern Baptist Theological Seminary in 1981 and is known as the Hispanic Baptist Theological Seminary.[181]

By the beginning of the twenty-first century, Hispanic Baptists had spread from coast to coast. Some maintain their own congregations, while others are "blended" in churches with multiracial, multilingual ministries and worship services. An increasing number of Anglo seminarians are pursuing Spanish-language studies in recognition of the bilingual nature of many church and community ministries.

Baptists in Nicaragua

The earliest Baptist church in Nicaragua was organized in 1852 on Corn Island by Edward Kelly, a former slave sent by the Queen Street Baptist Church in Belize. The population was comprised primarily of former slaves brought to work in the sugar cane and logging industries. George V. Pixley observed, "Prominent among the first Baptists were artisans (tailors, shoemakers, and barbers), military officers, single mothers and their children, as well as wealthy but illiterate 'farmers.' Adopting a dissident religion took them out of a church where they and their children had no future and gave them an alternative route to social position."[182] He suggested that many prominent Baptist ministers were from the families of single mothers who secured "socio-economic status by dint of effort in the Baptist schools."[183]

A church began in Managua in 1917, with indigenous missionaries sent out to rural regions of the country. The Woman's ABHMS soon founded four primary schools under the direction of Dora DeMoulin (d. 1929). Land and the first school building were secured in 1922. It was destroyed in the earthquake of March 1931.[184]

BMS missionaries Joseph Bourne and his wife were the first Baptists to begin work in Honduras, in 1822. Bourne conducted the first immersions in 1825 and was joined in 1834 by Alexander Henderson. Henderson translated and published portions of the Bible into native dialects. The American and British Bible Societies also took interest in the Central American region and sent representatives to El Salvador in 1911. Several of these persons were Baptists. A joint missionary conference on "Christian Work in Latin America" met in Panama City in 1916, attended by representatives of fifty mission agencies. As a result of these deliberations, Baptist mission societies were asked to "occupy" the Central American nations of El Salvador, Honduras, and Nicaragua.[185] Missionary preachers, physicians, and teachers were sent to El Salvador, and by 1931 there were sixteen missionaries and indigenous pastors, eighteen churches, and approximately 870 members.[186]

The Nicaragua Baptist Convention was founded in 1936. It joined with the ABHMS to support schools such as the Colegio Bautista in Managua, and the theological seminary transferred from El Salvador in 1941.

During the last quarter of the twentieth century, Nicaragua was plagued by civil war, economic distress, and other sociopolitical upheavals. The Marxist-based Sandinista regime overthrew the dictator Somoza in 1978 and remained in power until a new more democratically based system was attempted in 1990. During those years, Baptists were divided over supporting or opposing the revolutionary government. The Baptist Convention remained united, however.[187] Baptist ministries continued during the Sandinista era, including work instigated by Denis Centeno among the Miskito communities from Honduras. The Miskito Baptist Association united with the Nicaragua Convention in 1992. The BMS also began cooperation with the Convention in 1990.[188]

Baptists in South America

Baptist churches in South America began largely through the work of missionaries sent from English-speaking countries, particularly Great Britain and the United States. The strong Catholic presence in the region often created conflicts and persecution of religious minorities. Baptist work was slow but steady, with churches, schools, and missionary societies developing in various countries.

Baptists in Brazil

Southern Baptists sent their first missionary, Thomas Jefferson Bowen, to Brazil during the years 1859–1861, but he was forced to return home due to ill health. They expanded their work in Brazil when displaced Southerners immigrated to that country after the Civil War, founding a colony at Santa Barbara São Paulo. Baptists in the group began a church in 1871 and soon petitioned the SBC Foreign Mission Board to send missionaries. William Buck Bagby (1855–1939) and Anne Luther Bagby (1859–1942) were sent to Brazil in 1881. Joined by Zachary Clay Taylor and Kate Crawford Taylor, they founded the first Brazilian Baptist church in Bahia in 1882. Bagby began a church in Rio de Janeiro in 1884 with only four members. Amid some harassment from Catholic authorities, the missionaries developed plans for a Baptist presence throughout the country. Brazilians who became Baptists were often persecuted. When the Portuguese empire fell to the Brazilian republic in 1889, there were four churches claiming a membership of some three hundred converts. The first Brazilian Baptist, Antonio Teixeira de Albuquerque, was converted to Protestantism while studying for the Catholic priesthood. His book *Why I Left the Church of Rome* was widely circulated among Brazilian evangelicals for decades. By 1900, numerous Brazilian Baptists, including Thomaz da Costa, F. F. Soren, and Joaquim Paranagua, had become leaders in indigenous churches that spread to Belém, Manaos, and other towns in the Amazon Valley.[189]

The Brazilian Baptist Convention was founded in 1907. It fostered missionary activities at home and abroad, publication programs, and educational institutions. As indigenous pastors and churches developed, SBC missionaries took on more specialized tasks in publishing and education, subject to approval by the Brazilian Baptist Convention. *The Baptist Journal* was begun by missionaries in 1901. It came under Brazilian Baptist control in 1907. Like its SBC counterpart, the Woman's Missionary Union of Brazil, founded in 1908, was an auxiliary to the Convention. It provided literature, Brazilian female mission workers, and support for several training schools.[190] The Brazilian Baptist Foreign Mission Board developed its earliest work in Portugal and Bolivia.

The seminary of North Brazil was established in 1902 as part of the American Baptist College of Recife. The South Brazil Seminary of Rio began in 1908 as part of the John W. Shepard College. The two schools became independent in 1936. Faculties included both missionary and Brazilian professors.

In 1953, the Baptist Missionary Society (London) sent Arthur and Kathleen Elder to Brazil to work in Curitiba, the capital city of Paraná. The BMS agreed to work in areas where there was no extensive SBC missionary presence. Arthur Elder refuted false assumptions that Brazil was a "Catholic country" and insisted that religious life was characterized by popular superstitions and an eclectic blend of folk religions. The Elders promoted self-support from Brazilian Baptists, following certain Southern Baptist emphases on use of the Sunday school and encouragement of tithing. Evangelism was emphasized under the slogan "Every Baptist Home a Preaching Station," meaning that such efforts were highly localized. BMS missionaries generally were involved in evangelistic and church-planting activities.[191]

By the 1950s and 1960s, Pentecostalism was exploding throughout Brazil. For example, Baptists in Paraná grew from some five thousand members in 1955 to almost eleven thousand in 1965. During the same period, the Brazilian Assemblies of God grew from 9,200 to 38,450. Brian Stanley noted that while Brazilian Baptists kept authority for celebration of the ordinances with ordained clergy, the Pentecostals gave much more freedom for clergy and laity in such matters. He observed that the "secret of Pentecostal success in Brazil … lies in the offer of active leadership participation to ordinary, uneducated people."[192]

A Pentecostal movement known as Renovation developed among the Baptists in the 1960s. It promoted charismatic worship, glossolalia, and the baptism of the Holy Spirit.

These practices created a schism and the foundation of a new denomination, the National Baptist Convention, with connections to the Baptist World Alliance and the ABCUSA. Many Baptist groups, including Conservative Baptists, Swedish Baptists, Independent Baptists, and Free Will Baptists, have cooperative work with Brazilian Baptists.[193]

The Curitiba Bible Institute was founded in the 1940s, with BMS support, "to prepare students with little secular education for entry to the Rio seminary." It offered evening studies for bivocational ministers and training for the Baptist laity.[194]

The BMS mission work in Brazil expanded rapidly during the 1980s, with ministries involving both evangelical and social services. Particular attention was given to work in urban shantytowns, known as *favelas,* with programs in São Paulo, Curitiba, and other cities. In 1991, Brazilian mission work was the second largest missionary force in the BMS, with some fifty-nine individuals. That same year, the Brazilian Baptist Convention reported a membership of seven hundred thousand persons.[195]

Brazilian Baptists, generally apolitical throughout most of their history, did not participate in liberationist movements that developed among certain Roman Catholic *comunidades de base* (Christian base communities) during the 1960s and 1970s. In 1990, however, the Brazilian Baptist Convention began a program for social action, promoting "the principles of Christian justice, solidarity and love, with the purpose of establishing a social order that guarantees the well-being and fulfillment of the human race." It represented a more formal Baptist effort to confront social issues collectively.[196]

At the end of the twentieth century, there were at least fourteen distinct Brazilian Baptist groups, some located in a single congregation. The total number of Baptists in Brazil is around 1.2 million, with two organizations, the Baptist Convention of Brazil (902,000) and the Brazilian National Baptist Convention (200,000), claiming most of that figure.[197]

Baptists in Chile

The Baptist presence in Chile began with German immigrants who settled in the south and formed the first Baptist church in 1892. A revival ensued under the leadership of H. L. Weiss, a Mennonite who worked for the Christian and Missionary Alliance. He soon was joined by William David and Janet MacDonald, who also served with the Alliance. MacDonald (1852–1939), a supporter of believer's immersion, broke with the Alliance over infant baptism in 1907. In 1908, encouraged by Brazil missionary William B. Bagby, MacDonald helped to found the Evangelical Baptist Union, which became the Chilean Baptist Convention. MacDonald served as superintendent, exercising significant influence over the churches and their pastors. Funding from the SBC began in 1914. The SBC sent William E. and Mary Skidmore Davidson to Santiago as its first representatives. It also took over support for MacDonald's work.[198]

Efforts at promoting indigenous leadership led to an administrative board comprised of representatives from the Convention and the mission in 1926. It became the Cooperative Board in 1936. A Woman's Missionary Union began in 1923. The Colegio Bautista, an academy and high school established by missionaries in 1922, acquired its first Chilean Principal, Timoteo Gatica, in 1947. The Colegio was founded by SBC missionary Agnes Graham and three other women. A theological seminary was founded by missionaries in 1923 at Temuco and later moved to Santiago. In the 1940s, another Chilean, Honorio Espinoza, was named president. He also edited the periodical *La Voz Bautista,* started by missionaries and later taken over by Chilean Baptists.[199]

Disputes continued when William MacDonald's son-in-law, Ishmael Neven, turned away from Southern Baptist support and, with several other churches, founded the Chilean Mission, or National Baptist Church. At the end of the twentieth century, that group claimed a membership of 5,600 and maintained a connection with the ABCUSA.[200]

Baptists in Argentina

Baptist churches were first founded in Argentina through the work of Pablo Besson, a Swiss pastor who entered the country in 1881. As a "herald of Christian liberty," he called for religious freedom in Argentina and was instrumental in establishing three Baptist churches. Besson served as pastor of the Central Baptist Church in Buenos Aires. The first Argentine Baptist was immersed in the Rio de la Plata in 1883.[201]

Baptist missionaries came to Argentina in 1903 as representatives of the Southern Baptist Convention. These included Sidney M. Sowell, Joseph L. Hart, Tennessee Hamilton Hart, Frank James Fowler, Daisy Cate Fowler, King Wolsey Cawthon, and Lillian McCall Cawthon. Sowell preached his first sermon in Spanish on November 20, 1904. A Baptist church was founded in Buenos Aires in April 1905, and the first Argentineans to be baptized, Cosmo Misetti and Marcos Zambianco, received immersion a month later.[202]

The Argentine Baptist Convention was organized by five Baptist churches in December 1908. Juan Varetto was one of the early Argentine Baptist preachers and writers who shaped the directions of the church. He and his son-in-law, Santiago Canclini, were strong proponents of religious liberty and freedom of conscience in religious matters.[203]

Numerous Baptist missions have sent representatives to Argentina. These include the Conservative Baptist Convention, which began work in 1947 through cooperation with the Christian and Missionary Alliance. These activities involved the formation of the Mobile Bible Institute in 1961. The mission also cultivated activities with the Guaranis.[204]

Argentine Baptists have developed Sunday schools, women's missionary societies, and a variety of social ministries. Central Baptist Church, Buenos Aires, was the first congregation to ordain women to the ministry. The denomination numbers over sixty thousand members, with some 90 percent of them being related to the Convencion Evangelica Bautista Argentina.[205]

Baptists in the Americas

At the end of the twentieth century, Baptists in the Canada, the Caribbean, and South America confronted their own unique issues and challenges. In Canada, numerical declines were of great concern to churches and denominational groups. Discussions regarding mergers between Baptists and other Protestant groups became increasingly important for many. In the Caribbean and South America, issues related to poverty and politics dominated the landscape. The influx of Latino immigrants into the United States extended the influence of Spanish-speaking constituencies and created greater need for cooperation among Baptists in the northern and southern hemispheres. The influence of the charismatic movement also promised to have a major impact on individuals and communities of faith. Theologically, divisions continued over ways of understanding biblical authority, church polity, and doctrinal orthodoxy. Maintaining distinct Baptist identities remained one of the greatest challenges for churches throughout these regions.

Notes

1. Mark Noll, *A History of Christianity in the United States and Canada* (Grand Rapids, Mich.: Eerdmans, 1992), 246.
2. Ibid.
3. Ibid., 248–49.
4. George Edward Levy, *The Baptists of the Maritime Provinces, 1753–1946* (St. John, N.B.: Barnes-Hopkins, 1946), 1.
5. Ibid., 10–13.
6. Ibid., 13–14.
7. Robert G. Gardner, "Early Baptists of Sackville, New Brunswick," *American Baptist Quarterly* 4 (March 1985): 93.
8. Ibid.
9. Ibid., 20.
10. D. G. Bell, ed., *Newlight Baptist Journals of James Manning and James Innis* (Hantsport, N.S.: Lancelot Press, 1984), xiii.
11. Levy, *Maritime Provinces,* 23.
12. Ibid., 25.
13. Ibid., 33.
14. Bell, *Newlight Baptist Journals,* 6.
15. Ibid., 8.
16. Levy, *Maritime Provinces,* 46.
17. Bell, *Newlight Baptist Journals,* 21.
18. Ibid.
19. George A. Rawlyk, *Ravished by the Spirit: Religious Revivals, Baptists, and Henry Alline* (Kingston, Ont.: McGill-Queen's University Press, 1984), 54–55.
20. Ibid., 57–58.
21. Ibid., 90.
22. Ibid., 92.
23. Bell, *Newlight Baptist Journals,* 22–23.
24. Ibid., 24–25.
25. Ibid., 29.
26. *Massachusetts Baptist Missionary Magazine* (September 1812): 197.
27. Bell, *Newlight Baptist Journals,* 33.
28. Ibid., 26.
29. Ibid., 34–35.
30. Robert T. Handy, *A History of the Churches in the United States and Canada* (New York: Oxford University Press, 1976), 232.
31. Rawlyk, *Ravished by the Spirit,* 93.
32. Ibid., 95.
33. Ibid., 109.
34. Levy, *Maritime Provinces,* 119.
35. W. G. Pitman, "Baptist Triumph in Nineteenth-Century Canada," *Foundations* 3 (April 1960): 163.
36. Levy, *Maritime Provinces,* 121.
37. Bill J. Leonard, ed., *Dictionary of Baptists in America* (Downers Grove, Ill.: InterVarsity Press, 1990), 179.
38. Walter E. Ellis, "Baptists and Radical Politics in Western Canada (1920–1950)," in *Baptists in Canada: Search for Identity amidst Diversity,* ed. Jarold K. Zeman (Burlington, Ont.: G. R. Welch, 1980), 165–66.
39. Levy, *Maritime Provinces,* 239.
40. Handy, *History of the Churches,* 232–33.
41. Edward B. Link, "North American (German) Baptists," in Zeman, ed., *Baptists in Canada,* 88–89.
42. Ibid., 91.
43. Ibid., 93.
44. Ibid., 95.
45. Ibid., 99–100.
46. Levy, *Maritime Provinces,* 88–91.
47. Ibid., 100.
48. Ibid., 138–39.
49. Ibid., 156–159.
50. Ibid., 167–68.
51. Ibid., 168.
52. Winthrop S. Hudson, "The Interrelationships of Baptists in Canada and the United States," *Foundations* 23 (January–March 1980): 80.

53. Levy, *Maritime Provinces,* 139–40.

54. Ibid., 141.

55. Ibid., 153.

56. *The Baptist Year Book of the Maritime Provinces of Canada* (1904), 137 (cited in Philip Griffin-Allwood, *The Canadianization of Baptists: From Denominations to Denomination, 1760–1912* [Ann Arbor, Mich.: University Microfilms International, 1986], 142).

57. Harry A. Renfree, *Heritage and Horizon: The Baptist Story in Canada* (Mississauga, Ont.: Canadian Baptist Federation, 1988), 209.

58. Ibid., 209–10.

59. Handy, *History of the Churches,* 350–51.

60. Griffin-Allwood, *The Canadianization of Baptists,* 155 (citing Robert Gardner, *Baptists in Early America: A Statistical Survey,* 1639–1790 [Atlanta: Georgia Baptist Historical Society, 1983], 353).

61. Ibid., 175–78.

62. Ibid., 178, 121 n.

63. Ibid., 179.

64. Ibid., 183.

65. Ibid., 186–87.

66. Ibid., 192.

67. Philip Griffin-Allwood, "Canadian Baptist Christians" (typescript, n.d.), 11.

68. Griffin-Allwood, *The Canadianization of Baptists,* 197.

69. Ibid., 201.

70. Ibid., 208.

71. Ibid., 213.

72. Ellis, "Baptists and Radical Politics," 161, 164.

73. Ibid., 165.

74. Ibid., 166–68.

75. Renfree, *Heritage and Horizon,* 200–201.

76. Jarold K. Zeman, "They Speak in Other Tongues: Witness among Immigrants," in Zeman, ed., *Baptists in Canada,* 69.

77. Ibid., 74.

78. Ibid., 75–77.

79. Ibid., 81.

80. Renfree, *Heritage and Horizon,* 265–66.

81. Paul R. Dekar, "Baptists and Human Rights, 1837–1867," in Zeman, ed., *Baptists in Canada,* 111.

82. Ibid., 112.

83. Ibid., 113–14.

84. Ibid.

85. Ibid., 116.

86. Ibid., 117.

87. Ibid., 119.

88. Ibid., 121.

89. Ibid., 121–22.

90. W. Gordon Carder, "A View of Some Canadian Headlines, 1860–1912," in Zeman, ed., *Baptists in Canada,* 140 (citing *The Christian Messenger* [February 14, 1856]: 2).

91. Levy, *Maritime Provinces,* 194–95; Dekar, "Baptists and Human Rights," 122–23.

92. Levy, *Maritime Provinces,* 205.

93. Renfree, *Heritage and Horizon,* 195, 318–19.

94. Ibid., 125.

95. Ibid.

96. Carder, "Canadian Headlines," 141 (citing *Canadian Baptist* [January 22, 1901]: 8).

97. Renfree, *Heritage and Horizon,* 251.

98. Griffin-Allwood, *The Canadianization of Baptists,* 256.

99. W. Gordon Carder, "Controversy in the Baptist Convention of Ontario and Quebec, 1908–1928," *Foundations* 16 (October–December 1973): 355–57.

100. Ibid., 358–59.

101. Ibid., 359–60.

102. Ibid., 361.

103. Ibid., 365–73.

104. Robert S. Wilson, "Patterns of Canadian Baptist Life in the Twentieth Century" (paper presented at the International Conference on Baptist Studies, July 2000), 31–32.

105. A. Ronald Tonks, "Highlights of the Relationships of Southern Baptists with Canadian Baptists," *Baptist History and Heritage* 15 (April 1980): 10–11 (citing the *Southern Baptist Convention Annual* [1958], 72).

106. Wilson, "Canadian Baptist Life," 32.

107. G. Gerald Harrop, "Canadian Baptists in Their North American Context," *Foundations* 4 (July 1961): 220–22.

108. Ibid.
109. Walter E. Ellis, "A Place to Stand: Contemporary History of the Baptist Union of Western Canada," *American Baptist Quarterly* 6 (March 1987): 44–45.
110. Constitution of the Baptist Federation of Canada.
111. Ellis, "A Place to Stand," 46.
112. Wilson, "Canadian Baptist Life," 37–41.
113. Ibid., 43.
114. Brian Stanley, *The History of the Baptist Missionary Society, 1792–1992* (Edinburgh: Clark, 1992), 68.
115. Clement Gayle, *George Liele: Pioneer Missionary to Jamaica* (Kingston: Jamaica Baptist Union, 1982), 15.
116. Ibid., 18–19.
117. Henry N. Smith, "William Knibb and Baptist Missions in Jamaica until 1845, " *Quarterly Review* 44 (October–December 1983): 49.
118. Ibid., 51.
119. Ibid., 52.
120. Stanley, *Baptist Missionary Society,* 74.
121. Smith, "William Knibb," 52.
122. Thomas F. Abbott, *Narrative of Certain Events Connected with the Late Disturbances in Jamaica* (London: Holdsworth and Ball, 1832), 21.
123. Smith, "William Knibb," 55.
124. Ibid., 57.
125. Ernest A. Payne, *Freedom in Jamaica* (London: Carey Press, n.d.), 107.
126. Ibid., 109–10.
127. William G. Barrett, *Baptist Mission in Jamaica: An Exposition* (London: John Snow, 1842), 8.
128. Ibid., 2–3.
129. Stanley, *Baptist Missionary Society,* 260–61. See also Horace O. Russell, *The Baptist Witness* (El Paso, Tex.: Carib Baptist Publications, 1983).
130. Stanley, *Baptist Missionary Society,* 262–64.
131. Albert W. Wardin, ed., *Baptists around the World: A Comprehensive Handbook* (Nashville: Broadman & Holman, 1995), 304–5.
132. Ibid., 91–92.
133. Ibid., 94–95.
134. Stanley, *Baptist Missionary Society,* 252–53.
135. Ibid., 267–68.
136. Bertha Grimmell Judd, *Fifty Golden Years: The First Half Century of the Woman's American Home Mission Society, 1877–1927* (Rochester, N.Y.: Du Bois Press, 1927), 113–18.
137. Wardin, ed., *Baptists around the World,* 310.
138. Ruth E. Mooney, "Missionaries in Latin America: Agents of Empire or Partners in Mission?" *American Baptist Quarterly* 18 (September 1999): 64.
139. Howard B. Grose, *Advance in the Antilles: The New Era in Cuba and Porto Rico* (New York: Presbyterian Home Missions, 1910), 43–49.
140. Charles L. White, *A Century of Faith* (Philadelphia: Judson Press, 1932), 195.
141. Ibid., 200.
142. Ibid., 197.
143. George P. Beers, *Ministry to Turbulent America: A History of the American Baptist Home Mission Society, Covering its Fifth Quarter Century, 1932–1957* (Philadelphia: Judson Press, 1957), 117–18.
144. Ibid., 130.
145. Wardin, ed., *Baptists around the World,* 296.
146. Marcos A. Ramos, *Protestantism and Revolution in Cuba* (Miami: Institute for InterAmerican Studies, 1989), 48-51.
147. Ibid., 79-80.
148. Ibid., 80.
149. Ibid., 81-82.
150. Ibid., 84-85, 136.
151. Wardin, ed., *Baptists around the World,* 296.
152. Ibid.
153. White, *A Century of Faith,* 209
154. Stanley, *Baptist Missionary Society,* 94, 100.
155. White, *A Century of Faith,* 210-11
156. Stanley, *Baptist Missionary Society,* 105.
157. White, *A Century of Faith,* 184.
158. Ibid., 187.
159. Ibid., 190–91.
160. Beers, *Ministry to Turbulent America,* 138-41.
161. Wardin, ed., *Baptists around the World,* 309.

162. David L. Montemayor, "Historia de los Bautistas en México" (online: http://www.bautistas.org.mx/histbau.doc); Frank W. Patterson, *A Century of Baptist Work in Mexico* (El Paso, Tex.: Baptist Spanish Publishing House, 1979), 23–28.

163. Patterson, *Baptist Work in Mexico,* 36–37.

164. White, *A Century of Faith,* 173–75.

165. Ibid., 65–73.

166. Ibid. See also Montemayor, "Bautistas en México."

167. White, *A Century of Faith,* 46–47.

168. Ibid., 55.

169. Ibid., 55–57.

170. Wardin, ed., *Baptists around the World,* 323.

171. Ibid.

172. White, *A Century of Faith,* 176.

173. Ibid., 181–82.

174. Ibid., 183.

175. Wardin, ed., *Baptists around the World,* 323.

176. Ibid., 322.

177. Ibid., 324.

178. H. Leon McBeth, *The Baptist Heritage* (Nashville: Broadman, 1987), 735.

179. "ABCUSA: Hispanic Baptists Celebrate 100 Years," American Baptist News Service, June 11, 2001.

180. McBeth, *The Baptist Heritage,* 737.

181. Ibid., 738–39.

182. George V. Pixley, "Nicaragua Baptists: Reclaiming Repressed Cultures," *American Baptist Quarterly* 18 (September 1999): 68.

183. Ibid.

184. White, *A Century of Faith,* 206–7.

185. Ibid., 202–3.

186. Ibid., 205.

187. Wardin, ed., *Baptists around the World,* 326.

188. Ibid.

189. *Encyclopedia of Southern Baptists,* 3 vols. (Nashville: Broadman, 1958), 1:186–87.

190. Ibid., 1:188.

191. Stanley, *Baptist Missionary Society,* 479, 486–87.

192. Ibid., 480.

193. Wardin, ed., *Baptists around the World,* 338–39. See also José dos Reis Pereira, *História dos Batistas no Brasil, 1882–1982* (Rio de Janeiro: JUERP, 1982).

194. Wardin, ed., *Baptists around the World,* 484.

195. Ibid., 496–97.

196. Ibid., 500.

197. Ibid., 336–37.

198. *Encyclopedia of Southern Baptists,* 1:252; Wardin, ed., *Baptists around the World,* 341.

199. *Encyclopedia of Southern Baptists,* 1:252.

200. Wardin, ed. *Baptists around the World,* 341.

201. *Encyclopedia of Southern Baptists,* 1:59.

202. Ibid.

203. Wardin, ed., *Baptists around the World,* 333–34.

204. Ibid.

205. Ibid., 334.

Chapter 11
African American Baptists

Up from Slavery

THE CONVERSION OF AFRICAN SLAVES TO CHRISTIANITY HAS BEEN EXPLORED IN numerous works on the subject.[1] Scholars continue to debate questions regarding the relationship between African religion and slave religion as well as the extent of Christianity's influence on the slave population. It is clear, however, that large numbers of slaves were converted to Christianity, particularly during the awakenings of the eighteenth and nineteenth centuries. Those conversions had a powerful influence on the nature of religious experience among Africans in the American colonies. The Baptist movement thrived among these converts, who organized churches and denominations. Eugene Genovese suggested, "By the time of the antebellum period, most southern blacks who professed Christianity called themselves Baptists."[2]

The connections between white and black Christians in slavery time and throughout American history reveal deep tensions, contradictions, and racial strife. Concerted attempts to evangelize slaves were slow in developing, with some of the earliest initiated by Anglicans during the late eighteenth century. Even then, many clergy were compelled to assure slaveholders that conversion to Christianity changed only the eternal status of the Africans, with no effect on their earthly situation. As William Clebsch observed, baptism threatened to make the slave "so nearly a person that no Christian could hold him in slavery."[3] Evangelization was tolerated by the slave owners, who hoped that it would make slaves more obedient and less prone to rebel against their circumstances. By the late eighteenth and early nineteenth centuries, efforts to "Christianize" the slave population were well underway.

Slaves participated in the revivals and camp meetings that fostered religious awakenings in the colonial and frontier periods. Once converted, many were drawn to Baptist ways of religious experience and ecclesial organization. Walter Pitts suggested that the Baptist ethos appealed to blacks for several reasons. First, Baptists incorporated "magical power into church doctrine," creating a mystical community that "enabled a convert to heal and prophesy."[4] Second, baptismal immersion appealed to African Americans because of its similarity to "African water rites." Third, and perhaps most significant, was the autonomous nature of Baptist church polity that permitted the formation of a congregation without permission or jurisdiction from other ecclesiastical tribunals. Pitts asserted, "The single most important outgrowth of the Great Awakening was that blacks who had been converted at the revivals formed their own independent congregations, thereby beginning the political, social, and economic autonomy of the Afro-Baptist church."[5] Baptist churches became the central religious community for a large portion of the black Christian populace.

In the South, slaves were not allowed to have their own congregations, and so Southern churches generally were integrated until the end of the Civil War. Black preachers were carefully monitored to ensure that they did not encourage insurrection, something greatly feared by white Southerners. James Cone maintained that in spite of these sanctions, blacks were drawn to Christianity because of its undercurrent of liberation for all persons.[6]

James Melvin Washington concluded that until the Civil War, most black Baptists in the South "worshiped either in racially mixed churches under white ministers or in black-led secret conventicles (the 'invisible institution') or both."[7] Clandestine gatherings of slaves, sometimes known as "hush arbors," took place outside the sight and control of their white masters. Peter Randolph, a nineteenth-century slave in Virginia, described such a scene:

> Not being allowed to hold meetings on the plantation, the slaves assemble in the swamps, out of reach of the patrols. They have an understanding among themselves as to the time and place of getting together…. They first ask each other how they feel, the state of their minds, etc. The male members then select a certain space, in separate groups, for their division of the meeting … then praying and singing all around, until they generally feel quite happy…. The slave forgets all his sufferings, except to remind others of the trials during the past week.[8]

These assemblies, along with the "enthusiastical" religion engendered by revival movements, shaped the formation of numerous Afro-Baptist churches, North and South, during the early nineteenth century. Pitts commented, "By the end of the second period of the Revivals in 1822, thirty-seven Afro-Baptist churches existed in the United States, most of them in the South."[9] Yet the outbreak of various slave revolts, such as those led by Denmark Vesey (1822) and Nat Turner (1831), led to the closing of most of the independent black churches and the merging of African Americans into white congregations.

In those churches, slaves often were disciplined for failure to obey their masters in ways "commanded" in the Bible. In principle, they could request that the church take disciplinary action against churchgoing masters who failed to adhere to biblical admonitions regarding the treatment of slaves. Slaves also could be disciplined by the churches. One such case concerned a slave woman named Winney, who, with her mistress, Esther Boulware, was a member of Kentucky's Forks of Elkhorn Baptist Church in 1807. Church records state:

> The 2nd Saturday in January after divine Worship [disciplinary action was] brought against Sister Esther Boulwares Winney … for saying she once thought it her duty to serve her Master & Mistress but since the Lord converted her, she had never believed that any Christian kept Negroes or Slaves—2nd. For saying she believed there was Thousands of white people Wallowing in Hell for their treatment to Negroes—and she did not care if there was as many more—Refer'd to next Meeting.[10]

Charges also could be brought against slaveholders for abusing blacks, but apparently with little result. The Forks of Elkhorn Baptist Church records noted, "Bro. Palmer complains against Bro. Stephens and his Wife for not dealing with Nancy their Negroe Woman & bringing her before the Church and for puting her in Irons—Bro. Stephens was Acquited. A second Charge against Sister Stephens for giving their Negroe Woman the lye [lie]—She was Acquited from both Charges."[11]

Blacks were members of the congregations, received as members, and "lettered out" (transferred membership) to other churches upon request.[12]

The evangelistic emphases of the Methodists and Baptists made those two groups particularly successful in attracting African Americans. Their freewheeling forms of worship were both an influence upon and influenced by the presence of blacks in their midst. Many scholars contend that the decline of revivalist worship styles among certain white churches was one reason for the departure of blacks from white congregations.[13]

Like white women, blacks had second-class status in white churches. Generally, only white males were allowed to vote on the calling of pastors and other matters of church business. In some congregations, male slaves were permitted to vote on disciplinary matters. Slaves and free blacks often were compelled to sit in segregated sections, perhaps in the "gallery," located in the balcony of the church.

In spite of their ties to white churches, African American Baptists developed their own distinct religiosity. Mechal Sobel studied the religious experiences of "Afro-Baptists" and concluded, "Critics who maintain that all of the black Christian's practices can be traced to white Christianity are in error. They overlook the fact that blacks influenced white culture in significant ways. They err further in that a great deal of the content of black Christianity is not shared by whites."[14]

African American Baptists experienced opposition from whites when they attempted to establish ecclesiastical organizations. The Executive Board of the Virginia Baptist State Convention, an African American body, noted in 1869, "That there is opposition against us, cannot be disguised. Men prejudiced to our advancement, simply because of our sable hue, have held churches aloof from us, telling them that it is too expensive to join us, yet draining the churches of larger sums than we ask, or is necessary to act with us; and said sums that apply to their own selfish ends, and not to the interest of Virginia and her helpless."[15]

Early African American Churches

Autonomous African American Baptist congregations began to separate from white Baptist communions by 1805. Because the earliest black Baptist churches were in the South, they held tenaciously to their independence. On the eve of the Civil War, there were some 4.2 million blacks in the South, in contrast to around two hundred thousand in the North.

After emancipation, African Americans in many white-dominated congregations came to feel that their second-class status was perpetuated in the church. At the same time, many Southern whites resented what they saw as Northern interference in the religious life of the churches, particularly where blacks were concerned. This tension influenced the decision of blacks to go their own way.[16]

African American Baptist churches were formed, and with them new mission boards and denominational configurations. With these actions, Baptists became the largest denominational configuration of African Americans in the United States. In 1890, some 54 percent of all African American Christians claimed Baptist affiliation, numbering more than 1 million. Georgia was a case in point. In 1883, Baptists in that state were divided between 121, 216 blacks and 123,851 whites.[17]

Washington suggested that George Liele (ca.1750–1820) was "one of the first slaves to be deeply affected by the missionary zeal of these new revivals" in the late eighteenth century. Converted in 1772, Liele (or Lisle) was ordained, with his master's permission, by the Buckhead Creek Baptist Church in Georgia for the explicit purpose of doing missionary work among the slaves.[18] Liele was instrumental in the conversion of several other slaves in the Savannah region, including Andrew Bryan and his spouse, Hannah, along with Kate Hogg and Hagar Simpson. Bryan began preaching soon after and was permitted to hold forth in a meetinghouse for slaves on the plantation of his master, Edward Davis.[19]

Liele's endeavors led to the conversion of two other black preachers: David George and Jesse Galphin. David George, born in 1742, was a slave near Silver Bluff, Georgia. Although disputes continue as to which congregation was the first African American Baptist church in America, many signs point to the church at Silver Bluff, founded sometime between 1773 and 1775. Recalling the event, George wrote, "Brother Palmer appointed Saturday evening to hear what the Lord had done for us, and the next day he baptized us in the mill stream. Brother Palmer formed us into a church, and gave us the Lord's Supper at Silver Bluff."[20] "Brother Palmer," George stated, "was an ex-slave and itinerant preacher who gathered various slave groups for religious services on farms and plantations. George's master, George Galphin, permitted his ordination.

Carter Woodson claimed that the Silver Bluff Church was formed sometime between 1773 and 1775.[21] George served as pastor of the church until the British captured Savannah, at which point he and most of the congregation received their freedom.

In 1782, George and other Southern blacks went to Nova Scotia. Ten years later, he and a company of blacks moved to Sierra Leone, where they founded the first Baptist church in that colony. The Silver Bluff Church was reconstituted in 1782 under the leadership of a slave named Jesse Peter. The church was admitted to the Georgia (Baptist) Association in 1790, with a membership of some 381 persons.[22] The meetinghouse and adjoining property were not formally recognized as belonging to blacks when white citizens petitioned in behalf of the slaves. A document signed by D. B. Mitchell, a major in the local militia, read, "I do hereby give unto the said Andrew as Pastor and to his Elders and Society, my full approbation to meet and perform Divine Worship, in the Meeting-house at Yamacraw, on the Sabbath day, between Sun Rise and Sun Set, so long as they Conduct themselves with due decency and order; and that the persons attending thereon have a pass from their masters or Mistresses for that purpose."[23] By this act, the black Baptists had use of the property.

The First African Baptist Church, Savannah, Georgia, probably was the second Baptist church founded by Southern blacks. Led by Jesse Galphin and Andrew Bryan, it began in 1788. George Liele preached frequently in Savannah before leaving for mission work in Jamaica. Liele baptized Andrew Bryan and his wife, Hannah, as well as Kate Hogg and Hagar Simpson, each one a founding member of the Savannah church.[24] Bryan was ordained by Abraham Marshall, son of Baptist patriarch Daniel Marshall. The ordination occurred outside a local congregation and therefore was deemed "irregular."[25] Desiring official relationship with Georgia Baptists, and concerned about the validity of his Baptist congregation, Bryan asked the Georgia Baptist Association in 1790 to rule on the church's status. The Association chose to accept the church and agreed that Marshall's earlier action was an "extraordinary case."[26] Ultimately, the Savannah Baptist Association was formed in 1802 by two white congregations and Bryan's First African Baptist Church. Later that year, the Association reported that there were five "colored" Baptist churches among their number.[27]

The Savannah church was instrumental in the founding of numerous African Baptist congregations. It sent out "exhorters," or ministerial apprentices, to organize "praise houses" for praise and worship. Until the Civil War, black Baptists throughout the South "participated in the rapid growth of legal biracial congregations."[28] Presbyterian Charles Colcock Jones estimated in 1813 that some forty thousand blacks were members of Baptist churches. During this time, Virginia's black population was the largest in the South.[29]

In 1776, First Baptist Church, Williamsburg, Virginia, was instituted by whites as a separate congregation for blacks. In 1781, it was organized fully by Gowan Pamphlet, an African American Baptist. The church was admitted to the white Dover Baptist Association in 1791.

Blacks and whites worshiped together in Richmond's First Baptist Church until 1841, when a new church was constructed for whites. Blacks retained the old building, which they bought for about $3,500. Richmond citizens contributed an additional $2,700 toward the purchase.[30] Robert Ryland, the African church's pastor, wrote, "Some very fastidious people did not like to resort to a church, where so many colored folks congregated, and this was thought to operate against the growth of the white portion of the audience."[31]

Those Africans seeking conversion were urged to communicate their concern to pastor or deacons. Slaves then were required to bring from their masters "a testimonial" of their conduct, signs of improvement and spiritual transformation, after which they were examined as to their understanding of doctrine and faith. One such letter from a master read,

> My woman, Clarissa Hill, has expressed a wish to unite herself in Christian communion with the church of which you are the acting minister. She is a most faithful servant, and one, of whom it affords me pleasure to say, that I believe she endeavors to conform to the great principles of her faith, and I believe she will be an exemplary and honorable member of your church, should you think proper to receive her as such. She has belonged to me for sixteen years, during which time her conduct has been most unexceptionably moral, and therefore, I cheerfully consent to her being baptized and admitted to your communion.[32]

During the early nineteenth century, some predominately black churches were led by white pastors. In Virginia, Baptist churches at Gloucester and Portsmouth were served by black ministers William Lemon and Josiah Bishop.[33]

Some scholars suggest that these early churches demonstrated many African traits in worship and orientation. African American leader W. E. B. Du Bois believed that in the beginning these congregations were not peculiarly Christian, but "a mere adaptation of those heathen rites which we roughly designate by the term Obe Worship, or 'Voodooism.'"[34] Pitts remarked, "In spite of their Christian veneer, the first Afro-Baptist congregants retained many of the African characteristics of worship that their forebears had imported with them."[35]

During the early nineteenth century, white Baptists generally resisted public stands for or against slavery. There were some notable exceptions, however. In 1789, the Virginia

Association of Baptists declared slavery to be "a violent deprivation of the rights of nature and inconsistent with a republican government."[36]

The opposition to slavery by Southern Quakers also had an impact on various Baptist individuals and groups. These antislavery Baptists often were known as "Friends of Humanity." Indeed, the Baptized Licking Locust Association, Friends of Humanity, was a Kentucky antislavery association of churches formed in the 1790s by Baptist minister David Barrow, who had freed his own slaves in 1784. In a sense, white Baptists' response to slavery began with a concern to convert slaves to Christianity and bring them into white churches in the South. Ironically, it was that introduction to Christianity and its promise of liberation that empowered many African Americans to oppose slavery and segregation.

Northern Churches

Black Baptist churches also were founded in the North. Joy Street Baptist Church, Boston, Massachusetts, was founded in 1804; Abyssinian Baptist Church, New York City, began in 1808; and the African Baptist Church of Philadelphia was formed in 1809. The Joy Street and Abyssinian churches were organized through the work of Thomas Paul, a free black born in New Hampshire in 1773. Paul was pastor of the Joy Street Church for at least twenty-five years. When African American members left First Baptist Church, New York City, to found the Abyssinian Church, Paul served as their temporary pastor. Paul helped to negotiate an amicable split that enabled First Baptist Church to grant "honorable letters of dismission" to the four men and twelve women who left that congregation to form the Abyssinian Baptist Church.[37]

Prior to the Civil War, African American Baptist churches were organized in cities such as Cleveland, Columbus, and Cincinnati in Ohio, as well as Detroit and Chicago. In 1836, the Ohio churches formed the Providence Baptist Association—the first such organization of African American congregations.[38]

A second such body, the Association of the Regular Baptist Churches of Color in Ohio, also known as the Union Association, was formed in 1836 from churches in Cincinnati, Columbus, Chillicothe, and Brush Creek. David Nickens, the pastor of one of these churches, perhaps was the first ordained black Baptist preacher in the state of Ohio.[39]

In 1840, the Union Association broke its remaining connections to white associations and changed its name to the Union Baptist Antislavery Association in an effort to express greater opposition to slavery.[40]

Antislavery sentiments also were evident in the founding of the third black association in Illinois in 1839. Originally known as the Colored Baptist Association and Friends to Humanity, it was renamed the Wood River Association. The Association established the Colored Baptist Home Missionary Society in 1844—the forerunner of the Western Colored Baptist Convention, founded in 1853.[41]

James Washington observed that African American Baptist associations focused on many issues common to their white counterparts, including missions, education, fellowship, and mutual encouragement. Unlike most of the white associations, however, the African American organizations engaged in a variety of activities aimed at abolishing slavery.[42]

Theological Issues

Theologically, African American and Anglo Baptists were impacted by many of the same movements and doctrinal debates. Many African Americans were unashamed Landmarkists who supported successionist views of Baptist origins. Most understood their own persecutions as a direct link to earlier persecuted minorities—Novatians, Donatists, Waldenses, and others—who were descendants of the first Christians.

Calvinism made significant inroads into certain African American Baptist communities. In 1890, Charles O. Boothe, pastor of Dexter Avenue Baptist Church, Montgomery, Alabama, published *Plain Theology for Plain People,* in which he urged African Americans to accept Calvinist theology. Gregory Wills remarked that in many cases African American associations and churches were organized around the same Calvinist-based confessions of faith that white churches used.[43]

The Fortress Monroe Conference and African American Institutions

Funding and control of African American educational institutions was one issue on the agenda when representatives of black and white Baptists met in Fortress Monroe, Virginia, in 1894. As the African American denominations developed, white Baptists made efforts to encourage education of blacks, particularly ministers. Some of these local schools met with limited success. The 1894 Fortress Monroe meeting was attended by representatives of the Southern Baptist Convention, the American Baptist Home Mission Society, and certain African American Baptist state conventions. They proposed "to marshal the manpower of white southern Baptists and the financial capabilities of northerners to support black Baptist colleges through local committees and to conduct informal classes for untrained preachers."[47]

Known as "New Era Institutes," these well-intentioned but inevitably paternalistic endeavors were established to provide doctrinal instruction for black pastors and bring them under the guidance of local white pastors. The actions were resisted by black Baptists who welcomed the new funding but were reluctant to relinquish control of their fledgling institutions. Some white ministers opposed the programs because, as one minister commented, they fostered "social equality, and we cannot agree to that."[48]

Educational Institutions

In the aftermath of the Civil War, Baptists founded numerous schools across the South aimed at educating freed men and women, especially ministerial students. As early as 1862, the American Baptist Home Mission Society (ABHMS) established a commission that recommended "immediate steps to supply with Christian instruction, by means of missionaries and teachers, the emancipated slaves."[49] In his study of Baptists in the South, Paul Harvey noted that this support for higher education was "the linchpin of northern Baptist missionary efforts."[50] Some twenty-eight institutions were funded, including Selma University, Alabama (1878); Spelman Seminary, Georgia (1881); Shaw University, North Carolina

(1865); Roger Williams University, Tennessee (1866); Bishop College, Texas (1881); and Virginia Union University (1865).

In 1865, the ABHMS sent Henry M. Tupper (1831–1893) to begin a school in Raleigh, North Carolina, that became Shaw University. White opposition was extensive, but Tupper and his associates prevailed, first constructing a chapel and classroom building and later establishing a brick manufacturing company that provided funds and materials for additional construction projects.[51] Between 1865 and 1881, nine new institutions were begun. In 1865, Wayland Seminary was established in Washington, D.C., and later merged with Richmond Institute and Theological Seminary (1872) to become Virginia Union University. After Nashville, Tennessee, fell to Union forces in 1864, Northern Baptists soon established the Nashville Institute (1866) under the direction of the Tennessee Negro Baptist Convention. In Mississippi, Natchez Seminary was founded in 1876. Its president, Charles Ayers, asked, "When will the colored people do these things—build houses and steamboats, make books, gain wealth, instead of being the football of other men?" Ayers answered, "When they have education."[52]

Spelman Seminary for women was founded in Atlanta in 1881. Bishop College, in Marshall, Texas, was the first school for freed blacks west of the Mississippi. It was named for Nathan Bishop, corresponding secretary of the ABHMS, 1874–1876.[53]

African American Baptist Conventions

James Washington suggested that the lines between the earliest denominations often were blurred. Societies, conventions, and associations were not as distinct as they would later become. Conventions were less centralized, nongeographic associations, cooperating in specific ministries.[44] Many of the early African American Baptist conventions were short-lived, one merging with another or disbanding all together. Some began as mission societies and later expanded their activities.

The Richmond African Baptist Missionary Society was organized in 1815 by a white deacon named William Crane and African American ministers Lott Carey and Collin Teague. It established links to the Triennial Convention and provided a portion of the funds that enabled Carey and Teague to go to Monrovia, Liberia, in 1821. After the division in the Triennial Convention in 1845, the Richmond Society channeled funds through the Southern Baptist Convention (SBC) until 1880. During those years, the SBC appointed William W. Colley, an African American preacher from Virginia, to Nigeria as assistant to W. J. David, a white missionary. In 1878, Solomon Cosby, another Virginian, was sent as a missionary to Nigeria by joint appointment from the SBC and the Virginia Baptist State Convention, an African American organization.[45]

Cosby died in 1881, around the same time that differences between the black Baptists and the SBC became irreconcilable. Missionary W. J. David urged the Convention to reject shared appointments and assert supervisory control over black missionaries. David wrote, "I wish to divert the minds of the Board from depending upon colored laborers from the South too much. In equal proportion, it will do well, I hope, but will not do to let the colored force preponderate."[46] This attitude created conflict among Liberian churches and led African Baptists to form the Native Baptist Church in the 1880s.

The American Baptist Missionary Convention

African Americans founded their first national mission society in 1840 at the Abyssinian Baptist Church, New York. Known as the American Baptist Missionary Convention, its members came from African churches in New England and the Mid-Atlantic states. While committed to missionary endeavors, its leaders expressed unequivocal opposition to slavery and encouraged the Triennial Convention to do the same. Membership was offered to all individuals, slave or free, who would subscribe one dollar per year. Churches and associations were asked to contribute three dollars per annum. The society also brought together blacks from New England and the South in missionary endeavors. The society endured for twenty-six years but generally was unsuccessful in maintaining centralized coordination of programs. Blacks churches guarded their autonomy closely.

The Consolidated American Baptist Missionary Convention

The Northwestern and Southern Baptist Convention was founded by African American churches in those regions in 1866. It merged with the American Baptist Missionary Convention in 1866 to become the Consolidated American Baptist Missionary Convention in Richmond, Virginia. It claimed a membership comprised of six regional conventions, thirteen associations, and seventy-two congregations. The Convention soon founded a ministerial training school, also located in Richmond. The leaders were particularly concerned that blacks develop their own institutions, and they asserted, "Our very organization is our proclamation to the world that we are able to do this work, and that we ought to do it."[54]

Unfortunately, regional loyalties weakened the national body and contributed to the demise of the Consolidated Convention in 1879. Two of these regional conventions, the Baptist General Association of the Western States and Territories and the New England Missionary Convention, even instituted their own autonomous programs.

Following the Civil War, African American members of white Primitive Baptist Churches began to organize their own denomination. The Colored Primitive Baptists of America originated in the 1860s under the leadership of Thomas Williamson. Other African American Baptists established the Indian Creek Primitive Baptist Association in 1869.[55]

The American National Baptist Convention

In 1886, the American National Baptist Convention was formed in St. Louis, with William J. Simmons (1849–1890) as president. Simmons was a preeminent black Baptist leader in the post-Civil War era. In 1890, he became president of the Kentucky Normal and Theological Institute in Louisville, Kentucky, and by 1884 the school had become a university. It was renamed for Simmons following his death in 1890.

Simmons founded the Colored Press Association in an effort to bring African American voices into the public media. As an author, he published *Men of Mark: Eminent, Progressive and Rising* (1887), a biography of outstanding African Americans.[56]

The Foreign Mission Convention

The Foreign Mission Convention, founded in 1880, was another of the early African American Baptist denominations. It began, at least in part, because of African American frustrations with white Baptist missionary organizations and their treatment of black missionaries.

Black missionary William W. Colley returned from Africa in 1879 and traveled throughout the South encouraging Baptists of color to establish their own society. The Convention was formed in Montgomery, Alabama, on November 26, 1880. This was particularly important because the Consolidated American Baptist Missionary Convention, the first "truly national organization among black Baptists," had dissolved the year before.[57]

Six individuals were sent to Liberia during the years 1883–1884, the first group of black missionaries after emancipation. Like their white counterparts, these missionaries experienced the ravages of disease. Hattie Presley, one of the six original missionaries, died only seven months after her arrival in Liberia. Her husband, Joseph Presley, was forced to return home because of illness. William W. Colley returned to the field but died tragically in March 1886 after being shot by an African. The deaths of black Baptists in the mission field strengthened the resolve of their American supporters for the continuation of African evangelization. Leaders of these mission societies responded to invitations from African Christians to offer help. They acknowledged a sense of kinship and destiny with their African homeland.[58]

The Baptist Foreign Missions Convention (BFMC) was organized according to the society method, which permitted membership from churches, associations, women's missions groups, and Sunday schools. It appointed representatives to other denominational bodies in an attempt to create fraternal relations with other mission societies, black and white. Like other African American mission societies, the members of the Foreign Mission Convention directed their energies toward the evangelization of Africa.

In 1888, the BFMC joined with the Baptist General Association of Western States and Territories (founded 1873) in certain cooperative endeavors. It was then renamed the American Baptist Foreign Mission Convention of the United States of America—a designation that was not widely used.[59] In an effort to preserve its own identity and integrity, however, the BFMC resisted any connection with the Anglo-based American Baptist Missionary Union. The BFMC struggled for funds and membership until 1894, when it passed off the scene as its members helped form the National Baptist Convention in 1895.

Conflicts with white denominations were frequent and often heated. In 1890, a controversy over publishing developed among the Southern Baptists, the American Baptist Publication Society, and African American Baptists. The American Baptist Publication Society had given black leaders such as William J. Simmons, Edward Brawley, and Walter Brooks the right to publish Sunday school literature. SBC leaders complained that Simmons wrote materials that were too militant regarding the rights of blacks in the church.

At this point, the American Baptist Publication Society was publishing literature for the SBC as well. The Society then withdrew its invitation to publish the African Americans. These actions influenced the decision to form a new publishing house.

African American efforts to provide educational materials for their own churches influenced the formation of the National Baptist Educational Convention in Washington, D.C., in 1893. The Convention sought to "secure data and statistics of the Denominations; to assist graduates of the schools in securing positions; to provide a fund for the assistance of promising young men and women; and to bring together the educators of the Negro Baptists."[60] The Education Convention focused attention on the church's teaching ministry as well as denominational expansion.

Other mergers also were underway. In 1893, the Foreign Mission Convention merged with the Union of the New England Convention and the Baptist African Mission Convention to become known as the Tripartite Union. In 1894, at the annual meeting of the Foreign Mission Convention, a proposal for a new denomination was presented. It stated:

> *Whereas, the interests and purposes of the three National Bodies, namely, the Foreign Mission, the National, and Educational Conventions, can be conserved and fostered under the auspices of one body; and whereas the consolidation of the three bodies upon the following plan:*
>
> 1. *That there shall be one National organization of American Baptists.*
> 2. *Under this, there shall be a Foreign Mission Board, with authority to plan and execute the foreign mission work according to the spirit and purpose set forth by the Foreign Mission Convention of the United States of America.*
> 3. *That there shall be a Board of Education and a Board of Missions to carry into effect the spirit and purpose of the national and Educational Conventions, respectively.*[61]

The National Baptist Convention of America

The scene was set for the formation of a new national denomination. In 1895, representatives of the Baptist Foreign Mission Convention, the American National Baptist Convention, and the American National Baptist Educational Convention of the United States of America met in Atlanta to form the National Baptist Convention of America.

Elias C. Morris (1855–1922), a former slave born in Murray County, Georgia, was elected president and served in that position until 1922. During the 1870s, he moved to Arkansas, where he became pastor of Centennial Baptist Church in Helena. He also was president of the Arkansas Colored Baptist State Convention, an active Republican, and editor of an African American Baptist periodical.[62] In a presidential address to the National Baptist Convention in Nashville in 1899, Morris observed, "This Society entertains no ill will toward any other Christian organization in the world. It seeks to be on friendly terms with all, and the charge that this organization means to draw the color line, and thereby create prejudice in 'Negro' Christians against 'white' Christians, is without foundation. We admit, however, that practically, and not constitutionally, the color line has been drawn by the establishment of churches and schools."[63] Morris did not hesitate to speak out in behalf of civil rights. He often warned the white majority that blacks would not wait forever to receive the rights to which they were entitled under American law.[64]

W. B. Johnson was another black Baptist pastor who urged his white ministerial colleagues to stand for the "pure, unadulterated gospel" that would end racial divisions. Johnson, pastor of Second Baptist Church, Washington, D.C., was a founder of the National Baptist Educational Convention and the *National Baptist Magazine*. He exhorted white ministers to "rise above racial prejudice" but acknowledged that such courage was difficult, if not impossible, in the face of deep racial prejudices among white Christians. He declared, "So far as the Anglo-Saxon civilization is concerned it may be compared to the religion of Buddha, Brahmin, Confucius or Mahomet, for there is less Christianity in the Anglo-Saxon Civilization as PRACTISED than in those religions which are called heathen. Then brethren, let us preach Christianity and not Anglo-Saxon civilization."[65]

Amid these responses to American racism, black Baptists continued to organize institutions for home and foreign missions, publication, and education. A publishing house was established in 1896 by the Home Mission Board and became an independent entity in 1898. Eric Lincoln and Lawrence Mamiya noted that this show of unity was important for African Americans because the years 1890–1910 witnessed increased legal support for segregation and the "separate but equal" policies of Jim Crow laws, along with the infamous Plessy v. Ferguson case of 1896. They suggest that during this period "the ranks of the black churches, which constituted the sole place of sanctuary, expanded accordingly."[66] Likewise, religious leaders such as W. B. Johnson believed that segregationist statutes demanded a forthright response from the African American community. Johnson insisted that the caricature of the "patient, humble Negro" of earlier eras would be overcome by a "countless army of strong men, who know their rights and will contend for them."[67]

At the founding of the National Baptist Convention (NBC), Georgia pastor Emmanuel K. Love declared:

> I am a loyal Baptist and a loyal Negro. I will stand or fall, live or die, with my race and denomination.... It is just as reasonable and fair for Negroes to want [organizations] to themselves.... It never was true anywhere, and perhaps never will be, that a Negro can enjoy every right in an institution controlled by white men that white men can enjoy. There is not as bright and glorious a future before a Negro in a white institutions there is for him in his own.... We can more thoroughly fill our people with race pride, denominational enthusiasm and activity, by presenting to them for their support enterprises that are wholly ours.[68]

The Lott Carey Baptist Foreign Mission Convention

Unity was difficult to sustain, however. Other African American Baptists, who feared that the NBC was too separatist in its sentiments, met in 1897 to found the Lott Carey Baptist Foreign Mission Convention. Decisions by the National Baptists to drop almost all Virginia members from the Foreign Mission Board and to publish their own literature compelled the Virginians to form a new society. While developing its own programs, the Lott Carey Convention (LCC) maintained cooperation with Northern Baptist mission societies.[69] Its leaders retained connections with white Baptist publishing organizations while continuing the traditions of the old Baptist Foreign Mission Convention.

North Carolina pastor Calvin S. Brown urged the new board to confront the realities of race. He insisted that black Baptists were weak while white Baptists were strong, and commented, "We are a nonentity in politics while they rule with iron. Destiny has shaped the situation, and I must accept it."[70] Even the most basic attempts at cooperative endeavors between black and white denominations and societies were difficult to sustain.

The behavior of the American Baptist Missionary Union in appointing LCC missionaries led Calvin Brown to observe, "The brethren understand from the terms sent us that your board is willing to co-operate with us as a subordinate body instead of a coordinate body. This feature does not meet the approval of our board. From the terms sent us, the brethren seem to get the impression that all of our efforts and doings must be submitted for your approval, and at the same time, we shall be expected to assume all responsibility so far as expenses go."[71]

Nonetheless, the NBC and the LCC established cooperative enterprises during the early twentieth century. In 1905, the LCC moved toward greater cooperation with the NBC while retaining its own identity as an independent missionary board. As Sandy Martin noted, "The LCC retained the right to enter a cooperative arrangement with any other Baptist group," white or black.[72] Yet the settlement did not endure. When the National Baptists split into two conventions in 1916, the LCC and the National Baptists, Unincorporated, developed a working relationship, which ruled out cooperation with the NBC Incorporated group. As Martin commented, "Since 1924 the NBC-Incorporated and the LCC have followed separate paths."[73]

National Baptists and the Publishing House

The publishing house soon became a central institution for the NBC. In an 1893 address, Elias C. Morris called for the founding of such an organization and suggested that it would provide employment for black Baptists and aid in "race development." He asserted, "The solution of the so called race problem will depend in a large measure upon what we prove able to do for ourselves."[74]

The birth of an African American Baptist publishing house led to increased competition with the American Baptist Publication Society. Some black leaders opposed the effort and believed that "such steps would be construed as enmity against our white brethren and friends who had given so much, and endured so much for us."[75] Others, such as Emmanuel K. Love, denounced the "deceitful, disloyal Negroes and Hirelings" who were employed by the American Baptist Publication Society. These black Baptists, Love believed, opposed the establishing of the "laudable Negro (publishing) enterprise [in order to] curry the favor of white people and to be called a good sensible Negro."[76] Conflicts over control of the publishing house divided African American Baptists in the early twentieth century.

In 1915, the NBC Publishing Board became the center of a divisive controversy over denominational control. R. H. Boyd, corresponding secretary of the Home Mission Board and the Publishing Board, moved to incorporate the Publishing Board in documents that made no reference to the NBC. No immediate objection was made to this action, and Boyd built the agency into a multimillion-dollar enterprise, publishing Sunday school lessons and other literature for the churches. In this effort Boyd also received help from the head of the new SBC publishing house.

Boyd built a new building on land he owned personally and chartered it according to Tennessee law. He then became the owner of copyrights for many of the publications. Objections soon arose regarding his control of the Board. The Convention requested that Boyd permit a formal audit of the Publication Board's finances and attempted to bring the agency under greater control of the Convention. Boyd rejected their request, withdrew from the Convention, and founded a new denomination, the National Baptist Convention, Unincorporated. The denomination later became the National Baptist Convention of America. Members of the Boyd family continued to oversee the work of the publishing house throughout the twentieth century.[77]

The Convention soon developed connections to state conventions and regional associations. It established seven boards for Home and Foreign Missions, Foreign Missions, Training Union, Publishing, Evangelism, Benevolence, and Education. At the end of the twentieth century, it claimed approximately 2.5 million members in some 7,800 congregations.[78]

In 1986, the Convention was incorporated and sought greater control over the publishing house. This created yet another controversy and led to the formation of yet another Baptist denomination, the National Missionary Baptist Convention of America. This African American group was founded in 1988 in Dallas. It remains unincorporated but has developed several boards and agencies, including state conventions in California, Oklahoma, and Indiana.[79]

One curious institution related to the National Baptist Convention, Inc., is the denominationally owned Bath House, located in Hot Springs, Arkansas. Purchased from the Federal Government in 1950, it was used as a retreat center and spa for convention meetings and members. At a time when retreat centers, vacation spots, and hotels were closed to blacks across the South, the Bath House filled an important role for families and church groups. The National Baptist Convention participates in the National Council of Churches of Christ, the World Council of Churches, and the Baptist World Alliance.

African American Primitive Baptists

During the early twentieth century, African American Primitive Baptists developed certain denominational alignments while also seeking to maintain the centrality of local church autonomy. In July 1907, the National Association of Colored Primitive Baptists was begun at a gathering in Huntsville, Alabama. By 1916, the group numbered about fifteen thousand members. The name was changed to the National Primitive Baptist Church Convention of the United States of America, Inc. Although more traditional members objected, the denomination established benevolent societies, Sunday schools, and other programs for churches. In 1995, the movement claimed some 1,530 congregations.[80]

The Progressive National Baptist Convention

The Progressive National Baptist Convention was born of yet another controversy, this one relating to leadership in the National Baptist Convention. In 1952, D. V. Jemison retired as president of the NBC and was succeeded by Joseph H. Jackson (1900–1990). That same year, the Convention approved a revised constitution that ended unlimited terms for the president and stated, "A President of this Convention shall not be eligible for re-election after he has served four consecutive terms until at least one year has elapsed."[81] For the next several years, conflicts brewed pitting Jackson and his supporters against those who felt he was exerting too much control over the denomination. By 1956, efforts were being made to "lift" the article on term limits from the constitution. Debates flared, and the matter was tabled until the Convention meeting in 1957. The 1957 Convention reelected Jackson to a fifth term. In response, a group of clergy filed suit, charging, "Dr. Jackson was holding the office in violation of the organization's constitution."[82] The courts supported Jackson in the controversy, and his detractors continued to challenge his position by supporting Gardner C. Taylor for the presidency. This "Taylor group" included Martin Luther King Sr. (1899–1984), Martin Luther King Jr. (1929–1968), Ralph D. Abernathy (1926–1990), Benjamin Mays (1894–1984), L. Venchael Booth (1919–2002), and other well-known Baptist leaders.

In 1960, Jackson was presented by the nominating committee as the only candidate for president and installed in that office. When the dissenters requested a roll call to establish a specific number of votes, Jackson's supporters immediately declared the meeting adjourned.

Dissenting delegates remained and elected Taylor as the new president. These actions were rejected by the opposition. The matter was again taken to the courts, which ruled in favor of Jackson's election. A year later, at the convention meeting in Kansas City, Missouri, the confrontations continued, even to the point of physical attacks. Jackson and his supporters prevailed, and Taylor and members of his group accepted the validity of the election. Jackson then removed Martin Luther King Jr. from offices in the denomination and began a long campaign opposing many of King's methods in behalf of civil rights.

L. V. Booth, pastor of Zion Baptist Church in Cincinnati, one of the first to call for the establishment of a new denomination, held organizational meetings at his church. The dissenters met in Cincinnati in November 1961 to form the Progressive National Baptist Convention, with T. M. Chambers as president. Taylor succeeded him in 1967. Utilizing the motto "Unity, Service, Fellowship, and Peace," the new convention developed its own identity, promoting education and evangelism while supporting the civil rights movement and opposing the Vietnam War. The preamble to its constitution declared, "Therefore, we the members of the Progressive National Baptist Convention, USA, Inc., federate ourselves together in the name of and under the direction and guidance of God, sharing our common faith in Jesus Christ and our concern for strengthening God's work through our common activities."[83]

African American Baptist Women

Women have shaped African American Baptist church life significantly. M. Sobel wrote that early on, "Black women found much room for involvement, expression, and leadership in the Baptist churches, which was in keeping with both the Southern Separatist tradition and earlier African traditions." Many congregations permitted women to serve as deaconesses and some women even preached. With time, however, the women's "sphere" in African American Baptist churches did not include ordained ministry or participation in the pastoral office.[84]

Women participated in the creation and development of multiple institutions in the black Baptist community. Among the early African American missionaries were Lucy Coles and her husband, John J. Coles, of Virginia, appointed to Liberia by the Baptist Foreign Mission Convention in 1889. John Coles died as a result of illnesses contracted in the field. Lucy Coles continued to work actively in the missionary cause, lending her voice to conflicts over funding and connections between mission boards.[85]

Women occupied significant positions in the development of the American National Baptist Convention, founded by William J. Simmons in 1886. Lucy Wilmot Smith spoke for women's suffering in the slavery society as they endured "repression, limitation and servitude." She urged women to develop important occupations within their place in a farm economy. Harvey observed that for Smith, "individual success and racial solidarity were intertwined."[86]

Smith's friend Mary Cook Parrish, another leader in the American National Baptist Convention, insisted that once the "vitalizing principles" of Baptist life and thought were brought to bear on Christian religion, "women will become free." She suggested that women's traditional roles within the "bounds of propriety" would not need to be changed, however.[87]

Delores C. Carpenter wrote, "Baptist women were recognized in the early 1900s as elocutionists, lecturers, field secretaries for the Women's Conventions, missionary workers, teachers, writers, training school directors, Bible Band workers, and orators."[88] She identified a group of significant but little-known black Baptist women, including Ida Becks, who served as secretary of the Colored Women's League of Dayton, Ohio, in the early 1900s. Another, Ella Whitfield, was matron at Guadalupe College and later served as a field worker in Joanna Moore's Bible Band. In that capacity she gave 491 speeches and visited 823 homes and 312 churches.[89]

From the beginning, women were in the majority in most, perhaps all, African American Baptist churches, and they exercised considerable influence within the "sphere" that developed around them. Missionary activity was a vital part of women's activities in the black churches.

Women's Mission Societies

African American women formed mission societies during the late 1800s, first in local churches and associations and then in national organizations. During this period, some 154 societies were founded by African American women associated with the National Baptist Convention.[90] These societies were established "to promote the purity, intelligence, and happiness of our homes, and to educate the women of our Baptist churches in a knowledge of missions, to cultivate in them a missionary spirit, and thus lead them to help in mission work at home, in the State, in our country, and in foreign lands."[91]

Many of the members worked hard to retain the autonomy of these societies. They funded their own missionaries as auxiliaries related to the broader Baptist denominations. The societies met periodically for worship, mission education, and mutual encouragement. Their commitment to the mission enterprise fostered a variety of fundraising methods. At an Alabama Woman's Day service in the early 1900s, one woman observed, "I am president of a mission band which meets once a month to learn of our duty to missions. We tax ourselves one nickle [sic] a month, and this is our donation to the work." Another woman remarked, "I raise chickens. One hen in my yard I've given to God. This money is from her eggs and chickens."[92]

In 1900, the Baptist Women's Missionary League was established alongside the National Baptist Convention. In 1901, in spite of male opposition, the League became the Women's Missionary Auxiliary to the Convention. Even though women were not permitted to have official leadership posts in the Foreign Missions Board or state conventions, they continued to give considerable support to the missionary endeavor.

The Women's Society supported missions and education. In 1909, members helped organize the National Trade and Profession School for Women and Girls in Washington, D.C. It provided elementary and secondary education with a curriculum in liberal arts and training for commerce or missions. Its founder and principal was Nannie Helen Burroughs (1883–1961), one of the foremost female supporters of African American Baptist missions. Burroughs selected the land for the school and raised the $50,000 necessary to construct the first building. In 1901, she became president of the Women's Auxiliary, serving until 1920. Her efforts, it was said, encouraged black women "to stand together as women with common ideals of work, of standards of living, of service, and of self-respect."[93]

Many of the early colleges and academies founded to educate freed persons became coeducational in a relatively short period of time. For example, Shaw University (North Carolina) was opened to women in 1872, and by 1880 only two of the schools founded by whites for blacks were not coeducational.[94]

Spelman Seminary, Atlanta, founded in 1881 for training African American women, and Hartshorn Memorial College, begun in Richmond, Virginia, in 1884, were funded in part by the Women's Baptist Home Mission Society. Both were established to provide education for "colored girls."[95] The Hartshorn Seminary was founded by Carrie V. Dyer, who also raised monies for missionary work. The leaders of the American Baptist Home Mission Society, the sponsor of these schools, were committed to the education of black Baptist women. In an 1880 report on the issue, Charles Ayers, president of Natchez Seminary, insisted, "Give us the ministers and the women and we will lift the masses of our free people."[96]

Anglo-based mission societies in the North also commissioned African American women to serve as missionaries. The Women's American Baptist Foreign Mission Society appointed Louise (Lula) Celestia Fleming (1862–1899) to serve as missionary to the Congo in 1886. She was the first black woman appointed for full-time service by that agency. She also was the first female medical worker to receive appointment to a Baptist mission field. She initially worked as a nurse but returned to the United States and received training as a medical doctor. She went back to the Congo in 1895 and remained there until 1899, when illness forced her back to the United States, where she succumbed to a variety of sleeping sickness.[97]

Evelyn Brooks Higginbotham wrote that ABHMS leaders did not distinguish "between black and white women when integrating lessons of refinement and other 'ladylike' proprieties into the liberal arts curriculum." Rather, they founded schools for black women much as they had for whites. Such an action was surprisingly progressive, given the ridicule that came from many Northern and Southern whites who suggested that educated black women tried to put on "airs."[98]

The schools themselves were not without racial incidents. Many white Baptists were hesitant to hire black professors for the faculties of African American schools. Higginbotham noted, "African Americans waged power struggles in all of the schools established by the northern white Protestant denominations, but Baptists suffered the greatest dissension."[99]

Nannie Helen Burroughs led in the creation of a school founded by blacks for blacks. As noted previously, she was the first corresponding secretary of the National Baptist Convention, Women's Auxiliary, founded in 1901. (The Women's Missionary League had been organized the previous year.) Burroughs grew up in Washington, D.C., and worked for a time as bookkeeper and secretary in the offices of the National Baptist Convention Foreign Mission Board, located in Louisville, Kentucky. While in Louisville, she helped to found the Association of Colored Women.

In 1901, Burroughs called upon the NBC to establish a training school for black women. Initially ignored, she continued to press for such an institution until it was approved and founded as the National Trade and Profession School for Women and Girls in Washington, D.C., in 1909. Burroughs herself raised much of the money for the school. The school sought to train women in what Burroughs called the "three B's"—Bible, bath, and broom. When it was destroyed by a fire in 1926, Burroughs's fundraising skills enabled it to reopen just two years later.[100]

One of her most enduring contributions was in urging churches to hold Woman's Day services—a practice that became an important part of many African American Baptist churches. While the emphasis was on foreign missions, it became an important vehicle for encouraging women's leadership in churches that were often hesitant to ordain women to ministry.[101]

Women and Ordination

The ordination of women remains a matter of debate among many African American Baptists. Yet by the end of the twentieth century, many African American women sought ordination in Baptist churches, often to great controversy. In a survey conducted in the late 1990s, Lincoln and Mamiya found only limited enthusiasm among black Baptist clergy for the ordination of women. In a study of Progressive National Baptists, 42.7 percent approved of women's ordination, while 57.3 percent disapproved. Members of the National Baptist Convention, U.S.A., Inc., disapproved of women's ordination by 73.6 percent to 26.4 percent.[102] The ordination of women occurs most often among Progressive National Baptists or in the American Baptist Churches USA.

African American Baptists and the Civil Rights Movement

While African American Baptists were at the forefront of the civil rights movement in the United States, they did not always agree on the means for accomplishing those ends.

Black Baptists greeted with enthusiasm the 1954 Supreme Court decision in the case of *Brown v. the Board of Education* and the effort to desegregate Southern schools. In September 1954, Joseph H. Jackson, president of the NBC, proposed that a day of reflection, celebration, and mourning be held on the two-year anniversary of the ruling. These observances were held throughout the country in May 1956.[103] Jackson also suggested that May 17 be designated a national holiday to celebrate democracy, freedom, and the Constitution. The proposal was introduced by congressional representative and Baptist pastor Adam Clayton Powell Jr., but it never got out of the judiciary committee.[104]

When Rosa Parks resisted the demand that she move to the back of the bus in Montgomery, Alabama, on December 1, 1955, black Baptists moved quickly to support the Montgomery bus boycott. The Dexter Avenue Baptist Church and its pastor, Martin Luther King Jr., soon became the center of the movement. Although he would later break with King, NBC president Joseph H. Jackson affirmed the effort to break the back of segregation in Montgomery and offered denominational funds in support. At its 1956 annual meeting, the Convention praised the boycott and invited Ralph Abernathy, Baptist pastor and civil rights activist, to address the gathering.[105] As Andrew Manis has shown, King, Abernathy, and other African American Baptists believed that desegregation and civil rights were the ultimate expression of American freedom, enabling the nation, in King's words, "to live out the true meaning of its Creed."[106] Court decisions, changes in laws, and the triumph of their struggle for integration led many black Baptists to see "God himself" as an active participant in their struggle for civil rights.[107]

Martin Luther King Jr. was both a Baptist pastor and the primary leader of the civil rights movement in the United States. Educated at Morehouse College, Crozer Seminary, and Boston University, where he received a Ph.D. in 1954, King served as pastor of Dexter Avenue Baptist Church and, along with his father, Martin Luther King Sr., later served as co-pastor of the Ebenezer Baptist Church, Atlanta, Georgia. King's work in the Montgomery boycott, his participation in the founding of the Southern Christian Leadership Conference, and his powerful rhetorical skills propelled him to such leadership. King's "I Have a Dream" speech, delivered at a massive rally at the Lincoln Memorial in Washington, D.C., in August 1963, became one of the great addresses in American history.

His concern for nonviolent resistance, nurtured in the black Baptist churches of his youth and influenced by Mahatma Gandhi's work in securing independence for India, became a hallmark of his antisegregation efforts. Arrested for his participation in civil rights demonstrations in Birmingham, Alabama, King issued his famous "Letter from a Birmingham Jail," chastening moderate whites, especially local ministers, for failing to respond decisively to the cause of freedom and justice.

In September 1963, the bombing of the Sixteenth Street Baptist Church, Birmingham, causing the death of four young women at Sunday school, galvanized the nation and gave poignant recognition to the role of Baptists in the efforts to end segregation. Local black Baptist ministers, such as Fred Shuttlesworth at Bethel Baptist Church and John Thomas Porter at Sixth Avenue Baptist Church, though not always in agreement, worked throughout the movement in Birmingham. King received the Nobel Peace Prize in 1964 and was assassinated in April 1968 in Memphis, Tennessee, while preparing to participate in a demonstration in behalf of the town's sanitation workers.

The list of African American civil rights leaders is itself a history of black Baptists in the latter half of the twentieth century. Even a partial list illustrates the extensive presence of Baptist preachers and churches in the movement. These included King lieutenants Ralph David Abernathy, Jesse Jackson, and John Lewis. Fred Shuttlesworth, Wyatt Tee Walker, A. D. King, John Porter, Adam Clayton Powell, and Gardner Taylor all served local Baptist congregations, North and South, amid their work for civil rights. After King's death, African American Baptists continued to work for civil rights throughout American society, with civil rights leader Jesse Jackson going on to pursue the Democratic nomination for president of the United States in 1984 and 1988.

African American Baptists: Facing the Future

Writing at the beginning of the twentieth century, Wallace Smith delineated the challenges facing African American Baptists and their churches. He noted that many younger blacks were "abandoning" the civil rights legacy and entering numerous factions. Some, benefiting from the earlier movement, gained "upward mobility" but became "indifferent" to the continuing racism around them. Others have found new community among non-Christian movements, especially the Nation of Islam. Still others have been influenced by Pentecostal spirituality, often participating in "Full Gospel" Baptist churches. Questions of ministerial authority, women's ordination, and female leadership also provide significant challenges for African American Baptists.[108]

At the end of the twentieth century, some Baptist groups experienced new cooperation. For example, National and Progressive Baptists began various cooperative endeavors, including the Revelation Corporation, a joint program of the two denominations concerned for issues of economic development in African American communities.[109] "Dual alignment" became an option for many African American churches that maintain membership in more than one denomination.

By the latter part of the twentieth century, there were eight specific African American denominations evident in the United States. These included the three largest groups: the National Baptist Convention, U.S.A., Inc.; the National Baptist Convention of America; and the Progressive National Baptist Convention, Inc. Smaller groups included the Lott Carey Baptist Foreign Mission Convention; the National Primitive Baptist Convention, U.S.A.; the United Free Will Baptist Church; the National Baptist Evangelical Life and Soul Saving Assembly of the U.S.A; and the Free For All Missionary Baptist Church, Inc.

Within the American Baptist Churches USA (ABCUSA) there is also a significant segment of African American churches. Known as the American Baptist Churches of the South, it grew out of a grassroots effort to bring black and white churches together in direct relationship with the ABCUSA. By 1970, some one hundred congregations, black and white, had developed connectional relationships within the ABCUSA. The organizational meeting for this denominational subgroup was held at Myers Park Baptist Church in Charlotte, North Carolina. Leaders included, among others, Carlyle Marney, pastor of the Myers Park Church; Kelly Miller Smith, pastor of First Baptist Church, Capitol Hill, Nashville; and LeRoy Jordan, pastor of the First Baptist Church, Tulsa, Oklahoma.[110]

As the twentieth century drew to a close, leadership in African American churches passed to a new generation of clergy and laity. Female preachers such as Suzan Johnson Cook, pastor of Bronx Christian Fellowship; Carolyn Knight, professor of homiletics at the Interdenominational Theological Center, Atlanta; and Prathia Hall, director of the African American studies program at Boston University, gained prominence in Baptist pulpits and classrooms. New York preachers such as Johnny Ray Youngblood, Calvin Butts, and Al Sharpton provided religious leadership and political response to issues inside and outside the Baptist family, often with considerable controversy across a broad spectrum. Wallace Smith concluded,

> From our inception as a people we Baptists have been a fragmented lot. And we African Americans, in the words of James Melvin Washington, have been a 'Frustrated Fellowship.' We have struggled to gain access into the larger Baptist family, but also have found challenges getting along within our African American family. The new spirit of ecumenism has helped. Rigid lines between denominations are no longer as fearsome as once was the case. Now is the time for intradenominational walls to also come down.[111]

Notes

1. A representative collection of such works includes W. E. B. Du Bois, *The Negro Church* (Atlanta: Atlanta University Press, 1903); Carter G. Woodson, *The History of the Negro Church* (Washington, D.C.: Associated Publishers, 1921); Albert Raboteau, *Slave Religion: The "Invisible Institution" in the Antebellum South* (New York: Oxford University Press, 1978); Eugene Genovese, *Roll, Jordan, Roll: The World the Slaves Made* (New York: Pantheon Books, 1974); and Melville J. Herskovits, *The Myth of the Negro Past* (New York: Harper, 1941).
2. Genovese, *Roll, Jordan, Roll*, 235; Ralph Reavis, "The Development of Black Baptists in Virginia, 1867–1882," in Everett Goodwin, ed., *Baptists in the Balance* (Valley Forge, Pa.: Judson Press, 1997), 334.
3. William A. Clebsch, *From Sacred to Profane: The Role of Religion in American History* (New York: Harper & Row, 1968), 89.
4. Walter F. Pitts, *The Old Ship of Zion: The Afro-Baptist Ritual in the African Diaspora* (New York: Oxford University Press, 1993), 45.
5. Ibid.
6. James H. Cone, *Black Theology of Liberation* (Philadelphia: Lippincott, 1970), 38–39. See also David O. Moore, "The Withdrawal of Blacks from Southern Baptist Churches Following Emancipation," *Baptist History and Heritage* (July 1981): 12–13.

7. James Melvin Washington, *Frustrated Fellowship: The Black Baptist Quest for Social Power* (Macon, Ga.: Mercer University Press, 1984), 21.

8. Pitts, *Old Ship of Zion*, 38.

9. Ibid., 49.

10. Washington, *Frustrated Fellowship*, 24; William Warren Sweet, *The Baptists, 1783–1830*, vol. 1 of *Religion on the American Frontier* (Chicago: University of Chicago Press, 1931), 329.

11. Sweet, *The Baptists*, 320.

12. Ibid., 334, 337, 360–61.

13. Moore, "Withdrawal of Blacks," 17.

14. Mechal Sobel, *Trabel'n On: The Slave Journey to an Afro-Baptist Faith* (Westport, Conn.: Greenwood Press, 1979), 98. See also William H. Myers, *God's Yes Was Louder Than My No* (Grand Rapids, Mich.: Eerdmans, 1994), 212. Myers concluded, "Little doubt should remain today that continuity exists between African-American religious experience and African religions" (213).

15. Virginia Baptist State Convention, *Proceedings of Fifth Annual Session* (Petersburg, Va.: Jos. Van Hold Nash, 1872), 14 (cited in Reavis, "Development of Black Baptists," 337).

16. Mary R. Sawyer, "Sources of Black Denominationalism," in *Down by the Riverside: Readings in African American Religion*, ed. Larry G. Murphy (New York: New York University Press, 2000), 61–63.

17. Paul Harvey, *Redeeming the South: Religious Cultures and Racial Identities among Southern Baptists, 1865–1925* (Chapel Hill: University of North Carolina Press, 1997), 46.

18. Washington, *Frustrated Fellowship*, 9.

19. James M. Simms, *The First Colored Baptist Church in North America* (1888; reprint, New York: Negro Universities Press, 1969), 15–16. George Liele was something of a controversial figure among African American Baptists. Although he worked extensively to establish black Baptist missions, churches, and overall identity, many are critical of his actions relative to whites. For example, he seems to have hesitated to challenge white authority on any level.

20. Owen D. Pelt and Ralph Lee Smith, *The Story of the National Baptists* (New York: Vantage Press, 1960), 30.

21. Woodson, *Negro Church*, 34. Debates continue as to the actual date of the founding. The cornerstone of the church lists the original date as 1750. See also C. Eric Lincoln and Lawrence H. Mamiya, "The Black Baptists: The First Black Churches in America," in Goodwin, ed., *Baptists in the Balance*, 100.

22. Simms, *Colored Baptist Church*, 39, 51.

23. Ibid., 46–47.

24. Washington, *Frustrated Fellowship*, 10. Carter Woodson suggested that the Savannah church "flourished" from 1779 to 1782. Lincoln and Mamiya use the date 1788 as the founding year (see "The Black Baptists," 101).

25. Washington, *Frustrated Fellowship*, 10–11.

26. Ibid., 11.

27. Simms, *Colored Baptist Church*, 59–60.

28. Washington, *Frustrated Fellowship*, 11.

29. Ibid., 12 (citing Charles Colcock Jones, *The Religious Instruction of the Negroes in the United States* [Savannah, Ga.: Thomas Purse, 1842], 52–58).

30. "Reminiscences of the First African Church," *American Baptist Memorial* 14 (September 1855): 263.

31. Ibid.

32. Ibid., 265.

33. Lincoln and Mamiya, "The Black Baptists," 101.

34. Pitts, *Old Ship of Zion*, 46.

35. Ibid.

36. H. Richard Niebuhr, *The Social Sources of Denominationalism* (New York: Meridian Books, 1957), 192.

37. Woodson, *Negro Church*, 77–78.

38. James Washington suggested that this association was organized in 1834 by Robert Townsend (see *Frustrated Fellowship*, 28). H. Leon McBeth used the 1836 date (see *The Baptist Heritage* [Nashville: Broadman, 1987], 781).

39. Washington, *Frustrated Fellowship*, 29.

40. Ibid., 30. Washington dated the founding of this association to 1836, but McBeth preferred 1840 (see *The Baptist Heritage*, 781).

41. Washington, *Frustrated Fellowship*, 31.

42. Ibid., 28.

43. Gregory A. Wills, *Democratic Religion: Freedom, Authority, and Church Discipline in the Baptist South, 1785–1900* (New York: Oxford University Press, 1997), 76–78.

44. Washington, *Frustrated Fellowship*, 38.

45. Henry C. Gregory III, "Black Baptists," in B*aptists and the American Experience*, ed. James E. Wood (Valley Forge, Pa.: Judson Press, 1976), 313–15.

46. Sandy D. Martin, *Black Baptists and African Missions* (Macon, Ga.: Mercer University Press, 1989), 51.

47. Ibid., 183.

48. Ibid., 184.

49. Frederick Richardson, "American Baptists' Southern Mission," *Foundations* 18 (April–June 1975), 136–37.

50. Harvey, *Redeeming the South*, 65. Harvey lists the twenty-eight schools funded by the ABHMS (66). They include Selma University (1878), Spelman Seminary (1881), Shaw University (1865), and Virginia Union University (1865).

51. Richardson, "American Baptists' Southern Mission," 138.

52. Ibid., 142.

53. Ibid., 143–44.

54. Ibid., 63.

55. William L. Banks, *A History of Black Baptists in the United States* (Philadelphia: Continental Press, 1987).

56. Bill J. Leonard, ed., *Dictionary of Baptists in America* (Downers Grove, Ill.: InterVarsity Press, 1990), 249.

57. Sandy D. Martin, "The Baptist Foreign Mission Convention, 1880–1894," *Baptist History and Heritage* 16 (October 1981): 16.

58. Martin, *Black Baptists,* 176.

59. Ibid., 24.

60. Ibid., 95.

61. Pelt and Smith, *National Baptists,* 29–30.

62. Harvey, *Redeeming the South,* 189.

63. Elias C. Morris, *Sermons, Addresses, and Reminiscences, and Important Correspondence* (1901; reprint, New York: Arno Press, 1980), 93.

64. Harvey, *Redeeming the South,* 189.

65. Ibid., 191.

66. Lincoln and Mamiya, "The Black Baptists," 105.

67. Harvey, *Redeeming the South,* 193.

68. Edwin S. Gaustad, "Baptists and the Making of a New Nation," in Wood, ed., *American Experience,* 51.

69. Ibid., 73.

70. Martin, *Black Baptists,* 153–54.

71. Ibid., 156–57.

72. Ibid., 163.

73. Ibid., 163.

74. Ibid., 57.

75. Ibid., 71.

76. Ibid., 72.

77. Lincoln and Mamiya, "The Black Baptists," 109–12.

78. Ibid.

79. Albert W. Wardin, ed., *Baptists around the World: A Comprehensive Handbook* (Nashville: Broadman & Holman, 1995), 414–15.

80. Frank S. Mead, *Handbook of Denominations in the United States,* 9th ed. (Nashville: Abingdon, 1995), 70–71.

81. William D. Booth, *The Progressive Story: New Baptist Roots* (St. Paul: Braun Press, 1981), 2.

82. Ibid., 17.

83. Wallace C. Smith, "Progressive National Baptist Convention: The Roots of the Black Church," *American Baptist Quarterly* 19 (September 2000): 253.

84. C. Eric Lincoln and Lawrence H. Mamiya, "The Black Denominations and the Ordination of Women," in Murphy, ed., *Down by the Riverside,* 368.

85. Martin, *Black Baptists,* 159–62. Coles's conflicts were over funding from the various boards and are discussed in these pages.

86. Harvey, *Redeeming the South,* 239.

87. Ibid.

88. Delores C. Carpenter, "Black Women in Religious Institutions," in Murphy, ed., *Down by the Riverside,* 101.

89. Ibid.

90. Martia Bradley, "The Work and Witness of Southern Negro Baptist Women from 1865 until 1935," *Quarterly Review* 37 (October–December 1976): 54.

91. Ibid. (citing Charles O. Boothe, *Cyclopedia of the Colored Baptists of Alabama* [Birmingham: Alabama Publishing Company, 1895], 261).

92. Ibid., 55 (citing J. A. Whitted, *History of the Negro Baptists of North Carolina* [Raleigh, N.C.: Edwards & Broughton, 1908], 118).

93. Ibid. (citing L. H. Hammond, *In the Vanguard of a Race* [New York: Council for Woman for Home Missions and Missionary Education Movement of the Unites States and Canada, 1922], 61).

94. Evelyn Brooks Higginbotham, *Righteous Discontent: The Women's Movement in the Black Baptist Church, 1880–1920* (Cambridge: Harvard University Press, 1993), 21. The coed schools were Shaw University (North Carolina), Benedict Institute (South Carolina); Nashville Institute (Tennessee); Natchez Seminary (Mississippi); Leland University (Louisiana); and Wayland Seminary (Washington, D.C.). The two males-only schools were Richmond Institute in Virginia and Atlanta Baptist College (Morehouse) in Georgia.

95. Ibid., 57 (citing *Negro Education* I [Washington, D.C.: Government Printing Office, 1917], 130).

96. Ibid.

97. William H. Brackney, *The Baptists* (New York: Greenwood Press, 1988), 166–67.

98. Higginbotham, *Righteous Discontent,* 30.

99. Ibid., 51.

100. Ibid., 211–21.

101. Carpenter, "Black Women," 101–2.

102. Lincoln and Mamiya, "Ordination of Women," 372.
103. Andrew Michael Manis, *Southern Civil Religions in Conflict: Black and White Baptists and Civil Rights, 1947–1957* (Athens, Ga.: University of Georgia Press, 1987), 61–62.
104. Ibid., 62.
105. Ibid., 68.
106. Ibid., 77 (citing Martin Luther King's "I Have a Dream" speech).
107. Ibid., 97.
108. Ibid., 255–56.
109. Ibid., 257.
110. Leroy Fitts, *A History of Black Baptists* (Nashville: Broadman, 1985), 302–3.
111. Ibid., 258.

Chapter 12
Baptists in Greater Britain

THROUGH EMIGRATION, EVANGELIZATION, AND THE DIRECT WORK OF THE Baptist Missionary Society, a Baptist presence was extended to countries associated with English Baptists in "greater Britain" and in the British Commonwealth. It developed in various ways in situations that took shape around specific cultural, theological, and political realities. Controversies over open versus closed communion, polity, and associational relationships were evident in each of these Baptist communities.

Baptists in Ireland

The Baptist Union of Ireland

From their beginnings in the seventeenth century, Irish Baptists developed a distinct identity. When English Baptist leader Andrew Fuller visited the churches in 1804 and offered pastoral advice in matters of doctrine and polity, he generally was ignored. When Fuller departed after six weeks, he was convinced that the Irish Baptists were an undisciplined lot, absorbed by endless disputes and short on evangelistic fervor. He wrote to a friend, "And with respect to the Irish Baptists themselves, I am not without hope that a new description of Baptists will rise up among them, of the spirit of the Evangelical episcopalians who appear after all the best body of Christians in Ireland."[1]

Connectionalism among congregations evolved slowly and with some difficulty. The Irish Baptist Association was dissolved in 1821. Reorganized in 1862, it continued until 1895, when it became the Baptist Union of Ireland.[2] The Association fostered cooperation among churches along with the training and preparation of ministers. A "general meeting" was convened annually. Joshua Thompson commented that the Association encouraged "the proper administration of baptism and the Lord's supper, church membership and discipline, the orderly conduct of business and the observance of occasional days of fasting and prayer in the churches for specific needs. Annually it arranged a systematic supply of approved preachers for vacant churches." Thompson concluded, "It is clear that the IBA throughout the eighteenth century was an important focus of identity and solidarity for the scattered Baptist community, and that it was active into the nineteenth century."[3]

Associational worship services included baptisms, ordinations, and celebration of the Lord's Supper. Circular letters facilitated theological discussion among the churches.

Questions regarding requirements for church membership led to this 1812 response from the Irish Baptist Association: "Resolved that any person who we believe is truly converted to God, if they apply for baptism and church fellowship shall be received into the communion of our Churches."[4]

Baptist churches in Ulster, Northern Ireland, developed separately from the Irish Baptist Association. These Ulster congregations owed their origins to Alexander Carson (1776–1844) and David Cook (ca.1769–1847), both of whom had strong ties to the Scottish Baptists. Carson joined the Baptists due to the influence of the brothers Robert and James Haldane, evangelical preachers in Scotland who had formed independent churches throughout the country. These churches observed weekly communion and practiced strict discipline. Some Haldane churches in Scotland and Ireland accepted believer's immersion. Such a new Baptist community was founded in Ireland in 1809.[5] The Haldane influence led to the formation of several Baptist churches in Ulster, yet the impact was limited. Alfred Underwood observed that while Carson revived Baptists' witness in Ireland, "he was rather a solitary star, for Baptist principles have never made any great headway in that island."[6]

English Missions in Ireland

Among English Baptists, a concern for evangelization in Ireland led to the formation of the Baptist Society for Promoting the Gospel in Ireland (the Baptist Irish Society [BIS]) in 1814. Isaac McCarthy (ca.1780–1859) was employed as an itinerant evangelist. The Society, formed in London under the leadership of Particular Baptist minister Joseph Ivimey, was constituted "to employ itinerants [preachers] in Ireland, to establish schools, and to distribute Bibles and Tracts, either gratuitously or at reduced prices."[7] It maintained a close relationship with the Baptist Missionary Society (BMS).

Ivimey was an advocate of education. He encouraged the Society to found schools whose "fundamental object is, to teach the most destitute to read the Holy Scriptures without note or comment, in their own language.... And, that every possible obstacle may be removed, no Creed, Catechism, or Confession of Faith, can be introduced."[8] Through the work of the BIS, Baptists founded schools, organized evangelistic activities, and established new churches in Ireland.

As a potato famine descended on Ireland in the 1820s and 1830s, the BIS attempted to provide some relief. In County Mayo in 1831, a BIS itinerant named James Allen established a soup kitchen in his own house, and he reported, "The poor creatures are dropping down at our door daily, and we are obliged frequently to give them wine to revive them."[9] In the 1840s, as the famine became far more acute, Allen and others led the BIS in developing additional strategies for fundraising and food distribution.[10]

The famine led to a massive movement of Irish immigrants to America and Canada—a diaspora that had significant impact on the Baptist churches. Pastor Thomas Hassell, of County Tipperary and the Cloughjordan Baptist Church, noted, "Thousands of protestants have emigrated to America—Methodists and Baptists have directed their course to Canada."[11] Baptists who remained benefited from a revival that descended on Ulster in

1859, extending a spiritual renewal to the churches and increasing church membership.

Changing times and economic realities led to the decision in 1864 to merge the Baptist Irish Mission Society and the Baptist Home Missionary Society. The merger took effect in 1865 with the organization of the British and Irish Baptist Home Mission Society. In 1890, the organizations again divided, and the British and Irish Baptist Home Mission Society was renamed the Irish Baptist Home Mission, becoming a self-supporting body that promoted missionary activity in Ireland alone.[12]

The Irish Baptist Association was reactivated in 1862 to provide cooperative support for the missionary enterprise. In 1895, the name was changed to the Baptist Union of Ireland. These Baptists broke with the Baptist Missionary Society and formed the Irish Baptist Foreign Mission Society in 1924. John D. Rockefeller Sr. helped to fund the formation of the Irish Baptist Training Institute. It later became the Irish Baptist College, located in Belfast.

Theology in the Irish Baptist Context

Irish Baptists were not immune to internal divisions over theology and practice. As an evangelical Calvinist, Alexander Carson wrote extensively on theological topics, often igniting controversy over limited atonement, saving faith, and baptism. Like most Irish Baptists, Carson advocated the plenary verbal inspiration of Scripture. He insisted, "The Honour of Revelation, the comfort and edification of the believer, and the truth of the express statements of the Scriptures themselves, demand our belief that the Bible, as originally given, is DIVINE IN EVERY WORD."[13] Of limited atonement, he wrote, "If there is anything plainly taught in Scripture, it is that the sacrifice of Christ was made for those only who shall eventually be saved by it."[14]

Divisions over communion broke out in many Irish Baptist churches. Some opened communion to all believers, while others administered it only to the immersed. Like the Scots, they preferred a "plurality of elders" ordained and serving in each congregation, only one of whom was designated pastor. This was different from English Baptists, who preferred a pattern that utilized one elder and numerous deacons.[15]

A concern for ministerial education led Hugh D. Brown to found the Irish Baptist College in 1892. Its purpose was "to give young men, members of our Baptist Churches, who have been evidently called of God to the Ministry of the Word, an opportunity for systematic study which they could not otherwise obtain."[16] Brown was an advocate of Charles Haddon Spurgeon's positions in the English "Downgrade Controversy" and wanted a school to protect orthodoxy among Irish Baptists.

Irish Baptists and Home Rule, 1886–1922

Home rule, whether political or religious, did not come easily for Irish Baptists. For seventy-five years (1813–1875), a British Baptist committee had "direct rule" over the "Irish Mission." Governance of the mission finally was relinquished to the Irish Baptist Association in 1888. Of the political complications between Ireland and England, Thompson wrote, "Irish Baptists, consequently, believed in political change by constitutional means. They rejected the use of illegal force or threats of violence by Protestants and Catholics alike, and looked to parliament and the Crown to maintain law and order."[17] Like other Protestants, many Baptists feared that they would be drawn into a Catholic state and thus favored close alliance with the British. This led them to object to the possibility of political home rule. On the one hand, they accepted "denominational home rule," which transferred the Irish Mission from the Baptist Union to the Irish Baptist Association. This arrangement was acceptable because it permitted them to control their own evangelistic and ecclesiastical processes. Political home rule, on the other hand, meant Roman Catholic dominance and therefore was unacceptable.[18]

Irish Baptist Conservatism

When Eire attained independence in 1922, Irish Baptists did not recognize the border as an ecclesiastical boundary. The majority of the churches in the six northern counties that remained British continued to form part of the same Union as the churches of Eire.

The conservatism of Irish Baptists was evident in their actions throughout the nineteenth and twentieth centuries. In 1888, a conservative confession of faith was accepted and later expanded. To this day, member churches, pastors, and new converts are required to affirm its principles.[19]

Conservative ideals led Irish Baptists to eschew membership in both the Baptist World Alliance and the European Baptist Fellowship. In 1955, the Irish Baptist Union declared, "While we believe that a very large percentage of the leaders of the Baptist World Alliance, at the present time, consists of evangelicals, nevertheless so far as we know the Baptist World Alliance has no constitution that would exclude from its membership those who hold views contrary to our Basis of Doctrine. In view of this we recommend that the question of affiliation with the Baptist World Alliance be dropped."[20]

The organization maintained its public opposition to the "ecumenical movement," asserting that the movement's beliefs and practices undermined the theology of "conservative evangelicals."[21] The Union does not have membership in the World Council of Churches but does participate in the Fellowship of Evangelical Baptists in Europe and in the Conservative Baptist International Mission Fellowship based in the United States.[22]

During the 1960s, Irish Baptist opposition to ecumenism also was related to overtures toward Roman Catholics. A resolution unanimously adopted at the Baptist Union affirmed "opposition to the Movement and to the Romeward trend observable today in many quarters."[23] It suggested that the "union" sought by the ecumenical movement was "unscriptural," "would not work," and "would do more harm than good." The resolution restated the Irish Baptists' Basis of Doctrine insistence on "the verbal inspiration and the all and sole sufficiency of the Holy Scriptures of the Old and New Testaments as originally given." It declared, "An organization composed of such heterogeneous elements would not be a Christian church, but rather a caricature of that Church which is His body. For this reason, if for no other, Irish Baptists are not in membership with the World Council of Churches, or indeed with any organization affiliated to it."[24]

During the latter part of the twentieth century, numerical growth among Irish Baptists was slow but steady. In 1938, there were eighteen congregations, and by 1995 that number grew to over 150 with some fifteen thousand members. The Irish Baptist Union is comprised of representatives of two national Baptist groups, the National Association of Northern Ireland and the Southern Association for the Republic of Ireland. Most members and churches are in the North.[25]

Baptists in Scotland

The Sandemanians

The Baptist movement in Scotland was influenced by John Glas (d. 1773), a Presbyterian preacher released from his church in Tealing in 1730 for his views favoring Independency (Congregationalism) and his advocacy of religious liberty. Glas's views gained popularity and led to the formation of numerous churches. The English initially referred to the followers of Glas as Glasites and later as Sandemanians—a reference to Robert Sandeman, Glas's son-in-law and successor.

Sandeman's views were published in the popular work *Letters on Theron and Aspasio*. As Restorationists, the Sandemanians sought to replicate the practices of the New Testament church as closely as possible. They insisted that reconciliation with God through Christ was accomplished without any outward repentance or act of profession. The truth of the gospel could be accepted simply through passive assent.

Sandemanians encouraged church discipline, spiritual holiness, and separation from those who indulged in sin. Their leadership rested in a multiplicity of elders chosen by the congregation. They required that at least two elders be present when the Lord's Supper was celebrated and discipline administered. Sandemanians chose deacons and deaconesses to care for the daily needs of the faithful. They practiced infant baptism, observed weekly communion, and advocated certain biblical dietary regulations. While they rejected gambling, they permitted their members to attend theaters and other public gatherings.[26]

The first Scottish Baptist church came directly from the Glasite/Sandemanian community. Its founders, Robert Carmichael (d. 1774) and Archibald M'Lean (McLean) of Glasgow (1733–1812), served as elders in a Glasite congregation. By 1764, M'Lean had determined that believer's immersion was the true New Testament mode. Carmichael reached similar conclusions and received immersion from John Gill in 1765 in London. In June of that year, he returned to Edinburgh and baptized seven persons in Edinburgh. The group then constituted a Baptist church. Like the Glasites, they maintained a "plurality of elders" and required strict discipline and unanimity in admitting persons to membership. They administered the Lord's Supper weekly and promoted "spiritual exhortation" among the members.[27] Soon other Baptist churches connected to M'Lean were founded in England and Wales.

M'Lean wrote extensively, including a popular work entitled *The Commission Given by Jesus Christ to His Apostles Illustrated,* in which he outlined the nature of the gospel, along with the meaning of faith and baptism. M'Lean's biblicism led him to question certain traditional elements of Christology. Derek Murray described his views: "He took issue with the Westminster Confession on this point, fearing that the concept of eternal generation, which he could not find explicitly in scripture, might lead to Arianism. Therefore Scotch Baptists were taught that Christ is the Son of the Eternal God, not the Eternal Son of God. This led to dissension in the Edinburgh Church."[28]

M'Lean also insisted that conversion was a rational confession that Jesus was the Christ. Andrew Fuller responded that this approach would "render faith a mere bone of contention, and their zeal will be consumed in the tithing of mint and cummin."[29]

Scottish Baptists were intent on maintaining doctrinal unity among their congregations. As Brian Talbot commented, these Baptists were concerned that their "basic principles ...

be maintained, even if it guaranteed that their basic numerical strength would never rise above a few thousand individuals."[30] They seem to have been particularly committed to replicating the New Testament church. An 1808 treatise noted, "They also hold it their indispensable duty to follow entirely the pattern of the primitive apostolic churches, and all the directions given them."[31] Churches seeking admission to associations encountered extensive examination regarding their doctrinal positions.

Scottish Baptists in the Nineteenth Century

The nineteenth century witnessed the rise of influence of the Haldane brothers, Robert and James, who accepted Baptist views in 1808. They fostered debates over the nature of the church, believer's baptism, and other doctrines that divided Congregationalists (Independents) and led to the formation of Baptist churches in Grantown-on-Spey, Elgin, Arbroath, Falkirk, Dublin Street, Edinburgh, and elsewhere. By 1810, there were forty-one Baptist churches in Scotland.[32]

In 1824, the Home Missionary Society for Scotland was founded. Although intended for ministry throughout the country, its primary labor was in the Highlands and the coastal islands among poorer classes of "Gaelic-speaking labourers." Work in the cities began slowly and with difficulty.[33] In 1827, the Society united with the Baptist Highland Mission to become the Baptist Home Missionary Society for Scotland.

English Baptist churches also were founded in Scotland. Their single-pastor leadership gained increasing prominence among the Scottish Baptists. Unity was elusive to these diverse Baptist communions, which Whitley saw to be "as busy as beavers and as unsociable as otters."[34]

English Baptist churches in Scotland were closely aligned with Particular Baptists in theology and practice. This affinity for Calvinism made them compatible with Scottish Baptists, who seem to have considered them a "sister" communion and led to joint participation in missionary endeavors through the Particular Baptist Missionary Society.[35]

Denominational Organizations

In 1835, the Scottish Baptist Association was formed by representatives of Haldane churches and the Home Mission churches to encourage fellowship, evangelism, and effective communication among congregations. It was concerned to "educate young men of ability and piety."[36]

In 1843, the Scottish Baptist Association became the Baptist Union of Scotland through the leadership of Francis Johnstone (1810–1880). Born to a Baptist family in Edinburgh, Johnstone was educated at Edinburgh University and soon entered the ministry. After serving several Baptist churches in England, he returned to Scotland in 1842 as pastor of a church in Cupar. He founded a school for ministers there and moved it to Edinburgh in 1846. Johnstone was a central figure in the creation of the Baptist Union of Scotland. The new organization grew slowly and was subject to severe criticism from other Protestant groups. Many Baptists were suspicious of such unions, and the group disbanded when Johnstone left Scotland in 1856.[37]

A second Baptist Union was founded in Glasgow in 1869 with William Tulloch as its first secretary. The initial membership included some fifty-one congregations. According to its constitution, the organization brought together those who accepted "evangelical doctrines as distinguished from Rationalism and Socinianism on the one hand and from Ritualism and Romanism on the other."[38] Its members promoted missionary endeavors and mutual encouragement "to aid young men" in preparation for the ministry, and to provide for inter-church cooperation.[39] The Union fostered church extension and the construction of church facilities throughout the country.

By the 1870s, the Scottish Baptist Union had established programs, committees, and funds to provide ministerial annuity, provide support for ministers' widows, and assist churches in securing building funds. In 1872, the Union entered into cooperation with the Baptist Union of Great Britain and Ireland. Special attention was given to Sunday school and youth programs—all aimed at evangelizing and training Christian young people.

Many members of the Union disagreed over educational methods. Some Scottish Baptists objected to ministerial education altogether, convinced that it fostered pride and undermined genuine spirituality. Some preferred that candidates for ministry be tutored by individual pastors, while others insisted that they study in Protestant schools at home or abroad. Many desired that a new Scottish Baptist institution be established.[40]

In 1894, the Baptist Theological College of Scotland was founded in Glasgow to provide theological education for ministers. Baptist layman Joseph Coats, a professor of pathology at the University of Glasgow, was named president. Almost immediately, the school was attacked for teaching "higher criticism" in biblical studies. In response, faculty member Jervis Coats declared, "As well might we be afraid that the everlasting stars will fall because sharper eyes and more perfect instruments are being directed towards them ... as believe that the Word of God, which liveth and abideth forever, can possibly suffer in its vital essence from that modern treatment to which it is being subjected."[41] In its seventy-fifth year, the Theological College moved to the campus of the University of Glasgow. Some Scottish Baptists continued to criticize its curriculum and teaching methods as too liberal.

By 1906, the Scottish Baptist Union accepted the British Union declaration of principle, with its three points of unity. The Union originally voted to affiliate with the World Council of Churches, though by a small majority vote. In 1956, after extensive debate and discussion, the Union withdrew from the World Council because of fears similar to those entertained in Ireland.[42]

Scottish Baptist Women

In 1909, the Women's Auxiliary to the Baptist Union of Scotland was formed on the following principles: (1) organizing the Baptist women of Scotland for the spread of evangelical truth and Baptist principles; (2) assisting the Union in promoting any scheme for the advancement of the denomination in Scotland; (3) appointing and supporting deaconesses; and (4) organizing women's work generally in the churches. These goals were achieved except for the development of the office of deaconess in Scottish churches.[43] Later in its history, the Auxiliary supported the work of certain women evangelists.

Scottish Baptist Church Life

Scottish Baptist churches felt the impact of the Welsh revivals, as prayer and preaching services created a renewal of religious fervor throughout the country.[44] Eight congregations were founded in 1878 alone, described as "centres whence flow forth the most beneficent influences for the amelioration and regeneration of the race."[45] Sunday schools flourished, reporting 2,467 students in 1869 and 10,220 by 1889. Boys' Brigade clubs were founded in the 1880s to aid inner-city youth, organizing them in military-like bands. The group's methods were controversial. The Adelaide Place St. Clair Street Mission was among those churches that disbanded the organization, rejecting "anything that tends to foster a warlike spirit in boys."[46]

Many nineteenth-century Scottish Baptists were strong supporters of the temperance movement. The Scottish Baptist Total Abstinence Society was founded in 1881, and numerous churches established Bands of Hope to instruct young people regarding the dangers of liquor and the social problems it provoked.[47]

Baptists in Wales

Welsh Baptists began missionary societies as early as 1776, when they initiated specific work in North Wales with assistance from the (English) Particular Baptist Fund. About this time, some congregations began to send funds to the Baptist Missionary Society to aid William Carey and the other missionaries in India.[48]

A gathering of Welsh and English ministers in Swansea in 1815 ended with formal commitments to collect BMS funds in Wales. The Welsh Baptist associations apparently were divided into six districts. This complex arrangement had mixed impact on missionary funding in Wales. Thomas Bassett concluded that an examination of the years 1815–1830 revealed "that the intentions of the Swansea conference were never realised and that the organization set up was rather haphazard."[49]

During the eighteenth and nineteenth centuries, many Welsh Baptists were influenced by McLeanism (M'Leanism), which had its origins among the Scots. The group's claim to reconstitute the New Testament church had a strong appeal to many Welsh Baptists.[50]

McLeanism came to North Wales through the work of John (Richard) Jones (1765–1822), a well-known Baptist preacher who accepted these views by 1795. In 1801, he led an exodus of Welsh Baptists to break with the Particular Baptist churches and form a new association in relationship with the Scotch or McLeanist Baptist churches.[51]

Welsh Baptist Church Life
Church life among Welsh Baptists mirrored that of other Baptist communions in Britain with varying distinctives. Local churches placed great emphasis on nurturing their own members to ministry, and a succession of pastors came from the membership of specific congregations. For example, the church at Swansea "provided its own ministry for 127 years; Llanwenarth for 90 years until 1745." Ministers would discern gifts in certain youth (males), take them on pastoral "rounds," and give them opportunities to address church meetings in various ways. Theological education was passed on through formal and informal training from ministers to ordinands.[52]

Debates and divisions occurred over open versus closed communion, the laying on of hands to the newly baptized, and Calvinist versus Arminian views. Seventeenth-century Welsh Baptists were, for the most part, Calvinist in sentiment, but Arminian attitudes were evident among certain ministers and congregation, often causing great controversy. The

Welsh Association frequently was asked to mediate when congregations divided over theological questions, often related to the Arminian sentiments of their ministers. Some questioned traditional theological language. In the late 1770s, Nathaniel Williams challenged the use of the word "Trinity" and noted, "Father, Son and Holy Ghost, are Scriptural names ... but a Trinity of persons is not Scriptural."[53]

Baptists' refusal to baptize infants meant that their births were not officially registered by established churches. This required some Welsh Baptists to develop "naming" ceremonies in which children were registered by the church and their names announced publicly with witnesses. This represented an early form of infant "consecration"—a practiced criticized by some Baptists as "sham baptism."[54]

Baptisms were administered outdoors, often as a self-conscious witness in the face of ridicule and "hooliganism" from non-Baptist observers. Communion generally was held monthly as a second service following the preaching of the word and was attended only by members of the congregation. Churches used ordinary wine, distributed in a common cup. In most seventeenth-century Welsh churches, the laying on of hands was given to the newly baptized. In many Welsh congregations, the deacons seem to have had great authority—a fact often bemoaned by the ordained ministers.[55]

Eighteenth-century Welsh Baptists conducted services on Sunday and monthly prayer meetings on Wednesday. They did not observe Christmas, Easter, Lent, or Whitsun. Churches were meeting places in which tempers could flare—and not uncommonly did so. Noise from infants, children, and dogs in church interfered with many a minister's sermons.[56]

Theological Education in Wales

Welsh Baptists moved slowly in addressing issues of ministerial education. As Joshua Thomas observed, "It is the general opinion of the Baptists in Wales, that grace and ministerial gifts are given by God; and in the same way that God, in the time of the apostles called learned men, and men without much learning into the work of the ministry, so he sees good to do today."[57]

Around 1734, an academy for ministers established at Trosnant, Pontypool, and it lasted until around 1770. After that, many Welsh ministerial students went to the Baptist theological college in Bristol. In 1807, Micah Thomas (1778–1836?) was chosen tutor of a new school established at Abergavenny. The school was transferred to Pontypool in 1836, later to become South Wales Baptist College.[58]

The College was not without controversy. Some Baptists withheld contributions until assurances were given that the Welsh language would have significant place in the curriculum. In 1834, five students left the school amid complaints that the school monitored their behavior too closely and that the principal, Micah Thomas, favored a student who held Arminian sentiments. The Northern Association of Welsh Baptists agreed to continue funding the College, but only if it came under greater associational control. Micah Thomas soon resigned. Bassett commented, "This unpleasant bickering went on for years."[59]

By the early nineteenth century, many Welsh Baptists were retreating from earlier challenges to the political establishments. In 1817, a group of Baptist ministers in Anglesey presented a declaration to the local justice of the peace. It stated, "It is not the province of Christians, to debate and discuss politics—but to behave humbly towards our superiors...."

Sirs, we do not feel the least interest in the great noise about universal suffrage, annual Parliaments, reform of Parliament, abolishing of the tithe and many other things."[60]

Others disagreed. In 1834, the Monmouthshire Quarterly Meeting petitioned Parliament "that no specific form of religion be the subject of the government's exclusive recognition and legal support ... and especially that all dissenters be relieved from oppressive enactments."[61] These views apparently prevailed among some Welsh Baptists throughout much of the nineteenth century. In July 1891, the *North Wales Chronicle* commented, "We regret to say that the Baptist denomination has produced quite a crop of agitating ministers whose little knowledge has been the most dangerous thing with which the forces of law and order has had to contend."[62]

Baptists in Australia

Baptist Beginnings and Growth

The British settlement of Australia began in 1787, when Captain Arthur Philip and a group of convicts reached Botany Bay, now Sydney. Although there were a few Baptists among the early Australian settlers, no congregation was organized in Sydney until 1831, with the arrival of preacher John McKaeg. Controversy soon erupted over McKaeg's business practices, his drinking habits, and his time in debtor's prison, and the church experienced schism.[63] Another chapel was begun in Tasmania in the 1830s.

Appeals for help from England received little immediate response. The BMS suggested that its charter required them to send missionaries to non-Christian, not "civilized" (British), societies. The BMS finally sent John Saunders (1806–1859), who arrived in December 1834. Two years later, he organized Sydney's Bathurst Street Baptist Church. The congregation maintained open baptism and communion policies, and its constitution asserted that "all applicants who could produce satisfactory evidence of Christian experience and character irrespective of baptism" could be admitted to membership.[64] The church took the Baptist name but maintained a more generically Protestant orientation, thereby appealing to a religiously diverse community of settlers. Saunders acknowledged his concern to lead persons "to sacraments, by first leading them to Christ. Neither are we to attempt merely to turn men from one party to another or to proselyte them from one sect to another."[65]

Saunders's attempt to avoid sectarianism was important for developing a Christian presence in the new colony. Australian Baptist John Bollen wrote of Saunders's action, "A Baptist cause in Sydney had thus begun by ignoring Baptist particularity, by not differentiating itself, in membership at all or in doctrine clearly, from the rest of evangelical Protestantism."[66] In distinguishing its broad-church openness, the Bathurst Street Church proclaimed, "Obliged to take a denominational badge in an age of so many divisions, ours is indeed a Baptist communion; but we consider ourselves entitled to a higher distinction; we pursue a nobler aim than the extension and perpetuation of sectarian differences."[67]

Other early Baptist ministers included Henry Dowling (1780–1869), who came to Hobart Town about the same time as Saunders. Lay preacher David McLaren began work in South Australia, and William and Mary Gibson helped found churches in Tasmania.[68]

Baptist work in Queensland originated with former associates of the Presbyterian John D. Lang (1799–1878), who hoped to create a Christian commonwealth in the new colony. One of Lang's followers was Charles Steward, a Baptist minister who became pastor of the United Evangelical Church in Queensland. Likewise, Johannes Gossner's Berlin Mission of 1836 led German and British Baptists to the colony in the 1840s. Gossner's specific mission failed, but many of his efforts increased the Baptist presence.[69]

A Baptist congregation began in Brisbane in 1855, and in 1859 Wharf Street Baptist Church became the first official Baptist congregation in Queensland. This church, influenced by Charles Haddon Spurgeon, later became known as the City Tabernacle.[70] By century's end, there were more than thirty Baptist churches in the colony. The Baptist Association, later known as the Baptist Union of Queensland, was founded in 1877.

Association and Denomination

While these churches were Particular Baptist in theology and doctrine, they often reflected considerable diversity regarding open versus closed communion. Schisms over such matters soon emerged. In 1861, conservatives left the Wharf Street Church, with its open member-ship policies, and formed the Jireh Baptist Church. The new congregation limited its membership to immersed persons and permitted only church members to receive communion. Jireh was Queensland's only Strict and Particular Baptist church. The Jireh Church nonetheless participated in founding the Baptist Association—an organization that endured until 1978.[71] The Association was comprised of seven churches, and its first president was James Voller, pastor of the Bathurst Street Church.

As Australian Baptist churches took shape, some of their leaders continued to complain about the indifference of the BMS to their work. In his presidential address to the tenth session of the Baptist Association of Victoria in 1870, Pastor James Martin noted, "If other denominations at home had thought as little of the colonial possessions of Great Britain as our own, and had done as little in proportion as we to supply the means of grace as the population grew and multiplied, all the religious institutions of Victoria would have been confined to a mere handful of inhabitants, and the rest would have been left to hopeless ignorance and spiritual destitution."[72]

The formation of the Association of New South Wales was one of the early signs of Baptist denominationalism in Australia. The New South Wales Association blended traditional Baptist beliefs with certain broad-church sentiments. As Baptist leader James Greenwood observed in 1871, "God has filled the world with marvellous variety.… Ought we not then to expect the mind to be equally various?"[73]

Churches grew slowly. The Baptist Union reported eleven churches in 1868, with only six ministers. In 1882, there were only sixteen churches and no more than ten ministers. Church attendance among the Congregationalists doubled between 1871 and 1881, while Baptists experienced only a slight increase during the same period.[74]

During the late nineteenth century, Australian Baptists, along with other evangelicals, opposed parochial school education, especially as established by Roman Catholics. James Greenwood led in movements to develop "free, secular and compulsory" education in Australia.[75]

Baptists in South Australia worked to combine denominational identity with interdenominational cooperation, aided in their task by the British pastor Silas Mead, who arrived in 1861. Mead's commentary on Baptist beliefs was summarized in his response to questions from the chairperson of the Congregational Union. For Mead and other South Australian Baptists, the role of the individual in interpreting Scripture and doctrine was primary. He commented, "Our contention today is—Nothing between us and the written word and law of God. Baptist churches exist to plead the independence of personal judgement. We obey no collective body, whether within the Baptist circle or without, which assumes to define for us what we are to believe and what not to believe."[76]

South Australia was the one British colony effectively founded by a Baptist, the merchant George Fife Argus (1789–1878). He ensured that its constitution would make it a "paradise of dissent."

Baptist endeavors in South Australia brought forth fruit. In 1910, one in every 77 persons in South Australia was a member of a Baptist church; in Victoria, it was one in 171; and in New South Wales, one in 333.[77] By the early twentieth century, things had changed. New South Wales Baptist churches, asserting their Baptist identity more sharply, showed extensive growth, while Southern Australian Baptists experienced decline. Debates over open versus closed membership continued, further complicated by the rise of "modernism" in many churches. Proposals for a union of Methodists, Congregationalists, Presbyterians, and Baptists were widely discussed but were unsuccessful.[78]

Unity and Division

Debates over doctrine and Baptist distinctives were evident in the work of C. J. Tinsley, pastor of the Stanmore Church. Sent to study at Spurgeon's Pastors' College, London, in 1898, he returned to the Stanmore congregation in 1902. He warned that doctrinal divisions that had led to Charles Spurgeon's break with the British Baptist Union should not be permitted to divide Australian Baptists. In a 1912 address given while serving as chairperson of the Baptist Union, Tinsley distinguished between "evangelical," the formal stance of other denominations, and "evangelistic," a love for souls that should characterize the Baptist witness. He warned that the loss of doctrinal solidarity and evangelistic fervor would bring decline in both the spirit and the number of the Baptist community in Australia.[79] Tinsley, along with John Ridley and Wilfred Jarvis, was a well-known evangelist who helped extend Baptist numerical success in the early twentieth century.

Amid these doctrinal disputes, some Australian Baptists reasserted the centrality of Baptist distinctives. In a 1938 discourse entitled "The Call for a Very Distinctive Baptist Note in Our Preaching and Teaching," Pastor B. A. Rogers identified Baptists as the true heirs of New Testament Christianity. He argued, "It is not the question of the mode and subject of baptism that keeps us aloof from other denominations. Our separate identity is based on something much deeper than that. In order that we be not misunderstood, it is necessary to give utterance to the whole body of Baptist doctrine."[80]

At Century's End

Australian Baptists claim five theological colleges, spread across the country. Schools were founded at Melbourne (1891), Brisbane (1904), Sydney (1916), Adelaide (1952), and Perth (1963).

Australian Baptists participate in the Baptist World Alliance and the Baptist World Aid program. They spent several decades debating whether the Australian Baptist Union or any of its six regional unions should join the World Council of Churches. In 1961, the Executive Committee of the Baptist Union released a pamphlet that explored the cases for and against membership in that organization. Although the Baptist Union has no membership in the World Council, some regional bodies seem more involved in ecumenical relationships than others.[81]

At the end of the twentieth century, Australian Baptists claimed about sixty-five thousand members in almost one thousand churches. Besides the Baptist Union, there are at least nine other Baptist subgroups in Australia.[82]

Baptists in New Zealand

Founding Churches

Baptists were among the early settlers of New Zealand, largely due to emigration from Scotland. The Hanover Street Church, founded in 1863 in Dunedin, was the first Baptist congregation in the colony. Some fourteen different Baptist groups were organized over a period of thirty years. The Baptist Union of New Zealand was established in 1882 to "promote the union of Baptist churches throughout the colony."[83]

The Baptists who arrived in the 1840s generally came as individuals, not in groups. Like other settlers, they sought to improve their economic status in a frontier environment. New Zealand was an affordable place to "take the cure" from illnesses that plagued persons in Britain.[84] One such person was Thomas Kirk, who made the journey in 1862, in his thirty-fourth year, seeking to improve his health and his economic status. After years of hard labor, he became the first curator of the Auckland Institute and Museum. Moving to Wellington in 1874, he became a founding member of the Baptist church there and later one of the presidents of the Baptist Union of New Zealand.[85] From the 1850s through the 1870s, Baptist churches were established throughout the colony, largely by laity who immigrated to the region.

The early Baptist churches were founded by the laity. Paul Tonson observed, "Up to 1882 there were eighteen laymen who had particular pastoral responsibilities in the churches. Seven of these gained legal recognition as Officiating Ministers for marriage purposes."[86] Many took pastoral charge of specific churches, conducting baptisms, communion, and other ministerial duties. One lay pastor was James Wright Sawle, a British native who arrived with his wife and their seven children in the 1860s. Five more children were born to them in New Zealand. He served as pastor of two churches in Malvern County and lived to the age of eight-five. Contemporaries described him as "a vigorous man, half flame, half muscle."[87]

Mission Agencies

Early missionary efforts began with Silas Mead, minister of Flinders Street Baptist Church, Adelaide, Australia, who called a gathering to establish a missionary society. This meeting produced the South Australian Baptist Missionary Society in 1864, the first such organization to be founded in the southern hemisphere.[88] A concern for missionary work led South Australians to send missionaries to India in 1881. The society engaged two females, Ellen

Arnold and M. T. Gilbert, to become missionaries to zenana women. Arnold arrived in 1885. Mead wanted the united mission movement to link Australia and New Zealand Baptists in a mission to East Bengal, India.[89]

While Baptists in Australia and Tasmania joined in some missionary action, New Zealanders did not participate. William Carey, grandson of the well-known missionary, served for a time as minister in New Zealand at the Lincoln Church in Canterbury. He arrived in 1883 and departed a few years later for mission work in India. An Australian (Baptist) Board of Foreign Missions was founded in 1913.[90]

Conflicts between the native Maoris and the settlers eventually led to the "Maori Wars." Apparently, Baptists maintained better relations with the indigenous peoples than did most others. In his *History of New Zealand,* Alfred Saunders reported that Maori leader Wiremu Kingi advised his people to "respect the persons and property of the Baptist minister [Thomas Gilbert] and other persons who had refused to carry arms against him; and his followers required these gentlemen to wear white scarves so that they and theirs should remain unharmed in any destruction or pillage that might occur at any time."[91]

Baptist Ministers

The New Zealand churches reflected General, Particular, and New Connection Baptist sentiments but resisted those designations. Their early doctrinal statements included articles on biblical inspiration, a regenerate church membership, baptismal immersion, and the atoning death of Christ. Tonson noted, "The doctrinal statements in New Zealand Baptists constitutions have never provided more than a minimal definition of belief."[92]

Denominational Organizations

The first Baptist association in New Zealand was constituted at the Hereford Street Baptist Church in Canterbury in 1873, and it included six of the seven churches in the town. This association—a prelude to a wider Baptist Union—was founded "to advance the cause of the Lord Jesus Christ by promoting the formation of Christian Churches, by the sustenance of Evangelists, by the assistance of Pastors, by giving counsel if requested, touching matters connected with any of its associated churches, or by such other means as its Executive may deem fit."[93] Membership was composed of churches and individuals who offered financial support.

The Canterbury Association was instrumental in the formation of the Baptist Union of New Zealand in 1882. The new organization immediately approved a constitution containing eleven clauses of "principles" and six clauses of "rules." These ideas remain a part of the existing constitution of forty principles and thirty-one rules. Tonson remarked, "From the beginning until now [1982] the Baptist Union of New Zealand has not required churches or ministers to assent to any particular creed."[94] Charles Carter, a former missionary in Ceylon, was elected the first president of the Union.

The New Zealand Baptist Missionary Society was founded at Dunedin, October 1885, at the fourth annual meeting of the Baptist Union of New Zealand.[95] Its first endeavors included missions to the Maoris and to India. Support came from free-will offerings, some collected through "missionary boxes" placed in every Baptist home. *The New Zealand Baptist* reported, "Not only have we formed our New Zealand Baptist Missionary Society, but we are profoundly gratified to announce that, already, a lady-worker [Miss Fulton of

Dunedin] impelled by the love of the Lord, is offering herself for the Field. The thing now needful is that the Churches and schools should set their machinery to work to secure the necessary funds. Let us be as enthusiastic as we ought to be in so glorious a cause."[96] Fulton was sent to Bengal, India. The Society's early statistics were impressive. J. Ayson Clifford observed, "Between the years 1881 and 1886 the number of census Baptists expanded by 25% from 11,476 to 14,357, while the general population increased by 18%."[97]

The Maori mission was undertaken by Alfred Fairbrother, a minister sent out from Spurgeon's College in 1883. The Union supported the effort, largely through contributions from Auckland's Tabernacle Baptist Church. There were few conversions, and Fairbrother was continually frustrated by certain native customs, particularly the use of home-brewed liquor. His behavior toward the Maoris created controversy with the Missionary Society, and in 1885 charges were brought against him. They included these: "Native drunk at meeting, so Mr. Fairbrother would not preach there. Did not visit sick. Pulled pipes out of mouths of men and women and rebuked them in bad temper. Threw sticks at woman who disturbed public worship. Put lights out before meeting finished because he wanted to go to another meeting. Did not impress the men favourably, and attendances fell."[98] Fairbrother soon resigned, and the mission to the Maoris was discontinued.

Leaders among New Zealand Baptists

Decimus Dolamore was one of the first ordained ministers in New Zealand. He arrived in 1851 to serve a group of Baptists near Nelson. Charles Carter, a longtime BMS missionary to Ceylon, moved to New Zealand in 1882 to lead the Ponsonby Church in Auckland. Thomas Spurgeon, son of the renowned preacher, came to Auckland in the 1880s seeking "the cure" for health problems. He accepted a pastorate in Auckland and encouraged his father's church to send a missionary to the Maori people of New Zealand. The church complied, and Alfred Fairbrother went as missionary in 1883, ending his work in 1885.

England's Stepney College provided many of the colony's ministers, among them Charles Dallaston (d. 1934), who spent his life in New Zealand and served two terms as president of the New Zealand Baptist Union. Not all who came, however, remained. Many ministers returned to England or Australia after only a brief sojourn in New Zealand.[99] In an effort to attract new ministers, some Baptists turned to newspaper advertisements. Auckland Baptists published this ad in the *New Zealander*, in 1853:

> *The Christian Brethren, commonly called Baptists, desire to intimate to the Inhabitants and Strangers of Auckland, that they meet for divine Worship, in the school room, Albert Street, near Smale's Point every Lord's Day in the morning at eleven and in the evening at six o'clock. The services are for the present mutually conducted by the members of the church. The order of Worship is STRICTLY PRIMITIVE. In the morning the Lord's Supper, reading the Scriptures, Exhortation, Prayer and Praise are attended to; and in the evening, a discourse is delivered by one of the Brethren. The people are invited to attend.*[100]

In 1888, New Zealand Baptists faced a series of crises, including a general economic depression, declining numbers, and the residue of divisions produced by the Downgrade Controversy—Charles Haddon Spurgeon's dispute with the British Baptist Union. The latter situation was complicated by the presence of Spurgeon's son, Thomas, as pastor of the

Auckland Tabernacle. The New Zealand Baptist Union resisted the controversy and contributed to Thomas Spurgeon's support as a full-time national evangelist. He traveled throughout the country conducting revivals, and he attracted great crowds by his preaching and his famous name. When Charles Haddon Spurgeon died in 1892, Thomas Spurgeon returned to England and succeeded his father as pastor of the Tabernacle in London.[101]

Like his father, Thomas Spurgeon used a variety of "new methods" to reach the unchurched public. As a missioner in New Zealand, he often gave public lectures on popular themes that concluded with an invitation to Christian faith. In lectures such as "The Conquest of the Congo," he used a technological wonder called the "oxy-hydrogen limelight" to show photographs on a screen.[102]

Alfred North, another leader of the Union, was pastor of the Hanover Street Church, Dunedin, for eighteen years. From the 1880s to the 1920s, North held most of the major offices of the Union, presiding over many of its committees and programs. At age sixty-five he was named General Organiser for the Union, charged with founding new churches across the colony.

In 1887, the Union initiated a training program for New Zealand Baptist ministers. One of the first graduates was John James North, who served New Zealand churches from 1895 to 1945. North arrived in New Zealand when he was eleven and distinguished himself in the university and the ministerial training program. Elected president of the Baptist Union in 1905, his presidential address revealed the influence of Social Gospel leader Walter Rauschenbusch. Commenting on "the Socialism of Jesus," he asserted, "You can no more separate social activity from Christian faith than you can untwist light and heat plaited in a sunbeam."[103] One direct response to social needs came in 1914 when the Union founded the Remuera Children's Home. In its first fifty years, some eight hundred children benefited from its services.

Theological Studies

In 1924, John J. North proposed a theological college to be established in Auckland with funds secured from churches, individuals, and "legacies." The idea gained support, and the Baptist College began in March 1926, with North as principal. He taught courses in Bible, theology, dogmatics, ethics, and preaching until his retirement in 1945.[104]

He was succeeded by Luke H. Jenkins, a graduate of Regent's Park College, Oxford. He also taught a variety of courses, including Bible, theology, Greek, Hebrew, ethics, literature, and preaching, and was the only full-time instructor at the school. Controversy regarding Jenkins's appointment, methods, and beliefs created increasing difficulties, and he resigned in 1953. He was succeeded by E. Roberts-Thompson, an Australian pastor trained in England at Bristol Baptist College. During his tenure, the student body increased from eighteen students in 1954 to thirty-one in 1960. The curriculum was changed to allow for accredited degrees to be secured in conjunction with the licentiate and bachelor of theology at the Melbourne College of Divinity. In 1960, the school was renamed the New Zealand Baptist Theological College.[105]

Women in New Zealand Baptist Life

Early histories of New Zealand Baptists give only limited attention to the work of women in the churches. As in other Baptist communities, women were not full participants in the governance of Baptist organizations. Initially, only men were appointed as delegates to the

Baptist Union. New Zealand women received the right to vote in national elections in 1893, but it was not until 1908 that the Baptist Union voted "that women, equally with men, are eligible as delegates from churches to the meetings of the Union."[106]

Although women did not serve as preachers, they taught Sunday school, organized prayer meetings, and provided Bible instruction. Catherine MacDougall was named a "city missioner" by the Hanover Street Baptist Church, where she worked with street people, particularly women of ill repute.[107] A 1910 editorial in the *New Zealand Baptist* declared, "How delightfully illogical we are. We allow a woman [Queen Victoria] to grace the Throne of this mighty Empire, and forbid her a seat in our legislative halls. We make her pastor in all but name [missionary] of our most difficult charges in India, and shudder at the bare suggestion of the Rev. mrs Smith being pastor of Hanover St., Dunedin."[108]

The first Baptist Women's League was organized in Auckland in 1947, and a national women's society was formed in 1952. In 1956, the first deaconess course was offered in the Theological College. It included theological and biblical instruction along with home nursing, crafts, singing, "blackboard work," and "elementary automobile mechanics."[109] Pat Preest, the first deaconess student at the school, returned in 1972 for ministerial training and was ordained at Remuera, later serving as a hospital chaplain in Hawkes Bay. During the late 1970s, at least four other women were ordained by Baptist churches.[110]

In the early 1950s, the Baptist Union established a Maori Department and appointed Joan Milner to work with the tribe. In 1954, she organized Bible schools and other programs, beginning at Pukekohe. She was joined by Des Jones and Dora Whitehead, both recent university graduates. Maoris who joined the church through these efforts were encouraged to accept leadership in the churches.[111]

Growing Denominational Identity
In 1945, there were five regional "auxiliaries" of New Zealand Baptist churches. In 1957, these cooperative endeavors became known as "associations." Supporters suggested that "the new name expressed more clearly the fellowship that our churches enjoy in the various districts and it is also a term which is widely used in other Baptist Unions."[112] The Auckland Association was particularly active in various evangelistic and social service endeavors. It provided loans for the building of new churches, establishing a youth hostel and senior citizens' homes.

Concerns over membership in the World Council of Churches continued to confront the New Zealand Union, and in 1964 a new report evaluating membership was prepared, recommending continued membership in the World Council, but with periodic reviews. It was approved by a wide margin of the delegates to the national assembly.[113] At the end of the twentieth century, there were some twenty-five thousand Baptists in New Zealand, with approximately 225 churches.

Baptists and British Connectionalism

At the end of the twentieth century, the British Commonwealth was a loose connection of countries linked by heritage, economics, and democratic government. Baptist churches in the British Isles and in former colonies acknowledged their common history with British Baptist theological and ecclesiological church life. At the same time, Baptists in these British-related countries had long developed their own identities and responses to theology, polity, and government. At century's end, each confronted rising secularism, religious pluralism, and the need to extend Baptist identity to a generation uncertain as to the importance of certain Baptist distinctives.

Notes

1. B. R. White, ed., *Association Records of the Particular Baptists of England, Wales and Ireland to 1660*, 3 vols. (London: Baptist Historical Society, 1971–74), 2:8 (citing letter from Andrew Fuller to John Saffery [September, 8, 1813]).
2. Joshua Thompson, *Century of Grace: The Baptist Union of Ireland: A Short History, 1895–1995* (Belfast: Baptist Union of Ireland, 1995), 3.
3. Joshua Thompson, "Baptists in Ireland, 1792–1922: A Dimension of Protestant Dissent," (D.Phil. diss., Oxford University, 1988), 11–12. Thompson's research suggests that Irish churchgoers were more energetic in their faith than previously inferred.
4. Ibid., 20.
5. Ibid., 31–32.
6. Alfred C. Underwood, *A History of the English Baptists* (London: Baptist Union Publishing Department, 1947), 196.
7. Thompson, "Baptists in Ireland," 46 (citing *Baptist Magazine* [1814]: 218–19).
8. Ibid., 61 (citing Joseph Ivimey, *The Teacher's Guide in Conducting the Native Irish Schools* [London: 1816], 5–6).
9. Ibid., 108 (citing letter from James Allen to Joseph Ivimey [July 30, 1831]).
10. Ibid., 114.
11. Ibid., 125.
12. Ibid., 198.
13. Ibid., 235 (citing Alexander Carson, *Works*, 5 vols. [Dublin: William Carson, 1847–63], 3:93).
14. Ibid., 234 (citing Carson, *Works*, 1:321).
15. Ibid., 239.
16. Ibid., 242 (citing *Baptist Union of Ireland Handbook* [1899–1900], 5).
17. Ibid., 256.
18. Ibid., 262.
19. Albert W. Wardin, ed., *Baptists around the World: A Comprehensive Handbook* (Nashville: Broadman & Holman, 1995), 187–88.
20. Thompson, *Century of Grace*, 147.
21. Ibid., 148.
22. Wardin, ed., *Baptists around the World*, 188.
23. Baptist Union of Ireland, *Irish Baptists and the Ecumenical Movement* (Glasgow: Baptist Union of Ireland, 1964), n.p.
24. Ibid.
25. Wardin, ed., *Baptists around the World*, 188.
26. Thompson, "Baptists in Ireland," 29–31.
27. Ibid., 30.
28. David W. Bebbington, ed., *The Baptists in Scotland: A History* (Glasgow: Baptist Union of Scotland, 1988), 22.
29. Underwood, *English Baptists*, 191.
30. Brian Richard Talbot, "The Origins of the Baptist Union of Scotland, 1800–1870," (Ph.D. diss., University of Stirling, 1999), 33.
31. Ibid. (citing William Jones, "A Compendius Account of the Principles and Practices of the Scottish Baptists," *The Theological Repository* 4, no. 23 [April 1808]: 199–200).
32. Derek B. Murray, *The First Hundred Years: The Baptist Union of Scotland* (Dundee: Baptist Union of Scotland, 1969), 12; Bebbington, ed., *The Baptists in Scotland*, 32.
33. Rev. Dr. Patterson, "The Baptist Denomination in Scotland," in *The Baptist Denomination in England, Wales, Scotland and Ireland*, ed. Joseph Angus (London: J. Heaton and Son, 1863), 23.
34. Ibid., 13.
35. Talbot, "Baptist Union of Scotland," 127–30.
36. Patterson, "Baptist Denomination in Scotland," 13.
37. Bebbington, ed., *The Baptists in Scotland*, 43.
38. Ibid., 37.
39. Ibid., 37–38.
40. Ibid., 72.
41. "The Baptist Theological College of Scotland, Jubilee, 1894–1944," 4.
42. Bebbington, ed., *The Baptists in Scotland*, 115–17.
43. Murray, *The First Hundred Years*, 78.
44. Bebbington, ed., *The Baptists in Scotland*, 62.
45. Ibid., 52.

46. Ibid., 62–63.
47. Ibid, 53.
48. Thomas M. Bassett, *The Baptists of Wales and the Baptist Missionary Society* (Swansea: Ilston Press, 1991), 5–8.
49. Ibid., 12.
50. "The McLeanist (Scotch) and Campbellite Baptists in Wales," *Transactions of the Baptist Historical Society* 7 (1920–21): 147–50.
51. Ibid., 165–66. Some McLeanite churches in Scotland and Wales also were influenced by the Restorationist theology of Thomas and Alexander Campbell.
52. Thomas M. Bassett, *The Welsh Baptists* (Swansea: Ilston Press, 1977) 61–62.
53. Ibid., 70–71, 115.
54. Ibid., 72–73.
55. Ibid., 75–81.
56. Ibid., 80–82.
57. Ibid., 66.
58. E. W. Price Evans, "Rev. Micah Thomas, Abergavenny," *Baptist Quarterly* 14 (1951–52): 109–13.
59. Bassett, *The Welsh Baptists,* 126–27.
60. Ibid., 131–32.
61. Ibid., 147.
62. Ibid., 328.
63. John D. Bollen, *Australian Baptists: A Religious Minority* (London: Baptist Historical Society, 1975), 7.
64. David Parker, ed., *Baptists in Queensland: A Guide to Their Life and Faith* (Brisbane: Baptist Historical Society of Queensland, 1994), 26.
65. Bollen, *Australian Baptists,* 9.
66. Ibid.
67. Ibid., 10.
68. Ibid.
69. Parker, ed., *Baptists in Queensland,* 26.
70. Ibid., 27.
71. Ibid., 28.
72. James Martin, *Chairman's Address and Report of the Tenth Session of the Baptist Association of Victoria* (Melbourne: Mason, Firth, and McCutcheon, 1871), n.p.
73. Bollen, *Australian Baptists,* 17.
74. Ibid, 19.
75. Ibid., 20.
76. D. Mervyn Himbury, "Baptists and Their Relations with Other Christians in Australasia," *Foundations* 17 (January–March 1974): 29.
77. Ibid., 32.
78. Ibid., 33.
79. Ibid., 39–40.
80. Ibid., 35.
81. Ibid., 36–50.
82. Wardin, ed., *Baptists around the World,* 115.
83. E. P. Y. Simpson, "A History of the New Zealand Baptist Missionary Society, 1885–1947" (master's thesis, University of New Zealand, 1948), 16.
84. Paul Tonson, 1851–1882, vol. 1 of *A Handful of Grain: The Centenary History of the Baptist Union of New Zealand,* ed. Angus McLeod (Wellington: New Zealand Baptist Historical Society, 1982), 3.
85. Ibid., 5.
86. Ibid.
87. Ibid., 20.
88. Ibid., 27.
89. Ibid., 29–30.
90. Ibid., 35.
91. Ibid., 11.
92. Ibid., 38.
93. Ibid., 106.
94. Ibid., 111.
95. Simpson, "Baptist Missionary Society," 38a.
96. Ibid., 45.
97. J. Ayson Clifford, 1882–1914, vol. 2 of McLeod, ed., *A Handful of Grain,* 4.
98. Ibid., 5.
99. Ibid., 27.
100. Ibid., 59.
101. Ibid., 9–10.

102. Ibid., 24.
103. Ibid., 69.
104. G. T. Beilby, 1914–1945, vol. 3 of McLeod, ed., *A Handful of Grain,* 55.
105. Ibid., 18.
106. Ibid., 93.
107. Ibid., 23–24.
108. Ibid.
109. Ibid., 71
110. Ibid., 71–72.
111. Ibid., 43.
112. Ibid., 7.
113. Himbury, "Christians in Australasia," 40–41.

Chapter 13
Baptists in Europe

BRITISH BAPTIST LEADER JAMES RUSHBROOKE WROTE THAT WHILE THE BAPTIST movement originated in seventeenth-century Europe, it went largely unnoticed there for the first two hundred years. Baptist life in Germany did not begin until the nineteenth century, through the work of the German minister and missionary Johann Gerhard Oncken (1800–1884).[1] As Randall and Hulse observed, "Prior to 1834, Baptists as we know them were virtually non-existent on the continent of Europe (the Mennonites excepted). In that year Oncken was baptised."[2] For the next fifty years, Oncken extended Baptist organizations throughout the European scene.

In 1800, there were no Baptist churches on the European mainland. Oncken's work changed all that. By 1850, there were four thousand church members, and 220,000 by 1900. In 1922, European Baptists claimed more than 1.25 million members.[3]

Rushbrooke's own analysis of the "Baptist advance" in Sweden, Romania, Estonia, Latvia, and Czechoslovakia explored both the evangelical and the democratic nature of the Baptist identity. He wrote, "The explanation must be sought in the distinctive characteristics of our Baptist testimony, in our historic and fundamental principles." These, he said, included the separation of church and state, "no priestly caste," equality of community, the church as "spiritual democracy," and the "preaching of the cross."[4]

Baptists in Germany

Through the work of Johann Gerhard Oncken, Germany became a center of missionary outreach for Baptists across the European continent. Born in Varel, Oldenburg (North Germany), Oncken was reared in the Lutheran Church. As a youth, he encountered Scots evangelicals James and Robert Haldane, who recommended him for missionary service with the Continental Society for the Diffusion of Religious Knowledge. This pan-European evangelical organization appointed Oncken in 1823. Five years later, he married an English woman named Sarah Mann and became associated with the Edinburgh Bible Society. He also founded a bookstore and a publishing house known as *Oncken Verlag,* a business that became one of Germany's best-known religious presses.[5]

By 1829, Oncken was convinced of his own need for believer's baptism but could find no one in Hamburg to perform such a rite. During the 1830s, he met Barnas Sears, an American Baptist studying at the University of Halle. Sears, who later became president of Brown University, immersed the Onckens and five other persons in the Elbe River on April 22, 1834. The next day, Sears ordained Oncken as pastor of a new German Baptist church in Hamburg.[6]

Oncken and Julius Koebner, a Baptist convert of Jewish descent, drew up a confession of faith in 1837. Its emphasis on the "doctrine of the election of grace" split the little band of Baptists, and the dissenters formed another congregation. This Calvinist confession contained fifteen articles, including a statement on closed communion as given "exclusively and only for such as through God's converting grace have become his possession and have received holy baptism."[7]

In 1835, the American Baptist Triennial Convention named Oncken its representative and funded his work in establishing congregations in Germany. A decade later, his support was assumed by the American Baptist Missionary Union. Oncken traveled widely, founding numerous churches in Europe and visiting the United States during the years 1853–1854.[8]

The early German Baptists utilized lay preachers, many of whom were artisans spread about the country. Oncken's colleagues, Julius Koebner (1806–1884) and Gottfried Wilhelm Lehmann (1799–1882), also organized many European Baptist churches. Lehmann was baptized by Oncken in 1837 and did extensive work in Berlin. Oncken, Koebner, and Lehmann became the Kleeblatt, or "clover leaf," of German Baptist life.[9]

Their actions soon met with opposition. Persecution from the Prussian state led to arrests and compelled the baptism of infants into the established (Lutheran) church. In response, Gottfried Lehmann wrote a dramatic defense of religious liberty. Internal disputes also arose. Oncken insisted that new congregations were branches of the central Hamburg church, while Koebner and Lehmann viewed them as autonomous faith communities.[10]

Oncken's visit to Switzerland led to the formation of its first Baptist church in 1849, with Koebner's baptism of a Dutch Reformed minister named Feisser. F. O. Nilsson, baptized by Oncken in Germany in 1847, helped to establish the first Swedish Baptist congregation in Gothenburg in 1848. Oncken later founded the first Baptist church in Lithuania as a German-speaking congregation.[11]

In January 1849, some thirty Baptist churches constituted the Union of Baptist Congregations in Germany and Denmark, the first general body of European Baptists. The Union founded a training school for evangelists in Hamburg the same year.[12]

The Baptist presence was evident in regions of central and eastern Prussia and Württemberg. Baptists in Hamburg numbered 719 baptized members by 1865, with some sixty-four "preaching centers" in surrounding regions. A theological school was established in Hamburg in 1880. At Oncken's death, in 1884, there were 150 congregations and some 31,438 Baptist church members in Germany.[13]

By the early twentieth century, German Baptists had begun to lament the loss of their original zeal for the gospel. Writing in the 1920s, Herbert Petrick expressed concern over Baptist class-consciousness. He wrote, "We no longer reach the peasants from among whom the first Baptists drew their strength. The higher ranks of the middle classes have nothing in common with us, know, most of them, nothing about our existence."[14] That left room for growth only among "the lower middle-class." The reason for this, he suggested, "is the way we proclaim our message."[15] Petrick feared that Baptists of his generation offered the world "an ego-centric Christianity" that promoted rabid individualism. He concluded, "How much selfish religious enjoyment there is, how many people who want only 'edification' and emotional enjoyment, and who have no idea that Christianity involves surrender and sacrifice!"[16]

In an article entitled "Some Impressions of Germany," published in 1929, British Baptist Ernest Payne commented on the state of postwar Germany. He suggested, "The basis, tradition and outlook are far narrower than in England, so narrow indeed that comparatively few of us would be able to remain in the present Baptist organization were we living in Germany."[17] He observed that each year, "many able and keen younger men and women are being lost to the Baptist cause in Germany, who might be retained were it made clear that our faith can be intelligently grounded, and our organization made democratic, and that a cardinal Baptist principle has been intellectual and spiritual freedom."[18]

German Baptists generally kept their distance from the struggles that divided the German churches under National Socialism and the Second World War. The meeting of the Baptist World Congress in Berlin in 1934 was an occasion for Nazi propaganda. In 1938, the German Baptists began a relationship with a Pentecostal group known as the Elim Congregations, and in 1942 they added the Plymouth Brethren to form the Union of Evangelical Free Church Congregations. Following the war, the Pentecostals left the Union, as did some of the Plymouth Brethren. The remaining Brethren in the Union retain their own identity amid the Baptist majority.[19]

The war was devastating to all Germans, Baptists included. At least five thousand Baptists died, and more than forty thousand were made homeless. Postwar Baptist churches in East Germany experienced the culture of communist dictatorship in the German Democratic Republic. Unlike churches in other communist countries, however, East German Baptists were able to retain a certain degree of autonomy. State sanctions were enacted against Baptist youth and educational ministries, and a formal break with West German Baptists was required.[20]

German Baptists demonstrated concern for Lutheran and Calvinist theology, linked to a strong pietistic orientation. After the war, German Baptists were known for their pietistic spirituality, evangelistic emphasis, strong congregationalism, and missionary outreach. Their spirituality was particularly manifest in their hymnody, evident in the hymnbook *Gemeindelieder*, published late in the twentieth century.[21]

The Union accepted a new confession of faith, the *Rechenschaft vom Glauben*, in 1977. It was the work of Baptists in Switzerland, Austria, and both East and West Germany. During this period, German Baptists generally turned from closed to open communion. They retained the practice of admitting only baptized believers to church membership. Reunification of the two Baptist groups occurred with the reunification of Germany in the 1990s. Holiness and Pentecostal influences also found their way into Baptist life. Baptists divided over fundamentalism and liberalism, biblical interpretation, and the ordination of women. In 1992, the Executive Board of the Union recommended that questions of ordination for women be left to the individual congregation.[22]

Although the Union does not participate in the World Council of Churches, it maintains membership in the German Association of Christian Churches, the Baptist World Alliance, and the European Baptist Federation. At the beginning of the twenty-first century, German Baptists claimed 114,200 members in some seven hundred churches.[23]

Baptists in Denmark

The Baptist presence in Scandinavia began in Denmark when Julius Koebner, Oncken's Danish colleague, began a mission to his native land in 1839. A pietist layman named Peder C. Moenster became a Baptist and invited Oncken and Koebner to Copenhagen. The three constituted Denmark's first Baptist Church on October 30, 1839.[24] Five churches were formed by 1844. Danish Baptist churches remained in the German Baptist sphere until 1888, when they established a free-standing association.

Supporters of the Lutheran state church responded quickly, and Moenster was imprisoned for fostering sectarian nonconformity. His brother, Adolph Moenster, wrote to Oncken in 1840, "At present the persecution appears to be becoming serious.... The police forbade us to assemble last Sunday, but we met as usual. Tomorrow evening probably we shall be disturbed, and brother Ryding, in whose house we meet, and myself, taken into custody."[25] Both brothers were jailed and brought to trial. The court sought to determine if the two were Anabaptists, a sect still considered radical and revolutionary, or Baptists, an offshoot of a more acceptable Protestant communion in England and North America. Adolph Moenster explained:

> The court would not, and could not, consider Oncken and Koebner as Baptists, partly because they are not acknowledged to be so by the authorities of Hamburg, partly because they are known in this country as Anabaptists, partly because the court does not know whether the Baptists in Hamburg are a new and self-constituted sect, or whether they are a church planted on apostolic principles by the Baptists in England or America, who are recognised in this country as genuine Baptists.[26]

Certain Danish newspapers took up the Baptist cause and urged that the government grant dissenters full religious liberty.[27] Nonetheless, both Moenster brothers were sentenced to almost a year in prison.

British Baptists soon dispatched a delegation to Denmark to petition the release of their Danish colleagues. In response, the Danish authorities ruled that Baptists could have freedom to worship, but only in certain backwater towns. The Moenster brothers rejected those terms and remained in jail. In 1842, American Baptists also sent representatives to lobby in behalf of religious freedom, but to no avail. Instead, the Lutheran leader Bishop Mynster had Baptist children forcibly baptized in Lutheran churches.[28] Ultimately, a greater religious liberty was granted in 1849, but the Baptist minority did not receive full benefits until much later.

These sanctions endured well into the twentieth century. During the years 1937–1975, the nonconformist graduates of teacher's colleges received diplomas that read, "Is not a member of the People's [Lutheran] Church, and can therefore not have a teaching position in primary school which involves religious instruction." In 1975, religious instruction in Denmark's schools continued but was designated as "non-confessional."[29]

The Danish Baptist Union *(Danske Baptistamfund)* maintained strong ties to Baptists in the United States. The Union utilized the New Hampshire Confession of Faith as a basic doctrinal guideline rather than use the German Baptist Confession. During the late nineteenth and early twentieth centuries, many Danish pastors received their theological training at Morgan Park Seminary, Chicago. A Danish Baptist Seminary was established in 1918.[30]

The confession of faith was never officially required, and the Union's constitution contains no confessional statement. During the 1930s, Danish Baptists moved from closed to open communion, and by the latter part of the twentieth century, some churches had accepted members baptized as infants in other Christian traditions without requiring rebaptism. Danish Baptists joined the Baptist World Alliance in 1905 and both the European Baptist Federation and World Council of Churches in 1948. Baptist Knud Wumpelmann became president of the Baptist World Alliance in 1990. The Union participates in such national ecumenical organizations as the Danish Bible Society, Danish Church Aid, the Danish Mission Council, and the Danish *Kirchen Tage*. By 1928, they developed missionary work in the African countries of Burundi and Rwanda and continue to be involved with African Baptist Unions.[31]

At the beginning of the twenty-first century, Danish Baptists numbered approximately 5,805 persons in some forty-five churches. Though a small minority, they have worked diligently to facilitate dialogue among Lutherans, Catholics, and other Protestant groups in the highly secular environment of Danish culture.[32]

Baptists in Sweden

No formal Baptist organizations were developed in Sweden until the 1830s. One of the earliest Swedish Baptist leaders was Anders Wiberg (1816–1887), a former Lutheran minister whose book *Who Should Be Baptized? and What Is the Meaning of Baptism?* was the first in Swedish to address a believers' church.[33] Wiberg and his wife immigrated to the United States, but responding to an appeal from other Swedish Baptists, they returned to Stockholm in 1855. Wiberg organized a General Conference of Baptists, held in June 1857, and in that year Baptists reported some forty-five churches and 2,105 members.[34] Wiberg made another trip to America, returning with funds that helped build the *Betelkapellet* (church center) in Stockholm. It was opened in 1866, along with a *Betelseminariet* for educating ministers, supported in part by the American Baptist Missionary Union.

Swedish immigration to America created significant connections among Baptists in both countries. As a young sailor, Swedish Baptist leader F. O. Nilsson (1809–1881) was converted to Christianity while in New York in 1845. He soon began preaching and, while in Hamburg in 1847, was baptized by Oncken. Returning to Sweden, he organized a church in 1848 after immersing its first five members. Nilsson then received ordination in Hamburg as the Swedish church's first pastor.[35]

Baptist expansion led to debates over open versus closed communion and the decision that such matters would be left to the discretion of each local congregation. Although most nineteenth-century churches practiced closed communion, a trend toward open communion developed during the twentieth century. Baptist success soon provoked a response from the Swedish Lutheran establishment, as evidenced in a law known as the *Konventikel-plakatet* (Conventicle Placard) of 1726, which forbade religious meetings in homes. Widely applied to Baptists and other groups, it remained in effect until 1858. A subsequent act of religious toleration was not broad enough to benefit the Baptists. Direct appeals to the Swedish king from Baptists inside and outside Sweden aided passage of legislation in 1873 that offered toleration for religious dissenters. Formal and informal sanctions endured for almost another century. Nils Sundholm wrote, "Not until January 1, 1952, however, was it possible for Swedish Baptists to leave the Lutheran Church without loss of civic rights."[36]

These sanctions took many forms. Marriages outside the Lutheran Church were not recognized by the state, and children born of those unions were considered illegitimate. Several Baptist leaders were imprisoned for nonconformist activities, including Nas Pehr Pehrsson (1854–1917), an itinerant Baptist evangelist known for his revivalistic fervor.[37]

Baptists continued to grow even amid persecution, and by 1874 they claimed some ten thousand members in 225 churches. By 1914, these numbers had increased to 635 churches, twenty-one associations, and fifty-four thousand members.[38] One Baptist church, from the town of St. Tuna reported, "Our hearts are filled with thanks to God, when we see what He has done to us. Many have come to believe in Jesus, and our membership has more than doubled by those who have been baptized in the name of Jesus Christ."[39] Schism led to a break in the original Baptist Union and the formation of the Free Baptists in 1872. Concern about the role of women in the church led to the formation of a Society of Baptist Nurses and Deaconesses in 1922.[40]

Pentecostal influence divided Swedish Baptists in the early twentieth century when Lewi Pethrus of the Filadelfia Church, Stockholm, received the baptism of the Holy Spirit. The church was dismissed from its association in 1913 and became a center of Scandinavian Pentecostalism.

During the 1930s, further controversy developed when Pentecostal experiences broke out in the Filadelphia Baptist Church in Orebro. The pastor, John Ongman, led the church to break with the Baptist Union in 1936 in order to become an independent congregation. The Orebro Movement brought other Baptist churches into the Pentecostal sphere. However, many Orebro churches continued to participate in Baptist missionary and publishing endeavors.

The Swedish Baptist Union participates in the Baptist World Alliance, the Swedish Free Church Council, and the Swedish Ecumenical Council, but they do not participate in the World Council of Churches.[41]

In May 1998, Swedish Baptists celebrated 150 years of Baptist life in their country by observing the anniversary of F. O. Nilsson's 1848 baptism by Johann Gerhard Oncken and the founding of an "illegal" church at Vallersvik. In 1998, the Baptist Union of Sweden claimed 278 churches and 18,553 members and missionaries in Congo, Africa, Thailand, Japan, Austria, and France.[42] During that same period, the Free Baptist Union/Holiness Union numbered 150 churches and seven thousand members, and the Orebro Mission claimed 254 churches and 22,738 members.[43]

Baptists in Finland

Questions regarding the baptism of infants first arose among some Finnish pietist groups in the eighteenth century. Enforcement of the *Konventikel-plakatet* of 1726 led to the imprisonment of numerous religious nonconformists who resisted baptism of their infant children.[44]

Baptist ideas were introduced in Finnish territory in the 1850s by Karl Justus Mattias Mollersvard, a Swedish sailor who had become a Baptist during a brief visit to New York.

Mollersvard preached on the island of Fogolo, where his success brought him to the attention of Lutheran authorities, who had him expelled. Johan Erik Ostling, a Finnish farmer, first preached in Finland after receiving immersion from Swedish Baptists in 1855. This led to the formation of the Foglo Baptist Church. Soon Baptist work expanded to the island of Abo. These early Baptist enclaves developed among Swedes who lived on outlying Finnish islands.[45]

Women were a pivotal force in establishing a Baptist presence in Finland. Anna Heikel, daughter of a Lutheran vicar in Osterbotten, became a Baptist in 1866. A new Baptist community developed around the Bible studies and worship services that she conducted in her home.[46]

Anna Hellman, a friend of the Heikel family, became a Baptist and was baptized in 1870. Through their religious bookstore, she and her sisters were instrumental in circulating Bibles among religious nonconformists. She was the only Baptist in Vasa until 1877, when another woman received immersion there. In 1881, two others joined the group, and the four founded the first Baptist church in Vasa.

The Vasa church became a center for promoting Baptist views throughout Finland. In 1880, Baptist convert Staffan Johnsson, of Petalax, brought a group of evangelicals to Vasa, where they received immersion. Erik Jansson, another citizen of Petalax, received baptism in 1881 and became one of Finland's most active Baptist leaders. Through his efforts, a church was founded in Petalax in 1882. A large chapel was built there two years later, and the congregation soon averaged some thirty-three persons a year. Harassment from the state continued, and numerous Baptists were imprisoned for their failure to conform to the regulations of the established church.[47]

A strong concern for congregational autonomy delayed the development of Finnish Baptist associations. A District Union (association) of Finnish Baptist churches was formed in 1883 by representatives of three congregations. A decade later, this association became known as the Conferences of the Baptist Denomination in Finland. Finnish-speaking Baptists founded a national Union in 1903, and other denominational agencies soon followed. These included a theological training school constituted in 1924. After completing that two-year program, students were encouraged to attend the *Betelseminariet* in Stockholm.[48]

A publishing society, *Facklans Forlag*, also was instituted. It produced a denominational periodical entitled *Missionsstandaret*. The Finnish Baptist Mission Society sent missionaries to work in China and the Congo. Finnish and Swedish Baptists maintained close relations with Swedish Baptists as well as with the Swedish Free Church Council. The Swedish Baptist Conference in Finland maintained a separate association among Finnish Baptist congregations. Finnish- and Swedish-speaking Baptists were part of the same Baptist union until 1903, when regional and linguistic divisions made a break necessary.[49]

Twenty-first century Finnish Baptists maintain two distinct unions. The Baptist Union of Finland is a Swedish-speaking communion, while the Finnish Baptist Union uses the national language. The two unions claimed their largest numbers in the early twentieth century, with the Swedish-speaking group numbering twenty-five hundred members and the Finnish group claiming some thirteen hundred members. Declines began after the First World War. The rise of Pentecostalism had a significant influence on this Baptist communion.

The Finnish-speaking Union is the more conservative, practicing closed communion and demonstrating a strong charismatic influence. The Swedish-speaking Union ordains women to ministry, practices open communion, and also reflects the influence of the charismatic movement. Ministerial training for Finnish-speaking churches is provided through a Bible school. Swedish-speaking ministers are taught at the ecumenical Abo Academy or study abroad. The Swedish-speaking Union participates in the Finnish Ecumenical Council. The Finnish-speaking Union numbers approximately six hundred members, while the Swedish-speaking Union claims about sixteen hundred.[50]

Baptists in the Netherlands

Baptists in the Netherlands began as a result of two important influences: turmoil within the Reformed Church and the efforts of European Baptists to begin work among the Dutch. The first Baptist pastor in the Netherlands, Johannes Elias Feisser (1805–1865), personified these events. A minister in the Reformed Church, Feisser was educated at the University of Groningen, a school whose theological orientation represented a "middle way" between the more liberal and the more conservative schools. The Dutch Reformed Church experienced divisions over the religious awakenings of the nineteenth century, known in Holland as Reveil. These divisions helped to foster the earliest Baptist churches in the country.

Theologically intense and concerned to practice what he believed to be true Christianity, Feisser completed his doctor of theology degree at Groningen in 1828. He married about that time and served in several Reformed parishes. His wife and two children died in 1833. While working in a thriving congregation in the province of Drente, he became convinced that few people were "true Christians," that is, genuinely converted. Controversy erupted when he sought to evangelize and discipline members of the congregation, and he was subsequently forced to resign.[51] Feisser then came into contact with certain groups of Mennonites and Baptists, some of whom knew of his books on baptism and discipleship.[52]

In 1845, after a visit to Oncken, Feisser returned to Holland and was baptized by Julius Koebner on May 15. The two preached throughout the country, and in June they baptized three men at Zuften. Churches then were constituted in Amsterdam and other towns.[53] A Dutch Baptist Union was founded in 1881.

British and German Baptists had a strong influence on their Dutch counterparts. Many of their ministers were trained at the German Baptist Seminary in Hamburg, while others received theological education in England, Scandinavia, or the United States. The first attempt to form a Dutch seminary failed, but in 1958, a school De Vinkenhof, was begun in Utrecht Province.[54]

The Baptist movement in Holland thrived with no outside missionary aid. In 1908, the Baptist Union claimed twelve hundred members with seventeen churches, and by 1932 those numbers increased to over four thousand members. During the Second World War, amid the difficulties of Nazi occupation, the churches continued to grow.[55]

The Baptist Union aligned itself with the Ecumenical Council of Churches in the Netherlands in 1945 and the World Council of Churches in 1948. In 1963, when some Dutch Baptists raised concerns about the liberalism in the two ecumenical organizations, the Union withdrew its membership in order to avoid schism. Non-Union churches formed the Brotherhood of Baptist Churches in 1981, a more conservative alliance. At the end of the twentieth century, Baptists in the Netherlands claimed approximately fifteen thousand members.[56]

Baptists in Norway

Like other Scandinavian countries, Norway was solidly Lutheran when Baptists arrived in the nineteenth century. The constitution of 1814 made the Evangelical Lutheran Church the state-sanctioned religious establishment. As in other such countries, the Lutheran *Konventikel-plakatet* of 1726 forbade religious gatherings not under the control of the Lutheran clergy.

In 1851, G. A. Lammers, a Lutheran minister who had been influenced by the Moravians, formed the Free Apostolic Christian Church in Norway. The church rejected infant baptism but did not require rebaptism of its members. Some in the church supported baptismal immersion, and one of them, a watchmaker named Gulbrandsen, was immersed in Germany by J. G. Oncken in 1857. Many then renounced their earlier baptism as infants and received believer's baptism. A schism resulted when the immersionists founded a new congregation, the Christian Dissenter Church. Fearing an outbreak of "fanaticism," Lammers returned to the Lutheran fold.[57] These groups were Baptist-like, if not completely Baptist, in orientation.

The first Baptist preacher in Norway arrived by a surprisingly circuitous route with links to both Europe and America. Frederick L. Rymker, a seaman from Denmark, was converted, baptized, and licensed to preach by Baptists at the Mariner's Temple in New York City in 1848. In 1850, he was sent by the Baptist Women's Society, Bethel, as a missionary to Denmark. Rymker's efforts produced limited results, and after seven years he was prepared to return to the United States. At the encouragement of Anders Wiberg of Stockholm, Rymker then was sent as a missionary to Denmark, funded by the American Baptist Publication Society and the New York Seaman's Friend Society. He arrived in 1857 and baptized his first convert in 1858. Others followed, and the first Danish Baptist church was founded in Porsgrund in 1860. They were soon joined by a faction from the Free Church in Skein. Skein became a central location for Baptist work in Norway.[58]

A native Norwegian named Gotfred Hubert also was converted through seamen's ministries in the United States. He received baptism in Boston in 1861 at the hands of Phineas Stowe, pastor of the Seaman's Bethel Church. In 1863, the Baptist Missionary Society appointed him a missionary to Norway. Several Swedish Baptists were sent to Norway, their work funded by the Baptist Missionary Society. O. B. Hansson, a Swedish blacksmith, also began preaching in northern Norway in 1862.

Some of the early Norwegian Baptist leaders were educated at Bethel Seminary in Stockholm or the Baptist school at Morgan Park, Illinois. By the 1880s, Norwegian Baptists claimed some twenty-two churches with a total membership of 1,681.[59]

When the Baptist Missionary Society, London, ended support for the Norwegian Mission in 1892, new funding was provided by the American Baptist Foreign Missionary Society. The Baptist Union in Norway, *Det Norske Baptistsamfunn,* was officially organized in 1879. It included five district associations, a youth organization, and Norsk Litteratursel-skap, a Baptist publishing house. The Norwegian Baptist Theological Seminary was organized in Oslo in 1910, also funded by the American Baptist Missionary Society.

During the Second World War, Baptists joined other Norwegian Protestants in opposing Nazi occupation. Complete religious liberty was delayed until 1964, when it was granted by the Norwegian Constitution. During the late twentieth century, church attendance in

Norway in general remained relatively low. Surveys taken in the 1990s suggested that some 33 percent of the population never attended church. Amid the developing secularism, Baptists have continued to retain minority status while seeking to avoid minority sectarianism.[60]

Although the Norwegian Baptist Union does not maintain membership in the World Council of Churches, it does participate in the Norwegian Free Church Council, the Norwegian Faith and Order Forum, and the National Council of (Norwegian) Churches. It is a member of the European Baptist Federation and the Baptist World Alliance. By the early twenty-first century, Norwegian Baptists claimed approximately 5,600 members and sixty-six churches.[61]

Baptists in Italy

Baptist beginnings in Italy occurred with the development of Italian independence. In 1861, a united kingdom of Italy was formed, leaving only Rome and Venetia outside its sphere. That same year, "Baptists reported evangelistic activities in Naples, Florence, Leghorn, Pisa, Genoa, and Milan."[62]

In 1866, two British missionaries, James Wall (d. 1901) and Edward Clark, were sent to Italy by the Baptist Missionary Society, London. Wall went first to Bologna and then to Rome after the city came under control of Italian nationalists. Clark founded the Spezia Mission for Italy and the Levant—a program that worked with civilian and military constituents. He established an orphanage in 1884.[63] Concerned for evangelization, the Spezia Mission established numerous preaching stations throughout the country.

In 1870, when Pope Pius IX relinquished control of Rome to the Italian state, the Baptist Missionary Society sent additional missionaries to Rome and Genoa. The Italian Parliament passed the Law of Guarantees in 1871, recognizing the pope's spiritual leadership but affirming "a free church in a free state."

The Southern Baptist Convention began mission work in Italy in 1871 with a church in Torre Pellice, a center of the Waldensian movement. Its appointee, William Cote, joined Wall and Italian Baptist Gaetano Giannini in founding a Baptist church in Rome in 1871.[64]

During the late nineteenth century, the BMS work in southern Italy was turned over to the SBC. Southern Baptist ownership of property protected Italian Baptists when church-state laws made it difficult for Protestant organizations to own land. Italian Baptists would not regain control of their properties until late in the twentieth century. Southern Baptists sent George Boardman Taylor to Italy in 1873. His distinguished career continued until his death in 1907. Taylor and other associates divided their work between northern and southern Italy. Northern work included Trieste on the Adriatic and Mentone in France. A Baptist Theological College was established in Rome in 1901.[65]

The Apostolical Baptist Union, an organization linking all Baptist mission agencies in Italy, was formed in 1884. It published a periodical known as *Il Seminatore*, or *The Sower*. In 1908, the Union reported fifty-eight churches, forty-six pastors, and a membership of 1,591.[66]

Mission work in Catholic Italy forced some Baptists to question some of their own theological and practical positions. Southern Baptist George B. Taylor was perhaps the only missionary to suggest that believer's baptism made evangelism among the Italians particularly difficult. Taylor suggested that because Catholic Italians received infant baptism, they were more apt to enter those Protestant churches "which received them as they are with a simple enrollment, for if converts to a new religion often react against the old, it is no less true that they also long bear in them its influence."[67] The Baptist requirement of rebaptism was especially daunting for Italians reared in Catholic traditions. During the years 1946–1948, Italians voted on a new constitutional assembly, which approved a new constitution permitting greater religious liberty. Baptist church membership increased from twenty-five hundred to five thousand in only a few years.[68]

In 1944, Manfredi Ronchi was chosen executive secretary of the Opera Evangelica Battista d'Italia, the Baptist Union of Italy. In 1947, he was named president and general secretary of the general assembly of the Opera Evangelica Battista. In 1956, the group changed its name to the *Unione Cristiana Evangelica Battista d'Italia.*

Greater liberties enabled indigenous Baptist groups to develop their own ministries apart from the work of foreign missionary programs. *The Entre Patrimoniale* was constituted in 1961 as the Baptist organization responsible for "financial transactions both for the Union and for local congregations."[69]

The continued influence of Catholic and fascist establishments led many Italian Baptists toward certain socialist, even Marxist, positions. These political sentiments created conflict with American missionaries, who were intensely opposed to any compromise with communism. Tensions increased when some Italian Baptists voiced criticism of American involvement in the Vietnam War.[70] Italian Baptists continue to reflect more liberal theological and social positions than many other European Baptist communions. Toward the end of the century, they were among the first European Baptist communions to address the issue of homosexuality, in a resolution that recognized the right of local congregations to decide on specific responses toward homosexuality in general and homosexuals in particular.[71]

A reorganization of the Union, begun in 1983, led to an agreement *(Le Intese)* with the Italian state in 1995. It included an organizational structure for the denomination, a confession of faith, and a council of elders for dealing with controversies. The agreement affirmed congregational autonomy and religious liberty. In response to the document, the Italian Parliament recognized marriages performed in Baptist churches by duly recognized ministers associated with the Union. This meant that civil ceremonies were no longer required to validate marriages performed in Baptist churches.[72] Through this agreement, Baptists retained their distinctiveness among Italian Protestant groups while receiving recognition as a legally constituted religious communion.

As Italian Baptists moved toward greater political autonomy, they began negotiations with Southern Baptist missionaries for the transfer of property long controlled by the SBC. The transaction was complicated by Southern Baptist concern over the support for socialism and communism among some Italian Baptists. The property finally was turned over to the Italians in March 1993.[73]

Italian Baptists pursued various ecumenical relationships, including a 1995 partnership with the Waldensian and Methodist churches to "grant each other full and mutual recognition." After years of negotiation, the agreement allowed for the recognition of ministerial ordination and encouraged increased cooperation among the churches.[74]

As the twentieth century came to a close, Italian Baptists continued to reflect more liberal responses to social and political issues. In 1994, the president of the Union of Christian Baptist Churches in Italy joined sixty-five other Protestant church leaders in supporting a resolution approved in the European Parliament that recommended legal recognition of homosexual unions. On February 24, 1994, sixty-five pastors and lay leaders from four Protestant denominations—Baptist, Lutheran, Methodist, and Waldensian—signed a declaration affirming that they "welcome and appreciate" the resolution. Franco Scaramuccia, president of the Italian Baptist Union, and sixteen other Baptist pastors also signed the resolution. The group acknowledged that they did not speak for other Italian Baptists, nor was their vote a specific declaration of approval for homosexual lifestyles. It was, Scaramuccia noted, "limited to the question of equality before the law for all European citizens."[75]

Additional mission work among American, Spanish, German, and Chinese émigrés was instituted in the 1990s. At the beginning of the twenty-first century, Italian Baptists numbered approximately five thousand members.[76]

Baptists in France

The Baptist presence in Catholic France began after the Napoleonic wars and the religious activities of English Protestant soldiers in the district of Nomain. In 1819, when certain French citizens in the region were attracted to Protestant ideas, the Evangelical Missionary Society sent Henri Pyt to instruct them. Although Pyt was not a Baptist, his descriptions of the work of William Carey led some of his listeners to investigate Baptist beliefs and request immersion. Pyt refused their request, but the group was undeterred. By 1821, they had formed a Baptist community.[77] Soon other Baptist groups appeared in Brittany, Alsace, and Paris, each with little or no connection to the others.

In 1831, an American Baptist named Howard Malcolm encountered some of these Baptists while traveling in France. He returned to the United States and urged the General Convention to send a missionary to aid the fledgling Baptist congregations in France. The Convention then sent Ira Chase of Newton Baptist Seminary to investigate the situation.[78]

At Chase's recommendation, two Newton Seminary graduates, Isaac Willmarth and Erastus Willard, were sent to France in 1834. They settled in Douai, where they organized the first "official" Baptist church in France in 1835. Shortly thereafter, the two opened a school for ministers. In 1856, the school moved to Paris, and Edward Mitchell, another Newton graduate, joined the faculty. Willard spent twenty-one years as a missionary to France.[79]

By the 1850s, Baptists had attracted the attention of French authorities, who took legal action against them. As a result, several pastors were fined or imprisoned. French Catholics seem to have found the Baptists particularly scandalous. John Jenkins, Baptist missionary in Brittany, described the response to his baptism of three women in 1853: "You can hardly form an idea of the stir and the effect this event has created in this country far and wide.... Popery had not yet received so painful a blow in Brittany. Praise God with us for this work of his grace."[80] Reuben Saillens, a well-known French Baptist pastor, wrote, "There is one thing, in this world, of which Rome is afraid, and that is, the individual conscience. Any system, therefore, which tends to annihilate the individual, to absorb him in the mass, to make him a mere cipher incapable of independent action, is a sure ally of Rome."[81]

In 1870, Baptists claimed approximately two thousand adherents, seven hundred of whom were baptized church members. In 1908, at the first meeting of the European Baptist Congress, French Baptists reported twenty-seven churches, ten of which were self-supporting. Church membership in that year included 2,200 baptized adults. By 1908, there were two national associations, the Fédération des Églises Baptistes du Nord de la France (Franco-Belgian) and the Association des Églises Baptistes Franco-Suisses (Franco-Swiss).[82]

A Baptist church was established in Paris in 1850, and its first building was constructed in 1872 with the help from American Baptists. By the latter part of the nineteenth century, Baptist churches were found in Lyon, Marseille, and Nice. Welsh Baptists funded missionary work in Brittany.[83]

By the 1920s, three distinct groups of Baptists were evident in France, each created as a result of differences over doctrine and practice. In the north, Philemon Vincent (d. 1929) led the Federation of Baptist Evangelical Churches of France, a group devoted to Baptist principles amid "interdenominational cooperation, and a certain degree of doctrinal pluralism."[84] A second organization, the Evangelical Association of French Language Baptist Churches, led by Ruben Saillens, was located primarily in the south. It was concerned for orthodoxy and "a strong Baptist line."[85] A third contingent, located solely in one congregation, the Independent Baptist Church of Arthur Blocher (Paris), emphasized congregational autonomy and fundamentalist theology.

During the 1920s and 1930s, the magazine *La Solidarité Sociale,* edited by Philemon Vincent and Robert Farelly, promoted many ideals of the Social Gospel among Baptists. Two world wars and the Great Depression confronted French Baptists with a variety of social and political challenges. After France fell to the Nazis, many French Baptists joined the resistance movement. Baptist André Gueziec, the first Protestant resistor to be executed by the Nazis, died on May 12, 1941.[86]

Following the war, French Baptists expanded their connections with other Protestant evangelicals through the French Evangelical Alliance (1953) and the Association of Believer's Churches (1957). By the 1960s, the influence of the charismatic movement was evident among French Protestants, and in 1988 the Federation of Charismatic Churches was founded within the Baptist Federation.[87] In the year 2000, French Baptists claimed some forty thousand participants, only twelve thousand of whom were baptized church members.

Baptists in Spain

The first Baptist church in Spain was formed in Madrid by American William Knapp in 1870. Knapp, appointed by the American Baptist Missionary Union, remained in Spain until 1876. After his departure, however, the Baptist communities he founded in Madrid and Alicante could not be sustained. In 1877, a Baptist presence in Galicia was established by Erik Lund, a Swede whose mission soon was acknowledged by the Swedish Baptist Union. Support for his work came from the American Baptist Missionary Union. Lund organized a church in Barcelona in 1883. Swedish Baptists then sent Charles Haglund, John Uhr, and Nils John Bengtson to Valencia, where they began a church in 1888. The trio also renewed the earlier missions in Madrid and Alicante. Lund remained in Spain until 1900, after which he began a mission in the Philippines.

In 1920, a "London agreement" between Baptist mission organizations in the United States and Britain gave the Southern Baptist Convention extensive responsibility for mission work in Spain. Through these missionary endeavors, Spanish Baptists grew slowly but steadily. In 1920, they reported some six hundred church members, and by 1955 the membership had increased to 2,245.[88]

The Unión Evangélica Bautista Española was founded in 1922. In 1929, it became the Spanish Baptist Convention, and in 1953 the name was changed to that of the original organization. The struggling churches confronted many difficulties. Funding from America decreased during the Great Depression of the 1930s. The Spanish Civil War (1936–1939) brought dictator Francisco Franco to power in a fascist regime that endured until his death in 1975. Franco's government was not hospitable to Protestants, and in the early days of his dictatorship, many Baptist churches were closed. While toleration increased a bit after the Second World War, persons convicted of carrying out "public evangelism" were subject to fines and imprisonment. In 1956, Baptists joined with other Protestants in forming the Committee of Evangelical Defense, aimed at securing greater religious liberty in Spain. The Law on Religious Liberty finally was passed in 1967, but Baptists divided over participation in the required state registration of non-Catholics. Some Baptists chose to register, while others refused—a situation that created serious schism in the Union. New legislation, approved in 1980, gave greater liberty to all religious groups in Spain and removed the registration requirements.[89]

The growth of religious liberty encouraged several Baptist denominations to begin mission work in Spain. These included the World Baptist Fellowship, the Brazilian Baptist Convention, Strict Baptists, and Free Will Baptists. Nonetheless, Baptists remain a minority among Spanish Protestants. At they end of the twentieth century, they claimed some fifteen thousand members in fewer than two hundred churches.[90]

Baptists in Poland

Early in the twentieth century, A. H. Newman wrote, "The Polish anti-trinitarian Antipedobaptist movement is of great importance to Baptist history. From this party the English General Baptists derived much of their impetus, by it they have been greatly influenced, and between it and them there has always been a close affinity, from it through the Rhynsburgers, or Collegiants, of Holland, the Particular Baptists of England seem to have derived their immersion (1641)."[91] Although direct connections between Polish Baptists and the early "Antipedobaptist movement" cannot be ascertained, it is clear that religious dissenters in Poland had a powerful affect on the development of Protestantism.

Poland's national identity took many forms in the eighteenth and nineteenth centuries. The nation disappeared in partitions of 1793 and 1795 and reappeared after the Congress of Vienna. For a brief period, 1830–1831, Poland was annexed by Russia.

The Baptist presence in Poland dates from November 8, 1858, when a group of German émigrés professed Christian faith and received immersion. One of their leaders, G. F. Alf (1831–1898), helped organize several Baptist communities in Poland.[92] Persecution from the state and the threat of exile to Siberia forced him to flee to Germany, where he received ordination as a Baptist minister.[93] Returning to Polish territory in 1859, Alf baptized more than one hundred people within two years. He and two German Baptists formed the first Baptist church in Poland at Adamov on August 4, 1861.

German émigrés to Poland constituted the earliest Baptist communities. The first Slavic Baptist church in Poland was founded in 1872 in the town of Zelov, near Lodz. Because the Polish state was closely linked to the Roman Catholic Church, the Baptist presence soon led to persecution—activities particularly acute in the cities. No Baptist congregation existed in Warsaw or Lodz until 1922. That same year, Slavic and Polish Christians formed a "Union of Slavic Baptists in Poland"—an organization that included "Polish, Russian, Ukrainian, White-Russian and Bohemian" groups. In 1923, a seminary was founded in Lodz.[94]

Slavic Baptist churches grew rapidly, and by 1922 there were ten churches and over nine hundred members. A decade later, the membership had risen to more than five thousand persons in seventy-three congregations. Nonetheless, they remained a tiny minority amid a predominately, and sometime hostile, Catholic majority.[95]

The Second World War and the Nazi occupation brought extreme detestation to Poland and its people. Polish Jews were executed in camps that became a "killing ground" for Nazi pogroms against Jews, Christians, homosexuals, and the disabled. With the defeat of Germany, Poland became a "satellite" of the Soviet Union and developed its own communist-oriented government. State efforts to both dominate and undermine religion took their toll, and the total number of Polish Baptists declined to no more than fifteen hundred members.[96] When several Protestant denominations created a central organization known as the United Evangelical Church of Poland, Baptists refused to join lest they be identified with Pentecostals. They, like other Polish Christians, faced state opposition for over forty years.[97]

With the demise of the Soviet Union, Polish Baptists experienced greater freedom and new vitality. Old laws that required a religious group to be connected to "national identity" were abolished, and property once confiscated from Baptist churches was gradually restored. For example, in 1994, the Baptist church at Lodz regained property on which it had once maintained a seminary, a deaconess ministry, a printing house, a Jewish-Christian mission, and a printing house.[98]

In 1992, the Polish Baptist Union reported 3,217 baptized believers and over 1,900 "sympathizers"—persons who attended services but had not received baptism. That same year, construction was begun on a seminary at Radosc, near Warsaw, that included a training school, a theological school, and a youth camp.[99] Evangelistic endeavors were renewed in prisons, parks, and theaters. At the end of the twentieth century, the Union of Christian Baptists claimed some four thousand members in over sixty churches.[100]

Baptists in Romania

In Romania, as in other European countries, Baptist work was initiated by Johann Gerhard Oncken. In 1845, Oncken baptized a German carpenter named Karl Scharschmidt, who, with his wife, Augusta, moved to Bucharest and helped to form a Baptist church there in 1856. Russian émigrés founded a church in Cataloi in 1862.[101]

The evangelization of ethnic Romanians began with the work of Constantin Adorian (1882–1954) in Bucharest. Converted through the German Baptist Church in Bucharest, Adorian studied at the Baptist Seminary in Hamburg, joined the German Baptist Church in Bucharest, and became founding pastor of the Romanian Baptist Church in that city in 1912. The Baptist presence in Transylvania began with Antal Novak, a tailor and colporteur supported by the British and Foreign Bible Society. By 1910, Transylvania was the site of 147 Baptist churches of Hungarian or Romanian heritage.[102]

The Romanian Baptist Union began in 1919, comprised of churches from Moldavia, Wallachia, Bessarabia, and Transylvania. It soon numbered 598 churches with some 18,751 members, although ethnic differences created divisions. In 1920, separate unions were founded by Hungarian Baptists in Transylvania and by the Russian-Ukrainians in Bessarabia. A theological seminary was formed in Transylvania in 1920 and moved to Bucharest in 1921. In 1923, the Southern Baptist Convention assumed responsibility for missionary activity in Romania and contributed funds for the seminary's first building. Home missionary work was then begun among the Romanian Gypsies.[103] Romanian Baptists grew rapidly, with some forty-five thousand members by 1930. Baptist communions tended to be conservative, with strict regulations regarding temperance, tobacco, dress, and Sunday observances.

State oppression, often encouraged by the Orthodox Church, was common from the 1920s through the 1940s. During the years 1938–1939, all Baptist churches were ordered closed.[104] These actions produced outcries from various international Baptist bodies. James Rushbrooke, first European commissioner for the Baptist World Alliance, led many delegations to Romania to lobby for greater freedom of religion for Baptists and other religious minorities.[105]

When the Russian army attacked Romania in 1940, the country's leaders sought German protection. New laws, such as Decree No. 972, written in 1942, called for "the abolition of the Baptist cult," the confiscation of Baptist properties, and the closing of churches. State sanctions against Baptists endured until 1944, when a new constitution provided for a degree religious freedom.[106]

With the rise of communist domination in Romania, Baptist numerical growth continued and even received state recognition. From the 1950s to the 1970s, however, the communist leadership began a systematic effort to undermine, if not abolish, all religious organizations. These efforts included direct attacks on pastors and priests, harassment of individual Christians in the workplace, and attempts to "infiltrate and manipulate the leadership of the local church."[107] Again, many Baptist churches and facilities were closed and ministers' licenses were revoked.

Baptist dissenters such as Josif Ton (or Tson) challenged the actions of the state, even after his license was withdrawn. His *Present Situation of the Baptist Church in Romania*, although confiscated and denounced by Romanian officials, was widely circulated in the West. Ton responded fearlessly to state sanctions against Baptists and wrote, "The churches have a sacred right to reject any decision of the Union which affects their life and, consequently, they must reaffirm their legal right of autonomous decision on when and how often they will meet together for worship."[108] Ton was particularly critical of efforts to monitor baptismal practices. He observed, "How can we have sunk so low as to allow, as a church, someone outside the church to decide when and how we may hold a baptismal service, or if we can have it at all?"[109] Even before the fall of the government of Nicolae Ceaucescu, in 1989, Romanian attempts to secure aid from the West led to some loosening of antireligious laws and began a new period of Baptist expansion. Nevertheless, some harassment continued until the collapse of the communist state.[110]

The Baptist University in Bucharest opened in 1991 with funding from the Romanian Ministry of Education. It offered programs in both secular and religious studies. By 1995, there were 250 students training for government service or Christian ministry. Graduate programs offered studies for social workers, linguists, and teachers of religion. The school received full government accreditation in 1995.

A Baptist seminary was founded in 1921 in Buteni and moved to Bucharest in 1925. It trained 95 percent of all ministers in the Romanian Baptist Union. Prior to 1990, the seminary policies of the communist government restricted enrollment to Baptists and other Christian traditions. Nonetheless, the school survived with a small number of students. In the 1990s, under the leadership of president Vasili Talpos, the seminary gained full accreditation from the government. In 1995, it reported an enrollment of some 104 ministerial students.[111]

New freedoms brought new controversies, specifically regarding the ordination of Baptist women. In 1993, Romanian Baptists refused to attend certain meetings of the European Baptist Federation because the Federation's new president, Birgit Karlsson, was an ordained minister of the Swedish Baptist Union. The Romanian Baptist executive council was unanimous in deciding, "We consider the ordination of women as pastors unbiblical. Due to the fact that an ordained woman will be installed as President of the EBF in Kishinev, we decided that our Union will not be represented at the meeting." Federation leaders assured the Romanians that no national union would be compelled to accept women's ordination as a qualification for membership.[112]

Romanian Baptists remain one of the largest Baptist communions in Eastern Europe. By the late twentieth century, they reported 109,000 members in almost fifteen hundred churches.

Baptists in Bulgaria

Protestantism in Bulgaria began with Methodists and Congregationalists in the 1850s and 1860s. An 1880 article, "The Macedonian Cry Re-Echoed from Macedonia Itself," published in the German Baptist periodical *Der Wahrheitszeuge,* urged Baptists to send missionaries to the country. It included a letter from Congregationalists in Kazanlik appealing for help from Baptists. Led by Grigor B. Duminkov, an evangelical committed to believer's baptism, the Congregationalists urged German Baptists to aid in the evangelization of Bulgaria. These appeals generally went unheeded by the Baptists, however.[113]

In 1880, John (Ivan) G. Kargel (1849–1937), pastor of a German Baptist church in St. Petersburg, moved to Bulgaria. His missionary activities were funded by Russian Baptists at the recommendation of his friend V. A. Pashkov. Kargel founded a church in Ruse in 1884, and he carried out extensive evangelistic projects in surrounding regions. He then moved to Kazanlik, where he organized a congregation.[114] By 1888, the church in Ruse claimed some thirty-two members.

Bulgarian Baptist churches tripled in membership between 1918 and 1940 to upwards of seven hundred persons. The Bulgarian Baptist Union established numerous programs for churches, youth, and women's organizations. Following the First World War, the General Missionary Society of the German Baptist General Conference of the USA (North American Baptist Conference) agreed to provide resources and missionaries for Bulgarian Baptist work. It appointed several German-speaking missionaries to aid the churches.[115]

Persecution from the state continued into the 1940s and was particularly intense after the Second World War, when the communists gained dominance. As in other Soviet-bloc countries, the communist-dominated government attempted to thwart all religious activities in an effort to secularize the state. No national Baptist congresses were permitted, property was confiscated, and the baptism of persons under the age of eighteen was forbidden. In 1949, some fifteen evangelical pastors, including Baptists Nickola Michailoff and Ivan Angeloff (d. 1987), were accused of espionage and imprisoned. Although released, their activities continued to be closely monitored.[116]

During this period, religious books were smuggled into the country, secret religious services were held, and other clandestine meetings were conducted within the Baptist community. With the breakdown of the communist system, Baptist churches gained new ground. In May 1991, the Baptist Union held a national congress—the first such meeting in forty-five years.[117] The Union of Baptist Churches in Bulgaria moved quickly to propose new building projects, but the government refused to grant immediate approval. Bulgarian scientist Theodor Angelov, president of the Union, was a longtime Baptist leader and dissenter in behalf of religious liberty. His leadership continued as new Baptist programs took shape in the postcommunist era.[118]

Increased religious freedom often intensified old animosities among religious groups. Throughout much of the 1990s, Baptists were among several Free Church communions to claim that they were victims of harassment from the Bulgarian Orthodox Church. Alexey Ivanov, a regional court judge and member of Sofia's International Baptist Church, called on the government to uphold the constitutional declaration stating, "The practice of any religion shall be free."[119]

Following the communist collapse, Bulgarian Baptists developed relief programs for families in dire need of food and fuel. Theodor Angelov observed in 1997, "The financial system is destroyed; criminality is growing. The crisis is not only political and economic. It is deeper—a spiritual and moral crisis."[120]

In the 1990s, Bulgarian Baptist churches offered "full acceptance" to Baptist Gypsies—one of the more controversial subgroups in the region. Angelov reported, "Our Union has 35 churches and 30 missions with 2,900 members. Of the total number of churches, 4 are completely 'Gypsy churches,' that is, those in which all members are Gypsies (Romani)." Some congregations included mixed communions of Bulgarians and Romani. In other European countries, Gypsies are more isolated from traditional churches.[121] In 1996–1997, Bulgarian Baptists reported sixty-five churches and three thousand members.

Baptists in Russia

The Baptist movement in Russia began in the mid-nineteenth century. Following the collapse of the czarist regime, the period 1918–1921 provided some opportunity for independence for nonconformist churches outside the Orthodox Church. This was followed by some seventy-five years of communist control. The demise of the Soviet Union, in 1989, produced new nations along with a variety of challenges and opportunities for Baptist communities.

Baptist Beginnings in Russia

Johann Gerhard Oncken was the first of the European Baptists to enter Russia. He traveled to St. Petersburg in 1864 and warned the Russian minister of the interior that government persecution of Baptists in Eastern Europe would soon teach them "that it is a very difficult thing to try and destroy a genuine religious movement."[122]

The official beginning may be dated at August 20, 1867, with the baptism of a Molokan named Nikita Voronin (1840–1905) by Martin Kalweit, a German Baptist immigrant from Lithuania.[123] The baptism occurred in Tbilisi, a region that soon became a center of Baptist life. Voronin was an itinerant evangelist whose travels brought him into contact with Vasili Pavlov (1854–1924), then only sixteen years of age. The baptism of V. I. Ivanoff (1846–1919) soon followed. Pavlov received baptism in 1871. For a generation, he and Ivanoff were prominent leaders among Russian Baptists.[124] A zealous evangelist, Pavlov was also a linguist who developed proficiency in Hebrew, Greek, Latin, Arabic, Turkish, and numerous Russian dialects. Veronin organized a church in Tiflis that became a base for Pavlov and his friend M. Ivanov-Klishnikov, another Russian Baptist leader. In 1875, Pavlov went to Germany, where he spent a year studying with Oncken.

Russian Baptists were sometimes labeled "Stundists," or "Bible Readers," and equated with a group of charismatic visionaries opposed by the Russian Orthodox Church. Pavlov himself worked with the actual Stundist movement, yet he and other Baptist leaders denied a direct link to the Stundist movement.[125]

By the mid-1870s, a northern sect similar to the Stundists was begun through the preaching of British pietist Lord Radstock. His work attracted various Russian aristocrats, including Count Bobrinsky, Count M. M. Korff, and Colonel Pashkov.[126] The northern Stundists were centered in St. Petersburg under leadership from Colonel Pashkov and Count Korff. Baptists in the North sometimes were called "Pashkovites." Following the Revolution, a common confession of faith and order was affirmed by Baptists and Stundists.[127]

The Union of Evangelical Christians, a Baptist-oriented assembly, was founded in St. Petersburg in 1888 by Ivan S. Prokhanoff. Prokhanoff was well known by Baptists in Western Europe, having received theological education at the Bristol Baptist College in Bristol, England.[128]

The Stundists shaped the beginnings of two Russian denominations: the Evangelical Christians and the Russian Baptists.[129] At a gathering in St. Petersburg in 1884, Baptists from northern and southern regions entered into a fraternal relationship while acknowledging their continued differences over baptism. The conference attracted governmental attention and precipitated the exile of Pashkov and Korff. That same year, the All-Russian Baptist Union was founded.[130]

Persecution was extensive under the czarist regime. In 1905, P. V. Ivanov-Klishnikov was among certain Baptist leaders arrested at a conference in Odessa and sentenced to a lengthy prison term. When the government attacked him for turning Baptist youth against the state, Ivanov-Klishnikov was said to have replied, "Are the Baptists to blame if their children grow up without sympathy for a Government that persecutes their fathers?"[131]

Vasili Pavlov gained an international reputation through his activities at the First Baptist World Congress in London in 1905, the European Baptist Congress in Berlin in 1908, and the Second Baptist World Congress in Philadelphia in 1911. In 1923, he began mission work with Russian Muslims. A year later, he was wounded when the train on which he was riding was attacked by anarchists.

Baptists and the Soviet State

Writing in 1943, James Rushbrooke observed that the Russian Baptists generally remained aloof from the politics of the new communist regime. He concluded, "At the outset, except on one point [the emphasis on atheism], Soviet legislation and administration commanded the general support of Baptists."[132] Church and state theoretically were separated in the new constitution, and at first there was little attempt to interrupt Baptist activities. Gradually, however, government censorship affected the function of religious life.[133]

Questions regarding alternative military service also created tensions with the state. Many Baptists opposed conscription in the First World War and continued to resist service in the Soviet army.[134] Soviet officials viewed such actions as "counterrevolutionary" and ordered imprisonment or execution of conscientious objectors. The law later was modified to allow for certain kinds of alternative service.[135]

Persecution of religion from the new Soviet Stalinist government increased in 1928. The Baptist community was accused of the economic exploitation of its members while maintaining connections with John D. Rockefeller Jr., a prominent American Baptist and the epitome of Western capitalism. Persecution took the form of excessive taxation, expulsion from labor unions, and the loss of bread rations. The children of Baptists were expelled from school.

The early Leninist government had passed laws that made it illegal "to restrain or limit freedom of conscience" and suggested that "any citizen may profess any religion or none at all."[136] Stalin's decrees withdrew all such rights and retained only vague references to "freedom of worship." A 1929 law defined religious communions as existing solely to provide the populace with specific rites. It forbade religious groups from maintaining libraries or conducting lectures, Sunday schools, or Bible studies. The Preacher's School in Moscow was forced to disband, and the printing of Bibles was forbidden.[137] Baptists soon divided over the appropriate response to state actions against religion.

The All-Union Conference of Evangelical Christian-Baptists

In 1944, the Evangelical Christians and the Russian Baptists united as the All-Union Conference of Evangelical Christian-Baptists (AUCECB), an organization approved by the Soviet state. In the words of A. V. Karev, one of its general secretaries, it became a "multinational and multi-lingual baptist body, joining Russians, Ukrainians, Byelorussians, Germans, Letts, Estonians, Lithuanians, Armenians, Georgians, Osetians, Moldavians, Chuvashes, Romanians, Hungarians, Finns, Komi."[138] The AUCECB brought together

Evangelical Christians, Baptists, Christians of Evangelical Faith, fraternal Mennonites, Church Mennonites, and other evangelical groups.[139]

The AUCECB attempted to link its national organization with local, regional churches. The churches appointed presbyters and deacons, with particular concern for the "spiritual level" of the leaders.[140] Most preachers were self-educated, but theological schools were established in Moscow, Tallin, and Riga.

Baptists in the AUCECB debated many doctrinal and ethical issues that confronted churches in the Soviet state. These included the rebaptism of "those whose baptism was questionable," issues of divorce and remarriage, and the nature of congregational authority.[141] They generally followed a basic statement of doctrines composed by Johann Oncken. It was called "Confession of Faith and Organization, of Communities of Christians Baptized in Faith, Commonly Called Baptists." They also published a magazine, *Herald of Brotherhood*.

They described themselves accordingly: "The Union of Evangelical Christian-Baptists in the USSR is a voluntary association of churches (communities and groups), which preach Evangelical Baptism and wish to have brotherly links and work together in the service of God. The Union of the ECB is comprised of Evangelical Christians, Baptists, Christians of Evangelical Faith; and Mennonites."[142] The AUCECB goals included (1) "To promote incorporation in the life and activity of the churches of the principles and doctrine of Evangelical Christian-Baptists"; (2) "To promote unity among Evangelical Christian-Baptists, Christians of Evangelical Faith, Mennonites and other denominations which preach revival from the Word of God and the Holy Ghost and water baptism in faith"; (3) "To promote preservation of the churches of Evangelical Christian-Baptists in the purity of the Gospel teaching."[143]

The organization determined: "Membership of a parish church can be conferred on one who has come to believe in Christ as his personal Saviour, who has experienced revival from the Word of God and the Holy Spirit, who has come of age and has undergone water baptism in faith."[144] Those desiring to unite with a congregation "through water baptism in faith" were required to notify "the presbyter" and observe a time of "relevant spiritual probation."[145]

AUCECB representatives participated in the European Baptist Congress in Amsterdam in 1964, and the Eleventh Baptist World Congress in Miami in 1966, where Y. I. Zhidkov, I. I. Motorin, and A. N. Kiryukhantsev were elected to the executive committee of the World Council of Baptists. M. Y. Zhidkov was elected vice president and later president of the European Baptist Federation.

The AUCECB maintained communion with a group known as the Christians of Evangelical Faith—a relationship begun in the 1940s. In 1963, the fraternal Mennonites merged with the Evangelical Baptist Brotherhood.[146] The fraternal Mennonites accepted immersion, while church Mennonites retained affusion/sprinkling. The latter were allowed to participate in Baptist church life but not to receive communion.[147]

Like others before them, certain Russian Baptist leaders could not resist connecting their movement directly to the New Testament communities. Karev stated, "It can safely be said that our Evangelical Baptist Church remains the sole exponent of apostolic Christianity in the whole world. It is to see this example of apostolic Christianity that foreign Christians come here."[148]

Divisions over Church and State

In his study of Soviet church-state relations, John Anderson noted that the Soviet Council for the Affairs of Religious Cults was a government-funded agency charged with bringing religious groups under state dominance. In the late 1950s, the questions surrounding relationships with the state again perpetuated division between those who acceded to state regulations and those who opposed them. The 1959 session of the AUCECB was compelled to accept a "Statute on the Union of Evangelical Christians Baptists in the USSR and Instruction Letter to All Senior Presbyters of the AUCECB." The documents restricted senior pastors from visiting their congregations and from preaching or conducting religious services without permission. The minimum baptismal age was raised from eighteen to thirty, and congregations were instructed to provide only for their existing members, not to seek new ones.[149] A dissenting group known as the "Organizing Committee" protested against these actions and the Baptist leaders who conformed to them.

The underground Baptist movement was particularly strong in the 1960s in reaction to the state-related Evangelical-Baptist organization. Many of these Baptists had been or were sentenced to labor camps for failure to conform to religious regulations. Some were monitored by the KGB, the Soviet secret police. Conflicts between the AUCECB and the Organizing Committee arose as early as 1961, when the latter group declared that the parent body had become "the mouthpieces of Satan," having sold out to the state.[150] The Committee denounced subsequent AUCEBC statements as not binding on true Baptist believers.

The Organizing Committee ultimately became the Council of Churches (CCECB), better known as *initiativniki,* or "reform Baptists."[151] This movement was outlawed by the state from the moment it began, and many of its members were convicted of violating laws on church and state. Some were sent to labor camps. Two of the best-known dissenters, Gennadi Konstantinovich Kryuchkov and Georgi Petrovich Vins, often were imprisoned for years at a time. Vins, secretary of the CCECB, served numerous terms, and in January 1975 he was given five years in prison to be followed by five years in exile.[152]

These attacks were particularly hard on the unregistered Baptist communities. In a 1963 letter to Nikita Khrushchev, dissenters described their problems as illustrated in the attack on one of their prayer meetings. It was, they said, disrupted by "druzhiniki [czarist-era gangs that prowled the streets enforcing proper behavior of the youth] and militia under the guidance of the KGB. In Kharkov and Zivoto (Vinnitsa oblast) believers were beaten up, and then those arrested sentenced to 10–15 days. In Kiev the KGB also instigated the beating up of scores of believers…'. There have been cases where church buildings have been demolished by bulldozers in raids led by groups of young people and druzhiniki, for example in Vladivostok, Tashkent, Brest and other places."[153]

An article in *Pravda,* February 19, 1966, recounted the government's perspective on events surrounding a large gathering of dissenting Baptists in Rostov-on-Don. It reported:

> Recently sectarians in our country have been exceeding all bounds. They have not only been arranging meetings in houses, but also have been openly holding forth in public places. For example, in July last year here was a group of sectarians on the suburban Azov-Rostov train who sang religious music to the accompaniment of a guitar and balalaikas. Passengers were indignant and demanded that this

lawlessness should stop. But the leader of the sectarian group, a certain Kolbant-sev, started to object, maintaining that the Baptist—initiativniki sect acknowl-edges no Soviet laws because it has its own.[154]

Persecution continued against both Baptist groups. It was particularly concentrated against the reform Baptists, whose leaders Nikolai Kuzmich Khmara, Ivan Alfonin, and Alexei Iskovskikh died in prison camps in the 1960s and 1970s. The arrests led to the founding of the Council of Baptist Prisoners' Relatives in 1964. They attested to the innocence of their imprisoned comrades and attempted to make their situation known to Baptists around the world. Their infamous "prisoner lists" detailed the names and addresses of persecuted individuals, along with the charges leveled against them. In this way, the CCECB sought to document state harassment of individuals on the basis of their religious activities.[155]

AUCECB leaders, on the other hand, were quick to respond to their critics. They asserted, "As Christians and citizens of our country we, like everyone else, have duties and responsibilities imposed on us by the state. And the more ardent we are as Christians the more serious we are in acknowledging our responsibilities and the more zealous we are in fulfilling our duty."[156]

In 1966, the AUCECB issued a statement declaring, "In accordance with the Holy Scripture (St. Matthew. 22, 21; Rom. 13, 1-5; Tit. 3, 1-2) AUCECB and the churches affil-iated with the Union respect and abide by the laws of the country in all activities other than those involving the inner spiritual life of the faithful."[157] The document noted, "Evangelical Christian-Baptist churches conduct their services in special buildings made available by the state for free use by the church or in premises rented from the local authorities or private individuals."[158]

While dissenters were subject to state sanction, the more cooperative Baptists were given greater opportunities by the state. John Anderson wrote:

More overt forms of state interference appear to have eased after Khrushchev's fall and at the 1969 AUCECB Congress it was reported that some 10,000 individu-als had returned to the Union. Yet many, especially those with family members in hiding or in labour camps, remained intransigent, and increasingly the authorities dropped the requirement that congregations could only be registered within the Baptist Union, a body some deemed excessively compromised. This proved attrac-tive to a number of congregations which began to register autonomously, causing further splits within the ranks of the initsiativniki (dissenters).[159]

All-Union Baptists, sanctioned by the state, did receive permission to print Bibles, New Testaments, hymnals, and a journal called *The Fraternal Messenger.* Theological education in the 1960s and 1970s was offered primarily through correspondence courses approved by the state. Some Baptists were permitted to study abroad, and certain pastors were allowed to travel to international Baptist meetings.[160]

During the Brezhnev era, dissenting Baptist churches organized illegal youth camps, Sun-day schools, and a publishing company, Khristianin, which produced unauthorized religious literature. The discovery of these underground presses led to the arrest of numerous Baptist leaders at various times during the 1970s and early 1980s. The detention simply intensified underground activities.[161]

The Collapse of the Soviet Union

With the breakup of the Soviet Union in 1989, Baptists, like other religious groups, experienced significant transition and reorganization in their denominational organizations. Pentecostals and others withdrew from the All-Union Council of Evangelical Christians-Baptists and the name was changed to the Union of Evangelical Christians-Baptists. The development of new nation-states led to the growth of national Baptist denominations. Baptists in the Commonwealth of Independent States continued to cooperate through a network known as the Federation of Unions of Evangelical Christians-Baptists.[162] In Russia, the Union of Evangelical Christians-Baptists (ECB) became the Russian Baptist Union (RBU). The twenty-ninth Congress of the Union in October 1993 was attended by six hundred delegates and approximately three hundred observers.

The emigration of older Baptist leaders from the Soviet Union thrust younger Baptists into prominence. Some suggest that prior to 1990, at least 50 percent of the Baptist regional superintendents had emigrated to the West. Also, new regional divisions of the Union meant that more leaders were required.[163] The new president of the Baptist Union was Piotr Konovalchik, pastor of First Baptist Church of St. Petersburg. At age fifty-three, he was one of the youngest individuals to hold that office. Forty-three-year-old Alexander Kozynoko became president of the Moscow Theological Seminary in the 1990s. Sergei Sannikov, president of the seminary and Bible school in the Ukraine, was in his mid-thirties when elected.

Many Baptist churches expanded ministries they had maintained during Soviet rule. Central Baptist Church in Moscow was organized in 1882 and moved to its own building in 1917. It was one of the few churches to maintain continuous service throughout the communist era. Of those years, Pastor Ivan Korablev observed, "Not even the atheists could close down our church."[164]

Baptist Responses to Chernobyl

The meltdown of the nuclear reactor at Chernobyl occurred in April 1986, while the Soviet Union was still intact. With the collapse of the Soviet government, European Baptists established a direct response to the victims of the nuclear catastrophe. In 1992, the European Baptist Federation initiated a program known as "Children of Chernobyl," which provided a medical care program for groups of Chernobyl children. Baptist churches throughout Europe became hosts, providing treatment to as many as 180 children annually.[165]

Theological Education

The Moscow Baptist Theological Seminary opened on October 3, 1993. Seventeen students, between the ages of eighteen and twenty-nine, were admitted. The idea for a seminary began among Baptists in Moscow as early as the 1920s. The school developed an affiliation with the Euro-Asiatic Federation of Unions of Evangelical Christians-Baptists, the successor of the older AUCECB. Its first graduation occurred in May 1997.[166]

Outside Moscow, the Odessa Bible School and Seminary, founded near that Black Sea resort city, began in 1990, with Sergei Sannikov as president. The school at first offered only weekend courses, and soon it attracted as many as two hundred students. Eventually, a four-year seminary curriculum was developed with a largely part-time faculty.

The Women's Department

Changes in Russian Baptist life led to the creation of the Russian Baptist Women's Department in October 1993. Vera Kadaeva, literary editor for the Euro-Asiatic Federation of ECB Unions in the Commonwealth of Independent States, detailed the group's intention to organize women's ministries, establish Bible study programs for women, and encourage evangelism through youth work and Sunday schools. The formation of women's organizations encountered some opposition. A pastors' council in one region voted to disband "organized" women's mission groups, apparently because of concern that they might lead women to pursue ordination and pastoral ministry.[167]

Russian Baptists and the State

During the 1990s, Russian Baptists received increasing affirmations from their new government. In 1993, an attempted coup against Russian president Boris Yeltsin did not stop government representative Michailov Genrich from attending the Baptist Union Congress. In his address to the Congress, Genrich declared, "I would like to tell you that in the government, Baptists are well-known; your contribution for spiritual revival and for social service is great."[168]

Baptists in the Ukraine

John Onishenko of the village of Osnowa probably was the first Ukrainian Baptist. After his baptism in 1852, small churches were founded at Osnowa, Lubomirka, and Carlovka. In 1918, the first All-Ukrainian Baptist Conference was established, with a registered membership of one hundred thousand. An article in a 1952 edition of the *Watchman-Examiner* noted that the largest Baptist church in U.S.S.R. was not in Moscow but in Kiev (Ukraine), with more than four thousand members. Emigration also spread Ukrainian Baptist churches to the United States and Canada.[169]

Baptists represent the third largest religious group in the Ukraine, after the Orthodox Church and the Greek Catholics. On January 1, 1993, Evangelical Christians-Baptists had a total of 1,297 churches; these included 1,194 related to the Union of the ECB of Ukraine, 103 from the Religious Congregations of the Former Council of Churches of ECB, 6 congregations of the unaffiliated Evangelical Christians, and 2 congregations of "Pure Baptists."[170]

They divided into groups such as the All-Ukrainian Alliance of Evangelical-Christian Baptist Associations, once part of the All-Union Council of Evangelical Baptists. The alliance became a distinctly Ukrainian body in 1994 under the leadership of pastor Hryhorii Komendant. He also headed a loosely knit Euro-Asian Federation of Baptist Unions, the successor of the All-Union Council.

Ukrainian Baptists maintain numerous pastoral training schools (seminaries) as well as a Bible institute. They publish two periodicals, including the Ukrainian-language paper *Khrystians 'ke zhyttia (Christian Life)*, in Kiev, and the Russian-language *Slovo very (Word of Faith)* in Donets. In 1994, the denomination claimed more than 1,280 churches with some 106,600 members.

Autonomous Baptists, earlier known as the Council of Evangelical Christian Baptist Churches, split with the All-Union Council of Evangelical Baptists in the 1990s. They number fewer than forty churches.[171]

Baptists in Estonia

Estonia is one of the Baltic countries included in the Soviet Union during the period 1945–1989. The Evangelical Christian-Baptist Union of Estonia (ECBUE) began in 1945. It brought together several groups in the Free Church tradition, including the Evangelical Free Church, Baptists, the Revivalist Free Church, and certain Pentecostals. Estonian churches were devastated at the end of the Second World War. Membership in the four denominations associated with the Free Church dropped from fifteen thousand to about ten thousand. Many churches and "prayerhouses" had been destroyed.[172]

In 1945, the Estonian Union joined the Evangelical Christian-Baptist Union. The decision to participate in the group was encouraged by Estonian Baptist leader Osvald Tark, "the most influential theologian of Estonian Baptists during Soviet years."[173] Nonetheless, this Union came under the dominance of the Soviet state and its attempts to control religious communions. As in Russia, Estonian Baptists divided over the appropriate response to be given to Soviet demands on the churches.[174] The forty-three years of Soviet dominance caused significant numerical decline in the ECBUE. In 1989, there were seventy-eight churches and a membership of 5,870. Between 1945 and 1989, "the ECBUE lost approximately 40% of its membership."[175]

During the Soviet years, Free Churches often were referred to simply as Baptists and were caricatured as untrustworthy nonintellectuals who made little contribution to the society. The Estonian Baptists faced many of the same difficulties as Russian Baptists in their relationships with the Soviet government. Printing religious literature was forbidden. For many years, the only Estonian Baptist publication was an annual calendar. Evangelism did occur through weekly worship and seasonal revivals. Youth services, officially forbidden, often were promoted as "birthday parties" in homes. During the years 1969–1981, a revivalistic movement known as *Effattaa* created spiritual renewal among Estonian Baptists while provoking controversy over charismatic gifts among the churches.[176] Billy Graham's 1984 trip to Estonia contributed to renewed evangelistic efforts and brought Baptists to public attention. An evangelism textbook by Baptist leader Robert Vosu was disseminated in typescript form among the churches.[177]

The union with other Free Churches brought disagreements over infant versus believer's baptism. Ultimately, decisions regarding the mode of baptism were left with the individual, not the church. Questions of open versus closed communion remained, however. In Tallinn, for example, the Oleviste Church maintained two separate communion services, one for the immersed and the other for the nonimmersed.[178]

The Estonian Theological Seminary closed in 1940, at the beginning of the Soviet era. Ministerial training then took the form of short-term seminars and continuing education programs. Textbooks often were typewritten manuscripts prepared by local pastors.[179]

Following the demise of the Soviet Union, Estonian Baptists moved quickly to establish new educational institutions. The Union of Christian and Baptist Churches of Estonia founded a Theological Seminary in 1989. New facilities for the school were dedicated in September 1994 in Tartu, and forty-seven students were enrolled.[180] By the late 1990s, the Union of Baptist Churches of Latvia claimed over seventy-five churches and 6,056 members.[181]

Baptists in Georgia

The Republic of Georgia, once part of the czarist Russian Empire, was later incorporated into the Soviet Union. The first Baptist presence there came when a German Lithuanian, Martin Kalweit (1833–1918), moved to Tblisi (Tiflis) in 1862. Kalweit was a member of a German Baptist church in East Prussia. He conducted worship in the city and, as noted previously, baptized the first Russian convert, Nikita Voronin, in 1867.[182]

Kalweit and Voronin organized the first Georgian Baptist church. Persecution from the Orthodox establishment was intense, and the congregation was not formally constituted until 1880. Vasili Pavlov, one of major leaders of the early Russian Baptist movement, was baptized by Voronin in 1871. The church endured numerous controversies, including divisions over Pentecostal experiences. Armenian members formed two distinct Armenian congregations, one Evangelical Christian, the other Baptist. Native Georgians came by 1912, and by 1919, some of the services were conducted in the Georgian vernacular. The church closed down during the years 1937–1944, reopening in 1945 in union with an Evangelical Christian congregation in Tblisi. In 1988, the congregation reported 2,450 members, including 1,500 Georgians, 550 Russians, 150 Armenians, and 250 Ossetians.[183]

The church became part of the Russian Baptist Federation in 1921 and joined the AUCECB in 1944. In 1990, the Georgian Baptist Union came into existence as an autonomous national denomination.

In 1995, the Georgian Baptist Union reported forty-one churches, with over four thousand members and seven ordained pastors. A year later, that number had risen to over 4,500 members in forty-two congregations. During the 1990s, the European Baptist Federation donated some $30,000 to help purchase eleven houses for use by Georgian Baptist congregations.[184]

Church membership consisted of eleven nationalities. In 1996, a seminary was founded in Tblisi, with approximately seventy students in its initial class. Dr. Levan Akhalmosulishvili, physician and pastor, was general secretary of the Union.[185]

Baptists in Europe: A Tenacious Minority

European Baptists carved out distinct identities throughout the nineteenth and twentieth centuries. In every country, they were a minority Protestant presence, often subject to harassment, even persecution, by religious establishments or hostile states. While these actions are well known in communist countries, it is often forgotten that state Lutheranism in Scandinavia promoted second-class status for Baptists and other Free Church traditions well into the twentieth century. In Germany, Baptists remained strangely silent during the Nazi era—a silence for which they later would repent. For Baptists in Eastern Europe, the struggles created by two world wars, Soviet dominance, and a developing nationalism created innumerable challenges surrounding church-state relations, evangelical witness, and internal divisions. The breakup of the Soviet Union reshaped Baptist life in Eastern Europe to significant degrees as Baptists in new nation-states founded churches, established schools, and created national identities. At the end of the twentieth century, European Baptists sought new ways to work together amid divisions over Pentecostalism, ecumenism, evangelical methods, and global economics.

Notes

1. James H. Rushbrooke, "Baptists in Continental Europe," *Baptist Quarterly* 1 (1922–23): 197.
2. Ian Randall and E. Hulse, "Oncken: Pioneer Baptist of Europe," *Reformation Today* (1975): 10.
3. Rushbrooke, "Baptists in Continental Europe," 197.
4. Ibid., 201.
5. Richard V. Pierard, "Germany and Baptist Expansion in Nineteenth-Century Europe," (typescript, n.d.), 3. In this paper, Pierard made extensive use of Günter Balders, ed., *Ein Herr, ein Glaube, eine Taufe: 150 Jahre Baptistengemeinden in Deutschland, 1934–1984*, 3rd ed. (Wuppertal: Oncken Verlag, 1989). Particular attention is given to Balders's own chapter in that volume, "Kurze Geschichte der deutschen Baptisten," 17–167.
6. Ibid., 3.
7. Randall and Hulse, "Oncken," 13–14.
8. Pierard, "Germany and Baptist Expansion," 3–4.
9. Randall and Hulse, "Oncken," 18.
10. Pierard, "Germany and Baptist Expansion," 5.
11. Randall and Hulse, "Oncken," 17.
12. Pierard, "Germany and Baptist Expansion," 6.
13. John Hunt Cooke, *Johann Gerhard Oncken: His Life and Work* (London: S. W. Partridge, 1908), 3.
14. Herbert Petrick, "The Tasks of the Baptist Denomination in Germany," *Baptist Quarterly* 4 (1928–29): 161.
15. Ibid., 162.
16. Ibid.
17. Ernest A. Payne, "Some Impressions of Germany," *Baptist Quarterly* 4 (1928–29): 114.
18. Ibid.
19. Albert W. Wardin, ed., *Baptists around the World: A Comprehensive Handbook* (Nashville: Broadman & Holman, 1995), 200.
20. Ibid., 200–201.
21. Ibid., 201.
22. Ibid., 202.
23. Ibid., 198.
24. Johannes Norgard, "The Rise of the Baptist Churches in Denmark," in *Baptist World Congress, Baptist Work in Denmark, Finland, Norway and Sweden* (Stockholm: Westerberg, 1947), 18.
25. *Revival of Religion in Denmark* (London: Houlston and Stoneman, 1841), 26; A. K. Moden, "The Baptist Churches of Denmark, Sweden and Norway; Their Origin, Development and Present Position," in *Record of Proceedings, First European Baptist Congress* (1905), 142.
26. *Religion in Denmark*, 32.
27. Ibid., 40.
28. Norgard, "Baptist Churches in Denmark," 20–21.
29. Peder A. Eidberg, "Baptist Developments in the Nordic Countries During the Twentieth Century" (paper presented at the International Conference on Baptist Studies, July 2000), 7–8.
30. Wardin, ed., *Baptists around the World*, 238.
31. Ibid., 238–39.
32. Ibid.
33. Nils Sundholm, "Baptists in Sweden," *Baptist Quarterly* 15 (1953–54): 183–87.
34. H. Danielson, "The Swedish Baptist Union," in Baptist World Congress, *Baptist Work*, 66.
35. Sundholm, "Baptists in Sweden," 183.
36. Ibid., 184.
37. Danielson, "The Swedish Baptist Union," 69.
38. Wardin, ed., *Baptists around the World*, 251.
39. Danielson, "The Swedish Baptist Union," 70.
40. Sundholm, "Baptists in Sweden," 186.
41. Wardin, ed., *Baptists around the World*, 251–52.

42. "Swedish Baptists Celebrate 150th Anniversary," European Baptist Press Service (May 6, 1998).

43. Wardin, ed., *Baptists around the World*, 250.

44. Alfons Sundqvist, "The Baptist Movement in Finland," in Baptist World Congress, *Baptist Work*, 27–28.

45. Ibid., 29–30.

46. Ibid., 30–31.

47. Ibid., 36.

48. Ibid., 40.

49. Ibid., 40–44.

50. Wardin, ed., *Baptists around the World*, 241–43.

51. Jan A. Bradsma, "Johannes Elias Feisser and the Rise of the Netherlands Baptists," *Baptist Quarterly* 16 (1955–56): 10–12.

52. Bradsma, "Johannes Elias Feisser," 14.

53. Ibid., 16–20.

54. Wardin, ed., *Baptists around the World*, 205–6.

55. Ibid.

56. Ibid., 205.

57. Arnold T. Ohrn, "Baptist Work in Norway," in Baptist World Congress, *Baptist Work*, 49–52.

58. Ibid., 52–54.

59. Ibid., 55–56.

60. Peder M. Eiland, "Norwegian Baptist Ecclesiology in the Twentieth Century: A Historical and Theological Retrospective" (paper presented at the International Conference on Baptist Studies, July 2000), 16–18.

61. Wardin, ed., *Baptists around the World*, 248–49.

62. Salvatore Mondello and Pellegrino Nazzaro, "The Origins of Baptist Evangelism in Italy, 1848," *American Baptist Quarterly* 7 (June 1988): 113.

63. Dexter G. Whittinghill, "The Development and Position of the Baptists Among the Italians," *Record of Proceedings, First European Baptist Congress* (1905), 166–67.

64. Mondello and Nazzaro, "Baptist Evangelism in Italy," 117–18.

65. W. Kemme Landels, "The Baptists in Italy," in *The Baptist Movement in the Continent of Europe*, ed. James H. Rushbrooke (London: Carey Press, 1915), 120–29.

66. Whittinghill, "Baptists among the Italians," 167–70.

67. Mondello and Nazzaro, "Baptist Evangelism in Italy," 123.

68. Paolo Spanu, "Italian Baptists Since the Second World War" (paper presented at the International Conference on Baptist Studies, July 1997), 4.

69. Ibid., 6, 7 n.

70. Ibid., 9–10.

71. Ibid., 12.

72. Ibid., 12.

73. "Property Transfers to Italian Baptists Termed 'Historical Event,'" European Baptist Press Service (March 18, 1993).

74. "Italian Denominations Agree to 'Mutual Recognition,'" European Baptist Press Service (October 11, 1995).

75. "Strasbourg's Recommendation on Rights of Homosexual Citizens Approved by Some Protestant Church Leaders Contested," European Baptist Press Service (March 17, 1994).

76. Wardin, ed., *Baptists around the World*, 277–78.

77. S. Vincent, "The Baptist Movement in France," *Record of Proceedings, First European Baptist Congress* (1905), 161. Some suggest that Pyt was a Baptist, or at least sympathetic to them. See Robert DuBarry, "Baptist Work in France and Neighbouring French-Speaking Lands," in Rushbrooke, ed., *Baptist Movement*, 114.

78. "Baptists in France," *Baptist Quarterly* 14 (1951–52): 183–87.

79. Ibid.

80. John Jenkins, *Baptist Magazine* (December 27, 1852): 127 (cited in Sebastian Fath, "Another Way of Being a Christian in France: One Century of Baptist Implantation [Twentieth Century]," [paper presented at the International Conference on Baptist Studies, July 2000], 4).

81. Reuben Saillens, "Roman Catholicism and Modern France," *The Sword and the Trowel* (June 1901), 274–75 (cited in Sebastian Fath, "Another Way of Being a Baptist in France," 5).

82. Vincent, "Baptist Movement in France," 163.

83. Ibid., 185.

84. Fath, "Christian in France," 7.

85. Ibid.

86. Ibid, 10.

87. Ibid., 13.

88. *Encyclopedia of Southern Baptists*, 3 vols. (Nashville: Broadman, 1958), 2: 1,287.

89. Wardin, ed., *Baptists around the World*, 282–83.

90. Ibid., 281–82.

91. M. S. Lesik, "The Baptists in Poland," *Baptist Quarterly* 7 (1934–35): 79.

92. Ibid., 80.

93. Pierard, "Germany and Baptist Expansion," 14.

94. Lesik, "The Baptists in Poland," 81.

95. Ibid., 82–83.

96. Albert Wardin, ed., *Baptists around the World*, 207.

97. Ibid.

98. "Polish Baptists Receive Back Lodz Property," European Baptist Press Service (December 2, 1994).

99. "Polish Baptists Register Gains," European Baptist Press Service (March 31, 1992).

100. Wardin, ed., *Baptists around the World*, 206–8.

101. R. E. Davies, "Persecution and Growth: A Hundred Years of Baptist Life in Romania," *Baptist Quarterly* 34 (April 1991): 265–66.

102. Ibid., 266.

103. Ibid., 266–67.

104. Wardin, ed., *Baptists around the World*, 265.

105. Davies, "Persecution and Growth," 267.

106. Ibid., 267–68.

107. Ibid., 268.

108. Josif Ton, *The Present Situation of the Baptist Church in Romania* (London: Jubal Multiwrite: 1973), 7.

109. Ibid., 13.

110. Davies, "Persecution and Growth," 269–70.

111. "Baptist Seminary in Bucharest Achieves Accreditation," European Baptist Press Service (April 21, 1995).

112. "Rumanians Decide against EBF Council in Kishinev," European Baptist Press Service (September 15, 1993).

113. Albert W. Wardin, "The Baptists in Bulgaria," *Baptist Quarterly* 34 (October 1991): 148–49.

114. Ibid., 149.

115. Ibid., 152.

116. Ibid., 154.

117. Ibid., 156.

118. "Bulgarian Baptists Still Cannot Build Because Sofia Government Has Not Approved," European Baptist Press Service (February 1, 1996).

119. "Bulgarian Government Continues to Harass Evangelicals," European Baptist Press Service (March 19, 1996).

120. "Bulgarian Crisis Growing," European Baptist Press Service (January 30, 1997).

121. "Gypsies Are 'Full of Enthusiasm' Says Bulgarian President," European Baptist Press Service (December 6, 1995).

122. Ernest A. Payne, *Out of Great Tribulation: Baptists in the U.S.S.R.* (London: Baptist Union of Great Britain and Ireland, 1974), 13.

123. James H. Rushbrooke, "Vasili Pavlov: A Russian Baptist Pioneer," *Baptist Quarterly* 6 (1932–33): 361.

124. Some Russian Baptist historians insist that "the Russian Baptists are not the movement started by any professional missionary" but from German Baptists living in Russia. See Nikolai Kornilov, "Distinctiveness of Russian Baptists: Historical and Theological Survey" (paper presented at the International Conference on Baptist Studies, July 2000), 27.

125. Geoffrey Shakespeare, "The Persecution of Baptists in Russia," *Baptist Quarterly* 5 (1930–31), 49–54.

126. Ibid., 55.

127. Rushbrooke, "Vasili Pavlov," 362–63.

128. James H. Rushbrooke, *Baptists in the U.S.S.R.: Some Facts and Hopes* (Nashville: Broadman, 1943), 6.

129. *Documents of Moscow 1966 All-Union Conference of Evangelical Christian-Baptists* (Moscow, 1966), 6.

130. Rushbrooke, *Baptists in the U.S.S.R.*, 5–6.

131. Rushbrooke, "Vasili Pavlov," 364–65.

132. Rushbrooke, *Baptists in the U.S.S.R.*, 8.

133. Ibid., 10.

134. Ibid., 10.

135. Ibid., 11.

136. Michael Bourdeaux, "Baptists in the Soviet Union Today," *Baptist History and Heritage* 10 (October 1975): 221. This was done in a decree on the separation of the church from the state, and the school from the church, adopted January 23, 1918.

137. Ibid., 13.

138. *Documents of Moscow*, 7.

139. Ibid., 8.

140. Ibid., 10–15.

141. Ibid., 19.

142. "Statute of the Union of Evangelical Christian-Baptists in the U.S.S.R." (1966), 51.

143. Ibid., 52.

144. Ibid., 59.

145. Ibid., 60.

146. *Documents of Moscow*, 34–36.

147. Ibid., 38.

148. Ibid., 28.

149. John Anderson, *Religion, State and Politics in the Soviet Union and Successor States* (Cambridge: Cambridge University Press, 1994), 51.

150. Ibid., 72.

151. Bourdeaux, "Soviet Union Today," 222.

152. Ibid.

153. Anderson, *Religion, State and Politics,* 59.

154. Bourdeaux, "Soviet Union Today," 223 (citing *Pravda,* February 19, 1966, 2).

155. Ibid., 226–28.

156. Anderson, *Religion, State and Politics,* 75.

157. Ibid., 55.

158. Ibid., 59.

159. Ibid, 128–29.

160. Bordeaux, "Soviet Union Today," 226.

161. Ibid., 83–84.

162. "Evangelical Christians-Baptists in C.I.S. Federate," European Baptist Press Service (November 20, 1992).

163. "Young Leaders Emerge in the Russian Baptist Union," European Baptist Press Service (October 14, 1993).

164. "BR-E Project for Moscow Church Building," European Baptist Press Service (October 15, 1996).

165. "European Baptist Care for Chernobyl's Children," European Baptist Press Service (April 24, 1996).

166. "Moscow Baptist Theological Seminary Opens," European Baptist Press Service (October 14, 1993).

167. "Russian Baptist Women Organize in Moscow," European Baptist Press Service (October 14, 1993).

168. "Genrich Says Baptists Are 'Well-known' to Government," European Baptist Press Service (October 14, 1993).

169. J. Hominuke, *A Centenary of Ukrainian Baptists, 1852–1952* (Detroit: Ukrainian Evangelical-Baptist Alliance, 1952).

170. Bohdan Bociurkiw, "Orthodox and Greek Catholics in Ukraine," in *The Politics of Religion in Russia and the New States of Eurasia,* ed. Michael Bourdeaux (Armonk, N.Y.: M. E. Sharpe, 1995), 151.

171. Vasyl Markus, "Religious Pluralism in Ukraine," in Bourdeaux, ed., *Politics of Religion,* 169–70; Jane Ellis, *The Russian Orthodox Church: A Contemporary History* (Bloomington: Indiana University Press, 1986).

172. Toivo Pilli, "Evangelical Christian-Baptist Union of Estonia 1945–1989: Survival Techniques, Outreach Efforts, Search for Identity" (paper presented at the International Conference on Baptist Studies, July 2000), 1–2.

173. Ibid.

174. Ibid., 3.

175. Ibid., 4.

176. Ibid., 9.

177. Ibid., 10.

178. Ibid., 11–12.

179. Ibid., 13–14.

180. "Estonian Baptists Dedicate Their New Seminary Facility," European Baptist Press Service (October 23, 1994).

181. "Latvian Baptist Congress," European Baptist Press Service (April 12, 1996).

182. Wardin, ed., *Baptists around the World,* 222.

183. Ibid., 223.

184. "What Does the Georgian Baptist President Do in His Spare Time?" European Baptist Press Service (September 29, 1995).

185. "Georgian Baptists Enjoy Growth, but Times Are Hard," European Baptist Press Service (February 21, 1996).

Chapter 14
Baptists in Africa and Asia

THE BAPTIST PRESENCE IS A GLOBAL PRESENCE. MISSIONARIES, MOBILITY, and the growth of indigenous churches contributed to the expansion of Baptists worldwide. A survey of the development of Baptists across the world demonstrates commonalities and diversities in belief and practice.

Baptists in Africa

Early Christianity flourished in North Africa in enclaves such as Alexandria, Hippo, and Carthage. Coptic Christianity, with its emphasis on Christ's single nature, took shape in Egypt, Ethiopia, and elsewhere from the early Christian centuries. Western monasticism, both communitarian and eremitic, flourished in North Africa in the fourth century. Indigenous religious traditions were present throughout the entire continent. Beginning in the seventh century, Islam soon established significant influence in many African countries, especially in the north.

During the nineteenth century, European explorations brought numerous missionary endeavors initiated by Baptists and other Christian groups from Europe and the United States. Elizabeth Isichei observed, "In 1800, the dominant form of monotheism in Africa was clearly Islam. Apart from the Copts and highland Ethiopia, Christianity was confined to small enclaves on the coast, in the Congo basin and on the Zambezi."[1]

By the twentieth century, Christianity had expanded across much of the continent. The following "much-quoted, if somewhat unreliable, statistics" suggested that in 1900 there were some 10 million Christians in Africa and by 1970 there were 143 million. Some estimates indicate that by the year 2000 there were more than 393 million African Christians. This last figure suggests that one out of five Christians worldwide is in Africa.[2]

Until the middle of the nineteenth century, only limited contact took place between Europeans and Africans. The work of missionary and explorer David Livingstone, however, paved the way for trade, commerce, colonialism, and missionary endeavors in various regions. East Africa was the scene of British presence, missionary activity, and antislavery impulse. Some Baptist and other Protestant missionaries were concerned that African colonization by the French and the Portuguese would extend Catholic influence in the region.[3]

Missions in West Africa

The Baptist presence in Africa began in the nineteenth century with missionaries sent from Britain, Germany, the Netherlands, and the United States. The Baptist Missionary Society (BMS) was encouraged by its Jamaican missionaries to begin a mission to West Africa that would be led by West Indian Christians and would work to eliminate the slave trade. John Clarke and G. K. Prince were sent from Jamaica to begin work on the Niger River. Stopping on the island of Fernando Po in 1841, they encouraged the creation of a mission base station there. They visited Cameroon and returned to England to encourage the BMS to found new missions in those territories.

In 1844, Clarke, along with Alfred and Helen Saker, arrived at Fernando Po as part of a missionary task force and established a base at the town of Clarence. Two Jamaicans, Joseph Merrick and Alexander Fuller, went first to Fernando Po and then to Cameroon. Merrick died after four years. Fuller's son Joseph later served as a missionary in the region. One observer noted in 1879, "In dear old mr Fuller we could see what the grace of God could do in and through a son of Africa."[4] Thomas Horton Johnson, the first convert, later became the first African pastor of the Bethel Church, founded in Cameroons Town.

Disease and fever struck the missionaries and challenged the popular belief that black Jamaicans would have greater immunity to illness than white missionaries.[5] Sickness, internecine disputes, and political alignments that occurred when Cameroon was claimed by Germany impacted the work of the BMS in the region. German Baptists initiated mission endeavors, but their request for supplementary funding from the BMS was refused. By the 1890s, the BMS dissolved its official connection with the churches founded in Fernando Po and the Cameroons. German Baptists then moved into the region and founded the Missions-Gesellschaft der deutschen Baptisten in 1898.[6]

Mission Efforts in the Congo

The life and work of missionary and explorer David Livingstone (1813–1873) focused European attention on the Congo. Livingstone moved across the continent opening unexplored regions to Western colonization. The Congo Free State was established through an act of the Berlin Congress in 1885. It became the Belgian Congo in 1908 as a colony of Belgium. Independence was secured in 1960, and the country was named Zaire in 1971.[7] In the 1990s, it became the Republic of the Congo.

In 1878, the BMS sent Thomas Comber and George Grenfell to the Congo with specific responsibilities for the area in and around São Salvador. Grenfell was forced to resign when he was charged with fathering a child by Rose Edgerley, his housekeeper during an earlier missionary sojourn in Jamaica. He resigned the mission and married Edgerley, and the two returned to Africa to work with the BMS missionaries. In 1884, he became "the spearhead of the Society's forward policy on the upper [Congo] River."[8]

Using the newly acquired riverboat *Peace,* the BMS sent teams of missionaries along the Congo to make contacts that they hoped would result in churches. Martha Spearing, the first single female sent to Africa by British Baptists, arrived in 1886. Disease again decimated the mission, and Comber and six others died in 1887. An early African convert, William Mantu Parkinson, was baptized in 1886, and the first African church, at São Salvador, was founded in 1887.[9] Of those early African Baptists, Brian Stanley wrote, "As in much of

Africa, the very first Protestant converts thus tended to be individuals who had been uprooted from their own societies and placed in an environment artificially protected by missionary influence. The missionaries were not unaware of this fact, and as a result were strengthened in their conviction that the Christian education of the young held the key to the evangelization of the Congo."[10] Conversions did occur, and by 1900 the Ngombe Lutete and the São Salvador churches claimed a total membership of 492 persons. The church at Mbanza Manteke, whose support was assumed by the American Baptist Missionary Union (ABMU), witnessed a significant number of conversions.[11]

Christianization brought many ethical and cultural dilemmas, especially regarding polygamy. Missionaries and indigenous churches encouraged and often required new Christians to abandon the practice. Churches affiliated with the ABMU were outspoken opponents of the custom, and in 1898 the Ngombe Lutete Baptist Church initiated antipolygamy policies. As a result, families were torn apart, and many persons, particularly females, were ostracized from tribal life. The social disruption created by such measures made others hesitant to enforce a stringent policy. Brian Stanley observed that although the immediate issue in the Ngombe Lutete Baptist Church was not fully resolved, "an important step had been taken in the process of establishing within the African church a Christian concept of marriage in place of the traditional proprietary understanding which lay in the root of the polygamous system."[12] In spite of controversy, many welcomed the changes, especially as they affected the status of African women. One Baptist reported, "We lived apart. Many in our town had not been to the river towns. Women married as you might buy a pig; she knew nothing. Then white men brought us the light; great blessing, great cause for thanks. In the dark we did terrible things. Now the change has come thanks to God. You women, you ought to thank God, but you say, what did you give for [us]?"[13] Others disagreed, warning that evangelization was an effort to undermine traditional African customs and replace them with Western "values."

The American Baptist Presence in the Belgian Congo

The ABMU established work in the Western Congo when it took over the Livingstone Inland Mission of London in 1884. The early missionaries encouraged conversion, organized churches, and promoted Bible study. In 1894, there were ten mission stations, some forty-six missionaries, and more than twelve hundred church members. Fourteen of the missionaries were African Americans.[14]

Local autonomy prevailed in church government but not in indigenous leadership. No African in this region was ordained during the years 1884–1959. Kikama Kividi commented, "Reverend Colon Kapini, CBCO's first General Secretary, was ordained in 1959 in order to fulfill the government requirement that the legal representative of a religious institution must be an ordained minister."[15] This hierarchical model shaped the way many African Baptist laypersons understood the nature of the church. Local autonomy was present in principle, but the missionaries exercised considerable control beyond the congregation.[16] Concerning the clash of Baptist organizational models and indigenous communities, Kividi remarked, "American Baptist missionaries did not take into consideration Bantu traditional social and political organization when they created mission stations which united many tribes together.... Mission station structures and denominational allegiances ... were foreign impositions."[17]

Civil Unrest

African Baptists (and white missionaries) in Angola were caught up in civil uprisings and rebellions in the early twentieth century. In 1913, Tulante Buta led a revolt against the reigning chieftain Kiditu, king of the Bakongo tribe. This action led to Portuguese intervention and armed conflicts against Buta and his armies. Simao Seke, a Baptist, was his chief adjutant. For supposed collaboration with the rebels, many Baptist churches and farms were burned by Portuguese soldiers, and church life was disrupted.[18]

Well into the 1920s, Portuguese control of the colony created censures against the Baptists, forcing preachers to secure licenses, closing schools, and even attempting to ban the use of vernacular hymnals and Bibles. Nonetheless, Angolan Baptists experienced growth. Membership in the Kibokolo church expanded from 8 members in 1916 to 1,734 in 1933.[19]

With growth came controversy. In 1921, a movement arose in the Nkamba church when the congregation refused to license Simon Kimbangu as a Baptist evangelist. Soon afterward, Kimbangu claimed to have experienced a new revelation that conferred upon him a unique apostolic calling and healing powers. After exercising certain prophetic gifts, he was recognized as a prophet by the larger Ngombe Lutete (Baptist) Church. R. L. Jennings, a BMS missionary, and M. Morel, the Belgian colonial administrator, soon challenged his claims. Morel sought Kimbangu's arrest, but he eluded capture. While several of his supporters were arrested, Kimbangu continued his public ministry.

Ultimately, he was arrested by the Belgians, tried for treason, and condemned to death. The sentence was commuted to life in prison, and he died in 1951. This religiopolitical movement created divisions in the churches and strained relations between African and European Baptists. A schism among the Baptists and other African Christians led to the formation of an indigenous church, *L'Église du Jesus Christ sur la Terre par le Prophete Simon Kimbangu*. It became Africa's largest independent church.[20]

African Church Life: The Congo

Congolese Baptist churches grew steadily amid a variety of practices. Total membership in the Baptist churches of the Congo related to the BMS increased from 5,495 in 1914 to 50,336 in 1960.[21] Church discipline was a major concern of many congregations. During certain years, excommunicated (disciplined) church members exceeded the number of baptized new converts. Discipline for sexual immorality, polygamy, and the use of alcoholic beverages was particularly stern and often created tensions between African Christians and Baptist missionaries. For example, the churches in the Upoto region reported in 1923 some 101 baptisms, with 140 disciplinary suspensions of members.[22] During the 1930s, revival movements among Baptists in the Congo produced conversions, enthusiastic worship, and the "fullness of the Holy Spirit."

Indigenous Baptist leaders soon appeared on the scene. Jacques Nzakimwena (d. 1956) was a Baptist who attended the evangelical training school known as *L'Ecole de Pasteurs et d'Instituteurs* at Kimpese. In 1944, he became the "first ordained [African] pastor of the BMS Congo mission" and served as pastor of the church at Kingemba in the Ngombe Lutete district of the church.[23]

Nzakimwena's brother, Emile Disengomoka (d. 1965), was a Baptist educator, "the first Congolese to study in Belgium for the three-year teaching diploma, the Régent littéraire."

Returning to the Congo, he became headmaster at the Ngombe Lutete School and served on the Commission for the Protection of Native Rights and other national committees.[24]

An African Church: Changing Relationships

Brian Stanley documented the difficulty that many of the veteran missionaries felt in relinquishing control of church affairs to indigenous African Baptists in the latter half of the twentieth century. Well into the 1950s, decision making remained solely in the hands of the Anglo Baptist missionaries. While these missionaries acknowledged the importance of passing on control to the Africans, they insisted that it should be done gradually due to the "African mentality, and the Africans' own desire for a gradual process of devolution."[25] Some local and regional councils were comprised of both missionaries and Africans, while others were limited to one group or the other. Africans often complained that the missionaries did not take new organizational structures seriously and were refusing to relinquish organizational control. By the 1960s, nationalist politicians such as Patrice Lumumba, president of an indigenous political party, created additional impetus for the Africanization of church structures.[26]

In 1961, Baptists in the Congo constituted three regional churches, including *L'Église Baptiste du Bas Fleuve, L'Église Baptiste du Moyen Fleuve,* and *L'Église Baptiste du Haut Congo.* BMS mission work continued, but only with endorsement by these new church units. New emphases on education led to the founding of additional Baptist-based schools at Thysville and Leopoldville in 1962.[27] During the 1960s, increasing military conflicts created difficulties for the population and the churches.

In 1970, a new all-Protestant body, *Église du Christ au Congo* (later *Église du Christ du Zaire),* was established. The Baptists joined that Protestant union, with subdenominations known as the *Communauté Baptiste du Fleuve,* the *Communauté Baptiste du Haut-Congo,* and the *Communauté Baptiste du Moyen Fleuve.* These three Baptist bodies ultimately united to become the *Communauté Baptiste du Congo Occidental.*

Century's End: Civil War

Civil war again struck Zaire in the 1990s when a coup led to a new government that renamed the country the Democratic Republic of the Congo. In the early 1990s, the Communauté Baptiste du Congo Occidental (CBCO) reported significant growth, particularly in the capital, Kinshasa. From 1970 to 1990, the CBCO churches around Kinshasa claimed eighty-one congregations with a membership of 47,468.[28] This growth among the indigenous population further accentuated differences between the (predominately Bantu-language group) African Baptists and the American Baptist missionaries.

Besides the Roman Catholics and the Kimbangu Church, Baptists are the largest communion in the Republic of the Congo (Zaire), numbering almost eight hundred thousand total membership. At the beginning of the twenty-first century, there were at least thirteen distinct Baptist groups in the country.[29]

Baptists in Liberia

The first American missionaries to Africa were sent to Liberia. It was there that the American Colonization Society hoped to dispatch large numbers of freed slaves as a way of ending slavery in the United States. The first transplanted former slaves arrived in Liberia in 1822, the year the colony was founded. Resettlement efforts ended in 1866 with fewer than twelve thousand émigrés sent to Liberia at a time when the black population in the United States numbered some 1.75 million. Support for this effort came from Southern slaveholders who hoped to remove the free black population from the country and thereby reduce the possibility of rebellion among slaves.

Although Liberian independence was secured in 1847, the nation struggled economically and racially throughout its history. By 1848, four American denominations had missions in Monrovia, the capital. These included Baptists, Methodists, Episcopalians, and Presbyterians. Other denominations began work their after the turn of the century.[30]

During these years, the ABMU affirmed its commitment to African missions in Liberia and elsewhere. Acknowledging the high mortality rate among white missionaries, the ABMU (mistakenly) recommended that the "colored brethren" were better fitted for such missions because they could cope with the heat and disease more easily. One source declared that these "brethren, though natives of America, are, by nature and constitution, better adapted to endure the trials of its climate." The board advised sending African Americans "to establish gospel churches on an enlightened and solid basis." It also affirmed the need to work with "our Southern colored brethren" in raising funds for such endeavors.[31]

In 1846, William C. Crane, an African American Baptist deacon in whose home the First Baptist Church of Monrovia was formed, urged the Southern Baptist Convention (SBC) to continue support of the Liberia mission. His words were double-edged: "And whether we view this great subject in the light of simply sending the gospel to the heathen, or in light of repairing the wrongs of oppressed Africa, or in the light of employing and benefitting the piety and zeal of probably one hundred and fifty thousand cold-hearted Baptists in our own country, your committee cannot but earnestly urge that our enquiries, our prayers, and our efforts, may be energetically employed in this behalf."[32] The SBC acknowledged the good work of the missionaries of color, but urged the sending of Caucasian missionaries. The missions committee declared that it was "peculiarly important that at least two well educated, well qualified missionaries, fitted for the work, should be employed there [Liberia] as leaders in an African Mission; and they would affectionately inquire, whether some of our good southern pastors cannot feel that God had called them to this important service."[33]

Harrison N. Bouey, an African American minister, was sent to Liberia in 1879 by the South Carolina Baptist Convention. He later served as an agent of the Alabama Convention Foreign Mission Board and the National Baptist Mission Board. He left Liberia in 1881 and returned in 1902, remaining there until his death.[34]

African Americans in Liberia retained English and an identity distinct from that of the indigenous Grebo and Kru peoples. The African American missionary Lott Carey died as a result of an explosion of munitions used for protection against the indigenous population.[35] The Baptist presence became prominent through a series of political leaders personified in the Tolbert family and the True Whig Party. William Tolbert, a Baptist active on the world scene, became president of Liberia in 1971. From 1965 to 1970, he was the first African to serve as president of the Baptist World Alliance. Tolbert was killed in a 1980 coup instigated by the army led by Samuel Doe. Doe himself died in another coup in 1990 as Liberia was thrown into a period of civil unrest that endured through the end of the twentieth century.[36]

Baptists in Nigeria

Modern missionary work in Nigeria originated in 1842 when a Methodist mission was founded by Thomas Birch Freeman and William de Graft. The SBC sent Thomas J. Bowen, who arrived in Ijaiye in 1854. A Baptist mission in Ogbomosho was established in 1855. By the mid-1860s, eight missionaries had been sent, but six died soon after arriving. Thomas Bowen left Africa for a mission in Brazil in 1859. A civil war during the years 1860–1861 fostered a violent anti-Christian backlash and led to the abandonment of the mission in 1872.[37]

In 1874, the SBC sent William J. David to Nigeria to work with W. W. Colley, a missionary from the Colored Baptist Convention of Virginia. They soon joined with a Nigerian lay preacher named M. L. Stone in founding a church in Lagos. Stone's work in Ogbomosho helped make it the center of Baptist work in Nigeria. Forced to return home because of illness, David returned in 1878 with his new bride, Nannie Bland David. He wrote to H. A. Tupper, executive secretary of the mission board, "Mrs. David and I turned our faces toward the 'dark continent,' believing that he who hath lived and cared for us in the past, will order our future in that way, that will bring most honor to his name. Our desire is to glorify Christ whether in life or death. Mrs. David says I must put 'Amen' to the above for her."[38] Nannie David lost a daughter and a son before she died in Africa in 1885.

In 1893, the SBC Foreign Mission Board reported "forty-two white and six colored" had served in Africa, thirteen of whom died either in country or on the trip home. That year, there were only four single male missionaries and three missionary families in the field.[39]

Nigerian native churches took shape in the late nineteenth and early twentieth centuries. The earliest converts originated with Lagos Baptists, many of whom were frustrated by the control of foreign missionaries over church affairs. Baptist polity lent itself to divisions and the possibility of reunion. Independent and mission-related Baptists were reunited in 1914.[40]

The African Baptist Assembly was one of the earliest organizations founded by African Baptists. It was formed by Daniel S. Malekebu (1887–1978), medical missionary and leader of the Providence Industrial Mission (PIM), based in Chiradzulu, Nyasaland (now Malawi). This mission was supported by the National Baptist Convention, USA. Malekebu, a Zulu, received his education at Baptist-related schools in the United States. He was converted to Christianity through the influence of John Chilembwe, who formed the PIM in 1901. Chilembwe's failed revolt against British colonialism in 1915 led to his execution and the end of the PIM. The organization was not revived until 1926, with Malekebu as leader.

The Nigerian Baptist Convention organized numerous schools, among them a theological seminary in Ogbomosho and various pastors' schools in Oyo, Owerri, Eku, Jos, Kaduna, and Gombi. The Convention's publication department provides materials printed in English, Yoruba, and Hausa, as well as a monthly periodical, *The Nigerian Baptist.*

The African Baptist Assembly began in 1945, founded by Malekebu as a network of Baptists from various African peoples, and aimed at providing fellowship and guidance for African Baptists. By the 1970s, the group had some twenty thousand members. It became a member of the Baptist World Alliance in 1974. By the 1980s, the organization claimed 474 member churches and a membership of more than forty thousand people.[41]

South African Baptists

The first English settlers who arrived in the Cape Colony in South Africa in 1820 came to escape the economic and social depression brought on by the Napoleonic wars. William Miller (1779–1856), one of these settlers, was the founder of the Baptist movement in South Africa. At age forty-two, he came on the ship *Brilliant,* having received baptism in England, in 1808, at London's Edward Street Church.[42] Of his calling he wrote, "From the day that I was baptised by the Rev. Mr Simmons, in Edward Street Chapel April 6th 1808, I not only said of the people of God 'This people shall be my people and their God shall be my God' but that I was willing to take the Gospel to the beds of the sick and the dying, to prisons and work-houses, and this desire was strengthened by a strong impression made upon my mind, as though made by a voice above me saying 'You must fly with the Gospel.'"[43]

Soon a small congregation of Baptists was constituted at Salem, with Miller as pastor. Miller next went to Grahamstown, where he provided occasional preaching services. Disputes over Miller's Calvinism led to his resignation from the pastorate. The Grahamstown church requested that a new minister be sent from England, and the BMS sent William Davies, the first ordained Baptist minister to the Cape Colony.[44] Nonetheless, William Miller is considered the "founder of the Baptist Church in South Africa."[45]

For the Davies family, the trip to South Africa was fraught with peril. Their ship ran aground off the island of Las Palmas, and their infant child was swept from his father's arms. Davies wrote of the incident, "Mercifully, however, I was not washed overboard, but oh! my son! my only son! was carried away from my arms and perished in the waves—yes, little William is gone. Great God, how wonderful are Thy ways."[46]

Davies and his wife were not immune to the theological divisions of the times. Davies wrote of his wife's theological position and their disputes:

> She was a moderate Calvinist; one who with [Andrew] Fuller and with all who are
> moderate in their views held the sovereignty of God in connection with the respon-
> sibility of man—who held free grace on the one hand and full duty on the other.
> She had a very great aversion to antinomianism ... a system which lays waste every
> duty and moral obligation and which with all the malignity of a demon unchris-
> tianises and consigns to eternal death all the church of God except the few, scant-
> ling elect that are found within its own 'sanctum sanctorum'.... She had seen with
> her own eyes the many mischiefs which it had done in our own churches—how it
> crucified our ministers—how it had perplexed our deacons and how it had kept
> societies which otherwise would have been peaceful and harmonious in broils and
> everlasting fermentations.[47]

Another church was begun in Kariega, where attacks from native Gaikas and Galekas were so volatile that no building was completed until 1854. The conflict between blacks and whites began early, as Davies noted:

> I understand, that in our native land Christian sympathy is turned almost exclusively
> towards the native. Every instance of suffering amongst them is repeated in doleful
> accent in the parlour, in the pulpit, and on the missionary platform. But nothing is said
> about the Poor Settlers, only 'that they are wicked christians',—nothing is said about
> our houses burnt,—nothing is said about our wives and children driven to the bush
> in the dead of night to hide themselves from the point of the blood-stained assegai.[48]

Internal controversies divided the fledgling churches almost from the beginning. In 1843, a new congregation was founded in Grahamstown on Bathurst Street by G. Aveline. It reported a Sunday school for both English and native children numbering around a hundred. Yet a split soon occurred, leading to the formation of the Ebenezer Baptist Church in 1849. The two congregations were not reunited for another fifteen years.[49]

In 1857, a constitution was written for the first church at Grahamstown. It states, "Believing that Baptism, as instituted by our Lord Jesus Christ, is an immersion on a profession of faith in Him as the one and all-sufficient Saviour of sinners, we would receive into Church membership only those who have been thus baptised, but as we would not judge any man's conscience who may differ from us, we would cordially welcome at the Lord's table all who afford satisfactory evidence that they love the Lord Jesus Christ in Sincerity."[50]

The Baptist presence spread, and the Queen Street Church in Port Elizabeth was formed in 1856. It became the "mother church" for numerous congregations formed by Afrikaners, indigenous Africans, and "coloureds"—a racial category in South Africa of mixed white, black, and Asian ancestors.

The Walmer Road Church in Port Elizabeth was an interracial congregation until 1913, when the whites moved out to form another church.[51] These churches were part of the Cape Colony's Eastern Province, a group of congregations that formed the Baptist Union in 1877. Strangely, no association was established for almost a century. The Eastern Province Baptist Association finally was founded in 1940.[52]

During the late nineteenth century, British-based churches in South Africa often developed connections with Charles Haddon Spurgeon and the Metropolitan Tabernacle. A request from South African Baptist leaders led Spurgeon to send W. Hamilton to organize a church in Cape Town. The church was founded in 1876 with a simple statement of faith that declared, "The Church of Christ as set forth in the New Testament is composed of those who trust alone in Christ for Salvation, profess His name before the World, and obey the Ordinances of Baptism [by immersion] and the Lord's Supper." It also advised, "No person shall be received as a member of this church who does not appear to us to be a possessor of vital godliness."[53]

German Baptists in South Africa

German Baptists came to South Africa in 1857–1859, during the period of the Crimean War—a conflict that pitted England and France against Russia. The towns that they established—Berlin, Frankfurt, and Potsdam—were named for their old country. In Frankfurt, Baptists Carsten and Dorothea Langhein, Carl Gustav-Adolph and Maria Christine Schmidt, and Christian Friedrich Sandow founded a church, with Langhein as elder. English Baptist pastor Alexander Hay came to Frankfurt in 1861 and ordained Langhein to the ministry.

As the church grew, the members wrote to German Baptist patriarch Johann Oncken, urging him to help them secure additional pastoral assistance. Oncken sent Carl Hugo Gutsche (b. 1843), who, with his wife, Mary Lange, arrived in King William's Town in December 1867. Gutsche set his energies toward organizing new churches, and soon "the church of baptised believers" in British Kaffraria was founded. It claimed some 283 members, divided into three associations. The *Kaffrarian Watchman* in King William's Town noted in 1868, "The German Baptists will build three chapels during the present winter season, at Hanover, Frankfurt and Breidbach. These will be erected principally by the people themselves who are very numerous in the vicinity."[54] Gutsche lived and worked in King William's Town for sixty years, during which time he built twenty-five churches in British Kaffraria.

Funds from the churches were difficult to secure. Gutsche received a fixed salary of £150 for thirty years! Church donations aided the Baptist Theological College in Hamburg Horn, supported new churches, and provided funds for widows whose husbands were killed in the Zulu War.[55]

Conflicts and schism occurred with some frequency. One heated dispute involved securing additional ministers from Germany. One member warned, "Don't be trapped into calling another minister from Germany.... The European blood is so ... hot and wants to rule, but the Americans are meek and patient and serve well; the German bellows like an ox and bawls like a donkey."[56]

Some Dutch-speaking Afrikaners also developed an interest in Baptist beliefs and practices. Gutsche baptized an Afrikaner named J. D. Odendaal in December 1867. The church records state, "Jacob Daniel Odendaal, farmer of Witkop near Burgersdorp, examined by the brethren Langhein, Sandow and Grünewald, who recommended him for admission to the church, acknowledges before the congregation that he is a poor lost sinner, and could be saved only by the blood of Christ. His hope is centred in Jesus alone. For the last eight years he already knows the meaning of being born anew. He desires to join us and to be baptised. He was unanimously received and baptised."[57]

Later ordained to the Baptist ministry, Odendaal was the founder of *Die Afrikaanse Baptiste Kerk,* organized in the Orange Free State in 1886. By the time of the foundation of the Baptist Union, membership in the Dutch and German Baptist churches had doubled.[58]

Another of Odendaal's congregations, the *Mooiheid Ebenhaezer,* later called the Ebenhaezer Baptist Church of Cornelia, was founded in the 1880s and soon instituted mission activities among blacks. Within a decade, it claimed both black and white members. Some blacks had full membership, while others maintained a special status for "friends and the household of the congregation." Church discipline was strict, and members often were excommunicated. Disciplinary actions could be directed against "strained personal relationships, physical violence, disobedience to congregational rules, non-attendance, ... slackness in parental discipline, ... incorrectly interpreting God's Word, ... attendance at concerts, Sabbatarianism, ... arrear debts to the congregation."[59] The "mixed" congregation did not endure, as many whites who visited the church refused to return even if "brown" people were present. Special work with coloureds was thus begun in a segregated mode.

The *Afrikaanse Baptiste Kerk* remained a language unit of the Baptist Union. A constitution was approved in 1944 and revised in 1957, but the organization floundered with membership departures and divisions. A further revision occurred in 1972.

The Baptist Union of South Africa was founded in 1877 on the occasion of the installation of the new pastor of the Grahamstown Baptist Church, G. W. Cross. Hugo Gutsche, R. H. Brotherton, and W. Hamilton of Cape Town were among the ministers present along with numerous lay leaders. The fledgling Union was established July 11, 1877, to encourage those of like faith, to effectively witness to faith in South Africa, and to work with other "free churches in the land" in evangelization and proclamation of the gospel.[60]

The Baptist Union of South Africa

The union marked an attempt at cooperation between English and German Baptists in South Africa. Cooperation did not mean uniformity. South African missiologist John Jonsson delineated differences in the two communions: "Whereas the English Baptist observed open communion, the German Baptist practiced closed communion. Whereas the English Baptists were a loosely knit association of Churches within the Union, the German Baptists represented a closely knit unity within the German Bund. It is not without reason therefore that the vexed problem of the relationship of the autonomy of the local congregation and the need for interdependence in Union evoked much discussion."[61] English-speaking Baptist churches stressed the independency of the congregation, while German-speaking Baptists placed emphasis on a congregational connectionalism among churches. The Declaration of Principle, approved in 1877, stated, "While the Union is composed of Churches and individuals holding the immersion of believers to be the only Christian Baptism, it fully recognises the right of every separate Church to interpret and administer in and for itself the laws of Christ."[62] The purposes of the Union included the promotion of unity and love, evangelization, and Baptist principles. It was to assist churches, obtain accurate information on the work of the churches, develop common programs for denominational welfare, promote religious liberty, and cooperate with other Christian communions.

The Declaration of Principle (1875–1876) provided the basis for the Union: (1) "That the Lord Jesus Christ, our God and Saviour, is the sole and absolute authority in all matters pertaining to faith and practice, as revealed in the Holy Scriptures, and that each church has liberty to interpret and administer His laws"; (2) "That Christian Baptism is the immersion in water into the Name of the Father, the Son, and the Holy Ghost, of those who have professed repentance towards God and faith in our Lord Jesus Christ who 'died for all sins according to the Scriptures, was buried, and rose again the third day'"; (3) "That it is the duty of every disciple to bear personal witness to the Gospel of Jesus Christ, and to take part in the evangelisation of the world."[63]

In 1881, Hugo Gutsche used his presidential address to the Baptist Union to declare, "Each church remains independent but not so independent that it could not be influenced by an outside directing or modifying power.... An independency, where one church does not care for another, appears to us ungodly."[64]

Gutsche himself paid a price for his Union-mindedness. One German congregation at *Keiskamma Hoek* refused to allow him to take communion with them because he had participated in forming the Union, which admitted open communion churches to its membership.[65]

In South Africa, German Baptists traditionally preferred closed communion, while the British Baptist churches generally accepted open communion. They were, however, willing to allow for differences on the matter. Efforts to make open communion normative were rejected in 1894 "on the ground that it was a matter for the individual churches to determine, and not the Union." These questions continued into the twentieth century. By the 1970s, most new churches in the Baptist Union of South Africa accepted closed membership, requiring believer's baptism of all members.[66]

In 1873, a "Colonial Baptist Sustentation Fund" was established for the purpose of assisting "in the formation and support of Baptist Churches in the Colony." The Sustentation Fund was absorbed into the Baptist Union of South Africa when it was formed in 1877. The earliest statistical data prepared by H. J. Batts, secretary of the Baptist Union in 1880, indicated German Baptist church members numbering 452—the same number as the membership in English Baptist churches of South Africa. The 1891 report indicated 953 German church members compared with 1,244 English Baptists.[67] The Union worked to establish churches in newly opened regions. In 1889, with the opening of a railway between Cape Town and Kimberley, the Baptist Union initiated efforts to establish churches in the Kimberley region, the center of South African diamond mining. G. W. Cross and H. J. Batts ventured to Kimberley, where they held services in the local theatre, reporting, "Galleries, pit and all, [were] full with an apparently eager congregation."[68] Soon a church was constituted.

Most of the early South African Baptist pastors came from England, Wales, or Germany. Some emigrated for reasons of health; others, because of difficulties at home. Cross, the early missionary and pastor, wrote to English supporters in 1898:

Sick men cannot do the work required in South Africa.... You have sent us many sick men and we have never refused them. They have been gentle, winsome, patient, often heroic. Sometimes in our glorious climate they have recovered and returned to 'civilization' and 'a larger sphere' but much oftener we have seen them struggle proudly with poverty, we have seen them make mighty efforts to earn a livelihood, until pitiless disease cast them upon the charity of strangers for a death bed.[69]

Early in their history, South African Baptists opposed any form of state patronage for religious groups. Close collegial relationships were developed and maintained with Methodists, Congregationalists, and Presbyterians in the colony. Anglicans and Dutch Reformed communities were less interested in cooperation with more sectarian groups such as the Baptists.

The South Africa War (1899–1902) intensified pastoral demands and complicated Baptist Union programs. Efforts to raise money for ministerial annuity and church extension, begun in 1899, were dropped in order to promote a "War Losses Fund." British Baptists responded to the plight of the churches by establishing the South African Colonial and Missionary Aid Society in 1901, aimed at securing funds for the devastated churches of the colony. It helped secure ministers for South African Baptist churches, pay their expenses, and underwrite the Union's work.[70] In 1910, the Missionary Aid Society was expanded to include aid for Australian and New Zealand Baptist churches, under the name "Baptist Colonial Society."

The South African Baptist Missionary Society was founded by the Baptist Union on April 20, 1892, to advance the Baptist witness at home and abroad. Much of its early labor was with blacks and other people of color in South African society.

Baptist Women's Movements in South Africa

During the late nineteenth century, numerous women's societies were organized. The earliest included "women's meetings" founded to provide support for local churches and missionary endeavors. In 1885, the Woman's Visiting Committee was founded in Durban by Mrs. I. Cowley, the wife of the first Baptist minister there. It was later known as the Mother's Meeting and then the Ladies Sewing Meeting. This group brought women together for prayer, Bible study, and missionary action. The Baptist Ladies League brought together women from various churches. By 1906, it held its meetings in conjunction with the annual Baptist Union convocation.[71]

The Union of Baptist Women, established in 1912 under the leadership of Mrs. Tom Perry of Grahamstown, sought to encourage the work of local churches, cooperate with the Baptist Ladies League, and unite, if possible, "all the Women's Baptist Associations in connection with our various churches."[72]

Theological Education

The first Baptist Bible school was founded in South Africa in 1926 to provide for proper ministerial training. It endured until 1931. During the early twentieth century, additional Bible schools were founded throughout the country. In 1951, the Baptist Theological College of South Africa was established in Johannesburg. Financial difficulties forced its closing in 1954, but it reopened the next year.

Social Issues

Race, of course, was the dominant ethical, religious, and political issue in South African life, and it had significant implications for Baptists. Baptist gatherings occasionally addressed racial strife and the national policies of apartheid. During the late nineteenth and early twentieth centuries, the Baptist Union's annual assemblies condemned such public practices as the "wholesale flogging of natives in Johannesburg, for walking upon the pavements of streets, as an unjust, inhuman, un-Christian and cruel procedure" (1894).[73] In 1911, the Baptist Union Assembly called for jury trials in cases where one party was black and the other white (since all judges were white). That same year, the Assembly called for "more stringent legislation" regarding "indecent publications, pictures, bioscopes, etc." since "large number of uncivilized and semi-civilized natives" lived in the society.[74] The Union had a long history of promoting the right of conscientious objection relative to military service and armed conflict.

The South African society distinguished among whites, coloureds, and native black peoples. Apartheid, the legally sanctioned policy of racial separation, led to strict divisions of class, color, and labor. "Homelands" for blacks were created within the country, further perpetuating the racial divisions.

Some coloured Baptist churches were part of the Indian immigration by the early twentieth century. The Telegu Baptist Home Missionary Society sent John Rangiah to Durban in 1903 to begin Baptist work. The first congregation was begun on December 25, 1903. This represented work with Indians in South Africa, carried out by an India-based mission society. Affiliated membership was granted to these churches by the Baptist Union in the 1920s. In the 1950s, the South African Baptist Missionary Society appointed one of its missionaries to India, Miss J. Morck, to work among the Indian Baptist churches in South Africa. She carried out an extensive ministry in Natal among women and children, particularly in urban tenements.[75]

Early in the twentieth century, Mohandas K. Gandhi (1869–1948), the Indian reformer, began his legal career in South Africa and confronted apartheid by challenging the South African system in his own unique way. In some of his activities, Gandhi was joined by J. J. Doke, pastor of Central Baptist Church in Johannesburg. Doke helped edit Gandhi's periodical, affirmed his actions, and cared for him when he was attacked by Indians who found his methods too moderate. Gandhi spoke at Doke's funeral in 1913, recalling "the evening when, at my request, the whole family sang to me the beautiful hymn, 'Lead Kindly Light.' That tune will never die from my memory; it will never fade out.... The whole family was at my disposal in order to nourish me, ... to serve me, ... to soothe me, although I was a stranger to them and had never done a single service to them."[76]

Baptists themselves sought to explain the racial situation in terms that acknowledged the problems but accepted much of the situation of apartheid. Writing in the 1970s, Sydney Hudson-Reed stated:

The attitude which developed in the relations between White and Coloured churches was never one of discrimination on the part of the White, but it must be acknowledged, that the paternalism, which evolved, depended more upon social practice for its justification than it did upon Biblical principles. It must also be frankly state that within the Coloured Community, there were those who preferred the many benefits which accrued to them as a result of this paternalism, to the carrying of heavy financial and other responsibilities, which were involved in independence from the White mother churches.[77]

Even historians were not above seeking to explain away racist divisions.

In 1938, the Baptist Union Assembly attacked anti-Semitism and called

upon all associated with the Baptist cause to manifest the spirit of Christ in all matters involving race relationships ... and desires to express its abhorrence of anti-semitic propaganda, and urges members and adherents of our Baptist churches to maintain the New Testament attitude of mind and heart towards the Jewish people. This Assembly would also place on record at this particular juncture its joy in a fellowship that embraces Afrikaans, German, Indian, Bantu and British Christians.

The Assembly also continued to assail liquor sales and distribution, while demanding "the total prohibition of the import and manufacture of alcoholic liquors."[78]

An elaborate statement on race relations was passed in 1960. In 1976, riots and unrest in black and coloured townships led the Baptist Union Assembly to approve a resolution that deplored the violence, urged the state to use severe measures only when absolutely necessary, and recognized that many of the grievances were the result of governmental refusal to hear long-running complaints from the African, coloured, and Indian communities. It concluded, "We welcome the assurances given by the Government that these grievances will receive immediate attention and the preliminary steps taken in this direction. We consider this to be a matter of desperate urgency.... We urge the Government to expedite the removal of all petty apartheid, and those discriminatory laws which weigh most heavily upon our African, Coloured and Indian peoples."[79]

The 1976 Assembly issued a statement in which it reaffirmed "that the Baptist Union is open to all churches which qualify in terms of its constitution, regardless of race or colour; affirmed that such churches would be welcome into the Baptist Union, and charged the Executive to make known to all the Churches within Baptist Union Associations." It noted, "Scripturally, a local church should be open to all persons, irrespective of race or colour, in respect to membership and attendance at services."[80]

As the last great struggles to end apartheid descended on South Africa, white Baptists divided over the methods for eliminating racial discrimination. South African Baptist leader John Jonsson wrote, "Among Baptist membership were those who gave general consensus to virtually everything the ruling government enacted in implementations of

Apartheid policies, considering the ruling powers to be truly 'a Christian government.'"[81] Some also defended social policies out of "religious piety," insisting that "Christendom in Africa" depended the order and stability of South African society. Although some whites sought to encourage greater racial equality and cooperation inside the Baptist Union, their methods often were perceived by blacks to be patronizing and controlling. Yet another segment of the white Baptist community urged an increased mutuality among the varied racial groups both in governance and missionary action through the Baptist Union and the Baptist Missionary Society.[82]

In 1985, the Baptist Union Assembly approved a letter to the South African president that denounced apartheid as evil, urged repentance for the country's racist past, and demanded an immediate end to segregation. It urged the implementation of a policy of "one person, one vote," a national educational system, equal pay for equal work, and an end to the Group Areas Act—a primary component of apartheid segregation.[83]

In 1987, the Baptist Union and the black Baptist Convention (a subgroup of the Union) split apart as old wounds over paternalism and racism surfaced with the death of apartheid. In 1991, the Baptist Union Assembly approved a statement offering thanks to God for the end of legalized apartheid. It noted, "As Baptists we too have been guilty to our shame; as individuals and as churches, we have sinned in our actions and our attitudes, and have allowed them to be governed by the pattern obtaining in society. We have conformed when we ought to have confronted. Whilst we have condemned the legislation, many of us have enjoyed the economic and social privileges resulting form it. For this we humbly repent. We acknowledge that true repentance will go beyond mere words and will manifest itself in the change of attitude and in positive action."[84]

Efforts at reconciliation included a series of prayer retreats sponsored by the Southern Baptist Convention and the American Baptist Churches USA in 1996 and 1997. At apartheid's end, leaders of the Baptist Convention of South Africa acknowledged their gratitude to the activities of the American Baptist Churches USA and the Lott Carey Foreign Baptist Mission Society.

Black and coloured Baptists in South Africa were drawn from diverse segments of the society and from various African language traditions. In rural black Baptist churches, women had significant leadership roles. Urban black Baptists were found throughout the segregated townships, functioning in the "servant population" and often unrecognized by official Baptist bodies.[85]

Denominational Growth and Development

The South African Baptist Missionary Society was founded in 1892, and in 1919 the Baptist Union and the Missionary Society adopted a method of coordination of programs and work. Between 1898 and 1918, European members increased from 3,033 to 5,156, while native members increased from 172 to 4,185. Sunday school training was begun in 1911. Also in 1911, "lady delegates" to the Baptist Union Assembly met in a gathering aimed at strengthening women's work. In 1912, the South African Baptist Women's Association approved its first constitution, and a new pension scheme was initiated in 1910.[86]

Following the First World War, numerical growth was steady but not spectacular, with membership in European-based churches increasing from 5,165 in 1918 to 8,153 in 1947.

Native churches grew from 4,185 in 1920 to 11,888 in 1947. In 1935, funds were approved for a full-time evangelist "to visit our churches to conduct evangelistic campaigns and for the deepening of Spiritual life." In 1944, the Baptist Union developed a "Thanksgiving Fund" for money to "develop Baptist work and the furtherance of the Baptist evangelical witness in Southern Africa." Other special funds followed.[87]

In 1928, Ernest Baker opened a Bible school in Mowbray to provide some ministerial training. Baker gained a significant leadership role, serving as secretary of the Union from 1902 to 1905 and as secretary of both the Union and the General Assembly from 1935 to 1937. He was involved in multiple facets of the work as editor of the first magazine, the Union's first full-time missioner, and head of the training school for ministers.[88]

In 1951, the Baptist Theological College of South Africa began in Johannesburg, with C. M. Doke as acting principal. Soon after, A. J. Barnard of Birmingham, England, was appointed full-time principal, but questions surrounding his views on the inspiration of Scripture led to his termination in 1954. During the 1960s, members of the Afrikaanse Baptiste Kerk established Die Seminarium van die Baptiste in order to have lectures in Afrikaans.

As noted earlier, most South African Baptist associations were not established until the middle of the twentieth century. The Border Baptist Association was founded in 1940 by churches in King William's Town, Cambridge, and Berea. Its work included conducting joint worship services, founding new ministries, "providing moderators" for churches without pastors, mediating church disputes, promoting the South African Baptist Missionary Society, and "advancing [Baptist] principles." The Association was composed of local churches and "personal members." In 1955, the German Bund (Conference) was united with the Border Baptist Association to form one gathering of congregations.[89]

Racial issues were evident at every turn. Baptists often took positions against the government's racial policies, passing numerous resolutions aimed at racial reconciliation. These resolutions called for public education for children of all races, urged repeal of the Mixed Marriages Act, and called on Baptists themselves "to recognise their personal and individual responsibility for race relations."[90]

In 1977, the Baptist Union was restructured, and its membership was limited to local churches, not associations or individual members. Associations were given seats on the executive committee of the Union. In 1966, the Baptist Convention of South Africa was founded out of the black-based Bantu Baptist Church (1927). With the end of apartheid, some black churches left the Convention and became part of the South African Baptist Union. The first black president of the Union, George Motale Ngamlana, was elected in the late 1990s.[91]

Baptists in Asia

Baptists first entered Asia through India, Burma, and China. Missionaries introduced Baptist ideas, and with time indigenous communities of faith were born. Mission boards and local churches funded numerous persons sent out by Baptist groups in Britain, Europe, and the United States. In the early years, married couples and single women established mission outposts, often doing so with little training and education. Churches and schools were founded as national Baptist denominations were formed.

Baptists in Japan

Christianity was introduced in Japan as early as 1549 through the efforts of the Jesuit missionary Francis Xavier. The movement gained momentum, and by the 1590s Catholics claimed some three hundred thousand converts. Japanese fears of foreign intervention led to persecution against missionaries and indigenous Christians. These actions created thousands of martyrs and arrested the growth of the church. The nation then was closed to outsiders until the nineteenth century.[92] Protestant missionaries attempted an entry in 1827 but were rebuffed. In 1853–1854, Commodore Matthew Perry's expeditions led to the "opening of Japan" to Westerners, and missionary endeavors began anew. A treaty of commerce mediated by Townsend Harris included a provision that Americans could build churches and be free to worship.[93]

Baptists first went to Japan in 1860 through the work of Jonathan (1827–1896) and Eliza (d. 1882) Goble, sent out by the American Baptist Free Mission Society, an abolitionist organization. Jonathan Goble had accompanied Perry to Japan and brought to the United States the first Japanese Baptist convert, a man known as Sam Patch.

By 1872, support for the Gobles and Nathan and Lottie Brown was taken over by the American Baptist Missionary Union. These four founded Japan's first Baptist Church in Yokohama in 1873. Goble's volatile behavior toward Japanese converts and his own wife led to his dismissal by the ABMU, but he remained in the country until 1882 as a "freelance missionary."[94] In 1879, Brown published the first complete translation of the New Testament into Japanese.

Other Baptist missionaries soon followed. Australian Baptists established a mission that endured only from 1874 to 1877. The Baptist Missionary Society (BMS) appointed William J. White in 1878 with a mission that endured until 1890, when his support was taken over by the ABMU. Growth was slow, and by 1888 there were nine hundred members in Japanese Baptist churches. In 1898, the ABMU received the donation of a large "gospel ship," which took missionaries to coastal towns for evangelistic activities.[95]

During the 1880s, the ABMU sent George H. Appleton, former Episcopal missionary, to Japan to begin new ministries in numerous locations. He concluded, "Japan, as a point of missionary radiation, has no superior."[96]

Initial attempts by Southern Baptists to enter Japan were thwarted by weather and theology. John and Sarah Rohrer, the first SBC missionaries sent out in 1860, went down on the ship *Edwin Forrest* on their way to Asia. Crawford Toy, professor at the Southern Baptist Theological Seminary, asked the Foreign Mission Board for appointment to Japan but was refused because of his liberal theological positions.

The presence of SBC missionaries in Japan led to a comity agreement between Southern and Northern Baptists in the United States, dividing the country into areas of work. Northern (American) Baptists took the region north and east of Kobe, while Southern Baptists claimed responsibility for mission work south and west of Kobe.[97]

Some of the first Japanese Baptists came from other Christian denominations, including the Reformed Church and the Russian Orthodox Church. Two of the earliest converts were Kawakatsu Tetsuya and Chiba Yugoro, the latter sent to the United States for college and seminary education. Kawakatsu Tetsuya (d. 1915) was the first Japanese Baptist to receive ordination. He worked with Baptist missionaries on the southern island of Kyushu. Kawakatsu preached at the organizational service of the Moji church on October 4, 1893. This was the first Baptist congregation on Kyushu, a congregation of some thirty charter members.[98]

Southern Baptists organized Kyotaki Gakuin, a day school for Japanese children on Kyushu, while Northern Baptists founded a theological school in Yokohama. Generally, however, Baptists were hesitant to found educational institutions. The failure of Baptists to organize training schools for boys retarded their influence considerably. By 1899, Northern Baptists claimed some 1,885 members, while Southern Baptist work produced only 75.[99]

During the 1890s, Shinto and Buddhist leaders intensified their antagonism toward Japanese Christians by questioning national loyalties. Under this pressure, many Christians turned away from the faith.

By the early twentieth century, Baptist mission agencies began the transfer of leadership to the Japanese Christians. Southern Baptist missionary Nathan Maynard praised "the faithfulness and efficiency of our fellow workers, the native preachers."[100] In 1910, the seminaries in Yokohama and Kyushu united to form the Japan Baptist Seminary in Tokyo. In the south, Seinan Gakuin (Southwestern Academy) was founded in Fukuoka in 1916. Leadership of the school was shared by C. K. Dosier, Baptist missionary, and Japanese Baptist layman Jo Inohiko.[101]

As ultranationalism increased in Japan in the 1930s, Japanese Baptists, like other Christians, confronted the dilemma of maintaining loyalty to the state while preserving freedom of conscience. Schools such as Seinan Gakuin were required to revere a portrait of the Japanese emperor, and students were required to bow before the portrait, although teachers assured them that this was not idolatry.

The West Japan Baptist Convention was founded in 1918 from the Southwestern Association, related to the Southern Baptists. That same year, the churches related to the American Baptists established the East Baptist Convention. In 1919, the earlier comity agreements ended when Southern Baptists sent a missionary to Tokyo.[102]

These two groups merged in 1940 in response to increasing totalitarianism in the state. The first national meeting of the Nihon Baputesuto Kyodan (Baptist Convention of Japan) convened in Himeji. Some two hundred delegates attended at a time when the Convention claimed 6,863 members in eighty-nine churches. Chiba Yugoro, longtime Japanese pastor, was named president. The Convention approved three important goals: "to multiply the membership of the churches by means of evangelistic campaigns; to double the number of churches; to increase self-support by placing emphasis on tithing." These efforts would be increasingly difficult to realize as the war expanded, especially after the attack on Pearl Harbor.[103] A year later, all Protestant groups were forced to join the government-monitored Kyodan, the United Church of Christ, a federation of thirty-four Protestant denominations.

Japanese Baptists were suspect because of their links to Americans, their pacifist sentiments, and their devotion to a religion that was seen as predominately Western. Churches were required to post pictures of the emperor and show reverence to it before worship could begin. Most conformed to these precepts, but individuals such as Namioka Samuro, president of the girl's school founded by the Northern Baptists at Himeji, refused to reverence the shrines and was imprisoned as a traitor, serving over a year in felon's prison.[104]

Allied bombings brought great destruction to the entire country, and Baptist facilities were not spared. Baptists in Yokohama lost over twenty buildings related to Soshin Jo

Gakko and Kanto Gakuin, schools founded by Northern Baptists. While many Baptist schools continued throughout the war, some were used as sites for antiaircraft guns and other military facilities.[105]

With war's end, many Baptist congregations left the United Church and reasserted their Baptist identity. In April 1947, the Nihon Baputesuto Remmei (Japan Baptist Convention) was organized with Ozaki Shuichi as president and Kawano Sadamoto as executive secretary. The convention approved a "ten-article statement of faith" based on the New Hampshire Confession.[106] Thus there were three distinct indigenous Japanese Baptist groups, each related to mission organizations in the United States: the Japan Baptist Convention (Southern Baptist related), the Japan Baptist Union (American Baptist related), and the Japan Baptist Church Association (with connections to the Baptist General Conference of America). By 1950, the Japan Convention claimed sixty-seven churches and a membership of 13,035.[107] The Japan Baptist Convention also sent out missionaries, the first to Okinawa in 1955. Togami and Kimiko Nobuyoshi were sent to Brazil—a country with significant Japanese immigrant presence in 1964.

While retaining membership in the Kyodan after the war, East Japan Baptists also established the Shinseikai, or New Life Fellowship. In 1953, it became the Kirisutokyo Shinseiki and included Kyodan and non-Kyodan churches. During the 1950s, it served as a "shadow denomination" of Baptists inside or alongside the Kyodan. Ultimately, it passed off the scene.[108]

During the early 1960s, some Japanese Baptists and American missionaries united in the New Life Movement, an evangelistic effort surrounding a crusade to be conducted in Tokyo by evangelist Billy Graham. Although illness kept Graham from the meetings, the campaign went ahead with substitute preachers. It was the first such religious gathering to be held in postwar Japan. Some 10,402 decisions "for baptism" were recorded among the Japanese who attended. Follow-up, however, was another matter. Calvin Parker observed that in Tokyo, Japanese Baptist pastors surveyed those who had signed "decision cards" only to find that many had no intention of becoming Christians. Parker noted that the pastors "concluded that the sermons had been too direct and offensive and invitations too emotional and compulsive. For whatever reasons, the lasting results were meager."[109]

In 1970, the Baptist World Congress met in Tokyo, the first such gathering of Baptists in Asia. While many Japanese Baptists supported the meeting, a group of dissident churches challenged the gathering for ignoring Japanese church-state controversies, the Vietnam War, and other world problems. They charged that the conference's theme, "Reconciliation through Christ," had "nothing to do with elegant talks nor with gaudy national costumes." The dissidents, known as the "Joint-Struggle Council," staged protests outside the Congress meetings. Student disputes over Vietnam, American imperialism, and the Baptist Congress also spilled over to several Japanese Baptist schools.[110]

In 1989, when wartime emperor Hirohito died, some Baptists divided over the appropriate response to the national observances. Some felt that as good citizens they should honor the events memorializing the emperor, while others insisted that as advocates of religious liberty and justice, Baptists should refuse to honor one whose leadership produced war and exploitation throughout Asia.

Numerous Baptist mission groups—Southern Baptists, American Baptists, Conservative Baptists, Baptist General Conference, and Baptist Bible Fellowship, among others—have sent missionaries to Japan, each helping to form a variety of Japanese Baptist communions. By the end of the twentieth century, the Japan Baptist Convention numbered more than thirty-one thousand, with some three thousand members in the Okinawa Baptist Convention. The Japan Baptist Union claimed some five thousand members. The Conservative Baptist Association listed over two thousand members, as did the Japan Baptist Church Association and the Japan Baptist Bible Fellowship.[111]

Although a tiny minority, Japanese Baptists have developed many strong churches and organizations. Their church life reflects the impact of the charismatic and church-growth movements as well as efforts to relate to a highly secularized culture.

Baptists in China

With its huge non-Christian population and geographical expanse, China was a prime target for evangelism by American Protestants, including Baptists. The first missionary efforts began in 1836 when the Triennial Convention appointed William Dean to go to China. Unable to enter the country, Dean went to Bangkok, where he founded the first Baptist church in Asia. The Triennial Convention then appointed John Lewis Shuck (1814–1863) and his seventeen-year-old wife, Henrietta (1817–1844). They left shortly after their wedding, arriving on the island of Macao in 1837. In 1842, they settled in Hong Kong and extended Baptist mission work there. Henrietta Shuck died in 1844, leaving five children, one of whom died when Lewis Shuck returned to the United States.

The Treaty of Nanking (1842) opened ports in China to Western residents and transferred control of Hong Kong to the British. Baptists, like other missionary groups, soon attempted to evangelize the Chinese populace. At first, the BMS was unable to respond but provided a small amount of funding for the American Baptist Foreign Mission Society to begin work in Hong Kong. British General Baptists sent T. H. Hudson and W. Jarrom and their spouses to Ningbo in 1845, but death and illness brought this effort to a hasty end.[112]

Internal rebellions with anti-Western overtones made missionary activities dangerous throughout the nineteenth century. The Taiping Rebellion of the 1850s was waged against the Qing dynasty, rulers who had responded positively to the Protestant presence. BMS missionary Hendrik Kloekers was expelled from Nanjing and told not to return.[113] Charles Hall and his wife established BMS work in Shandong in 1861, but Hall died in a cholera epidemic in 1862. Other British Baptist appointees followed, most racked by disease and forced to return home. Converts came slowly, but by the late 1860s, R. F. Laughton counted thirty-five Chinese Christians from three villages as part of a church he founded in Yantai province. Laughton's intent was to lead indigenous churches to become self-sufficient, and he wanted no appearance of buying converts. He acknowledged that there was a "deep and wide-spread hatred to foreigners caused by the nefarious opium traffic."[114] Laughton died as a result of typhus in 1870.

The American Baptist Mission Society took responsibility from the BMS for the Yantai church in 1875. Timothy Richard, the BMS missionary there, moved further inland to Chingzhou and insisted that itinerant evangelism should be done only by the Chinese themselves. A church was founded, and pastor Qing, one of the earliest Chinese Baptist pastors, was brought from Yantai to lead the congregation.[115]

After the 1845 schism in the United States, Southern Baptists reappointed J. Lewis Shuck, who went to Canton in 1846. He was assisted by a native preacher named Yang Seen Sang, converted during Shuck's earlier term.[116] The first group of missionaries established missions and churches in Canton, Shanghai, and Shantung.

Matthew T. Yates (1819–1888), a Wake Forest College graduate, was one of the early appointees, arriving in Shanghai with his wife, Eliza Moring Yates, in September 1847. A gifted linguist, he was particularly successful in communicating with the Chinese. When the Civil War broke out at home, Yates wrote that its greatest evil was its interference with the missionary imperative and pleaded, "May the God of nations save our country from a fratricidal war! Viewing the whole matter from this distant point of observation our people, North and South, seem to be mad."[117] Yates baptized the first female Chinese Baptist in Shanghai in 1855. He resisted creating groups of "rice Christians," who joined the church only for food or funds. He commented, "My church of believers only, is attracting more and more attention. There seems to be something in the simple act of immersion that impresses the Chinese favorably. It carries with it the idea of truthfulness and stability." He insisted that new Christians should be encouraged to "become the disciples of Jesus Christ, and not the disciples of the missionary."[118]

The Republic of China took shape in 1911 with the removal of the last emperor and the installation of Sun Yat-sen as president. Internal struggles continued throughout the provinces, but missionary activity thrived. In 1900, there were some fifteen hundred Protestant missionaries in China. In 1925, the missionary population had reached its peak in approximately eight thousand persons.[119]

Baptists under Communism

In 1926, Chiang Kai-shek formed a Nationalist army and sought to unify the entire country. Japanese invasion and hegemony over Manchuria brought warfare and destruction during the 1940s. During these years, the Red Army was organized by Mao Tse-tung. In 1949, his forces defeated Chiang Kai-shek and united the country under communist rule. Chiang and his followers took up exile in Taiwan.

In the early days of the communist revolution, Chinese churches were permitted to remain open, but pastors and laity were harassed and some direct persecution occurred. Nonetheless, a truly Chinese church took shape. The Three-Self movement was founded in 1951 with governmental permission. Its purpose was to promote self-government, self-propagation, and self-support for churches in China. The government then moved to abolish denominations and reduce the number of congregations.[120]

The Cultural Revolution, instigated by Mao in 1966, continued until 1976 as an attempt to reinvigorate the revolution by destroying "old ideas, old culture, old habits, old customs."[121] This was a period of great violence against religious people and institutions. Churches were closed and leaders jailed. One Chinese Christian (reared a Baptist) in Guangzhou described a day when the Red Guard (young people committed to the Cultural Revolution) came to his house: "They took all my books and burned them in the street. They sat me on a stool, put a dunce cap on my head, and shouted at me. They called me an 'enemy of the revolution' and spit on me. They beat me with sticks. I covered my face with my hands to protect my eyes. They quit only when I fell off the stool, unconscious."[122]

With the death of Mao and the end of the Cultural Revolution in 1979, churches were reopened under a new policy that united all Protestants into one ecclesiastical organization. The effort to create a Chinese church, distinguished from foreign influence and domination, extended the work of the Three-Self Patriotic Church. House churches and "open churches" alike flourished with millions of adherents. Some estimate that there are over 20 million participants in the house churches.[123] Those influenced by Baptist beliefs and practices have now generally been absorbed into the Three-Self movement or other united Protestant communions in China.

Baptists in Taiwan

With the communist takeover of mainland China in 1951, many Christian missionary groups turned attention to the island of Taiwan (Formosa), then known as Free China or the Republic of China. Southern Baptists were particularly concerned to develop what one historian called "a viable Baptist church community" on the island.[124] In 1948, the SBC Foreign Mission Board sent a single female longtime missionary to China, Bertha Smith, and a Chinese Baptist colleague to work with the refugees who were streaming into Taipei. By 1961, the Baptist community included sixty-eight churches and a membership of more than six thousand eight hundred persons.[125] Chinese Baptist émigrés joined with missionaries in establishing a Baptist presence on the island. Internal tensions were high because the native Taiwanese (Formosans) felt their country to be co-opted by the mainland Chinese refugees. In their initial missionary efforts, Baptists chose to put most of their energy into work with the Chinese refugee population, leaving mission work with the native Taiwanese to the Presbyterians. Baptists were the first missionary group to initiate ministry among mainland Chinese on Taiwan.[126]

The Taiwan Baptist Theological Seminary was founded in 1952 to train indigenous ministers. Missionary and Chinese professors served on the faculty. During the 1950s, the school averaged about fifty students, graduating some fifteen persons each year.[127]

As the Chinese Baptist population expanded, the missionaries developed a plan for sharing leadership with indigenous Chinese. Early projections of growth did not materialize, and the decade after 1961 represented a period of stagnation in membership growth. Likewise, a new generation of missionaries had no experience in the old mainland culture.[128] Chinese Baptists complained that they were not treated as equal colleagues with the missionaries, who were perceived as controlling and at times condescending. Missionary attempts to change the relationship and create greater shared ministry with the Asian Christians provided some help for the situation.[129] The stagnation grew out of changing structures in Taiwanese life, including greater prosperity and the rise of folk religion and traditional Chinese spirituality, as well as the opening of new missions from other religious communions.[130]

Baptists in India

By 1843, fifty years after William Carey's arrival in Bengal, the membership in Indian churches founded by the Baptist Missionary Society was 1,449. Many of these were European émigrés living in India. Brian Stanley observed that although missionaries initially received a "polite reception" from the Indians, a "willingness to pay the price of conversion to Christianity was quite another matter."[131] Those few Indians who converted to Christianity were persecuted, ostracized, and often cast out of their communities.

The famous Sepoy Rebellion, waged against British colonialism in 1857, was seen by many Baptist missionaries as an attempt by the Hindu upper classes to thwart Christianity and its opposition to the caste system of Hindu culture. The rebellion failed, and Indian membership in Baptist churches increased. Some churches refused to accept those who were judged to be interested only in improving "their temporal lot" while retaining "heathen habits."[132] As in other missionary endeavors, difficulties arose over the boundaries of the missionary societies and the indigenous churches.

A mission in the Indian region of Orissa was begun by the General Baptist Missionary Society in 1822. Its steady increase led to a membership of two hundred by 1842. There were some seven "Christian villages" in the region by 1844, which provided sanctuary for those forced out of their native villages.[133]

Orissa became a center of Baptist influence. Brian Stanley observed that as late as the 1950s, the West Utkal District Union of Orissa Baptists was the "most encouraging instance of spiritual vitality in the [British] Indian mission." In the 1950s, Baptist influence increased in the Kond Hills of Orissa, with 58 churches in 1955 growing to 168 congregations by 1964.[134] In March 1968, the last British Baptist missionaries departed the South Mizo District of North India. At that time there were some two hundred churches claiming more than fifty thousand members.[135]

American Baptist missionaries reached India in March 1836, with the arrival of Nathan and Eliza Brown and Oliver and Harriet Cutter. They were joined by other missionaries, who served in northeast India in the regions of Assam, Nagaland, and Manipur. Their first Indian convert, Nidhi Levi, received baptism in 1841. A church—the first Christian communion in the northeastern region—was organized in 1845 in Guwahati. The Baptist Association of Assam was established in 1851.[136]

As rebellions at home, funding difficulties abroad, and the missionary death rate took their toll, the indigenous Indian Baptists were soon "on their own." Frederick Downs wrote of those early Indian leaders in the Assam region, "Kandura, the son of a blind fisherman, hence a member of the lowest of castes in the Assamese society of that time, became the instrument through which the first Baptist churches were established in the hills. With the baptism of forty Garos and the establishment of the Rajasimla church in 1867, the number of Baptists in the region almost doubled overnight!"[137]

Other indigenous Baptists instigated mission work in Nagaland by the end of the nineteenth century. Associations soon were formed, usually along linguistic and geographical lines. In 1914, the Assam Baptist Christian Convention was organized to bring these diverse linguistic associations together. Downs noted that its primary purpose "was to negotiate with the [American] Mission for the establishment of the indigenous denominational structure that we now know as the CBCNEI" (Council of Baptist Churches in North East India). Initially, the CBCNEI was a via media between the indigenous churches and the missionary board. Primary administrative authority was not ceded to the Indians until the 1950s and 1960s.[138]

In the early twentieth century, the American Baptist Board of International Ministries began the appointment of physicians to serve in India. A clinic was built in Tura in 1910, with larger hospitals founded in the region in 1925 and 1933. By 1950, there were five associational Bible schools—a number that rose to eleven by the 1980s. As the century neared its end, Edward Singha, general secretary of the CBCNEI, commented on the challenges facing Indian Baptists, "We are Christians but we are still too self-centered and we possess tribalistic attitudes.... Our vision needs to be broadened and horizon widened. We need to have a view of things in terms beyond ourselves, beyond our tribe, our geography. Let us include in our vision, other people, other states, the whole of India, other countries and even the whole world. We shall always be small, undeveloped and stagnant if we direct everything to ourselves."[139]

Southern Baptist missionary work in Karnataka state led to the founding of an eighty-bed hospital in Bangalore in 1973. By the 1990s, the hospital had increased its facilities to 143 beds in a city of 5 million persons. In the 1970s, there were 5 Baptist churches in the state—a number that increased to 450 churches by the 1990s.[140]

Downs suggested that the regions near the Bay of Bengal, moving from Burma (Myanmar) in the north to Sri Lanka toward the south, "have one of the largest conceltrations of Baptists in the Third World." He cites statistics published by the Baptist World Alliance in 2000 that indicate some 2,287,719 Baptist church members in 8,500 congregations in this area. While these figures may be a bit overextended, they reflect significant numbers, with most Baptists associated with one nf three denominations. All were influenced by the American Baptist Churches USA. They include the Myanmar Baptist Convention (631,511), Samavesam of Telugu Baptist Churches (475,639), and the Council of Baptist Churches, North East India (741,724). These groups have 80 percent of the total Baptist presence. Although these groups could qualify for membership in ecumenical groups such as the Asian Christian Council or the World Council of Churches, most have chosen not to do so.[141]

When the ecumenical Church of North India was founded in 1970, J. K. Mohanty, a Baptist minister in Orissa, was named its first bishop, and certain churches soon chose to join the new communion. By 1975, at least three-fourths of the Baptist churches in West Bengal and almost half the churches in Bihar, Delhi, Baraut, and Simla had become members of the Church of North India, relinquishing their Baptist classification. This led to serious divisions among the Baptists in those regions.[142]

The Baptist presence in North India was influenced by the so-called comity agreements worked out in the nineteenth century by various Protestant mission organizations. This meant that certain sections of the globe were divided among these denominations, with individual Christian groups taking primary responsibility for evangelizing specific regions. In the Indian state of Mizoram, churches in the north were developed by Welsh Presbyterians, while southern churches were the responsibility of British Baptists.[143] The development of Baptist missions in certain territories was shaped by this agreement. Baptists became so numerous in some of these districts that they constituted something of an unofficial religious establishment. This is the case with the Council of Baptist Churches in North East India. The CBCNEI is the largest of the Baptist groups in the region and is organized around local associations, regional conventions, and a central council.[144]

Baptist missionaries, among others, not only established churches but also influenced the development of a new "tribal identity" by standardizing languages, providing written texts, and extending links between autonomous villages.[145]

The ABMU helped to found a seminary at Ramapatnam near the Bay of Bengal in 1870. Its purpose was to train indigenous leaders for Indian Baptist churches. Initially, it was simply a preparatory school, offering basic literacy programs.[146] John E. Clough, one of the leading missionaries to India, raised endowments and secured four faculty members. His efforts met with some success. In 1874, the school claimed twenty-eight students, and its name was changed to Brownson Theological Seminary in honor of the largest donor to the endowment,

Mr. Brownson of Titusville, Pennsylvania. By 1886, the school asserted, "More than two hundred young men are here studying for the Christian ministry. Quite a number of the students are married, and the wives of many attend the lectures and take notes in order to help their husbands in their future ministrations.... They are chiefly from among the multitude of recent converts in the district of Ongole."[147] Students helped to found new churches and even established other schools. Famine, persecution, and other difficulties descended on the area during the late nineteenth and early twentieth centuries. There was a brief union with a struggling Canadian Baptist Seminary, and in 1929 the school was given its original Indian name, the Ramapatnam Baptist Theological Seminary.[148] By the 1960s, at least thirty-six Indians had served on the faculty of the school as professors, as deans, and in other administrative positions.

At the beginning of the twenty-first century, India had more Baptists than any country except the United States, with an approximate membership of 1.5 million persons.

Baptists in Burma

The beginnings of Baptist missionary activity in Burma have already been noted in the work of Adoniram and Ann Judson and others who came after them. Their ventures, and those of other early Baptist missionaries, were particularly directed toward the Karen tribe of the region. Some suggest that during the years 1840–1848, more than five thousand Karens received baptism as a result of Baptist mission enterprises, and an equal number of unbaptized believers also were present in Karen communities.[149]

Baptists among the Kachin People

The Kachins, present in a specific region of Burma, were the object of Baptist mission work during the latter part of the nineteenth century. Kachin Baptist churches developed and thrived into the twentieth century amid the difficulties posed by Japanese invasion and internal rebellions. The Kachin villages were in remote areas of "upper Burma" and manifested a distinctive tribal culture.[150]

American Baptist missionary Eugenio Kincaid, who arrived in Burma in 1833, was instrumental in establishing mission work with the Kachins. On a missionary journey in the Bhamo region, he encountered his first Kachins, concluding (mistakenly) that they were Karens, another native people. Kincaid was never able to revisit the Kachins, but he wrote to the American Baptist Missionary Society of his assurance that "their conversion will be rapid."[151]

It was not until 1877, fortx years after Kincaid's first encounter with the Kachins, that an actual mission was attempted. Josiah N. Cushing, already in Burma, began such a mission early that year. He was joined by Jacob A. Freidays and Albert J. Lyon, appointed by the American Baptist Missionary Society. Lyon died of fever barely a month after his arrival. Like others who confronted these early deaths, Cushing struggled to explain this ordeal. He wrote, "It was a mysterious providence, that the first KaKhyen [Kachin] missionary should lay down his life in sight of the mountains where he longed to preach the love of Christ."[152] The early missionary community in the region was struck by disease and emotional distress.

In spite of the difficulties, many Kachin people were converted, Baptist churches founded, and indigenous pastors ordained. The first ordination occurred when a Kachin named Damau Naw became the only native pastor in the region from 1901 to 1914.[153] The formation of churches led to questions regarding proper Christian behavior. Missionary records ask,

"Are we permitted to use alcohol and opium as medicine? Can we receive a woman who comes down from the mountains with her relatives and leaves her husband?" Missionaries moved quickly to encourage indigenous support in the churches, but as usual, questions arose regarding the shared leadership of the Kachins and the missionaries. By 1921, the Kachin Baptist churches claimed 1,565 members—a figure that reached 11,260 two decades later.[154]

Burmese Baptist Churches

The Japanese invasion of Burma during the Second World War brought great suffering to the region and to the Baptist churches. Missionaries were displaced, as were large numbers of native peoples. Churches were damaged and deserted. Nonetheless, Herman Tegenfeldt concluded, "Despite the dislocation and scattering of the churches and even the spiritual failure of some of the leaders, the Church emerged from the war showing a definite increase in membership."[155] Following the war, the role of the fledgling Kachin Baptist Convention expanded its indigenous leadership, linking itself with the larger Burma Baptist Convention.

Missionaries sent to Burma by the American Baptist Foreign Mission Society were forced to leave the country in 1941 due to the Japanese invasion. At war's end in 1945, three missionaries returned, including Gordon S. Jury, Gordon E. Gates, and David W. Graham. Burma gained independence from Great Britain in 1948, and an ensuing rebellion by the Karen tribe created civil unrest in the country (now Myanmar) that lasted into the twenty-first century. After a brief time of relative political stability, the army gained power in 1962 and promoted a socialist agenda for the "Burmese Way to Socialism."[156] This effort was largely unsuccessful, although it endured until 1988.

In 1966, the government decreed that all foreign missionaries, including Baptists, would be required to leave the country. Nonetheless, indigenous Baptist churches continued to exist, and their growth was slow but consistent. By the mid-1980s, a renewal of missionary and evangelistic enthusiasm developed among the Baptists. The Myanmar Baptist Convention developed programs for training evangelists and promoted missionary activities. For example, during the 1990s, the Bassein-Myaungmya Karen Baptist Association provided support for fifty-seven missionaries working among the Myos people in Rakhine state.[157] Also during this period, there were some thirty-three schools and seminaries spread throughout the country. Most used their own regional language, aimed at educating many of the some 120 different ethnic communities in Myanmar. In 1995, Myanmar Baptists counted approximately five hundred graduates of those schools.[158]

Writing of the Baptist presence in his homeland, Eh Wah, principal of the Myanmar Institute of Theology, commented, "As we approach the new century, we are still beset with difficulties and even threats. We may not have adequate freedom of speech, but we try to make positive contributions, because we love our country."[159] Those words might have been written by John Smyth and Thomas Helwys, exiled from England, in the earliest days of the Baptist experience.

Baptists in Africa and Asia: Facing the Future

Baptists in Africa and Asia face many challenges in the twenty-first century. In Africa, regional wars, famine, and the AIDS crisis threaten life on the continent as never before. Baptists worldwide must find ways to respond to the pressing needs of the region. In Asia, the changing economic situation, conflicts between religious groups, and rising populations provide major challenges. Baptists represent a strong but decidedly minority presence throughout the region.

Notes

1. Elizabeth Isichei, *A History of Christianity in Africa* (Grand Rapids, Mich.: Eerdmans, 1995), 98.
2. Ibid., 1. Statistics are difficult to confirm, given the number of small, indigenous churches in Africa and the difficulty of securing adequate counts.
3. Ruth Slade, "Congo Protestant Missions and European Powers before 1885," *Baptist Quarterly* 16 (1955–56): 200.
4. Ibid., 190.
5. Brian Stanley, *The History of the Baptist Missionary Society, 1792–1992* (Edinburgh: Clark, 1992), 106–8; Walter L. Williams, *Black Americans and the Evangelization of Africa, 1877–1900* (Madison: University of Wisconsin Press, 1982), 8–10. The first African American missionaries to Africa were sent to western and central regions, where whites died quickly. It was believed that blacks could endure the diseases more readily than whites.
6. Stanley, *Baptist Missionary Society*, 117.
7. Albert W. Wardin, ed., *Baptists around the World: A Comprehensive Handbook* (Nashville: Broadman & Holman, 1995), 35.
8. Stanley, *Baptist Missionary Society*, 119–23.
9. Ibid., 125–26.
10. Ibid., 127.
11. Ibid., 128.
12. Ibid., 130–31.
13. Isichei, *Christianity in Africa*, 190.
14. Williams, *Black Americans*, 19.
15. Kikama Kividi, "Church Growth in an African City: CBCO Kinshasa," *American Baptist Quarterly* 18 (September 1999): 10. Kividi provides an outstanding analysis of the tensions between the Baptist mission model, based on believing, and the Bantu family model, based on belonging, for understanding the differences in mission strategy and indigenous Baptist communities.
16. Ibid.
17. Ibid.
18. Stanley, *Baptist Missionary Society*, 336–39.
19. Ibid., 340.
20. Ibid., 341–44.
21. Ibid., 345.
22. Ibid., 346.
23. Ibid., 353–54.
24. Ibid.
25. Ibid., 365.
26. Ibid., 366–68.
27. Ibid., 442–43.
28. Kividi, "Church Growth," 7.
29. Wardin, ed., *Baptists around the World*, 34–35.
30. Isichei, *Christianity in Africa*, 165–66.
31. H. Leon McBeth, *A Sourcebook for Baptist Heritage* (Nashville: Broadman, 1990), 269–70.
32. William R. Estep, *Whole Gospel, Whole World: The Foreign Mission Board of the Southern Baptist Convention, 1845–1995* (Nashville: Broadman & Holman, 1994), 74 (citing Proceedings of the Southern Baptist Convention [1846]).
33. Ibid.
34. Williams, *Black Americans*, 66.
35. Isichei, *Christianity in Africa*, 165.
36. Ibid., 347.
37. Ibid., 171.
38. Estep, *Whole Gospel, Whole World*, 132.
39. Ibid.
40. Isichei, *Christianity in Africa*, 179.
41. Bill J. Leonard, ed., *Dictionary of Baptists in America* (Downers Grove, Ill.: InterVarsity Press, 1994), 18.
42. H. J. Batts, *The Story of a 100 Years, 1820–1920: Being the History of the Baptist Church in South Africa* (Cape Town: T. Maskew Miller, 1922), 4–5.
43. John Jonsson and Christopher Parnell, *Together for a Century: The History of the Baptist Union of South Africa, 1877–1977* (Pietermaritzburg, South Africa: Baptist Historical Society, 1977), 11.
44. Batts, *100 Years*, 5.
45. Ibid., 11.
46. Ibid., 16–17.

47. Jonsson and Parnell, *Together for a Century,* 11.
48. Ibid., 14–15.
49. Sydney Hudson-Reed, *By Taking Heed: The History of Baptists in Southern Africa, 1820–1977* (Roodepoort, South Africa: Baptist Publishing House, 1983), 18–19.
50. Jonsson and Parnell, *Together for a Century,* 17.
51. Hudson-Reed, *By Taking Heed,* 25–26.
52. Ibid., 32–33.
53. Ibid., 164.
54. Ibid., 36.
55. Ibid., 38.
56. Ibid., 39.
57. Jonsson and Parnell, *Together for a Century,* 21.
58. Ibid.
59. Hudson-Reed, *By Taking Heed,* 214.
60. Jonsson and Parnell, *Together for a Century,* 24–25.
61. Ibid., 39.
62. Ibid., 50.
63. Ibid.
64. Ibid., 66.
65. Hudson-Reed, *By Taking Heed,* 41.
66. Jonsson and Parnell, *Together for a Century,* 67.
67. Ibid., 69, 72.
68. Hudson-Reed, *By Taking Heed,* 148.
69. Ibid., 74.
70. Ibid., 79–80.
71. Ibid., 186.
72. Ibid., 191–92.
73. Ibid., 82.
74. Ibid.
75. Ibid., 277–78.
76. Ibid., 108–9.
77. Ibid., 237.
78. Jonsson and Parnell, *Together for a Century,* 102–3.
79. Ibid., 130.
80. Ibid., 137.
81. John N. Jonsson, "Baptists in Socio-Political Life in South Africa: Historical and Theological Reflections Covering the Past Thirty Years," *American Baptist Quarterly* 4 (September 1985): 244.
82. Ibid., 246–49.
83. Terry Rae, "Dialogue and Reconciliation on South Africa: Statements on the Journey," *American Baptist Quarterly* 18 (September 1999): 245.
84. Ibid., 246. See also Desmond Hoffmeister, "Address," *American Baptist Quarterly* 18 (September 1999): 248-53. Hoffmeister, general secretary of the Baptist Convention, briefly describes the reasons for the split between the two Baptist groups.
85. Jonsson, "Baptist in Socio-Political Life," 248.
86. Jonsson and Parnell, 87.
87. Ibid., 92–96.
88. Ibid., 104.
89. Hudson-Reed, *By Taking Heed,* 68.
90. Jonsson and Parnell, *Together for a Century,* 128.
91. Wardin, ed., *Baptists around the World,* 57.
92. F. Calvin Parker, *The Southern Baptist Mission in Japan, 1889–1989* (Lanham, Md.: University Press of America, 1991), 2–3.
93. Ibid., 3–4.
94. Ibid., 14–15.
95. Wardin, ed., *Baptists around the World,* 102.
96. Parker, *Mission in Japan,* 22.
97. Ibid., 23.
98. Ibid., 44.
99. Ibid., 19, 49–50.
100. Ibid., 62–63.
101. Ibid., 79–85.
102. Wardin, ed., *Baptists around the World,* 103.
103. Parker, *Mission in Japan,* 155.
104. Ibid., 170.
105. Ibid., 171–72.

106. Ibid., 176.

107. Ibid., 208.

108. F. Calvin Parker, "Baptist Missions in Japan, 1945–73: A Study in Relationships," *Japan Christian Quarterly* 40 (winter 1974): 35.

109. Parker, *Mission in Japan,* 216–17.

110. Ibid., 236–39.

111. Wardin, ed., *Baptists around the World,* 100–102.

112. Stanley, *Baptist Missionary Society,* 176–77.

113. Ibid., 178–79.

114. Ibid., 180.

115. Ibid., 183–84.

116. Estep, *Whole Gospel, Whole World,* 69–72.

117. Ibid., 96.

118. Ibid., 104–5.

119. Wayne Dehoney, *The Dragon and the Lamb* (Nashville: Broadman, 1988), 17.

120. Wardin, ed., *Baptists around the World,* 97.

121. Dehoney, *Dragon and the Lamb,* 22.

122. Ibid., 31–32.

123. Ibid., 64.

124. Murray A. Rubinstein, "American Evangelicalism in the Chinese Environment: Southern Baptist Convention Missionaries in Taiwan, 1949–1981," *American Baptist Quarterly* 2 (September 1983): 269.

125. Ibid., 270.

126. Ibid., 275.

127. Ibid., 272.

128. Ibid., 277–79.

129. Ibid., 28–29.

130. Ibid., 283–84.

131. Stanley, *Baptist Missionary Society,* 141.

132. Ibid., 146–47.

133. Ibid., 162–63.

134. Ibid., 407–9.

135. Basil Amey, *The Unfinished Story: A Study-Guide History of the Baptist Missionary Society* (London: Baptist Union of Great Britain, 1991), 125.

136. Frederick S. Downs, "Historical Reflections on the Changing Context of North East India," *American Baptist Quarterly* 15 (June 1996): 105.

137. Ibid., 106.

138. Ibid., 108.

139. Ibid., 117–18.

140. Estep, *Whole Gospel, Whole World,* 384.

141. Frederick S. Downs, "Baptists and Tribal Identity in North East India" (paper presented at the International Conference on Baptist Studies, July 2000), 1.

142. Stanley, *Baptist Missionary Society,* 419–20.

143. Downs, "Baptists and Tribal Identity," 3.

144. Ibid., 3–4, 8.

145. Ibid., 6–8.

146. James D. Mosteller, "Ramapatnam: Jewel of the South India Mission," *Foundations* 11 (October–December 1968): 309.

147. Ibid., 311.

148. Ibid., 314–15.

149. Herman G. Tegenfeldt, *A Century of Growth: The Kachin Baptist Church of Burma* (South Pasadena, Calif.: William Carey Library, 1974), 288.

150. Ibid., 61.

151. *Baptist Missionary Magazine* (1838): 299–300.

152. Tegenfeldt, *A Century of Growth,* 99.

153. Ibid., 144–45.

154. Ibid., 149–53, 180.

155. Ibid., 200.

156. Eh Wah, "A Personal Perspective: Thirty Years after the Western Missionary Era in Myanmar," *American Baptist Quarterly* 15 (June 1996): 97–98.

157. Ibid., 98.

158. Ibid.

159. Ibid., 102.

Chapter 15

Baptists in the British Isles and Europe: The Twentieth Century

Baptists in the United Kingdom and Ireland

British Baptists approached the twentieth century with great hopes for the future, moving quickly to improve various denominational programs and appeals. John Howard Shakespeare, pastor of St. Mary's Church, Norwich, was named secretary of the Baptist Union in 1898. In 1899, he led in introducing the "Twentieth Century Fund," a plan to raise £250,000. Half was to be used for church extension, with other portions to fund "village ministers," the ministerial annuity fund, and educational endeavors. Baptists in Wales were asked to raise £50,000, Scottish Baptists £20,000, and Irish Baptists £7,000. While this was the largest amount that British Baptists had ever attempted to solicit, the goal was achieved by 1902.[1] *The Baptist Times and Freeman,* a new denominational journal, was established early in the century. Shakespeare was aided in his early work by two longtime leaders of the British Baptist movement, Alexander Maclaren, and John Clifford, both of whom served as presidents of the Baptist Union at the beginning of the twentieth century.

The Baptist Union Assembly approved a revision of the denominational constitution in 1904, which included a new declaration of principles listing three points as the basis of the Union: (1) "That our Lord Jesus Christ is the sole and absolute authority in all matters pertaining to faith and practice, as revealed in the Holy Scriptures, and that each Church has liberty to interpret and administer His laws"; (2) "That Christian Baptism is the immersion in water, into the Name of the Father, the Son and Holy Ghost, of those who have professed repentance towards God and faith in our Lord Jesus Christ"; and (3) "That it is the duty of every disciple to bear personal witness to the Gospel of Jesus Christ, and to take part in the evangelization of the world."[2]

A new hymnal, *The Baptist Church Hymnal,* was published in 1900, and new denominational departments, including an office for publication, were begun by 1902. In 1908, the Baptist Women's Home Work Auxiliary was founded and reformed into the Baptist Women's League in 1910. The Baptist Total Abstinence Association continued to insist that churches relinquish the use of wine in communion. In 1904, the Association claimed that at least 2,077 churches were using grape juice in their observance of the Lord's Supper.[3]

The Baptist Forward Movement, an effort to extend the ministry of Baptist churches in high-poverty areas, began in September 1889. From the Forward Movement came the office of deaconess—women who lived or worked in the slums and tenements, caring for the sick, teaching the young, and offering help and comfort. The Baptist Deaconesses' Home and Mission was founded in London in 1894. Some twenty deaconesses were at work in London by 1907.[4]

British Baptists also hosted the international Baptist conference that led to the formation of the Baptist World Alliance in London in 1905. The Welsh Revival of 1904–1905, under the leadership of Evan Roberts, was a profound spiritual renewal that brought some thirty-two thousand persons into the Baptist fold. Such developments created a powerful sense of optimism that permeated Baptist life before the First World War. In 1903, the *London Daily News* counted 163,052 Baptists in London, the largest Free Church body in the city. Charles Booth concluded, "The Baptist Community [in London] is virile beyond any other Christian body."[5] In spite of these assertions, declines in Baptist membership began by 1905. Indeed, by 1909, the Union established a committee on "Baptist Arrested Progress" (later renamed the Spiritual Welfare Committee) to confront the issue.

As the century got underway, Baptist denominationalism continued to be refined by churches and associations. In 1904, the Council of the London Baptist Association approved new regulations requiring that all candidates for pastor of an associated church give "proof" of a call to the ministry by completing the course of a recognized college, passing the Baptist Union examination, or receiving the Council's approval of having fulfilled an acceptable ministry in one church for three years.[6] Ministers so recognized were added to the "accreditation list" of denominationally sanctioned clergy. Through Shakespeare's leadership, the Union was reorganized, with ten districts formed in England and Wales, each guided by a general superintendent, whose job it was to relate closely to pastors and congregations in behalf of the denomination. All of these changes encouraged a greater denominational connectionalism. The office of general superintendent paralleled certain aspects of the earlier office of messenger among British Baptists.[7]

Denominational development led to improved facilities. The Baptist Church House, London, the administrative center of the Baptist Union, was dedicated in 1903. It housed offices of the Union until the 1990s, when the headquarters was moved to Didcot, near Oxford.

British Baptists and the First World War

The First World War began in August 1914 when Britain and France declared war on Germany. The "Great War" lasted until 1918 and cost the lives of some 10 to 15 percent of European males. The shock of the war and its impact on the nation had profound effects on the Baptists. British Baptist churches experienced the loss, and churches soon developed memorials to their fallen members. Charles Johnson observed, "In the churches normal programmes gave way to the call to help refugees, provide social centres for the Forces and supply comforts for the men on the battlefield."[8]

In November 1914, Baptist leaders participated in a rally at the City Temple (Church), London, the center of English nonconformity, that affirmed support of the Allied cause. The Baptist Union Council sent a message to the Baptists of the British Empire urging them to unite in the "war to end all wars."[9] When the United States joined the war effort in 1917, John Clifford and John Shakespeare wrote to their American Baptist colleagues, "We are fighting for Christianity against paganism, for right against cruel might, for liberty against cruel tyranny; for humanity against the works of the devil."[10]

During the war, many Baptist leaders defended the right of conscientious objectors to resist military service—a very unpopular stance. While the number of Baptist conscientious objectors was relatively small, F. B. Meyer, John Clifford, and other prominent British Baptists signed a 1916 document supporting their right to dissent. Meyer summarized the Baptist ideal: "Conscience is the supreme authority on Right and Wrong. It is the viceregent of the Eternal Throne.... Even when it is dethroned, disgraced, mocked, silenced and consigned to the dungeon, it never abdicates—it never withdraws its claims. Men instinctively recognise them, and do them homage. Joseph's brethren spluttered, but his dreams came true."[11] Most Baptist conscientious objectors did alternative service rather than participate in combat.

The war raised spiritual and theological questions throughout Britain. Graham Scroggie (1872–1958), pastor of the Charlotte Chapel, Scotland's largest Baptist congregation, declared in 1916, "The war has widened our horizon, and increased our sympathies, and is leading us not to a new message, but to a proper adjustment of the old message to the new condition of things."[12]

After the devastation of the First World War, many Baptists turned to pacifism entirely. The Baptist Ministers' Pacifist Fellowship began in 1934 with 580 members. By 1935, it had become the British Baptist Pacifist Fellowship, with a membership comprised of both clergy and laity. In a statement released in 1935, its members declared, "We, members and adherents of Baptist Churches, covenant together to renounce war in all its works and ways; and to do all in our power, God helping us, to make the teaching of Jesus Christ effective in all human relations."[13]

Paul Dekar suggested that these pacifist ideals were based on a conviction that an essential human goodness ultimately would prevail, a belief in the centrality of "individual conscience," and an emphasis on "practical pacifism" lived out in daily life.[14]

Fundamentalism of the 1920s

During the 1920s, fundamentalism shook Baptist churches in the United States and Canada much more directly than it did those in Britain. Nonetheless, some British Baptists warned of the dangers of a rising liberalism. James Mountain, an evangelical minister, received immersion from F. B. Meyer and founded St. John's Free Church, Tunbridge Wells, as an evangelical congregation with Baptist sentiments. He was a fundamentalist, concerned that orthodox doctrines be affirmed by Baptists. Mountain became an advocate for the Baptist Bible Union (BBU)—an equivalent of the fundamentalist organization founded in Canada by T. T. Shields. The movement attracted certain Baptist leaders, several of whom ultimately withdrew. Other fundamentalists came from those whom David Bebbington calls the "heirs of C. H. Spurgeon," many associated with the Pastors' College founded by the great preacher. These conservatives recalled the "Downgrade Controversy" and feared that the legacy of liberalism remained inside the Baptist Union.[15]

Certain Baptist moderates also became associated with the early fundamentalist movement in Britain but soon became disillusioned with its abrasiveness and withdrew their support. In Wales, Baptist revivalist Rhys Bevan Jones, a leader in the Welsh Awakenings, lent his strong support to Mountain and the fundamentalist endeavors. As a vice president of the BBU, Jones wrote, "I dare to declare that the Baptist Churches of Wales are solid for orthodoxy."[16]

In 1922, the BBU and other fundamentalist groups convened an "All-Day Bible Demonstration" at the Metropolitan Tabernacle. During services in which the choir sang "Bible Battle-songs," speakers attacked movements that undermined biblical authority. Soon the *Bible Call,* published by the BBU, became the *Bible Call and Fundamentalist Advocate.* One editorial commented, "We are in hearty sympathy with the Fundamentalists of America and hope to work in co-operation with them."[17]

Fundamentalist alliances developed in segments of English Baptist life on a much smaller scale than those in America. Bebbington suggested that British Baptist fundamentalists were drawn together by issues such as "anti-Catholicism, Keswick teaching, premillennialism, crises in public affairs, secularizing tendencies, [and] the American example."[18] Mountain challenged the orthodoxy of numerous Baptist pastors, including F. C. Spurr, a Baptist Union evangelist and frequent speaker at Keswick (deeper life) meetings. Mountain was successful in getting Spurr removed from the Keswick programs.

A few fundamentalist Baptist churches withdrew from the Baptist Union. Yet in spite of these efforts, fundamentalism never really caught on in British Baptist life. It lacked the network, leadership, and aggressiveness of its American counterpart. Ian Randall suggested, "The fundamentalist conspiracy within English Baptist life in the 1920s lacked a significant leader," and thus created no major divisions in the Baptist Union.[19]

Revivals among the Baptists

In the aftermath of the First World War, periods of religious revival flourished among some British Baptist congregations. Touched by the inner religion and holiness emphasis of the modern Keswick movement, Hugh Ferguson, pastor of London Road Baptist Church, Lowestoft, invited Douglas Brown to conduct a preaching mission in 1921. Brown, pastor of Ramsden Road Baptist Church, Balham, was judged by some to be a "hypnotic preacher." The meetings lasted for more than a month, during which time some five hundred conversions were reported. Brown emphasized the Keswick doctrine of the baptism of the Holy Spirit in quietistic, not flamboyant, spiritual encounters. Seekers were invited to come forward to pray and receive counsel at the church's "quiet room."[20]

Brown preached for other Baptist pastors, with similar responses of huge attendance and numerous conversions. By the summer of 1922, it was estimated that Brown had spoken at seventeen hundred services in East Anglia and other regions. In 1924, at the Bloomsbury Baptist Church, London, Brown was commissioned an evangelist for the Baptist Union.[21]

As might have been expected, Baptists divided over the benefits of the revivals and the validity of the "enthusiasm" they provoked. Graham Scroggie warned against excessive emotionalism as a road to genuine conversion. He declared, "Faith is not credulity; faith is not ignorance; faith is intelligent; faith is open-eyed; faith has a reason as well as emotion, and the man is in grave peril who is resting on emotion rather than upon intelligent understanding."[22] Scroggie was particularly concerned about Brown's emphasis on Spirit baptism.

Ecumenism amid Denominationalism

During the war years, the Baptist Union instituted a "Sustentation and Ministerial Settlement" plan to bring greater equality to ministerial salaries. Married ministers were allotted £120 annually, with the congregation required to provide a minimum of £70. By 1920, grants were given to over five hundred churches, each of which was required to belong to the Baptist Union and conform to its regulations regarding use of the funds. This represented an important step in denominational centralization for English Baptists.[23]

Amid this denominationalism was also a growing sense of ecumenism—cooperation with other Christian groups—in British Baptist life. F. B. Meyer, a staunch evangelical elected president of the Baptist Union in 1906, was a strong proponent of interdenominational cooperation, particularly among British evangelicals. He was influenced by the nondenominationalism of American evangelist D. L. Moody as well as by the Holiness-related Keswick movement. Meyer served as pastor of the Regent's Park (Baptist) Chapel during the years 1888–1892, and then moved to Christ Church, a nonsectarian congregation in which he instituted baptismal immersion—a practice he never relinquished.[24] Indeed, after 1918, while his increasing involvement in Keswick and the premillennial movements led him away from denominationalism, he retained great loyalty to the Baptist "testimony" of immersion. Thus, one of Britain's best-known nondenominationalists had a Baptist identity at heart.

John Howard Shakespeare, a lifelong advocate of ecumenical connections, was instrumental in the founding of the Federal Council of the Evangelical Free Churches in 1919. That same year, Shakespeare published *The Churches at the Crossroads,* in which he encouraged formation of a United Church of England that would aim to achieve reunion with the Church of England. His positions on church union were not well received by many British Baptists who feared that the autonomy of Baptist churches and denominational organizations would be compromised by a new form of establishmentarianism.[25] John Clifford and T. R. Glover opposed Shakespeare's approach to "unionism." They agreed that interchurch cooperation was necessary, but not at the cost of Baptist principles.

Shakespeare's ecumenical concerns were taken up by Baptist Hugh Martin, who became one of the early participants in the British Council of Churches. He was one of the first Baptist supporters of the World Council of Churches. Martin's ecumenical commitments grew out of his involvement in the Free Church Federal Council, his own work as a writer and a preacher, and his position as general manager of SCM Press. Although Martin was an unashamed advocate of Christian unity, he consistently distinguished between "unity and uniformity."[26]

In 1932, he addressed the Federal Council concerning "The Unity of the Free Churches" and acknowledged the difficulties Baptists brought to any discussion of baptism. He noted, "I speak as a Baptist. I believe in the Baptist doctrine and practice, which I hold to be the New Testament doctrine and practice. I believe that here Baptists have a valuable contribution to bring to a United Church. But our fundamental witness, as I understand it, is to a belief in the spiritual character of the Church which is now shared, whatever may have been the case in the past, by those divided from us as to the administration of the ordinance."[27]

Martin's call for greater unity was opposed by some Baptists, among them H. L. Taylor and Gilbert Laws. Taylor warned that the rush to a United Free Church would severely compromise Baptist principles and identity among the young. Laws insisted that Baptists could not compromise on three essentials of their faith: regenerate church membership, believer's baptism, and the authority of the local congregation.[28]

In 1932, the Baptist Union Council appointed a special committee to examine the possibility of a union of Baptists, Presbyterians, and Congregationalists. The committee's report, issued in 1937, concluded that no real decision on Christian union could be possible until Baptists themselves gave thorough attention to "the question of baptism," which "has been somewhat neglected amongst us in these later years." The report noted, "Until we have considered it more fully, we are not ready to come to a decision on the issue of union with any other Christian Church. Believer's Baptism, whether it be called an ordinance or a sacrament, is a matter of the most serious import, since it is based upon the authority of our Lord Himself and has contributed, as we are convinced, to the welfare of the Christian community and the maintenance of Christian doctrine."[29] The Baptist Union Council welcomed the report, and a resolution was approved. It acknowledged the impossibility of formal union with other denominations while affirming the desire of Baptists to cooperate with other churches "to extend the Kingdom of God."[30]

These actions did not deter ecumenically minded Baptists such as Hugh Martin from their commitment to Christian unity. Martin spent his life in that endeavor, serving as moderator of the Free Church Federal Council (1952–1953). He attended the earliest gatherings of the World Council of Churches and, along with other Baptist leaders, remained an advocate of unity and cooperation throughout his life. Of these efforts, Morris West commented, "It is one of the continued ironies of British church life that Baptists, who on the whole are judged by most of the media to be extremely slow and backward ecumenically, have supplied a number of the leading officers within the organized ecumenical movement, particularly in the British Council of Churches and the Free Church Federal Council."[31]

A Theological Statement

The Declaration of Principle, a basic confession of faith of the Baptist Union of Great Britain, was revised in 1938. It stated that the basis of the Union was (1) "That our Lord and Saviour, Jesus Christ, God manifest in the flesh, is the sole and absolute authority in all matters relating to faith and practice, as revealed in the Holy Scriptures, and that each Church has liberty, under the guidance of the Holy Spirit, to interpret and administer His Laws"; (2) "That Christian Baptism is the immersion in water into the Name of the Father, the Son and the Holy Ghost, of those who have professed repentance towards God and faith in our Lord Jesus Christ who 'died for our sins according to the Scriptures, was buried, and rose again the third day'"; and (3) "That it is the duty of every disciple to bear witness to the Gospel of Jesus Christ, and to take part in the evangelization of the world."[32]

The initial basis of union among British Baptists, adopted in 1813, had strong similarity to the Particular Baptist Confessions. With the "formal amalgamation" with General, Particular, and New Connection Baptists in 1891, things changed. The Union then preferred the broader declaration as a basis for a wider gathering. "The Declaration, it becomes clear, was designed to hold together in covenant a wide Baptist family, rather than to create the kind of boundaries, more typically associated with a Confession, which largely serve to hold people apart."[33]

Worship Trends

The early stages of the ecumenical movement contributed to a renewed attention to worship practices in British Baptist churches. While Baptists remained cautious about any hint of elaborate liturgy that might smack of "Prayer Book" conformity, many churches moved toward new structures in worship format and theology. M. E. Aubrey's *Minister's Manual* was published in 1927, a work that provided resources for ministers for over twenty-five years.[34]

Political Sentiments between the World Wars

David Bebbington suggested that after the First World War, Baptist political sentiments turned from the Liberal to the Conservative Party in Britain. He found evidence of this transition in the editorial positions of the *Baptist Times,* the periodical of the Baptist Union. J. C. Carlile, who succeeded John Shakespeare as editor in the 1920s, did not share the pro-Liberal positions of his predecessor. In 1924, the paper expressed support for a Conservative government, excluding Labour.[35]

Bebbington concluded that the reasons for this departure from liberalism included the elimination of traditional nonconformist critiques of government policies toward religion, the changes from "communal politics" to "class politics," the decline of the social bonds created by the chapel system, and the Liberal Party's own self-destructive tendencies.[36] By the 1930s, Baptist disillusionment with British politics seemed evident. The *Baptist Times* was hesitant to acknowledge the developing economic difficulties that led to the worldwide Depression. In a 1931 article, M. E. Aubrey (d. 1957), general secretary of the Baptist Union, wrote, "It may yet take many of us time to realize the danger is real, and that, after an era of extravagance, a return to plainer living, simpler pleasures, hard work and unselfish service is the only way out." As economic dangers loomed, a return to a life of service and communal concern was the proper response.[37]

By the mid-1930s, leadership of the Baptist Union was "largely pro-Conservative but anti-Chamberlain," Neville Chamberlain being someone whose leadership skills they questioned. More affluent evangelical Baptist churches followed the Baptist Union's lead in supporting the Conservative policies. In working-class areas of the country, many churches supported the Labour Party more extensively, while larger, more urban congregations remained more sympathetic with the Liberal Party.[38]

Between the World Wars: Declining Numbers

British Baptists experienced significant numerical decline in the 1930s. Some suggested that their successes among the middle class had distanced them from the working classes. The Sunday school system was not as strong with the public as it had been before. As early as 1930, decreases were evident in both church membership and Sunday school attendance. Membership dropped from 411,389 to 406,954.[39]

Many Baptist leaders urged a renewed evangelism and improvement of denominational programs. Yet continued decline led to continued concern. In 1936, an outreach program known as the "Call to Advance" was implemented as part of a general Forward Movement of the denomination.

The numerical declines continued throughout the twentieth century. In 1981, the total membership of the Baptist Union had fallen to 170,000.[40] One scholar observed, "Baptist churches fell foul of their own social aspirations. As they became more and more respectable they unwittingly increasingly distanced themselves in ethos, worship and outlook from the working classes."[41]

After the Second World War: Celebration and Concern

With war's end in 1945, British Baptists celebrated their rich history and sought to stem the tide of denominational decline. Ernest A. Payne served as general secretary of the Baptist Union from 1951 to 1967. He became one of the best-known Baptist participants in the ecumenical movement, particularly in the World Council of Churches and in efforts to develop improved relationships between Baptists and other British religious traditions.

Payne also promoted the Ter-Jubilee (1959–1963), an effort to commemorate the sesquicentennial of the founding of the Baptist Union. Its purpose was to infuse Baptists with a greater appreciation for their heritage while promoting contemporary evangelism, economic development, and response to the decline in church membership.[42]

The Baptist Unions of Great Britain, Scotland, and Wales met with representatives of the Baptist Missionary Society in November 1994 to discuss strengthening ties among their respective organizations. They formed a four-point covenant for the Fellowship of British Baptists. The Baptist Union of Ireland chose not to participate. The Fellowship sought to move beyond mere exchange of information to direct action and common ministry. The covenant expressed unity "in our Baptist faith and heritage" amid the "diversity which enriches our fellowship." It concluded, "We hereby commit ourselves to the strengthening of fellowship and development of partnership in the service of Christ and his Kingdom." The Fellowship was a collective effort in promoting publication, encouraging mission, and shaping Baptist identity.[43] Nonetheless, these efforts proved to be largely abortive, and no publications ever emerged.

Patricia Took, of Cann Hall and Harrow Green Baptist Church, London, was named first female superintendent for the Baptist Union of Great Britain in 1998. The Baptist Union first ordained women in 1922, but no woman held a regional ministry position (superintendent) until 1998. Took's ministerial work was in the multiracial Cann Hall Baptist church in inner-city London.[44]

Worship Resources

Concerns for worship patterns among British Baptists were evident in several worship "manuals" published during the last decades of the twentieth century. W. M. S. West suggested that perhaps "the most influential Baptist publication of 1960 was *Orders and Prayers for Church Worship: A Manual for Ministers.*" Edited by Ernest Payne and Stephen Winward, it was used extensively by British Baptists and utilized materials that introduced many churches to a broader liturgical approach. West said of the book, "It figures significantly in any consideration of Baptist worship in the twentieth century."[45]

In 1980, a volume entitled *Praise God: A Collection of Resource Material for Christian Worship* provided worship resources focusing on the Christian year, prayers and litanies, and special services. Again, its approach reflected concerns to give greater attention to somewhat more specified liturgical order and activity.[46] In 1991, Bernard Green edited *Patterns and Prayers for Public Worship* in response to the changing worship practices in Baptist churches. Attention then was given to approaches that could be formal and informal, for larger congregations and house churches.[47]

Theological Explorations

The role of women in the church was only one of many theological and ecclesiastical issues addressed by certain British Baptists in the latter part of the twentieth century. Many addressed old themes with new eyes, all aimed at restating Baptist ideas inside an increasingly secular and nondenominational culture.

Ministers and academics connected with the British Baptist colleges, particularly Regent's Park College, Northern Baptist College, Spurgeon's College, and Bristol Baptist College, worked together to address theological and ecclesiological issues in a changing Britain. For example, Paul Fiddes, principal of Regent's Park College, called Baptists to rethink the meaning of covenant. He insisted, "A Baptist ecclesiology built on the concept of covenant must take a strong view of the Church Universal." The universal church, therefore, was not simply the composite of local churches, as Baptists sometimes thought. Rather, Fiddes believed, "There is a universal reality which preexists any local manifestation of it…. Covenant and Catholicity belong together." Fiddes contended that certain contemporary Baptist groups used the word "covenant" to describe their relationships (he cites Sweden and Germany) with limited "theological reflection" on the implications of the term. A reexamination of covenant concepts was necessary because the word "covenant" was used in various secular contexts and thus had become "a dead metaphor."[48]

Covenant became a major theme developed by the Baptist Union in approaching the third millennium. It published a collection of materials for use by churches entitled *Covenant 2001*, comprised of readings and services aimed at understanding the nature of covenant between God and Christian believers and the centrality of covenant for Baptists. The book included a covenant service that churches were encouraged to utilize as a way of entering the new millennium. The service included the Apostles' Creed as a statement for common belief and unity.

In 1999, a consultation sponsored by the principals of these four British Baptist colleges addressed aspects of Baptist theology and led to the publication of a booklet entitled *Doing Theology in a Baptist Way*. In the introductory essay, Brian Haymes, principal of Bristol Baptist College, called Baptists to consider theological distinctives beyond the ecclesiological distinctions usually set forth as the center of Baptist identity. He noted, "Given that we are unwilling to make creeds authoritative, and that we hold, as a matter of theological principle, that each church has liberty in the Spirit to interpret and administer Christ's laws, then each new generation must work at its theology as reflection upon practice. It is part of vocation."[49] Other essays placed emphasis on the nature of Baptist community, covenants (a major theme among British Baptists), and the need for Baptists to listen to new voices of liberation theology raised by churches in developing countries.

British Baptists also struggled with their relationship with the state, often with varying viewpoints. In 1948, Henry Townsend, principal of Manchester Baptist College, issued a scathing denunciation of the established church. Like the early Anabaptists, Townsend declared, "It was a sad day for the Church when the Empire of Constantine entered into official relations with it."[50] He identified his position with that of the Puritans, who "regarded the alliance of Church and State as a betrayal of the Gospel and a hindrance to the spiritual growth of the nation."[51] Ernest Payne, writing at the beginning of the reign of Elizabeth II, urged caution in moving too quickly toward disestablishment of the Anglican Church, as such a conflict would seriously damage the developing ecumenical movement in England. He also warned, "It would be disastrous at the beginning of a new reign to embark upon a religious controversy that would be complicated, prolonged and embittered, and which would, equally and inevitably, involve the status and powers of the Crown."[52]

Later scholars suggested that antiestablishment concerns became increasingly less essential in secular Britain due to the decline of the Anglican Church and the rise of religious pluralism. Writing in 1999, Alan Sell concluded that the presence of "Methodists and Muslims, Sikhs and secularists," among others, "calls into question any lingering establishment theology to the effect that to be English is to be a member of the Church of England, and that not so to belong implies subversion at best and treachery at worst."[53]

At the end of the century, a number of British Baptist scholars and pastors called upon their churches to revisit Baptist perspectives on the nature and theology of baptism. Serious discussion ensued, with particular attention given to the question of whether the term "sacrament" had been or could be applied to Baptists' understanding of this act of Christian initiation. Anthony Cross was among those scholars who suggested that although many nineteenth- and twentieth-century Baptists eschewed the term "sacrament" when referring to baptism or the Lord's Supper, seventeenth-century Baptists perhaps were less hesitant to do so. He contended that Baptist perspectives on what was commonly called an "ordinance" showed great diversity and even changes from one era to another. Cross acknowledged that a majority of nineteenth- and twentieth-century Baptists generally accepted the symbolic interpretation of baptism. Strict/Grace Baptists in Britain repudiated any idea of sacramentalism in baptism. They would have agreed with W. T. Whitley's condemnation of "sacerdotalism and sacramentalism" as "twin errors." Whitley concluded, "Believe one, and the other must follow; destroy either and the other must die."[54]

Cross cited several of his contemporaries who had revisited the question of sacramental terminology in early Baptist life. Philip E. Thompson, for example, insisted that there was a "serious misrepresentation of early Baptists by their modern descendants" when claiming that they were "non- or anti-sacramental." He challenged the idea "that Baptist theology has remained fairly constant throughout the four centuries of Baptist existence." Thompson contended that seventeenth-century Baptists' commitment to their place in the universal church kept them from rejecting "*a priori* a view of baptism as non-sacramental simply because it was used by those who baptized infants."[55]

Stanley K. Fowler wrote that although early Baptist writers opposed a sacramentalism that involved "an automatic bestowal of grace," they refused to "deny that baptism has an instrumental function in the application of redemption."[56] Fowler cited Benjamin Keach, who moved from the General to the Particular Baptists, as one who used sacramental language in his *Catechism* and elsewhere. Keach denied that water in and of itself conveyed grace, but he asserted that the Spirit through the water was regenerative. He wrote, "Baptism is a means of conveying Grace, when the Spirit is pleased to operate with it; but it doth not work a physical Cause upon the Soul … for 'tis the Sacrament of Regeneration."[57]

Anthony Cross thus concluded that by the early twenty-first century, while many Baptists continued to promote an antisacramental view of baptism, "the number who recognize baptism as a sacrament, a means of conveying God's grace, has grown significantly."[58] Baptist Union documents in the twentieth century reflect this growing baptismal sacramentalism. He pointed to a 1967 study, *Baptists and Unity*, which used the word "sacrament" throughout. The document, aimed at calling for greater ecumenical dialogue, defined sacrament as "a symbol through which the grace of God becomes operative where faith is present."[59]

Thirty years later, Paul Fiddes wrote, "Thus the baptism of believers does not merely *picture* these central experiences of being in the world; it actually enables participation in the creative-redemptive activity of God that is taking place in both the natural world and human community."[60]

In a volume published in 1996, Christopher Ellis noted that although "most Baptists do not refer to baptism as a sacrament," they have held "a wide range of views about baptism altogether." He suggested that the use of the term "ordinance" "side-stepped the issue of sacramental theology by placing the importance of the rite in the believer's and the church's obedience to the command of Christ."[61] At the same time, the hesitancy to use the word "sacrament" often was based on reaction to the use of the word in other traditions rather than an attempt to discern its possible usage inside Baptist communities.

Baptists, Ellis believed, turned their focus from baptismal theology to baptismal action, concerned with who is the proper subject of baptism and what is the proper method for baptism. Although these approaches may be understandable, Ellis argued, they have impoverished Baptists.[62] He concluded by proposing a definition that Baptists might use in revisiting the importance of baptism as sacrament. It stated, "The term 'sacrament' suggests the power of symbols to link us to the depths of reality, and points us to the use by God of material means to mediate His saving action."[63]

Ellis's article appeared in a volume on the subject of baptism produced by Regent's Park College as a resource that churches might use in reexamining the nature of baptism. It illustrates the renewed interest in distinguishing questions that are central to Baptist identity. These studies may well reflect the fact that at the beginning of the twenty-first century, British Baptists were less concerned about standing over against an established church than about distinguishing basic beliefs amid the need for interchurch cooperation, interfaith dialogue, and a de facto secular establishment in the broader culture.

These varied studies illustrate the efforts of some Baptists to revisit the traditions and theology endemic in basic Baptist practices. They reflected the concern of certain British Baptists to come to terms with pluralism and secularism in their own country, while at the same time reexamining ways in which Baptist identity could be cultivated and responsive to the changing world. Writing on the response of Baptists to liberation theology, Richard Kidd commented that in spite of their concerns about Baptist identity, he and others remained Baptist: "Why? Because one of the things that Baptists ... have in common is a proper sense of dissent, a non-conformism, which always keeps us living near an edge. The danger with edges, of course, is that it is all too easy to fall off; but it is, I believe, on the edge where the reality of God has been and is most strongly made known."[64]

Baptists in Scotland: The Twentieth Century

Baptists in Scotland began the century with energy and growth. Between 1844 and 1914, the number of Baptist churches increased from 97 to 137, with membership expanding from

5,500 to 21,053. These churches had an increasing sense of cooperation in varied ministries, including work with children, social ministries, and evangelistic outreach.[65]

The First World War (1914–1918) brought death and destruction, with some one thousand Baptists killed in the fighting. In the war's aftermath, however, new church buildings were constructed and old ones remodeled. The Second World War (1939–1945) also brought death to some thirty-four thousand Scots, soldiers killed in action and civilians killed in bombings. Many churches were damaged by bombs, and some had facilities confiscated for use by civil authorities. Following the war, the Scottish Baptist Union instigated new efforts at "pioneer ministries" in various locations. The economic devastation of the war affected church contributions significantly. Yet, as Ian Balfour noted, "Despite falling membership, an indifferent economic background and the terminal decline of Scottish heavy industry from the late 1950s, Scottish Baptists funded their thirty-four new buildings."[66]

Evangelistic concerns led to the development of a five-year plan called "Every Member an Evangelist," aimed at promoting spiritual maturity, youth ministry, and missions to the community and the world. Local churches used Sunday schools as their primary evangelistic organization. Evangelism aimed at young people was conducted through groups such as Bands of Hope, Young Worshippers' Leagues, and Christian Endeavour Societies.[67] Youth rallies and revival crusades (including a Billy Graham meeting in 1955) also had implications for evangelism. American attempts to evangelize in Scotland led Southern Baptists to send various missionary teams to the country by the 1960s.

Scottish Baptists and World Ecumenism

Although the leadership of the Scottish Baptist Union supported participation in the World Council of Churches from its inception in 1948, many clergy and laity in the churches were opposed to the action. The motion for affiliation in the Council was approved by only one vote. Concerns about the World Council's liberalism led ultimately to a decision to withdraw in 1955 and give seven years for the ecumenical group to change its ways. In 1963, the Union reaffirmed its decision to remain outside the World Council, and it continues to accept that position. This is not to suggest that Scottish Baptists have been oblivious to ecumenical overtures. Many local congregations continue to participate in various forms of cooperative conversation and ministry with other denominations in their communities.[68]

Scottish Baptists and the Charismatic Movement

The modern charismatic movement had a profound impact on Scottish Baptist churches from the 1970s into the twenty-first century. Debates over the baptism of the Holy Spirit and its influence on worship practices, theology, and piety have characterized much of the discussion of the issue in Scottish churches. Ian Balfour observed that the movement's earlier "emphasis on 'tongues' has given way to a new emphasis on 'prophecy,' 'tongues' being used now more for personal devotions. Along with 'prophecy' there came a greater interest in 'healing,' and a dedication to resisting the occult."[69]

Scottish Baptists and Social Christianity

The conservative theology of Scottish Baptists sometimes made them hesitant to become too involved in the Social Gospel movement with what seemed its accompanying liberalism.

Likewise, Scottish Baptists were concerned with personal morality, eschewing liquor, tobacco, gambling, and other "worldly" practices. The Baptist Total Abstinence Society, founded in 1881, promoted complete abstinence among Baptists, from temperance pledges to the use of unfermented grape juice in communion. In 1944, a committee of the Baptist Union acknowledged, "We have laid the emphasis too exclusively on personal salvation, to the neglect of the social implications of the Gospel."[70] Throughout the latter half of the twentieth century, Scottish Baptists moved to fund retirement facilities, youth centers, and housing for the homeless, among other social ministries.

One environment in which pastoral and social concerns were discussed among Scottish ministers was the ministers' "fraternals," gatherings of ministers in a town or region to discuss various problems, personal and theological. During the twentieth century, fraternals became places where ministers could conduct dialogue about divorce, homosexuality, the charismatic movement, liberation theology, and other controversial topics. Monthly meetings were held in restaurants and included ministers and professors related to Baptist churches.[71]

The 1979 minutes of the Edinburgh fraternal include references to a discussion of questions regarding churches "having an admitted homosexual in (church) membership." Several ministers mentioned cases of this issue in their churches. The minutes reflect the conclusion that "any discipline administered should be done with the utmost discretion and carefully minuted in Church records," and that "any charge of immorality likely to be regarded as defamation of character should be avoided." However, wide ranges of opinion were duly noted.[72]

Scottish Baptists and Christian Missions

Throughout much of the twentieth century, Scottish Baptists supported missions through the Baptist Missionary Society. A full-time Scottish representative of that organization was appointed as early as 1937. Scottish Baptist churches provided numerous missionary nurses, doctors, and ministers sent out by the Society. By the latter part of the twentieth century, support for other nondenominational missionary agencies also became popular in some Scottish Baptist churches. This reflected the interest of many churches in connecting with the broader evangelical community as well as a concern to support missions in areas where the BMS did not have specific work.[73]

Missions and ministry for women created controversy among Scottish Baptists, much as they did for Baptists throughout the world. In 1997, the General Assembly voted 260 to 171 to recognize women ministers, but the vote represented 62.6 percent, not the 66.6 percent required for the two-thirds majority needed to change the bylaws. A similar vote taken in the 1980s was essentially a draw. Although churches could call a woman as pastor, the female candidate was not given official recognition by the Scottish Baptist Union.[74] In 1999, the General Assembly approved a motion to allow female candidates for the ministry.

Irish Baptists in the Twentieth Century

Baptist work in Ireland was extended during the twentieth century, particularly in the region of Belfast, Northern Ireland. The urban shape of Baptist life in Belfast began as early as 1847 with the founding of the Great Victoria Street Church. When the First World War began, there were nine Baptist churches in Belfast, including Great Victoria Street (1847), Antrim Road (1867), Mountpottinger (1891), Shankill (1896), Milltown (1896), Cliftonpark Avenue (1901), Bloomfield (1903), East Eng (1904), and Grove (1915).[75]

These churches were committed to evangelism and the establishment of new congregations. They were started in working-class and middle-class neighborhoods. Between the world wars, nine additional churches were founded in Belfast. With few exceptions, these churches grew rapidly, and "there was a significant increase in the number of Baptists in Belfast."[76]

Following the Second World War, the Belfast population exploded. Suburban housing soon was under construction. Eleven new Baptist communions were founded in Belfast between 1951 and 1972. Political conflicts and civil unrest led to the decline of the inner city, so much so that by the 1970s, some social analysts were calling Belfast one of the most troubled cities in Europe.[77]

The "Basis of Doctrine" of the Baptist Union of Ireland was approved as a guide for churches in 1895. It continued to be the doctrinal statement of Irish Baptists throughout the twentieth century. It affirmed "The inspiration and all-sufficiency of the Holy Scriptures — The Trinity in Unity of the Godhead — The Deity of our Lord and Saviour — The Personality of the Holy Spirit — The depraved and fallen state of man — The substitutionary sacrifice of our Lord and Saviour Jesus Christ — and the eternal punishment of those who die impenitent." The statement was not intended to be "binding" or a "test of orthodoxy" but an effort to refute charges that Baptists did not accept those basic doctrines.[78]

Irish Baptist churches remain uniform in their membership policies and reject open membership and open communion. Those seeking membership in a congregation must attest to their faith in Christ and receive (or have received) immersion. Church membership is a prerequisite for receiving communion. In many Irish churches, children can receive baptism, but they cannot become full (voting) members until age eighteen.[79]

A Baptist college was founded in Dublin in 1892 as a Baptist Training Institute and Boys' School. It was intended as a school for ministers. Its founder, Dublin pastor Hugh Dunlop Brown, noted in 1905 that although "divinity schools cannot manufacture ministers," there was "a need to guard our pulpits from the intrusion of those who, neither from an educational nor spiritual standpoint, possess qualifications which will last the strain and wear of pastor work."[80]

As with most Baptist schools during the early twentieth century, the Dublin College struggled financially, often nearing the brink of collapse. Early attempts to move the school to Belfast were resisted by churches in Dublin, and funding was finally secured. During the 1930s, the college again faced financial difficulties and a declining enrollment.

In 1916, T. Harold Spurgeon, grandson of Charles H. Spurgeon, was named tutor in classics, English, and Hebrew at a salary of £40 per year. He later was named principal, and in 1935 was charged with heresy for his use of A. H. Strong's "dynamic" view of biblical inspiration. Some saw this as a challenge to the inerrancy of Scripture. Spurgeon was acquitted of the charges.[81]

Financial problems and declining enrollment finally took their toll, and the school was closed in Dublin in 1963 and reopened in Belfast the next year with support from the Baptist Union of Ireland. The Irish Baptist College continued into the twenty-first century in Belfast.[82]

The Irish Baptist Union has two associations, a northern association for Northern Ireland and a southern association for the Irish Republic. Approximately 90 percent of the churches and church members are in the northern association. Following the Second World War, various independent Baptist groups from the United States developed work in Ireland, most in some cooperation with the Irish Baptist Union. At the end of the twentieth century, the Union claimed about eight thousand members in ninety-one churches in Northern Ireland, and approximately four hundred members in eleven churches in the Republic of Ireland.[83]

Baptists in Wales

Society in Wales changed dramatically in the late nineteenth century with an expanding middle class, many of whom left nonconformist churches for Anglicanism. Welsh Baptists, like other nonconformists, gave serious attention to higher education. Yet controversies arose over modern science, higher criticism, and other signs of modernity. At the beginning of the twentieth century, Welsh Baptist Abel Parry praised the orthodoxy of Baptist ministers and "called for loyalty to traditional standpoints whether Calvinist or Arminian, seeming to imply that the new thinking was too dangerous to be aired before a congregation."[84]

In matters of public education, Welsh Baptists supported the use of public funds and opposed any effort to impose religious tests on potential teachers. Baptists also insisted that if public money were given to parochial schools, they would refuse to pay the appointed tax. Baptists themselves could not agree, however, on whether religious instruction should be offered in public educational institutions.[85]

The Welsh Revival

During the years 1904–1905, a dramatic revival of religion erupted in Wales. The first Baptist references to such a phenomenon appeared in 1904 in Ponciau concerning services conducted by Thomas Shankland and J. R. Jones. Conversions and emotional religious experiences soon were reported from other congregations. Prayer meetings were held throughout the country and often became occasions for revival. Evan Roberts, the Welsh Methodist who became a central leader of the revivals, preached frequently in Baptist churches. The revivals produced significant numerical growth among Baptists and other Welsh Protestants. For example, in 1905, Baptists in the Rhondda Valley reported an increase of some three thousand members.[86]

Social Upheavals

Welsh Baptists divided over participation in elements of the Social Gospel movement, especially as related to labor unions and efforts to organize miners. In 1910, for instance, the Monmouthshire Welsh Association urged approval of a "living wage" for all workers. While Baptists claimed certain labor leaders among their members, some pastors were concerned about the secular attitudes evident in socialist rhetoric.[87]

During the First World War, Baptists generally supported the Allied cause while championing the right of Baptist clergy and laity to conscientious objection. Following the war, efforts were made to recover lost members and momentum. However, the Great Depression and the Second World War also weighed heavily on Welsh Baptists, and declines continued.[88]

During the years 1950–1982, the numbers dropped from 740 churches to 600 churches, only 400 of which were Welsh speaking. At the turn of the century, there were 25,384 members in 544 churches.[89]

International Connectionalism among Baptists

Throughout the twentieth century, Baptists developed a variety of interdenominational relationships, evident in the work of the Baptist World Alliance (BWA) and the European Baptist Federation (EBF). As early as 1806, William Carey had called for a "general association of all denominations of Christians from the four quarters of the world."[90] This and similar declarations led to ecumenical missionary gatherings in India in 1825, during the 1860s, and at Madras in 1900.

The Baptist World Alliance
The missionary movement gave impetus to the decision in 1905 to form an alliance of Baptists worldwide. J. N. Prestridge (1853–1913), editor of the *Baptist Argus* (Louisville, Kentucky), used his periodical to call for a world Baptist organization. The paper published articles from Baptists around the world. Prestridge's call for a congress of world Baptists was supported by seminary professor A. T. Robertson (1863–1934), Baptist editor Robert H. Pitt, and Georgia Baptist pastor William Warren Landrum. In 1904, at the urging of John Shakespeare, John Clifford, and Alexander Maclaren, the Baptist Union of Great Britain and Ireland organized the first Baptist World Congress, held in London, July 11–19, 1905.

The meeting attracted Baptists from Britain and the United States as well as from Australia, New Zealand, India, China, and Japan. Scottish Baptist leader Alexander Maclaren served as the first president of the conference. The group approved a constitution that asserted that the time had come to express "the essential oneness in the Lord Jesus Christ … of the Churches of the Baptist order and faith throughout the world." The BWA was a fellowship, "recognizing the independence of each particular church and not assuming the functions of any existing organization."[91]

John Clifford, second president of the BWA and prominent British pastor, wrote, "The intrinsic catholicity of our fundamental ideas and principles impels us to unity and universality wherever they have free play." He insisted that for too long Baptists had stressed only one side of "the Baptist shield," emphasizing individual freedom for both the local church and the believer. "Now we realize that we must act together as a unit, move in the same direction, engage in the same work and become a world factor."[92] John Shakespeare, secretary of the British Baptist Union, and eastern secretary of the BWA, even advocated a union of Free Churches in England. In a work entitled *The Churches at the Crossroads* (1918), Shakespeare called for a United Free Church of England—an idea that was criticized strongly by other Baptists and that never materialized. Shakespeare served as general secretary of the BWA from 1905 to 1928.

The second World Congress, held in Philadelphia in 1911, was attended by Baptists in the northern and southern hemispheres, Africa, Australasia, and Europe. A Women's Committee of the BWA was established—the first attempt to organize Baptist women internationally.[93]

Following the First World War, BWA-related groups established relief endeavors in nine European countries. The European Baptist Conference insisted that while they would "do good to all men, especially to the household of faith, … we would go in the spirit of Christ with relief for all who suffer, regardless of religious or racial differences."[94]

The third World Congress convened in Stockholm in 1923. A "World Baptist Young People's Union" was instituted. The women's meeting appointed Mrs. F. C. Spurr as president and Helen Barrett Montgomery as secretary. The fourth World Congress met in Toronto, June 1928, with some 4,800 delegates in attendance. E. Y. Mullins, Southern Baptist leader and president of the BWA, was unable to attend due to illness. Nonetheless, he and British Baptist James H. Rushbrooke issued a paper clarifying BWA identity and responding to critics, noting that the Alliance was not an administrative, judicial, or legislative body but "a voluntary and fraternal organization for promoting fellowship and cooperation among Baptists."[95] Rushbrooke was named general secretary, and the position became a full-time administrative appointment. Later general secretaries included American Walter Lewis (1939–1948), Norwegian Arnold Ohrn (1948–1960), Norwegian Josef Nordenhaug (1960–1969), American Robert Denny (1970–1980), German Gerhard Class (1980–1988), and American Denton Lotz (1988 to the present).

The Baptist World Alliance in Berlin, 1934

The fifth World Congress, held in Berlin in 1934, thrust Baptists into the early turmoil surrounding the growth of the Third Reich. Over three thousand persons attended, representing over forty-three Baptist groups. As a portion of its business, the Congress went on record addressing "racialism," denouncing "as a violation of the law of God, the Heavenly Father, all racial animosity and every form of unfair discrimination towards the Jews, towards coloured people, or towards subject races in any part of the world."[96] At the same time, many delegates were impressed with the social and moral emphases of the Hitler regime. Boston pastor John W. Bradbury wrote, "It was a great relief to be in a country where salacious sex literature cannot be sold; where putrid motion pictures and gangster films cannot be shown. The new Germany has burned great masses of corrupting books and magazines along with its bonfires of Jewish and communistic libraries."[97] BWA pronouncements acknowledged, "Chancellor Adolf Hitler gives to the temperance movement the prestige of his personal example since he neither uses intoxicants nor smokes."[98]

Many delegates deplored the racial attitudes of the Nazis, while others seemed less concerned. M. E. Dodd, president of the Southern Baptist Convention, wrote after his return from Germany that Jews "were not to be blamed for the intelligence and strength, so characteristic of their race, which put them forward." Yet they were using their strengths of intellect and economics "for self-aggrandizement to the injury of the German people."[99] For Dodd, governmental aggression against the Jews in Germany was regrettable but perhaps necessary. He commented, "Since the war some 200,000 Jews from Russia and other Eastern places had come to Germany. Most of these were Communist agitators against the government."[100] The BWA assembly in Berlin brought out the best and the worst of Baptist responses to the social and political realities of their day. During the war, the BWA moved its headquarters from London to McLean, Virginia, where it remains.

Baptist World Alliance Expansions

The BWA met in Atlanta in 1939 as the world descended into war. It did not convene again until 1947 in Copenhagen, where American Baptist layman and congressman Brooks Hays insisted that the great appeals "of stricken Europe" demanded actions from governments. Churches did not have resources to provide adequate response alone.[101]

The congress in Toronto approved of a wide-ranging statement on human rights that called for human rights related to uncoerced worship, "privacy," "nationality," employment, "peaceful assembly," "leisure," and "education." The document urged Baptists to work together in evangelization, education, and actions that promoted human rights in the world.[102]

At the end of the twentieth century, the BWA described itself as "a fellowship of believers around the world." Its purposes included these: to (1) "encourage our brothers and sisters as they struggle under very difficult circumstances to proclaim the good news of Jesus Christ"; (2) "learn first-hand from believers around the world how God is working among them"; (3) "network with Baptist leaders from six continents and become conduits of hope"; (4) "pray with Baptists who suffer from religious, government or economic injustice and work with them for religious freedom and justice"; and (5) "deepen and strengthen our Baptist roots and identity."[103]

In 2002, the BWA claimed connection with 206 Baptist groups comprising a membership of more than 43 million people.[104]

Baptists in Europe: The Later Twentieth Century

In the late 1980s, the collapse of the Berlin Wall and subsequent fall of the Soviet Union produced significant changes for Europeans in general and Baptists in particular. New nation-states developed out of the former Soviet Union, with Baptist groups in those countries reorganizing and establishing new programs and institutions. Even a brief survey illustrates the changing environment for Baptists in the new nations.

The European Baptist Federation

Baptist cooperation in Europe began in conjunction with the founding of the Baptist World Alliance in the early twentieth century. The first European Baptist Congress was held in Berlin in 1908. The meeting was a consequence of the work of the Baptist World Congress held in London in 1905, a gathering that led to the formation of the BWA. Newton Marshall urged BWA president John Clifford to tour Europe and encourage Baptist cooperation there. The BWA subsequently sent both Clifford and Marshall on such a journey, encouraging the work of a European Baptist Congress.[105] At the time of the meeting in Berlin, there were ten Baptist churches and four thousand members. Clifford reported, "We meet as a section of the Baptist World Alliance," and noted that the "Congress itself, is a fruit of the spirit of Christian unity. It is the firstborn child of that prolific mother, the Baptist World Alliance; and that Alliance is the offspring of the Baptist World Congress held in London in 1905." Clifford contended, "A new day is dawning. No nation lives to itself now. They cannot. They reciprocate, supplement and complement one another. Internationalism is born, and will not die."[106]

Although two world wars and their aftermaths retarded the development of such a Baptist coalition, these early efforts contributed to the founding of the European Baptist Federation in 1950. The organization worked to provide fellowship and cooperation among Baptist bodies in Europe. With the fall of the Soviet Union, EBF membership expanded as new states and new Baptist unions appeared on the scene.

By the 1990s, the EBF was breaking new ground in many areas of European Baptist life. For example, in 1994, Brigit Karlsson, Swedish Baptist minister, was elected the Federation's first female president. In 1995, two new unions—the Baptist Union of Slovenia and the Union of Evangelical Christians-Baptists of Yugoslavia—were accepted for membership, an action indicative of the growing affiliations in Eastern Europe. That brought to forty-nine the number of unions in the EBF.

During the 1990s, the EBF issued a strong statement on religious liberty, affirming "as a basic human right, the right of all people to freedom of religious belief and practice." It also condemned those actions of "governments, majority churches and dominant religious groups" that undermined religious liberty.[107] In 1997, the EBF sponsored the first human rights forum aimed at responding to particular issues and informing member union about developments related to religious liberty.

In 1996, the EBF provided relief funds for projects in Albania, Chechnya, Moldova, Yugoslavia, and Chernobyl. The European Baptist Women's Union reported major initiatives in Uzbekistan, Georgia, Azerbaijan, Croatia, and Bosnia. The organization also established dialogue with leaders of the Orthodox Church in Eastern Europe.[108]

During the late 1990s, European Baptists worked together to aid relief efforts in response to local wars in Bosnia, Croatia, and Serbia. Among other things, they asked that (1) Baptist church property vacated by Serbs be protected by the Croatian Baptist Union and utilized by new groups settling these areas; (2) Baptists make a concerted effort to care for Serbian Baptist refugees forced to leave Serbia; (3) Baptists in the republic of Yugoslavia (Serbia) and Croatia get special assistance in responding to the needs of over 3 million refugees in those regions; (4) European Baptists seek funds to produce Bibles in the Serbian language; and (5) European Baptists provide aid in training pastors in the regions.[109]

In 1992, the EBF was given governmental permission to establish the first Baptist contact with Albania. This followed a forty-year effort by communist governments to remove all forms of religious expression. Laws opposing religion were relaxed after the fall of communism in 1991. The EBF opened a branch office in Tirana to aid in initiating a Baptist witness that would result in conversions and a formal Albanian Baptist Union. Chris and Mairi Burnett, both physicians, were appointed by the Baptist Missionary Society to begin the work.[110]

In 1997, British Baptist David R. Coffey became president of the EBF, succeeding Theodor Angelov of Bulgaria. Coffey was also general secretary of the Baptist Union of Great Britain, elected in 1991. Coffey pledged to "be a voice for the oppressed," "to discover the younger leaders in our European Baptist family," "to be an encourager of unity," "to occasion a wider vision of the church," and "to be a bearer of good news."[111] Theodor Angelov of Bulgaria was elected general secretary of EBF, succeeding Karl-Heinz Walter. His term began in January 2000. Angelov was the eighth general secretary of the organization and first eastern European to assume the post.

In 1995, the Division for Theology and Education of the EBF produced a document aimed at providing "an explanation as to who Baptists are." Although it outlined certain Baptist distinctives, it was not intended "to be a confession of faith." The EBF council received the document but was not required to give it official approval. It described elements of Baptist identity in Europe as follows:

1. *We are part of the whole, world-wide Christian Church and we confess faith in One God as Father, Son and Holy Spirit.*

2. *We affirm the need for personal faith in Jesus Christ and for discipleship in his likeness.*

3. *Our final authority in faith and practice is Jesus Christ, as revealed in the Scriptures and present among his people through the Holy Spirit.*

4. *We recognize the Scriptures of the Old and New Testaments as the primary authority for knowing God's revelation in Christ.*

5. *We understand the Church to be a fellowship of believers, sharing the table of the Lord.*

6. *We practice baptism, for believers only, into the Body of Christ.*

7. *We affirm the freedom and the responsibility of each local congregation to discover the purpose of Christ for its own life and work.*

8. *We affirm the "priesthood of all believers," in which all members of the church are called to ministry; some among them are called to exercise spiritual leadership, which is always understood as serving.*

9. *We believe that mutual commitment expressed in baptism and in membership of the local church should lead to wider partnerships between churches wherever possible.*

10. *We believe that every Christian disciple is called to witness to the Lordship of Jesus Christ, and that the Church as a part of God's Kingdom is to share in the whole mission of God in the world.*

11. *We affirm the need to preserve freedom of conscience, and so we accept differences among us.*

12. *We stand for the separation of church and state, rooted in the sole Lordship of Christ and concern for religious liberty.*

13. *As Christian believers, we live in hope of the final appearing of Christ in Glory, and the transforming of all creation.*[112]

At the beginning of the twenty-first century, the EBF claimed a membership of fifty Baptist unions located in some forty-six countries in "Europe, Eurasia and the Near East." These unions numbered approximately 775,000 "baptized members" in at least 10,600 congregations.[113]

The International Baptist Seminary

Conflicts between the Southern Baptist Convention Foreign Mission Board and the European Baptist Federation escalated in 1992 with the decision of the SBC body to defund the International Baptist Theological Seminary (IBTS) in Ruschlikon, Switzerland. Ownership of the seminary property was assumed by the EBF in 1988, but Southern Baptists had promised to continue financial contributions for at least fifteen years. Differences arose over what SBC leaders saw as the liberalism of some the seminary's professors as well as a willingness on the part of EBF leaders to work with new Baptist groups, including the Cooperative Baptist Fellowship. The latter group was begun in 1991 by SBC moderates displeased with the right-wing drift of their denomination.

The Hamburg Agreement of 1992 was a reaffirmation of cooperation between the SBC Foreign Mission Board and the EBF. The document recognized the freedom of the EBF to work with the newly formed Cooperative Baptist Fellowship and other Baptist agencies. It acknowledged the common belief "that Baptists are a people who believe in the complete trustworthiness of the Bible and are committed to Jesus Christ as Lord. Likewise, they are a people of a confessional faith rather than a creedal faith." This allowed for various emphases in joint mission endeavors. The document affirmed "mutual respect," "spiritual freedom," "genuine consultation," and "reciprocal sharing" in various mission tasks.[114] The decision of the SBC Foreign Mission Board to defund the Rüschlikon Seminary was denounced by all European Baptist Unions except that of Romania. Ultimately, even the Romanian Baptist Union refused to accept SBC funds and acknowledged its displeasure at the SBC action. In 1992, the Cooperative Baptist Fellowship voted to provide funding for the Rüschlikon school.[115]

In 1994, the Rüschlikon property was sold to a Swiss insurance company for around $20 million. The money was used to purchase property and renovate buildings in Prague, where the school was moved in August 1995, following the last graduation in Rüschlikon. Much of the renovation at the new campus was provided by volunteers from Baptist communities in Europe and the United States. Various degree programs are offered by IBTS through the Protestant Theological Faculty of Charles University in Prague and the University of Wales, all in partnership with Spurgeon's College, London.

By 1998, the decision was made to reconstruct the curriculum in response to changes in European Baptist life. Originally, the IBTS at Rüschlikon provided theological education for European Baptist students at a time when few other schools were available, particularly in Eastern Europe. During the 1990s, the EBF reported that more than thirty new seminaries and Bible schools had been founded by Baptists in Europe. These realities prompted revisions in the curriculum of the IBTS. Degree programs were minimized and emphasis was placed on programs of continuing education, with greater concentration on specialization in Baptist history and identity, missions and evangelism, and religious liberty.[116]

Other Baptist Federations

The European Baptist Federation was not the only federation of Baptists to be established in Europe and throughout the world. Other regional connections were formed, many in response to political and cultural changes in their respective regions. In May 1995, representatives of three Baptist Unions of Central Asia—Kazakhstan, Kyrgyzstan, and the Middle Asian Union of Tajikistan—convened their first joint mission conference. Four hundred people attended the event.

The All-Africa Baptist Fellowship established an office in Lusaka, Zambia, in 1996. Eleazar Ziherambere, general secretary of the Fellowship, was forced to relocate headquarters from Rwanda after 1994's genocidal warfare in that country. The organization, closely linked to the BWA, represents thirty-seven Baptist unions and conventions in twenty-two African countries.

Similar alliances were founded in Eastern Europe following the collapse of the Soviet Union. The Congress of the Euro-Asiatic Federation of Unions of Evangelical Christians, comprised of Baptists in the Commonwealth of Independent States, met in April 1996. A Kazakhstan pastor, Franz Tissen, was elected president. The conference gave extensive attention to the growth of "charismatic manifestations" in member churches and the controversies connected with certain evangelists and "healing prophets" from the West.[117]

The Twentieth Century: Working Together

The efforts of such federations illustrate attempts by twentieth-century Baptists to participate together in common tasks and concerns. The changing face of Europe in the latter part of the twentieth century and the rise of the European Union in the twenty-first century brought new relationships between countries and individuals across the region. Many churches were influenced by charismatic, nondenominational movements even as they sought to respond to increasingly secularized environments.

Notes

1. Ernest A. Payne, *The Baptist Union: A Short History* (London: Baptist Union of Great Britain and Ireland, 1959), 157–59.
2. Ibid., 162.
3. Ibid., 165.
4. Ian Randall, "Mere Denominationalism: F. B. Meyer and Baptist Life," *Baptist Quarterly* (January 1993): 24.
5. W. Charles Johnson, *Encounter in London: The Story of the London Baptist Association, 1865–1965* (London: Carey Kingsgate Press, 1965), 58.
6. Ibid., 59.
7. H. Leon McBeth, *The Baptist Heritage* (Nashville: Broadman, 1987), 501.
8. Johnson, *Encounter in London*, 63.
9. Payne, *The Baptist Union*, 180.
10. Ibid.
11. Paul Dekar, "Twentieth-Century British Baptist Conscientious Objectors," *Baptist Quarterly* (January 1993): 38.
12. Ian Randall, "Capturing Keswick: Baptists and the Changing Spirituality of the Keswick Convention in the 1920s," *Baptist Quarterly* 35 (July 1996): 333.
13. Dekar, "Conscientious Objectors," 39.
14. Ibid., 39–40.
15. David W. Bebbington, "Baptists and Fundamentalism in Inter-War Britain," in *Protestant Evangelicalism: Britain, Ireland, Germany and America, c. 1750–c. 1950*, ed. Keith Robbins (Oxford and New York: Blackwell, 1990), 303.
16. Ibid., 306.
17. Ibid., 298.
18. Ibid., 314.
19. Randall, "Capturing Keswick," 336.
20. Ibid., 338.
21. Ibid., 339–40.
22. Ibid., 340.
23. Payne, *The Baptist Union*, 184.
24. Randall, "Mere Denominationalism," 21.
25. Payne, *The Baptist Union*, 185–87.
26. Anthony R. Cross, "Revd Dr Hugh Martin: Ecumenist," *Baptist Quarterly* (April 1997): 72–73.
27. Ibid., 73 (citing "The Unity of the Free Churches," *Baptist Times* [December 22, 1932]: 913).
28. Ibid., 74–75.
29. Ibid., 77.
30. Ibid., 79.
31. Anthony R. Cross, "Revd Dr Hugh Martin: Ecumenical Controversalist and Writer," *Baptist Quarterly* (July 1997): 143–44 (citing Morris West, *To Be a Pilgrim: A Memoir of Ernest A. Payne* [Guildford, England: Lutterworth], 128).
32. Richard Kidd, ed., *Something to Declare: A Study of the Declaration of Principle of the Baptist Union of Great Britain* (Oxford: Whitley Publications, 1996), 10.
33. Ibid., 15–16.
34. Michael J. Walker, "Baptist Worship in the Twentieth Century," in *Baptists in the Twentieth Century: Papers Presented at a*

Summer School, July 1982, ed. Keith W. Clements (London: Baptist Historical Society, 1983), 23.

35. Michael Goodman, "A Faded Heritage: English Baptist Political Thinking in the 1930s," *Baptist Quarterly* 37 (April 1997): 58.

36. Ibid. See also David W. Bebbington, "Baptists and Politics," in Clements, ed., *Baptists,* 76–95.

37. Goodman, "A Faded Heritage," 60.

38. Ibid., 66–67.

39. Michael Goodman, "Numerical Decline Amongst English Baptists, 1930–1939," *Baptist Quarterly* 36 (January 1996): 249.

40. L. G. Champion, "Baptist Church Life in the Twentieth Century," in Clements, ed., *Baptists,* 4–5.

41. Goodman, "Numerical Decline," 249.

42. McBeth, *The Baptist Heritage,* 503

43. "British Baptists Strengthen Ties in 'Fellowship,'" European Baptist Press Service (December 15, 1994).

44. "First Woman Superintendent for British Baptists," European Baptist Press Service (December 12, 1997).

45. W. M. S. West, "The Child and the Church: A Baptist Perspective," in William H. Brackney and Paul S. Fiddes, eds., *Pilgrim Pathways: Essays in Baptist History in Honour of B. R. White* (Macon, Ga.: Mercer University Press, 1999), 97.

46. Alec Gilmore, Edward Smalley, and Michael Walker, *Praise God: A Collection of Resource Material for Christian Worship* (London: Baptist Union, 1980).

47. Bernard Green, ed., *Patterns and Prayers for Public Worship* (Oxford: Oxford University Press, 1991).

48. Paul S. Fiddes, "'Walking Together': The Place of Covenant Theology in Baptist LIfe Yesterday and Today," in Brackney and Fiddes, eds., *Pilgrim Pathways,* 47. Many of the essays in this fine volume explore the nature of covenant among Baptists past and present.

49. Brian Haymes, "Theology and Baptist Identity," in *Doing Theology in a Baptist Way,* ed. Paul S. Fiddes (Oxford: Whitley Publications, 2000), 3–4.

50. Alan P. F. Sell, "Doctrine, Polity, Liberty: What Do Baptists Stand For?" in Brackney and Fiddes, eds., *Pilgrim Pathways,* 42 (citing Henry L. Townsend, *The Claims of the Free Churches* [London: Hodder & Stoughton, 1949], 196).

51. Ibid., 43.

52. Ibid. (citing Ernest A. Payne, *The Free Churches and the State* [London: Carey Kingsgate Press, 1953], 28).

53. Ibid., 44.

54. Anthony R. Cross, "Dispelling the Myth of English Baptist Baptismal Sacramentalism," *Baptist Quarterly* 38 (October 2000): 367–68. See also Anthony R. Cross, *Baptism and the Baptists: Theology and Practice in Twentieth-Century Britain* (Carlisle: Paternoster, 2000).

55. Ibid., 369–70 (citing P. E. Thompson, "A New Question in Baptist History: Seeking a Catholic Spirit Among Early Baptists," *Pro Ecclesia* 8, no. 1 [winter 1999], 51–72).

56. Ibid., 370.

57. Ibid., 372.

58. Ibid., 381.

59. Ibid., 382.

60. Ibid., 385 (citing Paul S. Fiddes, ed., *Reflections on the Water: Understanding God and the World through the Baptism of Believers* [Macon, Ga.: Mercer University Press], 29–30). See also Cross, *Baptism and the Baptists.*

61. Christopher Ellis, "Baptism and the Sacramental Freedom of God," in Fiddes, ed., *Reflections on the Water,* 23.

62. Ibid., 27.

63. Ibid., 37.

64. Richard L. Kidd, "Baptists and Theologies of Liberation," in Fiddes, ed., *Baptist Way,* 52.

65. David Bebbington, ed. *The Baptists in Scotland: A History* (Glasgow: Baptist Union of Scotland, 1988), 64.

66. Ibid., 69.

67. Ibid., 71.

68. Ibid., 74–76.

69. Ibid., 77.

70. Ibid., 78.

71. Kenneth B. E. Roxburgh, "Edinburgh Behind Closed Doors: The Edinburgh and Lothian Baptist Association Fraternal, 1947–87, *Baptist Quarterly* 38 (January 1999): 34.

72. Ibid., 41.

73. Bebbington, ed., *The Baptists in Scotland,* 83–84.

74. "Scottish Baptists Vote Against Recognizing Women Ministers," European Baptist Press Service (December 12, 1997).

75. J. Warke, "Baptists in Belfast: The Twentieth-Century Challenge of Urban Growth and Decline," *Irish Baptist Historical Society Journal* 20 (1987–88): 13.

76. Ibid., 15.

77. Ibid., 17.

78. Joshua Thompson, "Covenants and Constitutions in Irish Baptist Churches," *Irish Baptist Historical Society Journal* 22 (1989–90): 7.

79. Ibid., 9.

80. Joshua Thompson, "Irish Baptist College: The Dublin Years, 1892–1963," *Irish Baptist Historical Society Journal* 23 (1990–91): 26.

81. Ibid., 33–34.

82. Ibid., 36. See also Joshua Thompson, "Irish Baptist College: 'The Belfast Years,'" *Irish Baptist Historical Society Journal* 24 (1991–92): 53–60.

83. Albert W. Wardin, ed., *Baptists around the World: A Comprehensive Handbook* (Nashville: Broadman & Holman, 1995), 187–88.

84. Thomas M. Bassett, *The Welsh Baptists* (Swansea: Ilston Press, 1977), 368.

85. Ibid., 374–75.

86. Ibid., 377–78.

87. Ibid., 384–86.

88. Ibid., 391–93.

89. Wardin, ed., *Baptists around the World*, 190–92.

90. William R. Estep, *Baptists and Christian Unity* (Nashville: Broadman, 1966), 30.

91. F. Townley Lord, *Baptist World Fellowship: A Short History of the Baptist World Alliance* (Nashville: Broadman, 1955), 10.

92. Ibid., 19.

93. Ibid., 29–30.

94. Ibid., 39.

95. Ibid., 57.

96. Ibid., 82.

97. *Watchman-Examiner* (September 13, 1934) (cited in William Lloyd Allen, "How Baptists Assessed Hitler," *Peacework* [May–August 1987]: 12).

98. Report of the Fifth Baptist World Congress (cited in Allen, "How Baptists Assessed Hitler," 12).

99. Allen, "How Baptists Assessed Hitler," 13.

100. Ibid.

101. Brooks Hays, "Baptists and World Tasks," in *The Life of Baptists in the Life of the World: 80 Years of the Baptist World Alliance,* ed. Walter B. Shurden (Nashville: Broadman, 1985), 135.

102. Ibid., 245–47.

103. Baptist World Alliance (online: http://www.bwanet.org/fellowship/index.htm).

104. Baptist World Alliance (online: http://www.bwanet.org).

105. *Record of Proceedings of the First European Baptist Congress* (London: Baptist Union Publication Department, 1908), 9–11.

106. Ibid., 44–45.

107. "EBF Council Adopts Strong Religious Freedom Statement," European Baptist Press Service (September 29, 1995).

108. "European Baptists Express Unity in Diversity at Council Meeting in Estonia," European Baptist Press Service (October 15, 1996).

109. "Baptists Meet to Coordinate Assistance for Bosnia, Croatia, Serbia," European Baptist Press Service (December 20, 1995).

110. European Baptists Are 'Welcome in Albania,'" European Baptist Press Service (April 16, 1992).

111. "Coffey Pledges Leadership in Five Areas as EBF President," European Baptist Press Service (October 27, 1997).

112. "Study Paper on Baptist Identity Asks, Who, or 'What,' Are Baptists?" European Baptist Press Service (October 11, 1995).

113. "About EBF" (online: http://www.ebf.org/about.html).

114. "The 'Hamburg Agreement,'" European Baptist Press Service (September 11, 1992).

115. "We Are Here to Say 'Yes' to You, Hewett Tells Seminary Community," European Baptist Press Service (March 2, 1992).

116. "EBF Executive Reaffirms New Directions of IBTS," European Baptist Press Service (May 6, 1998).

117. "Tissen, Firisiuk Elected to Head Federation of Unions in CIS," European Baptist Press Service (April 12, 1996).

Chapter 16
Baptists in the United States: The Twentieth Century

THE TWENTIETH CENTURY BROUGHT INNUMERABLE CHANGES TO AMERICAN life. In a mere one hundred years, Baptists, like the rest of the nation, confronted shifts from rural to urban to global economies, technological innovations beyond measure, and medical breakthroughs of astounding proportions. They participated in two world wars and a variety of "minor" ones, faced the realities of the nuclear age, and witnessed the rise and fall of Soviet communism. At the beginning of the century, religious Americans struggled to adjust to the pluralism of "Protestant, Catholic, Jew." By century's end, the growth of multiple world religions in America challenged the hegemony of Judeo-Christian identity as never before. While many Protestants began the century with debates over modernism, biblical criticism, reason, and science, they ended it with debates over postmodernism, narrative theology, feminism, and spirituality. Denominations—the "shape of Protestantism" throughout much of the century—were reshaped by ecumenism, pluralism, regionalism, and individualism.

Although Americans elected three Baptist presidents, Harry Truman, Jimmy Carter, and Bill Clinton (all Democrats), many conservative Baptists repudiated each of them in the role of chief executive. The election of the first Catholic president, John F. Kennedy, occurred over the opposition of many Baptists long fearful of "Romanist" influence in the United States. The world wars, the Great Depression, Vietnam, Watergate, and the Clinton impeachment created public crises that impacted all Americans. Ethical concerns arising from racism, sexism, homosexuality, sexual promiscuity, abortion, illegal drugs, violence, and firearms served both to galvanize and divide Baptists throughout the century. During the early 1900s, Baptist denominationalism evolved significantly, as evidenced in the changing organizational structure of numerous Baptist subgroups. At century's end, Baptists, like other Protestants, were compelled to reexamine denominational connections and identity.

The Northern Baptist Convention

A New Denomination

The twentieth century had barely begun when the three principal societies representing Baptists in the North were reconfigured to form the Northern Baptist Convention. The cumbersome nature of the society method had become increasingly evident as autonomous societies proliferated and competed. These self-perpetuating societies included the American Baptist Foreign Mission Society, the Woman's American Baptist Foreign Mission Society, the American Baptist Home Mission Society, the Woman's American Baptist Home Mission Society, the American Baptist Historical Society, the American Baptist Education Society, and the American Baptist Publication Society. Each autonomous society sought funds directly from congregations, associations, and individuals through an intricate process of solicitation. When added to the direct fundraising procedures of colleges and other benevolent agencies, churches often seemed inundated by financial requests.

Plans for a more unified denomination began in the 1890s and were formulated at the annual May meetings of the various societies. In May 1896, a conference at Asbury Park, New Jersey, led to the creation of a "Commission on Systematic Beneficence," charged with developing a unified budgetary program. The Foreign and Home Mission Societies and the Publication Society agreed to these resolutions. The following year, the Woman's Baptist Home Mission Society called Baptists in the North to combine their missionary periodicals into one magazine.

In May 1900, a "Commission on Coordinating" was appointed to correlate programs and enhance communication among agencies. The Chicago Baptist Association approved a resolution in 1906 calling for "more coherence in our missionary work" and greater "denominational unity." The Association encouraged "greater effectiveness in the conduct of our great annual meetings, known popularly as the Baptist Anniversaries."[1] The proposed organizational conclave was scheduled for May 1907, when provision would be made "for a permanent organization of a general association or convention representing all Northern Baptist churches."[2] Similarly, the executive secretaries of the American Baptist Foreign Mission Society, the Home Mission Society, and the Publication Society expressed a willingness to create a new denominational organization.

The preamble to the provisional constitution declared its belief in local church autonomy and the "representative nature of the local and state associations." It affirmed loyalty to "all our denominational organizations" and suggested that just as local churches served "their several constituencies," so the time had come for "a general body that shall serve the common interests of our entire brotherhood."[3]

In 1907, Baptists gathered in Washington, D.C., and established a provisional organization for a national denomination. It brought together numerous societies, including the Home and Foreign Mission Societies, the Publication Society, the Educational Society, Woman's Home Mission Societies (east and west), the Foreign Bible Society, and the Young People's Union. A committee of fifteen was appointed to "draft a plan of organization," and in Oklahoma City in 1908, the constitution and bylaws of the denomination were approved. The Northern Baptist Convention (NBC) was established "to give expression to the sentiment of its constituency upon matters of denominational importance and general religious and moral interest, to develop denominational unity; and to give increasing efficiency to efforts for the evangelization of America and the world."[4] The new denomination created a greater connectionalism among the societies and their supporters and made organizational structures more manageable, productive, and businesslike.[5]

Charles Evans Hughes, chief justice of the Supreme Court (1930–1934), was elected first president of the new body. Denominational cooperation was tempered by a commitment to congregational autonomy. Convention delegates represented their local churches but made no claim to speak for the entire congregation.

Ex officio membership was extended to representatives of state conventions, executive agencies, and officers of benevolent societies. Societies retained their identity, with boards of managers, "all of whom shall be elected by the society upon the nomination of the Northern Baptist Convention at its annual meeting."[6] Whereas previous society membership was permitted to individual contributors, this proposal allowed only for financial support directly from churches. Individuals contributed to their local church, which in turn forwarded the money to the denomination. The new Convention was responsible for approving the budgets of each society. The societies retained the right to terminate the new relationship with a year's advance notice.

No real provision for associations was made by the new denomination. Associations existed parallel to the convention networks. Direct connections between the denomination and the associations were not immediately established.[7]

Norman Maring noted that the formation of the NBC reflected the unending "tension between local churches and their corporate authority." This is evident in the earliest deliberations regarding the new denomination. Some "declarations" suggested that the NBC was "purely advisory," yet the NBC's act of incorporation stressed the role of the denomination in promoting unity and evangelization along with ethical, religious, and "denominational matters." One statement suggested that convention delegates could only "give advice, while the other implies that they could make decisions and express opinions for the constituent churches."[8] The organizational structure of the NBC was itself a compromise, linking elements of both the convention and society methods. The societies were not integrated into one system but were a "loose federation of societies and churches."[9]

Attempts to coordinate this unwieldy organization included the decision to hold the annual meetings of each society in the month of May, generally in the same location. Delegates to the national denominational meeting then served as representatives to the various societies. An executive committee comprised of thirty members plus convention officers and past presidents was charged with planning the annual convention and establishing links between the convention and its societies.[10]

The American Baptist Board of Education was formed in 1909, aimed at coordinating instructional programs and policies for the new denomination. Connections with American Baptist universities, colleges, and seminaries received only limited attention before 1930. In 1949, a Department of Theological Education was added, charged with relating to issues of ministerial education.[11] As boards were formed and structures set, the new Convention immediately confronted a variety of complicated relationships.

Denominational Funding Programs

Some Baptist denominations, North and South, soon developed collective funding procedures. Previous Baptist financial programs were based on "designated offerings" made by individuals or churches to specific Baptist societies.

Early in the century, Northern Baptists turned to an "apportionment program" whereby churches were asked to contribute specific amounts of money to the operation of the denomination and its societies. The first general apportionment in the NBC occurred in 1907–1908. The description of its purpose, although a bit arcane, demonstrates both the determination and the uncertainty of Baptist leaders in embarking on such a plan. It noted that the budget-apportionment plan was essential "to secure full, yet proportionate recognition of all the general objects of church beneficence; to eliminate the unworthy, but provide for the presentation of all suitable causes, even if not in the budget; to prevent 'competitive appeals by the substitution of a comprehensive, fair, and adequate scheme that shall do justice to all phases of our missionary work, substitute definite for hazy ideas of duty, and open new fountains of supply.'"[12] Denominational literature urged churches to encourage all members to make regular contributions, thereby reducing their dependence on single donors who provided large sums for the work of the church and the Convention.

In short, the early twentieth century marked a concerted effort to systematize funding to churches and ecclesiastical bodies. This approach often involved abandonment of pew rents and for direct funding through the "duplex envelope" system of weekly contributions.[13] As this process of cooperative funding took shape, F. M. Ellis, a pastor in Baltimore, remarked, "We have unified the denomination at the contribution box, and that is next to the throne of grace."[14]

Another funding mechanism began in 1913 with the chartering of the Ministers and Missionaries Benefit Board of the Northern Baptist Convention. This retirement agency administered funds to ministerial employees of the churches, the denomination, and the mission boards, and their "wives or widows, and their dependent children."[15] The dire financial straits of many retired ministers provided a major incentive for the program.

The Southern Baptist Convention

Southern Baptist Denominationalism

The Southern Baptist Convention (SBC), organized around a more centralized convention system in 1845, nonetheless retained a society method of funding until 1925. Before that time, individuals, local churches, or associations contributing to the work of the Convention could serve as official "messengers" to the annual meeting. In that year, the Convention approved a "Cooperative Program"—a giving plan by which churches funneled financial resources through the state convention to the national denominational structure.

Throughout much of the twentieth century, Southern Baptist denominational organization mirrored that of corporate business. In 1927, the Convention approved a report by the Committee on Business Efficiency that effectively increased the functions of the Executive Committee in administering denominational affairs.

A significant financial crisis struck the SBC in 1927 and 1928 when it became known that denominational employees at both the Foreign and Home Mission Boards had embezzled over a million dollars in funds. Austin Crouch, the first executive treasurer of the denomination, set about trying to regain some fiscal soundness for the Convention. Likewise, J. B. Lawrence became executive secretary of the Home Mission Board. During his twenty-five-year tenure, the board recovered its financial moorings.[16]

Twentieth-century Southern Baptists redefined the nature of representation to the annual denominational meetings, and with it "official" membership in the SBC itself. The early convention procedures allowed for representatives from "churches, Sunday schools, woman's missionary societies, ladies of the church, African missionary society, ministers' conference, associations, foreign missionary society of the state, women's missionary society (state body), colleges, young men's or young women's missionary societies (colleges organization), legacy to the convention, periodicals, [and] business firms."[17]

Efforts later were made to limit official representation to messengers sent from contributing churches. In 1931, the Convention approved a plan that allowed for one messenger for every Baptist church cooperating with the SBC and an additional three messengers for every $250 contributed. In 1933, this number was raised from three to ten messengers. That formula remained static throughout the rest of the century.[18] Financial struggles plagued the SBC until the 1950s. Numerical growth was steady, however, and by 1941 churches had added almost half a million new members to SBC Sunday schools.

During these difficult times, the denomination was guided by numerous pastors and professors from the South and the Southwest. One of the best-known Southern Baptist preachers of the time was George W. Truett, pastor of First Baptist Church, Dallas, who served as a president of the SBC and the Baptist World Alliance. Truett was a frequent target of criticism by fundamentalist J. Frank Norris, pastor of First Baptist Church, Fort Worth. During the 1930s and 1940s, several seminary and college presidents were also chosen as presidents of the SBC. These included Furman University president W. J. McGlothlin, Southern Seminary president John R. Sampey, and Southwestern Seminary president L. R. Scarbrough.

Southern Baptist Missions

During the 1930s, the Foreign Mission Board was reorganized by its executive secretary, Charles Maddry. China remained a strong mission field, with almost three hundred missionaries in that country in the 1920s and early 1930s. The Great Depression and the Japanese invasion of China created numerous problems for Southern Baptists and other missionary groups. Many missionaries were interned by the Japanese during the war in Asia. In 1938, the president of the Baptist University in Shanghai was assassinated, and the All-China Seminary closed down due to the war.[19]

Home missions work continued among Native Americans, in urban regions in the South, and in Appalachia. Extensive work in the Southwest and the West led Baptists to establish churches and other missions in California and elsewhere. The first Southern Baptist church in California was founded in Bakersfield in 1936. These actions led to conflicts with Northern Baptists and the need for "comity agreements" to define boundaries of work between various groups of Baptists.

Comity Agreements

During the early twentieth century, Northern and Southern Baptists expanded agreements reached at the Fortress Monroe Conference in 1894, a meeting that established geographic boundaries for the work of each denomination. At gatherings in Old Point Comfort, Virginia, in 1911, and at Hot Springs, Arkansas, in 1912, certain "Principles of Comity" were established to guide regional ministries outside the North and the South for the next thirty years. Robert Torbet observed, "In effect, they set forth the basic proposition that Baptist bodies should not injure the work of any other Baptist group, and that complete cooperation between the two conventions should be effected."[20]

Gradually, these cooperative measures were strained as Northern Baptists withdrew from Oklahoma, some Missouri Baptist churches joined the SBC, and Southern Baptists began work in Arizona. This action led to a reaffirmation of the Principles of Comity in 1925. By the 1940s, Southern Baptist expansion into the North and the West created tensions between the two denominations and the de facto collapse of the comity agreements. In 1951, the SBC disavowed any geographic limitations on missionary outreach, and its leaders insisted that denominational agencies should be "free to serve as a source of blessing to any community or any people anywhere in the United States."[21] These claims were not well received by Northern (American) Baptists, who considered such actions an "invasion," especially when they implied that there had been "no Baptist witness" in the regions until Southerners arrived.[22] The breakdown of the comity agreements contributed to a further division between Baptists North and South.

Evangelistic Efforts

In 1917, Northern Baptists began a five-year emphasis on evangelism implemented by the Home Mission Society. In 1919, a department of evangelism was created by the Society and was charged with "the development of every church into an evangelistic and social force in its community, and a resultant mighty impact of our denominational life upon the nation and the world."[23] The denomination continued to utilize traveling evangelists and citywide crusades but gave increasing impetus to evangelism through the local congregation. Likewise, the impact of the Social Gospel compelled Northern Baptists to pursue programs of personal evangelism and social action. For many, this meant addressing both individual and corporate sins, economics, unemployment, and the exploitation of workers.[24]

Throughout much of the twentieth century, many Baptist groups continued to use revival services as a method for conducting public evangelism. Seasonal revivals in the South and "preaching missions" in the North were occasions when local pastors and itinerant evangelists called sinners to repentance.[25]

Laymen's Movements

Concern for evangelism and stewardship led to programs aimed at reaching men with the gospel and encouraging them to provide financial support for the Baptist missionary endeavors. The International Laymen's Missionary Movement was an early interdenominational effort to enlist males in the service of the church's missionary calling. Baptists were among those present at its formation in 1906. Northern Baptists urged the organization to expand its work to both home and foreign missions—a recommendation approved in 1907.[26]

In 1908, the NBC established its own Baptist Brotherhood as a denominational department. The Brotherhood was "to promote the organization of men in ... churches, congregations and communities" toward "spiritual development, good fellowship, social betterment, civic and commercial righteousness, the reinforcement of the church, the evangelization of the world, and the brotherhood of man in Jesus Christ."[27]

The Laymen's Missionary Movement of the SBC was founded in 1907 through the encouragement of Joshua Levering, a Baptist layman from Baltimore. Its concerns were for evangelizing males, promoting missionary endeavors, and encouraging a "business-like system of giving" in Baptist churches.[28]

In 1926, the organization's name was changed to the Baptist Brotherhood of the South, and it continued an emphasis on missions, stewardship, and lay ministry. In 1950, it became the Brotherhood Commission of the SBC, an agency of the denomination. Its members were charged "to promote the work of their church and denomination, and enable the church through its leadership to develop, encourage, assist and guide the men in their Christian growth, influence and witness."[29]

Throughout the century, Baptist men's groups developed specific mission projects in areas such as disaster relief and medical treatment and other short-term experiences in missionary service. At century's end, most Baptist men's organizations were declining in number, and some had begun to connect with newly organized interdenominational men's movements such as Promise Keepers.

The First World War

The outbreak of the First World War brought other divisions to Baptist life and challenged them to respond to issues of nationalism and nonviolence. Like other Protestants, non-German Baptists generally were supportive of American involvement in the First World War. In 1918, the SBC issued a "Report on the World Crisis," which stated, "The issues at stake are not primarily personal or political. They are in essence religious. They are concerned with fundamental human rights and liberties. They touch the very foundations of moral law."[30] In the North, an editorial by W. I. Hargis in the *Watchman-Examiner* noted, "We are fighting for a principle that is dearer than life. We are fighting to establish in every land the things that Jesus brought to the world and for which he laid down his life."[31]

E. Y. Mullins, president of Southern Baptist Theological Seminary, served as a volunteer chaplain, working at Fort Knox, Kentucky, during the devastating influenza outbreak of 1918. He warned, "Wars deceive us by their nearness. They are like punctuation marks in a sentence, but never the sentence or history that God is writing."[32] War fever made most Baptists hesitant to encourage conscientious objection, largely because of the belief that the war would "make the world safe for democracy." Northern Baptist pastor and editor A. C. Dixon saw the war as further evidence of the evils of Darwinian evolution. He suggested, "Back of this war, and responsible for it is Darwin's pagan teaching that the strong and the fit have the right to destroy the weak and the unfit." Dixon believed that Darwin's ideas on the survival of the fittest had influenced Friedrich Nietzsche, "the neurotic German philosopher," whose views played on the warlike nature of the German state.[33]

Baptists' anti-German rhetoric came from fundamentalists such as Dixon as well as liberals such as Harry Emerson Fosdick. Delegates to the NBC in 1917 affirmed their "wholehearted allegiance and support" to the nation while insisting that "we war against war itself."[34] The resolution called churches to "care for the moral and spiritual welfare of our boys" and to work with the War Department to fight liquor and "all the evils that are allowed to infest the camp environment."[35]

Southern Baptists expressed strong support for the war effort. Some SBC leaders compared the Kaiser to the Antichrist and insisted that the war was a confrontation between forces of light and darkness. Writing at war's end, William Louis Poteat of Wake Forest College, acknowledged, "The German menace outraged us." He concluded, "We thank God that night has past [sic] and the day has dawned at length. We have achieved a signal victory which promises to be permanent for civilization against barbarism."[36]

Pacifism and the Second World War

Following the war, many Baptists joined other Protestants in a rush to pacifism and a refusal to support future armed conflicts. With the armistice, large numbers of Baptists pledged themselves never again to support another war. Harry Emerson Fosdick declared himself a pacifist, noting that while pacifists often were "wrongheaded, they were 'wrongheaded in the right direction.'"[37] As the world moved toward a second global conflict, Fosdick joined a "Ministers' No-War Committee," and he continued to affirm his pacifist views even after Pearl Harbor while acknowledging that he was not "neutral" in his sentiments against the Nazis. His concern, he wrote, was "to keep the church Christian despite the unchristian nature of war."[38]

Some Baptists promoted the World Disarmament Conference in 1931 and deplored "the continued assertion that preparedness is a means of peace."[39] A 1934 resolution by the Northern Baptist Convention urged Congress to impose embargoes on armaments and munitions. It called on churches and pastors to defend conscientious objectors, with military action undertaken only in the case of an invasion of United States territory.[40]

The Second World War and the Nazi menace sent many of those earlier affirmations spinning. In 1944, the Northern Baptists issued a "position" on "the present world war" that acknowledged the need to stand outside human conflicts while supporting the nation and the troops, "nearly a million" of whom were "Baptist youth." It concluded with caution, "We will not bless war, but we will not withhold our blessing from our sons who fight and from our country's cause."[41] Baptist churches generally united in support of the fight against world fascism, with Baptist ministers and laity serving in the armed forces.

Baptists and Fundamentalism: The Early Years of Conflict

The so-called Fundamentalist-Modernist Controversy brought conflict and division to many American denominations, including the Baptists. Although its roots stretch back to the colonial period in American religious life, the confrontation began in earnest during the late nineteenth century and flourished throughout the twentieth century in a variety of forms. Winthrop Hudson observed that during the early 1900s, "Northern Baptists were more deeply divided, distracted, and immobilized by the Fundamentalist controversy than any other denomination."[42] Many Northern Baptist clergy and laity responded positively to the scientific and theological analyses that informed the modernist-liberal movement. When conservatives responded, the denomination was thrown into a controversy that surfaced at each annual convention held from the 1920s to the 1940s.[43] Hudson noted that the debates between liberals and conservatives impacted the denomination's numerical growth and its reputation. Many moderates departed, and potential members turned to less argumentative communions. Thus the controversy gave the NBC "an unattractive public image."[44]

Baptist Liberals

William R. Hutchison described "the modernist impulse" in American life in three important emphases. Modernists attempted to adapt "religious ideas to modern culture," promoted "the idea that God is immanent in human cultural development," and believed that society was moving toward realization of the kingdom of God on earth.[45] They promoted historical-critical biblical studies, challenged the immutability of creeds, and championed religious experience as the abiding reality of faith beyond culture-conditioned dogma.

Baptist educators participated in the theological debates of the early twentieth century. In the North, these included William Newton Clarke (1840–1912), longtime professor at Colgate Theological Seminary; Alvah Hovey (1820–1903) of Newton Theological Institution; and Augustus H. Strong (1836–1921) of Rochester Theological Seminary. Modernist Baptists on the faculty of the University of Chicago included its president, William Rainey Harper (1856–1906), as well as Ernest DeWitt Burton (1856–1925), Edgar J. Goodspeed (1871–1962), and Shailer Mathews (1863–1941).

In the South, "progressives" included E. Y. Mullins (1860–1928), of Southern Baptist Theological Seminary; evolutionist William Louis Poteat (1856–1938), professor of biology and president of Wake Forest College; and Edwin McNeill Poteat Sr. (1861–1937), Baptist pastor and president of Furman University.

In 1896, Social Gospel advocate Walter Rauschenbusch responded to controversies surrounding the teaching of higher criticism by Baptist professors. He wrote that Baptists "have no authoritative creeds to which we pledge the teachers of our churches. We have never put the future under bond to the past. In taking the Bible only as our standard, we have taken … the record of a continuous and progressive unfolding of the truth…. Even if some of us do not belong to it ourselves, we assert the right of a liberal wing of the Baptist denomination to exist and to contribute its share to our development."[46]

Shailer Mathews, professor of New Testament history at the University of Chicago, was a layman elected president of the NBC in 1915.[47] In an attempt to blend new science and traditional faith, he insisted that religious experience, not dogma, was the heart of Christian faith. Mathews defined modernism as "the use of the methods of modern science to find, state and use the permanent and central values of inherited orthodoxy in meeting the needs of a modern world."[48] Christianity, he believed, was not "a hard and fast system of philosophy or orthodoxy" but "that religion which Christians believe and practice."[49]

Mathews and other Baptist liberals affirmed "organic evolution"; utilized the historical-critical method of biblical studies; appealed to the discoveries of sociology and psychology;

accepted certain philosophical methodologies, particularly "philosophical idealism"; and "recognized vital moral values in a fully socialized democracy."[50] To Mathews, and other liberals like him, Jesus Christ was central to life and faith.

Liberalism raised serious questions about the nature of the biblical revelation. Moderates such as Augustus H. Strong affirmed the veracity of biblical teachings while acknowledging the need to take seriously the discoveries of science. During his illustrious career, Strong served as president and professor of biblical theology at Rochester Theological Seminary (1872–1912). He accepted historical-critical methods of biblical interpretation but warned Baptists not to abandon biblical authority. Strong wrote, "Baptist churches are founded upon Scripture. Their doctrine of regenerate church membership, and of church ordinances as belonging only to believers, presupposes an authoritative rule of faith and practice in the New Testament."[51]

Strong later became an outspoken critic of the liberal movement. He cautioned, "The unbelief in our seminary teaching, is like a blinding mist which is slowly settling down upon our churches and is gradually abolishing, not only all definite views of Christian doctrine, but also all conviction of duty to 'contend earnestly for the faith' of our fathers."[52]

Baptist Conservatism

Baptist conservatives or fundamentalists readily mounted a counterattack on modernism. Indeed, the word "fundamentalist" was coined by Baptist Curtis Lee Laws (1868–1946), editor of the *Watchman-Examiner,* to describe those prepared "to do battle royal for the Fundamentals."[53] In 1928, Laws was among some 150 Baptists who demanded a "General Conference on Fundamentals" to follow the meeting of NBC. They warned that "rationalism" and "worldliness" were creating "havoc" among the churches.[54]

Laws represented a group of irenic conservatives within the NBC who rejected liberalism but hoped to avoid a split in the denomination. In a 1921 editorial he wrote, "Now, be it known unto all men everywhere that Baptist fundamentalism is a spontaneous movement within our beloved denomination which seeks to reaffirm and re-emphasize the age-long principles for which our fathers suffered and died. It seeks to unite our denomination rather than to divide it."[55]

Millennialism

Premillennialism, the belief that Christ would return before the thousand years of kingly reign, was especially influential on some fundamentalists. This view of eschatology gained ascendancy over postmillennialism, the belief that the church itself would help bring in a golden age of religious devotion, followed by the return of Christ. A series of Bible conferences, many held at Niagara, New York, served to extend premillennialist influence.[56]

Premillennialism found its way into the Baptist ranks through the work numerous fundamentalist leaders. One of the most outspoken Northern Baptist premillennialists was Adoniram Judson Gordon (1836–1895), pastor of Boston's Clarendon Street Church. Gordon defended the veracity of premillennialist eschatology and pointed to the "signs of the times" that set the scene for Christ's dramatic return. He was elected the first president of the Baptist Society for Bible Study in 1890, a group concerned for the promotion of Baptist millenarianism.[57]

Baptist Fundamentalists

Not all fundamentalists were premillennialists, however. Many supported an amillennial position that there was no literal millennium and that eschatological language should be interpreted symbolically. Fundamentalists agreed on traditional orthodoxy and often were as concerned as modernists to prove the rationality of their systems. These beliefs were extensive but often were summarized in a series of "points," including biblical inerrancy, the virgin birth of Christ, Christ's substitutionary atonement, his bodily resurrection, his miraculous powers, the need for all persons to receive him as Savior, and the uniqueness of the Christian revelation above all other world religions. Some included a belief in Christ's premillennial second coming.

Leading Baptist fundamentalists were articulate in their defense of the faith. William Bell Riley (1861–1947) founded a newspaper in 1918 entitled *Christian Fundamentals in School and Church,* which gave particular attention to the impact of liberalism on Baptist schools. Called as pastor of First Baptist Church, Minneapolis, in 1897, Riley founded the Northwestern Bible and Missionary Training School. By 1935, he had formed the Northwestern Evangelical Seminary, and, in 1944, Northwestern College. As a young man, Billy Graham (1918–) became president of the Northfield schools before moving into full-time evangelism. Riley was also founder of the World's Christian Fundamentals Association (1919), the group that secured the services of William Jennings Bryan in prosecuting the famous Scopes Trial of 1925.[58]

Amzi Clarence Dixon (1854–1925) was a Baptist pastor and revivalist who challenged liberal doctrines and evolutionary views of science early in the twentieth century. After serving as pastor of Ruggles Street Baptist Church in Boston, he became pastor of Chicago Avenue Church in Chicago, Illinois, in 1906. By 1910, he had met Milton and Lyman Stewart, two wealthy Californians who funded an elaborate series of essays known as *The Fundamentals,* the first six volumes of which were edited by Dixon. As pastor of University Baptist Church, Baltimore, he continued his efforts to provide a scholarly response to liberal ideology.[59]

J. C. Massee (1871–1965) suggested that no Baptist school should tolerate even a small percentage of liberals on its faculty. He feared that Baptist schools were turning away from "the ancient landmarks" of the faith through the influence of modernism, rationalism, and materialism.[60] Massee presided at a gathering of fundamentalists prior to the meeting of the NBC in 1920. Its intent was to "restate, reaffirm and re-emphasize the fundamentals of New Testament faith."[61] Massee's own disillusionment with the fundamentalists' methods and spirit led him to break with the movement in the late 1920s.

John Roach Straton (1875–1929), pastor of Calvary Baptist Church, New York, was another of the Baptist fundamentalists who attacked modernism in his own denomination. He denounced the immorality of New York City, its theaters, nightclubs, gambling, alcohol, and other vices.[62] Straton labeled fellow Northern Baptists Shailer Mathews, Harry Emerson Fosdick, Walter Rauschenbusch, and other liberals as "infidels" who "have departed from the faith, and their form of infidelity is far more subtle and seductive and ruinous than the old, outspoken, sneering infidelity of the past."[63]

A. C. Dixon, W. B. Riley, and Canadian conservative T. T. Shields organized the Baptist Bible Union in 1921. It challenged Baptist liberals and supported conservative mission efforts. In 1923, the three men produced a confession of faith that affirmed classic orthodoxy and condemned evolution and the social gospel.[64]

Denominational Conflicts

In 1920, Northern Baptists appointed a committee to investigate alleged liberalism in schools and colleges. The resolution requested "the trustees and faculties of all our schools carefully to examine their work, to correct evils which they may discover, and to put forth a statement of their purpose and work, which may give assurance to the denomination of their fidelity to the Saviour, and to the gospel as held and proclaimed by Baptists immemorially."[65]

The study, delivered to the 1921 meeting of the NBC, found only limited evidence of liberalism at the schools and concluded, "For the most part our schools of all grades are doing a work of which the denomination may well be proud.... It is the duty of the Baptist communities ... to displace from the schools men who impugn the authority of the Scriptures as the Word of God and who deny the deity of our Lord, but they must do it in prescribed ways."[66]

The report produced a volatile reaction. Curtis Laws wrote that it "created the wildest disorder. A sober, reverential body of men and women was transformed into a shouting, hissing, applauding bedlam. The disgraceful scenes witnessed at Buffalo should never be repeated."[67]

Baptist conservatives soon turned their energies to new institutions. In 1925, Eastern Baptist Seminary in Philadelphia was founded as a conservative response to Crozer Seminary. Earlier, Northern Baptist Seminary had been founded in Chicago, in part as a response to liberalism at the Divinity School of the University of Chicago.[68]

At the annual meeting of the NBC at Indianapolis in 1922, fundamentalists urged the denomination to adopt the New Hampshire Confession of Faith as its doctrinal statement. Instead, the assembly approved a statement that read, "The Northern Baptist Convention affirms that the New Testament is the all-sufficient ground of our faith and practice, and we need no other statement." The resolution passed by a vote of 1,264 to 637.[69]

Charges of liberalism among Northern Baptist missionaries sent Laws and other conservatives on a tour of mission fields. A 1925 investigative report praised the missionaries, their work, and their beliefs. Nonetheless, suspicions continued.[70]

In 1924, the Board of Managers of the American Baptist Foreign Mission Society announced that it would only appoint evangelical missionaries who affirmed the gospel as "the good news of the free forgiveness of sin and eternal life ... through vital union with the crucified and risen Christ, which brings men into union and fellowship with God."[71] Fundamentalists pressed for a commission to investigate missionary orthodoxy, and in 1925 four missionaries were dismissed for their theological views.

The Fosdick Case

The controversy over missions became even more explosive when Harry Emerson Fosdick (1878–1969) toured mission sites in Asia and discovered the deep divisions there. Returning to the pulpit of "Old First" Presbyterian Church, New York City, where he was the preaching minister, Fosdick delivered a sermon entitled "Shall the Fundamentalists Win?" The sermon challenged fundamentalist ideology and declared, "The new knowledge and the old faith had to be blended in a new combination. Now, the people in this generation who are trying to do this are the liberals, and the Fundamentalists are out on a campaign to shut against them the doors of the Christian fellowship. Shall they be allowed to succeed?"[72] Although Fosdick called for "toleration and Christian liberty," his sermon became a catalyst for further divisions. Steps were taken to remove him from his Presbyterian pulpit. The church refused to accept his initial resignation, but Fosdick ultimately departed to become pastor of Park Avenue Baptist Church. In the 1930s, with the help of Baptist philanthropist John D. Rockefeller Jr., he moved the congregation to a magnificent Gothic sanctuary known as Riverside Church, dually aligned with American Baptists and Congregationalists.

The Controversy Abates

The controversy between liberals and fundamentalists in the Northern Baptist Convention reached its apex in 1926. Moderate conservatives offered a resolution that the NBC be comprised of churches "in which immersion of believers is recognized and practiced as the only Scriptural baptism; and the Convention hereby declares that only immersed members will be recognized as delegates to the Convention." W. B. Riley sought to amend the motion to read that the Convention "recognizes its constituency as consisting solely of those Baptist Churches in which the immersion of believers is recognized and practiced as a pre-requisite to membership." The original statement passed, and Riley's amendment was defeated. This was the final confrontation over fundamentalist-liberal issues at the annual Convention meeting during the 1920s.[73]

Southern Baptists and Fundamentalism

During the 1920s, fundamentalism affected the Southern Baptist Convention in several ways. First, Texas Baptist pastor J. Frank Norris (1877–1952) accused numerous persons and institutions in the SBC of liberalism. Norris's antics and agendas challenged Southern Baptist leaders to investigate any liberalism in their midst. Second, questions about the orthodoxy of missionaries and seminary professors led many to call for a denominational confession of faith. A "consultative" gathering of representatives of the Northern and Southern Conventions convened in 1922 to explore the possibility of a shared confession. Northern "anti-creed convictions" contributed to the breakdown of the talks.[74] Third, a confession of faith known as the Baptist Faith and Message was approved by the SBC in 1925. Taken primarily from the New Hampshire Confession, it was the first such confessional document to be used by the denomination. Fourth, a 1926 antievolution resolution introduced by George McDaniel, pastor of First Baptist Church, Richmond, Virginia, was made binding on employees of all SBC-funded agencies. Enforcement was difficult and generally neglected.[75] Fundamentalism continued to impact the SBC throughout the century.

Independent Baptists

The Independent Baptist movement began as a direct result of the Fundamentalist-Modernist Controversy. Although shunning elaborate denominational organization, and placing emphasis on the independence of the local congregation, these Baptists created several new "fellowships" of conservative churches. Independent Baptists may be described as a coalition of fiercely autonomous congregations, with a strongly fundamentalist theology, a Baptist polity, and a separatist approach to other ecclesiastical bodies.[76] Theirs was a reaction, as one supporter commented, to the "worldliness, modernism, apostasy and compromise" in traditional Baptist denominations. They have maintained loose confederations of local churches, funding missionaries directly rather than through mission boards or elaborate denominational agencies. They also supported personal evangelism, church growth, and independent Bible schools. Their own leaders describe these churches as "Independent, Fundamental, Premillennial and Baptistic."[77]

Although Independent Baptists promoted many fundamentalist doctrines, they often used the "five points" of doctrine—biblical inerrancy, Christ's virgin birth, Christ's substitutionary atonement, Christ's bodily resurrection, and Christ's literal, premillennial second coming—to describe the nonnegotiable orthodoxy of their movement. Many stressed biblical separatism, the belief that orthodox Christians should avoid all contact with doctrinally impure churches and individuals. It was not enough to reject liberalism; true believers had to avoid all contact with liberals themselves. John R. Rice, editor of the *Sword of the Lord,* warned against "yoking up with modernists, having modernists on the platform [at Christian meetings], and calling them to lead in prayer, and sending 'inquirers' to modernist churches."[78]

They accepted Baptist distinctives such as regenerate membership, baptismal immersion, local autonomy, missionary outreach, and religious liberty, yet interpreted those ideas in light of fundamentalist orthodoxy and independent, separatist ecclesiology. One leader declared that the term "fundamentalist Baptist" was synonymous with orthodox Christian. "In fact," he continued, "one cannot truly be a Fundamentalist without being a Baptist with just as much emphasis on the 'Baptist' end of the name as on the 'Fundamentalist' end."[79]

In 1931, J. Frank Norris broke with the SBC to found the Premillennial, Fundamental Missionary Fellowship. In 1948, it became the World Fundamental Baptist Missionary Fellowship.[80] Norris was an inveterate critic of the Southern Baptist denominational "machine." He attacked its schools, specifically Texas-based Baylor University and Southwestern Baptist Theological Seminary, as seedbeds of liberalism. He wrote that denominationalism was "the curse of the hour," noting, "I have yet to see where there is anything else in the New Testament but churches and how these churches cooperated together, but not one single time was there any overhead, overlord centralized hierarchy."[81]

Independent Baptists were not without their own internal disputes. By 1939, Norris had established a Bible school, the Fundamentalist Baptist Institute, "to fight liberalism, save souls, train young men and women and turn out pastors, evangelists and missionaries." Its curriculum was centered in the English Bible and "practical Christian work." It later was renamed the Baptist Bible Seminary.[82] It was founded, as Norris said, according to "the New Testament method," by a local church, based in that church (First Baptist Church, Fort Worth), and funded by local churches, not by a hierarchical denominational system. This method, Norris believed, "guaranteed" the school's orthodoxy.[83] That did not mean that the school escaped controversy, however.

The Baptist Bible Fellowship

Disagreements over control of the Baptist Bible Seminary led to a schism among Independent Baptists and the founding of the Baptist Bible Fellowship on May 24, 1950. G. Beauchamp Vick (1901–1975), president of the seminary, charged that Norris retained veto power over the board of trustees by using an unauthorized set of bylaws. Norris attempted to dismiss Vick as the seminary president without a vote by the trustees. When some trustees refused to support his action, Norris appointed another board and a new president. Norris's opponents rejected his efforts and moved to develop their own fellowship. Organized in Fort Worth, the Baptist Bible Fellowship moved to Springfield, Missouri, and established Baptist Bible College and the *Baptist Bible Tribune* as part of a new network of Independent Baptists. It was not a denomination but a fellowship formed "to preserve the sanctity and sovereignty of local churches and provide an opportunity for local churches to labor together in supporting missionaries and establishing churches."[84]

In an early edition of the *Baptist Bible Tribune,* editor James Combs noted that the group broke with Norris because of autocratic attitudes evident in his efforts to control the school. He asserted that the new fellowship totally opposed "the Modernism now rampant in the Northern and Southern Baptist Conventions."[85]

The General Association of Regular Baptist Churches

The General Association of Regular Baptist Churches (GARBC) was founded in 1932, largely in response to liberalism in the Northern Baptist Convention and to the "elaborate machinery" of its denominational structures. The GARBC drew members from the Fundamentalist Fellowship, begun in 1920, and the Baptist Bible Union, formed in 1923.

In 1909, conservatives left the Grand River Rapids Association of Baptist Churches (Michigan) and founded the Grand River Valley Association. In 1920, the group was renamed the Michigan Orthodox Baptist Association, and its support for independent missions led to formal dismissal from the Michigan Baptist State Convention. In 1928, it became the Grand Rapids Association of Regular Baptist Churches. In 1928, Ohio conservatives formed the Ohio Association of Independent Baptist Churches.

Internal disputes led to the demise of the Baptist Bible Union and the formation of the General Association of Regular Baptist Churches.[86] Its earliest statement stressed efforts "to preserve a denominational order" and "to re-affirm the truths of Scripture historically believed by Baptists" as expressed in the Second London, New Hampshire, Philadelphia, and Baptist Bible Union confessions of faith.[87] The association established independent missionary agencies that routed funds directly from churches to missionaries on the field. This represented a "thoroughly Baptistic" principle that moved "from the local churches up and not from a convention board down."[88] The GARBC began with a doctrinal statement based on the New Hampshire Confession of Faith, with an addendum affirming premillennialism.

Independent Baptists in the World

As premillennialists, Independent Baptists were determined "not to 'reform the world'" but to preach and teach "the Gospel of salvation to each individual soul."[89] While they often rejected worldly political alliances, they did not hesitate to address moral and political issues.

John R. Rice wrote, "When moral questions enter into politics, the preacher ought to express himself and help people to know what is right." These included opposition to the New Deal, the New Frontier, socialism, welfare, racial intermarriage, and civil rights legislation.[90] In opposing Al Smith's campaign for the U.S. presidency in 1922, J. Frank Norris declared, "In the name of the American Flag and of the Holy Bible I defy the Roman Catholic machine of New York."[91]

During the 1960s and 1970s, Independent Baptist periodicals included editorials, sermons, and articles dealing with civil rights issues, civil disobedience, the role of the federal government, and the assassinations of John F. Kennedy, Robert F. Kennedy, and Martin Luther King Jr. While deploring the murders of John and Robert Kennedy, many preachers suggested that God "permitted" the assassinations due to the actions of their "liquor-selling" father (Joseph Kennedy), their socialistic tendencies, the sinfulness of a "communistic" assassin, and their plans to build a political "dynasty."[92]

Some Independent Baptists moved into the political realm with the founding of the "Moral Majority" by Jerry Falwell in 1979. Falwell (1933–), pastor of the Thomas Road Baptist Church in Lynchburg, Virginia, attempted to involve conservative Christians in the political processes in response to issues of abortion, homosexuality, prayer in public schools, pornography, and the overall collapse of American moral culture. While most Moral Majority supporters came from the ranks of the Independent Baptists and other fundamentalist-based churches, Falwell also claimed support from conservative Catholics, Mormons, and other groups. The Moral Majority was disbanded in 1989, when Falwell announced that it had achieved its goals. By century's end, some suggested that Christian conservatives should again eschew political entanglements and renew their energy for redeeming individuals for Christ.

The Thomas Road Baptist Church mirrored the methods of the Independent Baptist movement. Founded by Falwell in 1956 in a vacant building owned by the Donald Duck Bottling Company, it grew into a megachurch of over twenty thousand members. Media broadcasts of the *Old Time Gospel Hour* moved from radio to television in 1968. Falwell and the church founded Liberty University in 1971, and by 2000 it claimed more than ten thousand students. The church maintained relationships with the Baptist Bible Fellowship, the Southwide Baptist Bible Fellowship, and other Independent Baptist networks. In the 1990s, as conservatives gained control of the Southern Baptist Convention, Falwell led the church in developing a dual alignment with that denomination. Falwell himself first served as a messenger from his church to the annual meeting of the SBC in 1998.

The Conservative Baptist Association of America

The Conservative Baptist Association of America was born of a later schism in the Northern Baptist Convention. By the 1940s, many conservatives who remained in the NBC attacked liberalism in the denomination and the appointment of liberal missionaries. The denomination refused to appoint only fundamentalist-approved missionaries, but offered to examine the views of any missionary who came under question. The denomination acknowledged the right of fundamentalists to designate their monies away from programs that they could not support in good conscience.

Disputes over these policies led conservatives to found the Conservative Baptist Foreign Mission Society in 1943 as a parallel mission organization outside the NBC. This society became an important coalition for Northern Baptist conservatives. Meetings of the Conservative Baptist Fellowship just prior to each annual meeting of the NBC allowed conservatives to address concerns about the denomination.

In 1946, the Conservative Baptist Fellowship recommended that its members remain within the NBC in order to maintain a witness to the denomination. Three regional conferences approved a manifesto drafted by the committee of fifteen that affirmed orthodox doctrines on the virgin birth, the substitutionary atonement, and bodily resurrection of Christ. It declared that the Fellowship would no longer provide funds to the constituent bodies within the NBC that could in any way be appropriated for the support of missionaries, secretaries, or others having direction of the organization who refused to affirm such doctrines as the inspiration of Scripture, Christ's substitutionary atonement and his "visible return in glory," and other classic conservative ideals.[93]

In 1945, the General Council of the Northern Baptist Convention urged the fundamentalists to change the word "conservative" to "fundamental" in describing their new mission society, insisting that the NBC mission society itself was quite conservative. Fundamentalists continued to call for more formal doctrinal statements, changes in mission funding, and termination of associations with the World and National Councils of Churches. When their efforts again were unsuccessful, the scene was set for a more formal division.[94]

In 1947, the Conservative Baptist Fellowship, meeting in Atlantic City, voted to form the Conservative Baptist Association of America. The statement of purpose noted that the group would encourage "mutual assistance" among churches for promoting evangelism, missions, and Bible teaching. The new organization was based on biblical and Baptist principles, "unmixed with liberals and liberalism and those who are content to walk in fellowship with unbelief and inclusivism." It opposed liberalism and supported "the fundamentals of the Christian faith."[95] The denomination founded two schools, the Western Conservative Baptist Theological Seminary in Portland, Oregon, and Conservative Baptist Theological Seminary in Denver, Colorado. By 1953, the new Association claimed a membership of some 500 churches and an additional 240 that were connected to state associations of fundamentalist sentiments.[96]

By the end of the twentieth century, the group was known as Conservative Baptists of America and had some two hundred thousand members in twelve hundred congregations. The movement is described as a group of autonomous churches that "function interdependently" in planting churches, evangelism, and missionary outreach.[97]

Ethnic/Immigrant Baptist Communions

Numerous "foreign-speaking" Baptist conferences were founded in the twentieth century. These included the Swedish Baptist General Conference of America (1914), the Russian Baptist Conference (1919), the Danish Baptist General Conference of America (1910), the Rumanian Baptist Association of America (1913), the Norwegian Baptist Conference of America (1910), the Czecho-Slovak Conference 1912), the Finnish Baptist Mission Union of America (1901), the English and French-Speaking Baptist Conference of New England (1891), the Italian Baptist Association (1899), the American Magyar (Hungarian) Baptist Union (1908), and the Polish Baptist Conference (1912).[98]

During the late nineteenth century, Baptists in the U.S. West attempted to evangelize the flourishing Japanese immigrant population. A Baptist mission to the Japanese was opened in Seattle in 1892, and other operations followed in Tacoma and Port Blakely, Washington. The Japanese Baptist Church in Seattle became the state's largest Japanese Baptist congregation, with 66 members in 1907 and 615 members by 1941.[99] Concern for Japanese immigrants was encouraged by certain women who once served as Baptist missionaries to Japan.

They organized a Japanese Woman's Home in Seattle in 1903, funded by Japanese Americans and the Woman's American Baptist Home Mission Society.

In California, H. Y. Shibata founded five missions aimed at reaching Japanese immigrants. The Los Angeles Baptist City Mission Society worked with the Japanese in southern California. In northern California, Sacramento became a center of Japanese work, with the First Japanese Baptist Church founded there in 1926.[100]

In 1942, when Japanese Americans were sent to wartime internment camps, the Northern Baptist Convention protested the action. It expressed "deep concern in this situation where democratic rights have been infringed upon and racial discrimination placed above the law." Although the resolution did not call for disbanding the camps, it urged that boards be established to provide citizens with "their right to liberty" and called for immediate "post-war restoration."[101]

Years later, renowned Japanese leader Jitsuo Morikawa wrote, "When historical events suddenly made us an unwanted people to be avoided, it really wasn't the universities, the liberal press, the intellectuals and the artists, not even the Supreme Court which came to our support: it was the Church, and among the churches the American Baptists and the Quakers were the first to lay their commitment on the line without waiting to see what others would do.[102]

Ecumenical Relationships

As with other issues, Baptists in America were divided in their responses to various interchurch movements that took shape during the twentieth century. Some were among the early participants in what became known as the "ecumenical movement." Others developed cautious connections with other denominations, while still other Baptist groups eschewed all ecumenical connections.

The Federal Council of Churches

Northern (American) Baptists were early participants in the major ecumenical endeavors of the century. The denomination was a charter member of the Federal Council of Churches of Christ, founded in 1908 and formed to unite various churches in evangelical social activities in the new century. A report submitted to the Northern Baptist Convention meeting in 1909 suggested that Baptists should be particularly responsive to the new Council's stress on the "essential oneness of the Christian churches of America" as well as its constitutional assertion that the Council "shall have no authority over the constituent bodies adhering to it, but its province shall be limited to the expression of its counsel and the recommending of a course of action in matters of common interest to the churches, local councils and individual Christians. It has no authority to draw up a common creed or form of government or of worship, or in any way, to limit the full autonomy of the Christian bodies adhering to it."[103] The report concluded that such democratic ideals were something that Baptists could and should support in concert with other Christians throughout the nation.

The decision to participate in the Federal Council paralleled the NBC's increasing commitment to the social implications of the gospel. Northern Baptists created a Social Service Commission in 1908, and in 1909 its members urged Baptists to support improved working conditions for laborers, an end to child labor, suppression of the "sweating system," a living wage, and "the abatement of poverty."[104] The Commission's 1909 report concluded by asserting, "Social service is not the whole of Christianity, and Christianity is something more than humanitarianism; but it will be a sad day for the church and for the world when Christian men allow themselves to be outhumaned by the humanitarians."[105]

Not every activity met with approval, however. The NBC rejected the 1932 report of the Laymen's Foreign Mission Inquiry, an ecumenical mission study group composed of Northern Baptist representatives. Opponents criticized the report's emphasis on "religious syncretism" and lack of attention to personal evangelism.[106]

Northern (American) Baptists participated in numerous ecumenical endeavors in both the nineteenth and twentieth centuries. They were involved in the American Bible Society (1816), the American Sunday School Union (1824), and the Foreign Missions Conference of North America (1893). In 1911, the NBC voted to become part of the Faith and Order movement, an early stage in the organization of the World Council of Churches. Their representatives were present in Amsterdam in 1948 when the World Council was founded.

Not all Baptists approved of such ecumenical alignments. In 1960, for example, a large congregation in the Midwest asked the Convention to remove all references to the National Council of Churches and other ecumenical connections from its literature. The request was soundly defeated.[107]

Denominational Connections

One tangible effort to connect American Baptists with other denominations developed in conversations with representatives of the Disciples of Christ. That communion, linked to the Restorationism of Barton W. Stone and Alexander Campbell, shared many beliefs and practices with the Baptists. Interest in potential union began in the nineteenth century, and by 1908 there were conferences involving Free Will Baptists, Northern Baptists, and Disciples. In 1909, the Free Will and Northern Baptists merged, but discussions with the Disciples broke down.

In 1928, a more formal joint committee, drawn from the two denominations, was appointed but again failed, in part because of differences over the Disciples' belief in baptism "for the remission of sins." Additional efforts resurfaced in the 1940s with the appointment of a Joint Commission on Baptist and Disciple Relations. At its 1940 annual meeting, the Northern Baptist Convention approved a resolution directing its General Council, "if desirable, to authorize conversations with a responsible body from the Disciples of Christ to explore possibilities and difficulties that would result from closer conference understanding and co-operation between the two denominations."[108] This group even worked out a schedule for proposed union to be achieved in the 1950s. Although conversations were extensive, in the end such complex issues as the identity of each tradition, the relationship of Baptists to their schools and to organizations such as the Baptist World Alliance, and the threat of schism in the American Baptist ranks led to the demise of the effort.[109]

Relations between Baptist groups took shape during the 1950s and 1960s. In 1958, some seven Baptist denominations in North America joined in a program known as the Baptist Jubilee Advance, "for the purpose of fellowship, mutual aid, shared objectives, and a common passion for the redemption of men."[110] Particular concern was for a united evangelistic witness and effort among the groups involved.

The Baptist Joint Committee on Public Affairs

The Baptist Joint Committee on Public Affairs grew out of the concern of some Baptists to address political issues and to lobby in behalf of Baptist concerns. Its work began with the Committee on Public Relations, founded in 1936 under the chairmanship of Rufus Weaver (1870–1947), pastor of First Baptist Church, Washington, D.C. Its first Washington office opened in 1946 under the name the Joint Conference Committee on Public Relations, with James M. Dawson (1879–1973) as executive director. Dawson was an outspoken proponent of religious liberty, and he insisted that Baptist voices on such issues must be heard in the public square. He opposed state funding of parochial schools, whatever their denominational connections, and encouraged Baptists to take their tradition of religious liberty seriously.

The organization was renamed the Baptist Joint Committee in 1950. It soon became the best-known Baptist agency lobbying in behalf of religious liberty. Support comes from a variety of Baptist groups, including the American Baptist Churches USA; the Baptist General Conference; the National Baptist Convention, USA; the National Baptist Convention, USA, Inc.; the North American Baptist Conference; the Progressive National Baptist Convention; the Religious Liberty Council; the Seventh Day Baptist General Conference; the Alliance of Baptists; the Cooperative Baptist Fellowship; and various regional Baptist groups. The Southern Baptist Convention withdrew from the Baptist Joint Committee in 1990, preferring a more conservative response to these issues.[111]

The American Baptist Churches USA

During the latter half of the twentieth century, the Northern Baptist Convention experienced significant reorganization. In 1950, the denomination voted to change its name to the American Baptist Convention (ABC), a designation that paralleled those of its societies (e.g., American Baptist Foreign Mission Society). The change also reflected the national character of a denomination extended throughout the United States. Numerical declines, theological disputes, and other internal struggles led to significant reevaluation of the denomination's mission and identity. Efforts were begun to pursue biblical concepts of the church, a renewed sense of mission, concern for diversity, and improvements in organizational structures.[112]

A concern for denominational history led to the founding of a new journal entitled *Foundations* (later called *American Baptist Quarterly*) and the publication of Robert G. Torbet's monumental *History of the Baptists* in 1950. Likewise, denominational agencies were moved to a central headquarters in Valley Forge, Pennsylvania. The General Council, the denomination's chief administrative board, was enlarged to ninety-six members, and a full-time administrative officer, the general secretary, was selected.[113] Reuben E. Nelson was chosen for that historic position.

In 1962, a Commission for the Study of Administrative Areas and Relationships was established, charged with evaluating existing organizational systems with an eye toward significant restructuring. It recommended that the ABC be divided into selected regional, state, and city units linked for cooperation and mission.[114]

Another important commission was created at the denomination's meeting in Boston in

1968. Known as the Study Commission on Denominational Structure (SCODS), it developed specific proposals for denominational reorganization. The Commission's work was informed by a 1969 "Statement of Purpose," which set forth theological and ecclesiastical bases for any restructuring of the ABC. As one expression of the broader church, the ABC was called to witness to Christ and to seek the "mind of Christ" in matters of theology, ethics, and economics. The denomination itself was to "guide, unify, and assist" American Baptists in their mission in the world, while advancing relations with other members of Christ's body, the church.[115]

SCODS offered its final report at the denominational meeting in Denver in 1972. Delegates also approved a recommendation changing the name from the American Baptist Convention to the American Baptist Churches in the U.S.A. (ABCUSA) The term "American Baptist Churches" was preferred by many over "American Baptist Church," as the latter designation might imply an ecclesiology that undermined congregational autonomy.[116]

The SCODS committee, created at the 1968 meeting of the ABC in Boston, understood its principal purpose to be "to develop a more representative structure at the national level with clear lines of accountability."[117] In the preamble to the report, Robert Torbet observed of American Baptist polity:

> *Accordingly, we have come to see the need for a delegated body to increase the ability of elected representatives of the congregations to hear and to understand each other and so be able to act responsibly under the guidance of the Holy Spirit. Such a shift in polity is from the society concept to the churchly concept.... We need, therefore, to recognize that we, as a denomination, are as truly a church within the Body of Christ as any one of the congregations in which we hold our membership.*[118]

The reorganization involved major modifications in governance. First, the General Board, comprised of representatives of cooperating churches, was established. In order to increase diversity, specific quotas were set regarding the number of clergy and laity, men and women, youth and ethnic groups, and other segments of the denomination. Second, the biennial meeting of the denomination would deal with business, strengthen fellowship, and modify bylaws when needed. Third, members of the General Board would be selected from some 142 specific election districts delineated throughout the denomination. Member churches choose delegates, who in turn participate in the election of General Board members. One-fourth of the General Board members are "representatives-at-large" elected at the biennial meeting. Ex officio members include six persons from other societies and agencies, including the president of ABCUSA, the vice president of ABCUSA, the former president, and chief executives from the American Baptist Women's Ministries, American Baptist Men, and the Ministers' Council.[119]

During the last quarter of the twentieth century, American Baptists forged new endeavors inside and outside the "official" denominational structure. They give evidence of the diversity of groups and theological and ethical concerns in the denomination. In 1970, the ABC formed an "associated relationship" with the African American Progressive National Baptist Convention. That same year, Native Americans and Hispanics in the ABC formed their own ethnic-based caucuses. In 1971, the American Baptist Charismatic Fellowship was founded. In 1973, another associated relationship was formed between the ABC and the Church of the

Brethren. In the 1990s and early 2000s, similar connections were developed with the Alliance of Baptists and the Cooperative Baptist Fellowship. The American Baptist Women in Ministry held their first national conference in 1980 and began efforts to build networks among ordained women inside the denomination. In 1984, the Baptist Peace Fellowship of North America began with links to Baptists in multiple denominations in the United States, Canada, and Mexico. A growing concern among some ABCUSA churches to reach out to gays and lesbians led to the formation of the Association of Welcoming and Affirming Baptists in 1992. That year also saw the beginning of the American Baptist Evangelicals.[120]

Southern Baptists

In an article entitled "The Mystery of the Baptists," Daniel Day Williams remarked, "There is a paradox of the Southern Baptists here again with their declaration of the autonomy of the local congregation, but with what appears, at least to an outsider, to be one of the most highly centralized systems of denominational cooperation and control in the whole ecclesiastical picture."[121] Twentieth-century Southern Baptists established an elaborate denominational system that linked churches, agencies, and individuals in diverse missions and ministries. By century's end, the denomination was in major transition and reorganization due to theological controversies, changes in convention leadership, and massive realignments of churches and institutions.

Public Morality

During the twentieth century, Baptists addressed the moral issues of their times in a variety of ways. The Baptist pulpit was a major forum for challenging public morality. Likewise, conventions and denominations offered resolutions and reports that responded to the moral and ethical issues of the day. In 1923, for example, Northern Baptists received a report on "Moving Pictures" from their Social Service Committee. It noted, "That they [films] are improving in quality is undeniable. That they need further improvement needs no argument." The report recommended, "A film bulletin in the newspaper, briefly explaining the character of the picture, is a help in making the public discriminating. Ministers should not hesitate to bring their educational influence directly to bear upon community opinion. Interpretation of principles and constructive suggestions go farther than denunciation; on occasion unsparing condemnation may be necessary."[122]

The 1923 report from the NBC's Social Service Commission commented, "Churches created the conviction which made the Eighteenth Amendment possible. The churches must stir the conviction that will make prohibition a reality all over the land."[123] The denomination opposed alcohol because of the harm brought to families, the excesses it produces, and a general concern for temperance.

The rising problem of divorce also was addressed at the 1923 meeting of the NBC, with a report imploring pastors and churches to "ascertain the facts about the family and child welfare, and then by a program of education in the reasons for excessive divorce, family desertion, and child exploitation, create in the people an intelligent understanding of the situation and drive home to their consciences the meaning for them and their children of lax standards now and for the future."[124]

The concern for deteriorating morals was a theme echoed throughout the twentieth century by various Baptist groups. In 1949, the NBC approved a resolution stating, "There are on newsstands and in other places of business many publications filled with violence and obscenity; and ... this is degrading to the morals of the American People, especially children; ... and there are being shown in moving picture theatres many scenes dealing with divorce, crime, drunkenness, and immorality." The Convention pledged to "organize and develop public sentiment against these evils, with a view to eliminating them."[125]

In 1949, the NBC passed a resolution opposing "the present national policy of preparation for atomic war, and favoring the development of atomic energy along peacetime and constructive lines."[126] Issues relative to the Cold War and international relations were divisive for Baptists as well as for the entire nation.

Twentieth-century Baptists, North and South, were outspoken opponents of alcohol and tobacco. Members were urged to practice total abstinence from both substances. Abstainers insisted that the human body was the "temple of the Holy Spirit" and should not be defiled by alcohol, tobacco, or drugs. This position often posed a moral dilemma for some agrarian Baptists who grew tobacco or whose corn crops were sold to liquor companies.[127]

During the latter half of the twentieth century, Baptists confronted the changing public morality evident in sexually explicit motion pictures, increased divorce rate, cohabitation outside of marriage, abortion, and questions regarding homosexuality. The Moral Majority, founded by Jerry Falwell, was supported by Baptists and other conservatives who sought to make a stand for "traditional family values." Congregational diversity and local church autonomy meant that divisions over how to respond to these public moral issues were evident throughout numerous Baptist denominations. Some Baptists were active in "pro-life" opposition to abortion, while others were "pro-choice," affirming a woman's "right to choose" abortion or reject it.

Civil Rights

Baptists divided publicly and privately over the issues of segregation, Jim Crow laws, "separate but equal" facilities, and racism throughout the twentieth century. Although the primary battleground for such issues was located in the South, racial divisions were evident among Baptists nationwide.

Southern fundamentalists, many within the ranks of the Baptists, often voiced opposition to integration and the civil rights movement. Some suggested that changes in law and culture would result in racial "mingling," fostered social and political anarchy, were a tool of communists to undermine American democracy, and were led by theological liberals who were enemies of orthodoxy.[128]

Many Independent Baptists were outspoken critics of the civil rights movement and its leaders. Noel Smith (1900–1974), longtime editor of the *Baptist Bible Tribune,* Springfield, Missouri, wrote extensively on the subject, as did Tennessean John R. Rice (d. 1980), editor of the *Sword of the Lord*. Rice declared that "godly colored people, born again, would be in heaven," but speculated that even there, "we may see our loved ones and we may prefer to be with those we know than with those we do not know." Heaven could be integrated, however, since there would "be no preponderance of venereal disease or crime or immorality among Negroes in heaven as on earth."[129]

Noel Smith challenged the idea that government should "have by law different races to associate themselves together against their mutual desire and interests."[130] He denied that Martin Luther King's methods of nonviolence had biblical support, writing that King was "guilty of a palpable falsehood when he implies that the New Testament and the practices of the early Christians authenticate his objectives and methods."[131] Both Smith and Rice insisted that King's liberal theology made him a heretic, not a true gospel preacher. Rice wrote that although King claimed to be a Christian, he did "not believe in the Christian faith nor trust in the virgin-born Savior."[132]

T. H. Masters, editor of *The Fundamentalist*, stated that "when a Negro became a Christian and acted like one, he was to be treated as my brother," while also maintaining that "evidently there is a mental difference between the Negro and whites," and that "the Creator must have made the difference" in the races.[133]

Rice worried that integration would mix the races in violation of certain biblical commands. He wrote, "If you had a daughter, would you want her to marry a Negro? Even if the man were a fine Christian, ... why would you want grandchildren who were mulatto children, unacceptable to both Negroes and whites?"[134]

Some Southern Baptists also expressed opposition to the civil rights movement. In 1956, Texas pastor W. A. Criswell (1909–2002), in a speech to the South Carolina legislature, expressed support for racial segregation and the idea that religious groups should "stick with their own kind." He asserted that few blacks desired to join white churches. By 1968, Criswell had moderated his views for the sake of evangelism, and in 1970 he commented, "I came to the profound conclusion that to separate by coercion the body of Christ on the basis of skin pigmentation was unthinkable, unchristian and unacceptable to God."[135]

In 1954, the Christian Life Commission of the Southern Baptist Convention issued a report that urged the denomination to accept the Supreme Court's desegregation decision "in harmony with the constitutional guarantee of equal freedom to all citizens, and with the Christian principles of equal justice and love for all men."[136] Critics soon challenged the report and the Court's action. In 1956, the Christian Life Commission for the Alabama Baptist Convention addressed the integration of the University of Alabama. It suggested that compelling integration was not "the will of God for our state in 1956." It urged white and "independent negro ministers" to meet for discussion without the presence of members of the white citizens' councils or the NAACP.[137]

Certain Southern Baptist leaders did not hesitate to speak out against racial divisions. Clarence Jordan (1912–1969), Baptist minister and scholar, founded Koinonia Farms near Americus, Georgia, in 1942 as an effort to bring together blacks and whites in common labor and spiritual experience. Their integrated workforce was a matter of great controversy in the region, and it sparked acts of violence against the community. Southern Baptist professors, including ethicists T. B. Maston (1897–1988) at Southwestern Baptist Seminary, and Henlee Barnette (1911–) at Southern Baptist Seminary, were outspoken advocates of civil rights.

Southern Baptist Controversies

Race was not the only issue to divide Southern Baptists in the latter half of the twentieth century. Fundamentalist-liberal debates, long present in the denomination, but generally kept at bay by its inherent conservatism and unwieldy denominational structure, gained momentum throughout the 1960s and 1970s, creating full-scale conflict by the 1980s. At century's end, the denomination continued to struggle as the convention system experienced significant realignment, fragmentation, and schism.

The Elliott Controversy

In 1960, Broadman Press, of the Southern Baptist Convention, published a book entitled *The Message of Genesis* by Midwestern Baptist Theological Seminary professor Ralph Elliott. Elliott's use of the historical-critical method of biblical studies led many to attack him for denying the "historicity" of much of the book of Genesis and to call upon the publishing house to revoke the work. Nonbinding resolutions presented at the convention in 1962 reaffirmed Southern Baptists' "faith in the entire Bible as the authoritative, authentic, infallible Word of God." Other statements warned the seminaries to reject any professors whose views might undermine biblical authority. Broadman Press ceased publication of Elliott's book, but he was fired from his position in 1962 when he refused to withdraw the book from publication with another press.[138]

In the wake of the Elliott incident, the SBC revised its statement of faith in 1963, with particular attention to academic freedom. In the earlier document, SBC progressives led in formulating the statement on "education," stating, "In Jesus Christ are hidden all the treasures of wisdom and knowledge. All sound learning is therefore part of our Christian heritage." The revised confession declared, "The freedom of a teacher in a Christian school, college, or seminary is limited by the pre-eminence of Jesus Christ, by the authoritative nature of the Scriptures, and by the distinct purpose for which the school exists."[139] The boundaries of education were narrowed considerably in the revision.

The Broadman Bible Commentary Controversy

When the SBC's publication house, Broadman Press, introduced a new commentary series in the 1960s, the first volume angered conservatives who rejected the author's use of historical-critical methods. In 1970, the Convention passed a motion calling on the press to withdraw the first edition and produce a rewritten version that reflected a more literalist approach to the Genesis text.

The Inerrancy Controversy

Tensions increased, with conservatives continuing to attack denominational seminaries and state Baptist colleges and universities as seedbeds of liberalism. Much of the discussion centered in the doctrine of biblical inerrancy—the belief that the Bible is without error in any facet of its content, whether faith, ethics, geography, history, or anthropology.[140] "Fundamentalists" (they preferred the term "conservative") insisted that all SBC denominational employees should subscribe to inerrantist dogmas. "Moderates" (most eschewed the label "liberal") rejected the term "inerrancy" while affirming biblical authority. They charged that fundamentalists were less concerned with theology than with gaining complete control of the denominational system.[141]

In 1979, fundamentalists elected Adrian Rogers, pastor of Bellevue Baptist Church, Memphis, as president of the SBC. Rogers and a series of fundamentalist presidents succeeded in using the appointive powers of their office to place inerrantists on every trustee board and agency of the denomination. Moderates were consistently unsuccessful in their own attempts to elect candidates for president. The annual convention meeting in Dallas in 1985 brought out some forty-five thousand messengers, the largest group ever assembled. By 1990, fundamentalist control was secure, and moderates gave up in their efforts to retake the national convention.[142] Major exoduses occurred from denominational agencies, particularly the six seminaries. Three of the six seminaries—Southern, Southeastern, and Midwestern—replaced over 90 percent of their faculties in a five- to ten-year period.

While gaining control of the national convention network, fundamentalists were less successful in the state Baptist conventions. Indeed, in Virginia and Texas, moderate majorities were so dominant that some fundamentalists broke away in 1996 and in 1998, forming their own state convention alliances and creating formal splits in the denomination. Some state conventions (e.g., Georgia and Florida) were more fundamentalist-oriented, while others (e.g., North Carolina and Alabama) were divided between elements of moderates and fundamentalists.

By the last decade of the twentieth century, the SBC had reorganized many of its national agencies. The Foreign Mission Board became the International Mission Board, and the Home Mission Board became the North American Mission Board. The denomination ended its relationship with the Baptist Joint Committee on Public Affairs and established its own lobbying office in Washington, D.C. A revision of the Baptist Faith and Message in 2000 affirmed that women could not be ordained to the pastoral office.

During the 1980s and 1990s, many Baptist colleges and universities, long governed by trustees appointed by the state conventions, redefined their relationships and gained their own self-perpetuating boards. These included Richmond (Virginia), Wake Forest (North Carolina), Samford (Alabama), Baylor (Texas), Furman (South Carolina), and Stetson (Florida) universities as well as Carson-Newman (Tennessee), Meredith (North Carolina), and Ouachita (Arkansas) Baptist colleges.

As a result of the controversy, new moderate Baptist organizations emerged, providing connections for missionary work, education, publication, and fellowship. These included the Alliance of Baptists (1986), the Cooperative Baptist Fellowship (1991), and Texas Baptists Committed (1991). Each of these groups drew individuals and churches previously connected with the SBC. While small in number compared to the SBC, these organizations reflected a return to a society method of affiliation, and they brought together a variety of churches and ministry groups for fellowship, missionary work, and cooperative endeavors.

In 1998, the Baptist General Convention of Texas revised its bylaws to become a more self-contained Baptist entity, distancing itself from the SBC and expanding many of its own programs in missions, education, and publishing. With almost one-fifth of its churches belonging to the SBC, the Texas convention's actions had major implications for the Southern Baptist future. At the beginning of the new century, many Southern Baptists essentially had returned to a de facto society method, with local churches and state conventions utilizing a variety of venues, inside and outside the old SBC, for their supporting programs and denominational participation.[143]

Other Baptist Controversies

Educational Institutions and Government Funds

Another controversy, surrounding education, involved the use of government funds by Baptist institutions of higher learning. During the 1950s and 1960s, this became a particularly volatile question, with editorials in Baptist papers generally denouncing such practices. Baptist principles regarding separation of church and state collided with the fiscal needs of private schools and the use of tax money for facilities, student loans, or faculty grants. Some Baptist schools received government funds as loans or for use in nonreligious programs. Other schools rejected federal assistance entirely. Some schools took a middle way, accepting loans for individual students and permitting student ROTC units on campus.[144]

The Ordination of Ministers

During the latter half of the twentieth century, several Baptist groups were compelled to revisit the question of ministerial ordination, in part due to the growing number of Baptist women seeking pastoral ministry. In 1968, for example, the theological conference of the American Baptists, held annually at Green Lake, Wisconsin, addressed the issue of ordination. In March 1969, the Ministers' Council and the Commission on Ministry of the American Baptist Convention approved a new statement of highly elaborate procedures for ordination. Among other things, it required candidates to be licensed by the local congregation at least six months prior to ordination. It also required four years of college and three years of seminary (completion of college and seminary degrees) of all ordinands after January 1, 1965. A seminary course on Baptist history and polity also was required. Candidates also were to relate in specific ways to a local congregation, their state commission on ministry, and their regional association, and each of those entities had specific assignments relative to the ordination process. Provisions were also made for "recognition of Non-American Baptist Ordination."[145]

Baptist churches and denominations divided over the ordination of homosexuals to the ministry. At the beginning of the new millennium, some Baptist congregations sought to be "open and affirming" of gay and lesbian members, even granting ordination. Others rejected any effort to view homosexuality as anything less than sin and a violation of biblical mandates. This led to divisions in Baptist communities throughout the United States.

Although most Baptists acknowledge that homosexuals have been present in churches across the theological spectrum, debates erupted over response to homosexuals who "came out," publicly acknowledging their homosexuality. Churches that permitted unions of homosexual couples or the ordination of homosexual persons often were dismissed from their associations and denominations. The Southern Baptist Convention approved a constitutional change in 1993 that banned any churches that "affirm, approve, or endorse homosexual behaviour."[146]

Baptists in the United States: A New Century

At the beginning of the twenty-first century, Baptists in the United States confronted a variety of new challenges relative to theology, ecclesiology, and spirituality. By the late twentieth century, it was evident that fewer religious Americans thought of their primary religious identity in terms of a denominational heritage. Many moved through multiple denominations, looking for particular kinds of local churches rather than the "brand" they represented. Denominations were torn apart by theological and ethical debates over abortion, homosexuality, biblical inerrancy, and doctrinal distinctives. They found difficulty collecting funds and retaining connections with local congregations. At the same time, localism flourished as church members seemed to be more concerned with their specific congregation than with larger denominational networks.

Baptist churches, large and small, across the nation confronted another challenge to denominational identity: the megachurch, a congregation of several thousand members, often led by a strong and populist founder-pastor whose sermons attract multitudes to worship and Bible study. Megachurches provide specialized ministries to target groups in the church and community, are particularly concerned to reach "seekers" (persons unaffiliated with any church), and are organized around intentional marketing techniques. Although often affiliated with Baptists of one form or another, many of these churches eschew specific denominational names in order to reach those who reject sectarian ecclesiology. They function as "mini-denominations," providing in one congregation many of the services and ministries previously left to denominational connectionalism. These include missionary programs, education, publication, literature, and religious identity. Their worship styles tend to be more informal, often involving "praise worship" that includes a sermon, praise choruses (brief refrains displayed on large screens in the "worship center"), skits, and other less traditional approaches to worship. In some churches, such practices reflect the influence of the charismatic movement with an emphasis on the baptism of the Holy Spirit, spiritual gifts, and hands raised in public and private prayer. Megachurches often occupy expansive "campuses," with facilities that include family life centers, food courts, and other amenities for weekday ministries.[147]

At the end of the twentieth century, Baptists in America searched for theological identity in Reformed theology, liberation theology, process theology, evangelical theology, feminist theology, and other movements. Some combined elements of several theological systems, while others sought to restate or reclaim traditional Baptist confessional statements or beliefs.

Amid concerns about the rising secularism and religious nonaffiliation, Baptists, like other Protestants, experienced a growing interest in "spirituality"—a religious quest that took many forms, traditional and nontraditional, individual and corporate. Some Baptists pursued a variety of spiritual disciplines and utilized wide-ranging devotional literature, from Roman Catholic to charismatic, from evangelical to Buddhist. Others saw such efforts as evidence of an eclectic spirituality detrimental to traditional orthodoxy.[148]

This spiritual pluralism was evidence of an even greater challenge for twenty-first-century Baptists: the interaction with other world religions, many of them gaining prominence and numerical expansion across the United States and elsewhere. The destruction of the World Trade Center buildings in New York City on September 11, 2001, compelled Americans to confront Islam, in its many expressions, nationally and globally. It heightened discussions already underway regarding interfaith dialogue, the nature of salvation, and the uniqueness of the Christian revelation. Those issues created significant debates among Baptists about the meaning of the Christian revelation itself.[149] They challenged Baptists to reexamine their identity amid the pluralism and globalism of a new century.

Notes

1. William H. Brackney, ed., *Baptist Life and Thought, 1600–1980* (Valley Forge, Pa.: Judson Press, 1983), 287–88.
2. Robert A. Baker, *Relations Between Northern and Southern Baptists,* 2nd ed. (1954; reprint, New York: Arno Press, 1980), 181.
3. Robert G. Torbet, "Baptists in the North," in James Wood, ed., *Baptists and the American Experience* (Valley Forge, Pa.: Judson Press, 1976), 273.
4. Minutes of the Meeting for the Organization of the Northern Baptist Convention (May 16–17, 1907), 4.
5. Paul Harrison, *Authority and Power in the Free Church Tradition* (Carbondale: Southern Illinois University Press, 1959), 38–39.
6. Baker, *Northern and Southern Baptists,* 182.
7. Norman Maring and Winthrop Hudson, *A Baptist Manual of Polity and Practice,* rev. ed. (Valley Forge, Pa.: Judson Press, 1991), 189–90.
8. Norman Maring, *American Baptists: Whence and Whither* (Valley Forge, Pa.: Judson Press, 1968), 76.
9. Maring and Hudson, *Baptist Manual,* 204–5.
10. Ibid., 205.
11. Sanford Fleming, "The Board of Education and Theological Education, 1911–1963," *Foundations* 8 (January 1965): 3–10.
12. *Annual of the Northern Baptist Convention* (1909), 79.
13. Ibid., 90.
14. Minutes of the Meeting for the Organization of the Northern Baptist Convention (May 16–17, 1907), 7.
15. *Annual of the Northern Baptist Convention* (1913), 4–5, 175–82.
16. Jesse C. Fletcher, *The Southern Baptist Convention: A Sesquicentennial History* (Nashville: Broadman & Holman, 1994), 148–50.
17. Ibid., 151.
18. Ibid., 153.
19. Ibid., 167.
20. Robert G. Torbet, "Historical Background of the Southern Baptist 'Invasion,'" *Foundations* 2 (July 1959): 315.
21. Ibid., 318.
22. Blake Smith, "The Southern Baptist 'Invasion': Right or Wrong?" *Foundations* 2 (July 1959): 320–31.
23. Eldon G. Ernst, "The Baptist Jubilee Advance in Historical Context," *Foundations* 9 (January–March 1966): 8.
24. Ibid., 8–9.
25. Bill J. Leonard, "Getting Saved in America: Conversion Event in a Pluralistic Culture," *Review and Expositor* 82 (winter 1985): 111–28.
26. *Annual of the Northern Baptist Convention* (1908), 41.
27. Ibid., 137.
28. *Annual of the Southern Baptist Convention* (1913), 22.
29. George W. Schroeder, *The Church Brotherhood Guidebook: A Guide for Organizing and Operating a Church Brotherhood* (Nashville: Broadman, 1950), 36; Bill J. Leonard, "A History of the Baptist Laymen's Movement," *Baptist History and Heritage* 13 (January 1978): 35–44, 62.
30. Glenn T. Miller, "Baptist World Outreach and U.S. Foreign Affairs," in Wood, ed., *American Experience,* 168.
31. Ibid.
32. Ibid, 169.
33. Brenda M. Meehan, "A. C. Dixon: An Early Fundamentalist," *Foundations* 10 (January–March 1967): 57.
34. Eldon Ernst, "Twentieth-Century Issues of War and Peace," *Foundations* 15 (July–September 1972): 308. The article includes the entire document regarding response to the war.
35. Ibid., 309.
36. James L. Thompson Jr., "Southern Baptists and Postwar Disillusionment, 1918–1919," *Foundations* 21 (April–June 1978): 114.
37. Harry Emerson Fosdick, *The Living of These Days: An Autobiography* (New York: Harper, 1956), 294.
38. Ibid., 303.
39. Ernst, "War and Peace," 310–11.
40. Ibid.
41. Ibid., 313.
42. Winthrop S. Hudson, *Baptists in Transition: Individualism and Christian Responsibility* (Valley Forge, Pa.: Judson Press, 1979), 120.
43. Ibid., 121.

44. Ibid.

45. William R. Hutchison, *The Modernist Impulse in American Protestantism* (Cambridge: Harvard University Press, 1976), 2.

46. LeRoy Moore Jr., "Academic Freedom: A Chapter in the History of the Colgate Rochester Divinity School," *Foundations* 10 (January–March 1967): 67.

47. H. Shelton Smith, Robert T. Handy, and Lefferts A. Loetscher, *American Christianity*, 2 vols. (New York: Scribner, 1960–63), 2: 238.

48. Shailer Mathews, *The Faith of Modernism* (New York: Macmillan, 1924) (cited in Smith, Handy, and Loetscher, *American Christianity*, 2: 240).

49. Ibid.

50. Smith, Handy, and Loetscher, *American Christianity*, 2:256.

51. Augustus H. Strong, *Outlines of Systematic Theology: Designed for the Use of Theological Students* (Philadelphia: Griffith & Rowland, 1908), 59–60 (cited in Hudson, *Baptists in Transition*, 132). See also Grant Wacker, *Augustus H. Strong and the Dilemma of Historical Consciousness* (Macon, Ga.: Mercer University Press, 1985).

52. George M. Marsden, *Fundamentalism and American Culture: The Shaping of Twentieth-Century Evangelicalism, 1870–1925* (New York: Oxford University Press, 1980), 166.

53. Ibid., 159.

54. Ibid.

55. Curtis L. Laws, "Fundamentalism Is Very Much Alive," *Watchman-Examiner* (July 28, 1921): 941.

56. Timothy P. Weber, *Living in the Shadow of the Second Coming: American Premillennialism, 1875–1925* (New York: Oxford University Press, 1979), 10–11. Premillennialists include several subgroups. "Historicists" believed that the biblical prophecies gave symbolic descriptions of the church's history and clues to the nature of Christ's return. "Futurists" asserted that the fulfillment of the prophecies were "signs of the times" indicating the immediate return of Christ. Futurists themselves disagreed as to the nature of the "rapture," in which the true believers would be taken up from earth. The *Scofield Bible* helped popularize the idea of "dispensations" leading to Christ's return. See also Bill J. Leonard, "The Origin and Character of Fundamentalism," *Review and Expositor* 79 (winter 1982): 6–7.

57. Ernest Sandeen, "The Baptists and Millenarianism," *Foundations* 13 (January–March 1970): 21–22.

58. C. Allyn Russell, *Voices of American Fundamentalism: Seven Biographical Studies* (Philadelphia: Westminster, 1976), 80. Billy Graham grew up inside fundamentalism. Through his work as America's most famous evangelist, Graham became the center of a renewed evangelicalism, concerned for orthodoxy but without the rancor of the old fundamentalism. His public ministry spanned sixty years and drew hundreds of thousands to crusades throughout the world. Graham is a Baptist whose evangelical ecumenism linked him with many Protestant communions.

59. Brenda M. Meehan, "A. C. Dixon: An Early Fundamentalist," *Foundations* 10 (January–March 1967): 55–58.

60. Russell, *Voices of American Fundamentalism*, 160.

61. *Watchman-Examiner* (May 20, 1920): 652.

62. Russell, *Voices of American Fundamentalism*, 162–63.

63. Joseph D. Ban, "Two Views of One Age: Fosdick and Straton," *Foundations* 14 (April–June 1971): 157.

64. Meehan, "A. C. Dixon," 58.

65. *Annual of the Northern Baptist Convention* (1921), 50, 60–75. The schools investigated included Berkeley Seminary, Chicago Divinity School, Colgate Seminary, Kansas City Seminary, Newton Seminary, Rochester Seminary, Philadelphia Seminary, Baptist Missionary Training School (Chicago), Institute for Christian Workers (Pennsylvania), Norwegian Seminary, Bethel Seminary, Grand Island College, Redlands, Broaddus Jr. College, Colorado Woman's College, Bethel Academy, Keystone Academy, Maine Central Institute (Free Baptist), Suffield School, Pillsbury Academy, Vermont Academy, Crozer Seminary, and Northern Seminary. Colleges and universities included Brown, Bucknell, Chicago, Denison, Des Moines, Franklin, Kalamazoo, Ottawa, Bates, Colby, Hillsdale, Rochester, Shurtleff, and William Jewell. Additional junior colleges and training schools included Frances Shimer, Coburn, Colby, Higgins, and Wayland.

66. Ibid., 93.

67. *Watchman-Examiner* (July 1, 1920): 845. See also C. Allyn Russell, "The Northern (American) Baptist Experience with Fundamentalism," *Review and Expositor* 79 (winter 1983): 48.

68. Ferenc M. Szasz, *The Divided Mind of Protestant America, 1880–1930* (University, Ala.: University of Alabama Press, 1982), 98.

69. Norman Maring, *Baptists in New Jersey: A Study in Transition* (Valley Forge, Pa.: Judson Press, 1964), 332.

70. Ibid., 333–34.

71. Russell, "Experience with Fundamentalism," 50.

72. Harry Emerson Fosdick, "Shall the Fundamentalists Win?" in Smith, Handy, and Loetscher, *American Christianity*, 2:298.

73. Szasz, *Divided Mind*, 98.

74. Fletcher, *Southern Baptist Convention*, 141.

75. Ibid., 144.

76. Bill J. Leonard, "Independent Baptists: From Sectarian Minority to 'Moral Majority,'" *Church History* 56 (December 1987): 504–17.

77. Nancy Tatom Ammerman, *Bible Believers: Fundamentalists in the Modern World* (New Brunswick, N.J.: Rutgers University Press, 1987), 21.

78. John R. Rice, "Bible Questions: Yoking with Modernists," *Sword of the Lord* (November 1, 1957).

79. George Norris, *Fundamentalist* (July 19, 1956): 3.

80. James O. Combs, ed., *Roots and Origins of Baptist Fundamentalism* (Springfield, Mo.: Baptist Bible Tribune, 1984); Russell, *Voices of American Fundamentalism*, 37–40.

81. J. Frank Norris, *The Fundamentalist* 8 (January 1932): 1; idem, "The New Testament Method of Financing," *Fundamentalist* (November 4, 1927).

82. R. O. Woodworth, "Baptist Bible Seminary," *Fundamentalist* (May 27, 1949); George W. Dollar, *A History of Fundamentalism in America* (Greenville, S.C.: Bob Jones University Press, 1973), 33–34.

84. Granville La Forge, "Has the BBFI Become Another Convention?" *Baptist Bible Tribune* (December 5, 1986): 49.

85. James Combs, "Reasons for Baptist Bible Fellowship," *Baptist Bible Tribune* (June 23, 1950).

86. H. Leon McBeth, *A Sourcebook for Baptist Heritage* (Nashville: Broadman, 1990), 570–71.

87. Ibid., 572.

88. R. T. Ketcham, *The Answer* (Chicago, n.d.), 49.

89. *Fundamentalist* (May 4, 1956); John R. Rice, "Moral Principles in National Politics," *Sword of the Lord* (July 24, 1964).

90. Rice, "Moral Principles," 7.

91. J. Frank Norris, *Searchlight* (April 14, 1922); idem, "Six Reasons Why Al Smith Should Not Be President," *Searchlight* (November 18, 1927).

92. "Why Did God Allow Kennedy's Death?" *Sword of the Lord* (January 24, 1964); "What Was Back of Kennedy's Murder?" *Sword of the Lord* (January 31, 1964); Tom Malone, "What Means the Death of President Kennedy?" *Sword of the Lord* (January 31, 1964); John R. Rice, "Senator Robert F. Kennedy's Death," *Sword of the Lord* (June 28, 1968).

93. McBeth, *Sourcebook*, 573–74.

94. Russell, "Experience with Fundamentalism," 55–57.

95. Ibid., 57–78.

96. Ibid., 57.

97. Conservative Baptists of America, "Who Are We?" (online: http://www.cbamerica.org).

98. *Annual of the Northern Baptist Convention* (1921), 226–29.

99. Salvatore Mondello, "The Integration of Japanese Baptists in American Society," *Foundations* 20 (July–September 1977): 255.

100. Ibid., 255–56.

101. Ibid., 257.

102. Ibid., 261.

103. *Annual of the Northern Baptist Convention* (1909), 140. The minutes of the NBC annual meetings also demonstrate continued explanation for membership in the Federal and World Councils of Churches. See *Yearbook of the American Baptist Churches* (1950), 158–59.

104. *Annual of the Northern Baptist Convention* (1909), 134.

105. Ibid., 136.

106. Charles G. Gilger, "Northern Baptists and the Laymen's Foreign Mission Inquiry," *Foundations* 6 (July 1963): 233–43.

107. John E. Skoglund, "American Baptists and the Ecumenical Movement After 50 Years," *Foundations* 4 (April 1961): 112–14.

108. *Yearbook of the Northern Baptist Convention* (1940), 130.

109. Franklin E. Rector, "Behind the Breakdown of Baptist-Disciple Conversations on Unity," *Foundations* 4 (April 1961): 120–37.

110. Minutes of the Baptist Jubilee Advance Committee (1958).

111. Bill J. Leonard, ed. *Dictionary of Baptists in America* (Downers Grove, Ill.: InterVarsity Press, 1990), 48.

112. Maring and Hudson, *Baptist Manual*, 206–7.

113. *Yearbook of the Northern Baptist Convention* (1949), 115–18.

114. Ibid., 208–9.

115. Ibid., 210–11.

116. Ibid., 211.

117. "Final Report of the Study Commission on Denominational Structure of the American Baptist Convention" (1972), 11.

118. Ibid., 100. See also Hudson, *Baptists in Transition*, 15.

119. Maring and Hudson, *Baptist Manual*, 212–13.

120. Eldon G. Ernst, "American Baptists—Twentieth-Century Denominational Chronology," in *Baptists in the Balance*, ed. Everett C. Goodwin (Valley Forge, Pa.: Judson Press, 1997), 216–18.

121. Daniel Day Williams, "The Mystery of the Baptists," *Foundations* 1 (January 1958): 8.

122. *Annual of the Northern Baptist Convention* (1923), 234.

123. Ibid., 236.

124. Ibid., 242.

125. *Yearbook of the Northern Baptist Convention* (1949), 144.

126. Ibid., 147.

127. George D. Kelsey, *Social Ethics among Southern Baptists, 1917–1969* (Metuchen, N.J.: Scarecrow Press, 1973), 131–47.

128. Bill J. Leonard, "A Theology for Racism: Southern Fundamentalists and the Civil Rights Movement," in *Southern Landscapes*, ed. Anthony J. Badger et al. (Tübingen: Stauffenburg, 1996), 165–81.

129. John R. Rice, *Dr. Rice, Here Is My Question: Bible Answers to 294 Important Questions in Forty Years' Ministry* (Murfreesboro, Tenn: Sword of the Lord, 1962), 241.

130. Noel Smith, "Constitutionally It Was Obscene," *Baptist Bible Tribune* (April 2, 1965).

131. Noel Smith, "Martin Luther King Wants a Revolution," *Bible Baptist Tribune* (April 23, 1965).

132. John R. Rice, *Sword of the Lord* (August 19, 1964): 3.

133. T. H. Masters, "I Examined My Conscience," *The Fundamentalist* (July 1963): 1.

134. John R. Rice, "Christian Fellowship with Negro and White, Not Intermarriages," *Sword of the Lord* (July 1, 1965).

135. C. Allyn Russell, "W. A. Criswell: A Case Study in Fundamentalism," *Review and Expositor* 81 (winter 1984): 122.

136. Andrew Manis, *Southern Civil Religions in Conflict: Black and White Baptists and Civil Rights, 1947–1957* (Athens: University of Georgia Press, 1988), 65.

137. Ibid., 69.

138. Robert G. Torbet, "Baptist Theological Education: An Historical Overview," *Foundations* 6 (October 1963): 330–32. See Ralph H. Elliott, *The "Genesis Controversy" and Continuity in Southern Baptist Chaos: A Eulogy for a Great Tradition* (Macon, Ga.: Mercer University Press, 1992).

139. McBeth, *Sourcebook,* 514–15.

140. Robison B. James, ed., *The Unfettered Word: Southern Baptists Confront the Authority-Inerrancy Question* (Waco, Tex.: Word, 1987).

141. Gordon James, *Inerrancy and the Southern Baptist Convention* (Dallas: Southern Baptist Heritage Press, 1986); Robison B. James and David S. Dockery, eds., *Beyond the Impasse? Scripture, Interpretation, and Theology in Baptist Life* (Nashville: Broadman, 1992).

142. Much has been written about the controversy. Studies include Nancy Tatom Ammerman, *Baptist Battles: Social Change and Religious Conflict in the Southern Baptist Convention* (New Brunswick, N.J.: Rutgers University Press, 1990); Bill J. Leonard, *God's Last and Only Hope: The Fragmentation of the Southern Baptist Convention* (Grand Rapids, Mich.: Eerdmans, 1990); E. Luther Copeland, *The Southern Baptist Convention and the Judgment of History: The Taint of an Original Sin* (Lanham, Md.: University Press of America, 1995); and David T. Morgan, *The New Crusades, The New Holy Land: Conflict in the Southern Baptist Convention, 1969–1991* (Tuscaloosa, Ala.: University of Alabama Press, 1996).

143. Bill J. Leonard, "One Denomination, Many Centers: The Southern Baptist Situation," in Goodwin, ed., *Baptists in the Balance.*

144. Alvin C. Porteous, "Church-Related Colleges and Government Aid," *Foundations* 7 (July 1964): 254–64.

145. "Ordination to the Christian Ministry in the American Baptist Convention Recommended Procedures," *Foundations* 12 (April–June 1969): 172–82.

146. Fletcher, *Southern Baptist Convention,* 322, 357.

147. Bill J. Leonard, "Perspectives on Baptist Denominationalism: Anticipating the Future," in *Findings* (Atlanta: Cooperative Baptist Fellowship, 1996), 102–11.

148. Bill J. Leonard, "Forum: American Spirituality," *Religion and American Culture* 8 (summer 1999): 152–57.

149. Diana L. Eck, *A New Religious America: How a "Christian Country" Has Now Become the World's Most Religiously Diverse Nation* (San Francisco: HarperSanFrancisco, 2001); Bill Moyers, "Democracy at the Crossroads: We Have Work to Do," *Christian Ethics Today* 8 (April 2002): 3–11.

Epilogue

THE FIRST BAPTIST CHURCHES BEGAN AS DISSENTING COMMUNIONS THAT SET
themselves over against the prevailing religious establishments of their day. They were bib-
licists, jettisoning those theological and doctrinal ideas that in their view could not be supported by Scripture. Born of Puritanism, they brought together numerous dogmas that were
present in seventeenth-century Protestantism, uniting them in peculiarly Baptist ways and
often delineating these beliefs in confessions of faith. Yet their concern for conscience, their
emphasis on individual conversion, their mistrust of "hierarchies," and the centrality of their
congregational polity made Baptists a Peoples' Movement in which division was imminently
possible. A theological diversity that ran from Arminian to Calvinist meant that even common dogmas had divergent definitions. Baptists were "deep water" Christians, with a mode
of baptism (immersion) that was the most distinctive outward and visible sign of their
theological and ecclesial identity. Their popularity amid the social and economic underclass
often brought derision upon them from critics inside and outside the Standing Order. Likewise, their internal divisions were not lost on their critics. Observing Baptist practices in the
"Carolina back-country" of eighteenth-century America, Anglican clergyman Charles
Woodmason wrote scornfully:

> They don't all agree in one Tune. For one sings this Doctrine and the next some-
> thing different—So that Peoples Brains are ... turn'd and bewilder'd.... Then
> again to see them Divide and Sub divide, Split into Parties—Rail at and excom-
> municate each other—Turn out of one meeting and receive into another... must
> give High offence to all Intelligent and rational minds.[1]

At the beginning of the twenty-first century, Baptist movements worldwide reflect both a
similarity and diversity not unlike that of their early forebears. Many of the distinctive characteristics manifested in the earliest Baptist churches remain present, in varying degrees, among
contemporary Baptists. Biblical authority and liberty of conscience, regenerate church membership and immersion baptism, local autonomy and associational cooperation, the priesthood
of the laity and the ordination of ministers, as well as support for religious freedom amid loyalty to the state, are apparent in various Baptist communions throughout the world. The Baptist World Alliance with its extensive international membership illustrates that Baptist groups
can work and worship together in a variety of ways. Yet as an essentially sectarian movement
worldwide, Baptists still "don't all agree in one Tune." Common or distinguishing marks exist
in churches that run the gamut from fundamentalism to liberalism, creedalism to non-creedal-
ism, missions to anti-missions, denominationalism to non-denominationalism, ecumenism to

anti-ecumenism, and Calvinism to Arminianism. Debates continue as to what constitutes a genuine—even orthodox—Baptist perspective. Divisions continue.

Indeed, certain Baptists have looked askance at others of their number whose definitions of "Baptistness" differed from their own. Baptist denominationalism thus remains a central identifying mark of a people who organize their Christianity around specific—sometimes varying—doctrines and actions. This diversity means that there are multiple voices claiming and articulating a Baptist identity, most with some form of historical authenticity. While core beliefs are discernible, identifying a common Baptist center remains at best elusive. Essentials vary from group to group and may include divergent theories of biblical inspiration, confessions of faith, conversionism, immersion, pietism, evangelicalism, congregationalism, voluntarism, soul liberty, and the centrality of Jesus Christ as Savior and Lord. Since these prototypes are present in other Christian communions, delineating what is distinctively Baptist poses a challenge for those who would assess and understand the movement.

While comprehensive membership statistics are difficult to calculate, by the year 2000 there were upwards of 45 million Baptists spread throughout the world, with over 30 million of that number located in the United States. Outside the U. S., only in India and Brazil do Baptists claim a million or more members. In Africa and certain areas of Asia, however, growth seems steady and substantial. Nonetheless, in most countries Baptists remain a small part of the overall population.

At century's end, most, if not all, Baptist communions found themselves impacted by transitions in culture, economics, globalism, pluralism, and other aspects of national and international life. These issues compelled Baptist groups, implicitly or explicitly, to confront their own historical and theological identities.

Globalism—the development of a worldwide nexus of cultures, economics, religions, mobility, and media—has created new opportunities for contact and cooperation among many Baptists through the Baptist World Alliance and other international and national groups. Increased opportunities for travel have enhanced the possibility for mission-oriented Baptists, both laity and clergy, to have firsthand short- or long-term experiences on previously "foreign" fields. Indeed, during the latter twentieth century, short-term missionary encounters increased substantially among a wide variety of Baptists. Many countries that once received Baptist missionaries from the West—Europe, Great Britain, and North America—consistently send out their own missionaries to countries around the world.

Globalism extended the boundaries of religious pluralism, increasing the presence and proximity of Christians and non-Christians across the globe. Baptist response to pluralism is certainly nothing new. In their call for religious liberty, not mere toleration from establishments political or religious, early Baptists in England and America anticipated pluralism as did few other seventeenth-century religionists. Contemporary religious pluralism means that beliefs previously foreign to particular countries and locales have been increasingly present next door. If in an earlier period marriage "outside the faith" meant Methodists or Catholics, in the twenty-first century it could easily include Muslims, Hindus, or Buddhists. Modern religious diversity again has compelled Baptists to confront with new intensity the nature of pluralism, salvation, mission, and religious liberty, as well as implicit and explicit religious establishments.

Twenty-first century Baptists also confront a changing ethos in many of their own communions. In certain parts of the world, Baptist churches and individuals have been greatly influenced by the Pentecostal or Charismatic movements, evidenced in varying manifestations of Spirit baptism, spiritual gifts, and even *glossolalia* (speaking in tongues). In many regions Baptists continue to divide over such issues as the role of women in ministry, the nature of biblical inspiration, the ordination of homosexuals, the content of Christian higher education, and the quality of racial and ethnic relationships. If earlier Baptists debated questions related to baptism and communion, slavery and segregation, socialism and capitalism, more recent disagreements have centered on divorce, abortion, homosexuality, biblical inspiration, and church/state issues. While various Baptist traditions persist in the development of elaborate denominational connections, a growing number have renewed the classic Baptist emphasis on localism and the centrality of the individual congregation. Some have even developed "non-geographical associations" with Baptists and other Christians in other regions or nations. Some Baptists participate in ecumenical and interfaith endeavors while others warn that dialogue with other religious communities might weaken Baptist identity or promote an incipient universalism. A concern for theological specificity and order led some Baptists to reassert traditional Calvinist doctrines. Indeed, the influence of Reformed Theology among many Baptists seems increasingly prominent at the beginning of the twenty-first century. Others have been drawn to so-called "post-modern" approaches to belief and practice with greater emphasis on narrative, reader-response to texts and traditions, and suspicion of "Enlightenment rationalism." Still others reassert Baptist evangelicalism with an abiding concern to "win souls for Christ," even while dividing over the nature of salvation and the means of securing it. Baptist groups on the right and the left debate responses to their respective governments. Some resist state infringements wherever they appear, while others continue to call for religious liberty in countries where it is denied. Still others challenge what they believe to be the ultimate modern establishment: secularism. These diverse responses to developments in church and society will continue to inform and divide Baptists throughout the twenty-first century. They challenge Baptists worldwide to revisit their history in search of identity old and new.

Amid these differences, however, there are ideals and emphases that seem endemic to Baptist individuality, certain common marks that characterize specific points of reference.[2] They include the following:

- God is the Creator of life and the object of faith.
- Jesus Christ, the living Word of God, is the Savior of the world.
- The Bible is the written Word of God.
- Faith in Jesus Christ is both personal and communal.
- Baptism in "deep water" dramatically portrays the union of believers with Christ and the Church.
- The Lord's Supper is a powerful symbol of Christ's continuing presence with the individual and the community of faith.
- God alone is judge of conscience.
- The people can be trusted to interpret Scripture aright
  … in the context of Christian community
  … under the guidance of Holy Spirit.
- Doctrines can and should be articulated by communities of faith.
- Dissent is a worthy and dangerous pursuit.

- Ideas are worth debating, even when they divide communities.
- There are many ways to be Baptist and many Baptist stories to be claimed.
- Being Baptist is messy, controversial, and divisive.[3]

That is the way it is, in the Deep Water.

Notes

1. Richard J. Hooker, ed., *The Carolina Backcountry on the Eve of the Revolution: The Journal and Other Writings of Charles Woodmason, Anglican Itinerant* (Chapel Hill, N.C.: University of North Carolina Press, 1953), 109; and John G. Crowley, *Primitive Baptists of the Wiregrass South 1815 to the Present* (Gainesville, Fl.: University of Florida Press, 1998), 8.

2. This list grew out of the research related to this book. Other Baptist readers, being Baptists, will surely find it wanting.

3. Bill J. Leonard, "Being Baptist: Hospitable Traditionalism," in Cecil P. Staton, Jr., editor, *Why I Am a Baptist* (Macon: Smyth & Helwys Publishers, 1999), 88.

Selected Bibliography

Abbott, Thomas F. *Narrative of Certain Events Connected with the Late Disturbances in Jamaica.* London: Holdsworth and Ball, 1832.

Ahlstrom, Sydney. *A Religious History of the American People.* New Haven: Yale University Press, 1972.

Allison, William H., and William W. Barnes. *Baptist Ecclesiology: An Original Anthology.* Ed. Edwin S. Gaustad. New York: Arno Press, 1980.

Amey, Basil. *The Unfinished Story: A Study-Guide History of the Baptist Missionary Society.* London: Baptist Union of Great Britain, 1991.

Ammerman, Nancy Tatom. *Bible Believers: Fundamentalists in the Modern World.* New Brunswick, N.J.: Rutgers University Press, 1987.

———. *Baptist Battles: Social Change and Religious Conflict in the Southern Baptist Convention.* New Brunswick, N.J.: Rutgers University Press, 1990.

Anderson, John. *Religion, State and Politics in the Soviet Union and Successor States.* Cambridge: Cambridge University Press, 1994.

Angus, Joseph, ed. *The Baptist Denomination in England, Wales, Scotland and Ireland.* London: J. Heaton and Son, 1863.

Armstrong, O. K., and Marjorie Armstrong. *The Baptists in America.* Garden City, N.Y.: Doubleday, 1979.

Backus, Isaac. *Church History of New England from 1620 to 1804.* Philadelphia: American Baptist Publication Society, 1844.

———. *A History of New England, with Particular Reference to the Denomination of Christians Called Baptists.* 2nd ed. 2 vols. Newton, Mass.: Backus Historical Society, 1871. Reprinted as *A History of New England, with Particular Reference to the Baptists.* 2 vols. in 1. New York: Arno Press, 1969.

———. *The Diary of Isaac Backus.* 3 vols. Ed. William McLoughlin. Providence: Brown University Press, 1979.

———. *Isaac Backus on Church, State, and Calvinism: Pamphlets, 1754–1789.* Ed. William McLoughlin. Cambridge: Belknap Press of Harvard University Press, 1968.

Baker, Robert A. *A Baptist Source Book, with Particular Reference to Southern Baptists.* Nashville: Broadman, 1966.

———. *The Southern Baptist Convention and Its People.* Nashville: Broadman, 1972.

———. *Relations Between Northern and Southern Baptists.* 2nd ed. 1954. Reprint, New York: Arno Press, 1980.

Ball, Bryan W. *The Seventh-Day Men: Sabbatarians and Sabbatarianism in England and Wales, 1600–1800.* Oxford: Clarendon Press, 1994.

Ban, Joseph D. "Two Views of One Age: Fosdick and Straton." *Foundations* 14 (April–June 1971): 153–71.

Banks, William L. *A History of Black Baptists in the United States.* Philadelphia: Continental Press, 1987.

Baptist Missionary Society. *A Brief Narrative of the Baptist Mission in India.* London: Button and Burdett, 1808.

———. *Memoir Relative to the Translations of the Sacred Scriptures to the Baptist Missionary Society in England.* Dunstable, England: J. W. Morris, 1808.

———. *Jubilee 1867–1917: Fifty Years' Work among Women in the Far East.* London: Carey Press, 1917.

Baptist World Congress. *Baptist Work in Denmark, Finland, Norway and Sweden.* Stockholm: Westerberg, 1947.

Barber, Edward. *A Small Treatise of Baptisme, or, Dipping.* London, 1641.

Barebon, Praise-God. *A Discourse Tending to Prove the Baptisme in or under the Defection of Antichrist to Be the Ordinance of Jesus Christ.* London, 1642.

———. *A Defence of the Lawfulnesse of Baptizing Infants.* London: M. Bell, 1645.

Barnes, William W. *A History of the Southern Baptist Convention, 1845–1953.* Nashville: Broadman, 1954.

Barrett, William G. *Baptist Mission in Jamaica: An Exposition.* London: John Snow, 1842.

Bassett, Thomas M. *The Welsh Baptists.* Swansea: Ilston Press, 1977.

———. *The Baptists of Wales and the Baptist Missionary Society.* Swansea: Ilston Press, 1991.

Batts, H. J. *The Story of a 100 Years, 1820–1920: Being the History of the Baptist Church in South Africa.* Cape Town: T. Maskew Miller, 1922.

Beasley-Murray, Paul, ed. *Anyone for Ordination? A Contribution to the Debate on Ordination.* Tunbridge Wells, England: MARC, 1993.

Beaver, R. Pierce. *All Loves Excelling: American Protestant Women in World Mission.* Grand Rapids, Mich.: Eerdmans, 1968.

Bebbington, David W., ed. *The Baptists in Scotland: A History.* Glasgow: Baptist Union of Scotland, 1988.

Beebe, B. L., comp. *The Feast of Fat Things.* Middletown, N.Y.: G. Beebe's Son, n.d.

Beers, George P. *Ministry to Turbulent America: A History of the American Baptist Home Mission Society, Covering Its Fifth Quarter Century, 1932–1957.* Philadelphia: Judson Press, 1957.

Begaye, Russell. "The Story of Indian Southern Baptists." *Baptist History and Heritage* 18 (July 1983): 30–9.

Beilby, George T. *Road to Tomorrow: A Popular Account of One Hundred Years of Baptist Work in New Zealand.* New Zealand Baptist Historical Society, 1957.

Bell, D. G., ed. *Newlight Baptist Journals of James Manning and James Innis.* Hantsport, N.S: Lancelot Press, 1984.

Benedict, David. *A General History of the Baptist Denomination in America.* New York: Colby, 1848.

Bochenski, Michael, ed. *Evangelicals and Ecumenism—When Baptists Disagree.* Didcot, England: Baptist Union of Great Britain, 1993.

Bollen, John D. *Australian Baptists: A Religious Minority.* London: Baptist Historical Society, 1975.

Booth, William D. *The Progressive Story: New Baptist Roots.* St. Paul: Braun Press, 1981.

Bourdeaux, Michael. "Baptists in the Soviet Union Today." *Baptist History and Heritage* 10 (October 1975): 220–32.

———, ed. *The Politics of Religion in Russia and the New States of Eurasia.* Armonk, N.Y.: M. E. Sharpe, 1995.

Bourdeaux, Michael, and Michael Rowe, eds. *May One Believe—in Russia? Violations of Religious Liberty in the Soviet Union.* London: Darton, Longman & Todd, 1980.

Brackney, William, H. *The Baptists.* New York: Greenwood Press, 1988.

———, ed. *Baptist Life and Thought, 1600–1980.* Valley Forge, Pa.: Judson Press, 1983.

Brackney, William H., and Paul S. Fiddes, eds. *Pilgrim Pathways: Essays in Baptist History in Honour of B. R. White.* Macon, Ga.: Mercer University Press, 1999.

Bradley Martia. "The Work and Witness of Southern Negro Baptist Women from 1865 until 1935." *Quarterly Review* 37 (October–December 1976): 53–60.

Briggs, J. H. Y. *The English Baptists of the Nineteenth Century.* Didcot, England: Baptist Historical Society, 1994.

Brown, Raymond. *The English Baptists of the Eighteenth Century.* London: Baptist Historical Society, 1986.

Brumberg, Joan Jacobs. *Mission for Life: The Story of the Family of Adoniram Judson, the Dramatic Events of the First American Foreign Mission, and the Course of Evangelical Religion in the Nineteenth Century.* New York: Free Press, 1980.

Bunyan, John. *Differences in Judgment about Water-Baptism; No Bar to Communion.* London, 1673.

———. *The Whole Works of John Bunyan.* Ed. George Offor. London: Blackie & Sons, 1882.

Burgess, Walter H. *John Smith the Se-Baptist, Thomas Helwys, and the First Baptist Church in England; with Fresh Light upon the Pilgrim Fathers' Church.* London: James Clarke, 1911.

Burkitt, Lemuel, and Jesse Read. *A Concise History of the Kehukee Baptist Association, from Its Original Rise Down to 1808.* Rev. ed. 1850. Reprint, New York: Arno Press, 1980.

Burrage, Champlin. *The Early English Dissenters in the Light of Recent Research (1550–1641).* 2 vols. Cambridge: Cambridge University Press, 1912.

———, ed. "Early Welsh Baptist Doctrines, Set Forth in a Manuscript, Ascribed to Vavasor Powell." *Transactions of the Baptist Historical Society* 1 (1908–9): 3–20.

Butler, Jon. *Awash in a Sea of Faith: Christianizing the American People.* Cambridge: Harvard University Press, 1990.

Byford, Charles T. *Peasants and Prophets: Baptist Pioneers in Russia and South Eastern Europe.* London: Kingsgate Press, 1911.

Carder, W. Gordon. "Controversy in the Baptist Convention of Ontario and Quebec, 1908–1928." *Foundations* 16 (October–December 1973): 355–76.

Carter, James E. "Dealing with Doctrinal Conflict in Associational History." *Baptist History and Heritage* 17 (April 1982): 33–43.

Cathcart, William. *The Baptists and the American Revolution.* Philadelphia: S. A. George, 1876.

———, ed. *The Baptist Encyclopaedia.* 2 vols. Philadelphia: L. H. Everts, 1880.

Clarke, William Newton. *An Outline of Christian Theology.* 20th ed. New York: Scribner, 1912.

Clebsch, William A. *From Sacred to Profane: The Role of Religion in American History.* New York: Harper & Row, 1968.

Clements, Keith W., ed. *Baptists in the Twentieth Century: Papers Presented at a Summer School, July 1982.* London: Baptist Historical Society, 1983.

Clipsham, E. F. "Andrew Fuller and the Baptist Mission." *Foundations* 10 (January–March 1967): 4–18.

Combs, James O., ed. *Roots and Origins of Baptist Fundamentalism.* Springfield, Mo.: Baptist Bible Tribune, 1984.

Cone, James H. *Black Theology of Liberation.* Philadelphia: Lippincott, 1970.

Conwell, Russell H. *Acres of Diamonds.* Philadelphia: Columbian Advertising and Distributing Co., 1892.

Cooke, John Hunt. *Johann Gerhard Oncken: His Life and Work.* London: S. W. Partridge, 1908.

Cooper, Robert E. *From Stepney to St. Giles': The Story of Regent's Park College, 1810–1960.* London: Carey Kingsgate Press, 1960.

Copeland, E. Luther. *The Southern Baptist Convention and the Judgment of History: The Taint of an Original Sin.* Lanham, Md.: University Press of America, 1995.

Crosby, Thomas. *The History of the English Baptists.* 4 vols. London: 1738–40.

Cross, I. K. *The Battle for Baptist History.* Columbus, Ga.: Brentwood Christian Press, 1990

Cuthbert, James H. *Life of Richard Fuller, D.D.* New York: Sheldon, 1879.

Davies, R. E. "Persecution and Growth: A Hundred Years of Baptist Life in Romania." *Baptist Quarterly* 34 (April 1991).

Davis, Lawrence B. *Immigrants, Baptists, and the Protestant Mind in America.* Urbana: University of Illinois Press, 1973.

Dekar, Paul R. *For the Healing of the Nations: Baptist Peacemakers.* Macon, Ga.: Smyth & Helwys, 1993.

———. "Twentieth-Century British Baptist Conscientious Objectors." *Baptist Quarterly* 35 (January 1993): 35–44.

Deweese, Charles W. "The Rise of the Separate Baptists in North Carolina." *Quarterly Review* 37 (October–December 1976): 72–7.

———. "Deaconesses in Baptist History: A Preliminary Study." *Baptist History and Heritage* 12 (January 1977): 52–7.

———. "The Role of Circular Letters in Baptist Associations in America, 1707–1799." *Quarterly Review* 36 (October–December 1975): 51–60.

Documents of Moscow 1966 All-Union Conference of Evangelical Christian-Baptists. Moscow, 1966.

Dollar, George W. *A History of Fundamentalism in America.* Greenville, S.C.: Bob Jones University Press, 1973.

Dorgan, Howard. *Giving Glory to God in Appalachia: Worship Practices of Six Baptist Subdenominations.* Knoxville: University of Tennessee Press, 1987.

———. *The Old Regular Baptists of Central Appalachia.* Knoxville: University of Tennessee Press, 1989.

———. *In the Hands of a Happy God: Primitive Baptist Universalists of Central Appalachia.* Knoxville: University of Tennessee Press, 1997.

Dowley, T. "Baptists and Discipline in the 17th Century." *Baptist Quarterly* 24 (October 1971): 157–66.

Downs, Frederick S. "Historical Reflections on the Changing Context of North East India." *American Baptist Quarterly* 15 (June 1996): 103–19.

Du Bois, W. E. B. *The Negro Church.* Atlanta: Atlanta University Press, 1903.

Durasoff, Steve. *The Russian Protestants: Evangelicals in the Soviet Union, 1944–1964.* Rutherford, N.J.: Fairleigh Dickinson University Press, 1964.

Edmonds, David. A *Sharp Arrow Darted against the Anabaptists.* London: 1652.

Edwards, Jonathan. *The Great Awakening: A Faithful Narrative.* Ed. Clarence C. Goen. New Haven: Yale University Press, 1972.

———. *The Life of David Brainerd.* Vol. 7 of *The Works of Jonathan Edwards.* New Haven: Yale University Press, 1985.

Eidberg, Peder A. "Baptist Developments in the Nordic Countries During the Twentieth Century." Paper presented at the International Conference on Baptist Studies, July 2000.

Eiland, Peder M. "Norwegian Baptist Ecclesiology in the Twentieth Century: A Historical and Theological Retrospective." Paper presented at the International Conference on Baptist Studies, July 2000.

Elliott, Ralph H. *The "Genesis Controversy" and Continuity in Southern Baptist Chaos: A Eulogy for a Great Tradition.* Macon, Ga.: Mercer University Press, 1992.

Ellis, Walter E. "A Place to Stand: Contemporary History of the Baptist Union of Western Canada." *American Baptist Quarterly* 6 (March 1987): 31–51.

Encyclopedia of Southern Baptists. 3 vols. Nashville: Broadman, 1958.

Ernst, Eldon G. "The Baptist Jubilee Advance in Historical Context." *Foundations* 9 (January–March 1966): 5–36.

———. "Twentieth Century Issues of War and Peace." *Foundations* 15 (October–December 1972): 298–318.

Estep, William R. *The Anabaptist Story.* Nashville: Broadman, 1963.

———. *Baptists and Christian Unity.* Nashville: Broadman, 1966.

———. *Whole Gospel, Whole World: The Foreign Mission Board of the Southern Baptist Convention, 1845–1995.* Nashville: Broadman & Holman, 1994.

"Extracts from the Diaries of Rev. William Ward, of Serampore." *The Baptist Magazine* (May 1879).

Falls, Helen Emery. "Baptist Women in Missions Support in the Nineteenth Century." *Baptist History and Heritage* 12 (January 1977): 26–36.

Fath, Sebastian. "Another Way of Being a Christian in France: One Century of Baptist Implantation (Twentieth Century)." Paper presented at the International Conference on Baptist Studies, July 2000.

Featley, Daniel. A *True Relation of What Passed at a Meeting in Southwark, between D. Featley, and a Company of Anabaptists.* London, 1642.

———. *The Dippers Dipt, or, The Anabaptists Duck'd and Plung'd over Head and Eares, at a Disputation at Southwark.* London: Nicholas Bourne and Richard Royston, 1646.

Fitts, Leroy. *A History of Black Baptists.* Nashville: Broadman, 1985.

Fleming, Sanford. "The Board of Education and Theological Education, 1911–1963." *Foundations* 8 (January 1965): 3–10.

Fletcher, Jesse C. *The Southern Baptist Convention: A Sesquicentennial History.* Nashville: Broadman & Holman, 1994.

Fosdick, Harry Emerson. *The Living of These Days: An Autobiography.* New York: Harper, 1956.

Fuller, Andrew Gunton. *The Complete Works of the Rev. Andrew Fuller, with a Memoir of His Life.* 5 vols. London: Holdsworth and Ball, 1831–32.

Gardner, Robert G. *Baptists in Early America: A Statistical History, 1639–1790.* Atlanta: Georgia Baptist Historical Society, 1983.

———. "Baptists and the Indians of North America, 1674–1845." *Baptist History and Heritage* (July 1983).

———. "Early Baptists of Sackville, New Brunswick." *American Baptist Quarterly* 4 (March 1985): 90–9.

Garrett, James Leo. "Restitution and Dissent among Early English Baptists: Part 1." *Baptist History and Heritage* 12 (October 1977): 198–210.

Gaustad, Edwin S. *Historical Atlas of Religion in America.* Rev. ed. San Francisco: Harper & Row, 1976.

———. *Baptists, the Bible, Church Order and the Churches: Essays from Foundations, a Baptist Journal of History and Theology.* New York: Arno Press, 1980.

Gayle, Clement. *George Liele: Pioneer Missionary to Jamaica.* Kingston: Jamaica Baptist Union, 1982.

Genovese, Eugene. *Roll, Jordan, Roll: The World the Slaves Made.* New York: Pantheon Books, 1974.

George, Timothy. *Faithful Witness: The Life and Mission of William Carey.* Birmingham, Ala.: New Hope Publishers, 1991.

Gilger, Charles G. "Northern Baptists and the Laymen's Foreign Mission Inquiry." *Foundations* 6 (July 1963): 233–43.

Gill, Athol, comp. *A Bibliography of Baptist Writings on Baptism, 1900–1968.* Rüschlikon-Zürich: Baptist Theological Seminary, 1969.

Goen, Clarence C. *Broken Churches, Broken Nation: Denominational Schisms and the Coming of the American Civil War.* Macon, Ga.: Mercer University Press, 1985.

Goodman, Michael. "Numerical Decline Amongst English Baptists, 1930–1939." *Baptist Quarterly* 36 (January 1996): 241–51.

———. "A Faded Heritage: English Baptist Political Thinking in the 1930s." *Baptist Quarterly* 37 (April 1997): 58–70.

Goodwin, Everett C., ed. *Baptists in the Balance.* Valley Forge, Pa.: Judson Press, 1997.

Graves, James R. *The Watchman's Reply.* Nashville: Graves and Shankland, 1853.

———. *Old Landmarkism: What Is It?* Memphis: Baptist Book House, 1880.

Griffin-Allwood, Philip. *The Canadianization of Baptists: From Denominations to Denomination, 1760–1912.* Ann Arbor, Mich: University Microfilms International, 1986.

Grose, Howard B. *Advance in the Antilles: The New Era in Cuba and Porto Rico.* New York: Presbyterian Home Missions, 1910.

Handy, Robert T. *A History of the Churches in the United States and Canada.* New York: Oxford University Press, 1976.

Hardesty, Nancy. *Great Women of Faith: The Strength and Influence of Christian Women.* Grand Rapids, Mich.: Baker, 1980.

Harrison, Paul. *Authority and Power in the Free Church Tradition.* Carbondale: Southern Illinois University Press, 1959.

Harrop, G. Gerald. "Canadian Baptists in Their North American Context." *Foundations* 4 (July 1961): 216–24.

Harvey, Paul. *Redeeming the South: Religious Cultures and Racial Identities among Southern Baptists, 1865–1925.* Chapel Hill: University of North Carolina Press, 1997.

Hayden, Roger. "Kettering 1792 and Philadelphia 1814." *Baptist Quarterly* 21 (January 1965): 3–20.

———. "Bristol Baptist College and America." *Baptist History and Heritage* 14 (October 1979): 26–33.

Helwys, Thomas. *A Short Declaration of the Mystery of Iniquity (1611/1612).* Ed. Richard Groves. Macon, Ga.: Mercer University Press, 1998.

Herskovits, Melville, J. *The Myth of the Negro Past.* New York: Harper, 1941.

Heyrman, Christine Leigh. *Southern Cross: The Beginnings of the Bible Belt.* New York: Knopf, 1997.

Higginbotham, Evelyn Brooks. *Righteous Discontent: The Women's Movement in the Black Baptist Church, 1880–1920.* Cambridge: Harvard University Press, 1993.

Himbury, D. Mervyn. "Baptists and Their Relations with Other Christians in Australasia." *Foundations* 17 (January–March 1974): 36–50.

Hiscox, Edward T. *Principles and Practices for Baptist Churches.* 1894. Reprint, Grand Rapids, Mich.: Kregel, 1980.

Hoad, Jack. *The Baptist: An Historical and Theological Study of the Baptist Identity.* London: Grace Publications, 1986.

Hominuke, J. *A Centenary of Ukrainian Baptists, 1852–1952.* Detroit: Ukrainian Evangelical-Baptist Alliance, 1952.

Hopkins, Charles Howard. *The Rise of the Social Gospel in American Protestantism, 1865–1915.* New Haven: Yale University Press, 1940.

Hopkins, Mark. "The Down Grade Controversy: New Evidence." *Baptist Quarterly,* vol. 35, no. 6 (April 1994): 262–78.

Howard, Victor B. "The Baptists and Peace Sentiments During the Mexican War." *Quarterly Review* (April–June 1978).

Howells, George, and Alfred C. Underwood. *The Story of Serampore and Its College.* Serampore, India: 1918.

Hudson, Winthrop S. "Stumbling into Disorder." *Foundations* 1 (April 1958): 45–71.

———. *Baptists in Transition: Individualism and Christian Responsibility.* Valley Forge, Pa.: Judson Press, 1979.

———. "The Interrelations of Baptists in Canada and the United States." *Foundations* 23 (January–March 1980): 22–41.

———. "Church Growth in an African City: CBCO Kinshasa." *American Baptist Quarterly* 18 (September 1999): 217–42.

Hudson-Reed, Sydney, ed. *By Taking Heed: The History of Baptists in Southern Africa, 1820–1977.* Roodepoort, South Africa: Baptist Publishing House, 1983.

Hughes, Richard, and William Adrian, eds. *Models for Christian Higher Education.* Grand Rapids, Mich.: Eerdmans, 1997.

Hutchinson, Lucy. *On the Principles of the Christian Religion.* London: Longman, Hurst, Rees, Orme, & Brown, 1817.

————. *Memoirs of the Life of Colonel Hutchinson, Governor of Nottingham. Rev. ed.* London: G. Routledge & Sons, 1906.

Hutchison, William R. *The Modernist Impulse in American Protestantism.* Cambridge: Harvard University Press, 1976.

Isichei, Elizabeth. *A History of Christianity in Africa.* Grand Rapids, Mich.: Eerdmans, 1995.

Ivimey, Joseph. *A History of the English Baptists.* 4 vols. London, 1811–30.

James, Gordon. *Inerrancy and the Southern Baptist Convention.* Dallas: Southern Baptist Heritage Press, 1986.

James, Robison B., ed. *The Unfettered Word: Southern Baptists Confront the Authority-Inerrancy Question.* Waco, Tex.: Word, 1987.

James, Robison B., and David S Dockery, eds. *Beyond the Impasse? Scripture, Interpretation, and Theology in Baptist Life.* Nashville: Broadman, 1992.

Johnson, W. Charles. *Encounter in London: The Story of the London Baptist Association, 1865–1965.* London: Carey Kingsgate Press, 1965.

Jones, J. William. *Christ in the Camp, or, Religion in the Confederate Army.* 1887. Reprint, Harrisonburg, Va.: Sprinkle Publications, 1986.

Jonsson, John N. "Baptists in Socio-Political Life in South Africa: Historical and Theological Reflections Covering the Past Thirty Years." *American Baptist Quarterly* 4 (September 1985): 243–56.

Jonsson, John, and Christopher Parnell. *Together for a Century: The History of the Baptist Union of South Africa, 1877–1977.* Pietermaritzburg, South Africa: Baptist Historical Society, 1977.

Judd, Bertha Grimmell. *Fifty Golden Years: The First Half Century of the Woman's American Baptist Home Mission Society, 1877–1927.* Rochester, N.Y.: Du Bois Press, 1927.

Judson, Ann H. *A Particular Relation of the American Baptist Mission to the Burman Empire.* Washington City: John S. Meehan, 1823.

Keach, Benjamin. *The Child's Delight: or, Instructions for Children and Youth.* London, 1664.

————. *The Gospel Minister's Maintenance Vindicated.* London, 1689.

Kidd, Richard, ed. *Something to Declare: A Study of the Declaration of Principle of the Baptist Union of Great Britain.* Oxford: Whitley Publications, 1996.

Kiffin, William, with Hanserd Knollys. *The Life and Death of That Old Disciple of Jesus Christ, and Eminent Minister of the Gospel, Mr. Hanserd Knollys.* 1692. Reprint, London: E. Huntington, 1812.

Kimbrough, Bradley T. *The History of the Walnut Street Baptist Church, Louisville, Kentucky.* Louisville: Press of Western Recorder, 1949.

Kirkwood, Dean, ed. *European Baptists: A Magnificent Minority.* Valley Forge, Pa.: American Baptist Churches USA., n.d.

Knollys, Hanserd. *The Rudiments of the Hebrew Grammar in English.* London: M. Bell, 1648.

Kornilov, Nikolai. "Distinctiveness of Russian Baptists: Historical and Theological Survey." Paper presented at the International Conference on Baptist Studies, July 2000.

La Forge, Granville. "Has the BBFI Become Another Convention?" *Baptist Bible Tribune* (December 5, 1986).

Lamb, Thomas. "An Appeal to the Parliament Concerning the Poor, That There May Not Be a Beggar in England." *Baptist Quarterly* 1 (July 1922): 128–30.

Lambert, Byron C. *The Rise of the Anti-Mission Baptists: Sources and Leaders, 1800–1840.* New York: Arno Press, 1980.

Laws, Curtis L. "Fundamentalism Is Very Much Alive." *Watchman Examiner* (July 28, 1921).

Laws, Gilbert. "Andrew Fuller, 1754–1815." *Baptist Quarterly* 2 (April 1924): 76–89.

Leland, John. *The Writings of John Leland.* Ed. L. F. Greene. 1845. Reprint, New York: Arno Press, 1969.

Leonard, Bill J. "A History of the Baptist Laymen's Movement." *Baptist History and Heritage* 13 (January 1978): 35–44.

———. "The Origin and Character of Fundamentalism." *Review and Expositor* 79 (winter 1982).

———. "Getting Saved in America: Conversion Event in a Pluralistic Culture." *Review and Expositor* 82 (winter 1985): 111–28.

———. "Independent Baptists: From Sectarian Minority to 'Moral Majority.'" *Church History* 56 (December 1987): 504–17.

———. *Community in Diversity: A History of Walnut Street Baptist Church, 1815–1990.* Louisville: Simons-Neely, 1990.

———. *God's Last and Only Hope: The Fragmentation of the Southern Baptist Convention.* Grand Rapids, Mich.: Eerdmans, 1990.

———. "A Theology for Racism: Southern Fundamentalists and the Civil Rights Movement." In *Southern Landscapes,* ed. Anthony J. Badger et al. Tübingen: Stauffenburg, 1996.

———, ed. *Early American Christianity.* Nashville: Broadman, 1983.

———, ed. *Dictionary of Baptists in America.* Downers Grove, Ill.: InterVarsity Press, 1994.

———, ed. *Christianity in Appalachia: Profiles in Regional Pluralism.* Knoxville: University of Tennessee Press, 1999.

———, ed. "Unity, Diversity, or Schism: The SBC at the Crossroads," *Baptist History and Heritage* 16 (October 1981): 2–8.

Letsinger, Norman H. "The Status of Women in the Southern Baptist Convention in Historical Perspective." *Baptist History and Heritage* 12 (January 1977): 37–44.

Levy, George Edward. *The Baptists of the Maritime Provinces, 1753–1946.* St. John, N.B.: Barnes-Hopkins, 1946.

Lord, F. Townley. *Baptist World Fellowship: A Short History of the Baptist World Alliance.* Nashville: Broadman, 1955.

Lumpkin, William L. *Baptist Confessions of Faith.* Chicago: Judson Press, 1959.

Lynch, James R. "Baptist Women in Ministry in 1920." *American Baptist Quarterly* 13 (December 1994): 304–18.

Mallard, I. "The Hymns of Katherine Sutton." *Baptist Quarterly* 20 (January 1963): 22–33.

Manis, Andrew Michael. *Southern Civil Religions in Conflict: Black and White Baptists and Civil Rights, 1947–1957.* Athens: University of Georgia Press, 1987.

Maring, Norman. *Baptists in New Jersey: A Study in Transition.* Valley Forge, Pa.: Judson Press, 1964.

———. *American Baptists: Whence and Whither.* Valley Forge, Pa.: Judson Press, 1968.

Maring, Norman, and Winthrop Hudson. *A Baptist Manual of Polity and Practice.* Rev. ed. Valley Forge, Pa.: Judson Press, 1991.

Marsden, George M. *Fundamentalism and American Culture: The Shaping of Twentieth Century Evangelicalism, 1870–1925.* New York: Oxford University Press, 1980.

Martin, Hugh. "The Baptist Contribution to Early English Hymnody." *Baptist Quarterly* 19 (January 1962): 195–208.

Martin, Sandy D. "The Baptist Foreign Mission Convention, 1880–1894." *Baptist History and Heritage* 16 (October 1981): 13–25.

———. *Black Baptists and African Missions.* Macon, Ga.: Mercer University Press, 1989.

Masters, Frank M. *A History of Baptists in Kentucky.* Louisville: Kentucky Baptist Historical Society, 1953.

Masters, Victor I. "Baptists and the Christianizing of America in the New Order." *Review and Expositor* 17–18 (July 1920): 280–98.

Mathews, Donald G. *Religion in the Old South.* Chicago: University of Chicago Press, 1977.

Mathews, Shailer. *Christianity and Social Process.* New York: Harper, 1934.

May, Lynn E., Jr. "A Brief History of the Baptist Associations." *Quarterly Review* 37 (October–December 1976): 31–44.

McBeth, H. Leon. "The Role of Women in Southern Baptist History." *Baptist History and Heritage* 12 (January 1977): 3–25.

———. *The Baptist Heritage.* Nashville: Broadman, 1987.

———. *A Sourcebook for Baptist Heritage.* Nashville: Broadman, 1990.

McCauley, Deborah Vansau. *Appalachian Mountain Religion: A History.* Chicago: University of Illinois Press, 1995.

McGoldrick, James Edward. *Baptist Successionism: A Crucial Question in Baptist History.* Metuchen, N.J.: Scarecrow Press, 1994.

McKibbens, Thomas R. "The Life, Writings, and Influence of Morgan Edwards." *Quarterly Review* 36 (January–March 1976): 58–70.

McLeod, Angus, ed. *A Handful of Grain: The Centenary History of the Baptist Union of New Zealand.* 4 vols. Wellington: New Zealand Baptist Historical Society, 1982.

McLoughlin, William. *Modern Revivalism: Charles Grandison Finney to Billy Graham.* New York: Ronald Press, 1959.

———. *Revivals, Awakenings, and Reform.* Chicago: University of Chicago Press, 1979.

———. *Cherokees and Missionaries, 1789–1839.* New Haven: Yale University Press, 1984.

———. *Soul Liberty: The Baptists' Struggle in New England, 1630–1833.* Hanover, N.H.: University Press of New England, 1991.

Mead, Frank S. *Handbook of Denominations in the United States.* 9th ed. Nashville: Abingdon Press, 1995.

Mead, Sidney. *The Lively Experiment: The Shaping of Christianity in America.* New York: Harper & Row, 1963.

Meehan, Brenda M. "A. C. Dixon: An Early Fundamentalist." *Foundations* 10 (January–March 1967): 50–63.

Meredith, Albert R. "Spurgeon and His Times: The Christian's Social Responsibility." *Quarterly Review* 35 (January–March 1975): 77–82.

Miller, Glenn T. "Baptist Businessmen in Historical Perspective." *Baptist History and Heritage* 13 (January 1978): 55–62.

Mills, Randy. *Christ Tasted Death for Every Man: The Story of America's Frontier General Baptists.* Poplar Bluff, Mo.: Stinson Press, 2000.

Moden, A. K. "The Baptist Churches of Denmark, Sweden and Norway: Their Origin,

Development and Present Position." 1905. In *Record of Proceedings, First European Baptist Congress.*

Moisey, S. W. A. "Marriage Covenants of the General Baptists." *Baptist Quarterly* 12 (April–July 1947): 202–7.

Mondello, Salvatore. "Baptist Churches and Italian-Americans." *Foundations* 16 (July–September 1973).

———. "The Integration of Japanese Baptists in American Society." *Foundations* 20 (July–September 1977): 222–38.

———. "Isabel Crawford, the Making of a Missionary: Part 1." *Foundations* 21 (October–December 1978): 322–39.

Mondello, Salvatore, and Pellegrino Nazzaro. "The Origins of Baptist Evangelism in Italy, 1848." *American Baptist Quarterly* 7 (June 1988): 110–27.

Moon, Norman S. *Education for Ministry: Bristol Baptist College, 1679–1979.* Bristol: Bristol Baptist College, 1979.

Mooney, Ruth E. "Missionaries in Latin America: Agents of Empire or Partners in Mission?" *American Baptist Quarterly* 18 (September 1999): 288–92.

Moore, David O. "The Withdrawal of Blacks from Southern Baptist Churches Following Emancipation." *Baptist History and Heritage* 16 (July 1981): 12–18.

Moore, LeRoy, Jr. "Academic Freedom: A Chapter in the History of the Colgate Rochester Divinity School." *Foundations* 10 (January–March 1967).

Morgan, David T. *The New Crusades, The New Holy Land: Conflict in the Southern Baptist Convention, 1969–1991.* Tuscaloosa, Ala.: University of Alabama Press, 1996.

Morris, Elias C. *Sermons, Addresses, and Reminiscences, and Important Correspondence.* 1901. Reprint, New York: Arno Press, 1980.

Mosteller, James D. "Ramapatnam: Jewel of the South India Mission." *Foundations* 11 (October–December 1968): 308–25.

Mueller, William A. *A History of Southern Baptist Theological Seminary.* Nashville: Broadman, 1959.

Mulder, John M., and John F. Wilson. *Religion in American History: Intrepretive Essays.* Englewood Cliffs, N.J.: Prentice-Hall, 1978.

Murray, Derek B. *The First Hundred Years: The Baptist Union of Scotland.* Dundee: Baptist Union of Scotland, 1969.

Murton, John. *A Description of What God Hath Predestinated Concerning Man.* London, 1620.

Music, David. "Psalmody and Hymnody in the Broadmead Baptist Church of Bristol, England." *Quarterly Review* 37 (October–December 1976): 66–71.

———. "The Introduction of Musical Instruments into Baptist Churches in America." *Quarterly Review* 40 (October–December 1979): 56–61.

Nelson, Clyde K. "Russell H. Conwell and the 'Gospel of Wealth.'" *Foundations* 5 (January 1962): 39–51.

Newman, Albert H. *A History of the Baptist Churches in the United States.* Philadelphia: American Baptist Publication Society, 1898.

Nicholson, J. F. V. "The Office of 'Messenger' amongst British Baptists in the Seventeenth and Eighteenth Centuries." *Baptist Quarterly* 17 (January 1958): 206–25.

Niebuhr, H. Richard. *The Social Sources of Denominationalism.* New York: Meridian Books, 1957.

Noll, Mark. *A History of Christianity in the United States and Canada.* Grand Rapids, Mich.: Eerdmans, 1992.

Norris, J. Frank. "The New Testament Method of Financing." *Fundamentalist* (November 4, 1927).

Olson, Virgil A. "Neither Jew nor Greek: A Study of an Ethnic Baptist Group, the Swedish Baptists, 1850–1950." *Baptist History and Heritage* 25 (January 1990): 32–42.

Owens, B. G., ed. *The Ilston Book: Earliest Register of Welsh Baptists.* Aberystwyth: National Library of Wales, 1996.

Parker, Daniel. *Views on the Two Seeds Taken from Genesis.* Vandalia, Ill.: Robert Blackwell, 1826.

Parker, David, ed. *Baptists in Queensland: A Guide to Their Life and Faith.* Brisbane: Baptist Historical Society of Queensland, 1994.

Parker, F. Calvin. *Jonathan Goble of Japan: Marine, Missionary, Maverick.* Lanham, Md.: University Press of America, 1990.

———. *The Southern Baptist Mission in Japan, 1889–1989.* Lanham, Md.: University Press of America, 1991.

Patterson, James A. "Motives in the Development of Foreign Missions among American Baptists 1810–1826." *Foundations* 19 (October–December 1976): 298–319.

Patterson, W. Morgan. "Changing Preparation for Changing Ministry." *Baptist History and Heritage* 15 (January 1980): 14–22.

Payne, Ernest A. *Freedom in Jamaica.* London: Carey Press, n.d.

———. "Some Impressions of Germany." *Baptist Quarterly* 4 (July 1928): 104–15.

———. *The Baptist Union: A Short History.* London: Baptist Union of Great Britain and Ireland, 1959.

———. *Out of Great Tribulation: Baptists in the U.S.S.R.* London: Baptist Union of Great Britain and Ireland, 1974.

———. "British Baptists and the American Revolution." *Baptist History and Heritage* 11 (January 1976): 3–15.

Pelt, Owen D., and Ralph Lee Smith. *The Story of the National Baptists.* New York: Vantage Press, 1960.

Pendleton, James M. *Distinctive Principles of Baptists.* Philadelphia: American Baptist Publication Society, 1882.

Petrick, Herbert. "The Tasks of the Baptist Denomination in Germany." *Baptist Quarterly* 4 (1928–29): 160–65.

Pierard, Richard V. "Germany and Baptist Expansion in Nineteenth-Century Europe." Typescript, n.d.

Piggin, Stuart. *Making Evangelical Missionaries, 1789–1858.* London: Sutton Courtenay Press, 1984.

Pilli, Toivo. "Evangelical Christian-Baptists Union of Estonia, 1945–1989: Survival Techniques, Outreach Efforts, Search for Identity." Paper presented at the International Conference on Baptist Studies, July 2000.

Pitman, W. G. "Baptist Triumph in Nineteenth-Century Canada." *Foundations* 3 (April 1960): 157–65.

Pitts, Walter F. *The Old Ship of Zion: The Afro-Baptist Ritual in the African Diaspora.* New York: Oxford University Press, 1993.

Pixley, George V. "Nicaragua Baptists: Reclaiming Repressed Cultures." *American Baptist Quarterly* 18 (September 1999): 293–97.

Poe, Harry Lee. "John Bunyan's Controversy with the Baptists." *Baptist History and Heritage* 23 (April 1988): 25–35.

Porteous, Alvin C. "Church-Related Colleges and Government Aid." *Foundations* 7 (July 1964): 254–64.

Price, Seymour J. *Upton: The Story of One Hundred and Fifty Years, 1785–1935.* London: Carey Press, 1935.

Prim, C. Clinton, Jr. "Colporteurs: Propagandists and Revivalists in the Confederate Army." *American Baptist Quarterly* 2 (September 1983): 228–35.

Proceedings of the Convention Held in the City of New York on the 27th of April, 1832, for the Formation of the American Baptist Home Mission Society. New York, 1831.

Purefoy, George W. *A History of the Sandy Creek Baptist Association, from Its Organization in A.D. 1759, to 1858.* 1859. Reprint, New York: Arno Press, 1980.

Raboteau, Albert. *Slave Religion: The "Invisible Institution" in the Antebellum South.* New York: Pantheon Books, 1978.

Randall, Ian. "Mere Denominationalism: F. B. Meyer and Baptist Life." *Baptist Quarterly* 35, no. 1 (January 1993): 19–34.

———. "Capturing Keswick: Baptists and the Changing Spirituality of the Keswick Convention in the 1920s." *Baptist Quarterly* (July 1996).

Randall, Ian, and E. Hulse. "Oncken: Pioneer Baptist of Europe." *Reformation Today* (1975): 9–18.

Rauschenbusch, Walter. *Christianity and the Social Crisis.* Ed. Robert Cross. New York: Harper & Row, 1964.

Rawlyk, George A. *Ravished by the Spirit: Religious Revivals, Baptists, and Henry Alline.* Montreal: McGill-Queen's University Press, 1984.

Rector, Franklin E. "Behind the Breakdown of Baptist-Disciple Conversations on Unity." *Foundations* 4 (April 1961): 120–37.

Reid, Adam A. "Benjamin Keach, 1640." *Baptist Quarterly* 10 (April 1940): 67–78.

Renault, James Owen. "The Changing Patterns of Separate Baptist Religious Life, 1803–1977." *Baptist History and Heritage* 14 (October 1979): 16–25.

Renfree, Harry A. *Heritage and Horizon: The Baptist Story in Canada.* Mississauga, Ont.: Canadian Baptist Federation, 1988.

Report of the Ladies' Association for the Support of Zenana Work and Bible Women in India, in Connection with the Baptist Missionary Society for 1877–78. London, 1878.

Revival of Religion in Denmark. London: Houlston and Stoneman, 1841.

Rhees, Morgan J. *Our Privileges, the Measure of Our Responsibility: Substance of a Discourse Preached on the Day Appointed for Public Thanksgiving.* Wilmington, Del.: Porter and Naff, 1846.

Rice, John R. "Bible Questions: Yoking with Modernists." *Sword of the Lord* (November 1, 1957).

———. "Christian Fellowship with Negro and White, Not Intermarriages." *Sword of the Lord* (July 1, 1965).

———. "Senator Robert F. Kennedy's Death." *Sword of the Lord* (28 June 1968).

Richardson, Frederick. "American Baptists' Southern Mission." *Foundations* 18 (April–June 1975): 136–45.

Riley, William B. "Why the Baptist Bible Union?" *Searchlight* (May 4, 1923).

Robbins, Keith, ed. *Protestant Evangelicalism: Britain, Ireland, Germany and America, c. 1750–c. 1950.* Oxford and New York: Basil Blackwell, 1990.

Robert, Dana L. *American Women in Mission: A Social History of Their Thought and Practice.* Macon, Ga.: Mercer University Press, 1996.

Robinson, H. Wheeler. *The Life and Faith of the Baptists.* London: Methuen, 1927.

Rogers, Albert N. "Ministerial Training and Seventh Day Baptists." *Foundations* 16 (January–March 1973): 57–67.

Roper, Cecil. "Henry Denne and the Fenstanton Baptists in England." *Baptist History and Heritage* 16 (October 1981): 26–38.

Rowe, David L. "Elon Galusha and the Millerite Movement." *Foundations* 18 (July–September 1975): 252–60.

Rubinstein, Murray A. "American Evangelicalism in the Chinese Environment: Southern Baptist Convention Missionaries in Taiwan, 1949–1981." *American Baptist Quarterly* 2 (September 1983): 269–89.

Rushbrooke, James H. *The First European Baptist Congress.* London: Baptist Union Publication Department, 1908.

———. "Baptists in Continental Europe." *Baptist Quarterly* 1 (January 1923): 196–202.

———. *Some Chapters of European Baptist History.* London: Kingsgate Press, 1929.

———. "Vasili Pavlov: A Russian Baptist Pioneer." *Baptist Quarterly* 6 (October 1933): 361–66.

———. *Baptists in the U.S.S.R.: Some Facts and Hopes.* Nashville: Broadman, 1943.

———, ed. *The Baptist Movement in the Continent of Europe.* London: Carey Press, 1915.

Russell, C. Allyn. "Rhode Island Baptists, 1825–1931." *Foundations* 14 (January–March 1971): 33–49.

———. *Voices of American Fundamentalism: Seven Biographical Studies.* Philadelphia: Westminster, 1976.

———. "The Northern (American) Baptist Experience with Fundamentalism." *Review and Expositor* 79 (winter 1983): 45–61.

———. "W. A. Criswell: A Case Study in Fundamentalism." *Review and Expositor* 81 (winter 1984): 107–31.

Sandeen, Ernest. "The Baptists and Millenarianism." *Foundations* 13 (January–March 1970): 18–25.

Sanford, Don A. *A Choosing People: The History of Seventh Day Baptists.* Nashville: Broadman, 1992.

Santee, R. Virgil. "Sallie Paine Peck." *American Baptist Quarterly* 3 (September 1984): 225–34.

Sawatsky, Walter. *Soviet Evangelicals since World War II.* Scottdale, Pa.: Herald Press, 1981.

Schroeder, George W. *The Church Brotherhood Guidebook: A Guide for Organizing and Operating a Church Brotherhood.* Nashville: Broadman, 1950.

Seventh Day Baptist General Conference. *Seventh Day Baptists in Europe and America.* 1910. Reprint, 2 vols., New York: Arno Press, 1980.

Shakespeare, Geoffrey. "The Persecution of Baptists in Russia." *Baptist Quarterly* 5 (April 1930): 49–54.

Shurden, Walter B. "The Baptist Drive for a Missionary Consciousness: Associational Activities Before 1814." *Quarterly Review* 39 (April–June 1979): 59–66.

———. "The Baptist Drive for Denominational Unity: Associational Activities Before 1814." *Quarterly Review* 40 (October–December 1979): 50–54.

———. *Associationalism among Baptists in America, 1707–1814.* New York: Arno Press, 1980.

Simms, James M. *The First Colored Baptist Church in North America.* 1888. Reprint, New York: Negro Universities Press, 1969.

Simpson, E. P. Y. "A History of the New Zealand Baptist Missionary Society." Master's thesis, University of New Zealand, 1948.

Skoglund, John E. "American Baptists and the Ecumenical Movement After 50 Years." *Foundations* 4 (April 1961): 112–19.

Slade, Ruth. "Congo Protestant Missions and European Powers before 1885." *Baptist Quarterly* 16 (January 1956): 200–14.

Smith, Blake. "The Southern Baptist 'Invasion': Right or Wrong?" *Foundations* 2 (July 1959): 320–31.

Smith, H. Shelton. *In His Image, but … : Racism in Southern Religion, 1780–1910.* Durham, N.C.: Duke University Press, 1972.

Smith, H. Shelton, Robert T. Handy, and Lefferts A. Loetscher. *American Christianity.* 2 vols. New York: Scribner, 1960–63.

Smith, Henry N. "William Knibb and Baptist Missions in Jamaica until 1845." *Quarterly Review* 44 (October–December 1983): 49–60.

Smith, Michael A. "Baptist Deacons in the Nineteenth Century." *Quarterly Review* 43 (October–December 1982): 67–76.

Smith, Noel. "Constitutionally It Was Obscene." *Baptist Bible Tribune* (April 2, 1965).

———. "Martin Luther King Wants a Revolution." *Baptist Bible Tribune* (April 23, 1965).

Smith, Wallace C. "Progressive National Baptist Convention: The Roots of the Black Church." *American Baptist Quarterly* 19 (September 2000): 245–59.

Smyth, John. *The Works of John Smyth.* 2 vols. Ed. W. T. Whitley. Cambridge: Cambridge University Press, 1915.

Spain, Rufus. *At Ease in Zion: Social History of Southern Baptists, 1865–1900.* Nashville: Vanderbilt University Press, 1961.

Spanu, Paolo. "Italian Baptists since the Second World War." Paper presented at the International Conference on Baptist Studies, July 1997.

Sparkes, Douglas C. *The Home Mission Story.* Didcot: Baptist Historical Society, 1995.

Spilsbury, John. *Gods Ordinance, the Saints Priviledge.* London: M. Simmons, 1646.

Spurgeon, Charles Haddon. *A Catechism with Proof, Compiled by C. H. Spurgeon.* London: Passmore & Alabaster, 1864.

Spurgeon, Charles Haddon, with Susannah Spurgeon and Joseph Harrald. *C. H. Spurgeon: The Early Years, 1834–1859.* London: Banner of Truth Trust, 1962.

Stanley, Brian. *The Bible and the Flag: Protestant Missions and British Imperialism in the Nineteenth and Twentieth Centuries.* Leicester, England: Apollos, 1990.

———. *The History of the Baptist Missionary Society, 1792–1992.* Edinburgh: Clark, 1992.

Stealey, Sydnor L., ed. *A Baptist Treasury.* New York: Crowell, 1958.

Steeley, John E. "Ministerial Certification in Southern Baptist History: Ordination." *Baptist History and Heritage* 15 (January 1980): 23–9.

———. "Associational Messengers in Baptist History." *Baptist History and Heritage* 17 (April 1982): 3–10.

Stepp, Nicholas D. "The Downgrade Controversy: Following Jesus and Frequenting Theatres." Unpublished paper, Regent's Park College, Oxford, 2000.

Stiansen, Peder. *History of the Norwegian Baptists in America.* Wheaton, Ill.: Norwegian Baptist Convention of America and American Baptist Publication Society, 1939.

Strong, Augustus H. *Outlines of Systematic Theology: Designed for the Use of Theological Students.* Philadelphia: Griffith & Rowland, 1908.

Sundholm, Nils. "Baptists in Sweden." *Baptist Quarterly* 15 (1953–54).

Sweet, William Warren. *The Baptists, 1783–1830.* Vol. 1 of *Religion on the American Frontier.* Chicago: University of Chicago Press, 1931.

———. *The Story of Religion in America.* New York: Harper & Row, 1950.

———. *Religion in the Development of American Culture, 1765–1840.* New York: Charles Scribner's Sons, 1952.

Szasz, Ferenc M. *The Divided Mind of Protestant America, 1880–1930.* University, Ala.: University of Alabama Press, 1982.

Taylor, Adam. *The History of the English General Baptists.* 2 vols. London, 1818.

Taylor, Dan. *A Catechism, or, Instructions for Children and Youth, in the Fundamental Doctrines of Christianity.* Leeds, England: G. Wright and Son, n.d.

———. *A Compendious View of the Nature and Importance of Christian Baptism, for the Use of Plain Christians.* London, n.d.

———. *A Charge and Sermon Delivered at the Ordination of the Rev. Mr. John Deacon.* London: J. Buckland, 1786.

———. *The Christian Religion: An Exposition of Its Leading Principles, Practical Requirements, and Experimental Enjoyments.* London: J. Smith, 1844.

Taylor, George Braxton. *Southern Baptists in Sunny Italy.* New York: Walter Neale, 1929.

Taylor, John. *New Preachers New!* London, 1641. Republished as *A Word to Fanatics, Puritans, and Sectaries; or, New Preachers New!* London: Baynes & Son, 1821.

Taylor, John. *A History of Ten Churches.* Frankfort, Ky.: J. H. Holeman, 1823.

Tegenfeldt, Herman G. *A Century of Growth: The Kachin Baptist Church of Burma.* South Pasadena, Calif.: William Carey Library, 1974.

Terrill, Edward. *The Records of a Church of Christ in Bristol, 1640–1687.* Ed. Roger Hayden. Bristol: Bristol Record Society, 1974.

Thompson, James L., Jr. "Southern Baptists and Postwar Disillusionment, 1918–1919." *Foundations* 21 (April–June 1978): 113–22.

Thompson, Joshua. "Baptists in Ireland 1792–1922: A Dimension of Protestant Dissent." D.Phil. diss., Oxford University, 1988.

———. "Covenants and Constitutions in Irish Baptist Churches." *Irish Baptist Historical Society Journal* 22 (1989–90): 5–13.

———. "Irish Baptist College: 'The Belfast Years.'" *Irish Baptist Historical Society Journal* 24 (1991–92): 53–60.

———. *Century of Grace: The Baptist Union of Ireland: A Short History, 1895–1995.* Belfast: Baptist Union of Ireland, 1995.

Throgmorton, W. P. *The Throgmorton-Potter Debate.* St. Louis: Nixon-Jones, 1888.

Tise, Larry E. *Proslavery: A History of the Defense of Slavery in America, 1701–1840.* Athens: University of Georgia Press, 1987.

Ton, Josif. *The Present Situation of the Baptist Church in Romania.* London: Jubal Multiwrite, 1973.

Tonks, A. Ronald. "Highlights of the Relationships of Southern Baptists with Canadian Baptists." *Baptist History and Heritage* 5 (April 1980): 5–13.

Torbet, Robert G. *A Social History of the Philadelphia Baptist Association: 1707–1940.* Philadelphia: Westbrook, 1944.

———. "Historical Background of the Southern Baptist 'Invasion.'" *Foundations* 2 (October 1959): 314–19.

———. "Baptist Theological Education: An Historical Overview." *Foundations* 6 (October 1963): 311–35.

———. *A History of the Baptists.* 3rd ed. Valley Forge, Pa.: Judson Press, 1973.

———. *The American Baptist Heritage in Wales.* Part 1. Lafayette, Tenn.: Church History Research and Archives Affiliation, 1976.

Tull, James E. *Shapers of Baptist Thought.* Valley Forge, Pa.: Judson Press, 1972.

Underwood, Alfred C. *A History of the English Baptists.* London: Baptist Union Publishing Department, 1947.

Vail, Alvert L. *The Morning Hour of American Baptist Missions.* Philadelphia: American Baptist Publication Society, 1907.

Wacker, Grant. *Augustus H. Strong and the Dilemma of Historical Consciousness.* Macon, Ga.: Mercer University Press, 1985.

Wah, Eh. "A Personal Perspective: Thirty Years after the Western Missionary Era in Myanmar." *American Baptist Quarterly* 15 (June 1996): 97–102.

Walker, F. Deaville. *William Carey: Missionary Pioneer and Statesman.* Chicago: Moody Press, 1960.

Walker, Michael J. "The Relation of Infants to Church, Baptism and Gospel in Seventeenth-Century Baptist Theology." *Baptist Quarterly* 21 (April 1966): 242–62.

Walker, Williston, et al. *A History of the Christian Church.* 4th ed. New York: Scribner, 1985.

Wamble, Hugh. "The Concept and Practice of Christian Fellowship: The Connectional and Inter-denominational Aspects Thereof, among Seventeenth-Century English Baptists." Ph.D. diss., Southern Baptist Theological Seminary, 1955.

Wardin, Albert W. "The Baptists in Bulgaria." *Baptist Quarterly* 34 (October 1991): 148–59.

———, ed. *Baptists around the World: A Comprehensive Handbook.* Nashville: Broadman & Holman, 1995.

Warke, J. "Baptists in Belfast: The Twentieth-Century Challenge of Urban Growth and Decline." *Irish Baptist Historical Society Journal* 20 (1987–88).

Washington, James Melvin. *Frustrated Fellowship: The Black Baptist Quest for Social Power.* Macon, Ga.: Mercer University Press, 1986.

Wayland, Francis. *Elements of Moral Science.* 4th ed. Boston: Gould, Kendall, and Lincoln, 1848.

———. *A Memoir of the Life and Labors of the Rev. Adoniram Judson, D.D.* 2 vols. Boston: Phillips, Sampson, 1853.

———. *Notes on the Principles and Practices of Baptist Churches.* New York: Sheldon, Blakeman, 1857.

Weber, Timothy P. *Living in the Shadow of the Second Coming: American Premillennialism, 1875–1925*. New York: Oxford University Press, 1979.

Wesley, John. *The Journal of John Wesley.* Chicago: Moody Press, 1952.

White, B. R. "The Frontiers of Fellowship Between English Baptists, 1609–1660." *Foundations* 11 (July–September 1968): 244–56.

———. "Early Baptist Arguments for Religious Freedom: Their Overlooked Agenda." *Baptist History and Heritage* 24 (October 1989): 3–10.

———. "The Origins and Convictions of the First Calvinistic Baptists." *Baptist History and Heritage* 25 (October 1990): 39–47.

———. *The English Baptists of the Seventeenth Century.* Rev. ed. Didcot, England: Baptist Historical Society, 1996.

———, ed. *Association Records of the Particular Baptists of England, Wales and Ireland to 1660.* 3 vols. London: Baptist Historical Society, 1971–74.

White, Charles. *A Century of Faith.* Philadelphia: Judson Press, 1932.

White, Ronald C., Jr., and C. Howard Hopkins. *The Social Gospel: Religion and Reform in Changing America.* Philadelphia: Temple University Press, 1976.

Whitley, W. T. *A History of British Baptists.* Rev. ed. London: Kingsgate Press, 1932.

Williams, A. D. *Benoni Stinson and the General Baptists.* Owensville, Ind.: General Baptist Publishing House, 1892.

Williams, Daniel Day. "The Mystery of the Baptists." *Foundations* 1 (January 1958): 7–9.

Williams, George Hunston. *The Radical Reformation.* Philadelphia: Westminster Press, 1962.

Williams, Walter L. *Black Americans and the Evangelization of Africa, 1877–1900.* Madison: University of Wisconsin Press, 1982.

Wills, Gregory A. *Democratic Religion: Freedom, Authority, and Church Discipline in the Baptist South, 1785–1900.* New York: Oxford University Press, 1997.

Wilson, Charles Reagan. *Baptized in Blood: The Religion of the Lost Cause, 1865–1920.* Athens: University of Georgia Press, 1980.

Winter, E. P. "The Lord's Supper." *Baptist Quarterly* 17 (April 1958): 267–81.

Wood, James E., ed. *Baptists and the American Experience.* Valley Forge, Pa.: Judson Press, 1976.

Wood, James H. *A Condensed History of the General Baptists of the New Connexion; Preceded by Historical Sketches of Early Baptists.* London: Simpkin, Marshall, 1847.

Woodson, Carter G. *The History of the Negro Church.* Washington, D.C.: Associated Publishers, 1921.

Woodworth, R. O. "Baptist Bible Seminary." *Fundamentalist* (May 27, 1949).

Young, Doyle. "Andrew Fuller and the Modern Missions Movement." *Baptist History and Heritage* 17 (October 1982): 17–24.

Yuille, George, ed. *History of the Baptists in Scotland from Pre-Reformation Times.* Glasgow: Baptist Union of Scotland, 1926.

Zeman, Jarold K., ed. *Baptists in Canada: Search for Identity amidst Diversity.* Burlington, Ont.: G. R. Welch, 1980.

Index